KEITH GRANT

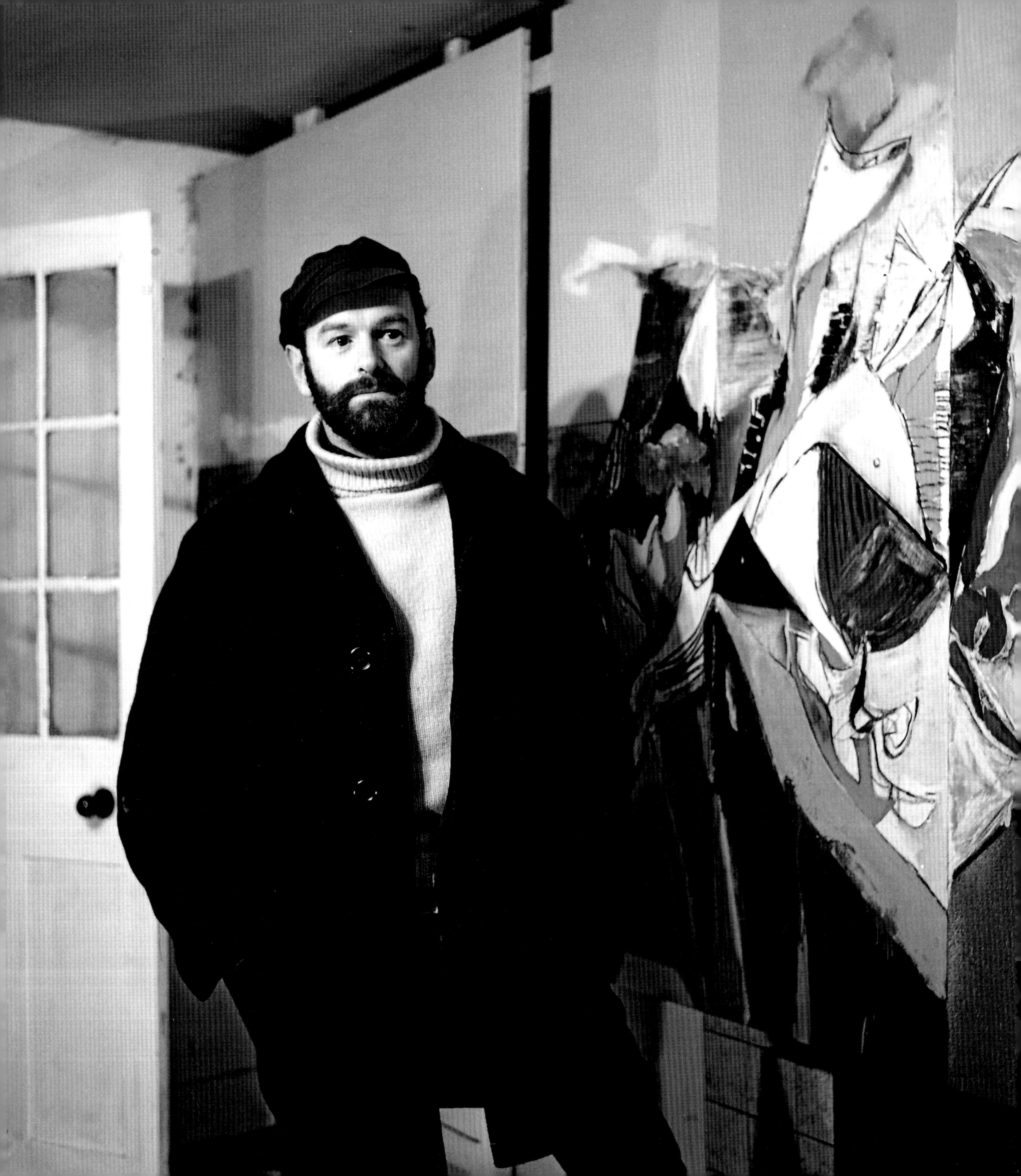

KEITH GRANT

Judith LeGrove

LUND
HUMPHRIES

First published in 2023 by Lund Humphries

Lund Humphries
Huckletree Shoreditch
Alphabeta Building
18 Finsbury Square
London EC2A 1AH
UK
www.lundhumphries.com

ISBN: 978-1-84822-627-2

A Cataloguing-in-Publication record for this book is available from the British Library

Designed and project managed by Crow Books
Set in Sofia Pro and Dunbar
Printed in Estonia

FRONTISPIECE: Photograph of Keith Grant at the Abbey Art Centre, *c.*1966
FRONT COVER: *Sea Drift by Moonfleet*, 2020, oil on linen, 100 × 150 cm, collection of the artist

Contents

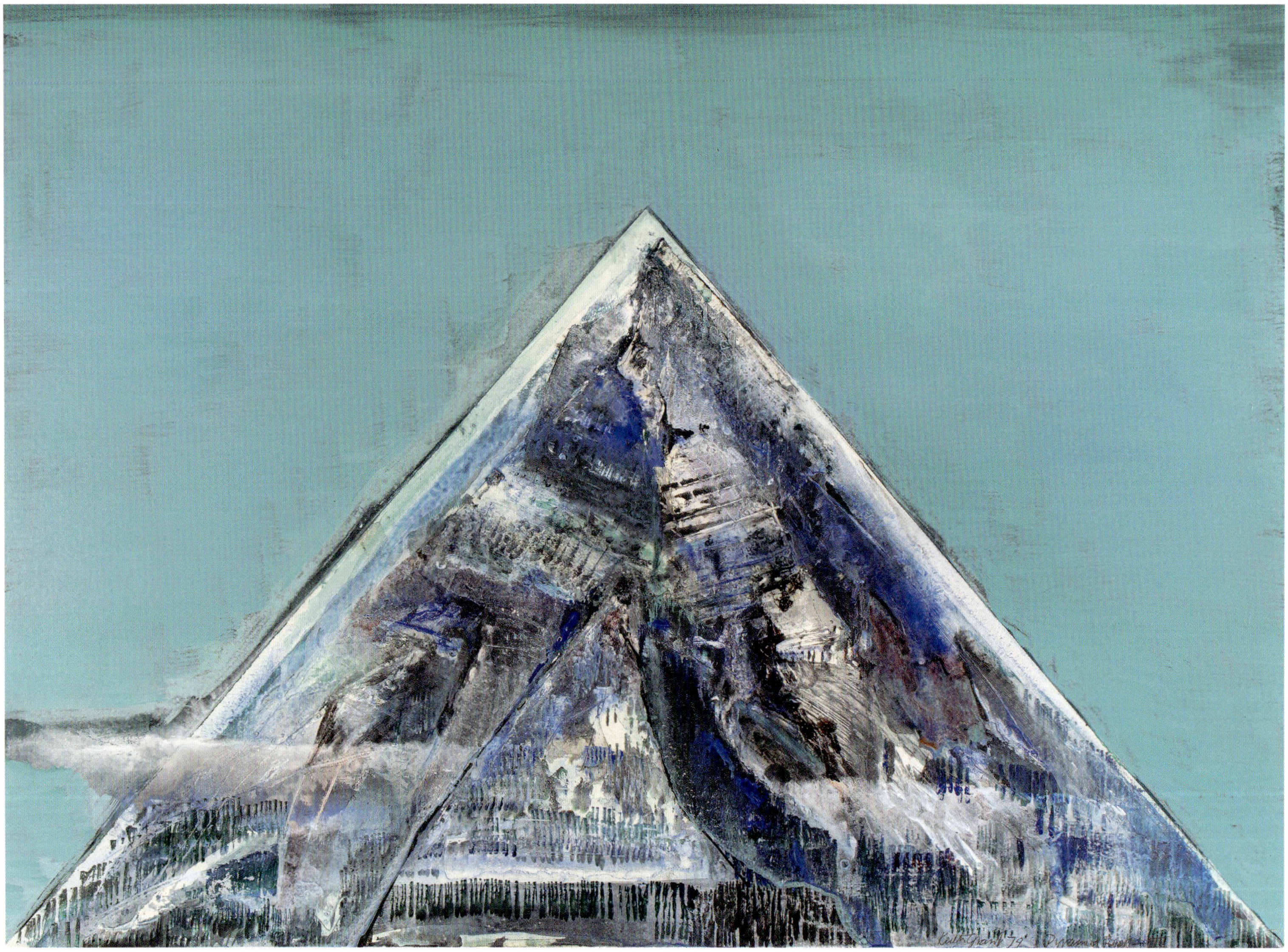

Introduction

Elemental, Radical

The Landscape Paintings of Keith Grant

1
Pyramid Peak IV, 1979
Oil on canvas
86.5 × 117 cm
Towner Eastbourne

In May 2022, as this book was taking shape, the exhibition *Radical Landscapes* opened at Tate Liverpool. Publicised as 'a revelatory exploration of art and our connections to the rural landscapes of Britain', it proved stimulating, frustrating, provocative, confusing and, at times, confused. What emerged was less a survey of radical responses to landscape than a manifesto for landscape used as a means of protest, sometimes to address its own destruction, but frequently to draw attention to marginalised, oppressed or minority communities. Perhaps this is as it should be, proving that landscape has lost none of its potency to arouse deep passions. *Radical Landscapes* certainly provides an intriguing framework to introduce the work of Keith Grant (b.1930).

Walking through galleries filled with conceptual art, installations, films, textiles and documentary evidence from campaigns such as those at Greenham Common, it was clear that Grant's work would have found little traction in such company. Examples of painting in *Radical Landscapes* were rare – viewers might have spotted Eric Ravilious, or Eileen Agar, co-opted for different purposes – but near the entrance two canvases signalled a pertinent response and counter-response to landscape: John Constable's *Flatford Mill ('Scene on a Navigable River')* (1816–17) and Stephen McKenna's *An English Oak Tree* (1981). There is plenty to explore in both of these pictures. Constable depicted workers in a rural landscape with which he was intimately familiar. The backdrop to his paintings included the Enclosure Acts and the mechanisation of agriculture that drove rural workers towards cities. *Radical Landscapes* suggested, furthermore, that by portraying an idealised view of the English countryside, Constable's paintings became 'almost a propagandist tool for the British Empire'.[1] McKenna's *An English Oak Tree*, on the other hand, deliberately combines different specimens and lineages to address a national symbol. Working from a small tree in Dulwich Park, and from studies of foliage and branches, McKenna presented a larger tree painted in the tradition of Gustave Courbet, John Crome and Caspar David Friedrich. Where might we begin to place Grant in relation to these examples?

That Grant succeeded in pursuing a career as a professional artist, despite his upbringing, may be attributed to the strength of his determination. He would not want this background to be dwelt upon, much though it shaped his political orientation and independence. He describes himself not as an artist 'with a capital "A"', but as someone whose sole motivation is to convey an overwhelming response to nature and landscape: a response that since childhood has supplied him with more than ample inspiration for his work. Asked how he approaches this, he states that he 'interprets' rather than 'depicts' what he sees, since 'if you try to depict nature, it will always win'. Comparing McKenna's *An English Oak Tree* with Grant's almost contemporary *Spring, The 'Pells', Lewes* (1982; fig.115, p.138) highlights their different tactics. McKenna creates a portrait of a tree, which while seeking to communicate its essential 'oakness' and through it a relationship to national identity, is nonetheless anchored in realism. Grant, to a far greater degree, selects, abstracts and moulds what he sees to represent what he regards as its essence. It is in this sense that we might describe his work as 'radical', from the word's origin, *radix* or 'root'.

Pyramid Peak IV (1979) shows the most extreme consequence of this approach (fig.1). Grant, throughout his life, has been drawn irresistibly towards landscapes of the North. Seeking to convey their power and underlying structure, he alighted upon the symbol of the pyramid. The mountain thus becomes a triangle, textured to represent rocks and forests and delineated uncompromisingly against a turquoise sky. This is not an especially large work, yet Grant indicates scale through a layer of cloud near the base of the peak. Indubitably, this painting possesses considerable impact. Rarely does Grant relinquish his thrall to abstraction, one of the consequences of which is the strong formal basis to his work even when it seems closest to traditional representation.

This fascination with abstraction and the North can be seen unfolding across multiple media – painting, constructions, mosaics, murals – but nowhere as inventively and revealingly as in a four-act 'fantasy', *Maritime Polar* (*c*.1972).[2] Unpublished and unperformed, this is essentially a Beckettian drama of the absurd, featuring as its main character 'Turnon', an artist recognised for a 'third eye' that endows special vision. He begins his quest by encountering an old harbour master, Okan, who holds a bright, illuminated orange rope. Close to the denouement, the shadowy forms of a cube, tetrahedron, octahedron and icosahedron, made from Perspex or welded aluminium, assemble about him: these are the four elements, their geometrical forms containing dancers, nude or in body stockings, whose bodies are painted green and white (for earth), red/orange with black patterning (fire), purple and ultramarine with turquoise (water) and pale blue with white cloud forms (air). The drama closes with Turnon, by now so cold that his eyelids freeze and his hands can no longer hold the rope, sinking to the ground, to be overwhelmed by an avalanche. Grant's imagination is a force never to be underestimated.

Grant's lifelong attraction to the North is the principal lens through which his commitment to landscape is understood. If it began with a first visit to Norway in 1957, it continues to this day, since from 1996 he has made Norway his home. An early painting of a fjord shows through its breadth, stillness and fierce structural clarity what compelled him to return (fig.2).

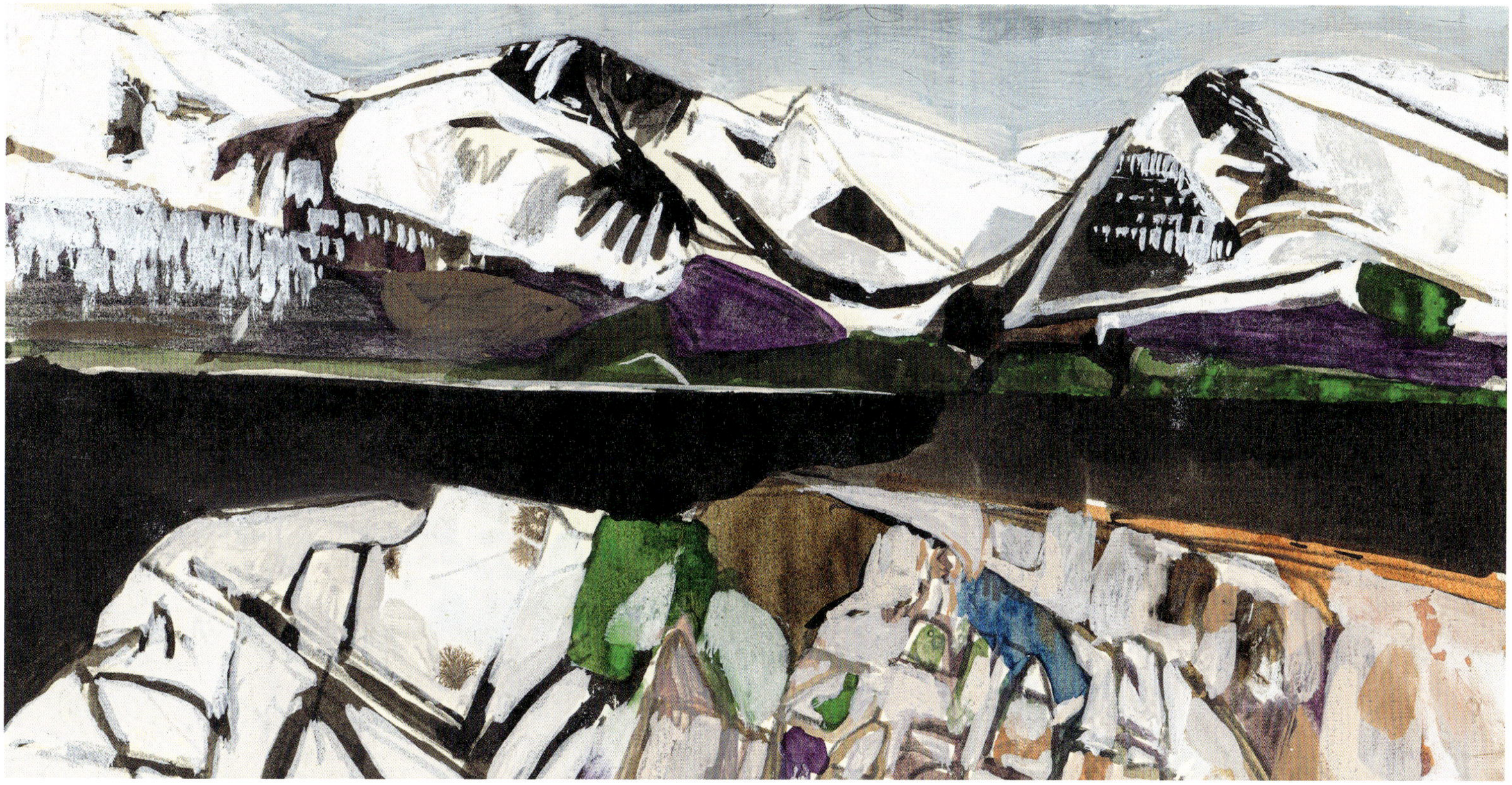

2
Fjord, 1961
Gouache, black ink and watercolour on paper
10.9 × 22 cm
Art Gallery of South Australia, Adelaide

Yet is this landscape radical? It is certainly elemental, in the way that its fissured rocks are defined by snow and by crystalline pockets of colour. It has a definite sense of place. We can be sure that if we found this view, its spirit, if not its precise colouration or formal detail, would match Grant's interpretation.

Another adjective to describe Grant's preference in landscape might be 'extreme'. During a career of over seven decades, he has travelled to the desert, to tropical rainforests, the Arctic and Antarctica, experiencing challenging, sometimes life-threatening, terrain. He has consistently been attracted to violent phenomena such as immense waterfalls or active volcanoes. Following a first sight of Mount Etna in Sicily, in 1964, he travelled repeatedly to Iceland to study volcanoes, most notably the eruption of Eldfell in 1973. An extended sequence of work from the mid-1960s focused on Surtsey, whose explosive imagery fractures his painted landscapes into molten, time-spliced visions (fig.3).

If Courbet, Crome and Friedrich are McKenna's artistic forebears, whom might Grant invoke? The artists he admires are many and various. He is well-acquainted with and admires the Romantic tradition in landscape, from J.M.W. Turner to Friedrich, John Martin to F.E. Church, while he draws repeated sustenance from Surrealism. Nearer to his own generation are Graham Sutherland, Paul Nash, Peter Lanyon, Alan Reynolds and John Minton, the last two of whom he knew well through their connection with the Royal College of Art. It should never be assumed, much though Grant is drawn to desolate landscapes, that he has not enjoyed the acquaintance of a wide circle of artists. While living in London, particularly, he organised impressive exhibitions on behalf of Medical Aid for Vietnam by encouraging friends and colleagues to participate. He has exhibited in many countries, and continues to enjoy a dedicated and extensive circle of collectors. Sir Kenneth Clark first saw and admired his work in the late 1950s, while

3
Midnight Sun, Surtsey, 1966
Gouache, watercolour and
polymer on board
54.5 × 112 cm
Private Collection,
Luxembourg

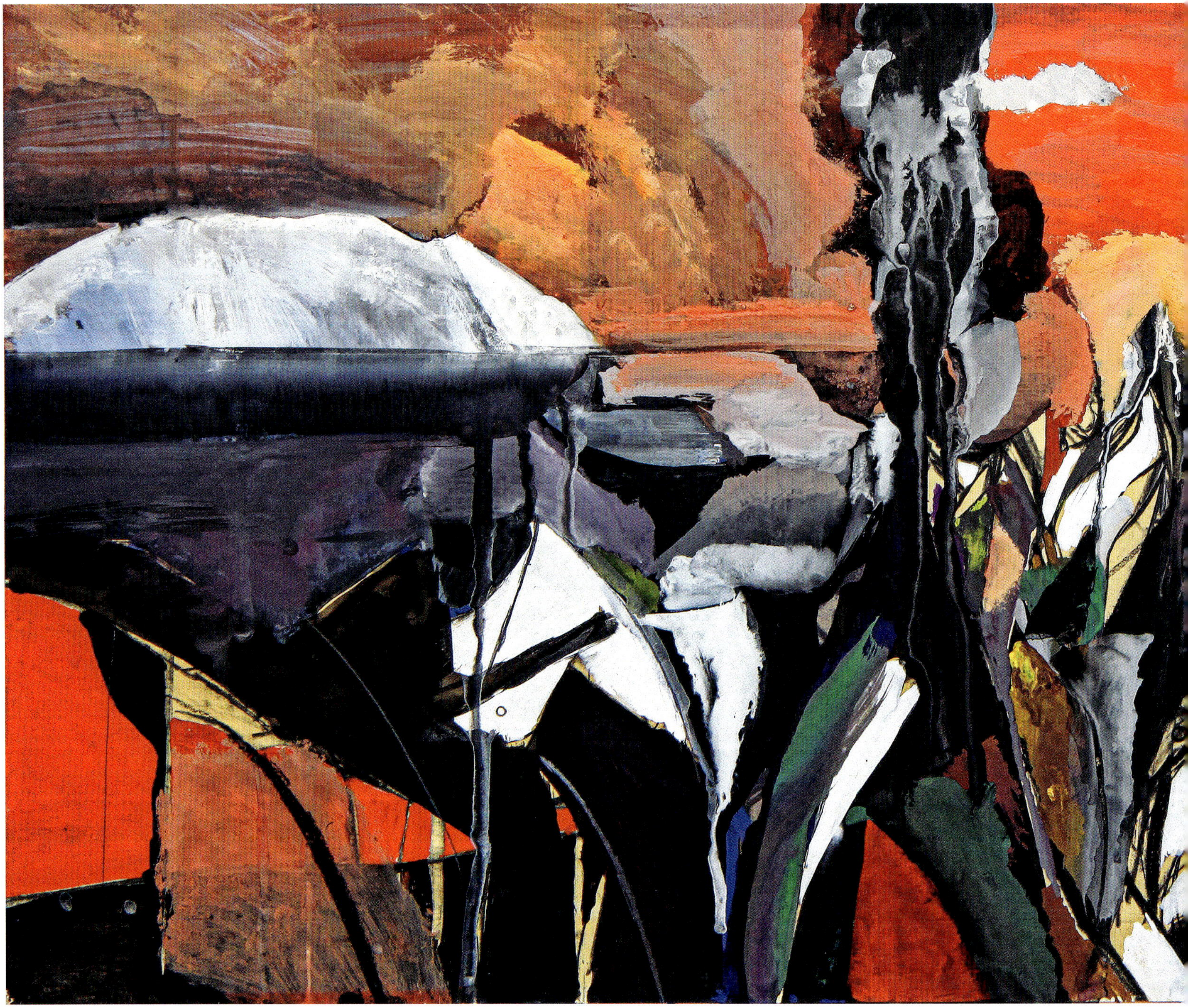

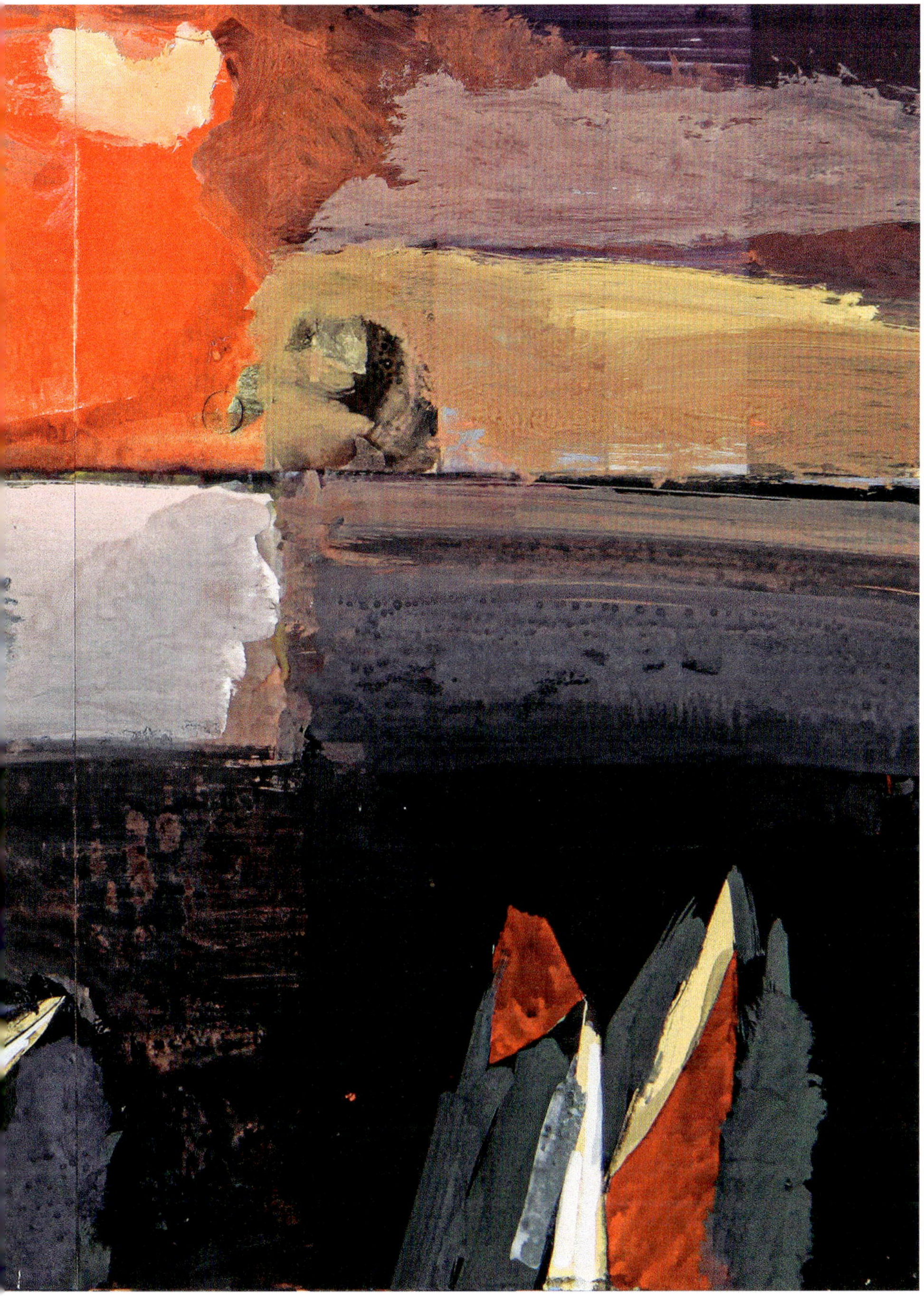

Sir David Attenborough, first encountering it in the 1980s, wrote of Grant's skill and vision 'to convey the awesome mystery of nature at its most monumental and dramatic'.[3] Conversely, Grant has proved unsuccessful in penetrating bastions of the British art establishment such as the Royal Academy or Tate. Irritated each time a setback occurs, Grant simply shrugs it off as peripheral to his desire to paint and to explore landscape.

Yet there are further aspects of Grant's work that disqualify him for consideration as an isolated figure. He bought a house in Lewes, Sussex, in 1973, but retained close contact with London's art scene until moving to Norway. For over thirty years he worked as a respected and influential teacher, most notably at Hornsey and Maidstone Colleges of Art, at Newcastle Polytechnic and Roehampton Institute. He has made numerous public works of art, sometimes involving educational projects, and has worked collaboratively on stage designs. In all of these, landscape has remained his focus. And while he has largely resisted political activism, during the 1960s his sense of outrage over Vietnam permeated his painting, his writing and his participation in non-combative assistance. He considers writing to be an integral aspect of his creative work, regularly keeping journals, some of which have been published as extracts.[4] *Maritime Polar* contains a satirical image of this inseparability of life, art and landscape when Turnon is advised that his journey will lead him onward by sea, snow, ice, by rope or 'in the throat of the volcano'. A display of the northern lights is then announced, and as they flicker and dance, 'Italic', the news seller, appears dressed in newspapers and distributes placards. Only, as he explains, the newspaper has no politics – no news of Vietnam,

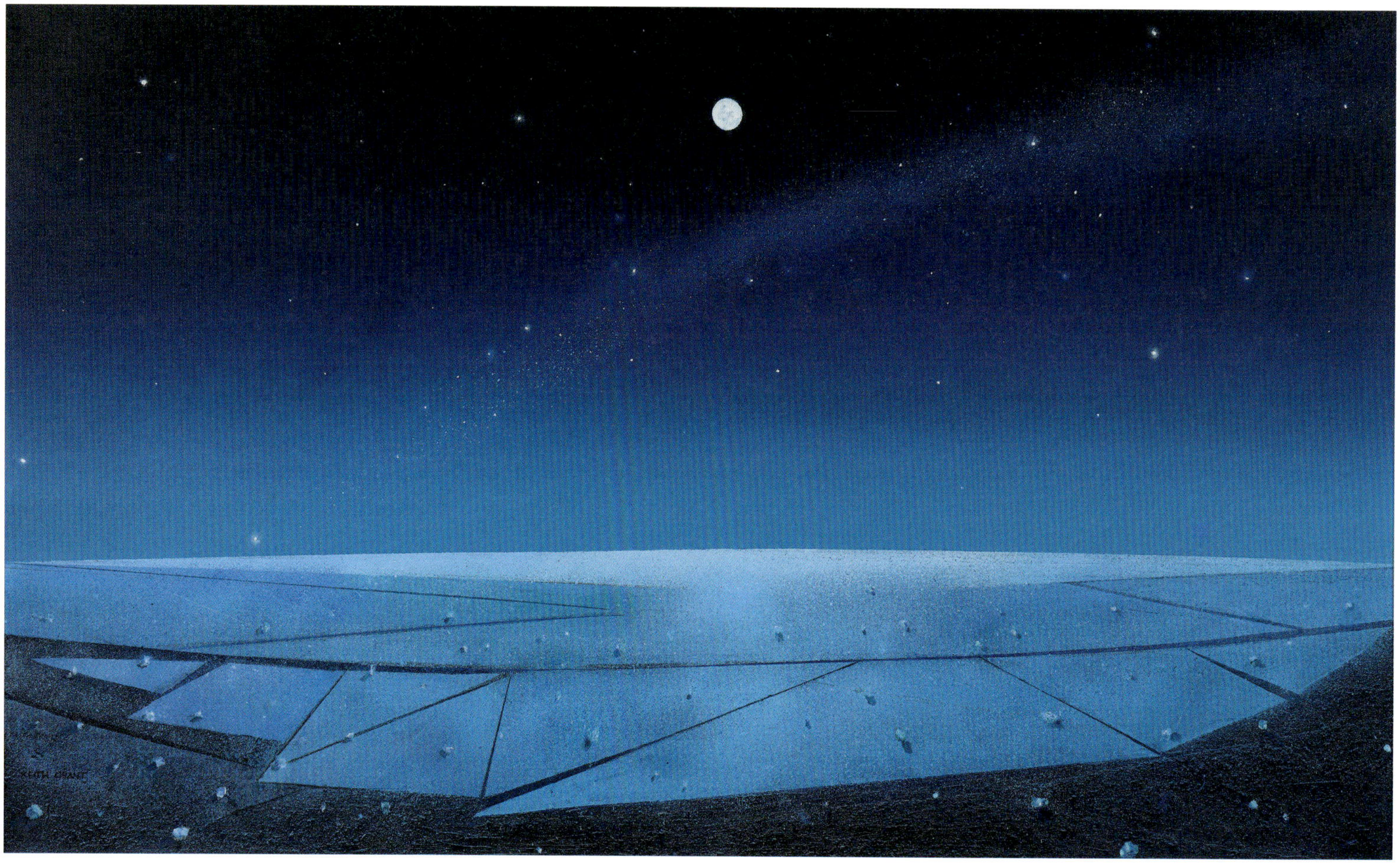

4
Last Ice, Horizon and the Milky Way, 2022
Oil on linen
87 × 147 cm
Collection of the artist

Israel, Russia or America – but focuses instead on the 'natural extremes' his readers find most interesting: an avalanche, a fierce snowstorm, an especially large catch of cod.

This is the Grant whom those who have met him will recognise: whom Gerald Forty recalled in 1980 as having the same 'mischievous twinkle' in his eye as when they met twenty years earlier. Forty, a former Director of the British Council's Fine Art Department, found it almost impossible to classify Grant, settling finally for 'visionary realist': an artist of integrity and inexhaustible energy, of his time yet unafraid to diverge from current trends.[5] Jack Hazan, a film director who has known Grant since the mid-1960s, adds to this, equally perceptively, Grant's ability to 'reinvent' himself several times during his life.[6]

While this is not a biography but a study of Grant's creative response to landscape, Hazan's comment is resonant nonetheless. The threads of nature, the North, the elements and a concern for the entire world in which we live are explored by Grant through sometimes widely divergent modes of expression, restlessly and inventively. These different phases are reflected in the structure of this book by exploring themes rather than by following a strict chronology. Thus, Chapter 1 outlines Grant's earliest years through an emphasis on English landscape. Chapter 2, the longest by virtue of its significance, addresses his engagement with the North, whether Norway, Iceland, the Faroe Islands or Scotland. In Chapter 3, attention shifts to the North's opposite: to rainforests and the desert. Chapters 4 and 5 explore the themes of ice and night. Chapter 6 is entitled 'Metamorphosis', denoting Grant's often surrealistic transformation of what he sees within nature, while Chapter 7 demonstrates how differently Grant approaches British landscape when he revisits it from 1980 onwards. Chapter 8 considers the impact of music on Grant's painting, and Chapter 9 his work for the public sphere. Finally, Chapter 10 focuses on the capacity of art to serve as protest or memorial.

In mid-August 1987, Grant began a large painting depicting Norway's Nordland region from the air, using the distant white walls of Lofoten to 'describe the stretched horizon's curvature . . . [and] patches of fjord to create a cubistic spatial effect.'[7] He was pleased with the painting's grandeur and spatial consciousness, as it neared completion, but not entirely satisfied. Contemplating it at his studio in Lewes, he wrote,

It is surprising how a rudimentary knowledge of perspective enables the imagination to place itself in any position relevant to landscape, either on the lowest plane – so that the horizon is on the eye-level or miles above the clouds. An artist with imaginative vision can place himself in the skins of animals, birds or fishes and see the world as they do.[8]

Grant continued work on the painting, altering it again after its inclusion in the Royal Academy *Summer Exhibition* in 1989, where it was 'skyed' – hung far above the line of vision. He has no qualms about revising work. It is not quite a case of 'never finished, only abandoned' (W.H. Auden's paraphrase of Paul Valéry), but often a matter of expediency: working to an exhibition deadline, then – sometimes years later – seizing the chance to reassess a painting. The process is frustrating for those who seek a definitive version, yet also exciting, rendering the works alive. In the revised version of *Islands of the North, 'Lofoten Islands'* (1987/9), Grant adduced further experiences of Lofoten as well as new satellite photographs of the earth's surface seen from space. In some ways he considered the final effect too photographic. What matters is the horizon: a beckoning signal, for Grant, of Shakespeare's 'undiscovered country from whose bourn no traveller returns'.[9]

The horizon divides two worlds, the real and the unattainable. It is also a symbol of discovery familiar from the bird's-eye vantage and wide horizons of 17th-century Dutch marine paintings. In autumn 2022, painting again an archetypal iceberg whose form continues to haunt him, Grant achieved an unexpected treatment of the reflected afterglow. His following painting, *Last Ice, Horizon and the Milky Way* (2022), acts as counterpart (fig.4). Removing the iceberg, while signifying its absence by scattered remnants of ice on a basalt shore, denotes anxiety for a landscape under threat. Attention focuses now on the horizon: softly curved, elusive in its distance and location. Is this what will remain?

Last Ice, Horizon and the Milky Way is a potent image with which to embark on a study of Grant's work. It demonstrates a cumulative vision by one of the most gifted landscape painters working today, one who remains as attuned as ever to nature's beauty, constancy and capriciousness. Framing its subject distinctively, radically even, this painting shows precisely why such art continues to matter, and why, in this era of climate change, we must value such elemental landscapes more than ever.

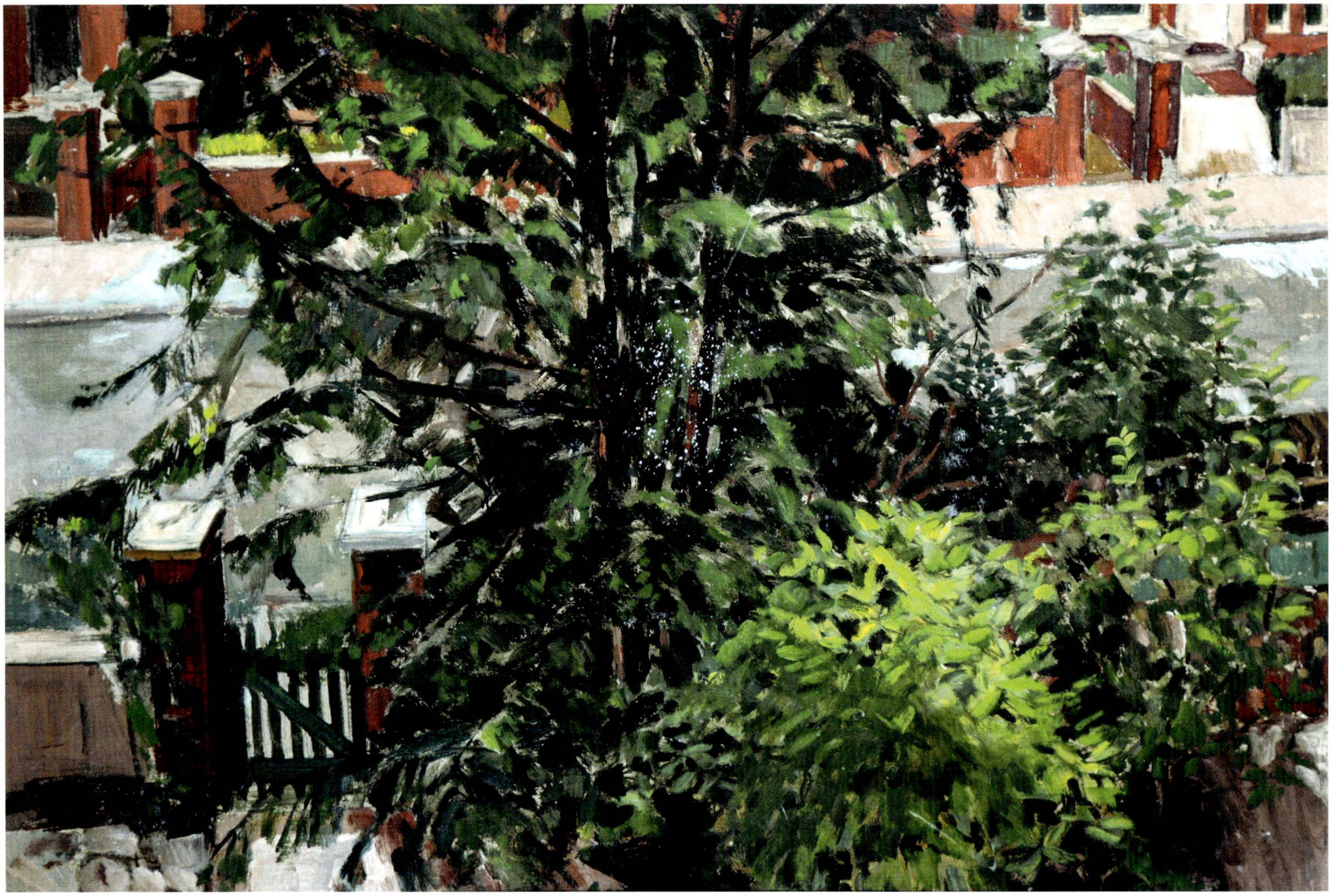

1

A Land

5
View from the Bedroom Window, *c.*1953
Oil on board
63.5 × 89 cm
The Atkinson, Southport

Early Years

One of Grant's earliest surviving oil paintings, *View from the Bedroom Window* (*c.*1953), shows the outlook from rented lodgings near Willesden Green (fig.5). A tree spreads across the street, screening the houses opposite just as – presumably – it screened Grant's intense observation from passers-by. Placing the tree centrally implies its dominance, yet its effect is to filter and diffuse the view. The windows opposite are darkened and half-cropped, the garden occluded by foliage and an elevated vantage, the gate closed. Thwarted, the eye notices instead the light, deducing a source from the sun, high overhead, to the right.

Frederick Nall and his twin brother, Roy, were born on 10 August 1930 at Walton Hospital in Liverpool. Unable to keep them, their unmarried mother placed them in a children's home. When she discovered their ill-treatment, however, she offered them for adoption. Charles and Gladys Grant thus became the twins' foster parents in 1932, adopting them legally in 1935. Long before this, Frederick became known as 'Keith', a name he liked because of its Scottish origins.

Charles Grant worked as a French polisher, principally in banks and on ships at Liverpool docks, barely earning sufficient money to support the household. Gladys's romanticised ideas about helping those in need inspired her desire to adopt four boys: Keith, Roy, Alistair and David, the last of whom stayed only briefly before returning to his parents. While the state's financial support provided welcome additional income, Gladys treated the boys with little warmth, trying unsuccessfully to maintain discipline. This pattern continued until Keith and Roy rebelled, burning the raspberry canes used to beat them, as well as perpetrating more insidious acts such as cutting the flowers from Gladys's prize fuchsia and wedging them between the piano strings. There was a dark undercurrent to this relationship. For the first years of the twins' lives, Gladys had allowed their birth mother to visit, introducing her as an aunt. Then, as the three grew close, she forbade them to meet. This subterfuge – such that Keith and Roy never traced their mother, or discovered the true history of their adoptive family – left a legacy of distrust that would shape Keith's independence.

Keith Frederick Grant grew up in Bootle at number 21 Patrick Avenue, an interwar house close to fields and countryside. His twin passions were nature and drawing, fostered by art lessons at the Roberts Primary School. When he made a painting of an eagle, his teacher, Miss Filshie, showed him how to temper it by applying a milky wash, unifying and transforming the picture. Grant learnt to remove excess paint with a newspaper or rag, a practice known as 'Tonking', after Henry Tonks, the influential teacher at the Slade School of Fine Art. He first heard of Antarctica through Miss Filshie, who was related to an Antarctic explorer, a member of Ernest Shackleton's team. Complimented on his pen and ink drawing of a crane at Liverpool docks, Grant became enthused by their mechanical forms, recalling 'a boyish frisson' about how beautiful they looked when encrusted with snow and ice, transformed by winter.[1]

In 1940, the twins were evacuated briefly to Peak Dale in Derbyshire, where they explored the countryside and quarries until their Uncle Walter sent them home because of their unruliness. Grant then won a two-year scholarship to Bootle Grammar School for Boys, from 1941 to 1943. At that point his schooling ceased. Required to contribute to his upkeep, aged 13, he took a job at the Co-op in Stanley Road, Bootle, where he packaged and shifted groceries, advancing eventually to counter work. He submitted illustrations to the Liverpool Co-op magazine: line drawings of mills, docks, historic buildings and local churches. Among the earliest was Sefton Church, then surrounded by fields, where Grant walked often, eagerly anticipating what he might encounter – whether a brightly patterned viper coiled in the sun under a hedge, a skylark's nest or the unforgettable sound of hundreds of skylarks cascading through the sky.[2] In 1947, Grant's watercolour of Willaston Mill was included in an open exhibition at the Hugo Lang Gallery, a framing and fine art business in Liverpool. Although he had chosen an alternative career as a weather forecaster, should his plans fail, he knew already that he wanted to become an artist.

Gladys's one concession was to allow Grant, aged 15 or 16, to receive weekly lessons in watercolour painting with Rose, Winifred and Edith Isaacs in nearby Litherland. He recalled their house as dark and Victorian and the sisters as 'old-fashioned ladies', one of whom had exhibited once, years ago, at the Royal Academy. Yet by setting him 'vigorously' to paint candlesticks, apples, tomatoes and damask covers, they encouraged concentration and a certain fluency.[3] The sisters owned a cottage near the Berwyn Mountains in the Welsh village of Glyn Ceiriog, which Grant's family borrowed for summer holidays. This was his first experience of abundant, precipitous nature, where clouds suspended halfway between mountain tops and the valley floor anticipated his discovery of Norway.

Grant's watercolours focused on landscape and architecture. He painted trees, structured to show trunks dividing into branches then twigs, reflected in water or arching across paths. Although the brushstrokes were sometimes hectic, there was a strong sense of space in the depiction of sharply defined foregrounds, ceding first to middle distance, then to an elusive hinterland. Such depth characterised Grant's approach to architecture too, as shown by a watercolour from 1946 of St Matthew and St James at Mossley Hill in Liverpool. Bombed in 1940, the church was portrayed as a cavernous void cross-shafted with light, in a palette extended through warm reds and purples from that of his landscapes. The vaulted timber roof, meanwhile, suggested proximity to a woodland interior.

Having attended evening classes at Bootle School of Art for less than a term, in October 1948 Grant

6
1954 copy of Paul Cézanne's
Le Bassin du Jas de Bouffan en hiver, c.1878
Gouache on paper
14.5 × 17 cm
Collection of the artist

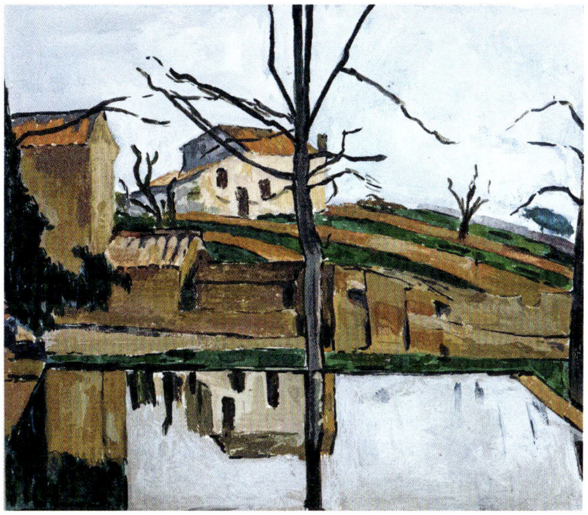

was called up for National Service in the Royal Air Force, where he spent months undertaking clerical duties. When he outspokenly criticised a painting in the canteen, he was challenged to do better. The Warrant Officer ordered materials from the workshop and instructed Grant to complete two six-foot wall panels by 8 am the following morning. Undaunted, he replicated in every detail a pair of Victorian watercolours of Thames barges that hung either side of the fireplace at home in Bootle. He repeated the ruse by painting the Bay of Naples onto the dining room wall of an officer's house, thus winning exemption from clerical work. From then on, Grant was responsible for decorating all the canteens, a task he enjoyed for the opportunity to invent large-scale designs featuring disparate elements. His work was rewarded in 1949 by a commendation from Group Captain Morton Swan Shapcott, the officer in charge of the 16th Maintenance Unit in Stafford, who was also a first-class cricketer.

Demobbed in 1950, Grant moved to London where he worked as a window dresser for the Co-op at Wood Green. A chance conversation with a seller of the *Daily Worker* encouraged him to enrol at the Working Men's College in St Pancras, founded in 1854 by members of the Christian Socialists and Co-operative Movement to provide adult education. Painting classes had been an important feature from the outset, attracting teachers such as John Ruskin, Dante Gabriel Rossetti and Lowes Dickinson. Post-war, the head of the art department, Francis Cromwell Cooke, employed young painters who were nearing the end of their studies, to give them teaching experience but also to benefit from their enthusiasm and experimental approaches.[4] Grant's evening drawing classes were taken by Cromwell Cooke, a painter and graphic designer, and Ivor Fox, who had organised the first *Young Contemporaries* exhibition in 1949 while still studying at the Royal College of Art (RCA). At the end of a year's study, in July 1952, Grant received the Lowes Dickinson scholarship to travel to France. The report commended his inquisitive frame of mind, command of space, sensitive observation and lively interest in the textural quality of paint, concluding by praising Grant's drawings for their 'response to landscape and the evolution of techniques valid to the problem in hand'.[5]

Grant did not travel immediately, however. Having assisted since 1951 at the Mountview Theatre in Crouch End, he was seriously contemplating a career in stage design. Before he could apply to study at the Byam Shaw School of Art, he needed to improve his knowledge of the figure, for costume design, and to gain sufficient O and A levels. Thus, in autumn 1952, he enrolled simultaneously at Kilburn Technical College and Willesden School of Art, where Fox also taught.

Grant's teachers at Willesden included William Brooker, Head of Painting and a passionate advocate of French artists such as Édouard Vuillard and Pierre Bonnard, and Edward Middleditch, a recent graduate from the RCA. Clifford Wilkinson was a skilled printmaker who taught lithography, but it was Cyril Kent, an artist with a keen sensitivity to nature and an instinct for form, whose teaching proved most inspiring to Grant. In composition classes, Kent encouraged students to begin with a spontaneous, gestural approach before gradually developing marks into an intentional pattern, selecting and colouring those that felt most personal to their own work. Although the results remained abstract, Grant started to see how the process might reveal shapes expressive of natural forms, triggering a response in the memory. The exercise functioned as a creative release: a licence to balance figuration and realism against Grant's always vivid imagination.

Influences and Early Exhibitions

If Willesden broadened Grant's knowledge of art and art history, travelling 'rough' through the south of France in the fiercely hot summer of 1953, using the Lowes Dickinson scholarship, deepened his knowledge of French painting and its relationship to landscape. At Fontainebleau, he visited the immense forest where Théodore Rousseau worked. At the Musée de Lyon he was struck by a painting from the *Femme assise* series, in an exhibition of Pablo Picasso's work, yet shocked by the casualness with which Roman urns and sarcophagi were 'strewn haphazardly' around the museum's courtyard outside. In Aix-en-Provence he saw an exhibition of Paul Cézanne's paintings, watercolours and drawings, climbed Mont St Victoire and sketched. Taking a boat from Cannes to the small Île Sainte-Marguerite, he snorkelled, marvelling at the myriad darting fish, anemones and sea urchins. In Antibes he saw the Picasso museum, with its superb ceramics and drawings, in Vence he visited the Matisse chapel and in Paris the Musée Rodin. Summing up, in an illustrated lecture given at the Working Men's College, he considered French art to be 'no better' than British.[6] It was at this point that he painted *View from the Bedroom Window*, a work that still surprises him for its uncharacteristically impressionistic approach to texture and light.

To complete his National Diploma in Design (NDD) at Willesden, Grant compiled a thesis on Cézanne, consisting of a written analysis interleaved with three pencil drawings, two gouaches and one watercolour copied from reproductions. It is a carefully crafted object: a handmade book with illustrations and a typewritten text mounted onto buff-coloured sugar paper. Between 1953 and 1954, Grant had seen exhibitions of Cézanne's work in Lyon and at the Tate Gallery in London, studying also examples of his painting in the Musée d'Art Moderne and Musée d'Orsay, in Paris, and at London's National Gallery. Most striking among the paintings he chose to copy is Cézanne's *Le Bassin du Jas de Bouffan en hiver* (*c.*1878), which features a central tree, extended in height by its reflection in water (1954; fig.6). Geometry is paramount in the strong vertical and horizontal axes, the bisection of the composition by the tree and the mirroring of the house and barn in the water. All of these strategies would continue to resonate through Grant's work as it developed.

The influence that began to exert itself most profoundly, however, was that of Paul Nash

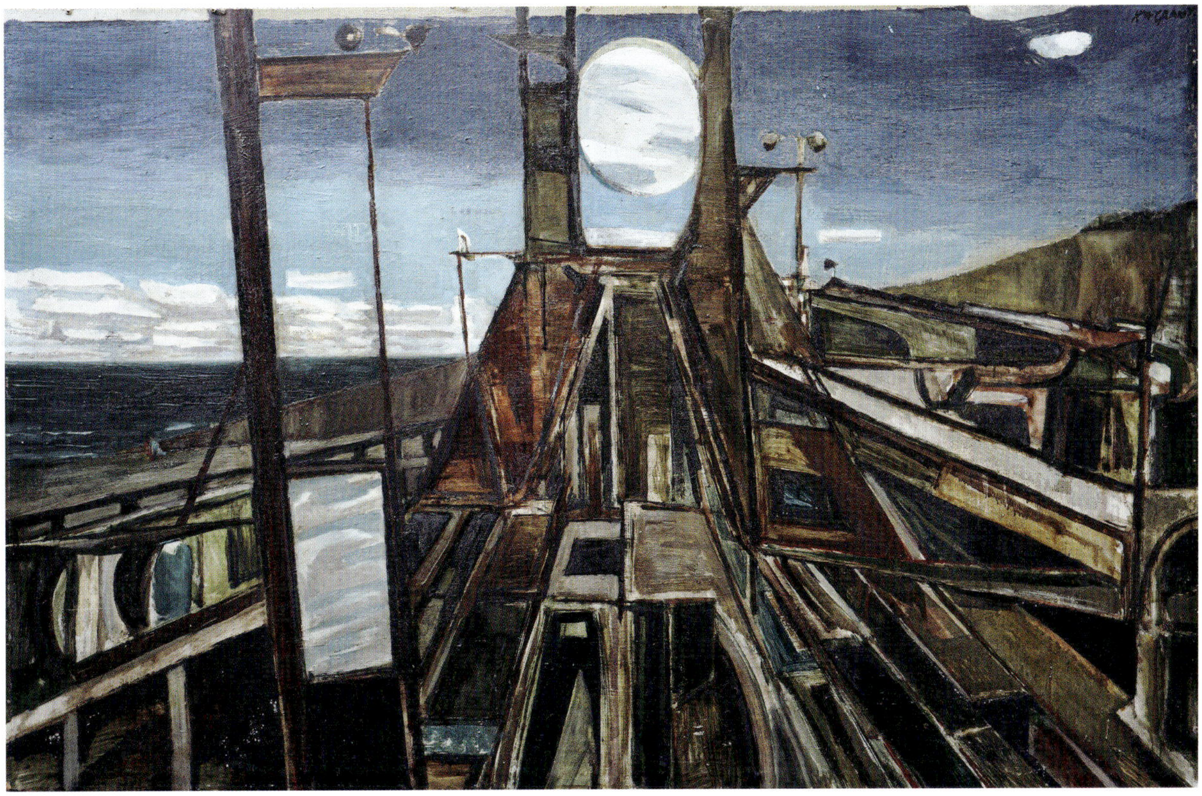

7
Marinescape, 1953–4
Oil on board
75 × 107 cm
Private Collection, UK

(1889–1946). *Marinescape* (1953–4) evokes the interior of a boat, steering between open sea and headland (fig.7). Yet Grant instantly subverts the straightforwardness of the scene by inserting the Surrealist motif of two mirrors – one rectangular, one circular – whose reflections reiterate stratified clouds at the horizon. There is a dialogue between the seen and unseen, the solid and the permeable, as the mirrors disclose a possible past and the boat's hull, seemingly solid, contains blocks of tone indistinguishable from the sea. Even the sky darkens across the composition, lending it an unsettling tilt. During walks in Orrell, a suburb of Liverpool, and across the golf links at Southport, Grant had witnessed similar clouds stacked in the distance. Other details in the painting, such as the small transmitters mounted on masts, derive from lamps seen on winding gear in coal mines. Elements culled from experience are thus transformed in a manner that would become characteristic, if seldom predictable. The structure resembling a boat was completely invented, however: Grant remembers almost 'building' it from wood as he painted it.

In *Road Through the Wood* (1954), a circular mirror is wedged into a framework blocking a road, which winds uphill before disappearing into a cluster of trees (fig.8). The conjunction of events is uncanny; the shapes and symbols – trees, scaffolding, a mirror – recalling Nash's painting *Landscape from a Dream* (1936–8) or his sculpture *Moon Aviary* (1937). Grant's visual prompt was sunlight on the new timber of a half-built house, seen while cycling into the countryside, whose context he transformed by adding a dark wood surmounted by an impending cumulonimbus thundercloud. If he intended (as he avowedly did) to convey a sense of entering into a mystery, there is a paradoxical lack of ambiguity in the painting's execution: the diagonals and crossings of light against dark within the composition are realised with sculptural rigour. It is precisely this

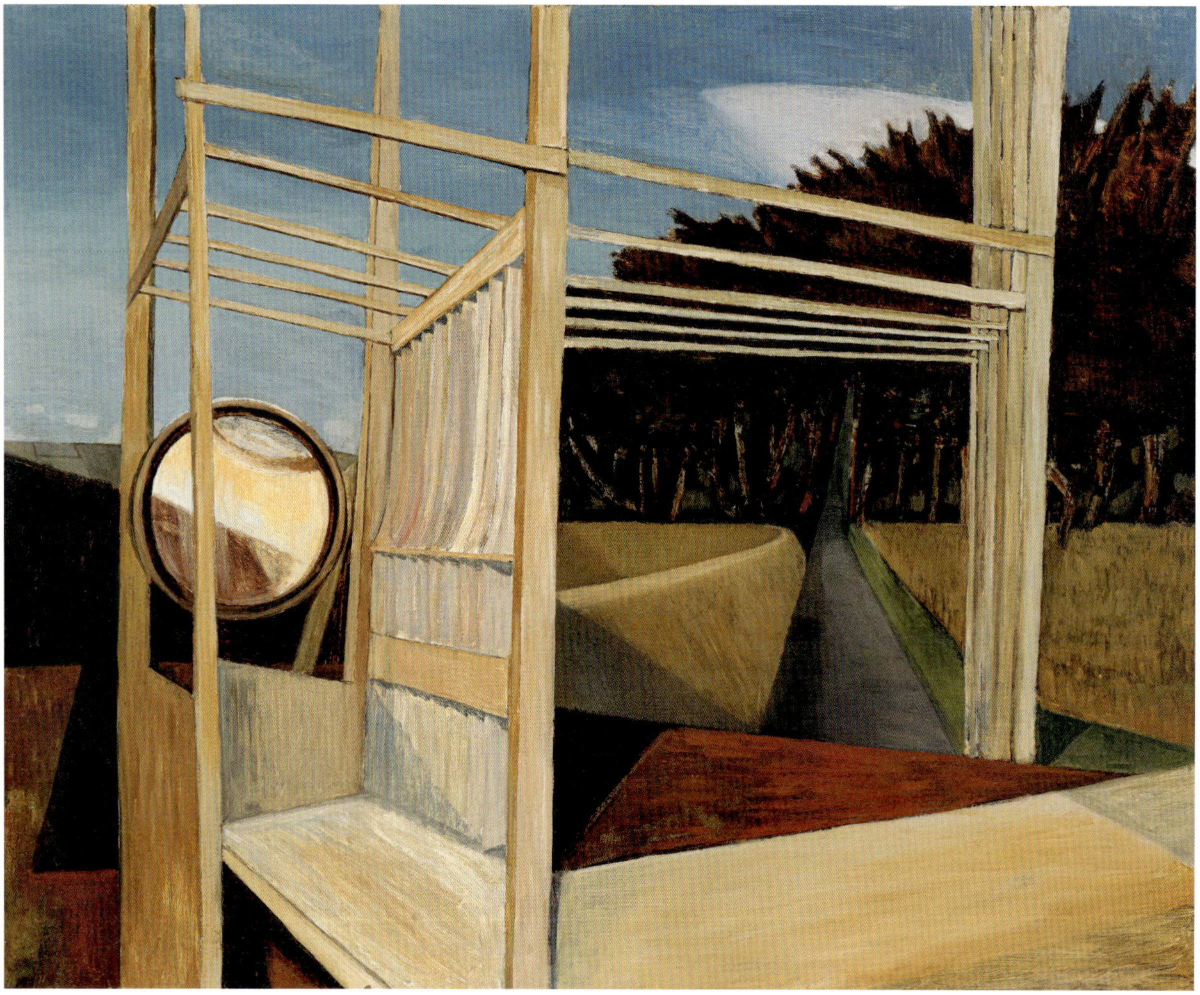

8
Road Through the Wood, 1954
Oil on board
91.4 × 121.9 cm
Beaverbrook Art Gallery,
Fredericton, Canada

strange juxtaposition of objects and circumstances, lit with the clarity of a stage set, that gives the painting such power.

Grant's work was beginning to attract attention through exhibitions such as the *Young Contemporaries* (1954), for which he acted as student chairman. In February 1954 he participated in a BBC televised discussion about the exhibition, using his paintings of Welsh and pit landscapes as illustrations, and that same month his work was discussed on the BBC's radio programme *The Critics*.[7] The selection committee for *Young Contemporaries* included William Coldstream, William Scott, L.S. Lowry, Ruskin Spear, Carel Weight and Prunella Clough, of whom Spear and Weight would become Grant's tutors at the RCA and Clough a valued mentor and friend. From the 556 works exhibited, a further selection committee consisting of Denys Sutton (critic), Louis Le Brocquy (artist), Howard Bliss (collector) and Charles Gimpel (art dealer) selected six artists to exhibit, with the sculptor Hubert Dalwood, at Gimpel Fils in August 1954. Grant, whose work had already been purchased by Bliss, was represented by four English and Welsh landscapes.[8] In spring 1955, *Road Through the Wood* was purchased from the *Daily Express Young Artists' Exhibition* by Lord Beaverbrook, thus entering his collection in Canada. Reviewing the exhibition at the New Burlington Galleries, Stephen Bone noted 'a large number of forceful canvases hung very close together', with the show overall 'full of a sort of lively gloom'.[9] Two months earlier, in March 1955, Grant's impressive first solo exhibition, *A Students Progress* [*sic*], at Bootle Art Gallery, consisted of 25 oil paintings (including *Marinescape* and *View from the Bedroom Window*), ten watercolours, numerous drawings and photographs of stage designs.

Grant had by now decided against a career in stage design. He completed his Intermediate certificate and NDD at Willesden in three years instead of four, with a place already secured to study painting at the RCA in September 1955. In the preceding summer, however, he made one of several visits to help with the archaeological dig at Verulamium, a Roman town south of St Albans. The 'car park' phase of the excavations, to investigate an area of land adjacent to the Verulamium Museum, required a large team of volunteers co-ordinated by the museum's director, John Lunn. It was through Lunn that Grant would receive a commission to paint six large mural panels for the interior of the museum.

The RCA and Mural Painting

Why did Grant apply to the RCA rather than the Slade, with its reputation for painting and drawing under the leadership of Coldstream? Answers lie in Grant's background, his already strongly formed attitude to the place of art in society and his attraction to the style of work associated with the RCA. Grant was articulate, self-reliant, had already achieved success in exhibiting and selling his work and proven his aptitude for working outside the studio. He chose window dressing because it seemed closer to art than anything else, and because the Co-op's ethos fitted with his socialist principles. In practice, it afforded little opportunity for creativity – Grant remembered a black-draped memorial for King George VI, as well as nearly suffocating while arranging a display of blankets – but he did derive a certain detached amusement in studying the power struggles between departments in what was effectively a microcosm of society. Window dressing, stage designs and murals, each to a different extent, conformed with the ideology of the RCA under the post-war leadership of Robin Darwin, who encouraged artists to earn their living in ways other than teaching. As for the style of realist painting practised there, it has been characterised by James Hyman as 'passionate, earthy and crude', in opposition to the 'intellectual, cultured and individualistic' version cultivated at the Slade.[10] Grant, who would become a friend of the realist painter, writer and critic John Berger, a lecturer at the RCA, was attracted particularly to the work of John Minton, a tutor there from 1949 to 1956.

Grant's teachers at the RCA included Minton, Weight, Spear, Colin Hayes and Kenneth Rowntree, who headed the Mural Department. While several of Grant's tutors had been involved in mural design, or had contributed large-scale paintings to the Festival of Britain's exhibition *60 Paintings for '51*, only Rowntree was actively involved with mural painting during Grant's studies, relying on assistance from past and present students to realise commissions. It was Rowntree who suggested that Grant should join the Mural Department, and who invited Grant to help execute a mural to his design (although Grant recalls involvement in this, too) for the 1958 Universal and International Exhibition in Brussels. Darwin encouraged such ventures. In 1956

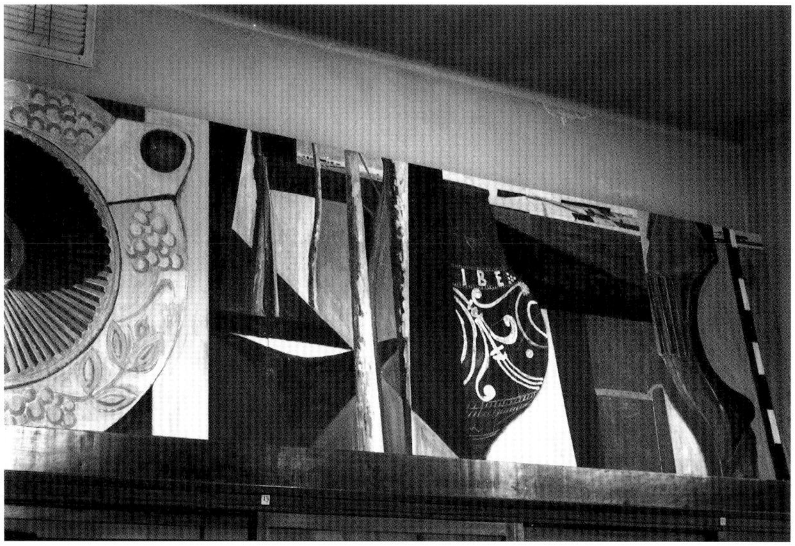

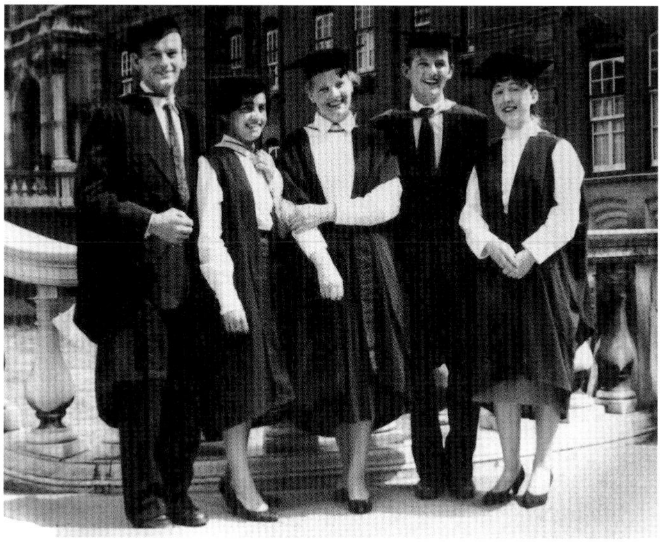

he had amalgamated the Mural and Composition departments into a single studio, to allow more space for the former (which had accommodated only a few students) and to discourage any 'artificial difference between easel and mural painting'.[11] Yet although the RCA's Annual Reports record considerable success in attracting commissions, none of Grant's exact contemporaries, who included Graham Arnold, Olwyn Bowey, William Green, Ken Howard and Sonia Lawson, pursued the medium (fig.10).

Grant positively relished working on a large scale. His designs for Verulamium depicted the Roman occupation from 25 BCE to the fifth century, with each panel fixed above a museum case displaying relevant finds. Particularly striking, for Grant, were the remains of shattered glass vases containing funerary flowers, discovered inside two lead-lined coffins. Placed in glycerine, the flowers expanded and began to float, becoming identifiable as wild rose sepals. One panel thus featured roses in a slender vase, or growing, entwined with ivy. In another, Grant depicted a serrated mortarium (used to extract juice from fruit), a piece of castor-ware inscribed 'Bibe' (Latin for 'drink'), a Kimmeridge shale table-leg and an archaeologist's striped measuring rod (fig.9). A *Guardian* review noted the murals' abstract dignity, their adherence to known data and their weaving of recurring motifs – poles, pegs, string and trenches – to sustain 'the immense perspective in time'. As the panels progressed chronologically, neutral colours yielded to warmer tones to imply the ascent and climax of the Roman civilisation.[12] The ingenuity of Grant's approach lay in its multiple depictions of time – through colour, through linear narrative (the settlement of the Ver Valley, its decay then rediscovery through archaeology), and through vertical layering. Along the top of the mural runs the horizon of a distant landscape, differentiating man's activity from the timelessness of the land. Is there any common ground with Sutherland's Festival of Britain commission, *The Origins of the Land* (1950–51), which sliced time to present the earth's interior, the ravaging effects of the elements and a menacing sense of pre-history in monumental, muralesque form? Certainly Grant knew this work as well as studies for it, which were exhibited alongside his own *Welsh Landscape* in the Arts Council's touring exhibition *Thirty Contemporary Paintings* in 1954.

Verulamium also provided the subject for a series of paintings. In *Village Landscape* (*c.*1959), an image bathed in spring sunlight, Grant reordered the scene by gathering houses and trees close behind the Roman wall where none stands in reality (fig.12). There is a telling contrast between the crisp gables

9 (left)
Panel from *The Verulamium Mural*, The Verulamium Museum, St Albans, 1957
Oil on board
120 × 730 cm (destroyed)

10 (right)
Keith Grant, Sonia Lawson, Elizabeth Keys, Ken Howard and Olwyn Bowey, after their graduation from the Royal College of Art, 1958

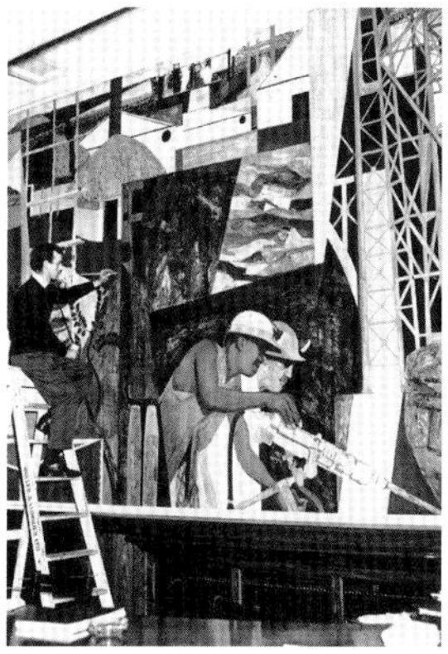

11
Keith Grant painting a mural at Rhodesia House, London, *c.*1958, photographer unknown, Royal College of Art Archive

and ragged clinker wall; between the erect measuring rods and the cushions of apple blossom; between the single column, remnant of a theatre, and the softly textured sky. Yet an insistent horizontality brings attention back to the rogue presence of the wall.

Taking the Roman wall as a constant, Grant pushed elements of the landscape towards radically different conclusions. Most contrarily, in *Verulamium Trees* (*c.*1958) he placed a tree so close to the centre of vision as almost to prompt an involuntary sidestep to look around it (fig.14). The three nearest trees become abstract verticals, individualised by their bark yet abbreviated by the limits of the frame. The wall, meanwhile, pales to a snaggle-edged foil against the trees' foliage. And if we return, again, to *Village Landscape*, we see a mesmerising interplay between the central motifs of column and tree: the one historic, reconstructed and distant, the other living and brought decisively to the fore. With *Roman Wall, Verulamium* (1959), however, the format is upended (fig.13). The wall, clearly displaying its layers of kiln-fired tiles between flints and mortar, carves a path through the wood, whose trees suggest a recollection of Nash's paintings of Wittenham Clumps in Oxfordshire. Studied further, Grant's composition yields a strangeness of vision. An occasional blue disturbs the rhythm of the grey-brown trunks. The levels of the road and verges are disconcertingly off-kilter, the wall recalling a trench defence. Among trees to the right of the road, a dark diagonal proves impossible to decipher.

In 1958 he won a commission to create murals for Rhodesia House, in the Strand in London: a building designed by Charles Holden, originally for the British Medical Association, that achieved notoriety through the desecration of Jacob Epstein's allegedly obscene carvings. Grant's designs depicted the major tea, copper and tobacco industries of (what was then) Rhodesia and Nyasaland against a background of villages, ancient sites and landscapes (fig.11). Writing about the project two years later, he felt that although some of the painting was better than the Verulamium panels, the difficulty of expressing the mood of a country he had not visited 'inhibited the integrity of the whole scheme'.[13] Terence Mullaly, present at the unveiling, largely disagreed. Admiring innovative passages that 'recall the action painters', he concluded that the mural largely succeeded in satisfying the demands of illustration and decoration, in response to a difficult brief, 'without being hackneyed'.[14] Although Grant received a first-class diploma and Silver Medal at the 1958 RCA Convocation specifically for painting his Verulamium and Rhodesia House murals, neither work has survived.

One consequence of Darwin's restructuring of the RCA, which involved the introduction of a Graphic Design Department led by Richard Guyatt, was a highly commercial vision of 'Englishness' blending folk art, landscape and Victorian revivalism into a style typified, at worst, by nostalgia and whimsy. Encapsulated by the student magazine, *ARK*, this 'Festival of Britain' idiom spread to advertising, lithographs, book illustration and painting. Grant, who was perfectly capable of mimicking this style, did not regard it seriously, although it might be argued that there was some overlap in the figurative aspects of his Rhodesia House mural. As *ARK* evolved towards a leaner, more experimental graphic style in the later 1950s, his work was included in an article entitled 'Ten Drawings – the Sky', which took its cue from the mysterious skywriting of the word

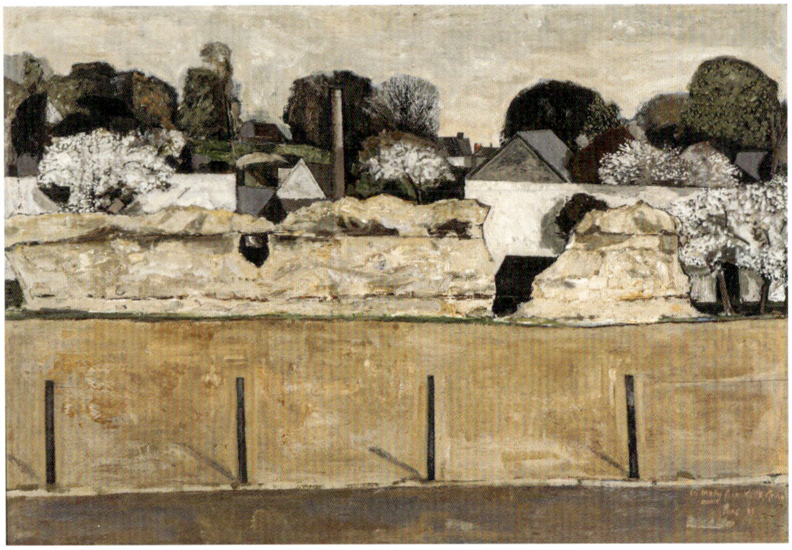

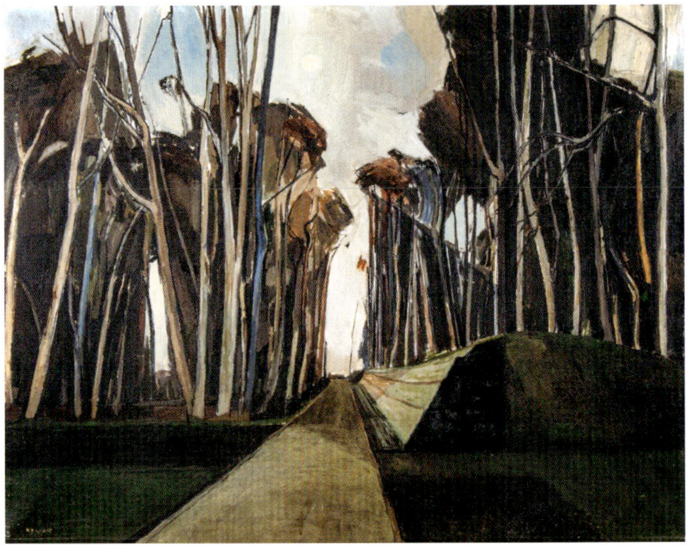

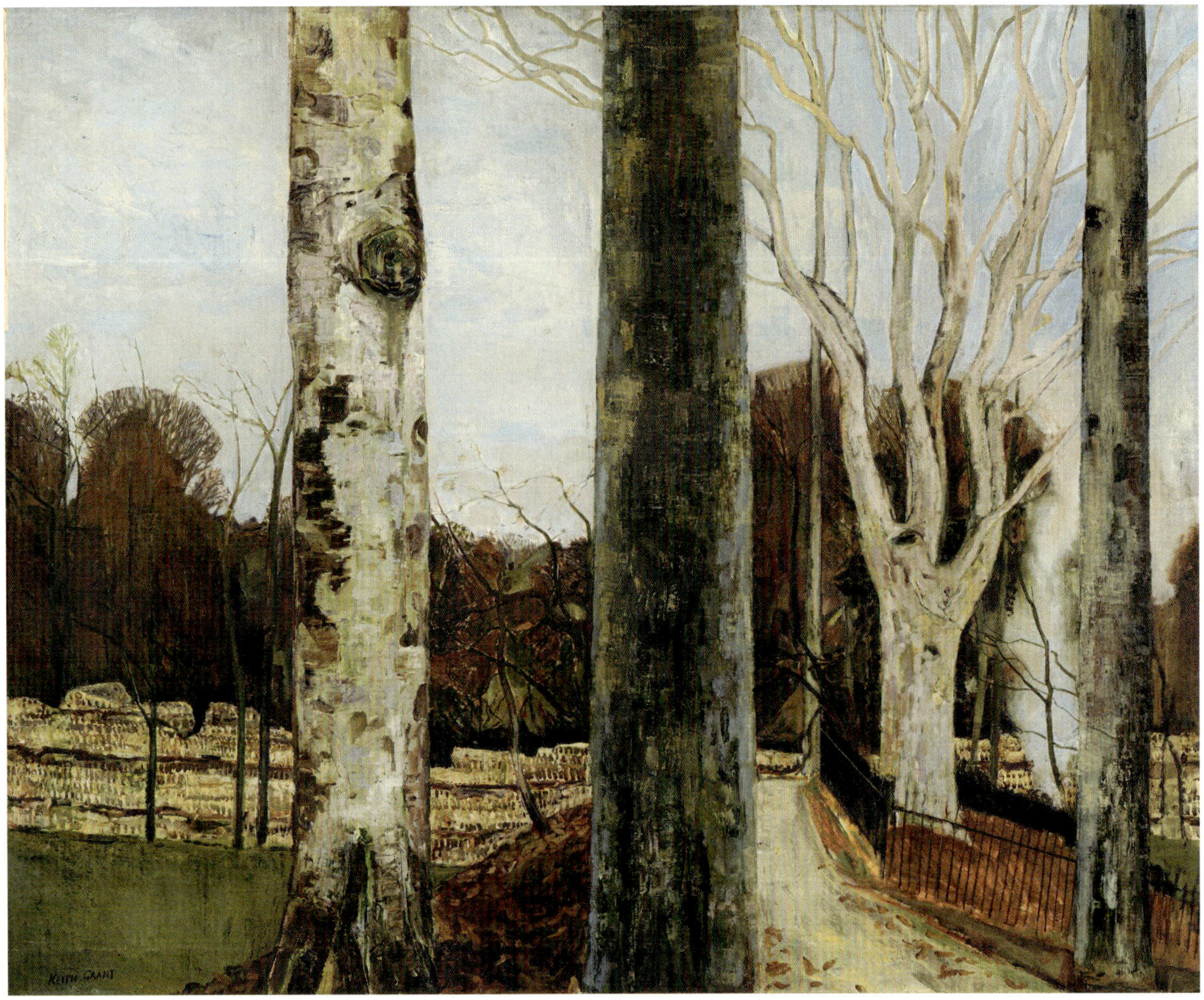

12 (above left)
Village Landscape, *c.*1959
Oil on board
72 × 108 cm
Collection of the artist

13 (above right)
Roman Wall, Verulamium,
1959
Oil on canvas
68.5 × 89.5 cm
Chris Beetles Gallery,
St James's, London

14 (left)
Verulamium Trees, *c.*1958
Oil on board
101 × 126 cm
The David Game Collection,
UK

'Lexington' by a red aeroplane on the first day of autumn term in 1957. Alongside work by William Green, Derek Hyatt and Julian Trevelyan, Grant's 'Above Verulamium' was an account of a flight with Lunn, accompanied by photographs, blurred by the aeroplane's jarring, that revealed the strange geometry of the site.[15] This abstract, aerial mode would have significant consequences for Grant's vision of landscape.

One of his earliest paid assignments, however, was located squarely in the illustrative approach of the Graphic Design Department. Through Rowntree, Grant was commissioned in 1958 to create a design for the *Shell Guide to Wiltshire*, to be reproduced on wallcharts and later as the cover of the *Shell Shilling Guide*. He undertook meticulous research, compiling an album of photographs including Avebury, Silbury Hill and the Ridgeway. From these, he devised a composition combining Avebury's standing stones, the White Horse at Westbury, a tractor, thatched cottage, a profusion of elderflower, poppies and white cranesbill, and a carved bust of Sir Christopher Wren, who was born at East Knoyle in Wiltshire (fig.15). Grant made further designs for Shell in the early 1960s, depicting Cardiganshire and Breconshire, and Shetland, each adopting a similar mode of placing symbols within the landscape. Although his contributions stand in a long line of work by eminent artists – for instance John and Paul Nash, John Piper, Cedric Morris, Edward McKnight Kauffer, Tristram Hillier and Graham Sutherland, as part of a history of advertising that continues to receive increasing attention[16] – Grant prefers to disregard his Shell designs as 'illustration'. They do, however, fulfil the brief perfectly: as bright, attractive and educational interpretations of their subject.

Grant first encountered the neolithic site of Avebury in 1956, through reading Jacquetta Hawkes's *A Land* (1951), published to coincide with the Festival of Britain to which Hawkes was archaeological adviser. *A Land* was envisaged as a popular introduction to geology and archaeology. Juxtaposing images of fossils, maps, rock formations and reproductions of work by Constable, Ben Nicholson and Henry Moore with a text alive with its own visual imagery, it proved particularly inspirational to artists and writers. Hawkes takes the reader back to the origins of the sarsen stones at Avebury: the hardest fragments of a layer once covering the chalk downs, quarried by water, frost and wind, shaped by stone mauls and antler wedges, shifted and ordered into circles and avenues of sacred significance.

Seeing Avebury in 1925 had so impressed Paul Nash that thereafter he 'hunted' stones. Their quiet, antithetical presence in the landscape spurred *plein-air* photographs, still lifes of flints and paintings such as *Equivalents for the Megaliths* (1935), in which he stripped the stones of their antiquity to focus simply on their form, grouped within space. Grant made at least three paintings of Avebury in 1958, all of which emphasise the stones' monumentality by proximity. Two show sarsens in front of houses or with the landscape spreading towards Silbury Hill. A third brings the stones so close as to leave space only for roofs, treetops and a thin strip of hills and sky (fig.16). This scale encourages a loose-brushed technique, rendering the craggy, lichen-textured surfaces of the stones as smears of paint, some applied with a palette knife to leave ridges and knurls. The approach has a captivating spontaneity, a sense of reflecting scenes

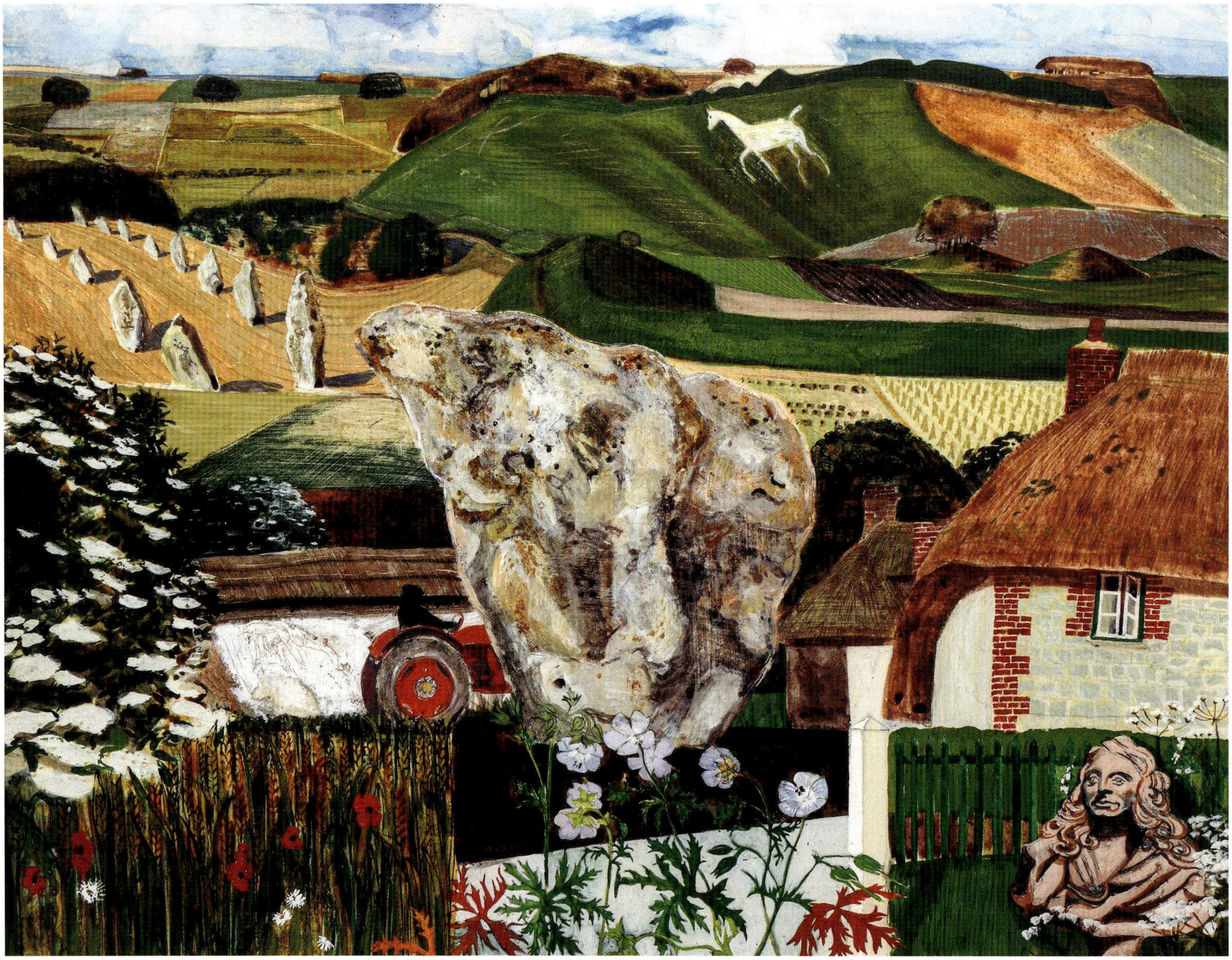

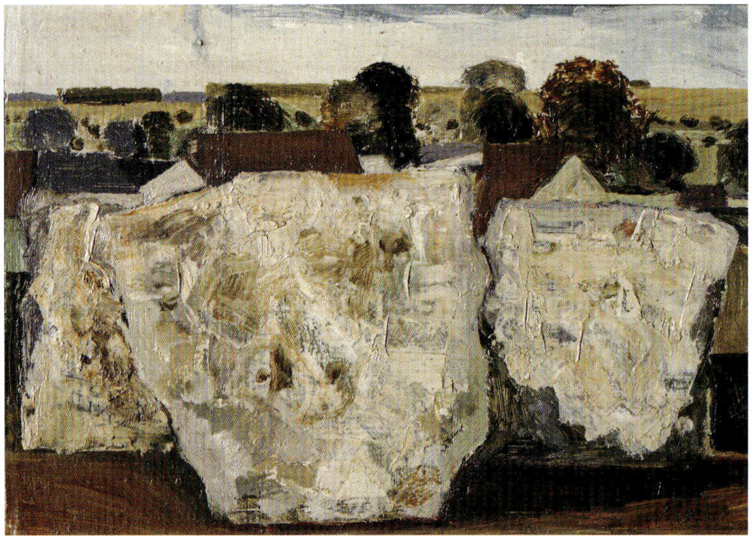

15 (above)
Design for the *Shell Guide to Wiltshire*, 1958
Watercolour and gouache with ink on paper
30 × 40.5 cm
Private Collection, UK

16 (left)
Landscape, Avebury, 1958
Oil on board
29 × 38 cm
Royal College of Art Collection, London

17
Landscape with Haystacks, Selborne, 1959
Oil on board
64 × 83.5 cm
Private Collection, UK

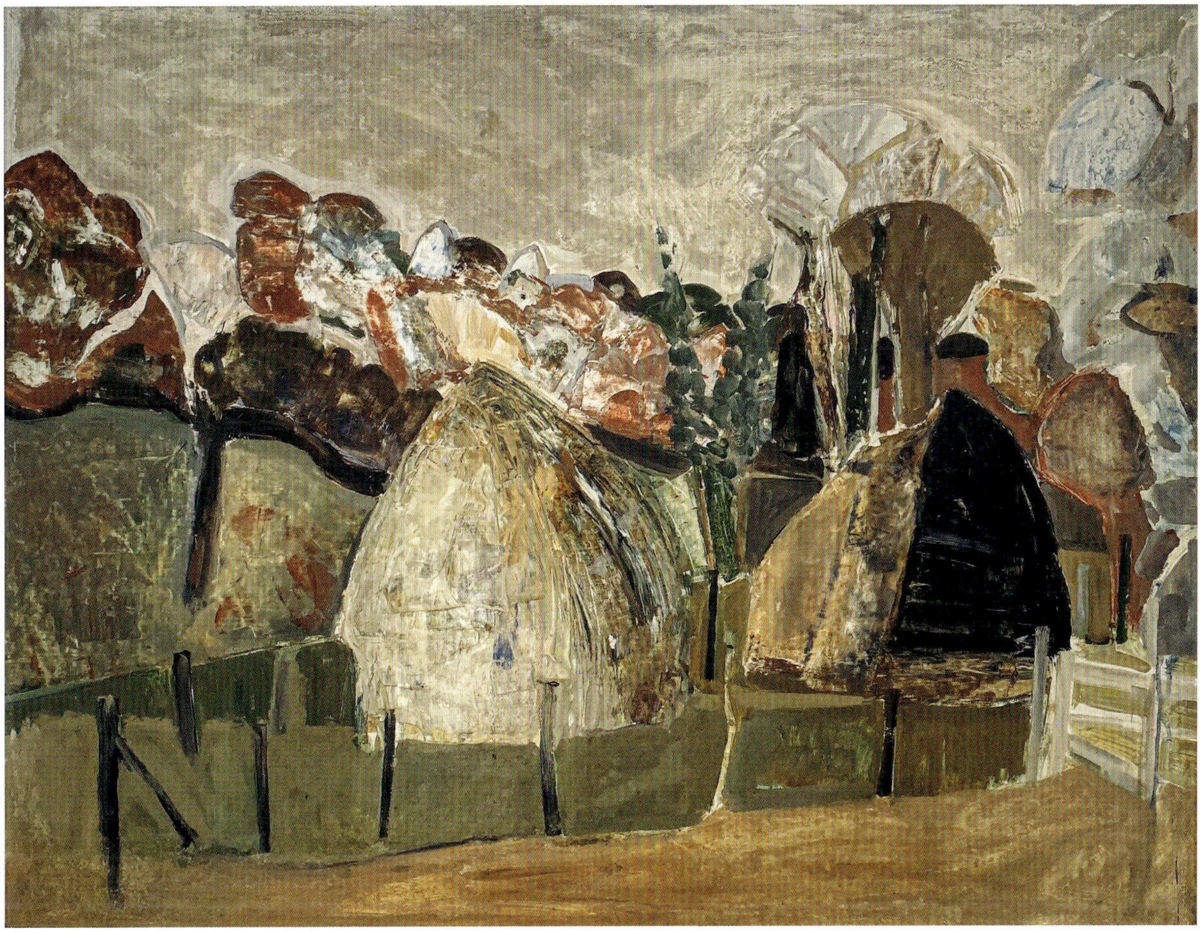

glimpsed and imprinted that is all the more powerful for its lack of documentary detail.

Literary Landscapes

Grant channelled his antiquarian interest in landscape into his third-year thesis, 'Of Men, Monuments and Myths' (1958), which began with a study of Avebury, its pioneering investigator, the Reverend William Stukeley (1687–1765), and a history of the druids. He was deeply interested in writing as a means of exploring landscape. Thomas Hardy's novels were one particular inspiration; another was Gilbert White's *The Natural History and Antiquities of Selborne* (1789), which he first read at Willesden. With two former students also from Willesden, Valerie Owen, whom he married in 1956, and Gerald Whybrow, Grant began to explore literary landscapes that would form his first series of paintings after leaving the RCA.

Grant documented these works through black and white photographs, listing details of their sale and exhibition history and often also their sources. *A Shropshire Idyll* (1959) acknowledges the influence of A.E. Housman's poetry while containing two figures identified as Sue and Jude, from Hardy's *Jude the Obscure*, on their walk from the register office. *Dorchester "Moonlight"* (1959) draws its imagery from the landscape of Dorchester-on-Thames, Oxfordshire, and its mood from a poem by Walter de la Mare, while *The Dark Wood, Dorchester* (1959), purchased by Sir Kenneth Clark, originates from a description in D.H. Lawrence's *The White Peacock*.

The coloration of these works could be unexpected. *Blue Cloud* (1959), for instance, recasts the Wiltshire landscape in blue and russet, Silbury Hill being the only feature to retain its original green. Some of the trees within it are goblet-shaped. Others, taking the form of a leaf, embody the principle of fractal geometry that Grant would return to time and again when structuring his compositions: a detail that when repeated or enlarged signifies the whole.

On leaving the RCA, Grant took a teaching post in the painting department at Kingston School of Art, from where he began to direct his students to the New Art Centre as a possible venue to exhibit their work. Founded by Madeleine Grand and Caryl Whinnery in 1958 as a charity to support emerging artists, the New Art Centre, at 41 Sloane Street, Belgravia, numbered among its trustees Kenneth Clark, Robin Darwin and John Sainsbury. Soon the gallery enquired after Grant's own work, initiating a relationship that would last until the mid-1960s. *Landscape with Haystacks, Selborne* (1959) was shown at the Royal Academy's *Summer Exhibition*, then in September at the New Art Centre (fig.17). Inspired by White's *Natural History* and Grant's own visits to Selborne, the painting suggests a pre-mechanised landscape. Its colours are muted, the receding landscape unruly with trees and hedgerows. To the fore, human intervention orders the composition: hay, raked and pitched into gently peaked stacks, is protected by a fenced enclosure.

The Dorset Mural

Grant's concentration on landscape, meanwhile, was gathering strength from a new direction. Travelling to Norway for the first time, in 1957, he discovered an elemental, expansive topography. On a second visit in 1960–61, he studied Edvard Munch's mural paintings for the University Assembly Hall in Oslo (begun in 1910), which are dominated by a sunrise over a fjord and rocks. At the centre of *The Sun* is a searing white disc, from which radiate splinters of colour, prismatically transmitting rainbows of red, yellow, blue, green and magenta across the landscape. Grant mentally superimposed Munch's imagery onto a landscape familiar from the Dorset coast, and when the opportunity arose to realise it on a large scale he seized the chance. The view was one seen from the house of Caryl Whinnery and her husband, the artist John Hubbard.

An undated sketch shows the sun cradled in a cleft between rocks, the landscape intensified as blocks of colour. When Grant began the mural, however, he altered his approach. A black and white photograph shows him roughing out the composition, standing precariously on a chair, dwarfed by the scale of the canvas (fig.19). What becomes apparent, immediately, is the fluidity of approach. The linear mapping is supple, and already there is evidence of the dripping that would characterise the finished work.

Reviewed in an exhibition at the New Art Centre, shortly after its completion,

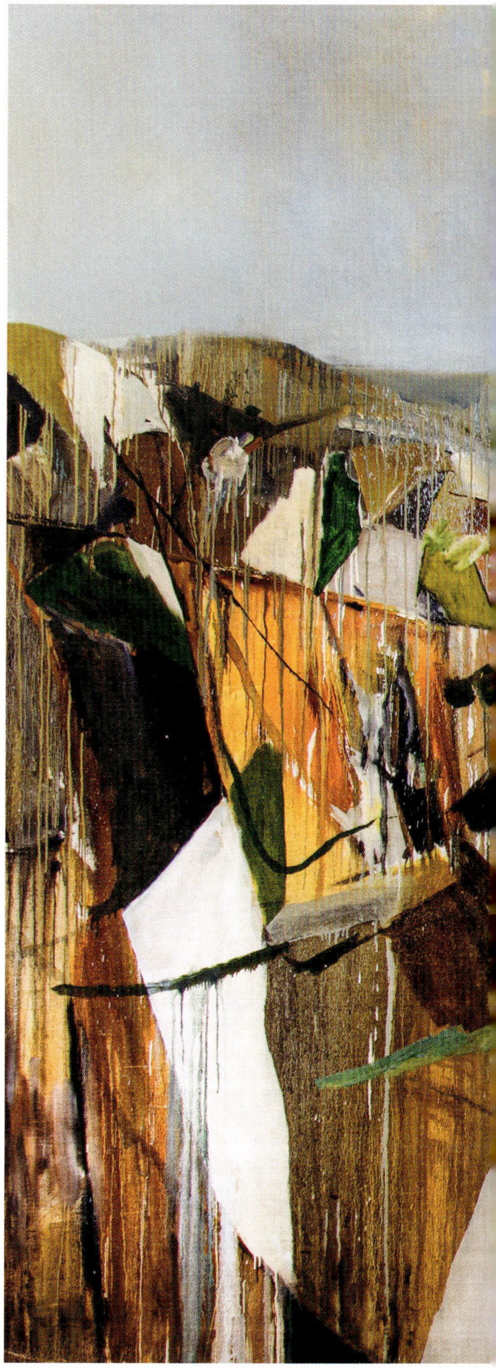

18
The Dorset Mural, 1962,
restored 2019
Oil on canvas
246 × 411 cm
Chris Beetles Gallery,
St James's, London

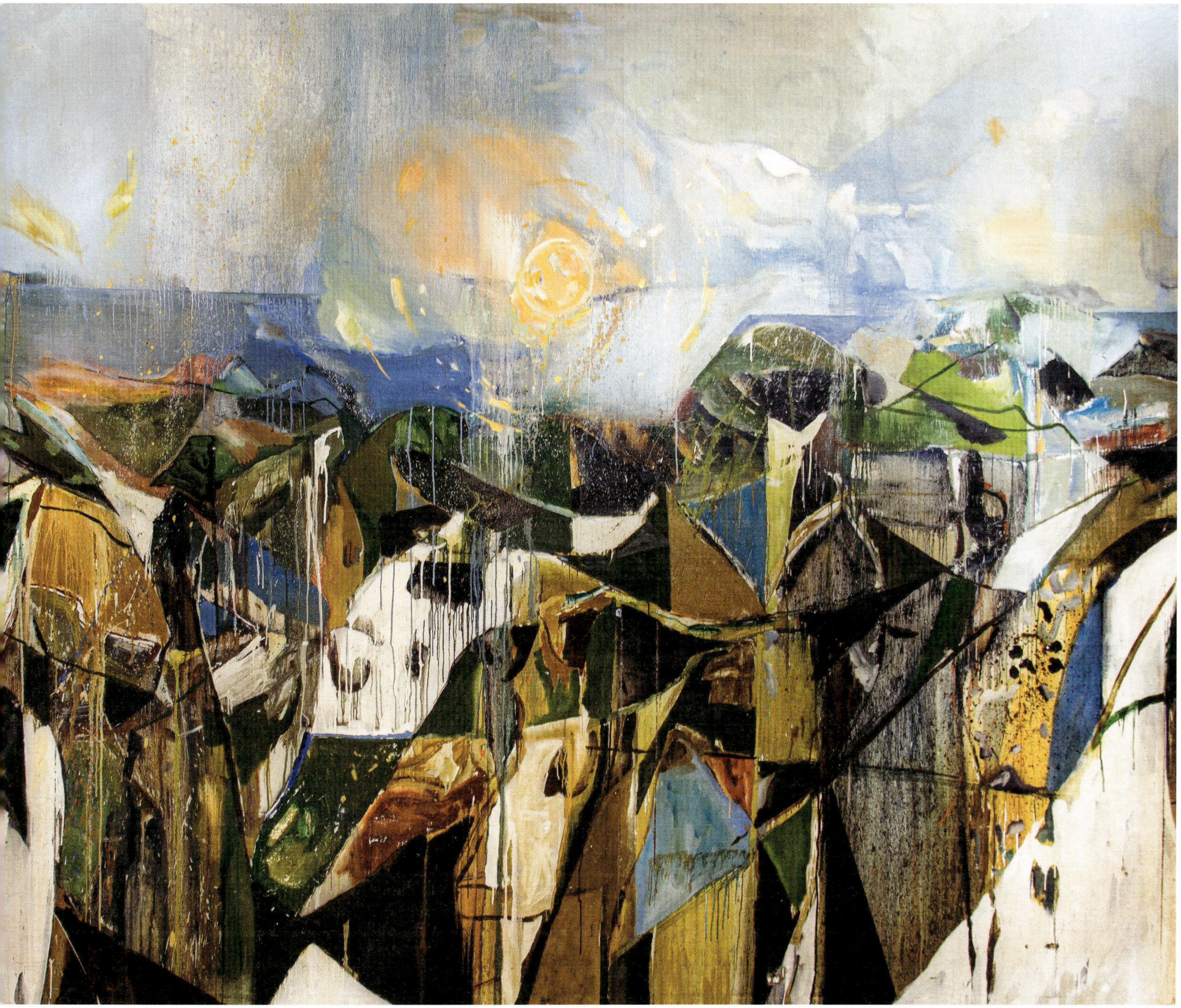

The Dorset Mural (1962) was described as 'a notable achievement, abstract in character, but full of visual incident, containing beautiful passages of colour and contriving also to convey much of local feeling'.[17] It depicts the sun rising over the sea at Swyre; to the left, the backbone of Portland stretches over the horizon (fig.18). The radical shift in style, even taking into account the scale of the painting, prompts questions. What had Grant been looking at? One obvious answer is Abstract Expressionism, following the small but much-discussed selection of works in the Tate Gallery's *Modern Art in the United States* (1956). Yet, as Margaret Garlake has noted, the paintings exhibited – by Mark Rothko, Jackson Pollock, Willem de Kooning, Robert Motherwell and Franz Kline – offered not so much a new direction to British artists, but a confirmation and a critical context for changes already underway.[18] Among the new works that would transform the prospects of British landscape art were the gliding paintings of Peter Lanyon and garden series by Patrick Heron, paintings created in defiance of the shadow cast by Kenneth Clark's indictment of a genre without future.

Clark based his death-knell upon a belief that the conditions 'in which great landscape painting grew up, no longer exist, and are not likely for some time to recur'.[19] His reservations – which were numerous – related to modernism's incompatibility with landscape, the threat to British tradition from continental influences ('one could not imagine Constable on the Riviera'),[20] and his concern over the disappearance of a human scale in painting, whereby a thistle might assume monstrous proportions (Sutherland) or the microscopic become a world view (Paul Klee). These tendencies, viewed less fearfully, could be seen as reinvigorating landscape depiction, particularly when allied to phenomenological approaches, multiple viewpoints or the rebalancing of abstraction versus literal representation, in paintings by William Gear, Terry Frost, Ivon Hitchens, Alan Reynolds, Lanyon or Heron. Reynolds's *Farm Buildings, A View* (1958), for instance, segments the composition through a series of watercolour washes to suggest a periodisation of time, slicing the landscape into irregular, geometrical forms. In Lanyon's *Airscape* (1961), the viewpoint is literally within the composition, the enveloping stratosphere conveyed by loaded brushstrokes, thin trails of paint, mutable washes. Lanyon ascribed a narrative to his imagery: 'a spiral current on the left, quiet air in the middle, and stormy weather conditions – an approaching rainstorm – on the right'. Out of range, below, was the landscape of St Agnes in Cornwall. A specific trigger for the painting was the act of disturbing a nesting bird when flying over a cliff. Such was the range of experience – 'from the immediate to the historical' – that Lanyon sought to include.[21]

While *The Dorset Mural* was among the earliest of Grant's paintings to evince a distinctly individual style, it is important to contextualise it within these shifts. Grant acknowledges the importance of Lanyon, while remaining unsure whether his work might have influenced him at the time. At the very least, an exploration of parallel strategies can be detected. The effect of sunrise is conveyed through dripped paint, bleeding one colour into another across vaporous washes, condensing downwards. Although there is a definite vertical–horizontal orientation to the composition, the viewpoint is unclearly defined. Standing in front of such a large work, the viewer looks upwards to the sun and is

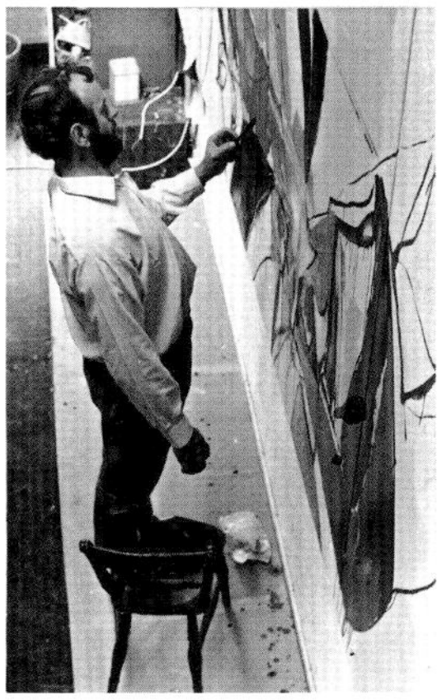

19
Keith Grant painting *The Dorset Mural*, c.1962, photographer unknown, archive of the artist

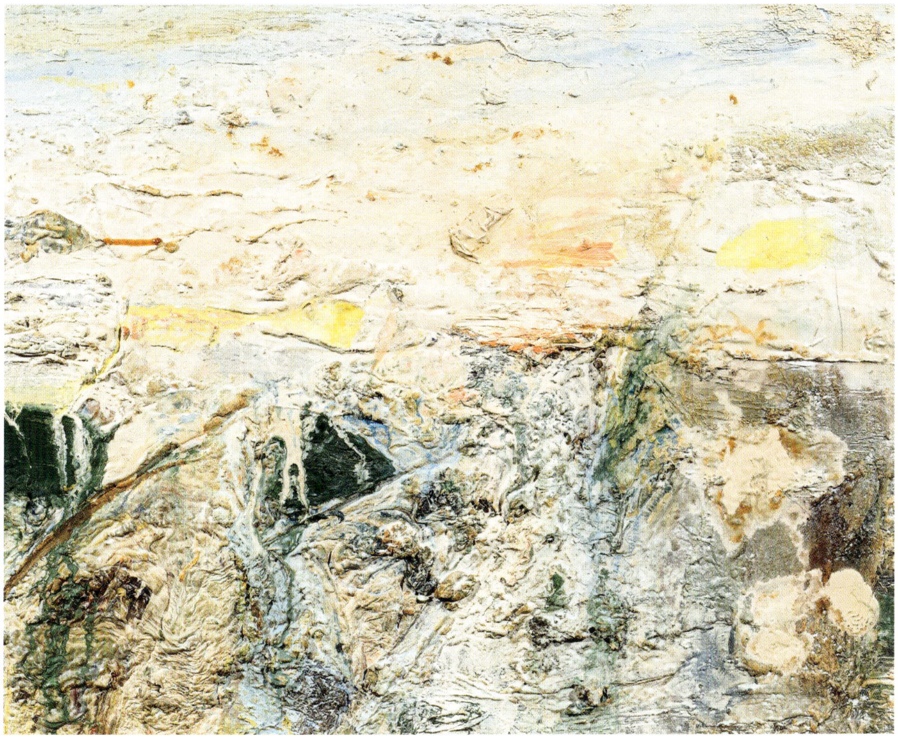

20
Morning near Vereux, *c.*1963
Oil on canvas
44 × 54.5 cm
Alfred East Art Gallery, North Northamptonshire Council

overwhelmed by rocks brought unfeasibly close to the picture plane.

In the six years since leaving the RCA, Grant had travelled extensively, taught at Kingston, Goldsmiths and Hornsey, acquired his first studio and, divorced in 1963 from Valerie, had married Gisèle Djouadi, whom he met while she was working in London. Grant was now living at the Abbey Art Centre in New Barnet, Hertfordshire: an artists' colony established in 1947 by William Ohly as a non-profit organisation with an attached ethnographic museum. In 1942, Ohly had opened the Berkeley Galleries, close to Gimpel Fils in Davies Street, specialising in non-western art, contemporary British painting, sculpture and studio pottery. Henry Moore, who exhibited there, was among artists including F.N. Souza and Hans Coper who visited the Abbey Art Centre to see Ohly's ethnographic collection. It was a vibrant place to live. Several artists arrived from Australia; other early residents included the painter Alan Davie, then focusing on making jewellery, and the sculptor Peter King, who set up a foundry to cast his own work. Among those whom Grant met were the émigré German filmmaker Carl Koch and his wife, the animator Lotte Reiniger.

In early 1964, Grant's solo exhibition at the New Art Centre demonstrated the confident direction his work had taken. Focusing on paintings of the sea, rocks and elements at different seasons and times of the day, it included several works related to *The Dorset Mural*, in which waves break or the coast unfolds, panoramically, across triptychs. A new feature of these compositions was the use of impasto, creating areas of heavily encrusted texture where paint swirls or congeals. Grant used the technique to powerful effect in his seascape *Hommage to Carl Koch* (1963–4), a triptych united by a single horizon. These and other paintings were likened by the critic John Russell to seascapes by the playwright August Strindberg: thickly, glisteningly, painted.[22]

Visiting France with Gisèle, Grant stayed with her family at Vereux, a village on the River Saône, on which he based the painting *Morning near Vereux* (*c.*1963; fig.20). Its horizon is reticent, the near-abstract composition converting the landscape to molten lava. The sky thickens until it seems palpable: only the palest dawn light leavens the effect. Grant painted with such impasto for little more than a year. Although landscape remained his focus, the subject for his painting had already veered away from the historic, the pastoral and the literary towards the North.

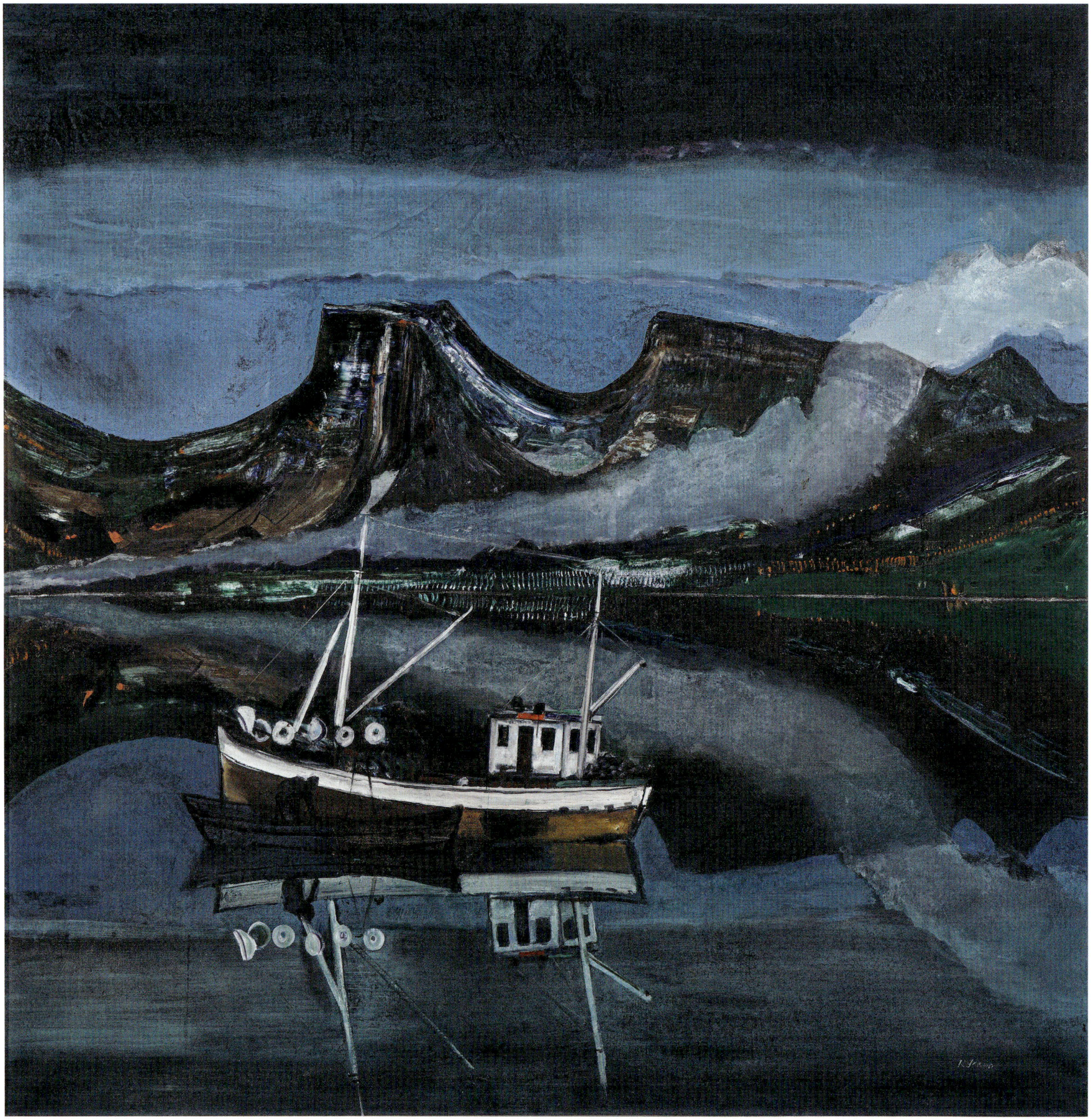

2

The North

21
Lofoten, 1971
Oil on canvas
120 × 121 cm
The David Game Collection, UK

What is North? According to Peter Davidson's *The Idea of North*, it is a point on an inner compass: an idea carried within each individual, plotted and framed according to experience and apprehension.[1] For Grant 'north' is identified most potently with Norway, although it encompasses the multiple landscapes of Iceland, Greenland and Antarctica, Scotland and the Faroe Islands. But why? In his journals, writing in 1964, Grant attributed his discovery of the North not to Wagner, or to William Morris, but to a quest to understand the point at which British painting had turned from classical subjects to the weather – 'how our island's position on the map made it an observatory of the transient rather than the timeless'. Since a child he had wondered where the weather came from, and had delighted in 'snow, pine trees and Christmas'. Travelling north in reality, he encountered glaciers, icebergs, mountains, avalanches, auroras and nightless days: 'a ground relatively unexplored' on which to base a lifetime's work.[2]

Norway

Grant's first visit to Norway in summer 1957, just before his final year at the Royal College of Art, was in the company of Gerald Whybrow: they spent two weeks in the western fjords, during which they walked and Grant photographed and sketched ideas for future work. Grant's second visit, for several months in 1960–61, was funded by a Norwegian Government Scholarship administered by the British Council. He was the first painter to win such an award. Leaving with two students from Kingston School of Art in July 1960 on a 9-metre pilot cutter, without previous experience of open-sea sailing, he became stranded on Dogger Bank for a week, drifted for three days on high seas, and was forced to turn back, sell the boat and travel by other means. When he did reach Norway, he spent one month in Oslo studying folk art and mural decoration. He then travelled to Bergen, Haugesund, Skien, Tønsberg, Lillehammer, Lom, Vaga, Trondheim, Bodø, the Lofoten Islands, Harstad and the Arctic, before buying the *Oswald*, a 15-metre motor fishing boat, to return to England with his wife, Valerie, and her brother, Nigel, who had flown to Norway to help with the voyage.

Grant had lived on a boat even while he was a student at the RCA, captivated by the sense of freedom it brought. In 1957 he purchased *Argo*, a small converted World War II landing craft, moored at Cheyne Walk, followed in 1958 by the motor cruiser

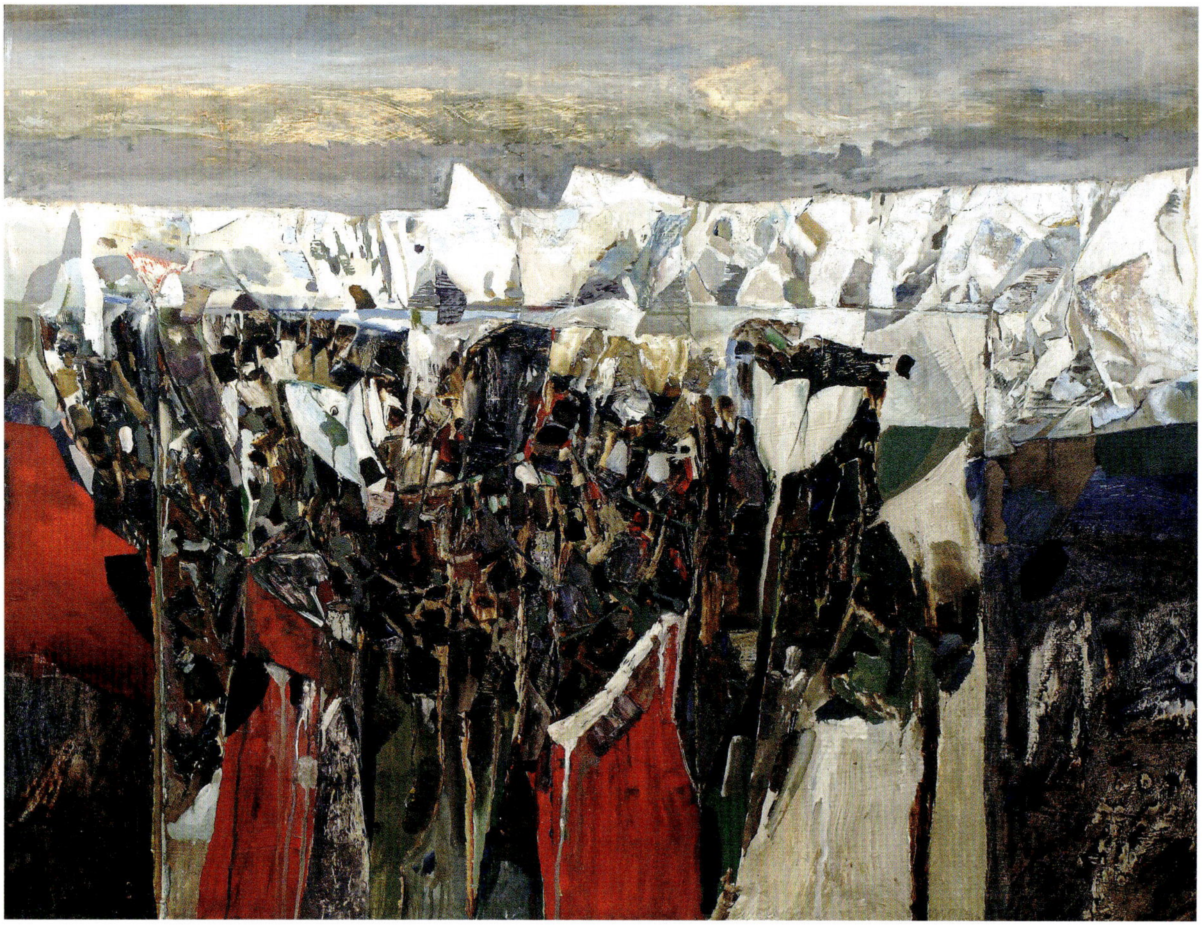

22
Landscape of a Landscape, Harstad, *c*.1961
Oil on board
91 × 122 cm
Chris Beetles Gallery, St James's, London

Anne VII, moored at Hampton Wick, Kingston upon Thames. The vessel that failed to reach Norway, *Gaumont*, built in 1906 and by 1960 past its prime, was designed by the Norwegian shipbuilder and naval architect Colin Archer, whose most famous boat, *Fram* (1892), was commanded on polar expeditions by Fridtjof Nansen and Roald Amundsen. In the summer of 1987 Grant bought *Marie of Itchenor*, a relatively new gaff-rigged vessel that rekindled his enthusiasm. As he restored the boat to peak condition, he marvelled at its aesthetic, the sensuous smell of tarred twine, lustre of varnish and polished brass, noting that 'boats are felt by some to be almost living beings'.[3] Distracting him for a time, this fascination with boats provided an intimate connection with the sea, the knowledge of which underpins many of Grant's paintings.

In *Lofoten* (1971), a water-bound landscape in north Norway, Grant included a rare depiction of himself (fig.21). Almost hidden within the shadow of the fishing boat is a black rowing craft in which Grant leans forward, silhouetted, wearing his characteristic bobble hat. The detail is easily overlooked, camouflaged by reflections and dwarfed by a landscape of mountains, funnelling cloud and a dark sky. Seemingly naïve, it is a composition of considerable power.

Paintings derived from Grant's visit to Norway in 1960–61 formed a substantial exhibition at the New Art Centre in March 1962. Roger Berthoud, critic for the *Evening Standard*, observed how their foreground detail gave way to a contrasting simplicity of mountains, glaciers and sky, finding

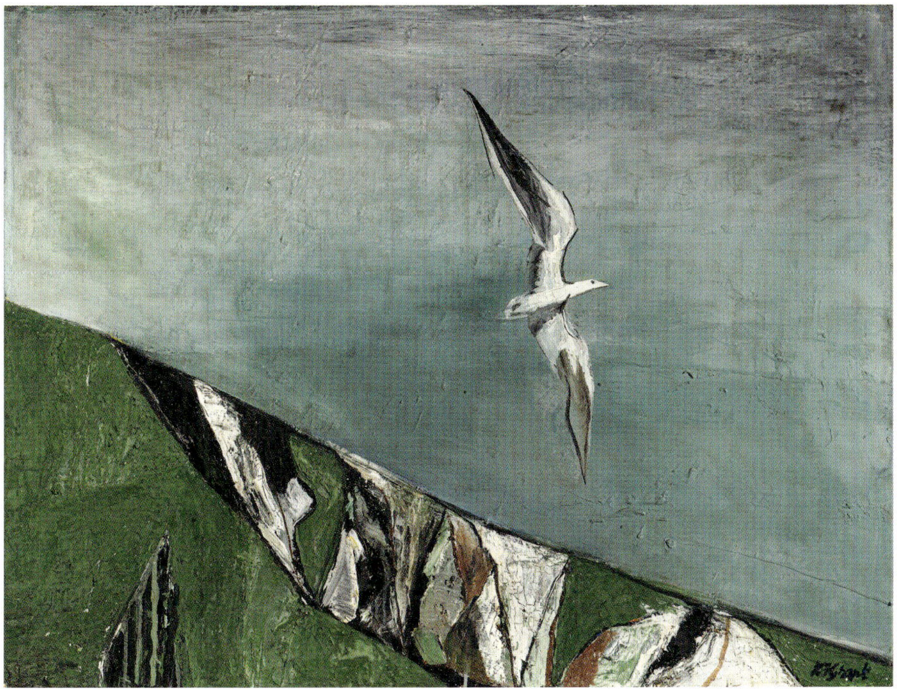

23
Gull in the North, *c.*1962
Oil on canvas
91 × 121 cm
Private Collection, UK

the overall effect 'stimulating and evocative'. His review was based on an interview with Grant, thus providing a valuable insight into the artist's views. Grant was keen to distance himself from the seduction of 'the Mediterranean' that drew Norwegian painters constantly to Italy and to a house maintained by the Norwegian Artists' Association in Paris. He maintained, furthermore, that the 'English sensibility' responds most profoundly to the scenery and colours of the North.[4] This was an attitude deep-rooted at the RCA in the years prior to his arrival. In an article entitled 'Chiefly concerning landscape', illustrated by Derrick Greaves, Edward Middleditch and Carel Weight, published in *ARK* in 1952, John E. Blake identified not only the 'intense consciousness of nature' underlying the best of English painting, but its stimulus, noting, 'we shun the hard revealing light of the Southern sun, we peer into the gloom and find mystery, the mystery of ourselves, the mystery of growing things, the strangeness of death'.[5] This dark identification of self with landscape would undoubtedly be an important facet of Grant's new work based on Norway.

Looking at *Landscape of a Landscape, Harstad* (*c.*1961), one of the largest paintings exhibited in 1962, the foreground is exquisitely tessellated, confirming Berthoud's observation of complexity ceding to simplicity (fig.22). The palette inhabits a spectrum of grey, rust-red and blue, while the composition reflects the topography of Harstad in north Norway, where splintered rocks yield to expanses of water, cliffs and broad skies. Making a pencil study, *en plein air*, Grant had become aware of the drawing merging with its subject – becoming a landscape within a landscape. The relationship recalls René Magritte's *La Condition Humaine* (1933), in which an easel painting placed before a window blends almost seamlessly with the view beyond. In *Landscape of a Landscape* Grant draws less attention to the dislocation: after all, both elements occupy the same space, without any division between interior and exterior. Yet the conceit remains intriguing. When *Landscape of a Landscape* was seriously damaged, Grant restored it, and in the process modified some details of the composition. What remains deeply satisfying, however, is the work's tonal harmony, the congruity of texture and the relationship of microcosm to macrocosm. In the inserted 'painting', a snow-white flower links to the mountains behind.

At the core of his New Art Centre exhibition in 1962 was a series of four paintings titled *Gull in the North*. Grant, like Peter Lanyon, was fascinated by watching gulls appear then vanish over the edges of cliffs. His paintings capture a split second in flight: the birds airborne or spread-winged, before they veer or plummet. While Grant's vantage point for observation was land, the grey expanse in *Gull in the North* (*c.*1962) is not sky but sea, although it might plausibly be either – such is the perspectival ambiguity (fig.23). The precise, dynamic outline of the gull and its colouring are mirrored in the strata of the rocks, creating an intentional unity between subject and context. At the time, Grant was reading *The Story of My Heart* (1883) by the 19th-century nature writer Richard Jefferies, whose space-conscious descriptions of lying on the ground, looking up to the sky or out to sea, informed paintings such as *Gull in the North*.[6]

Reading Grant's journals from 1963 onwards, earlier volumes having been destroyed, gives a stereoscopic view of the creative dilemmas he was facing. The journals provide a consistently poetic, often confessional account, tempered only rarely by revision or redaction. The paintings, meanwhile, show a continual refinement of approach. In June 1963, in one of the earliest journal entries to survive, Grant wrote, 'As a painter it is of the North that I will speak – more articulately now for I have at last contained the experience.'[7] He tends to describe this process of containment as 'formalism', denoting the abstraction of an image from its subject: an approach that would prove both ongoing and fluctuating throughout his career.

On his first visit to Norway in 1957, Grant travelled north to the western fjords, seeing Geiranger, Olden, Sandane and Briksdal. The mountain glaciers and waterfalls he encountered were reflected by large-scale oil paintings created on his return. There is an overwhelming physicality to these works, which depict a terrain visibly sculpted by ice and water to create terraces, peaks and plateaux. *Briksdal, Norway* (1959), for instance, is quasi-expressionistic in its heightened colouration, gouged surfaces and clouds depicted as knots of dense, solid matter (fig.24).[8] Nonetheless it remains largely representational. By contrast, *Landscape of a Landscape* is a tightly organised

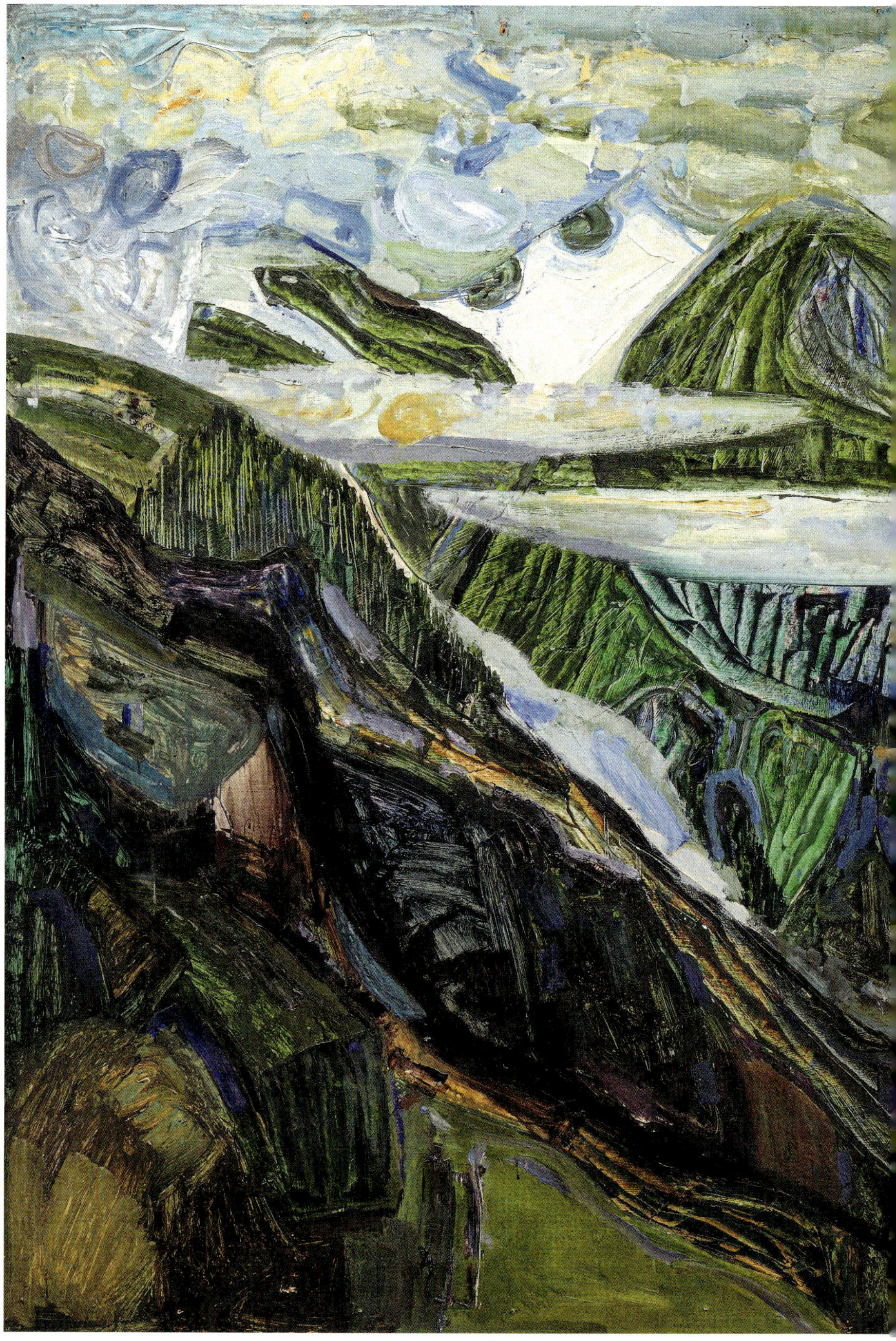

24
Briksdal, Norway, 1959
Oil on board
122 × 247 cm
Private Collection, UK

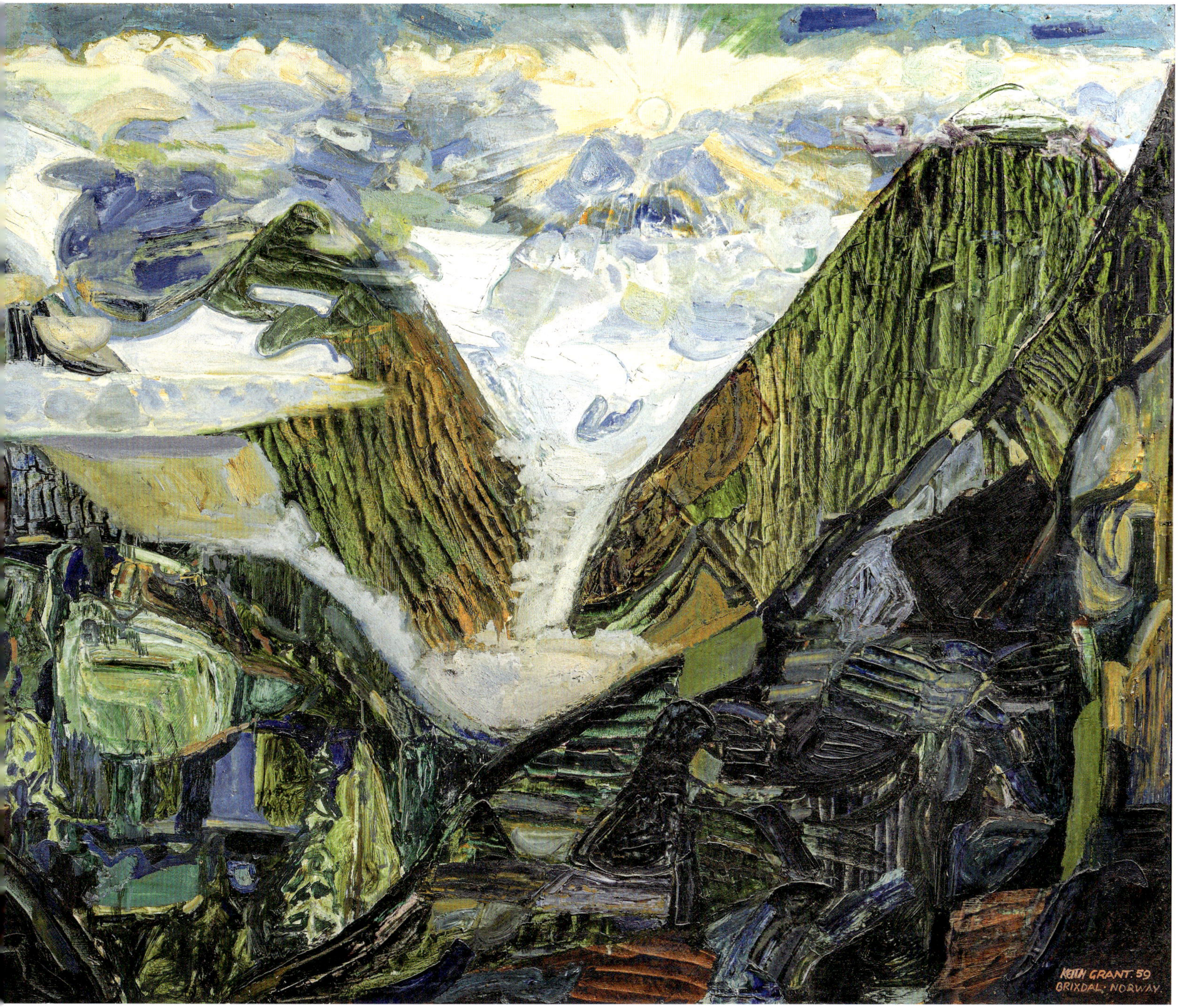

abstraction from its subject. Both are expressive of landscape, although the painting of Harstad is undeniably more 'contained'.

These paintings, in their sense of stasis and silence, embody aspects of landscape that drew Grant mesmerically towards the North. Yet these very qualities seemed to demand a counterpart. As if in acknowledgement, Grant began to circle a phenomenon that would act as a defining symbol in his work. First, and completely imaginatively, he painted *Volcano in the Sea* (1963): an impressionistic composition worked, like *Morning near Vereux* (fig.20; p.31), in a palette of dawn colours.[9] There is little in this large-scale canvas to suggest its subject. Mysterious and reticent, it makes no attempt to match the theatricality with which Joseph Wright, for instance, projected the eruption of Vesuvius upon what he actually observed in Naples in 1774.[10] Wright heightened the effects of light on dark by encircling the volcano with clouds, a just-visible moon rendering the sea glimmering.

Iceland

Grant had been encouraged to travel to Iceland by his tutor at the RCA, Colin Hayes, whose encounter with the landscape, during a wartime posting with the survey section of the Royal Engineers in 1942, aligned him with the war artists Eric Ravilious and Thomas Hennell. Ravilious, who described flying over 'mountain country that looks like craters on the moon',[11] lost his life in a failed rescue mission; Hennell was sent in 1943 as his replacement. Grant, despite having won a grant from the Icelandic Government in 1962, decided instead to travel with his future wife Gisèle to Vereux. Thus it was not until spring 1965 that he and Tony Buckingham, a friend from the Working Men's College, finally reached Iceland.

Arriving on 13 May 1965, Grant spent his first day in Reykjavik. In the National Museum he was shown a collection of watercolours by the English artist W.G. Collingwood, made in 1897 as illustrations for a travel volume about the Icelandic Saga-Steads, which struck him 'for the freshness of the colours'.[12] The following day he drove to the lava fields south-east of Reykjavik, a desert landscape punctuated by tufts of grass and white lichen under a brittle white light. There, he registered

the flow of the lava undulating like the sea . . . Caves appeared under vaults of contorted and twisted lava – red blue and orange pigments flowed from great wounds on the sides of old volcanoes – each time the eye left a particular detail the distance and the desolation so evacuated one of any feeling save that of disbelief . . . In this scene was the complete and most beautiful negation of landscape. A beauty incomprehensible without the taste of the lava-dust and the stench of rotting cod and the elixir of the salt-laden air.[13]

Experienced through all the senses, the lava fields were also as tactile as sculpture. Resembling a series of upturned bowls shattered by a weight, they were connected by narrow, deep crevices, some containing snow. This was the landscape whose sterility Grant depicted in *Lava Field* (*c.*1965) (fig.25). Taking the passage of time as a framework, he divided the canvas vertically into 'hours' marking changes to the landscape effected by light or cloud. The sequencing is relatively gentle, reflecting the slow movement

25
Lava Field, *c.*1965
Oil on canvas
122 × 122 cm
Te Papa Tongarewa Museum of New Zealand, Wellington, New Zealand

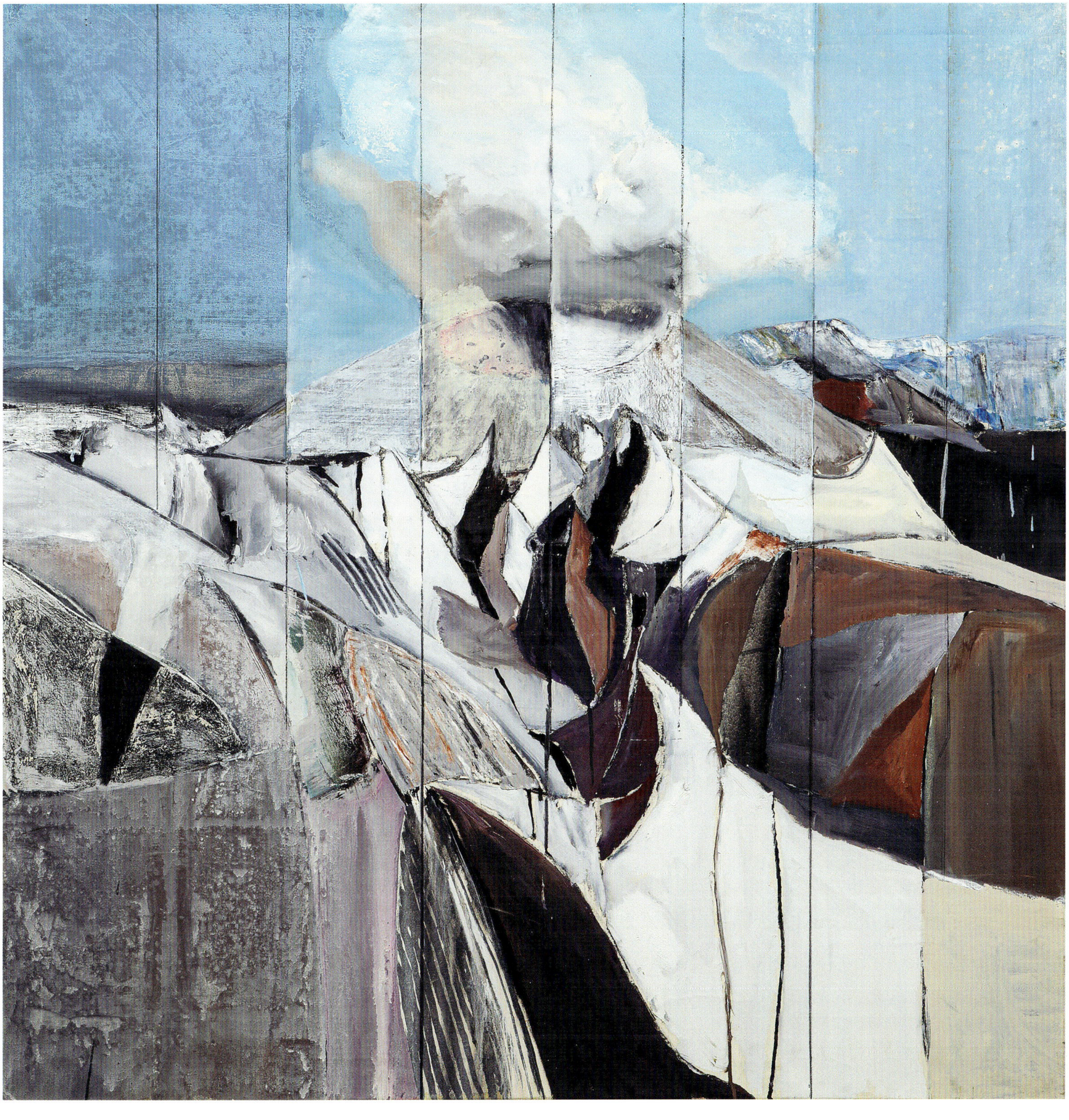

of the lava fields themselves. Yet, alerted by the divisions, the eye begins to register the ghosting of forms and mismatches within planes of colour. The sky shifts from ash-laden to clear blue; the landscape from textured grey to smooth purple, brown and black. This formal innovation was one of several new approaches evident in Grant's solo exhibition at the New Art Centre in May 1966, which consisted entirely of work derived from Iceland.

This, the most raw, elemental landscape Grant had yet encountered, drew from him extremes of emotion that overlaid and amplified his predispositions: elation, awe, loneliness, fear, sadness as well as despair. He described in terms of horror the force once required to set the lava fields in motion. There was a fragility of existence inherent in a landscape that might change catastrophically with little warning, but also a grandeur and a pent-up energy. Arriving by boat, he sailed close to the volcanic island of Surtsey, created fifteen months earlier at Iceland's southernmost point. He was startled by its size, its brooding menace and the scale of its activity, resolving that to honour the gravity of this inspiration would require an expression approaching that of 'the great religious pictures . . . a pieta of our world'.[14]

Thus, beginning work in a basement studio in Chiswick in November 1965, it was with a sense of responsibility freighted by history. Grant had witnessed skies the colour of Giotto's and Nicolas Poussin's, reflections as if through the eyes of Edvard Munch, colour-patterns recalling Alfred Manessier or Serge Poliakoff, and a mountain so fissured it resembled a citadel by Max Ernst, before wondering, finally, how Paul Nash might have responded.[15] *Lava Field* he regarded as a requiem to landscape. With *Surtsey* (*c*.1965), likewise segmented into vertical divisions, he framed the composition within a circular canvas, pulling the volcano to the fore and heightening its clouds of ash and steam against a blue sky (fig.26). This time the colours are vivid: rust through ginger, ochre, red, juxtaposed with a disquieting emerald suggesting the gradual colonisation of the island by plants. With its jewelled colours and the resonance of its tondo format, it evokes an altar painting. Indeed,

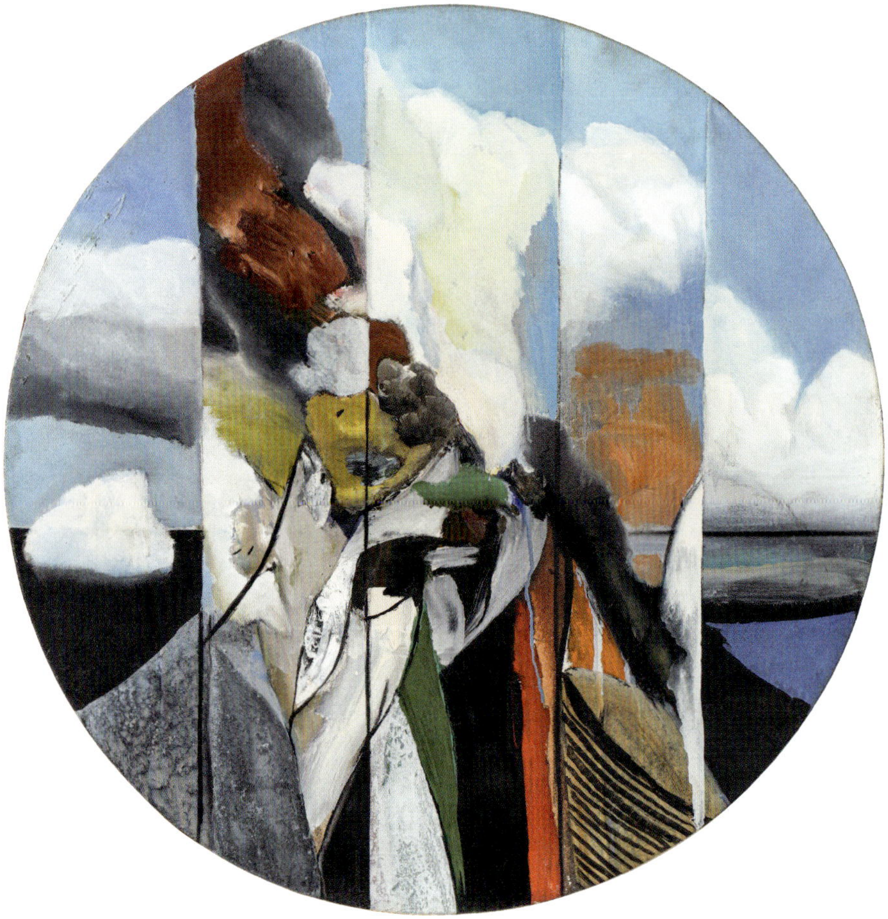

26
Surtsey, *c*.1965
Oil on canvas
91 cm diameter
The Red House Aldeburgh Collection (Britten Pears Arts), Aldeburgh

when it was purchased by Peter Pears, it was once hung in a niche in the entrance hall to The Red House in Aldeburgh, on the Suffolk coast.

If *Surtsey* plays dramatically with time, spliced into five 'hours' across which clouds drift and shape-shift, *Twenty-Four Hours of the Day, Surtsey* (*c.*1965), acquired by the Norwegian Embassy in London, not only embraced a day's complete cycle but broached for the first time the third dimension of space. A horizontal canvas is divided by outcrops of double-sided mirror glass. Walking its length, the viewer experiences 'a flickering representation of landscape whose changing colours and shadows show the passage of time throughout a day'.[16] The ploy proved contentious, some considering it tricksy. Yet for the art critic and ex-aviator Max Wykes-Joyce, its intelligent refinement of expression led him to commend Grant's exhibition 'unreservedly to all who enjoy cerebral pleasure equally with sensual in the visual arts'.[17]

What Wykes-Joyce responded to most was Grant's use of an aerial viewpoint in three of the large canvases depicting Surtsey. Hovering low above its subject, *Surtsey from the Air* (*c.*1965) superimposes the target-like circles of an aeroplane's drift-indicator at one remove from the crater, the imagery broken further by shadows, steam and the edges of crags. *Marine Volcano* (*c.*1965), surveyed from a higher vantage, presents the volcano slipping to starboard, while in *Drift Indicator (Triptych)* (*c.*1965), the highest yet, the circles of the indicator are present in only one of the panels, to suggest 'an eye freely moving in space'.[18] These works, with their oblique relation to the land below, continue the parallel with Lanyon's glider paintings. Both draw from the exhilaration of being airborne – identifying, too, with the freedom of birds in flight.

Films and Constructions

Ten days after the exhibition opened, on 13 May 1966, Grant made a sudden decision to return to Iceland to film the new eruption at Surtsey, taking with him the photographer Peter Amsden, a lecturer at Hornsey College of Art. They arrived in Reykjavik having flown through a cyclonic storm over the Atlantic in an unpressurised DC-6 last serviced ten years earlier. To explore remote areas of the landscape, Grant borrowed a Land Rover from the British Consulate and drove into the hills. The roads were little more than compressed grit on top of permafrost: staying too long in one place, the vehicle sank and had to be towed free by a passing truck with chains.[19] The Icelandic Government lent a twin-engine Bonanza, in which they circled over Surtsey. The new, nearby island of Jólnir was struggling to throw up enough ash to maintain its solidity. Engaged in a cycle of 'mushrooming explosions', before the emerald sea once more engulfed the crater, the nascent landmass was crested by arcs of steam and surrounded by drifts of pumice.[20] Grant combined the imagery with the recollection of an earlier volcanic island, Syrtlingur, also a vent from Surtsey, that had appeared and disappeared in 1965. *Syrtlingur from Surtsey* (1966) replaces the hard edges of the recent volcano paintings with veils of aqueous colour (fig.27).

Part of the purpose of the journey was to acquire footage for Jack Hazan's documentary about Camden Studios, a newly completed complex of purpose-built artists' studios designed around a communal courtyard and garden by the architect Peter Shepheard. Grant was among the original residents, who would include the designer Peggy Angus and painter Adrian Ryan. Hazan's documentary,

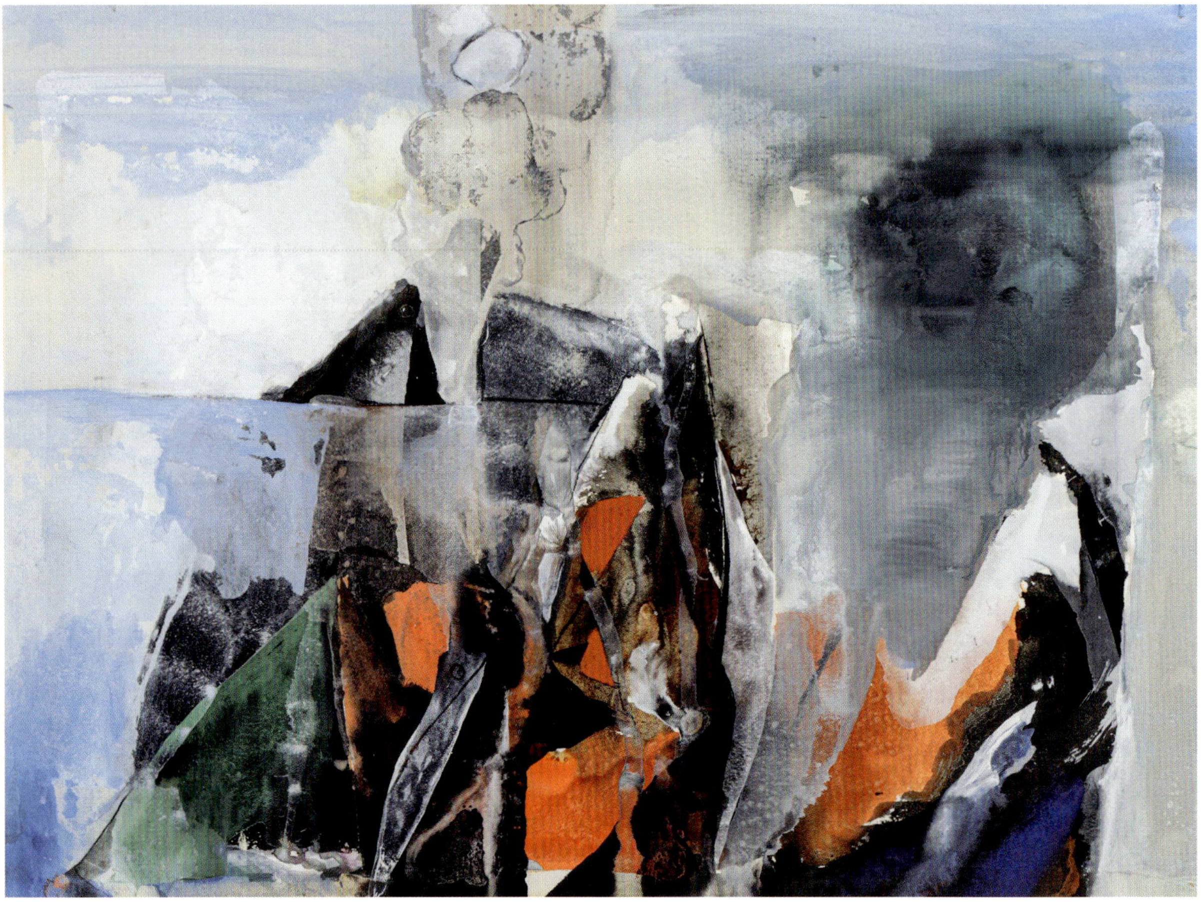

27
Syrtlingur from Surtsey, 1966,
Watercolour on paper
54.5 × 75 cm
The Hepworth Wakefield

Especially at My Time of Life (1969), focused on Grant, the sculptors Peter Peri and Peter Logan, and textile designer Natalia Marks talking about and making their work.[21] It featured the private view of Grant's exhibition at the New Art Centre in 1966, with his recent volcano paintings, aerial footage of Surtsey erupting, and Grant drawing two female models at Camden Studios, surrounded by his work. *Especially at My Time of Life*, screened at the Academy Cinema in 1969, was shot over an extended period, during which a further film about Grant took shape. *Grant North* (1969) would be Hazan's first documentary to focus on a single artist, predating by several years his best-known film, *A Bigger Splash* (1973), about David Hockney.

Both films are significant not just in preserving contemporary footage of Grant but in posing serious questions about his work. *Grant North*, which opens provocatively with a satellite dish cross-cut with images of Grant's recent constructions and a transparent rhombicuboctahedron, against the backdrop of *musique concrète*, positions Grant as an artist of the technological age. Weighed against this, however, is footage of Grant on a desolate winter beach at Bootle, rowing, scrambling across rocks, landing in a helicopter on snow and walking, away from camera, into a white-out. Hazan plays with time, reversing and rotating imagery with gentle burlesque but also serious intent. A Welsh pool is reflected in a Norwegian fjord; painted landscapes depict mountains perfectly mirrored in water. Romantic, contemporary or avant-garde? The soundtrack posits Grant as a 'traveller': an idea to which we shall return.

The constructions featured in *Grant North* resulted from Grant's visits to north Norway and Iceland,

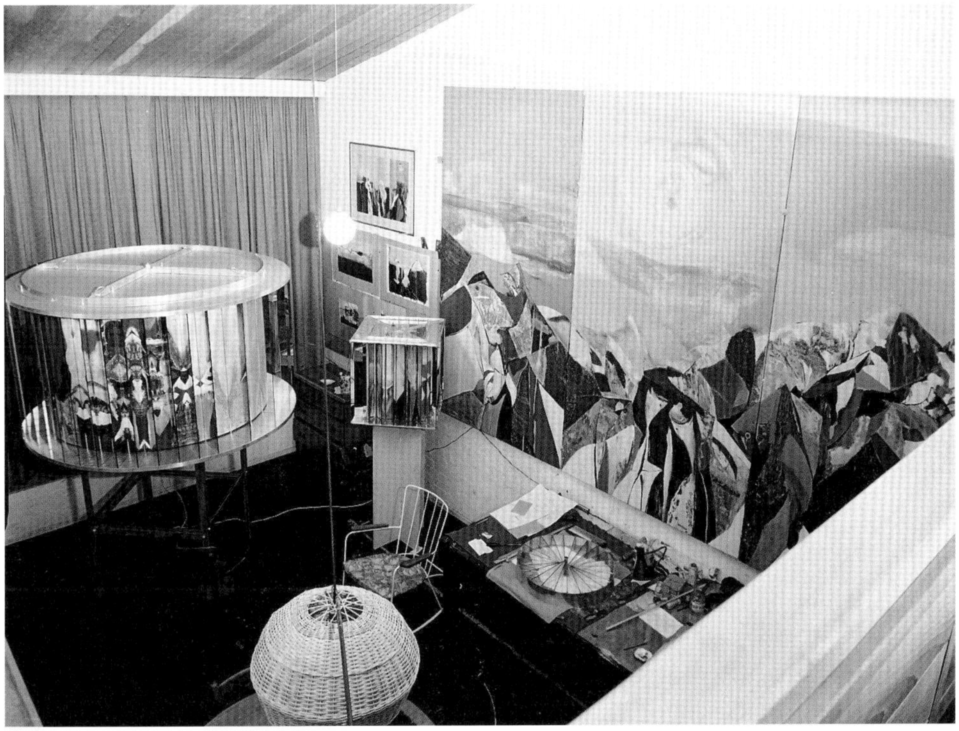

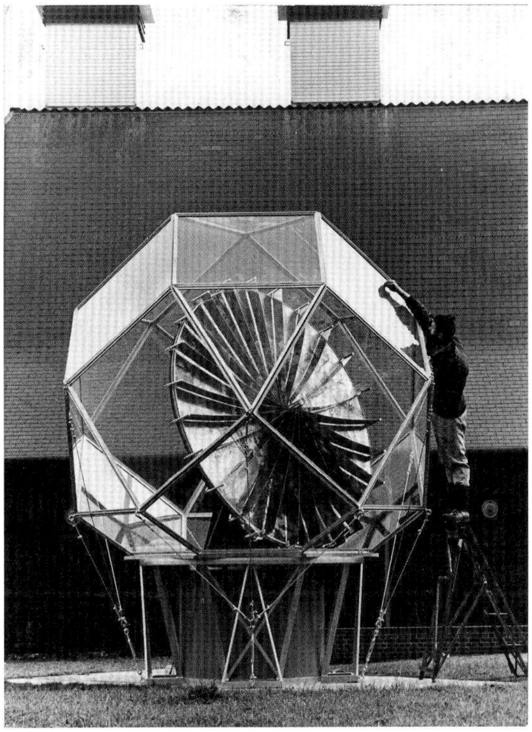

28 (left)
Keith Grant's studio, Camden Studios, London, 1967, photograph by Peter C. Amsden

29 (right)
Keith Grant working on *Earth Time Space – The North* at Snape Maltings, Suffolk, 1969, photographer unknown, archive of the artist

as attempts to recreate the shifting 'pageantry of effect' experienced near or above the Arctic Circle.[22] Beginning with the painted landscape, he had extended the genre incrementally until it became kinetic sculpture. *Twenty-Four Hours of the Day* (1967), a painting mounted onto a drum, ringed by twenty-four mirrors at right angles, was motorised to rotate slowly through a cycle from day to night, passing from white to violet to black. Purchased by Pears, and suspended in the foyer of Snape Maltings concert hall, newly opened for the Aldeburgh Festival in June 1967, it was described by Benjamin Britten as 'ravishing'.[23] The much larger *Twenty-Four Hours of the Day* (1967–8), exhibited in the City of London Festival in 1968, was installed at the Starcross School in Islington where Kathleen Mitchell, a friend of Britten and Pears, was headmistress. It is this version that features prominently in *Grant North*, where pupils candidly describe the effect of the landscape unfolding as it rotates. Evidently well versed on the work's materiality and intent, one pupil comments, 'It's a waste of time, really, because he painted a good picture then spoilt it by putting mirrors round it.'[24] The environment in which these works evolved, at Camden Studios, was captured by the photographer Peter Amsden (fig.28). On the wall is a triptych commissioned by the head of Midland Dairies, Arthur White, for his new, modernist house, The Folly, in Wolverhampton. A square construction rests on a pedestal, to the left is the large, circular *Twenty-Four Hours of the Day* and on the desk is the centrepiece of a model for the future work, *Idomeneo* (1969–70; fig.154, p.183).

Earth Time Space – The North (1967–9), the largest construction in this series, was commissioned by Britten and Pears to stand outside Snape Maltings during the 1969 Aldeburgh Festival on a site occupied previously by sculptures by Henry Moore and Barbara Hepworth (fig.29). It evolved slowly, benefiting from Pears's encouragement and financial support. In January 1969, having finished the circular canvas, on which was painted an aerial view of the Lofoten Islands, Grant wrote, 'It must create many problems.

The surface is that of the earth seen from above, and the painting is the most natural and the best I have produced. It is a patchwork like the surface of the earth I have flown over. It must affect the work I produce in future.'[25]

Grant not only set himself a complex technical challenge, but was positively courting aesthetic dilemmas to inspire further work. *Earth Time Space – The North* conflates painting with sculpture, tradition with technology, the natural with the constructed. A painted disc, fragmented by twenty-four stainless steel mirrors, rotates clockwise on a motorised turntable. Each element is predicated on time and space – the disc angled at 23 ½° (the tilt of the earth's axis), the mirrors representing the hourly points of the sun during an Arctic summer day. Yet Grant's field of reference ranges further, to the heliotropism of *convolvulus* (bindweed), William Blake's visionary 'sunflower, weary of time', radio telescopes, solar mirrors and satellites. The construction was protected by a Perspex case based upon the rhombicuboctahedron, a polyhedron drawn as a diagram by Leonardo da Vinci and seen by Grant in a portrait of the Renaissance mathematician, Luca Pacioli, where it hangs, half-filled with water, in a darkened room. Hazan took this idea and presented Grant's Perspex model rotating slowly, describing a trajectory across the night sky. In *Grant North*, key aspects of *Earth Time Space – The North* are explained and demonstrated. We see its landscape painting in detail, John Piper assisting with varnishing, and Britten and Pears finally setting the work in motion.

Although Grant's constructions are little known – the example inside Snape Maltings was destroyed by fire, the one outside irrevocably damaged by students following its relocation to Bath – they form a compelling counterpart to the exploration of landscape and time by artists considered more radical than Grant: Keith Arnatt, John Latham, Robert Smithson or Richard Long, whose interventions, happenings or journeys are preserved through a discrete legacy of film or photography. The obstacle to Grant's work being assimilated in this canon is plausibly his use of painting, tying him to a tradition he seemed less fearful to escape than keen to extend. This is where we can begin to understand him as a traveller: an artist committed to landscape, but searching restively; unsure, perhaps, of what he was seeking.

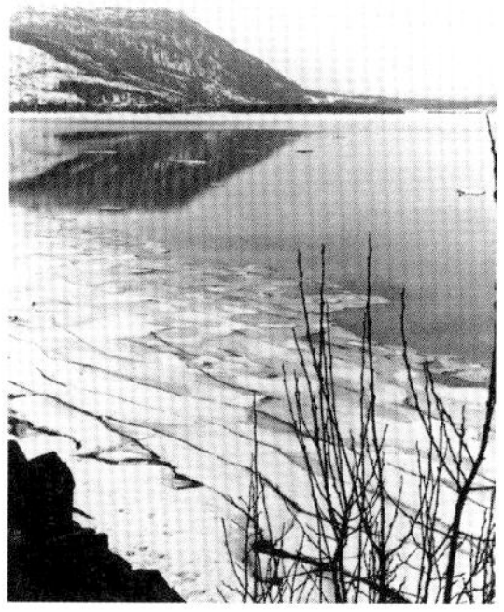

30
Landscape in north Norway, *c.*1964, photograph by Keith Grant

Mirror Reflections and *The North Lands*

The North Lands – Paintings, Grant's first exhibition with Roland, Browse and Delbanco, in January 1967, took place less than a year after his New Art Centre show. Featuring work based on Iceland and Norway, it sold well. The *Evening Standard* applauded Grant as 'a virile Nordic offshoot of the strongest tradition of British art – romantic landscape painting'.[26] Terence Mullaly acknowledged Grant's talent while remaining unconvinced by his 'abstract' landscapes and rotating construction (nothing more than 'an amusing toy'), while Bruce Laughton, who was diffident about the segmentation of landscape ('perhaps too easy a formula . . . more acceptable as mural decoration'), was intrigued by the circular construction, expanding and contracting 'with a dreamy pulsation, orgasmic in effect', but considered its mechanical ingenuity too obtrusive.[27] More sympathetically, James Burr praised Grant's emphasis on 'the remoteness and mystery of natural forces', his ability to convey landscape without

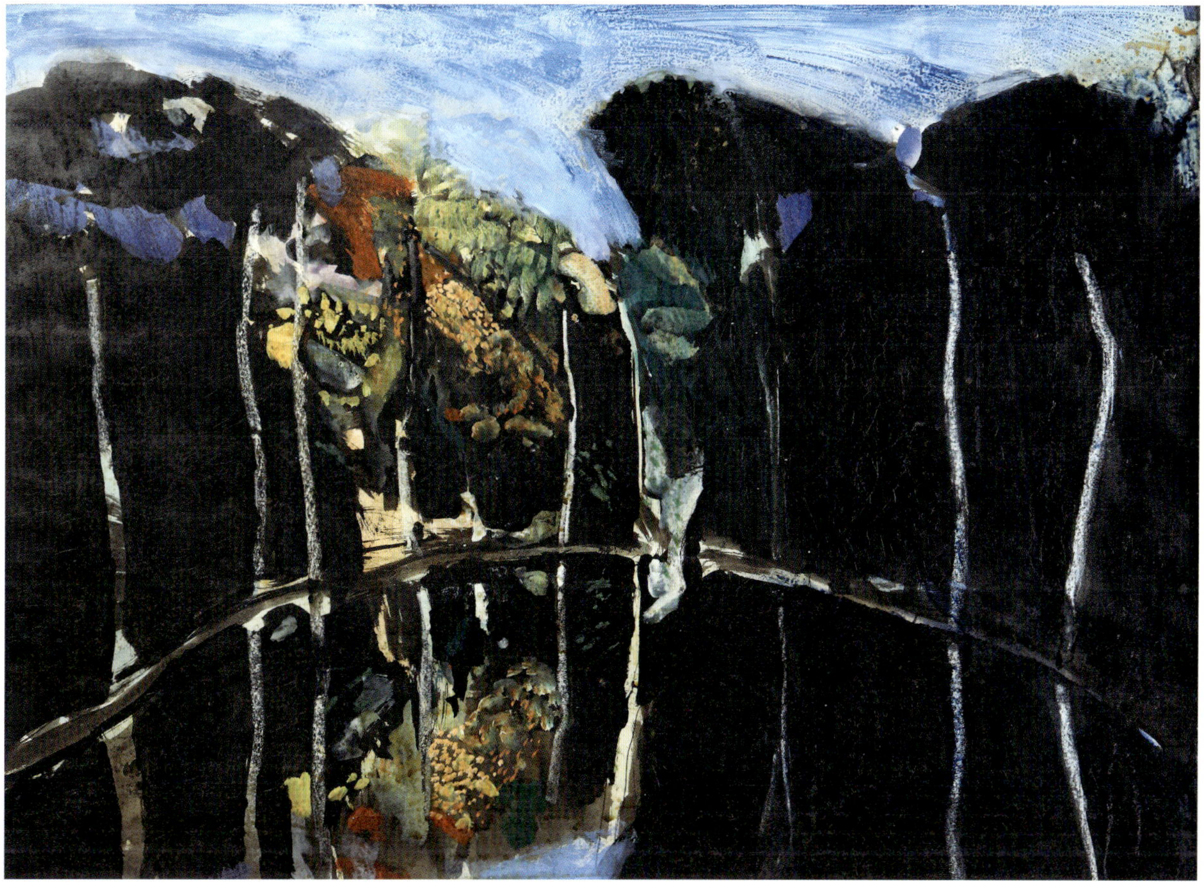

31
Northern Pool – Autumn, 1967
Gouache on paper
51.1 × 70.8 cm
The Red House Aldeburgh Collection (Britten Pears Arts), Aldeburgh

depicting it explicitly, and his 'sense of infinite space' communicated in a vital and unique way.[28]

By focusing on Grant's response to 'remoteness and mystery', Burr identified the core of the sustenance he received from the North. Landscape's visual form might be lodged in the memory, yet there was something beyond it – an intangible essence – that could prove unnervingly ephemeral. Separation from the landscape, once back at his studio in London, would manifest itself in symptoms of physical unease. Grant's journals record being unable to settle, nervous about being able to recapture or consolidate his experience. Such self-reflecting passages allow the reader to glean the artist's thoughts as he prepared to embark on new work.

In his Camden studio in May 1967, recently returned from Norway, Grant recalled photographing the sun's reflection in a forest lake, on whose surface floated twigs and insects: 'the pool became another medium in which were suspended strange light-bearing vessels, brilliant in a dark solution.'[29] Among the resulting paintings would be *Northern Pool – Autumn* (1967), showing a forest tarn at Nordmarka, north of Oslo (fig.31). Silver birches rim the water, while the landscape wraps immersively around the composition in tones of graphite, gold and emerald. The effect is fluid, dripping downwards from the loosely brushed sky into what Grant described as 'the serum of nature'.[30]

The vision of a reflected landscape, which had been set rhythmically into motion in the mirrored constructions, was beginning to formalise in Grant's compositions. Photographs he took while travelling recorded imagery that he would not copy but that might serve as a prompt for future work. A black and white photograph of north Norway, for instance, shows a snowy mountain reflected in a fjord. The lack of colour emphasises form: the smudged reflection of the land, tessellated ice gathering at the water's edge. A strong zigzag, leading downwards across the fjord to the shoreline rocks, is countered by bristling twigs in the foreground (fig.30). In the same journal entry where he described the forest pool, Grant recalled a narrow inland lake in the early morning, mirroring the surrounding slopes to create a profound 'valley of peace'.[31]

Figures in the Landscape

The human figure weaves an occasional presence through these painted landscapes, alongside a more constant practice of drawing portraits: not to commission (as would be his formal portraits), but as gifts, impromptu acts or following a creative impulse. The subject of these informal portraits is almost invariably female, and Grant has written frankly in his journals about the inspiration he derives from life drawing. From his descriptions it seems incontrovertible that the practice has both sustained his painting of landscape and distracted him, casting the role of his sitters – who might be chance acquaintances, travelling companions or as part of a longer-term relationship – as that of the problematic female 'muse'. How the figure relates to the landscape is an important aspect of Grant's work, nonetheless. It is quite unlike the example of John Piper, where a nude might become one with the landscape, absorbed in its geological structure, tone or mood of the weather. Grant's figures, informed by an eye attentive to the individual subject, have a lucidity and directness allied to his abstraction from landscape.

These issues came to the fore in the summer of 1970 as Grant focused on the 'mirror reflection' theme in landscape. He was looking intently at Henri Rousseau's *The Sleeping Gypsy* (1897), in which a lion stands over a sleeping woman, silhouetted against an arid landscape, water, mountains and a star-pierced sky. Although there is a soft unity to the colouration of Rousseau's painting, there is no blurring of definition: the curved forms of the figure, mandolin and vase are counterpointed sharply by the striped dress, instrument's strings and wooden staff. By March 1971, Grant was planning a set of '*études*' each featuring a girl in a boat, to juxtapose the transience of youth with the permanence of landscapes seen on his most recent visit to Norway.[32] One model would be Pia Khan, a young woman from Pakistan who worked at the St Pancras Library (fig.32). Seeking a unity between landscape and figure, and also between east and north, Grant focused on the 'jewel-like' colours and patterning of Pia's sari, as part of a wider fascination with the fashion and individuality of women's dress. He painted two large compositions: one of Pia standing before a reflected fjord, another a diptych comprised

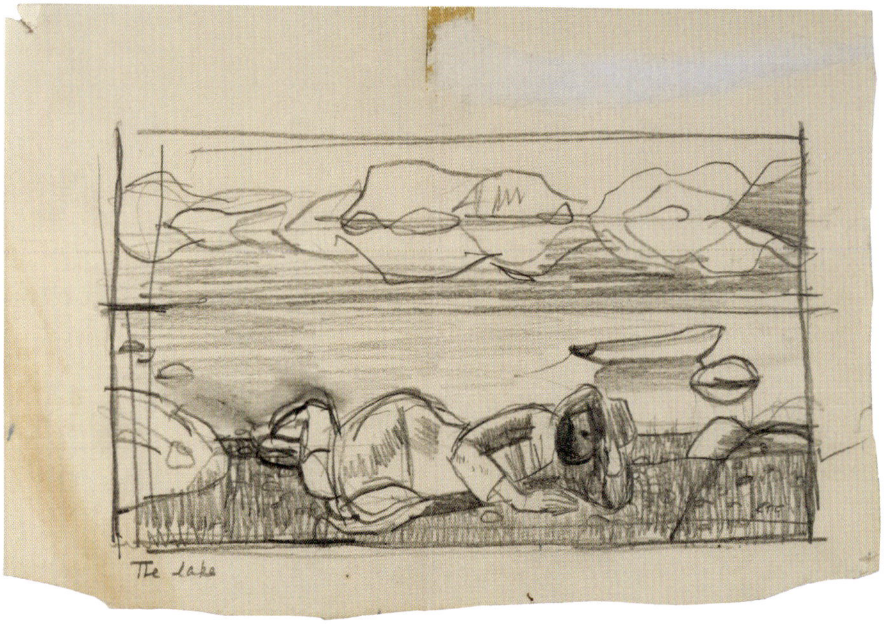

32
The Lake, 1971
Pencil on paper
16 x 24 cm
Private Collection, UK

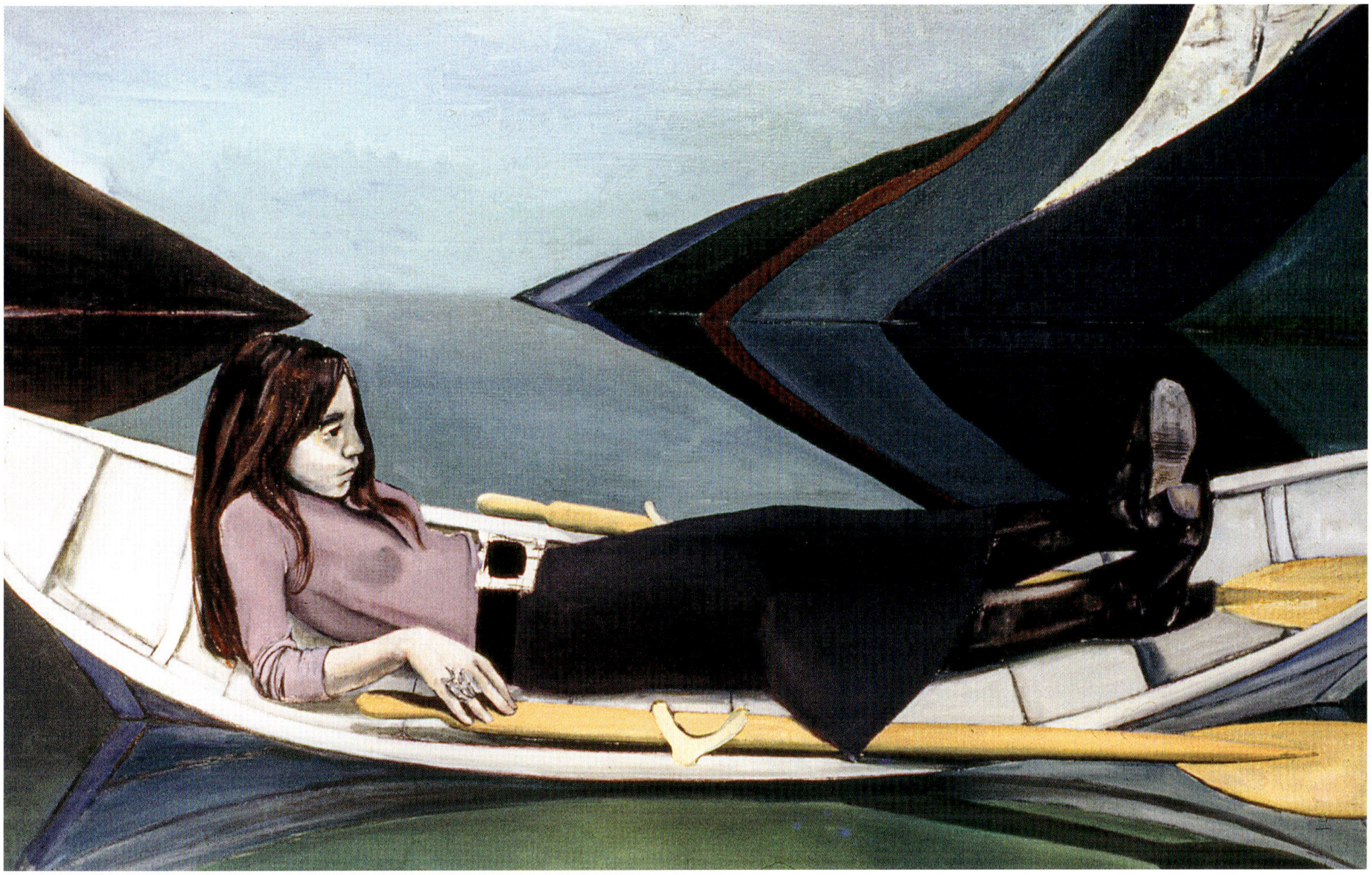

33
Cathy in a Norwegian Boat, *c.*1971
Oil on canvas
122 × 152 cm
Private Collection (location unknown)

of a fjord above a reclining figure, the landscape's profile consciously echoing the human form.

Grant had become captivated by the stylisation of Indian miniatures studied at the V&A, the British Museum and the India Office, which he described as 'essays in stillness and archaic association'.[33] In his painting of Pia, standing, this influence is unmistakable. The composition's treatment is enchanting, yet there is an almost too-conscious focus on the sari's decorative patterning, the diagonal symmetry of the figure and the reflected landscape that render it static. A painting of Catherine Ashmore, a photographer and daughter of the actress Rosalie Crutchley, is more abstract and in many ways more successful (fig.33). Grant's literary source was *Pan* (1894) by the Norwegian writer Knut Hamsun, in which the character of Edvarda, 'a fragile yet stubborn girl', represented for him the mysteriousness and transience of life.[34] The composition derived from separate sources: Cathy, wearing a sculptural ring, large buckled belt and quirky black boots from studio drawings, and the boat, mountains and fjords from sketches during a recent visit to western Norway. There is an intentional sense of the figure's intrusion, reinforced by the awkwardness of Cathy's posture, in a composition that is otherwise tranquil, inviolate. Grant was eager to maintain an honesty of approach, eschewing the decorative or academic, reaching to the core of landscape and figure.

In the autumn of 1971, Grant remained intent on the figure, his thoughts directed now towards portraits of fishermen or farmers, workers in the landscape, through reading for the first time the Scottish poet and novelist George Mackay Brown. He had recently seen the Royal Academy's exhibition *Ensor to Permeke: Nine Flemish Paintings 1880–1950*, dominated by Constant Permeke's monumental depictions of peasant workers. In *Black Bread* (1923), a painting of two figures at a table, the subject and its rendering fuse so indivisibly that, as one Belgian critic commented, Permeke seemed 'to have grubbed in the paint like a peasant grubbing in the soil'.[35] Grant, in his journals, commented merely that the exhibition helped identify forms that might enable him to integrate figures into the landscape without self-consciousness.[36] He envisaged an entire summer and autumn travelling to Lofoten by way of the Faroe Islands, including a winter in the far North. This was the context in which he painted *Lofoten* (fig.21):

It is all there: the calm in the cold mornings when the grey light (or blue like a whale's back) is the dull luminosity of the sun that does not set. A breathless chill greyness when a sound carries across the water. An oar dropping into a boat startles the cormorants on a far distant rock. A cough as the man in morning sullenness bends to lift the nets into the large vessel alongside. The eminence of great mountains, diaphanous breath issuing from forest and fissure. The hours of suspended life: a great codfish deep in the glassy depths of the fjord: upwards a cold lens-eyed stare.[37]

The Narrow Road to the Deep North

Lofoten may be seen as a crossroads. Grant might have pursued the Socialist Realist agenda of portraying workers in the landscape, as planned. Instead, he refocused his attention on the act of travel itself, harnessing to it an incipient interest in Japanese art and literature that would fundamentally reshape his response to the North. He began by working from drawings of Norway from 1961, linking each to lines from Matsuo Bashō's *The Narrow Road to the Deep North*, a prose and verse diary recording a hazardous journey through Edo Japan in the late 17th century. The ensuing watercolours possess a Blakean luminosity and intimacy enhanced by the handwritten inscriptions rimming their imagery. Using acrylic and Indian ink, Grant offset vibrant colour against areas of deep black, expressing landscape through washes and broad strokes. That Blake was a conscious model is evident from dated annotations in his copy of the *Selected Poems*.[38] Yet Grant was looking at other traditions of landscape painting, too, noting a visual parity between the 'subtle mistiness' of the western fjords and Chinese watercolours.[39] In his paintings, responding afresh to Norway's landscape, he encapsulated fleeting effects of weather or light, often featuring cloud or mist over water. The catalyst for *Cloud over Lofoten* (1971) was a verse by the poet Isshō, included in notes to the Penguin edition of *The Narrow Road to the Deep North*:

How beautiful it is,
The snow on the ground,
And the cloud in the west
That brings more of it.[40]

The painting's format is circular, the landscape identified as Lofoten (fig.35). Translating *The Narrow Road* into ink and acrylic paintings on paper, Grant noticed that 'something of the humility of Bashō's reflections on nature and his sublimely ordered

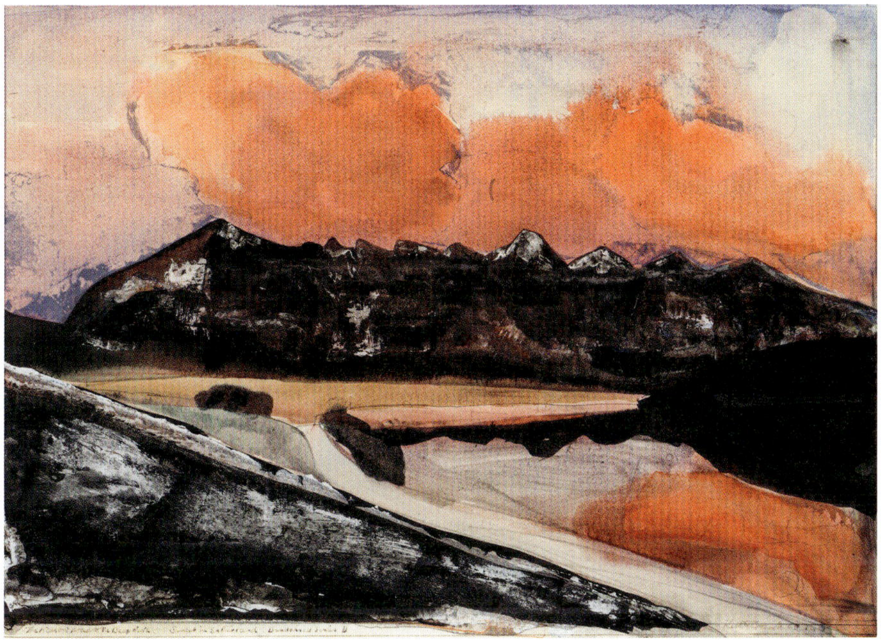

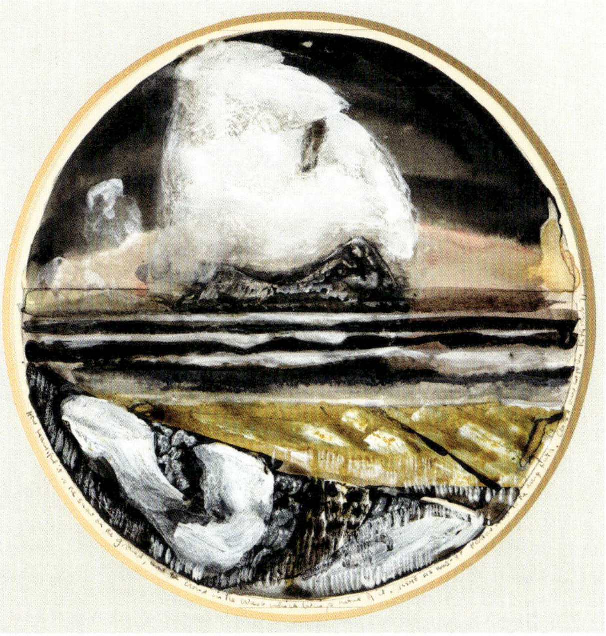

34 (left)
The Narrow Road to the Deep North: Sunset in Sutherland, 1972
Acrylic on paper
32 × 18 cm
The David Game Collection, UK

35 (right)
The Narrow Road to the Deep North: Cloud over Lofoten, 1971
Acrylic on paper
29 × 29 cm
Private Collection, UK

means of expression' influenced them.[41] Mapping each halting-point on his journey through Norway against a counterpart in Bashō – Bergen representing Edo, Narvik becoming Kurobe, Svolvær Kurikara – he invoked also Yasunari Kawabata's 1948 novel *Snow Country*, which he had just finished reading. In his journal he copied verses attributed to Han Shan about a journey to 'Cold Mountain', commenting, 'more and more I see the relationship between my "Northern awareness" and that of Japanese & Chinese Poets'.[42] Travelling by boat to Norway, on New Year's Eve 1971, he wrote a long poem concerning the North. And as he journeyed around the coast, north to the Arctic, he would continue to see landscape through the eyes of Bashō. Rain fell, dirtying the snow and making the sky seem 'to breathe out black soot through every rift in the hanging clouds'.[43]

The literary sources Grant cited appeared to rein in his response to the landscape: not by lessening its impact, but by tempering any residual influence of the northern Romantic tradition with a more controlled approach. There was no escaping that this was an intensely autobiographical project. Grant saw himself shunning the temptation to create large pictures or ones 'that "vibrate"' (that is, constructions) to 'speak of nature closing in on an individual':

As the temperature drops and the darkness becomes more complete, I hope that stage by stage the essence of the North will be revealed . . . I will find more out about myself. I will feel more bodily in that intense cold and I will observe the night of blizzards, stars and ephemeral light.[44]

Leaving his young daughter, Dominique, he imagined the glaciers winking back at him 'confirming the action of Bashō', who, discovering a child crying by the River Fuji, offered food yet abandoned it to 'the irresistible will of heaven'.[45] The crystalline descriptions in Kawabata's *Snow Country* form a persuasive parallel. Travelling by train, the protagonist, Shimamura, notices the alteration in the window's reflection as lights inside are turned on and the landscape outside darkens. The window becomes a mirror to the girl's face opposite. Sending its ray through the pupil of her eye, a distant, cold light transforms it into a 'beautiful bit of phosphorescence on the sea of evening mountains'.[46] Located at the beginning of the narrative, as Shimamura travels towards the snow country unaware that Yoko, the girl opposite, will play an important role in his life, the moment's poignancy is emphasised. Some years before encountering this passage, Grant recorded a similar sensation when he worked all afternoon,

as if seeing the reflections in windows of skies and scenes that collectively make up a pattern of the world outside myself. Today the mood is pitched in silence – evening and morning . . . when there are no more barriers and no more rewards one may turn to a window and see the infinite as an everyday thing and perhaps find inexpressively moving a sense of ones [sic] own individuality before timelessness.[47]

Was there any further context to Grant's thinking, in 1971? Perhaps the solitary traveller in Schubert's song cycle *Die Winterreise*, an archetype of German Romanticism, although Britten's *Curlew River* (1964), a highly ritualised reworking of the Japanese *Nō* play *Sumidagawa*, forms a more stimulating analogy. In *Curlew River*, Britten relocates *Sumidagawa* as a Christian parable in fenland East Anglia, where a Madwoman, seeking her son, finds only his grave. Grant knew *Curlew River*, and had seen Britten's second church parable, *The Burning Fiery Furnace* (1966), at Orford Church during the Aldeburgh Festival in 1967. Describing the production as 'wonderful', he responded to the contrast between the stylised costumes and the beauty of the singers' heads. The choir boys, in particular, were 'exquisite, angelic'.[48]

Inherent in the church parables, as in Bashō, was the process of travelling towards a spiritual or psychological goal, a process which for Grant was playing out simultaneously on multiple levels. *The Narrow Road to the Deep North* series extended beyond Norway to Scotland. In August 1972, Grant made one of his frequent visits to Dundonnell House to stay with Alan Roger, a noted collector of Chinese art and expert on bonsai. Situated at the head of a valley on the west coast of Scotland, Dundonnell is not far from Little Loch Broom and the sea: a landscape with a parity to the coast and fjords of north Norway. Roger recalled watching Grant lie on a rock for nearly an hour watching the sun set over the Hebrides, 'impressed by his passionate and intense concentration'.[49] *Sunset in Sutherland* (1972; fig.34), while lacking a quotation from Bashō, is a sibling to paintings based on Narvik and Svolvær.

The clearest way to consider these and the works that followed is through two solo exhibitions based around them: *The Narrow Road to the Deep North* (touring, 1973–4), organised by the Scottish Arts Council, and *The Way to Cold Mountain* (1976), held at Rochdale Art Gallery. A third exhibition, *The Volcano in the North* (1977), at Portsmouth Museum and Art Gallery, will be addressed later.

The Narrow Road to the Deep North was the boldest indication, to date, that Grant was working serially to create extended bodies of work. While few examples from *The Narrow Road* sequence itself were included, 32 paintings titled *The Road to Snæfjellsnes* (1973) continued their scope and materiality. These were paintings begun in Iceland during a visit in June: works Grant described as 'colour studies', bearing handwritten inscriptions identifying their subject. Contrasting with their intimate scale were the 24 canvases of *Maritime Polar* (1973) charting the hours of the day. The title, also used by Grant around this time for his four-act play (see p.8), identifies a type of air mass bringing showers or sleet first introduced to him in the 1940s by the Reverend Eric Fairfax Robson, weather correspondent for the Liverpool Co-op magazine, who was advising him on a possible career as a weather forecaster. Although the canvases were displayed on screens arranged in a circle, creating an immersive cyclorama, the constituent paintings function equally well as groups. For instance, the four-part *Snow Drift, Clear Sky* charts a continuous expanse of sea, cloud and mirror-glass reflections (1973; fig.36). The landscape is imaginary: assembled and stitched from observation. Marina Vaizey's catalogue essay drew attention to the paintings' northern inspiration without mentioning Bashō or how concepts of time – the hours of the day, or the days of travelling – were structuring Grant's work.

The Way to Cold Mountain

The notion of a journey through landscape had embedded itself in Grant's psyche. In 1976, over a hundred works were presented chronologically in *The Way to Cold Mountain*, titled after a place in the poetry of Han Shan (*fl.*9th century) where mist is impenetrable and ice never melts. To travel to Cold Mountain, Grant wrote in the catalogue introduction, 'is a lonely progression to a state of inner being; those who set out on this journey have few followers'.[50] *The Way to Cold Mountain* was popularised by Jack Kerouac's novel *The Dharma Bums* (1958), in which he based scenes on meeting the American Zen poet Gary Snyder as he translated Han Shan, then hiking past California's Twin Lakes to ascend the jagged, glittering Matterhorn Peak (Snyder reached the summit, Kerouac gave up just below).[51] Grant located his own way to Cold Mountain as 'the desolate E.6.', a route from south Norway to the borders of the Russian Arctic. Was the white peak of *Snow Drift, Clear Sky*, reproduced as the catalogue's cover image, a symbol for Cold Mountain?

There was a core of imagery relating to Iceland in both exhibitions. A watercolour inscribed 'Snow pattern frieze behind old volcanoes – snow melt pool in foreground – Iceland' (June/July 1973) depicted a landscape marked by scoured white forms resembling ancient chalk figures on downland. Grant characterised them as 'a monumental script, an alphabet of signs tying the land to the belly of the clouds'.[52] This sketch contained the germ of a work Grant, returning from Iceland, was still unsure how to tackle. In his journal he glued two reproductions of Japanese woodblock prints, seemingly cut from a newspaper colour supplement. Hokusai's woodcut *Mount Fuji in Clear Weather* (1823–9) shows the sacred mountain as a reddened peak, capped with rivulets of snow, against a sky delicately layered with cloud. Hiroshige's *The Bow Moon* (1830–35), in a vertical format, depicts a waterfall and moon

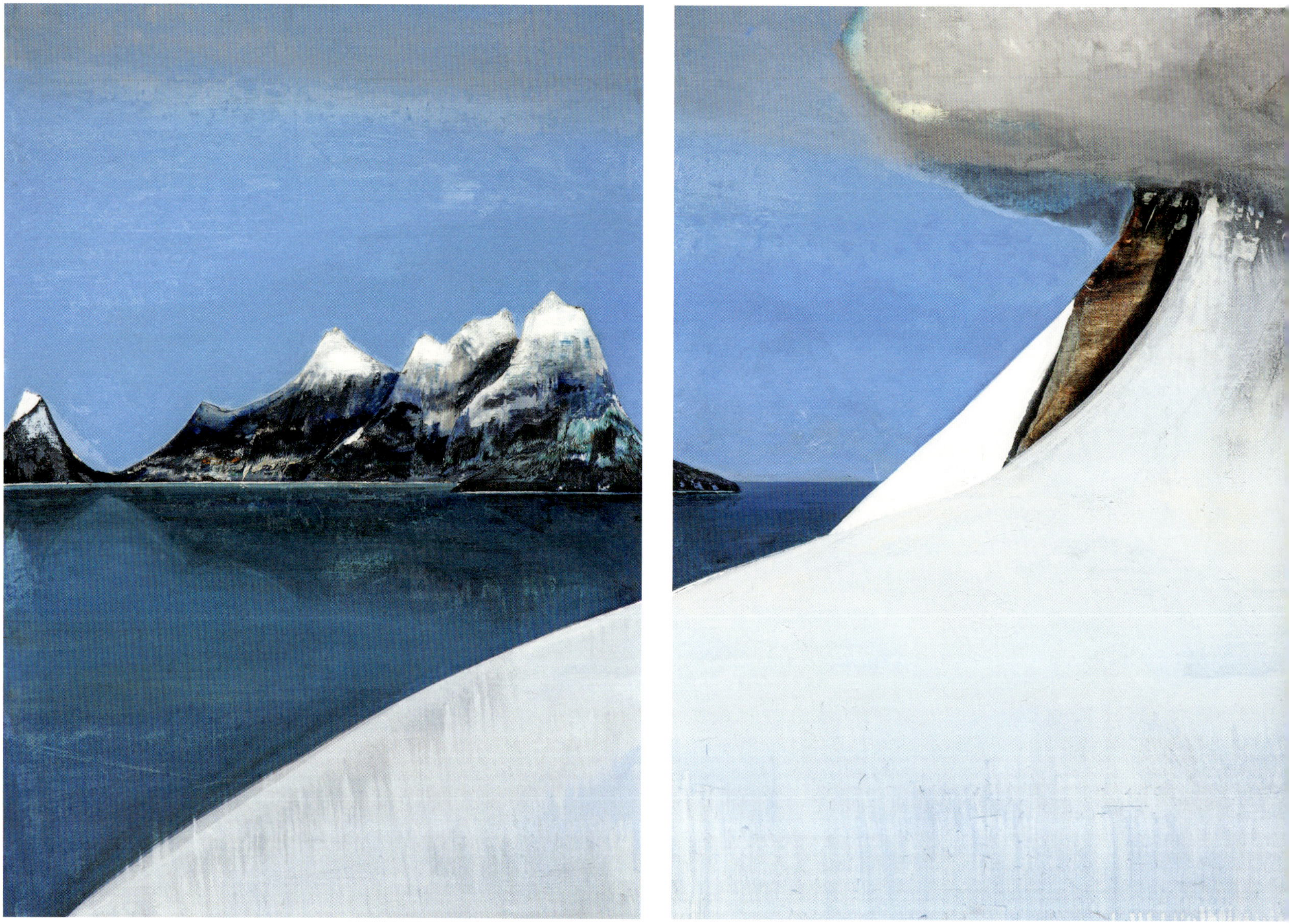

36
Maritime Polar: Snow Drift,
Clear Sky, 1973
Oil on canvas
four panels, each 121.5 × 91.2 cm
Touchstones Rochdale Art
Gallery

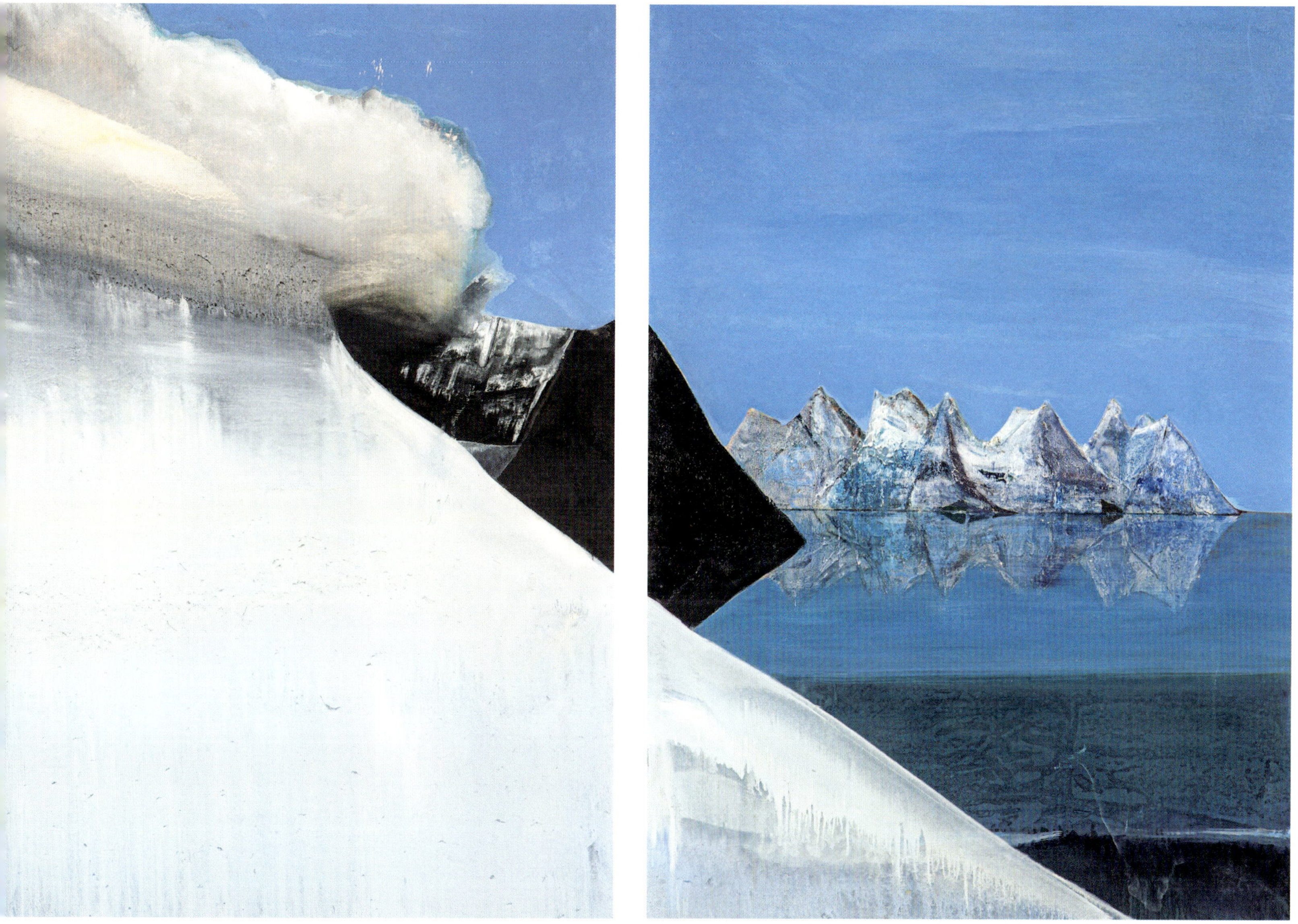

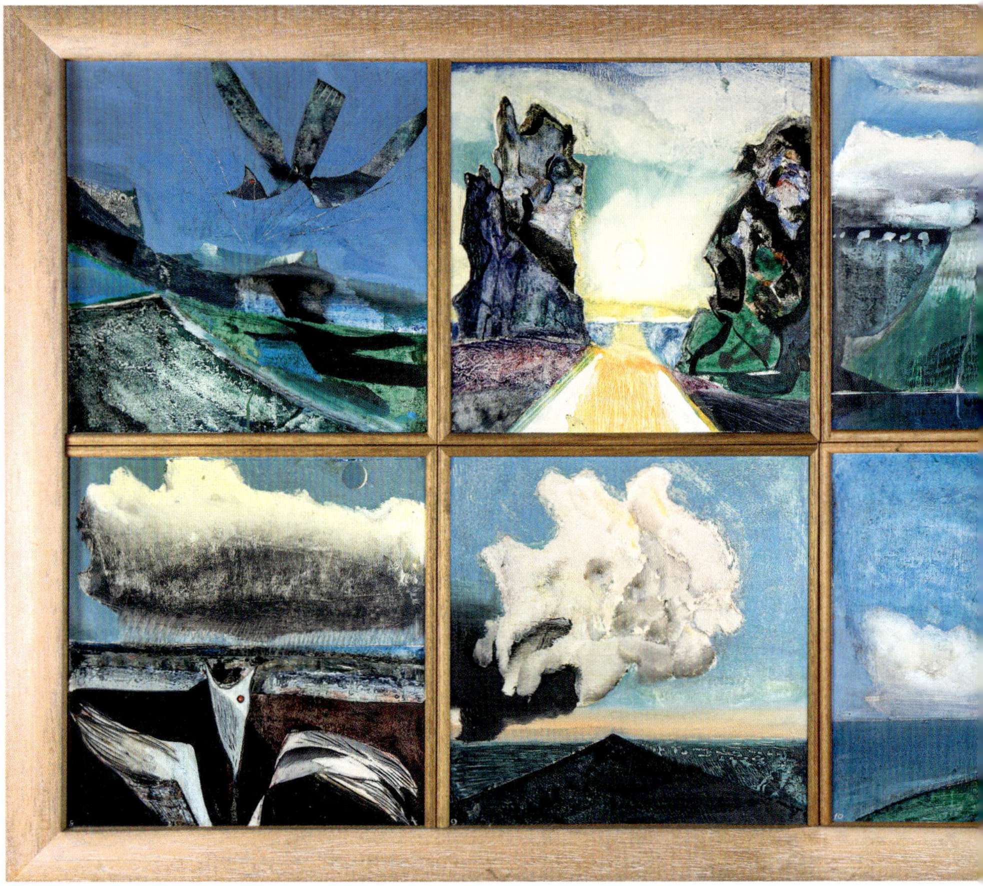

37
Fourteen Stations on a Road, Iceland, 1974
Oil on board
14 panels, each 30 × 30 cm
Private Collection, UK

glimpsed through a cleft in rocks joined precariously by a twisted bridge. Each resonates intriguingly with compositional strategies Grant had already used and would continue to develop. Beneath these images, Grant wrote, 'The chance sight of the Fuji print and the little Hiroshige reminds me of the 101 views of Snæfjellsjökul which I would like to do', not based entirely on the glacier, 'most will simply be of Iceland'.[53]

Fourteen Stations on a Road, Iceland

Among ideas still unresolved were illustrations to the stations of the cross, of which only drawings as yet existed, and a volcano series. 'Iceland', as Grant concluded portentously, remained 'neither near me nor far away.'[54] Grant had met George Mackay Brown in his hometown of Stromness, Orkney, through Colin Hamilton and Kulgin Duval, who were collectors of his paintings but also dealers in rare books and manuscripts. Through this connection arose the idea of illustrating Peter Maxwell Davies's song cycle *From Stone to Thorn* (1971), a setting of the first section of Mackay Brown's *Stations of the Cross*. At the time, Grant had not read the poems, yet he immediately questioned the subject's relevance: '14 Stations expressed by landscape, but what does it mean?'[55] Meditating upon the witnessing of cruelty and repeated crushing of humanity, his thoughts paralleled the narrative of Christ's stumbling, falling and struggling to rise again as he bears the cross. A sheet of drawings (surviving as a 35 mm slide) presents 12 strongly composed graphic ideas within circular frames. As well as the characteristic symbols of the volcano and sun, Grant experimented with incorporating the cross, for instance in the cast shadow of a bird's wings. Although Hamilton and Duval commissioned editions of artists' illustrated books, this particular project was not pursued.

Instead, Grant developed his ideas as *Fourteen Stations on a Road, Iceland* (1974), gathering literary and cultural references around an intensely personal core of imagery (fig.37). 'Stations', historically, relate to trade, religion or military usage, sharing a common purpose as places for sustenance or reflection. In Grant's mind was undoubtedly Hiroshige's *Fifty Stations of the Tōkaidō* (1833), a sequence of woodcuts illustrating a journey from Edo (Tokyo) to Kyoto. Hiroshige treats the scenes dramatically throughout the seasons, the viewpoints chosen – some corresponding with published travel guides, others never identified – suggesting an imaginative mode of working. *Stations of the Tōkaidō* ostensibly depicts a pilgrimage to offer thanks for a successful harvest, a

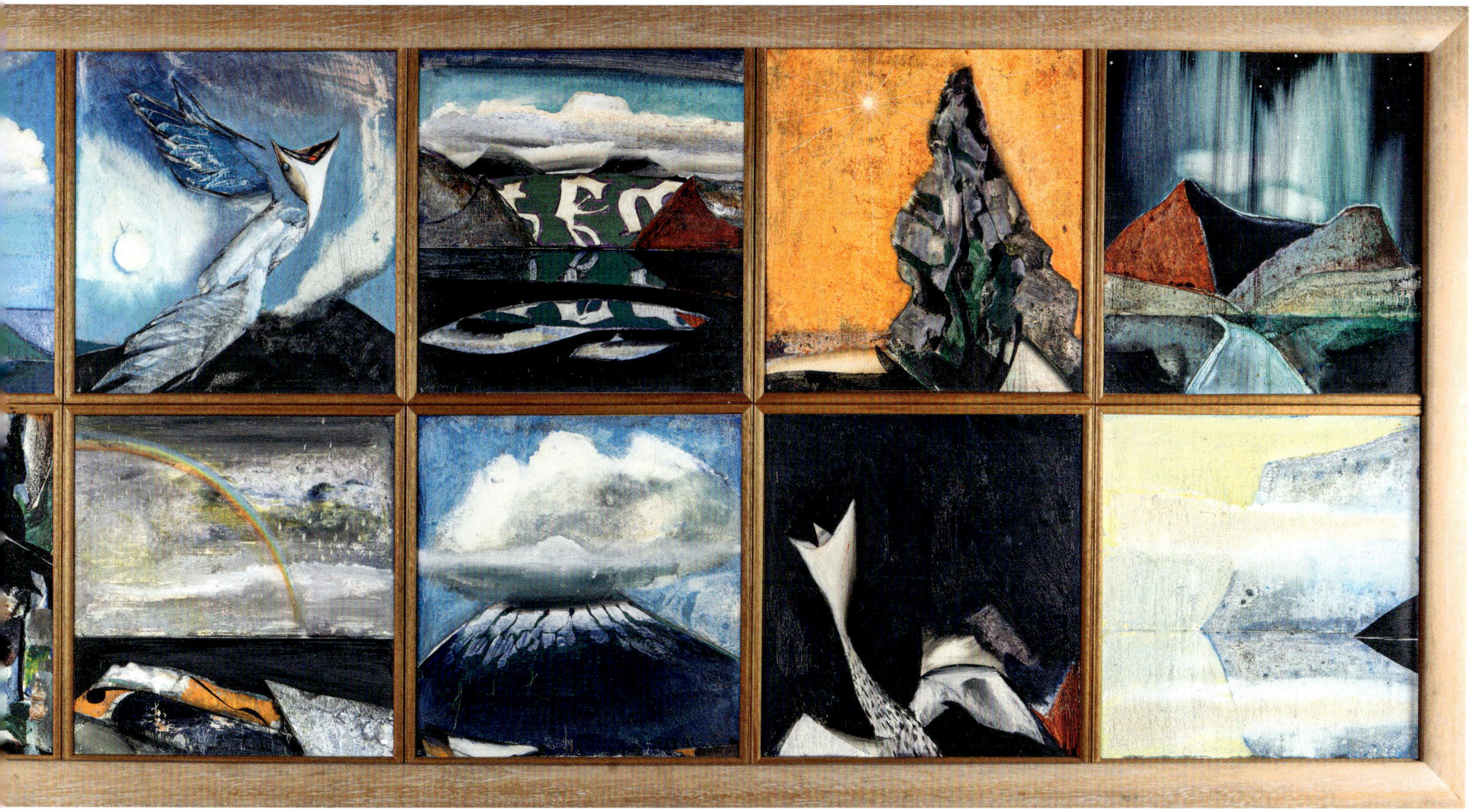

motive that parallels Mackay Brown's *Stations of the Cross* in binding the seasons to the landscape and to a profound faith.

In Grant's paintings, Christ is symbolised by a white bird: falling, with limp wings, then earthbound, gaping skywards. This embodiment of pain and loss, which recurs throughout Grant's work, deliberately evokes D.H. Lawrence's 'strange white bird', blown, with a broken wing, from the frozen seas of the North.[56] Interspersed are tableaux of exquisite beauty. Light, whether from the sun, northern lights, a rainbow or diffusing mist, illuminates a landscape of rocks and volcanoes: effects that elsewhere in his journals Grant likens to 'a continuous tapestry' lining the walls inside his skull.[57] Some of the paintings, such as that of reflected snow patterns (fifth from top left), derive from specific examples of the 'colour studies' made during or following Grant's visit to Iceland in June 1973. The journey within a landscape that compelled him for its strangeness, distance and climate had assumed the mantle of a penance.[58]

Imagery from this landscape remained fertile as source material. In 1973, Grant received sponsorship from the Calouste Gulbenkian Foundation to work as artist-in-residence at Bosworth College, Desford, in Leicestershire, constituting the first such appointment to a state school. Allocated a studio where students could watch and discuss the progress of his work, Grant gave talks at Bosworth and at local schools, the experiment proving so successful that the appointment was extended for a further year. Among the first works completed was the *Bosworth Triptych* (1973), derived from the second of the *Fourteen Stations*. Two basalt laval rocks on Iceland's Reykjanes peninsula stand sentinel on either side of a panorama dominated by clouds. Split by the tripartite format, the landscape appears framed within the cockpit window of an aeroplane, tilting as it banks over land. Realised on a vast scale (approximately 6 m wide), and dedicated to Britten and Pears, the *Bosworth Triptych* hung for many years in the foyer of the Guildhall School of Music in London.[59]

The Volcano in the North

In his autobiography, Patrick Procktor commented on the persistent attraction of certain subjects in painting, such as volcanoes or Venice, which always sell no matter how well executed or by whom. Having himself painted Venice, he concluded, 'The volcanoes I leave to Keith Grant.'[60] The two had remained friends since Procktor taught Grant at the RCA, to the extent that in 1980 Grant contemplated accompanying him to China. Procktor's comment, slight in itself, reinforces the extent to which Grant had become associated with the imagery of volcanoes. His engagement intensified further when, hearing of an eruption on the island of Heimæy, on 23 January 1973, he flew the following day to Iceland to document it. The studies made during six visits that year formed the basis of an entire exhibition, *The Volcano in the North*, at Portsmouth Museum and Art Gallery in 1977.

Heimæy means 'island of fire' in Icelandic. The catastrophic eruption of Eldfell in 1973 necessitated the urgent evacuation of the island's 5300 inhabitants, burying houses, petrol stations and playgrounds, and shutting down the fishing economy on which the population depended.[61] Grant took 700 photographs on his first visit alone, and less than a month later returned – through seas raging in a Force 9–10 gale – with a BBC film crew to document the eruption further. He had received a commission from Icelandair, facilitating an unparalleled opportunity to observe the volcano from above. Back in his Camden studio, in February 1973, Grant recalled the violence of the phenomenon:

The monumental and giantesque beauty of the eruption cloud, the charcoal cone and the red lava flakes falling, twisting and trailing like comets down the outer walls of the crater. And then the quiet moments after the tempestuous days of wind and sea, of hail and ash caught in the updraught around the volcano rushed into the sky spiralling and waltzing into baroque convolutes.[62]

Approaching perilously close to the cones of active volcanoes to take photographs, at one point he lost his rucksack and several reels of film, but captured the explosive power that propelled ash and steam through the earth's crust (fig.38).

In the catalogue for the Portsmouth exhibition, describing a volcano's cycles of expansion, contraction and explosion, the volcanologist John Guest likened his discipline to that of a doctor monitoring a sleeping giant's temperature, blood pressure and pulse rate. Yet he observed that such data can be 'felt' emotionally, too, concluding that Grant's paintings, made from direct experience, express the sensation of being close to a live volcano with greater intensity than is possible in photographs.[63] In May 1973, Grant had spent the night on Helgafell looking down on the erupting volcano on Heimæy. Lava bombs launched high into the air exploded 'with flashes like anti-aircraft shells':

The ash veil fanned out in graceful curves. The uprush of gas and flame many colours side by side broke through the dense clouds of black and blue smoke – enormous fires glared in the cavities of these clouds

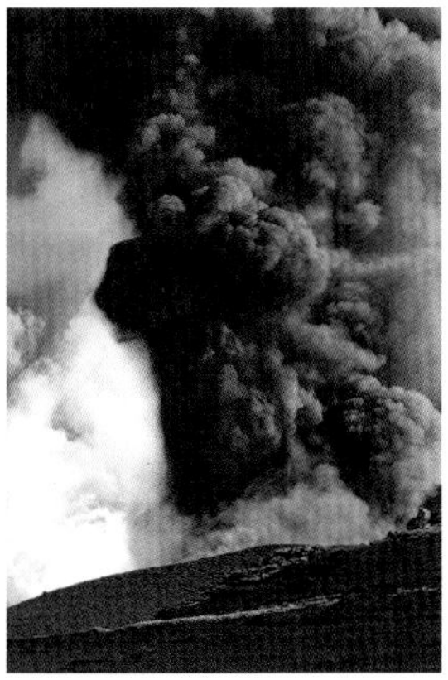

38
Volcanic eruption, Heimæy, Iceland, 1973, photograph by Keith Grant

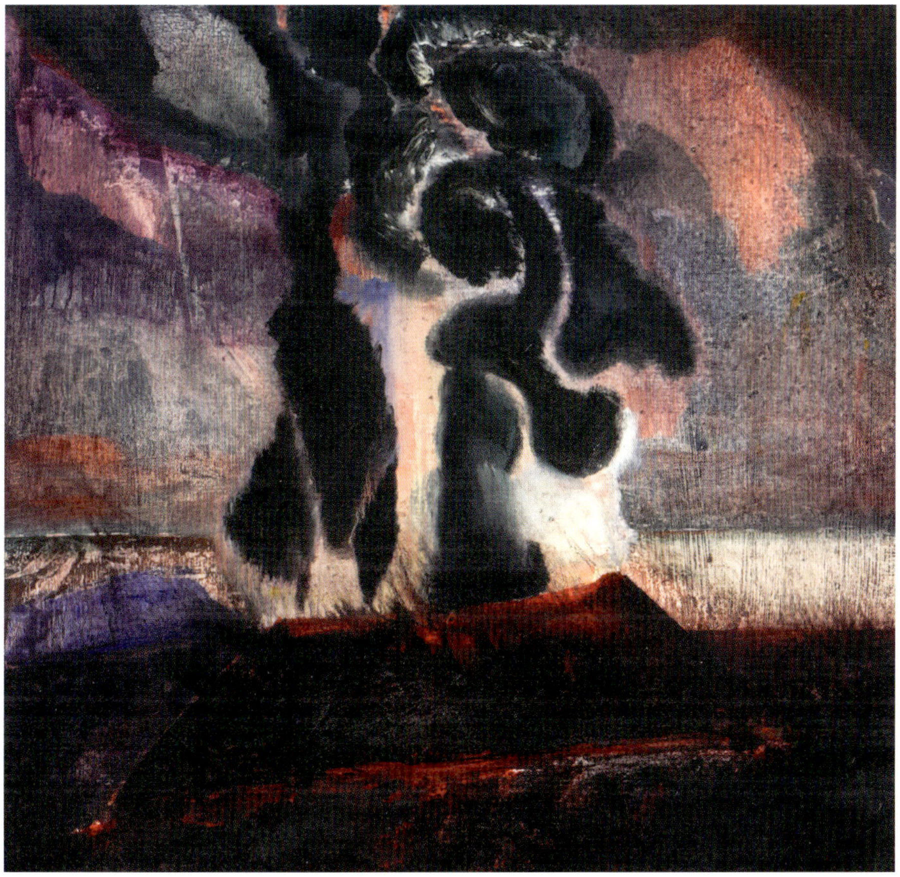

39
Volcano in the North, Heimæy, 1975
Oil on board
61 × 61 cm
Imperial Health Charity Art Collection, London

– at about 4000 feet the black gave way to yellow brown and then to steam of the purest white. The great clouds drifted towards the east and threw an immense shadow over the sea – under white tornados and waterspouts weaved fantastic swaying columns of pure white.[64]

The variety of means with which Grant expressed these sights demonstrates both the profundity of his response and adroitness of his imagination. Moreover, the distance of time opened the possibility of more radical or abstract equivalents. In Brighton, in January 1975, Grant based his first etching on the volcano, while at the Bosworth College he began a series of 12 studies showing the volcano either close or distant, with rock and bird forms to the foreground. A visit to Ireland interrupted his work. Only in December, fleeing a personal crisis, did he return to the series, sensing that the hiatus enabled him 'to draw only those essential forms necessary to express the apocalyptic nature of the subject'.[65] To what extent should biography be linked to art? Grant admitted the potential of the 'writhing black forms', which had invaded his dreams after Heimæy's eruption in 1973, still to colour his mood.[66] The set of studies begun in January have a directness yet foreboding that is hard to quantify. In some, the volcano smoulders ominously at night; in others, the intensity of the eruption sears the sky (fig.39).

As he worked on a large triptych, *Volcano in the North, Heimæy* (1976/77/82), Grant strove to embody the sensation of his visual memory through form and paint. The painting's three panels show the volcano at night from the air (fig.40). Grant tried new tactics to depict the stars, seeking to match the intensity he was achieving concurrently in smaller acrylics. Although the triptych was exhibited at Portsmouth in 1977, it was altered again before reaching the version shown in 1983 in *Pintura británica contemporánea* (*Contemporary British Painting*) at the Museo Municipal in Madrid. The layering of paint, taking days to dry, belies the immediacy of an image rivalling the scale and ambition of *The Dorset Mural* of 1962 (fig.18; pp 28–9). Broad swathes of colour are speckled with black, red and white; steam swells behind the crater. Yet there is a delicacy and mystery in Grant's vision that renders the volcano's

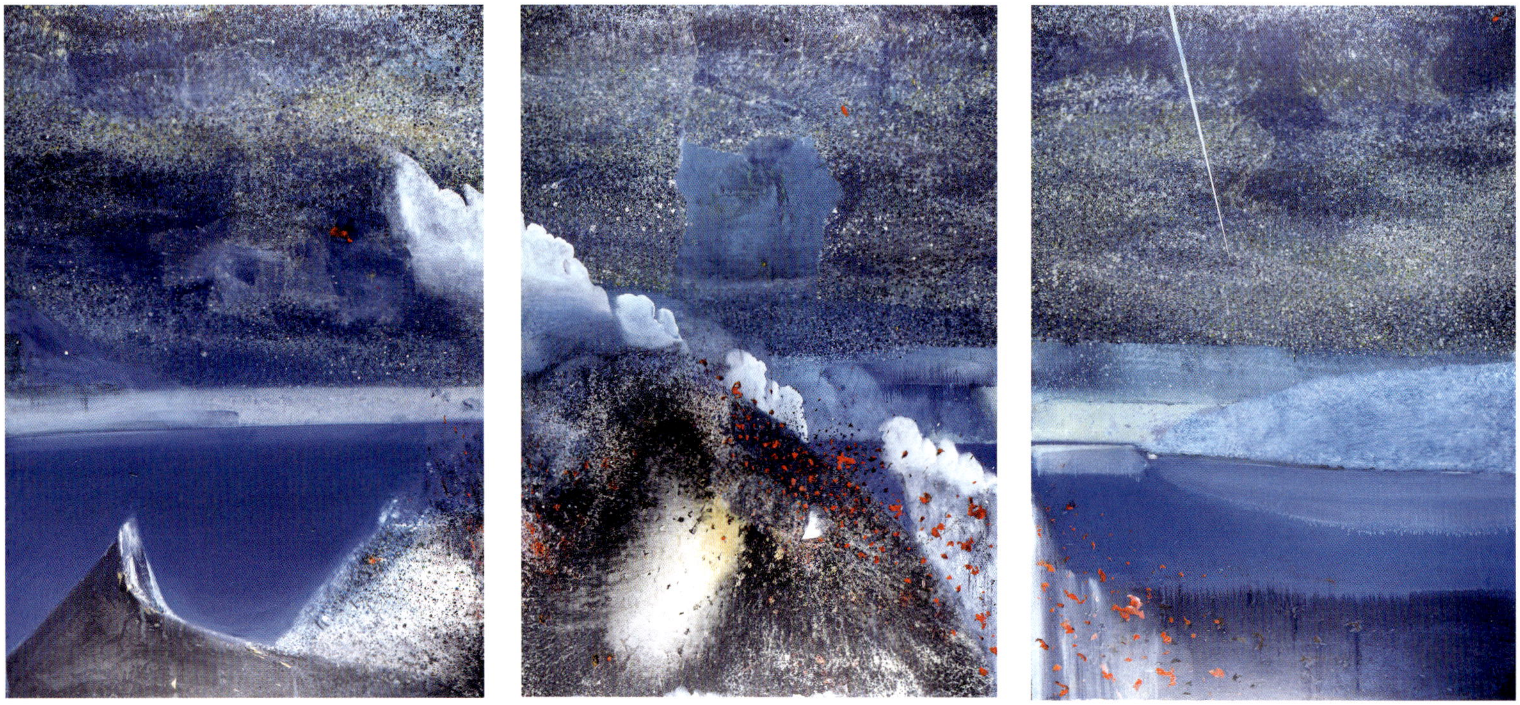

40
Volcano in the North, Heimæy, 1976/77/82
Oil on board
triptych, 213 x 456 cm (each panel 213 x 152 cm)
Private Collection, Australia

movement ethereal rather than violent, stylised rather than explicit. Considering Grant's photograph of the eruption alongside his paintings demonstrates graphically the transmutation of the experience.

At certain points in Grant's life he witnessed a phenomenon so cataclysmic that it formed a persistent theme within his work. Such was the case with the Icelandic marine eruption seen from the air in 1973. In 2015, he recast his recollection by incorporating a bird into its ash column (fig.42). *Marine Eruption* transforms the imagery of *Lava Field* and *Surtsey* (figs 25, 26) through a surrealistic orchestration of cloud and ash veils, further countering the menace Grant had sensed when watching Heimæy erupt.

A Winter Journey

Seven years after his extended travels to the 'deep north', Grant prepared to embark on an expedition to north Norway to create a visual chronicle for his exhibition, *A Winter Journey*, at Browse & Darby in July 1979. He began at Svolvær in March 1978, originally intending to travel south, lightening his palette, thereby controlling colour as Bashō controlled his narrative. If it is easy to forget the strenuous physical nature of such a venture, a snapshot of Grant sketching, with snow nearly reaching the top of his boots, serves as a potent reminder (fig.41). Face to face with the landscape, Grant felt an underlying 'crystalline geometry' from which compositions such as *Moon and Fjord, North Norway* (1978) derive their archetypal simplicity. Not for the first time, the language he used to describe what he saw, and how he wanted to process this visual information, was arrestingly contradictive. He sought, as he recorded in his journal, to convey the 'passionately extreme juxtaposition of soft-curve and hard-edge; the fullness of snow-form and the angular face of granite'.[67] Geometry thus coexists with fervour, just as Grant's cubistically abstracted landscape in *Moon and Fjord* is coloured impulsively in tones of orange, purple and viridian.

Despite his plans, Grant did not travel south on his visit to Norway in 1978 but stayed mainly near Svolvær, where an exhibition, held in an 'improvised gallery',

41
Keith Grant sketching, north Norway, May 1978, photographer unknown, archive of the artist

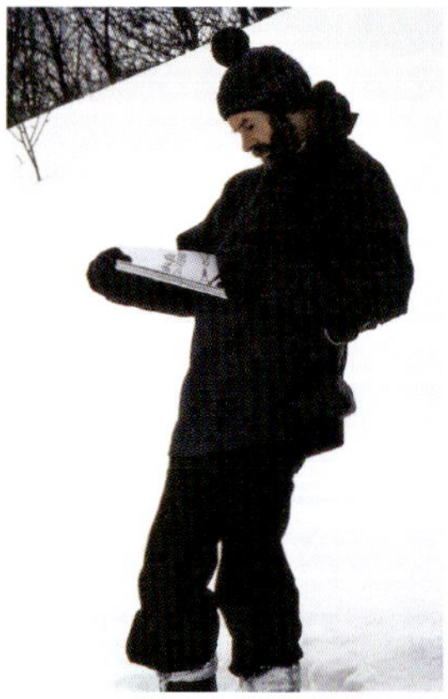

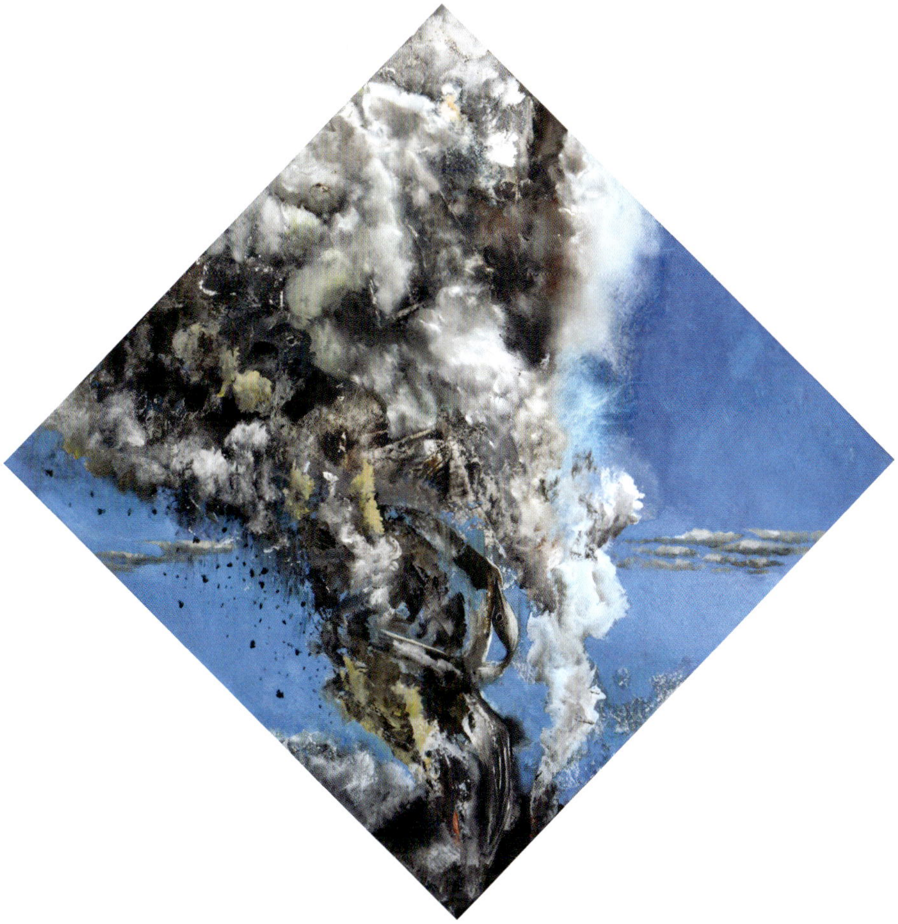

42
Marine Eruption, 2015
Oil on canvas
79 x 79 cm
Collection of the artist

sold successfully.[68] Instead he travelled further north to the Norwegian archipelago of Svalbard in the Arctic Ocean. The landscape was characterised by ice, silence and an 'elemental horizontality', reminding Grant of Mahler's orchestral song cycle *Das Lied von der Erde* or Vaughan Williams's *Sinfonia Antarctica*.[69] On the desolate beach at Longyearbyen, at the edge of the ice, he discovered a beacon constructed from wind-eroded wood, once painted a warning red, now bleached pink. The beacon was crudely formed as a tetrahedron. At its centre was a tree trunk surmounted by a rusting iron drum, also faded pink, peppered with gunshot holes to resemble a 'time ravaged mask'.[70] This beacon, with its associations of warning and assurance, haunted Grant.

The idea lay fallow for over a year. In January 1980, Grant finished the first version of a stormy seascape with a thin structure supporting a faded flag: a beacon, dividing the white and black landmasses, casting a shadow on the ice. Grant titled it *Between Two Fixed Points*, recognising it as a profoundly personal work (fig.43). Even without probing the symbolism, it is clear that this painting possesses an unusual quality, perhaps deriving from the inversion of timbre (brown clouds, white ground) and the delicate overlaying of the beacon. The softly rendered landscape gradually asserts its geometry, insistently reiterating the form of the triangle against a horizontal substructure. Ronald Alley, Keeper of the Modern Collection at the Tate, was so taken by the painting, in its revised version, that in May 1983 he proposed it and a drawing for purchase. Two months later, Grant received a letter from the Director asking him to collect his works, following their rejection.[71]

Haiku of the North

Over the next decade, multiple readings of Bashō fuelled Grant's desire to visit Japan, the inspirational force of which he believed (at the time) might sustain the 'final phase' of his work.[72] He laid foundations diligently through literature: recollecting *Snow Country* and reading for the first time the poems of the *Man'yōshū* (*Collection of a Thousand Leaves*, CE 759) and Alan Watts's *The Way of Zen*. In Bashō's *The Narrow Road* he sensed now 'an intimate connection with the mystery of life of which the phenomena of nature are images and signs'.[73]

Amid this reawakened interest, in March 1989 he completed the first of a projected series, *Haiku of the North* (fig.44). The painting's imagery is explicitly biographical in its mapping of nature to the symbolism of Grant's inner landscape. A motionless

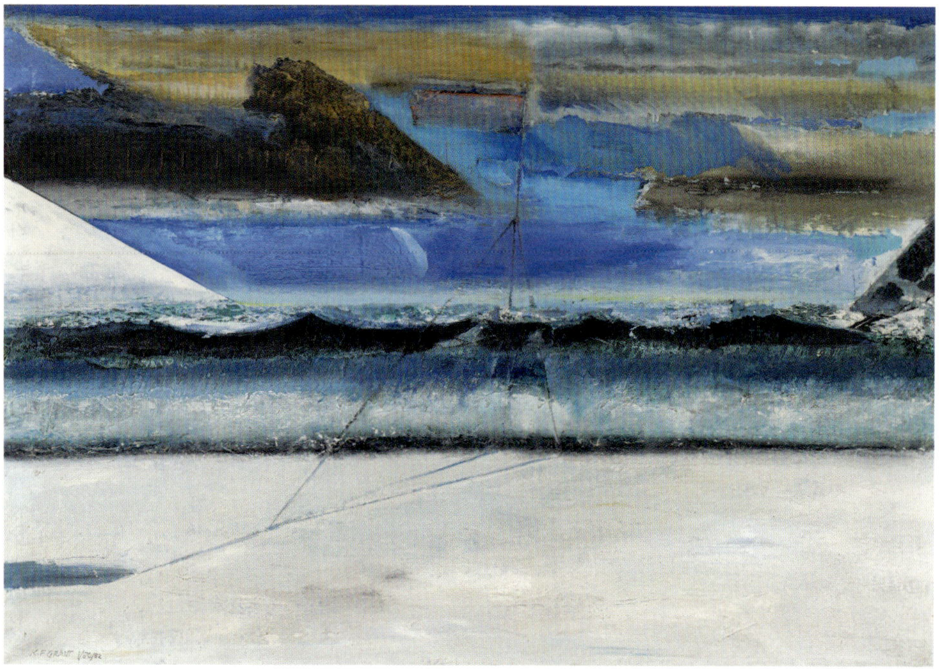

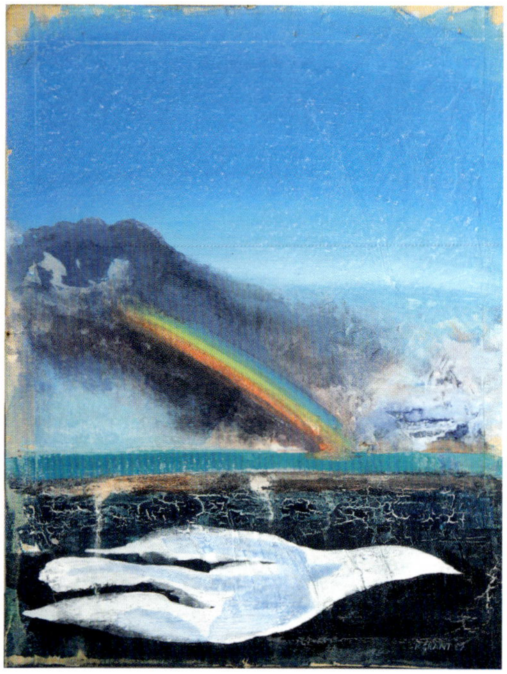

43 (left)
Between Two Fixed Points, 1980/82
Oil and acrylic on canvas
91 × 122 cm
The David Game Collection, UK

44 (right)
Haiku of the North, 1989
Mixed media on card
27 × 20 cm
Private Collection, Canada

white bird lies in the foreground, its essence a blue shadow, its support a bed of blackened, cracked rocks. Beyond, the sea, azure sky and storm cloud are dominated by a rainbow. The promise of the North? If the symbolism appears trite in description – as Grant feared when he abandoned the series – the execution is poignant in its expression of ephemerality. The sky is rain-bright with a shaft of colour, the painting's surfaces blurred and crackling.

From *The Way of Zen*, Grant identified concepts relevant to his work, specifically the metaphorical depth of darkness, the infinite continuum of colour and the Sanskrit words *matr* ('to measure, farm, build, lay out a plan') and *dva* (division and duality). A month after completing the first *Haiku*, he mooted a series titled *Rainbow, Moon, Islands and Clouds*, inspired by his long admiration for the Japanese artists Hiroshige and Kunisada. The proposed division of each painting into six vertical panels would evoke the folded screens of artists such as Sōtatsu (*fl.*1600–30) and Ogata Kōrin (1658–1716).

Once more, the realisation of the idea brought aspects of Grant's Japanese sources into proximity with Western landscape. Once more, too, there was the anticipated stimulus of companionship from a young woman, Saoli, with whom he hoped to travel. Each work would take its cue from a single form, such as a rainbow or moon, echoing the simplicity of Hiroshige's naming of his works. In the first completed study for the series, *Suilven, Sutherlandshire* (1989), a 'hastily sketched bow' arches over a distant image of the Scottish peak (fig.45). A flock of sea birds punctuates the space of one panel, a single white bird is defined in another. The painting was described by Grant as the busiest of a set of preliminary sketches, with 'movements of light and cloud against large simple areas of sky . . . bordered by massive elongated triangles of black rock'.[74] Grant never travelled to Japan, yet its art and poetry would remain a touchstone.

The Faroe Islands

At last, in 2008, Grant reached a landscape he had conjectured nearly forty years earlier. The

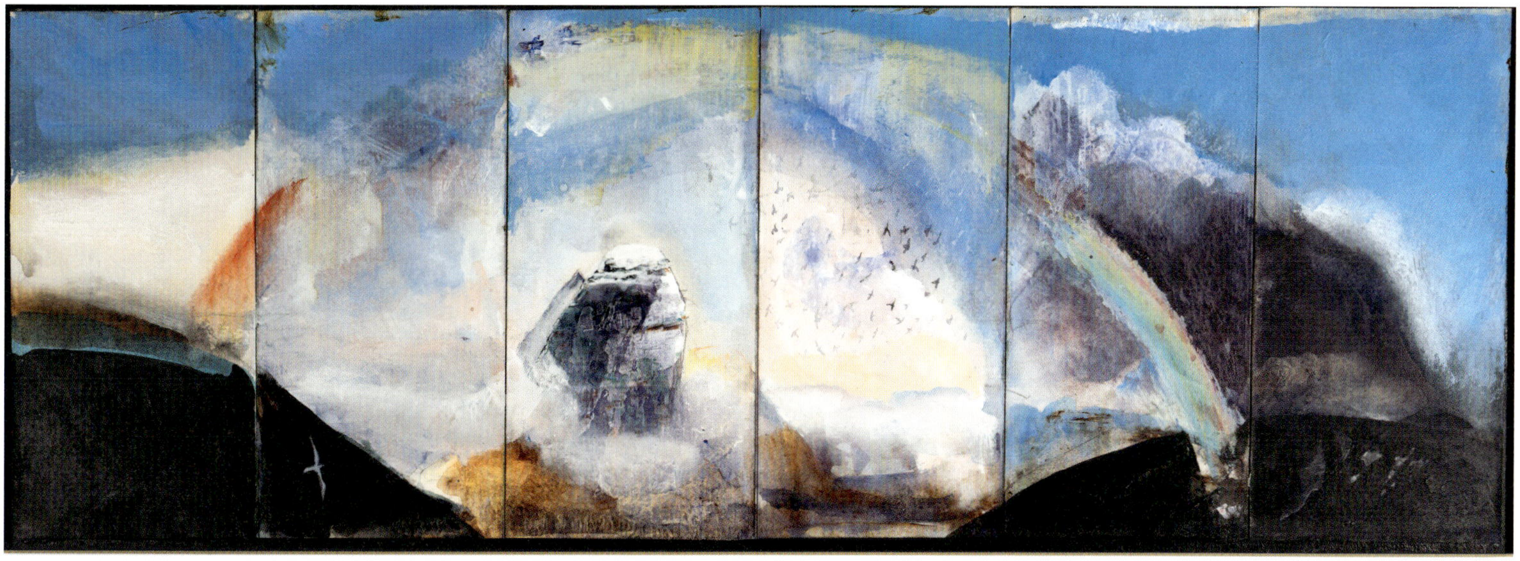

45
Suilven, Sutherlandshire,
1989
Acrylic and gouache on paper
21.6 × 60.5 cm
Private Collection, UK

Faroe Islands, a cluster of 18 volcanic landmasses between Iceland and Norway, attracted Grant for its fragmented topography and extreme contrast between volcanic cliffs and the sea. The islands are connected by a network of road tunnels, causeways, bridges, as well as harbours and piers at the sea's rim. Concrete, an alien presence in the landscape, Grant perceived as harmonising with the rocks and sea as it decayed. An old jetty fascinated him, 'clothed in tightly fitting though threadbare sheets of bright green sea-weed . . . the eroded concrete stairs, pitted surfaces and cracked walls [retaining] the original though much degraded functional geometry of the small harbour'.[75]

In *The Old Helicopter Landing Pad, Gjogv, Faroe Islands* (2009), the geometry is that of a circle: a concrete disc bearing radial incisions to resemble a sundial, but also the form of a cloud-topped island (fig.46). Such comparisons unify the composition – the precise lines of the horizon, the disc's markings, cliff's striations and diagonal rain against the splashed rocks and tempestuous sea. The colouring is unusual if not atypical. At the turn of the millennium Grant had painted several sunrise pictures showing reflections in the ice at Norsjø, a lake in Telemark, Norway. The blue-tinged reds of these works were followed by the clear tones of *Red Sunrise* (2007), whose reasserted geometry heralds that of *The Old Helicopter Landing Pad.*

Grant's second visit to the Faroe Islands, in 2016, consolidated his approach to the landscape, bringing more surrealistic interpretations to the fore. As he wrote in his journals, shortly after returning, it was a question of setting aside popular preconceptions and allowing the landscape to work freely upon the imagination. Once done, 'I found that the elements combined in a deeply mysterious series of configurations which at once eliminated the picturesque and which harmonised so completely with the surface geometry of the islands.'[76] The point is made visually by a comparison with Grant's illustration for the *Shell Guide to Shetland* (1962), which uses a comparable landscape as backdrop to its defining symbols, from broch to spinning wheel, archaeology to intricate knitting patterns.

But there are more specific examples of this altered approach. In 2009, Grant painted *The Bay of Birds, Faroes*, a vertical landscape in which two gannets fly low over rocks, the bay curving gently towards a vertical cliff. The viewpoint is intriguing yet not sufficiently skewed to be disquieting. In *The Faroe Islands Suite, No. 10: Bay of Birds* (2016), the

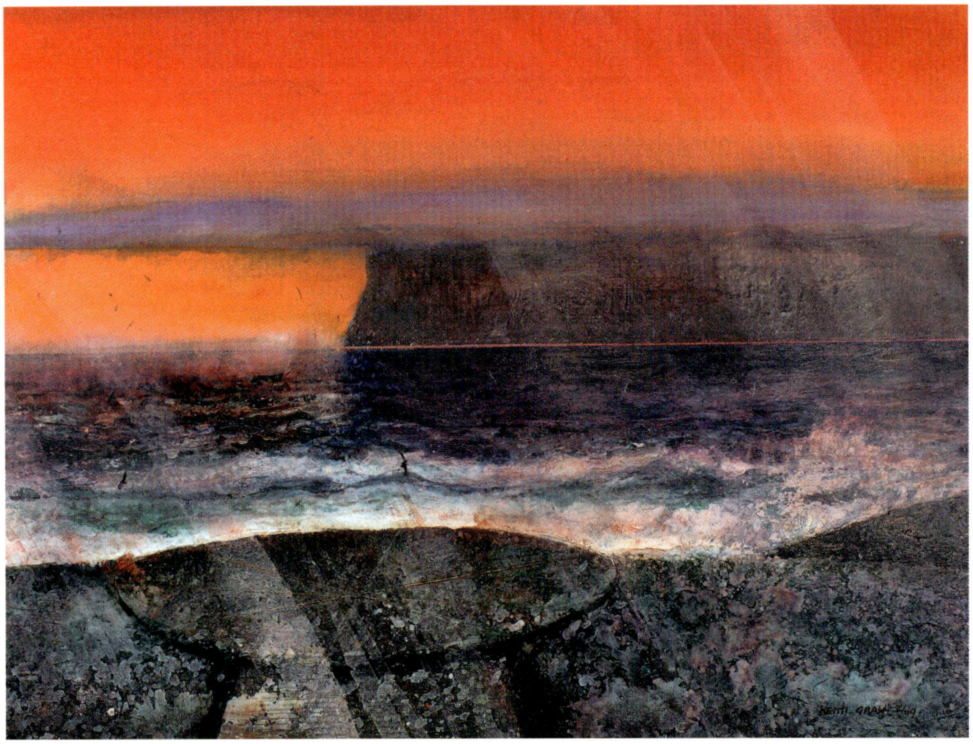

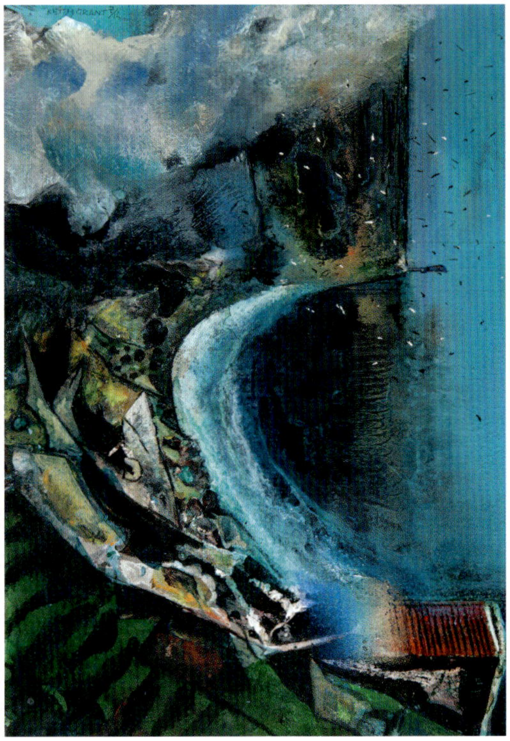

46 (left)
The Old Helicopter Landing Pad, Gjogv, Faroe Islands, 2009
Acrylic, ink and watercolour on card
25 x 34 cm
Private Collection, UK

47 (right)
The Faroe Islands Suite, No. 10: Bay of Birds, 2016
Acrylic, ink and varnish
41 × 28 cm
Private Collection, UK

effect is quite different (fig.47). Painted as if from the air, it looks down on the bay, which rears up vertiginously. Immediately below is a stepped jetty. On this second visit, Grant had only three full days for sketching, so worked rapidly: the result 'seemed to set the landscape itself in motion'. Everywhere was movement – the rhythm of the sea, but also the light, washing the sky in 'swathes of pulsating blue . . . palest cerulean to a deep throbbing hue of cobalt / ultramarine'.[77] *Bay of Birds* contains a spectrum of blues and a disorienting sense of being airborne. There is a direct line from *Gull in the North* (fig.23) to this painting, but with no sense of repetition. The later painting loosens its attachment to the solidity of landscape, which dissolves in cloud and luminous sea mist above the jetty.

The tiny sea birds, almost beyond sight, appear weightless. In August 1995, Paul Grant, Keith and Gisèle's second child, died aged 21 in a bicycle accident. The symbol of the bird, which began as autobiographical, now became associated with Paul: a spirit, or soul, set free. *Winter Storm, Vesterålen* (*c.*1995) bears the weight of this meaning (fig.48). Based on the coastal landscape of an archipelago in north Norway, it is a study of light and its absence. The sky is sulphurous yellow, the sea flecked with white, and the bird visible only by dint of the black cloud behind it. Among the paintings that have remained important to Grant is Caspar David Friedrich's *The Monk by the Sea* (1808–10), depicting a solitary figure on the land's edge, facing the sea.[78] The inconsequential scale of the monk emphasises his transitory presence in the landscape: however deep his footprints, Friedrich observed, the wind will soon erase them. *Winter Storm, Vesterålen* suggests a similar humbling before nature. It also acknowledges the inescapably human impulse to invest landscape with emotion. Loneliness, tragedy, a journey, freedom – all are projected onto the vast canvas of the North.

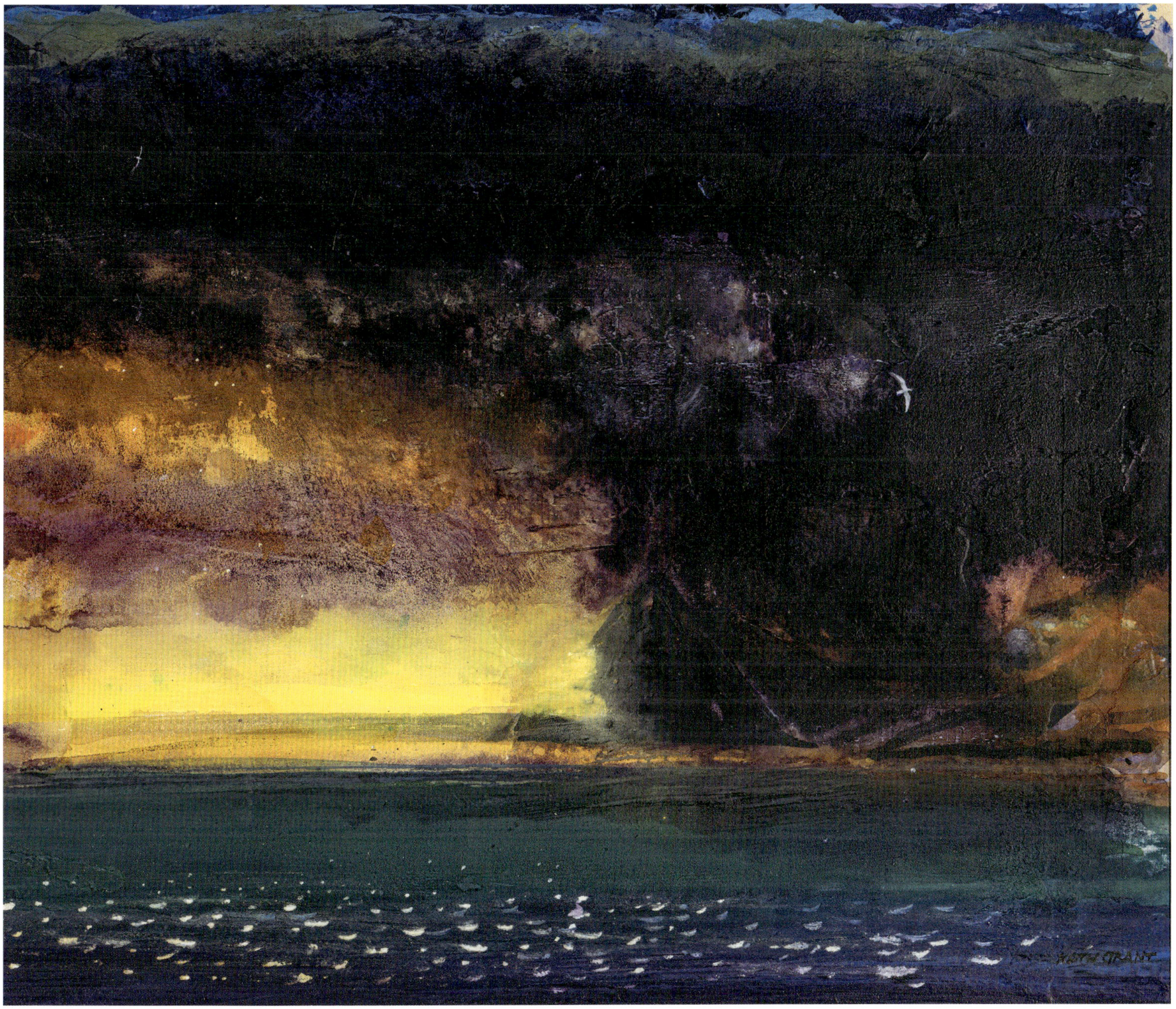

48
Winter Storm, Vesterålen,
*c.*1995
Acrylic on paper
25 × 30 cm
Private Collection, UK

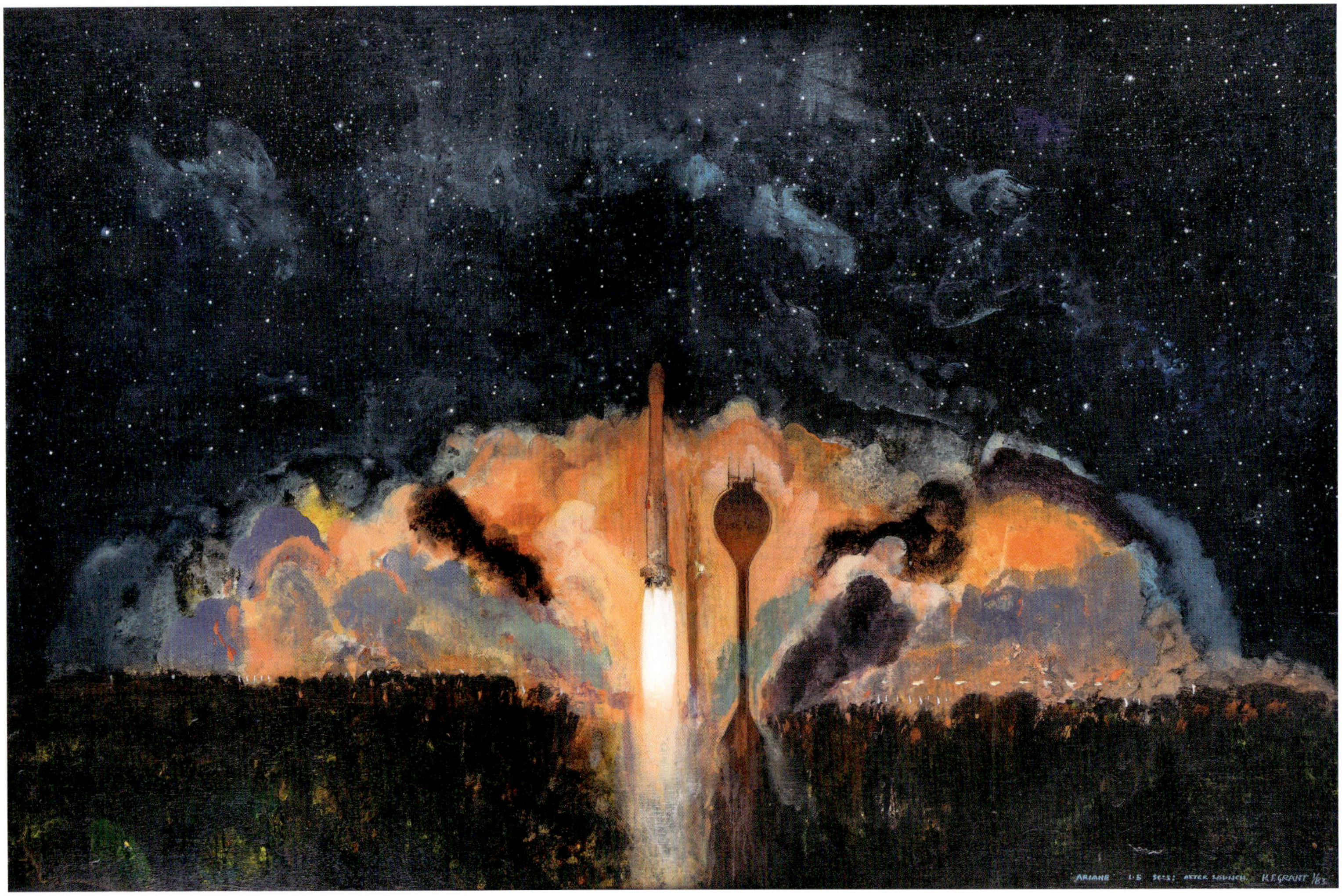
ARIANE
GRANT 1/83

3

The Tropics and Desert

French Guiana

On the night of 9 September 1982, Grant was in Kourou, French Guiana, having accepted a joint commission from the Department of Science, Information and Technology, British Aerospace and Logica plc to document the first commercial launch of the rocket *Ariane*. He watched the distant glitter of the Centre Spatiale Guyanais and the illumination of the savannah by tinsel-like fires that flared then extinguished their luminous green light: these were savannah fireflies, not to be confused with the larger, glowing variety of the forests.

As *Ariane* launched, a white flare was followed by a red-orange glow, spreading beneath the rocket and from the launch pad 'like rapidly unfolding wings'.[1] Seconds of silence passed, then the sound of the blast reached those watching, rising in crescendo as the earth vibrated and the air shimmered with fireflies. *Ariane* ascended vertically, its motors leaving short trails of blazing light against the night sky. That the launch failed, because of misfiring, in no way diminished the spectacle.

Ariana 1.5 Secs After Launch (1983) places the rocket centrally amid the landscape (fig.49). On the day before take-off Grant made several detailed drawings of the site, concentrating on the structure of the tower and launching apparatus, with a ribbon of scrub and vegetation in the foreground. Depicting the dramatic illumination of the sky seconds after launch, Grant emphasised the form of the spherically topped water tower, a striking feature of three paintings completed by January 1983. These were the first 'space'-themed works by Grant since the rocket paintings he had made in the mid-1950s – one of which, ironically, had been bought by former Verulamium Museum director John Lunn shortly before he emigrated to Canada in fear of atomic war. The rocket blast at Kourou contrasts intriguingly with Grant's interest in volcanoes: the former highly controlled, the latter utterly unpredictable.

Because of this artificial origin, the launch of *Ariane* interested Grant far less than the promise of a new landscape. Preparing to travel to South America, he read the Cuban writer Alejo Carpentier's *The Lost Steps* (1953), a novel describing a suffocatingly claustrophobic journey to penetrate the jungle by boat, beset by insects, vegetation, snakes and oppressive humidity.[2] Grant was seeking co-ordinates with which to frame his forthcoming work. Among them would be the Expressionist painter Chaïm Soutine, whose exhibition at London's Hayward

49
Ariana 1.5 Secs After Launch, 1983
Oil on board
94 x 147 cm
Chris Beetles Gallery, St James's, London

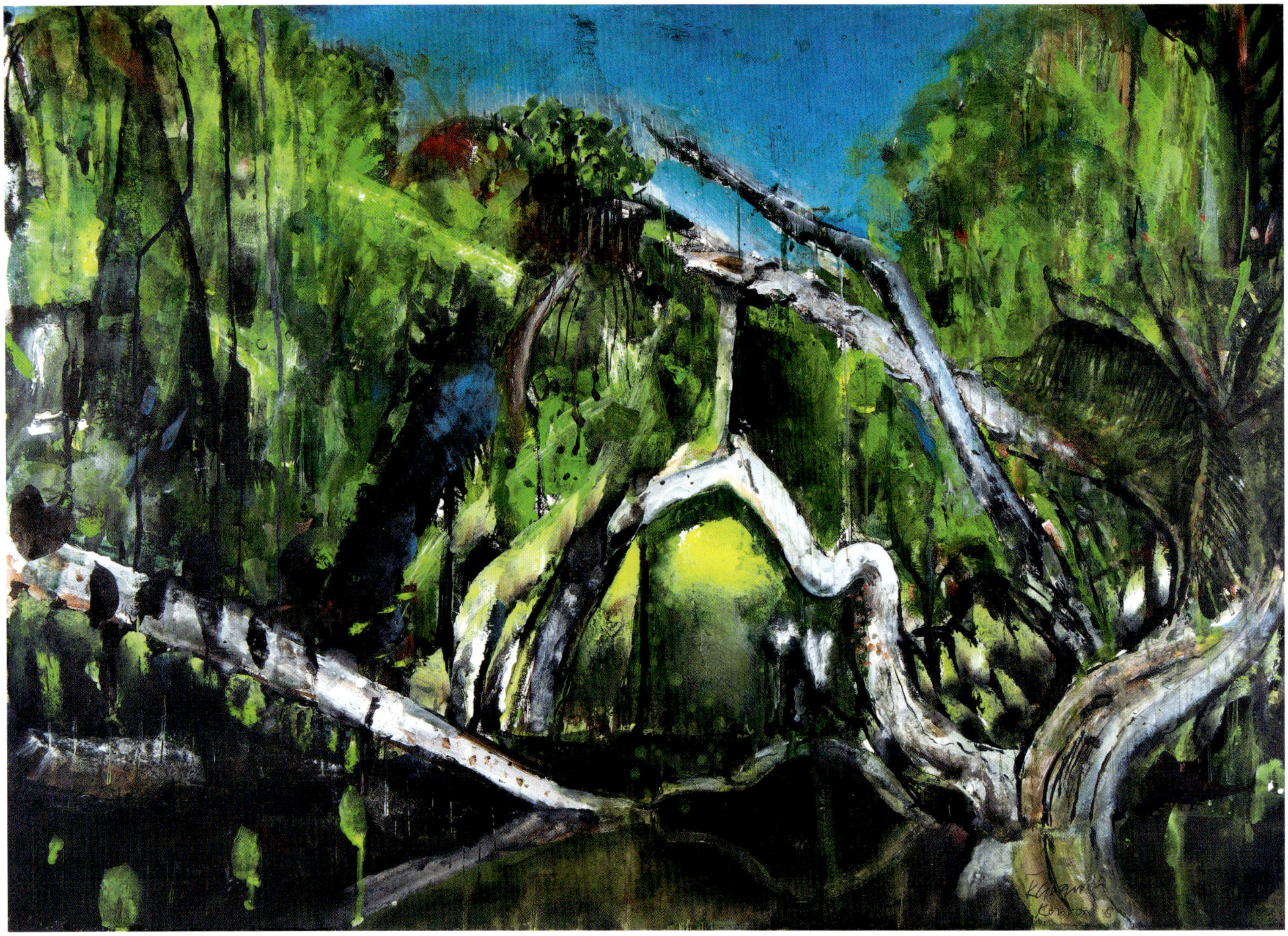

50
Kourou, 1983
Acrylic on paper
58 × 86 cm
Private Collection, UK

Gallery in summer 1982 he visited three times, pasting into his journal a postcard of *Group of Trees* (1922), depicting trees twisting about a house, warping it to their shape. In this painting, nature's proximity is conveyed powerfully by the thickly brushed tree trunks that conceal but also modify their surroundings. Carpentier wrote graphically of the 'inexhaustible mimetism of virgin nature', whereby alligators resemble rotten logs, vines seem like snakes and aquatic plants mimic solid ground. In this world of deceit, everything speaks of artifice: it is 'the world of the lizard-cucumber, the chestnut-hedgehog, the cocoon-centipede, the carrot-larva, the electric fish that electrocutes from the dregs of the slime'.[3]

Grant, immediately prior to departing for Kourou, was engaged in a study of English landscape that resulted in paintings such as *The Sun: River Ure, Yorkshire* (1982) and *Spring, The 'Pells', Lewes* (1982; fig.115, p.139). In the ensuing series of jungle paintings, this painstakingly detailed depiction of nature became an increasingly forbidding, untamed vision of what he had experienced. *Kourou* (1983) shows trees rising menacingly from the swamp, their sinuous forms resembling cobras (fig.50). Palm fronds, which in the rocket painting formed a stiff counterpoint to the night sky, here mingle with the vegetation, doubling as the ribbed wings of bats. Humidity is expressed in the dripped facture of the paint – equating rain with falling leaves – in blurred, myriad greens. Grant wrote in his journal of 'huge trees with roots that spread as far as one could see, so-called cathedral trees, with trunks like moulded columns, trees with great fin-like roots, like the tails of rockets, but more massive, and trees that soared without lateral branches into the dense confusion of the canopy high overhead'.[4] At the centre of his painting, dappled with green, is a golden light.

In the contorted trunks, bent yet continuing to grow, there is an echo of Graham Sutherland's depictions of trees that resemble limbs, or bombed buildings split open to reveal their twisted, damaged interiors. Grant, in the only surviving fragment of his original Kourou journal, stated a desire to penetrate deeper into the 'dark, inexpressibly sad, silent interior' of the jungle.[5] As he did so, in September 1982, French Guiana's history affected him oppressively. Offshore from Kourou was Devil's Island, the site of a French penal colony notorious for its harsh confinement of political prisoners, most famously Alfred Dreyfus, falsely accused in 1894 of spying for the Germans. Devil's Island, one of three islands where punishments ranged from relative freedom to solitary confinement in darkness, operated for a century between 1852 and 1952. Further along the coast, at Sinnamary, was a prison for priests and political prisoners established during the French Revolution in 1792. Grant stopped between Kourou and Sinnamary to sketch a swamp near the road. He recalled the almost comical incident of being plagued by a hornet, swiping it into the path of a Mercedes, then, having seen it run over, watch it twitch, move its wings and fly again. The painting Grant made from this landscape was *Swamp on the Road to Sinnamary, French Guiana* (1983; fig.51), inscribed 'Crique près de Kourou' ('Creek near Kourou'). Asked about it in 2022, he recalled the place as 'horrible', clouded by knowledge of those who had suffered nearby. The painting's clear blue water and golden reflections belie this memory. Beyond them, the impenetrable wall of the jungle recalls the prison witnessed by Grant on Saint Joseph Island, its remains slowly enveloped by tropical plants, flowers and palm groves.

The sketchbooks kept while Grant was in French Guiana record source material for later use. Swift pencil studies express the confusion of close-pressed vegetation, while more detailed drawings document dragonflies, seeds and flowers, annotated

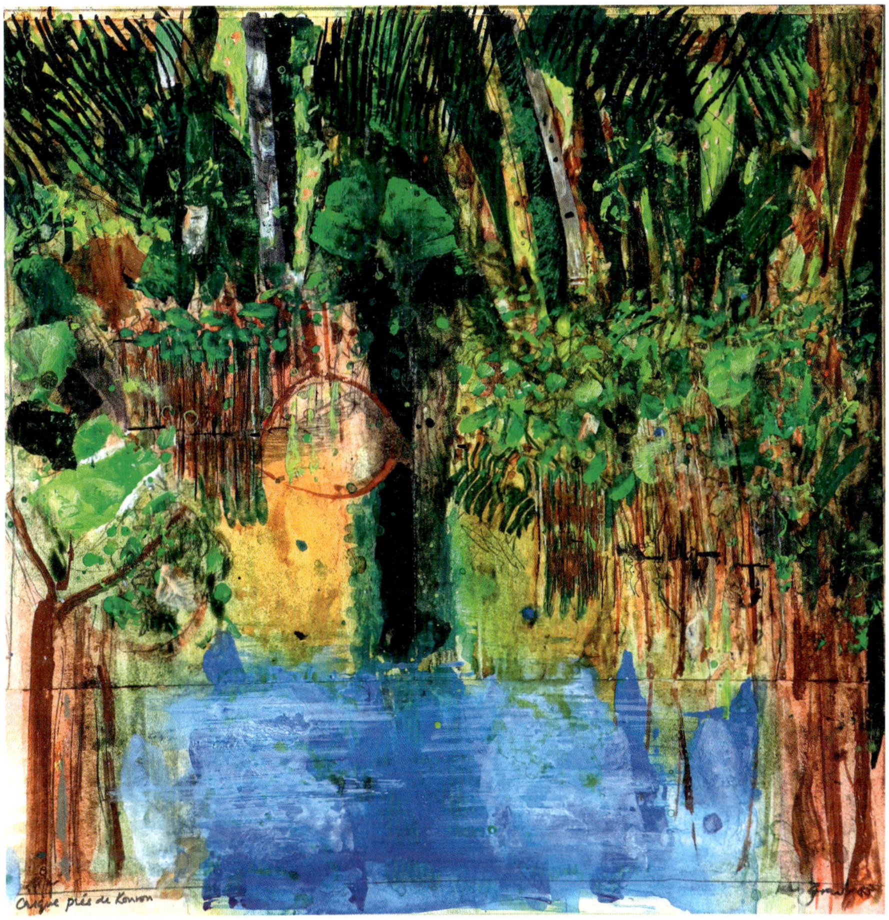

51
Swamp on the Road to Sinnamary, French Guiana, 1983
Acrylic on paper
58.5 × 57 cm
Leicestershire County Council Artworks Collection

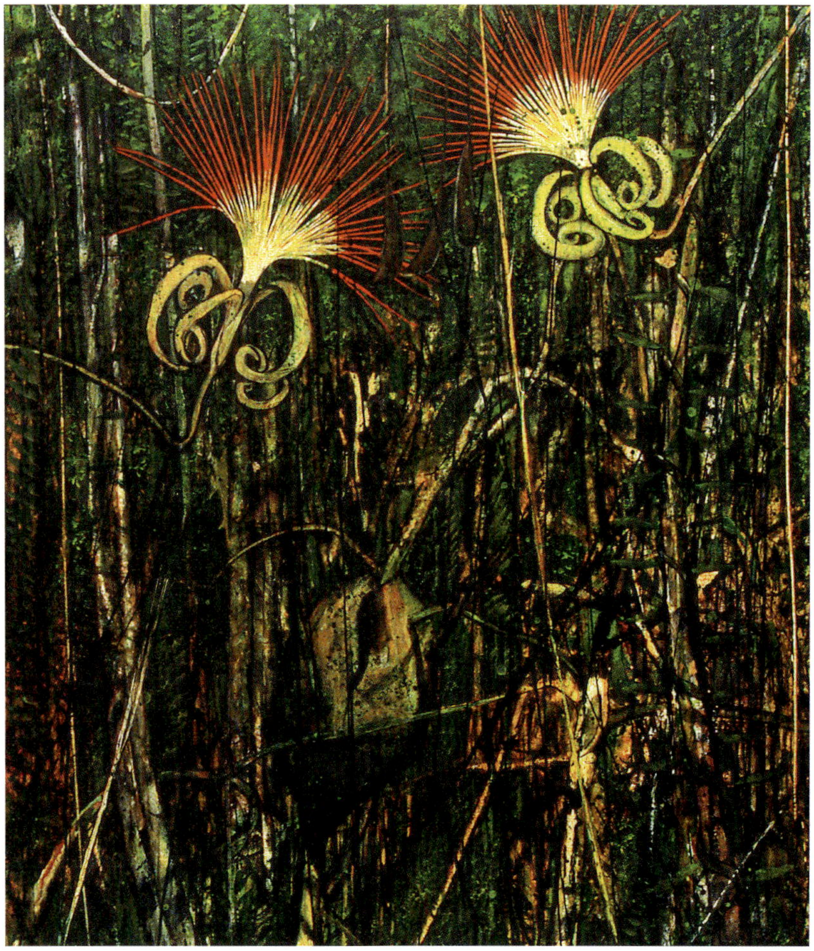 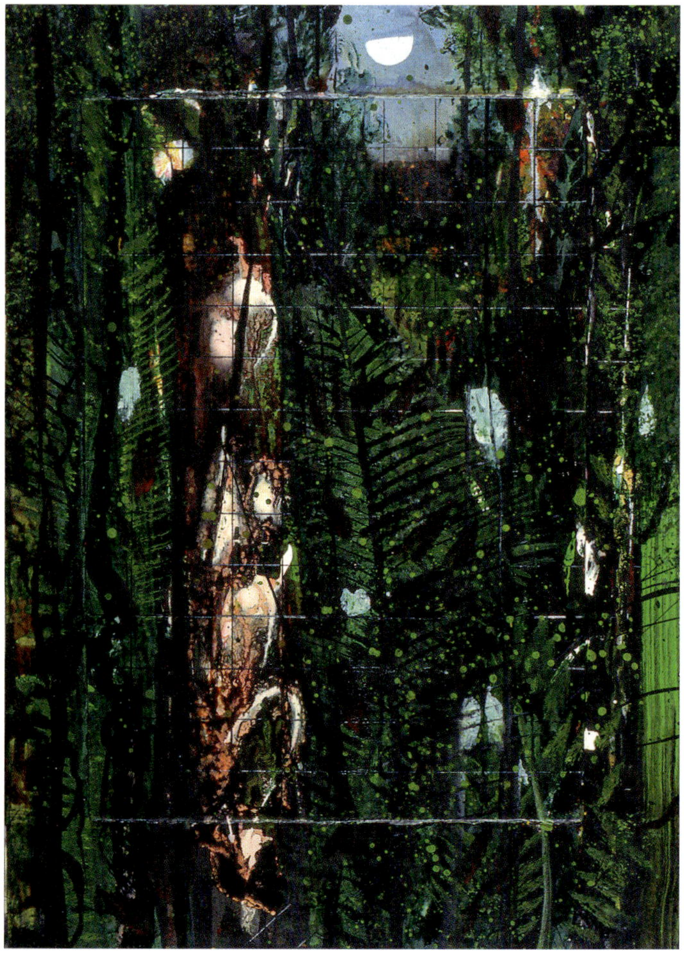

to recall specific colours. A later development, used in drawings of Venezuela in 1992, was to insert small circles within the drawing – functioning as magnifying glasses – within which Grant might enlarge the texture of a tree trunk or lichen. In *Termites' Nest with Parasitic Blooms* (1983), he depicted the exotic flowers of *Pachira aquatica*, a tropical swamp-growing tree native to South America (fig.52). Scarlet-tipped flowers blaze to the foreground, while the termites' nest recedes into a thicket of plant stems. Grant was developing techniques of painting with broader brushes to suggest the foliage of plants such as ferns, effects he considered 'both painterly and botanical'.[6] In his journals he described the luxuriant surface of the jungle as 'expressing caverns deeper than those of the lower deities of Norse mythology'.[7]

The contrast with the landscape of the North affected Grant powerfully. It was an experience of abundance so overwhelming that all individual identity seemed lost. As he wrote, 'In the North I am an observer . . . In the jungle I am a participant active in an enclosed environment. All senses engaged.'[8] He lodged in a wooden hut built on poles: an open platform with a corrugated iron roof and hammocks, below which dogs patrolled a wire-netting puma fence. This physical barrier, practical in keeping wild animals at bay but also symbolic in repelling the encroachment of the forest, became the subject of several paintings. In some, Grant extended the surface of the card to enlarge the composition, creating a raised, collaged area emphasising the matrix of the fence (fig.53). The imagery translates an effect described in his journal, where the sunlit

52 (left)
Termites' Nest with Parasitic Blooms, 1983
Acrylic on board (detail)
approx. 122 x 76 cm
Private Collection (location unknown)

53 (right)
Forest Moon and Puma Fence, 1983
Watercolour and acrylic on card and paper
approx. 51 x 37 cm
Private Collection (location unknown)

half of the moon was parallel with the horizon: 'as the light increased, the forest resolved into an uncountable number of vertical trunks of different thicknesses – light in colour, patterned with lichens and moss – browns, reds, buffs, yellows, but with the off-white of the bark predominating'.[9] Attention is drawn to the distance by the curious presence of the moon, yet the materiality of the raised grid and glossy surface draw the eye back to the picture plane, keeping the observer within its congested textures.

Grant's *Ariane* paintings were shown at the Salon internationale de l'aéronautique et de l'espace (Paris Air Show) in 1983, and thereafter in exhibitions organised by, among others, Browse & Darby and by Logica, who sponsored Grant's visit. Jacquetta Hawkes praised the extent to which Grant surrendered himself to this landscape, discovering 'the strange forms and brilliant colours of its vegetation, and the sense of the enfolding darkness beyond'.[10] Terence Mullaly, reviewing Browse & Darby's exhibition for the *Daily Telegraph*, admired not only the exotic exuberance of the jungle landscapes but the paintings of the rocket launch, where 'technology is invested with poetry'.[11] Did Grant agree?

His journals reveal only partial satisfaction with these new paintings: a diffidence stemming from a desire to understand and reveal landscape ever more profoundly. This was the urge that drew him repeatedly to the North and, at this point in the early 1980s, to deepen his engagement with an utterly unfamiliar landscape. While Grant intended to return to French Guiana, and made tentative plans to travel to Peru, his next journey would be to Sarawak in Malaysia, an opportunity that arose from an introduction forwarded by the British Council.

Sarawak

To depict foreign landscapes, particularly those as distant as the tropics, invokes specific concerns. John Minton made several paintings of Jamaica in the early 1950s, based on drawings and watercolours created while visiting the island. As he explained, 'the travel-folder romanticism is all there in Jamaica . . . the air hangs heavy, there is a sense of watchfulness, of waiting, which belongs to the tropics . . . with a disquiet that is potent and nameless'.[12] Minton painted lush, stylised vegetation in a vibrant palette of greens and acid yellows, punctuated by figures wearing flamboyantly coloured clothing and straw hats silhouetted against the light. Dismissing the paintings as generalisations, a review in the *Manchester Guardian* observed that Minton had 'fastened on the banana tree almost as tightly as Sutherland had clasped the more uncomfortable thorn-tree'.[13] Yet landscapes such as these were far from familiar in the early post-war period, and John Berger, for one, was convinced. Reviewing Minton's Lefevre Gallery exhibition, he wrote, 'One senses Jamaica as a definite place in these pictures – the alternating dryness and dampness of the vegetation, the nights of unreal moonlight.'[14]

Grant's two visits to Sarawak, in 1984 and 1985, were of a different level of intensity to Minton's relatively brief stay in Jamaica. Travelling by longboat along the river, and significant distances by foot, he stayed in longhouses and settlements, often sleeping on the bare floor. On one particularly perilous part of the journey, he walked far into the jungle, made the sheer and tangled ascent of the sacred mountain, Gunung Mulu, and spent an almost fatal night, lost in the cold, before being rediscovered by guides. Grant

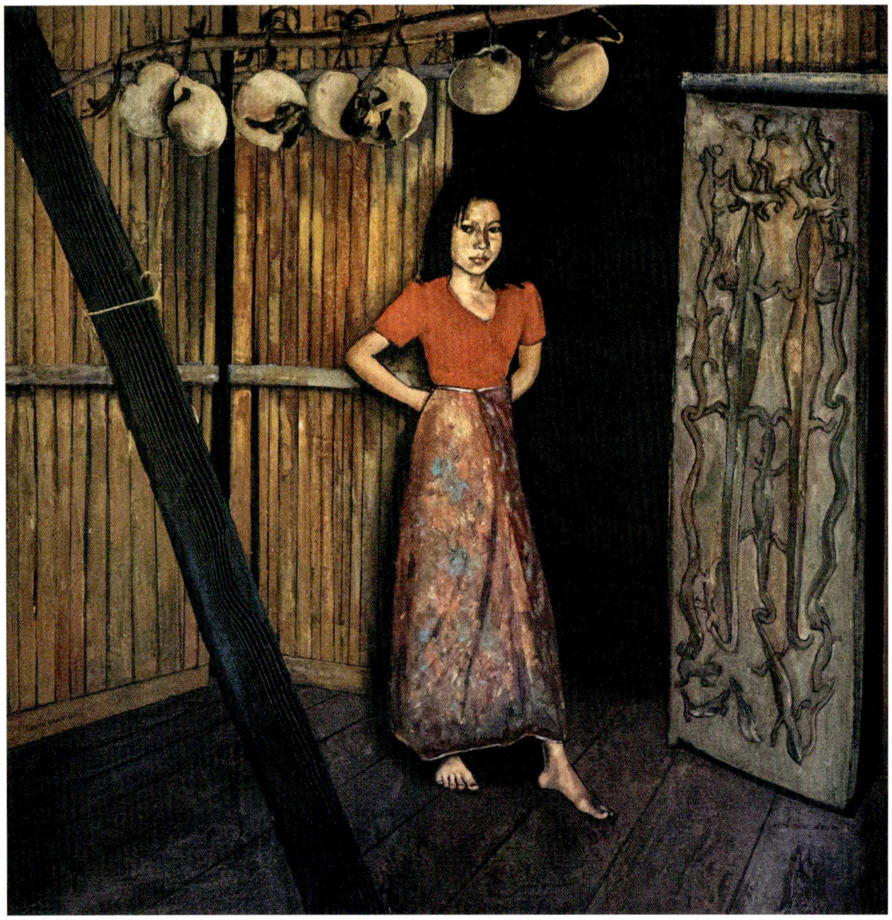

54
Tuah of the Batu Bungan,
1985/90/2009
Oil on board
102 × 102 cm
Collection of the artist

described in detail the types of plants that alternated profusion with 'almost architectonic' order. Each leaf bore a different form: 'blades, spatulae, fronds, cinquefoil, trefoil, feathers, hands, fans, etc.'[15] A similar attention to detail can be seen in the closely observed paintings of plants made by Lucian Freud while staying with Ian Fleming in Jamaica, in 1953.

Among the most significant aspects of Grant's visits to Sarawak was a reawakening of interest in the human figure. He drew children and women in particular, recalling how his sketchbook became almost 'a passport' among those who welcomed him into their homes.[16] Drawing at night in Long Miri he experienced, as earlier in Lio Matoh, the sensation of 'people behind me gently blowing on to my neck as I worked. I presumed this was to cool me.'[17] In July 1985, three months after his second visit to Sarawak, he began an uncompromising painting of Tuah, the young wife of the head of the village, who had acted as a guide on the ascent of Gunung Mulu (fig.54). Initially included in the composition was the bloodied corpse of a monkey, its eyes blank and mouth propped open to reveal fangs. The door towards the dark forest is ornamented with ancient carvings of snakes and lizards; above head-height is a slung row of human skulls. The subject, Tuah, reflected for Grant 'the reality of life in the jungle': beauty and pride, often amid decay, corruption, injury or early death.[18] While painting, he sensed her presence linger elusively on the easel, changing expression. The implication is fascinating, not least since in the finished composition Tuah's face proves difficult to read. Originally her eyes looked towards the monkey; after Grant's revision of the painting in 1990, removing the animal, her gaze falls upon something unseen. Jacquetta Hawkes interpreted the original version as a plea 'to us all to spare these last rain forests and their people'.[19] Once titled *Death and the Maiden*, it remains a beautiful yet disturbing image.

Grant painted certain subjects repeatedly, varying the detail or emphasis. Several paintings record the Salo Bridge, built to take children to school across a ravine containing king cobras. In one version, using a high-key palette, he introduced a segment of azure sky at the top, straightened the bridge and hardened the outlines of the leftmost tree trunk, serrated palm fronds and leaves that frame the image. Another version softens the light and removes the glimpse of sky to stress a sense of enclosure beneath the tree canopy (fig.55). The treatment of light, here, is subtle and mysterious, dappling the trunks and creating textures that dissolve their solidity. To the right, an area of darkness implies the snake-filled ravine.

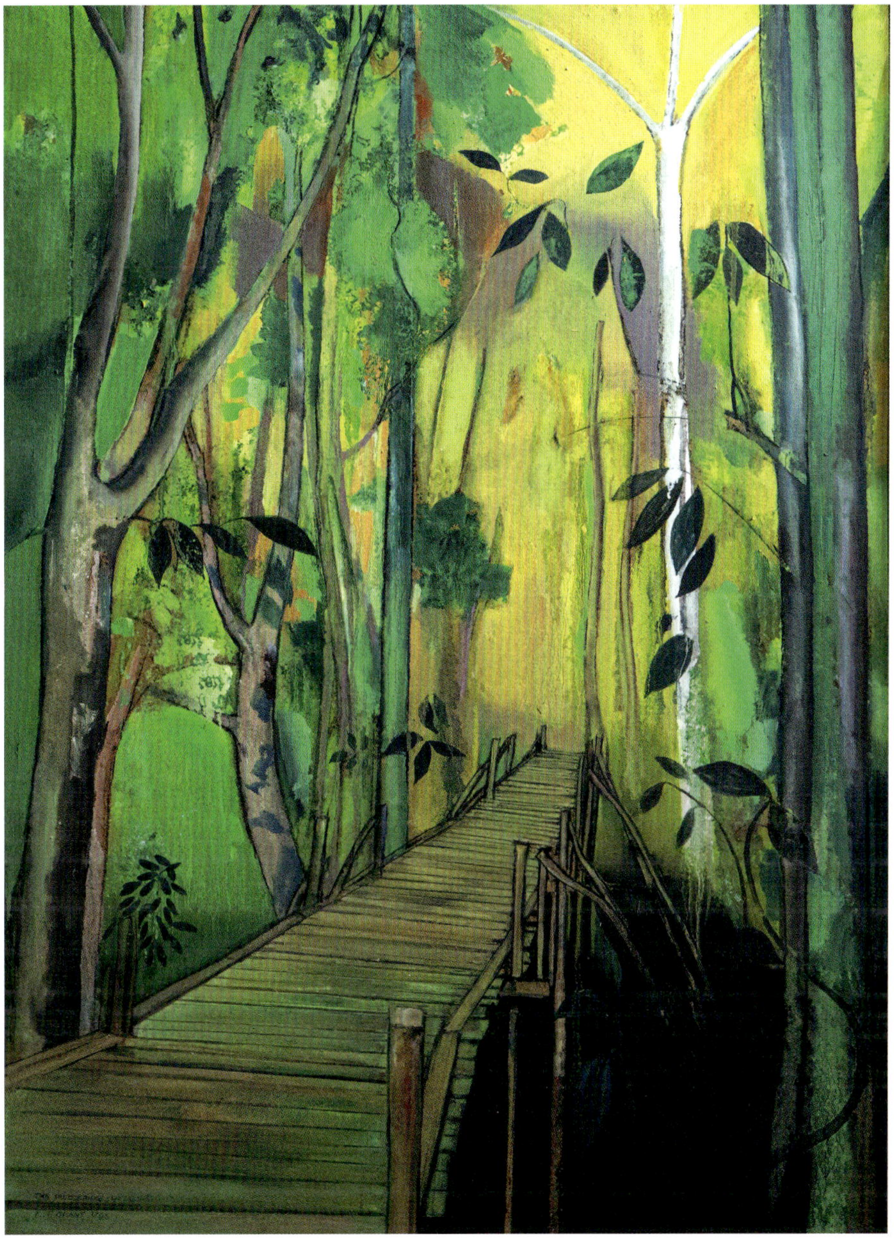

55
The Salo Bridge, Lio Matoh, Sarawak, 1985
Oil on board
123 × 91 cm
Collection of the artist

As Grant was painting these works he remained conscious of Paul Gauguin's Tahiti paintings, which, in their portrayal of an untouched paradise, sidestep questions about the impact of sexual exploitation and colonialism. Grant described Gauguin's stance as 'genuine dishonesty', resulting in 'a kind of history painting . . . bound to appeal to the amateur anthropologist in us' – masterpieces based on the foundation of a lie.[20] Gauguin's was an uneasy if inescapable creative companionship. Living among the people in Sarawak, as Grant did for a brief period, he was an attentive observer. He noted among the children often an intense, fixed stare that gave their faces the beauty of sculpted masks. Physically, they possessed immense grace, crouching without awkwardness, able to negotiate rock or mud and to climb with ease the notched tree trunks or poles giving access to their houses. An inner strength allowed the adults to remain motionless for long periods while children wove intricate patterns among them.[21]

These glimpses from Grant's journals inform an understanding of the resulting paintings. One of his finest figure studies, *The Visitation, Sarawak* (1985), derives from seeing two young girls – the left-hand figure again being Tuah – meet one another (fig.56). Perhaps because of being watched, the friends' shyness and intimacy seemed to imply a spiritual connection, recalling for Grant the paintings of the Annunciation by Fra Angelico. In Grant's composition, a strong structural framework is created by the wooden platform, diagonal beam and arches of broad-leaved banana leaves. The detailing of Tuah's dress echoes the nearby foliage. Unity between nature and existence is a powerful message; yet it is equally a sense of mystery – in the areas of darkness and the figures' oblique glances – that charges the composition.

Through his visits to Sarawak, Grant attracted the attention of conservationists. Paintings such as *Gunung Api* and *Gunung Mulu* (1985), exhibited at the Francis Kyle Gallery in 1985, were reproduced and sold in aid of the environmental organisation Earthlife Foundation. Among those working for Earthlife was

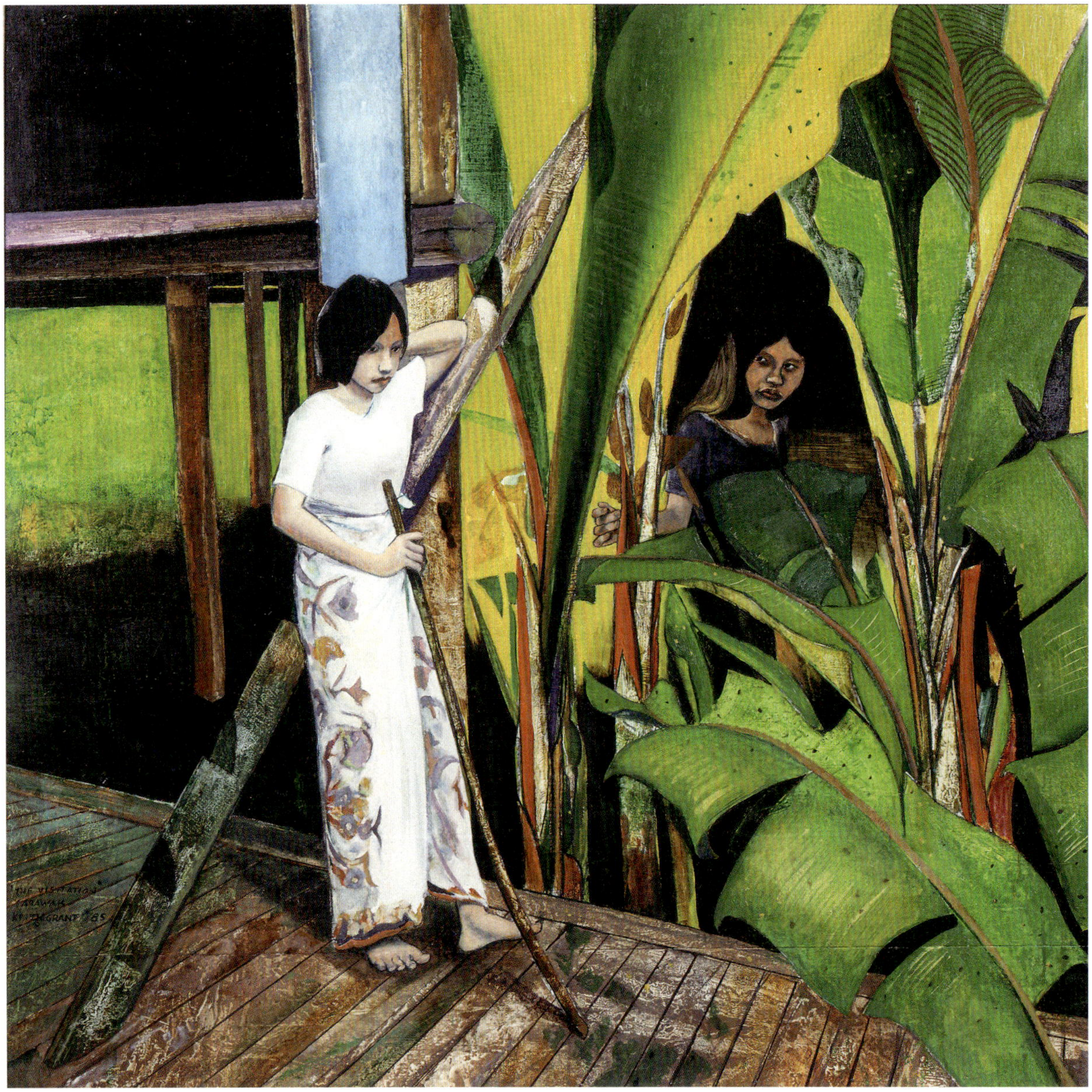

56
The Visitation, Sarawak, 1985
Oil on board
122 × 122 cm
Private Collection, Norway

Phil Agland, whose award-winning documentary *Korup: An African Rainforest*, filmed over a span of five years, was shown during Channel 4's first week of broadcasting in November 1982. Agland and Earthlife spearheaded a ten-year campaign to protect Korup's rainforest, securing the first British Government contribution of £440,000 towards conservation and resulting in the forest's designation as a National Park. It was through this connection that Grant travelled to Cameroon in April 1985: his first experience of Africa.

Cameroon

Grant's Cameroon sketchbook pays particular attention to plants and trees, often depicting them as isolated specimens. A flowering frangipani tree is carefully recorded, standing squat and densely foliated. In a drawing made on the same day, 8 April, a tall fringe of elephant grass screens the distant jungle under a leaden sky. Days later Grant travelled to the lava fields of Mount Cameroon, which in 1959 had

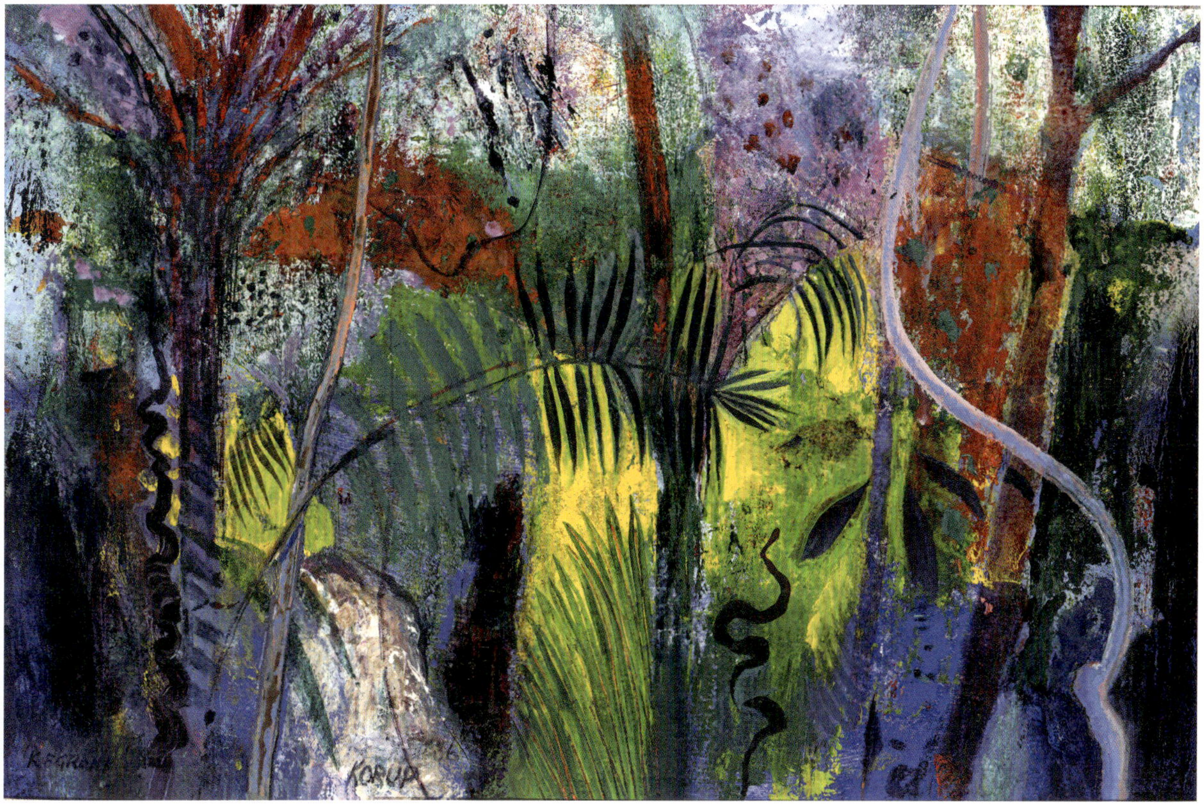

57
Landscape at the Foot of Mount Cameroon, Korup, 1986
Oil on canvas
dimensions not known
Private Collection (location unknown)

stopped a kilometre short of the town of Ekona. There, he drew the dominating canopy of the *Ceiba* (or kapok), having been forbidden from photographing it because the tree is sacred. He noted the blue smoke from small fires lit to create clearings where bananas and yams might be planted. As he drew, a brilliant butterfly – 'dark purple black with white insignia on the wing tips and two pools of iridescent aquamarine/turquoise on each main wing' – alighted and rested on his hand.[22] Grant stayed only two weeks, yet worked intensely to return with as many photographs, drawings and memorised images as possible.

It was ten full days into the visit before Grant arrived at Korup, where, having fulfilled the stringent immigration obligations, he was permitted to enter the rainforest. Too tired by then to write descriptively, he simply filled six pages of his journals with a list of impressions: hornbills, a poacher, fruit, monkeys, a rattan basket, flowers, termites' nests, roots, a second poacher, the common toad, a shotgun cartridge, varieties of liana (belt, twisted, looped, plaited, coiled), insect stings, illicit gin, ants, fish, deer, birdsong, the detail and texture of the bush. Many more sensations were itemised – not least the bee sting – and remained with him, 'as if a recurring dream'.[23]

The paintings realised on Grant's return to England surpass those of Sarawak in vividness, tapping a palette frequently invoked in his journals. Night skies glowed 'orange and pink, peach, lemon and pale violet' between indigo clouds; the air heavy with humid heat.[24] In a painting inscribed 'Korup' (1986), the composition is blocked into reds, blues, yellows, greens and purples, creating a structure over and through which the forest vegetation twines (fig.57). Colour coruscates, applied in fluid strokes, thinly brushed or as speckles to suggest the insect-filled air. Although the palm fronds and trunks confirm the subject as landscape, Grant's rendering is close to abstraction. The path he followed through the rainforest threaded narrowly around rocks, roots and trees, across sandy soil that provided

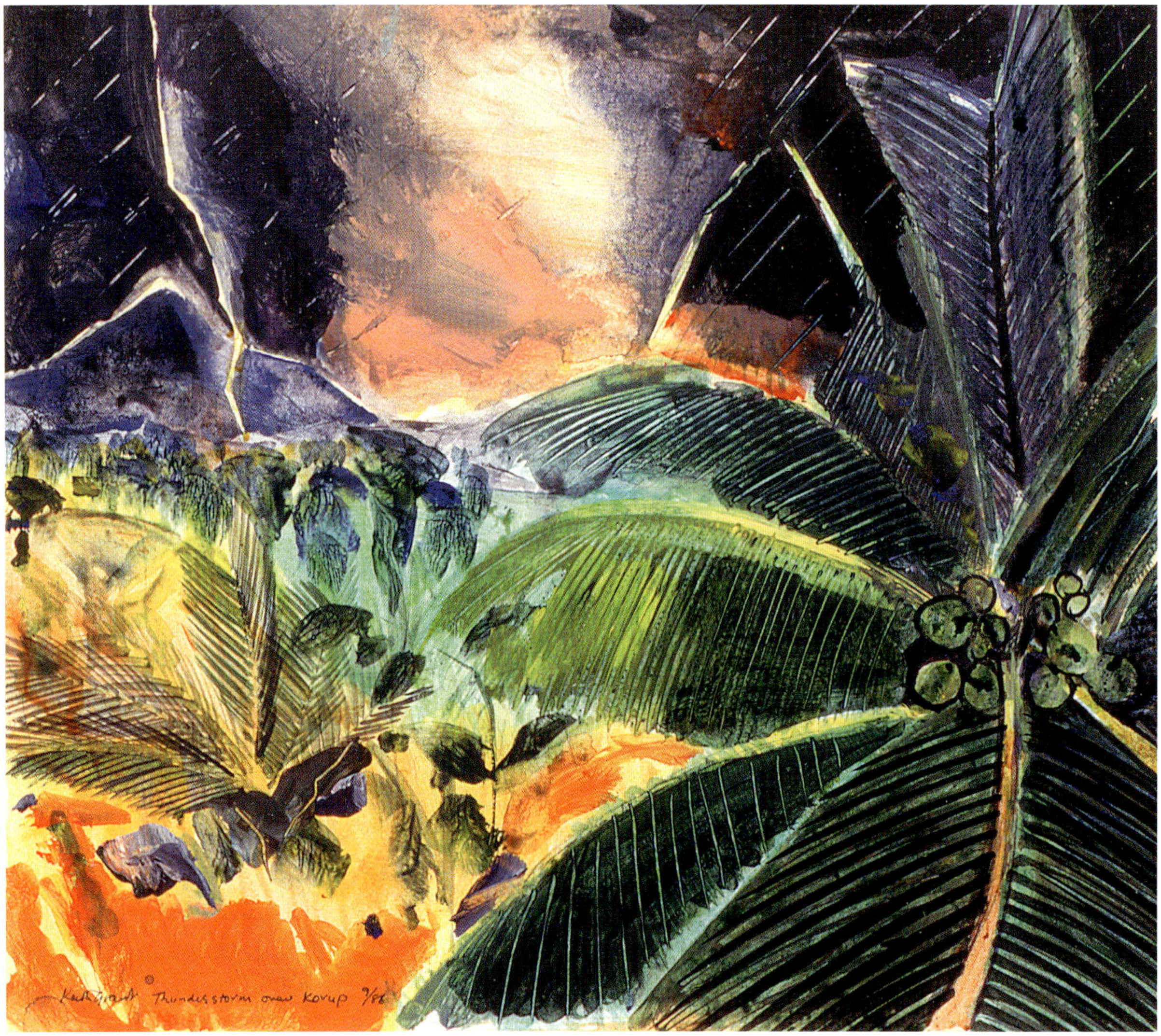

58
Thunderstorm over Korup, Cameroon, 1986
Watercolour, acrylic and ink on paper
approx. 20 × 25.5 cm
Private Collection (location unknown)

little anchorage for trees. Aerial roots formed arches like 'flying buttress of eccentric and varied design'. Penetrating deeper into the forest, Grant noted that the 'sheer variety of greens and the confusion of branches and lianas created a staggeringly beautiful textural quality. The growth was in the main vertical towards the canopy in which hornbills, squirrels and monkeys could be seen. Some of the trees displayed the most lovely shades of red/purply-red/orange and yellow.'[25] A painting of a thunderstorm captures the elemental transformation of landscape (fig.58). Lightning illuminates the rain, while the wind, violently strong, whips the trees into a fantastical shadow-dance. Again, colour flashes the landscape.

Israel

Despite over thirty years' experience of working in the landscape, Grant's particularity of response was such

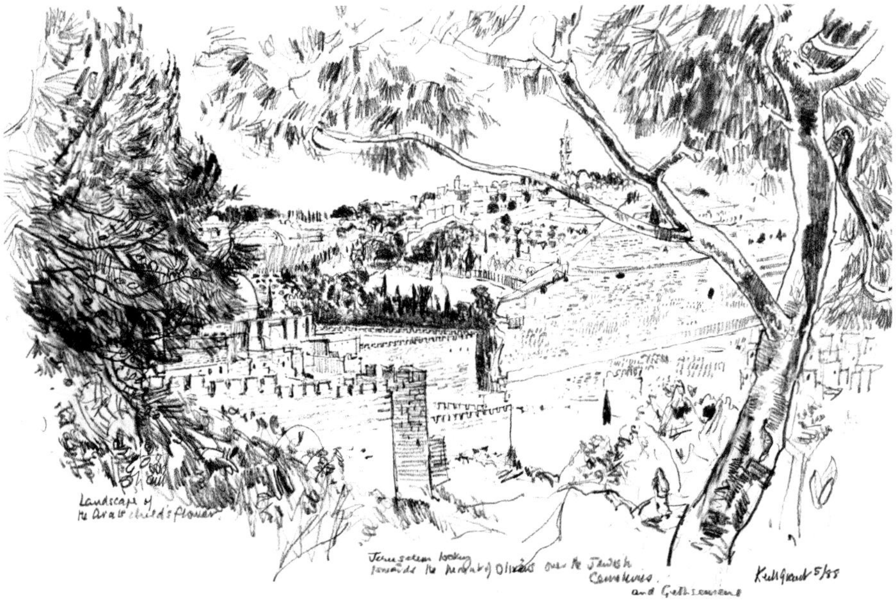

59
Landscape of the Arab Child's Flower, May 1988
Pencil on paper
28.5 × 40.5 cm
Collection of the artist

that he never relied upon a single approach: each new terrain demanded a different way of working. Sarawak elicited paintings he felt in retrospect to be unduly illustrative; those from Cameroon developed more imaginatively from their source material. Yet even as Grant was coming to terms with the rainforest, he was already envisaging the desert, possibly the Sahara. Was this a compulsion to experience an antithesis to the North, and thus, contrarily, to precipitate a return to its frozen landscapes? An invitation from the British Israel Arts Foundation and Ben Gurion University Trust in April 1988 presented an opportunity to visit Israel, and with it the Negev desert.

Grant's sketchbooks depict barren landscapes that contrast diametrically with the enclosure of the rainforest. In these new drawings, the horizon reasserts itself: high, to emphasise the sere, stony habitat, or low, to emphasise the immensity of sky. Grant described in his journals the psychological effect of the desert as an 'arena' to test the strongest wills, asking,

How could I expect to come here and remark upon the strange topography as might a visitor passing through? I have not – there is a power here, more devastating than the volcano in Iceland infinitely more terrifying than the Arctic storm. Each rock shadow which falls across the sand is a metaphor; of harrowing loneliness and death. The geological reality of this place contributes little to lessening my subjectivity, for it is of the force behind the forms that I think.[26]

In the desert, Grant read the rocks' architectonic forms as if a 'cubistic' code: a naturally scrawled calligraphy of pyramids and cones. A monster rock, so named by him after Paul Nash's surrealistic findings, resembled a giant reptile twisting its 'bulk high above the valley in a spectacular flurry of petrified gills and fins'.[27] Jerusalem, however, provoked a creative impasse, with Grant daunted both by the wealth of topographical depiction that preceded him and the concern that creating drawings specifically for an exhibition constituted working to order. Yet whether premeditated or spontaneous, Grant did create a portfolio of topographical compositions while in Israel. These differed from his sketchbook drawings in their degree of finish: where the former indicated the outline of landscape, featuring only selected details and notes, the latter were realised in detail.

A view of Jerusalem looking across the Jewish cemeteries and Gethsemane towards the Mount of Olives was titled *Landscape of the Arab Child's Flower*, after a gift of a marigold made while Grant

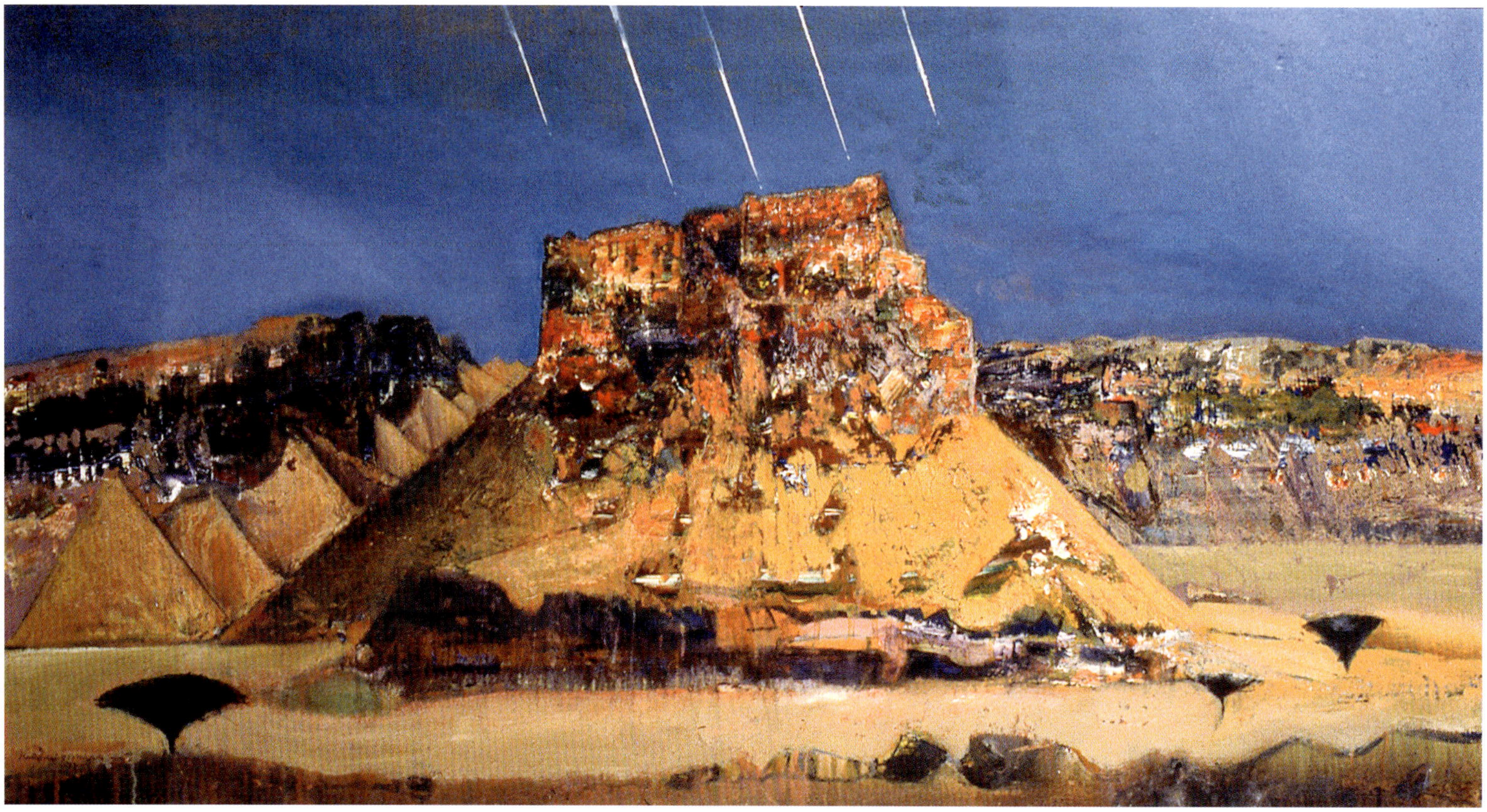

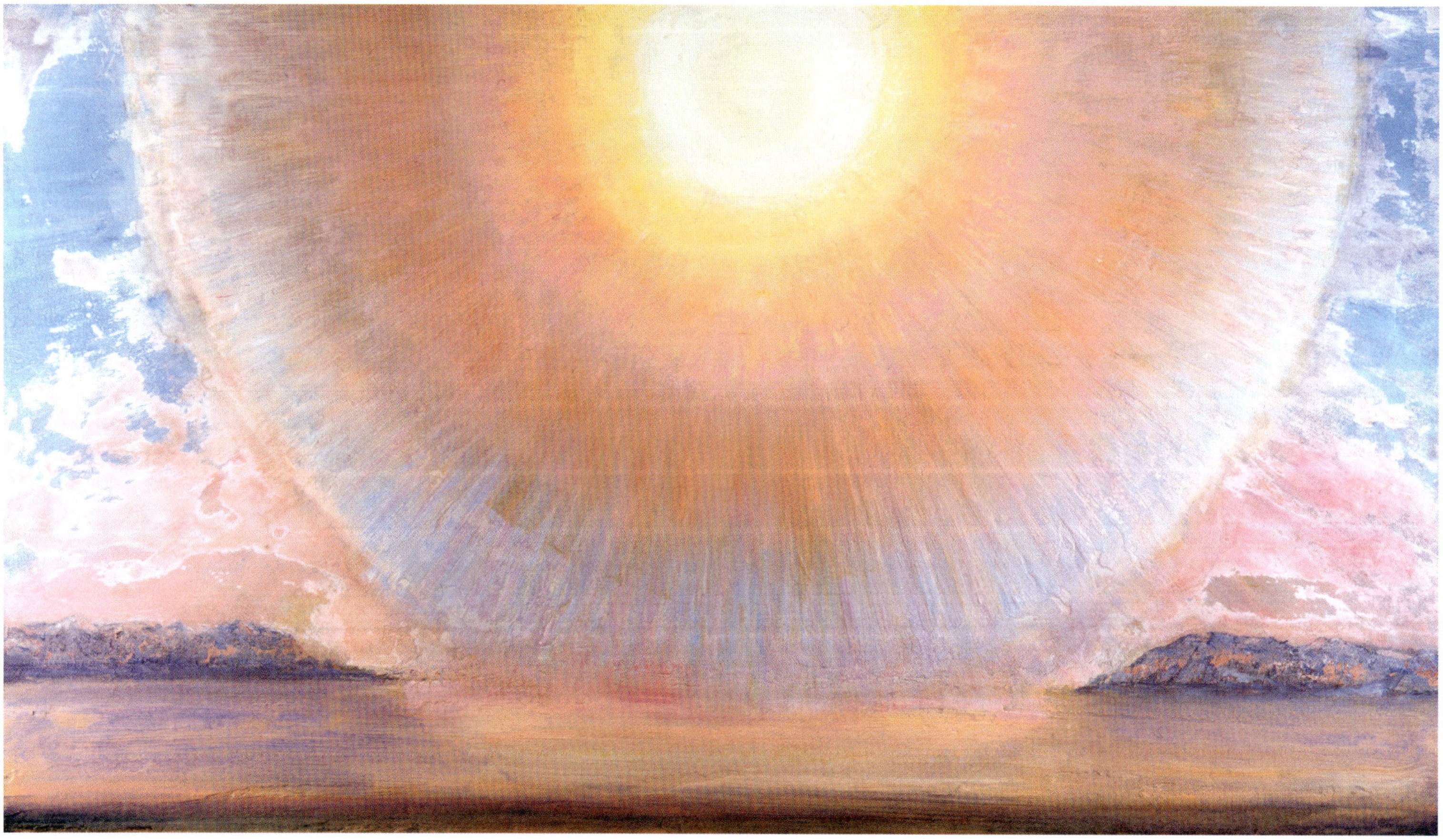

60
Masada with Jet Streams, Israel, 1989
Oil on canvas
59.7 × 133 cm
Private Collection (location unknown)

61
Sunburst over the Negev, Israel, 1989
Acrylic over gesso on board
68.6 × 122 cm
Private Collection, UK

was drawing (1988; fig.59). In the foreground are the city's crenellated walls. As the view extends, it encompasses the garden of Gethsemane and Jewish cemetery. Grant had read Joseph Ernest Renan's popular *Life of Jesus* (*Vie de Jésus*, 1863), praised facetiously by the theologian Albert Schweitzer for its 'skill to make [readers] see blue skies, seas of waving corn, distant mountains, gleaming lilies, in a landscape with the Lake of Gennesareth for its centre'.[28] The key was Renan's ability to transport the imagination to a timeless landscape in which history is enacted. From his window in Jerusalem, Grant looked out over the massive city walls screening the Armenian Quarter, with, to the left, the 16th-century Jaffa Gate. Drawing Jerusalem, he framed his composition as landscape, curtained by trees and scrub, sloping upwards to the distance.

In drawings of the Sea of Galilee, *en plein air*, Grant used oil pastel for the first time. The medium was ideally suited to depicting light, which Grant described as 'deeply mysterious and of blinding intensity at midday'.[29] Around the lake's edges flourished thistles and bell-like flowers the size of hollyhocks, mauve-pink in colour. In *The Eastern Shore of Galilee*, a drawing made on 7 May 1988, Grant recorded exactly this scene: the lake dusted with silver, an iridescent sky and a foreground implying an abundance of flowers. The novelty of the approach proved liberating: 'I found I was working practically automatically and selecting from the colours those most capable of conveying the light, heat and diffused distance.'[30]

Back in England, Grant faced the routinely difficult task of retaining the impetus of what he had seen. He resumed a triptych of the sea left unfinished before departure. Its subject now counterbalanced his recent experience: the sea as the region where life started, the desert its negation. A period of organisation, as he prepared boards and bought paints for the new work, provided an interlude of calm. Arranging his photographs suggested the desert as 'a landscape of panoramas, of series of architectonic forms ranked one behind the other until the broken horizon merges with the sky'.[31]

The ancient fortress of Masada, on the eastern edge of the Judean desert overlooking the Dead Sea, was among Grant's most vivid experiences, forming the basis of at least five paintings. Masada stands on an isolated plateau amid a landscape of such silent loneliness that Grant felt detached, as if 'looking into the past through some beautiful and inexplicable metaphysical system'.[32] While the landscape's antiquity is felt in paintings containing little except stone outcrops, there are also ciphers for a continuing human presence. Masada has a rich history of occupation. At the palace of King Herod the Great, seeds from the extinct palm forests of the Jordan valley were discovered in 1963 and germinated forty years later by a scientist in Tel-Aviv, to raise a tree named Methuselah. Herod's palace endured a year-long siege by the Romans, after which its Jewish occupants committed suicide rather than surrender. The fortress became a symbol of resistance. While Grant was there, a military presence remained visible at Masada: recruits for the Israeli Armoured Corps were required to ascend to the fortress at dawn, in order to swear allegiance to the nation of Israel. In *Masada with Jet Streams, Israel* (1989) Grant included five vapour trails from the Israeli Defence Force's aeroplanes that patrol the region (fig.60). He followed the siege walls built to encircle Masada, and experienced intense sadness at the thoroughness of

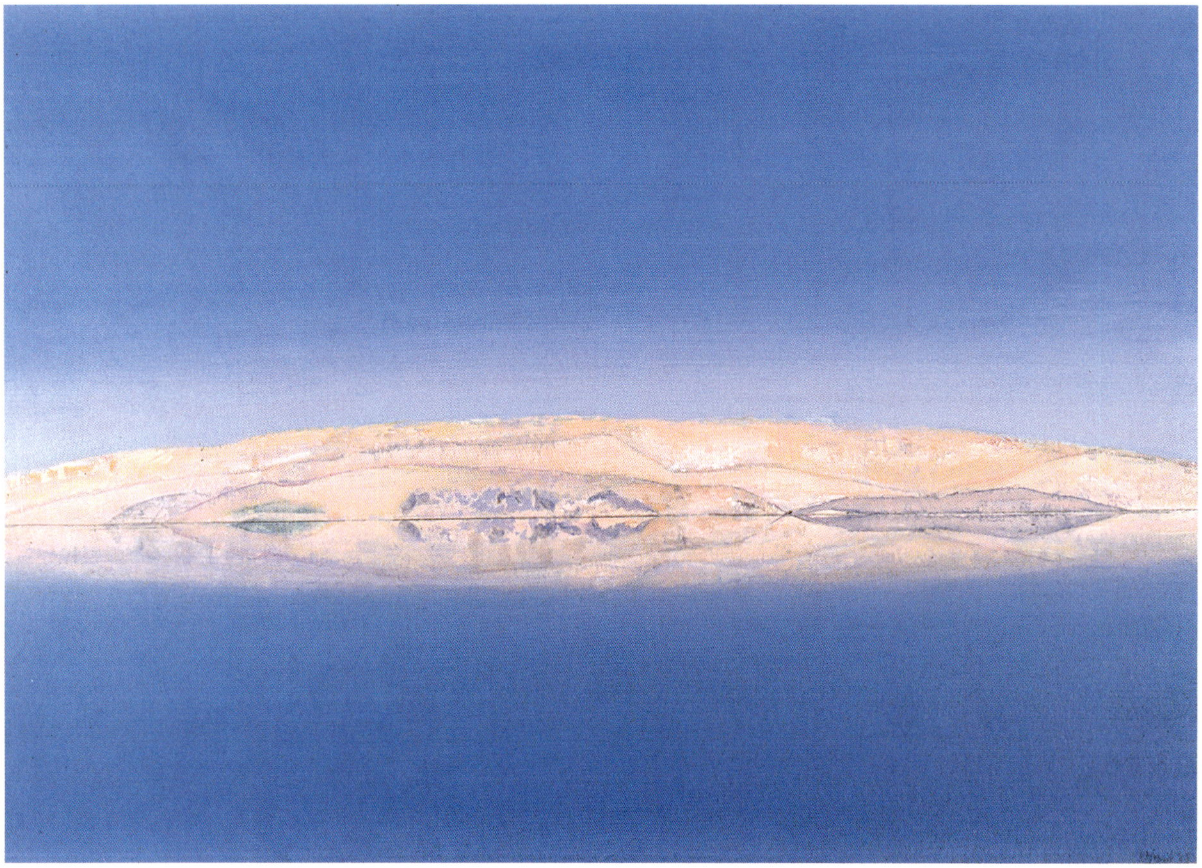

62
Reflections, The Dead Sea, Israel, 1988
Acrylic on canvas
51 × 91 cm
Private Collection (location unknown)

their construction. His Israel journal is suffused with alternate questioning, outrage and empathy for what he encountered, juxtaposed with the quotidian threat of danger. Roads were subject to frequent ambush. Near the Sea of Galilee, in a landscape of light, birds and 'sublime blues', Grant suddenly observed a fine, vertical vapour trail – 'an accent like a white incision in the taut cerulean membrane of heaven.'[33] A detonation echoed on the mountainsides, muffled by the burning air.

Heat pervades Grant's descriptions and paintings of Israel. Although he had painted the sun repeatedly, and with particular focus since the early 1980s, the new works possessed a specific intensity. As Grant described, 'Here . . . it is no distant phenomenon to be viewed, it is as if a million suns are bursting in the bloodstreams of my body.'[34]

Sunburst over the Negev, Israel (1989) crops the sun to emphasise the overwhelming proximity of its presence (fig.61). The sun appears like an immense eye, a rainbow of heat pulsing from the searing pupil at its centre. Only much later does landscape itself become apparent. Rocks that are monumental in actuality recede as a jagged horizon, bleached by light. Grant was reminded, while in the desert, of the apocalyptic landscapes of the 19th-century painter John Martin, and contemplated making works possessing formal simplicity and a careful calculation of colour, texture and facture in relation to scale. A painting of the Jordan mountains reflected in the Dead Sea becomes a strip of landscape, glowing brown-pink and rose-violet as the sun fell (fig.62). Jacquetta Hawkes wrote admiringly of Grant's Israeli desert paintings, with their 'oxidised colours of dryness and heat'.[35]

Guyana

In April 1991, as Art Director of Operation Raleigh, Grant underwent a weekend of strenuous physical tests to qualify for a forthcoming visit to Guyana, in South America. He was required to plunge fully clothed into a freezing lake, cross it by tightrope, climb an electric fence using three logs and some rope without touching it, locate a position with incorrect map co-ordinates and run for 3 miles. Having passed with some pride, aged 60, he accompanied Operation Raleigh's expedition to compare the survival of fish from the lower and higher regions of the Potaro River.

The focus of his own work became the Kaieteur Falls, the largest volume single-drop waterfall in the world. Prior to departure, Grant discussed Guyana with David Attenborough, who had noticed and admired his paintings of French Guiana before knowing him as an artist. Attenborough opened Grant's exhibition in May 1991 at Roehampton Institute, where he had recently been appointed artist-in-residence. A fortnight later Grant showed the exhibition to the poet Kathleen Raine. Without knowing of his impending visit to South America, Raine recommended the Guyanese writer Wilson Harris, in whose first novel, *The Palace of the Peacock* (1960), the river and waterfall, presumed to be Kaieteur, are principal symbols.

Photographs of Grant sketching at Kaieteur show him kneeling on a narrow overhang adjacent to the immense vertical downflow of water. He is immersed in the scene, such that you can almost hear the thunder of the waterfall and feel its spray. Grant remained for many hours lying flat on this rock, later recording:

I could see the complete length of the plummeting river until it disintegrated into a vast cauldron of roaring explosions and rioting tidal waves . . . Above this maelstrom the delicate spectrum of a rainbow trembled silk-like within diaphanous veils of descending vapour. The tropical evening advanced into night as if a colossal dimmer-switch rapidly and steadily reduced the light. Suddenly from the deepening sky thousands of swifts in precisely timed squadrons dived to their nightly roosts in the great cave behind the falls. The birds shot down the columns and folds of water almost faster than the eye could see and pulling out of their frenzied dive veered round and soared upwards behind the great curtain of the falling river, the river which now incessantly roared into a black void of vaporised space.[36]

Grant began with a series of paintings in acrylic, trying with each work to express the varying effect of the waterfall according to angle and distance. On some days he watched vapour rising from the cauldron at the foot of the waterfall to fill the entire valley. In *Kaieteur* (1991), the fall is depicted from directly in front, crashing into the river below and barely screening the cave behind (fig.63). Paint is applied mercurially to suggest the texture of rock caught by light, the movement of clouds or the veiling of water-haze. Working on a large canvas of the same subject, Grant began to capture different aspects of the phenomenon he had studied for over two weeks, memorising its 'detail of light shattered mist and curtained space'.[37] He then decided to extend the canvas by adding two side panels to create a span of 182 x 320 cm. The column of the falls divided the void of the cave, which appears

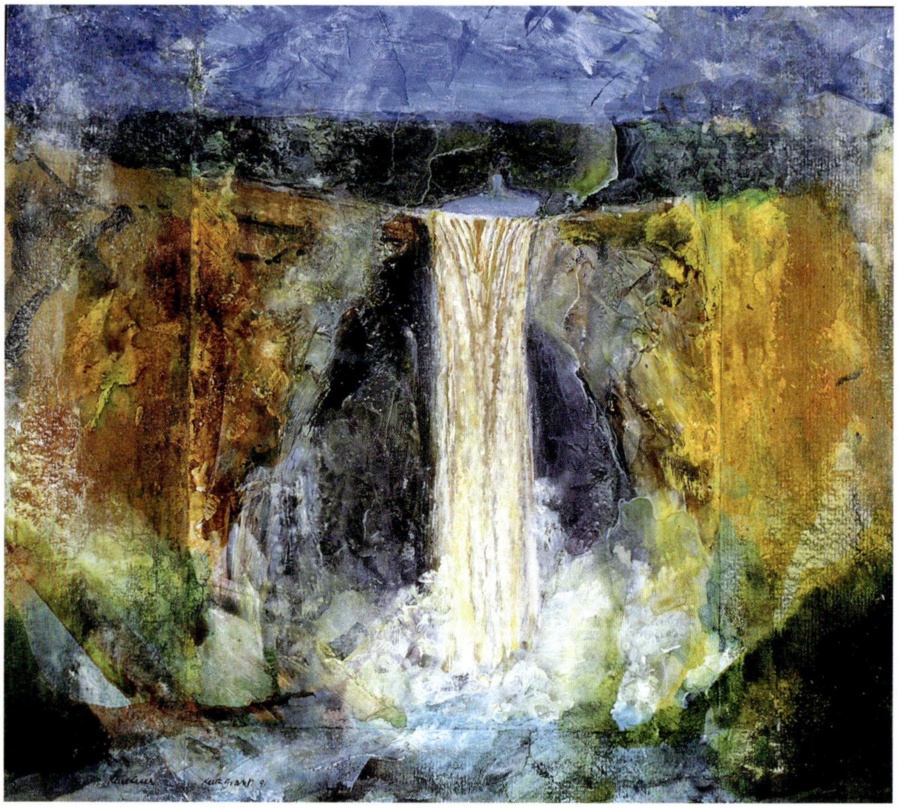

63
Kaieteur, 1991
Watercolour and acrylic on card
27 × 32.5 cm
Private Collection, UK

gouged into the cliff wall, flanked on either side by shafts of broken and continuous water. This masterly depiction of vapour, melding with water and blurring the edges of the rock, recalls his vision of the haze filling the valley.

Writing about Grant's recent paintings, at the Gillian Jason Gallery in February 1992, Attenborough drew attention to the tradition of British explorers as mountaineers and travellers, particularly to the polar regions, South America and Africa. William Hodges, in the 18th century, revealed 'visions of a new paradise in the Pacific' through his paintings of voyages with Captain Cook. But who had followed his example? Attenborough identified Grant as rare in embracing the gamut of landscape, paralleling a growing realisation by naturalists of the environment's interconnectivity: that pollution on one continent poisons woodland on another, that destroying equatorial forests may impel polar climate change, and that 'the extermination of an animal or plant, no matter where it takes place, impoverishes us all'.[38] Attenborough admired the 'perfection and vividness' with which Grant conveyed extremes of landscape, particularly the enclosure of the rainforest, changing colour throughout the day, then suddenly breaking to provide a vista of a waterfall.[39]

It was not that Grant had never painted waterfalls before: he had, in studies extending as far back as his paintings of Norway in 1959. Yet the works based on Kaieteur captured something entirely new through their prolonged engagement with a single example. By dint of this experience he was able to short-circuit his approach, creating waterfall paintings striking in their abstraction and immediacy. In *The Hanging Forest, Guyana* (1991) there is no firm sense of orientation (fig.64). A curved rock resembles the surface of a planet; to its left is a thin white line of water, behind it a green curtain, below a pool of concentrated blue. Discussing Kaieteur, before Grant's visit there, Attenborough mentioned that he could imagine the rocket trails of his *Ariane* paintings transmuted into waterfalls. The suggestion excited Grant. Visiting Venezuela with Earthlife in 1992, and journeying through the rainforests with the natural history illustrator John Norris Wood to see Angel Falls, the highest waterfall in the world, provided the visual data to test the idea.

64
The Hanging Forest, Guyana,
1991
Acrylic on paper
27 × 32.5 cm
Collection of the artist

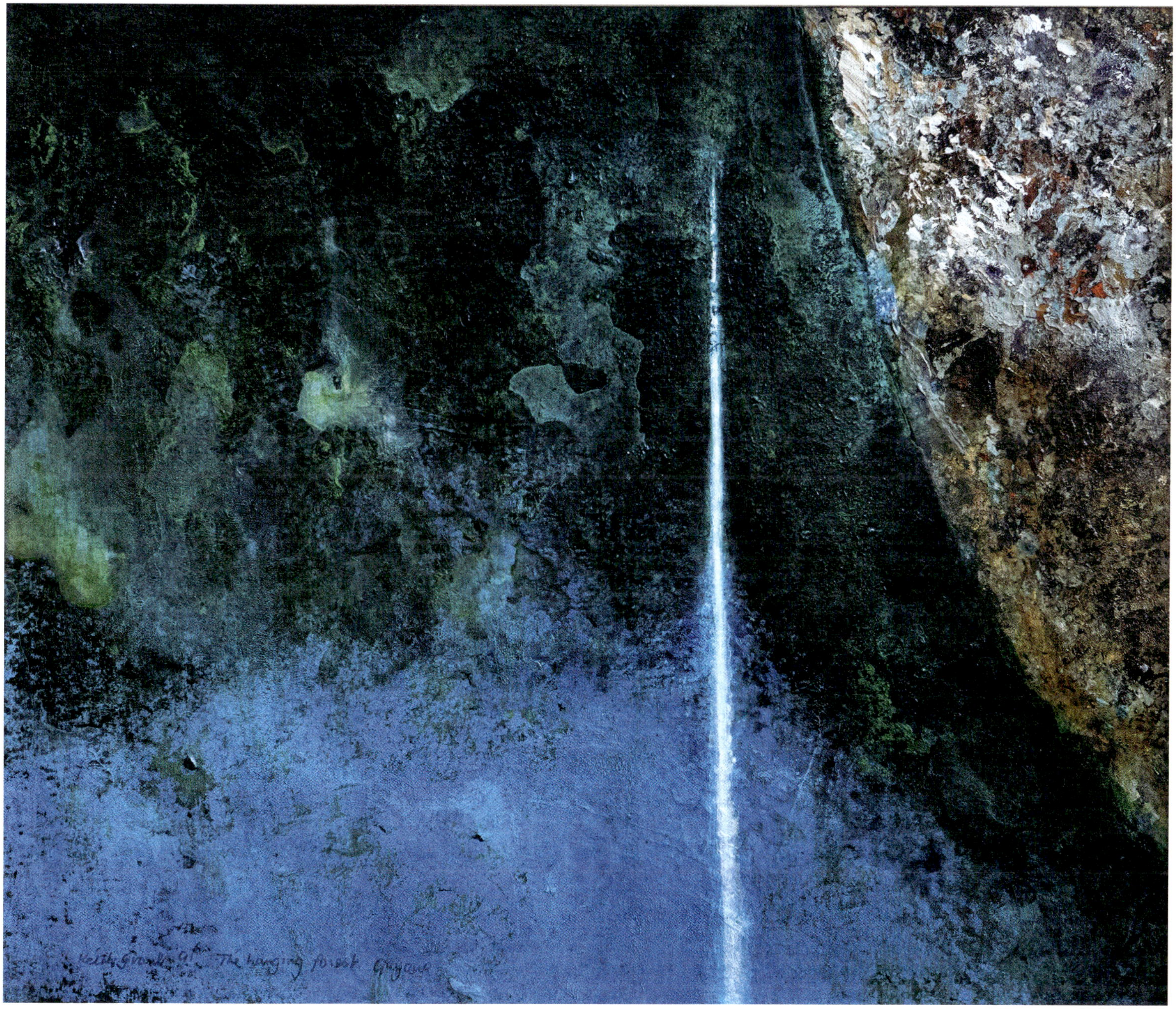

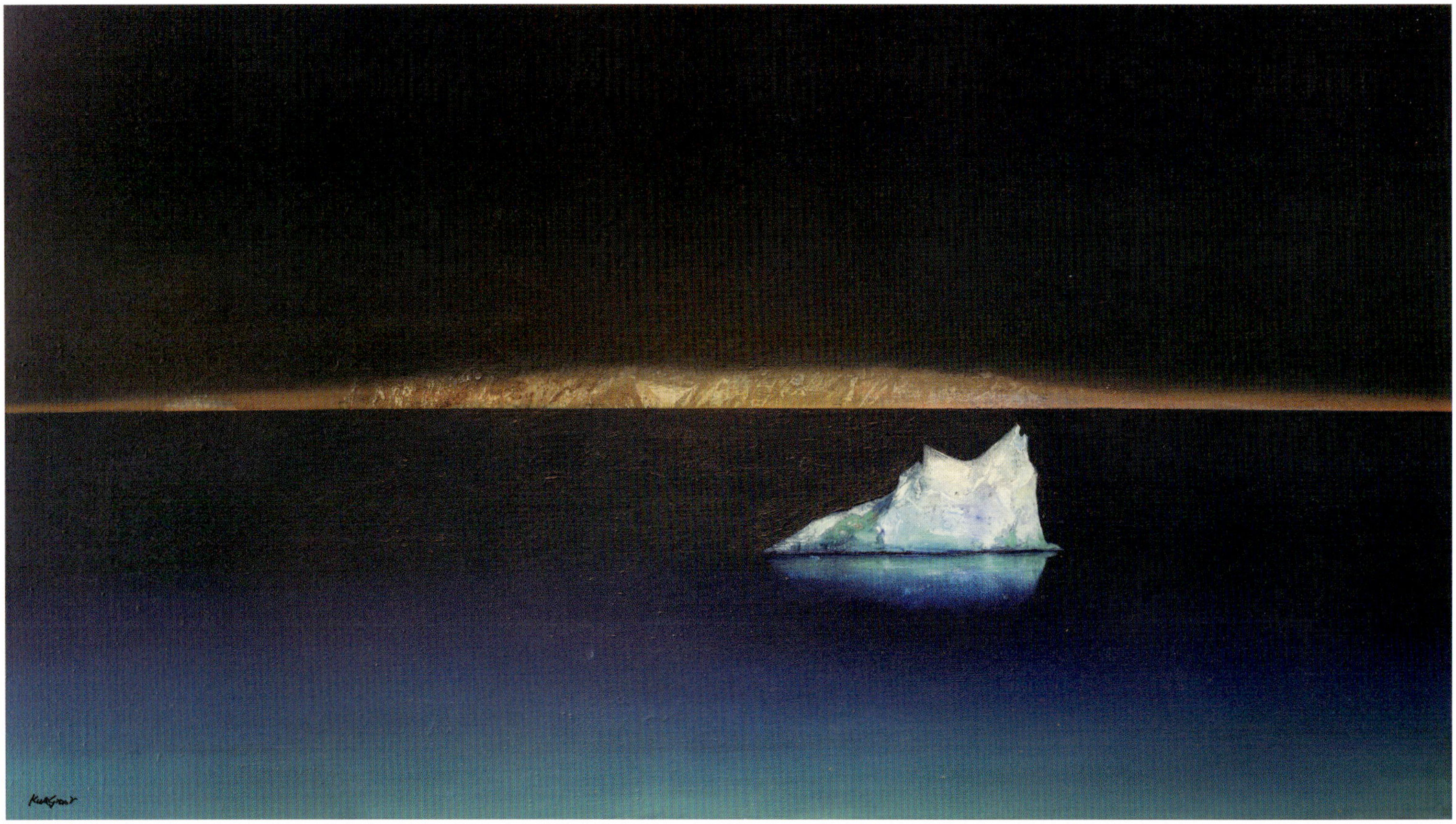

4

Ice

Greenland

On 30 August 1989, a day after poor visibility had prevented all flights, Grant flew from Reykjavik to Narsarsuaq, at the head of the Tunulliarfik Fjord in southern Greenland. As soon as the aeroplane crossed the coast, the ice cap became visible. Everywhere there were signs of geological stress. Glaciers threaded towards the sea between snow-buried mountains; furrows appearing no more than wrinkles from the air became 'terrifying crevasses' on descending to snow level. Settled into his hotel, Grant walked to the fjord and for the first time encountered icebergs: exquisite, jewel-like forms, whose sharp edges possessed a diamond transparency. Deeper within them, the low evening sun was transmuted into a spectrum of colour. Viridian greens, Prussian and cobalt blues, pinks and mauves, pale violets, yellows, iridescent pearl, umber and madder appeared as an 'almost super-natural expression' in the flotillas of ice, motionless upon the dark water.[1]

65
Beyond Silence, 1989
Oil on canvas
68.5 × 118 cm
Private Collection, UK

Beyond Silence (1989) locates a solitary iceberg in a night sea (fig.65). There are no stars or moon, yet a pale light spreads along the horizon and illuminates the iceberg in colours from palest blue to aquamarine. Preparing to travel to Greenland, Grant had asked, 'How will my viewing icebergs affect my future work?'[2] He had long known Caspar David Friedrich's *Das Eismeer* (*The Sea of Ice*, 1823–4), depicting a ship crushed by shattered Arctic pack ice but painted from observing the frozen River Elbe in Germany.[3] By 1989 he was studying paintings by the 19th-century American landscape artist Frederic Edwin Church based on sketches made during a month-long journey to the North Atlantic coasts of Newfoundland and Labrador. Church's *The Icebergs* (1861), seen by Grant first in reproduction then in January 1990 at the National Gallery of Art in Washington DC, in an exhibition he travelled expressly to see, depicts solid and hollowed ice masses against a roseate sky. Monumentally and romantically conceived, it nonetheless contains a human scale in the addition of a broken mast in the foreground.

There is no such contrast in Grant's painting, which communicates its subject's desolation and inherent loneliness through minimal means. Although Grant felt a kinship with Church, he noted his own advantage in knowing the modernist work of Georges Braque, Picasso, Nicolas de Stäel and Mark Rothko:

For there must surely be an innate sense of the abstract geometry of natural form and an awareness

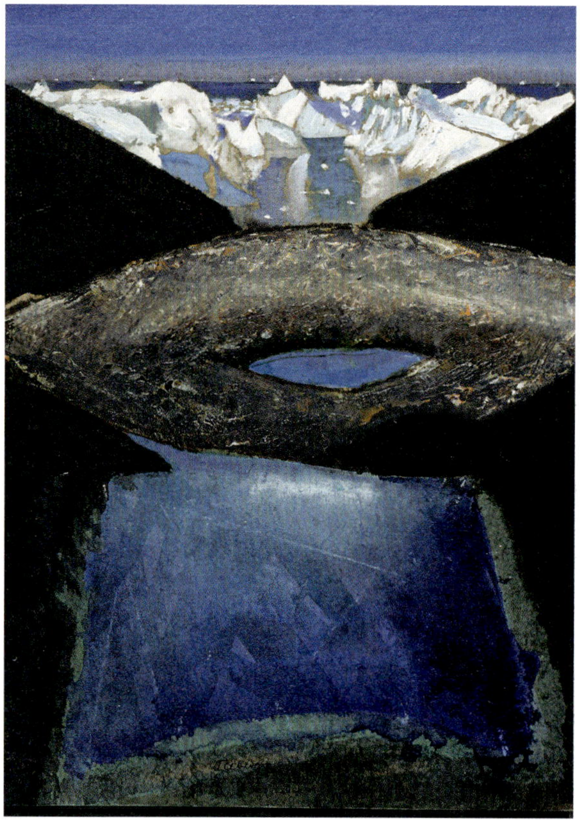

66 (left)
Icebergs Seen through a Valley with Frozen Pools, Jakobshavn, Greenland, 1990
Acrylic on paper laid on card
34.2 × 24.1 cm
Private Collection, UK

of the tactile quality of paint and how it might, as in a Strindberg [painting], be used fortuitously and intuitively. If painting such an awesome subject as icebergs newly carved from the parent glacier is to be free of idiosyncratic sentimentality or over-elaboration, then the abstract element is essential.[4]

Resolving to be as objective as possible, Grant was undoubtedly alive to intimations of the sublime in the work of the Abstract Expressionists. *Beyond Silence*, among his early iceberg paintings, perhaps comes closest to this in its distillation. Against a ground of limitless darkness, the horizon appears as a spectral 'zip' across the canvas.

By early September Grant had reached Jakobshavn, recommended to him by the British polar explorer Wally Herbert as having the most spectacular icebergs anywhere in the Arctic.[5] Jakobshavn, named after the Danish merchant Jakob Severin, who in 1739 repelled a Dutch fleet in Disko Bay, was later re-named Ilulíssat, meaning 'icebergs'. Grant spent all day at the ice-fjord, watching icebergs glisten in the sun: 'doomed vessels' already in the process of dissolution. The following day he discovered a valley giving a strikingly framed view of the icebergs. Underfoot was granite, glacier-scoured, patterned by quartz veins and coloured with yellow, russet, black and white lichen. The bay ahead was defined by an almost black shoreline that contrasted starkly with the ice crushed against it. To complete the 'pitilessness' of these elements, the landscape's stillness was broken by thunderous detonations as the ice shifted, creating an eerie cannonade that set dogs howling throughout the day.[6] In a composition based on this experience, Grant deftly marshalled the elements he had seen: a pool of viridian-turquoise water, in a black-rimmed stone nest, topped by icebergs in a sea of blue (fig.66). The view would be almost symmetrically balanced were it not for the ice, fragmented irregularly into larger and smaller floes, accentuating the perceived distance to the horizon.

After some difficulty, having been warned of the danger, Grant hired a small boat belonging to the Greenlander Henrik Petersson to venture into the icefields. The vessel was old, unprotected by guard rails, equipped only for solitary journeys into the sealing grounds. On deck was a large anchor and harpoon with an ivory tip and retractable barb.

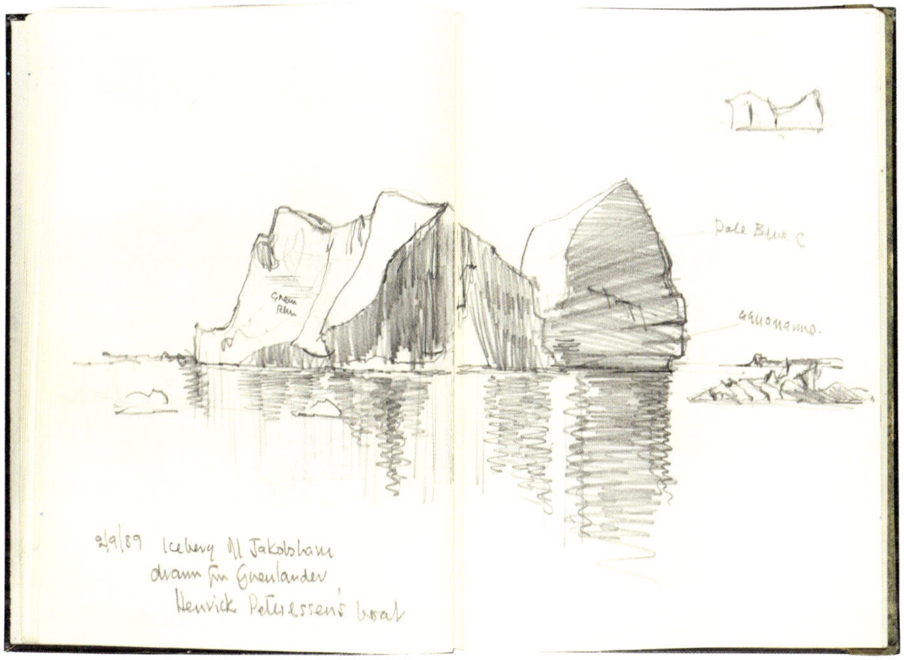

67
Icebergs off Jakobshavn, 1989, from the 'Greenland sketchbook'
Pencil on paper
29.5 × 40 cm
The Fitzwilliam Museum, Cambridge

Leaving the harbour, the sky began to cloud. The boat headed for two large icebergs some distance away, scraping its keel on submerged ice as it passed close to smaller icebergs, undercut and carved into caves by the sea. From these grottos, whose ceilings were hung with icicles resembling glass teeth, exhaled a cold breath.

F.E. Church kept no written account of his travels, and Grant marvelled at his ability to memorise colour. Grant's own journals contain detailed descriptions, matched by notes in his sketchbook recording the location on the ice of particular greens, aquamarines and blues. One page shows a large tabular iceberg seen from Petersson's boat, its form clearly delineated to show the smooth faces where it had broken free from a larger ice mass (fig.67). Above, on the righthand side, a smaller drawing indicates the placement of two vertical lines, described in his journal as light cobalt and cerulean blue, formed on the ice wall by melt water frozen in narrow fissures. Grant was reminded of a Barnett Newman painting: 'the lines were ruled and very thin in comparison with the mass they divided and . . . spoke of the divine geometry of this whole area'.[7]

Grant's journey to Greenland was prefaced by a premonition that the iceberg might supplant the volcano as a symbol in his paintings, to become a more 'natural' unifier of sky and sea. He perceived elegant parallels between the lava and vaporised seawater emitted from a marine volcano and the frozen precipitation released as an iceberg slowly dissolves: both are sublime, easily legible signs of the transformation of matter.[8] Jacquetta Hawkes, in her catalogue preface to the first exhibition of Greenland paintings, at the Crane Kalman Gallery in February 1990, considered the frozen landscape to have inspired some of Grant's finest work. Instead of monotony, she saw variation: a series of detailed character or portrait studies that contrasted with seascapes ('bergscapes') showing flotillas of ice on the water. Icebergs, for Hawkes, made ideal subjects for the transfiguration of nature, 'for they tend towards the abstract, sometimes approaching a natural cubism'.[9]

Antarctica, 2001–2

The Arctic landscape, with its formalised language of ice and water, had bitten deeply into Grant's visual imagination. In 1995 he received an invitation to accompany the British Antarctic Survey to the South

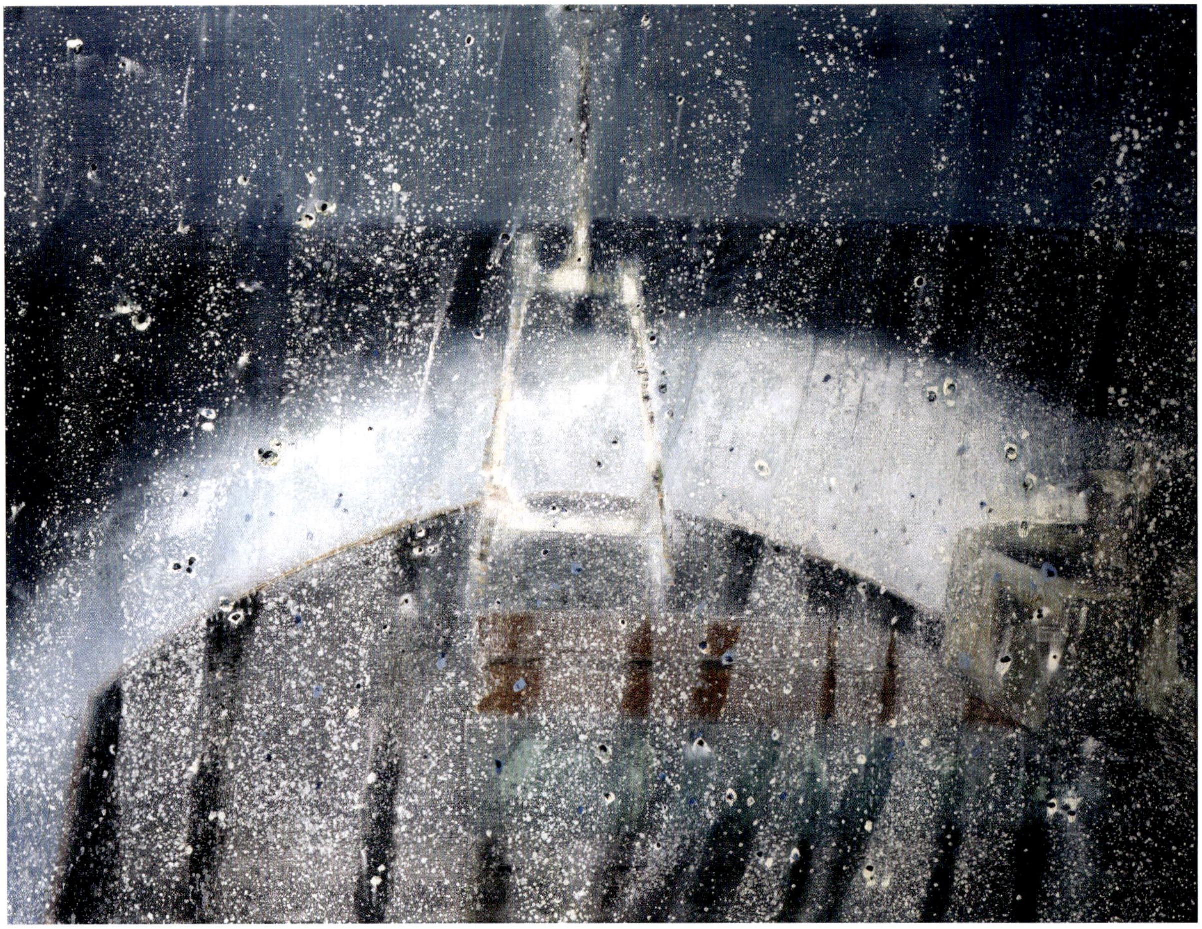

68
RRS James Clark Ross Entering Southern Ocean, 2002
Oil on canvas
110 × 120 cm
Private Collection, Australia

Pole, which, in the turmoil following his son's death in August that year, he felt unable to accept. Six years later he applied successfully for the inaugural Artists and Writers Programme of the British Antarctic Survey. Also present would be the artist Philip Hughes, although to Grant's disappointment there was no writer that year. In November 2001 Grant flew by RAF aeroplane from Brize Norton to the Falkland Islands, where he joined the research ship RRS *James Clark Ross* for a two-month trip to the Antarctic.

During periods of 'down time' during the voyage, discussions with the crew, scientists and journalists took place. While Grant felt obliged to articulate his stance towards landscape and the environment with authorities such as Professor David Walton, a botanist and ecologist who had worked with the British Antarctic Survey since 1967, he refuted any intentionally ecological bias to his work. Equally, to honour the spirit of the commission, he felt it vital to resist a documentary or illustrative approach, but instead to take time to respond to 'the mysteries' he began to perceive in the landscape.[10] His objective was a formalisation of 'the implication of wilderness in the 21st century.'[11]

This scope might be compared informatively with the work of a much younger artist, Mariele Neudecker, who in the 1990s began to create 'tank works' – miniature environments containing forests, mountains and the effects of mist – to explore the legacy of the Romantic sublime. Neudecker's indebtedness to Caspar David Friedrich is overt, particularly in *After Life* (2016), an installation incorporating the

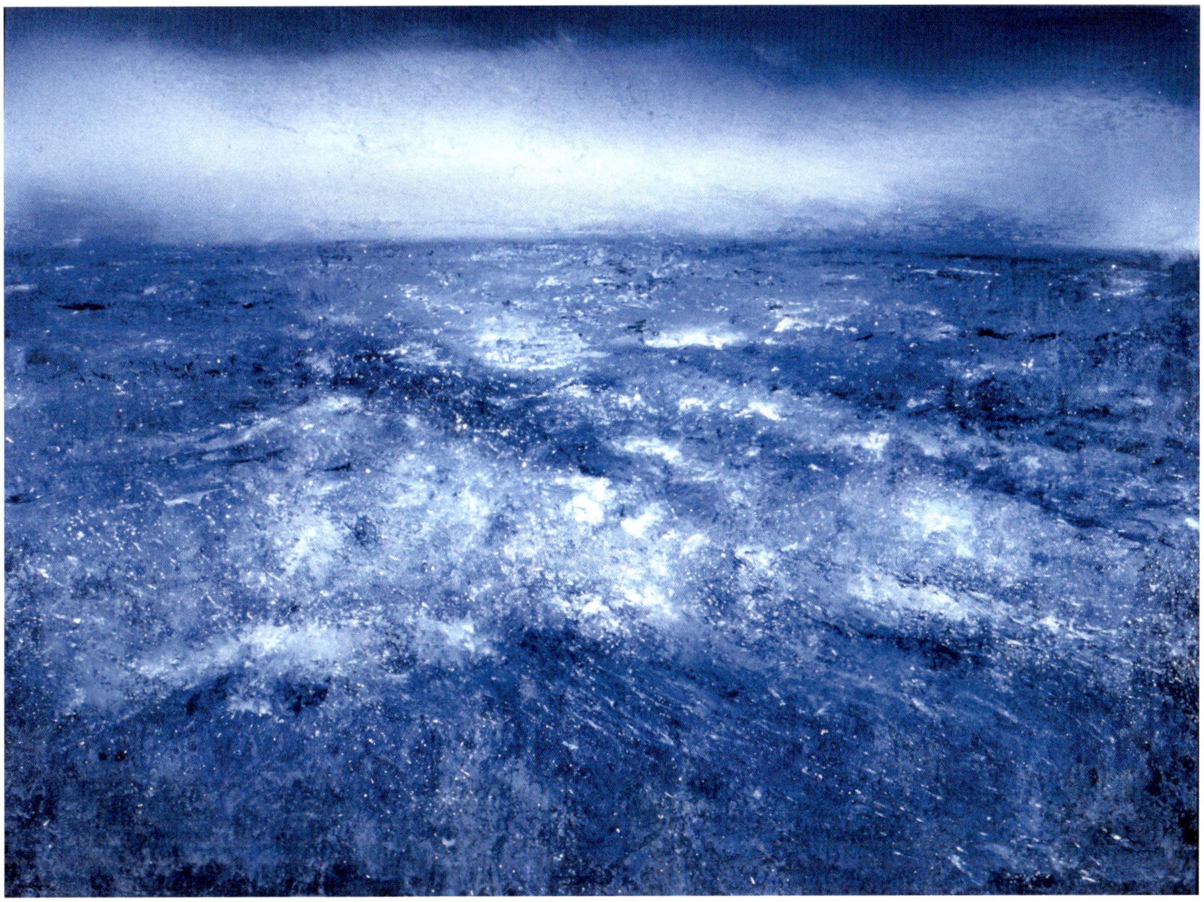

69
Off Elephant Island, 2002
Oil on canvas
112 × 152 cm
Private Collection, UK

structure of a ship, half-submerged, amid icebergs. In 2012, travelling to northwest Greenland, reaching Arctic field stations using dog sleds, she questioned whether 'pure nature' still existed. The answer proved negative: climate change had affected the livelihood of the Inuits by shortening their hunting season, while no region seemed totally untouched by culture. *There is always something more important* (2012), created as a result, features a fibreglass iceberg, sliced and reduced to human scale, reflecting the damaging impact of contemporary existence.

To consider Grant's own response, we can begin by seeing the journey unfold through his eyes. A constant, during the months away, was the environment of the RRS *James Clark Ross*, a vessel equipped with laboratories and a low noise signature to allow sensitive acoustic equipment to be used. Many hours spent on the bridge provided a physical frame to his view. Back in Norway, in a newly created studio, in May 2002 he began a series of paintings based on this imprinted view. *RRS James Clark Ross Entering Southern Ocean* (2002) shows the ship's blurred foremast through the wheelhouse windows (fig.68). Rain lashes and settles momentarily in beads and fine vapour. Ahead the swell is white where the ship carves its way through water. This was the entrance to the Neumayer Straits, where the most violent weather of the entire journey was encountered.

The impact of this painting lies in its layering of texture: fine washes to denote mist, stippling for downwashes that fleck and veil the imagery. Looking closely, raindrops that appear three-dimensional transpire to be circles with black eyes, suggesting a minute reflection of the darkened landscape. Even while witnessing this effect, Grant's mind was exploring precedents that deepened his response to the experience. The beacon-mast he likened to Alejo Carpentier's description, in the opening pages of *Explosion in a Cathedral*, of a guillotine erected on deck while the crew slept: a presence 'resembling, in the necessary precision of its parallel lines, its implacable geometry, some gigantic instrument of navigation'.[12]

In late November 2001, as the RRS *James Clark Ross* neared Elephant Island in the South Shetland Islands near Antarctica, the sea altered from a glassy swell to rolling waves. The island is mountainous and icebound, taking its name both from its shape and as the location of an early sighting, in 1851, of elephant seals. In Grant's large-scale *Off Elephant Island* (2002), however, the focus is the sea (fig.69). Working on it, Grant discovered new techniques:

On the surface the work is a flux of amorphous forms but there is a taut spatial geometry below this surface so that the power of the Southern Ocean is expressed by a constraining tension which I felt when on the J.C.R. [James Clark Ross]. The cold water was not far from congealing into ice and it seemed to direct a terrifying weight and chaotic force against the ship.[13]

Geometry is a surprising description for a painting almost impressionistic in its depiction of the sea and mist-obscured island. Yet beneath the water's turbulence is indeed a perceptible matrix, cross-shaped in outline, just as the sky is characterised by air currents sweeping towards a node to the right of the horizon. Detail and implication ally to create a compelling evocation of the subject, taking the spectator, with Grant, to the ship's bridge amid the freezing, featureless sea. Completing the painting, towards the end of August 2002, Grant dedicated it to Ernest Shackleton, paying homage to the pitiless weather he and his companions faced on their mission to South Georgia in 1916.

The challenge of depicting icebergs had preoccupied Grant since his visit to Greenland. There, he described in detail their colour and responsivity to light. In the new Antarctic paintings, he was preoccupied with movement. Despite their apparent stillness, he knew the icebergs to be shifting, imperceptibly, as if pieces upon a vast chequerboard. Within a landscape typified by absence, Grant was forced to register sensation on a different scale. He equated stillness with silence. On the ice at Fossil Bluff, when he stopped walking, there was a silence of such transcendental power that all he could hear was his own breathing then a scarcely audible hiss akin to the background radiation of the universe. Whether this came from inside his head, or from the vast ice fields, he was unable to tell.[14] Returning to Norway, and working on a series of canvases depicting icebergs in the summer of 2002, Grant probed this aspect single-mindedly. His aim was to create an image of suspended time, between movement and immobility: 'To take stillness beyond any natural manifestation. To transcend absolute zero!'[15]

Stillness, Antarctica (2002) is aptly titled to measure his success (fig.70). The iceberg is profiled against an intense blue sky. A sense of calm is realised through the composition's softness and depth: the immense distance between foreground snow and the almost invisible icebergs on the horizon. The principal iceberg's facets are distinct yet not unduly sharp. Its reflections blend into sea. Is

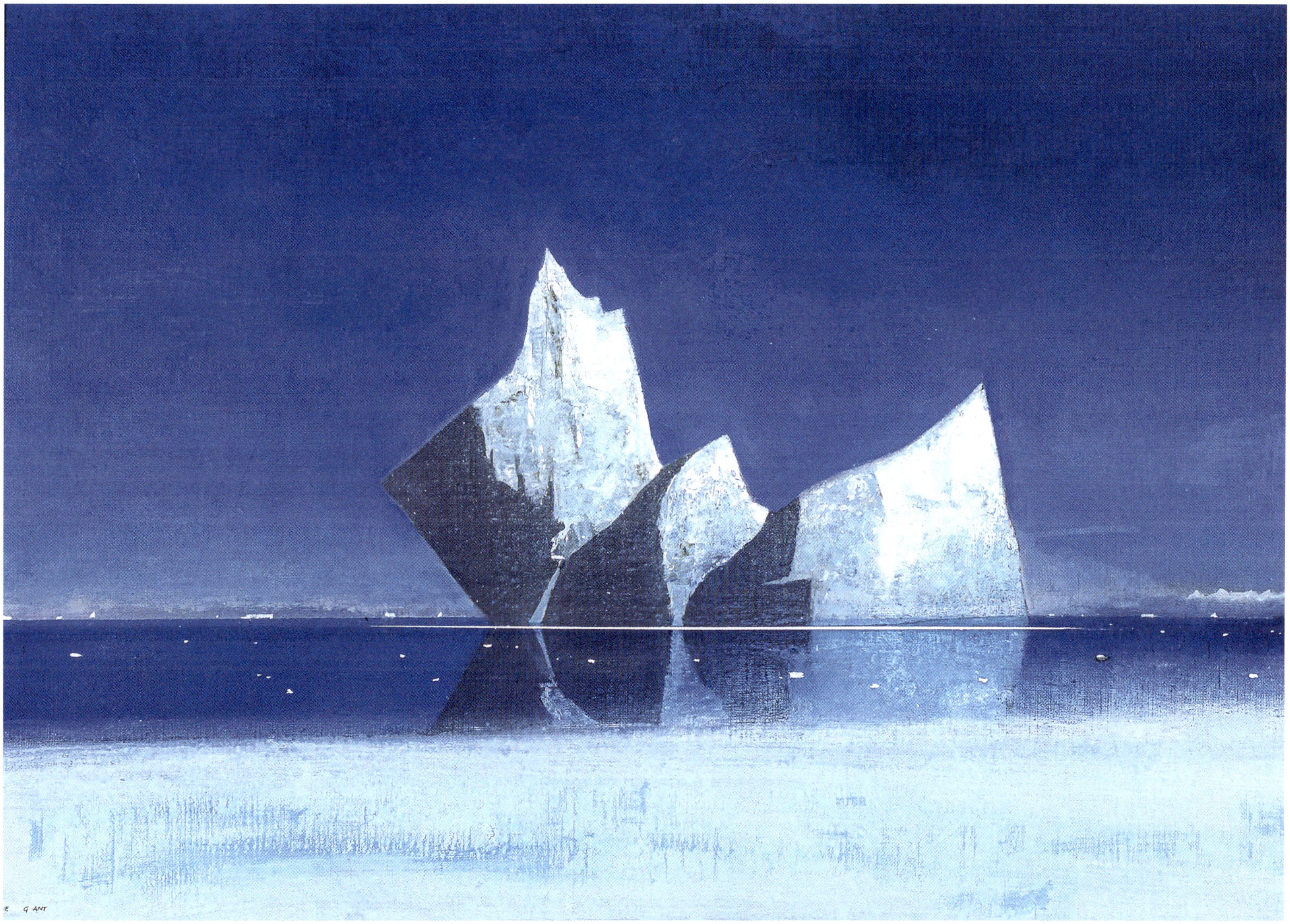

70
Stillness, Antarctica, 2002
Oil on canvas
90 × 180 cm
Private Collection, France

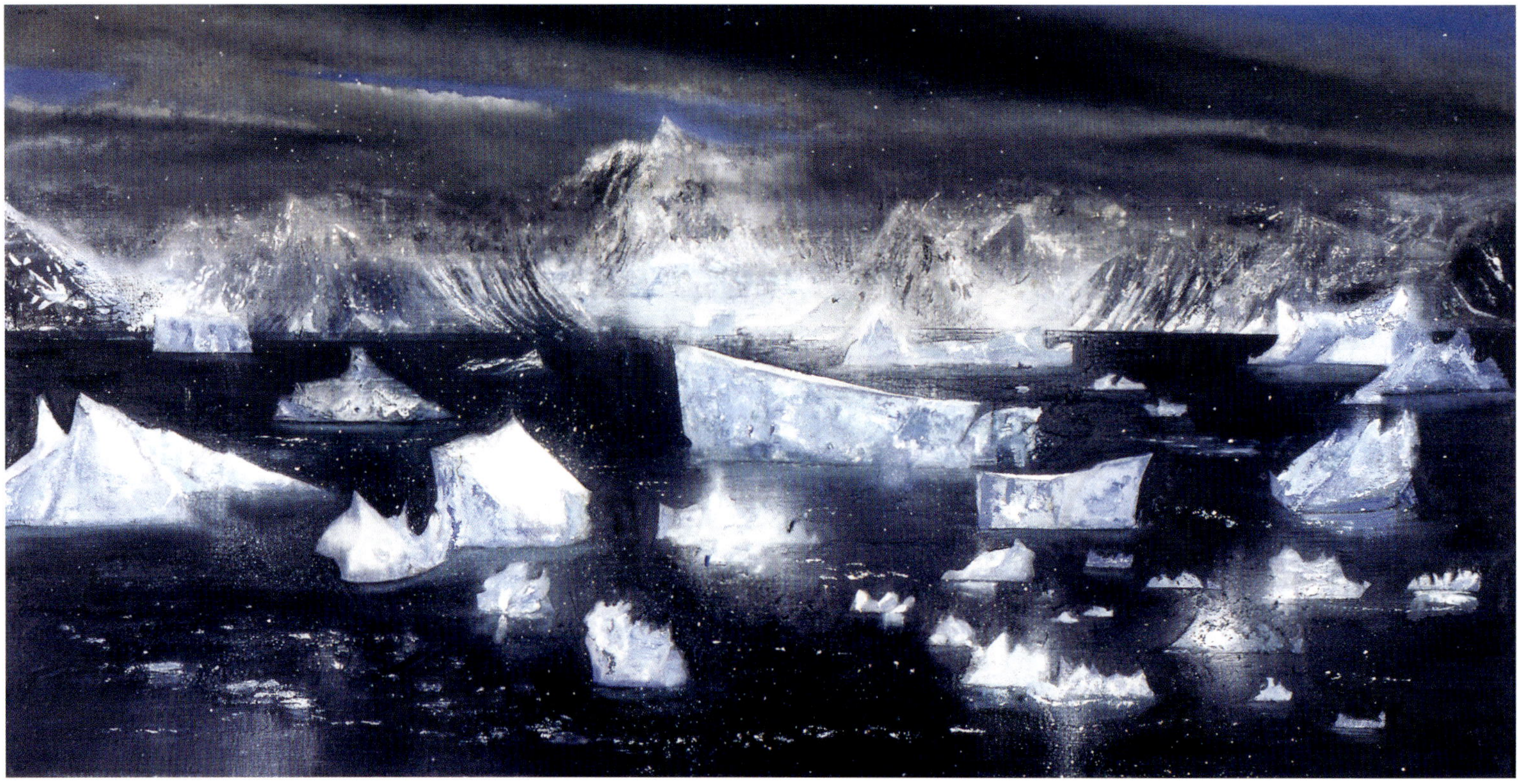

it through this lack of harsh division that the merest movement is suggested, or through our knowledge, now, of Grant's intention to explore the liminality of landscape? The edges within the composition are paramount, whether blurred, as between land and water, horizon and sky, or ruler-sharp, as in the singular white division emphasising the juncture between the iceberg and its reflection.

In the Neumayer Channel, Grant witnessed a chaotic dance of snow mingling with spray, spiralling over the deck, in a storm unremitting in violence. The icebergs that passed appeared unlike those seen previously. Here they were degraded, 'bergy bits' (as the crew called them), floating white against the darkened sea. Grant felt something eerie in their repetition:

The waves pound into them and spray drenches and obscures them from sight – they loom up in the half light and then appear to gather speed passing us at a real 'lick'. Certainly these icebergs are different from those I viewed objectively in Greenland – they are animated not just by their motion in the water but by the weather and atmosphere which plays over them.[16]

A Nameless Scene (2002) draws elements from this experience, showing shattered icebergs on a black-slicked sea (fig.71). The sky is leaden yet streaked with blue, while across the composition a sparse speckling of white denotes falling snow. David Walton dubbed the painting 'North Bay' for its proximity of mood and atmosphere to the landscape near the research station at Rothera, although there was no topographical exactitude to the comparison. Grant, however, felt it to be the closest yet interpretation of the powerful visions he had encountered every day in the Antarctic.

71
A Nameless Scene, 2002
Oil on canvas
90 × 180 cm
Private Collection, Australia

72
Glass Blue, 2007–8
Oil on canvas
101 × 117 cm
Private Collection, UK

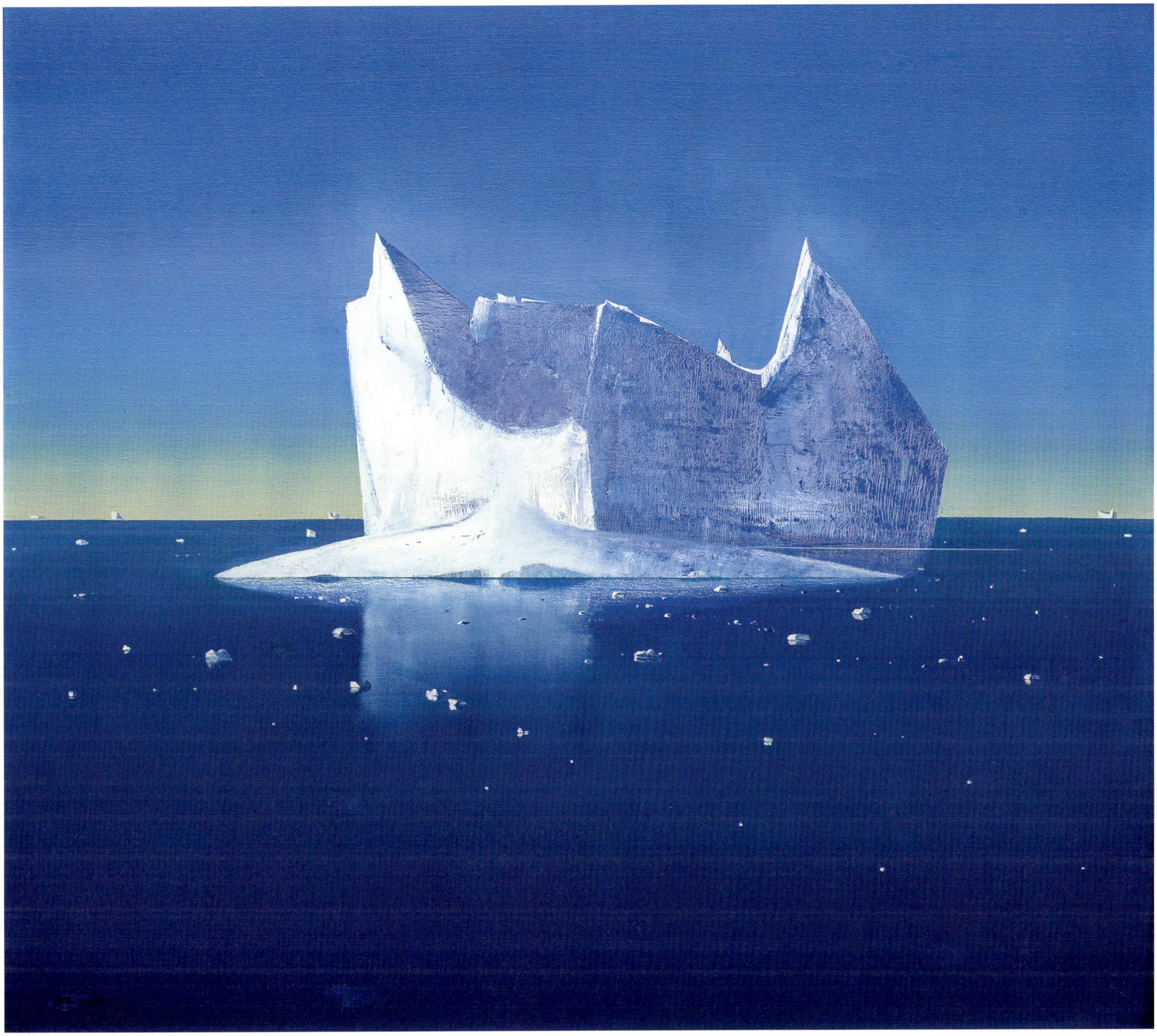

The more mundane routine of living onboard ship forms a pendant to Grant's experience of the landscape. He got on well with the ship's crew, making portrait drawings of many of them as records or tokens of friendship. On Christmas Eve, the cook accidentally shattered one of the large cakes. Grant was summoned to the kitchen, where he transformed the pieces into models of icebergs and mountains using food colouring and vast quantities of sickly meringue. He observed, 'Everyone seemed to think it looked good – the taste will be another matter however!'[17] Grant was constantly thinking through how he might render the landscape, materially, on his return. Crumpled foil was one idea, 'marouflaged' onto a prepared gesso surface in very shallow relief, to allude to the waves' formations. But he also compared the landscapes he saw to works by other artists. Rothko came to mind as he looked at the horizon below dense grey clouds, 'the ice stretching to the ruled distance with the same clarity one would create by resting a half-square of pristine white paper onto a grey/black full square'.[18] Certain icebergs reminded him of Henry Moore's best work ('almost all surface finishes are displayed'), while others resembled 'classical sculpture in bas-relief decoration even to the waves in the hair of a god'.[19] Shortly before arriving home, Grant recalled Kenneth Clark saying that Sidney Nolan 'had as completely failed to express the mood of Antarctica through his art as I had completely succeeded in expressing the reality of the Arctic'. Correct or not, Grant sympathised with Nolan's predicament in facing so implacable a vision.[20]

The paradox of Nolan's paintings of the Antarctic is their proximity to his paintings of the desert and outback: there is a sense that only the palette need be altered to effect a change from one to the other. Grant's landscapes never exhibit this fickleness, yet they continued to show a modified response to their subject matter. In *Glass Blue* (2007–8), the iceberg seems sharpened in focus, increased in monumentality (fig.72). The title invokes Gerard Manley Hopkins's lines on the colour blue, associated with the Virgin Mary,

The glass-blue days are those
When every colour glows,
Each shape and shadow shows.[21]

In Hopkins's poem, the heaven is blue, the air 'azured', the sky 'sapphire-shot'. Grant, in *Glass Blue*, redoubles the intensity of his earlier iceberg paintings in what is a composite rather than a specific depiction of an iceberg. The spur was a visit to Ilulíssat in 2006, where he saw many of the same sites he had discovered in 1989, but processed their imagery quite differently. Through an imaginative reworking, the ice-fjord now cradled a shark's tooth range of peaks, a white bird hovered low over a reflected moon, while a full moon nestled in the arc of an iceberg. Extending the idea of the *Fourteen Stations on a Road* (fig.37, pp 54–5), Grant made a series of small, square paintings entitled *20 Stanzas of the Arctic Moon, Ilulíssat* (2007). Several of these small 'stanzas' were enlarged as independent paintings. From them, *Glass Blue* exemplifies the distillation of Grant's thoughts, encapsulating the shimmering presence of the iceberg and the frozen clarity of the seascape. Although it would not be his final statement on the theme, it relayed its essence in terms he had not previously achieved.

73
Icy Coast, *c.*1964
Oil on canvas
110.4 × 74.9 cm
Leamington Spa Art Gallery & Museum (Warwick District Council)

Antarctica, 2017

In 2017, when an opportunity arose for Grant to visit Antarctica for a second time, his motivation in accepting was specifically to study icebergs. What resulted was a series of over seventy paintings depicting all manner of phenomena – avalanches, squalls, glaciers, sunrise, rainbows, moonlight, pack ice, waterspouts, as well as icebergs. Again, the depiction was altered and extended. But was it not, also, that Grant now registered different aspects of the landscape?

If we return to a much earlier painting, there is a fascinating anticipation of the work Grant was about to commence. *Icy Coast* (*c.*1964) depicts its theme abstractly and economically (fig.73). It was inspired by the landscape of Norway, although its location is immaterial. The crux is indicated by the title: each brushstroke inscribes cold, whether ice on the rocky coast or the ice-cold wind that moves the air. In the works based newly on Antarctica, Grant adopted a thrillingly bifocal approach. Some use the quasi-expressionist mode prefigured in *Icy Coast*, while others return to the surrealist-tinted vision of *Road Through the Wood* (1954; fig.8, p.20).

One of the first canvases, in November 2017, was *Squall on a Nameless Coast* (fig.74). Grant recorded in his journal, 'I have begun the first oil of the Antarctic series. A seascape that is largely from memory. The essential thrust of these new paintings – if I am to sustain the Antarctic theme – must be totally in respect of imaginative interpretation.'[22]

Grant had taken photographs on his recent journey as well as compiled a sketchbook, yet he was seeking to amalgamate this information with data from his visit in 2000 to 2001: neither, in itself, would

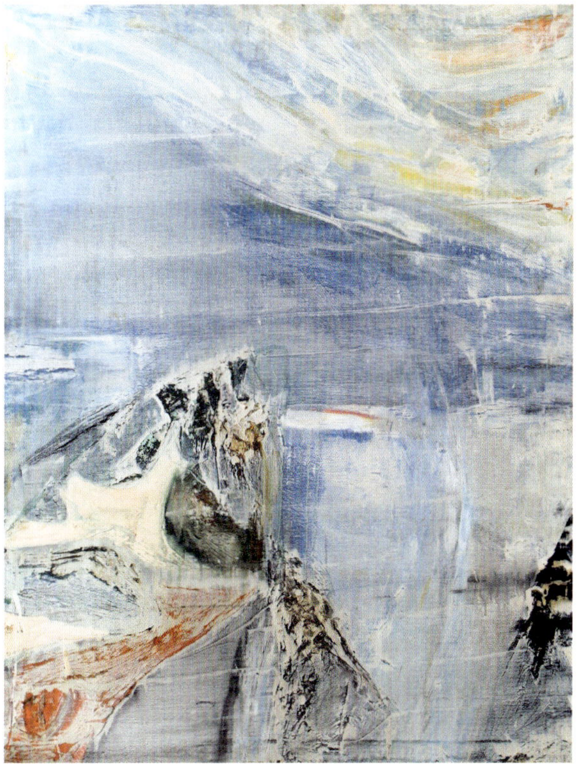

give sufficient inspiration for the extensive body of work he now contemplated. In *Squall on a Nameless Coast*, he openly admitted the lack of specificity of the subject. Instead, he reached to the core of his memory by working spontaneously and intuitively. The canvas is small, the brushstrokes pronounced. The result is immediacy: the viewer is drawn towards the imagery, which whips and scours with quixotic force. Each area of the canvas demands attention. From the momentary clearing of the sky, where the bird flies, to the churning sea and fret driving from the east, there is not a second of stasis.

Turning, then, to the slightly larger canvas, *Small Bergs in Rough Sea, off South Shetlands* (February

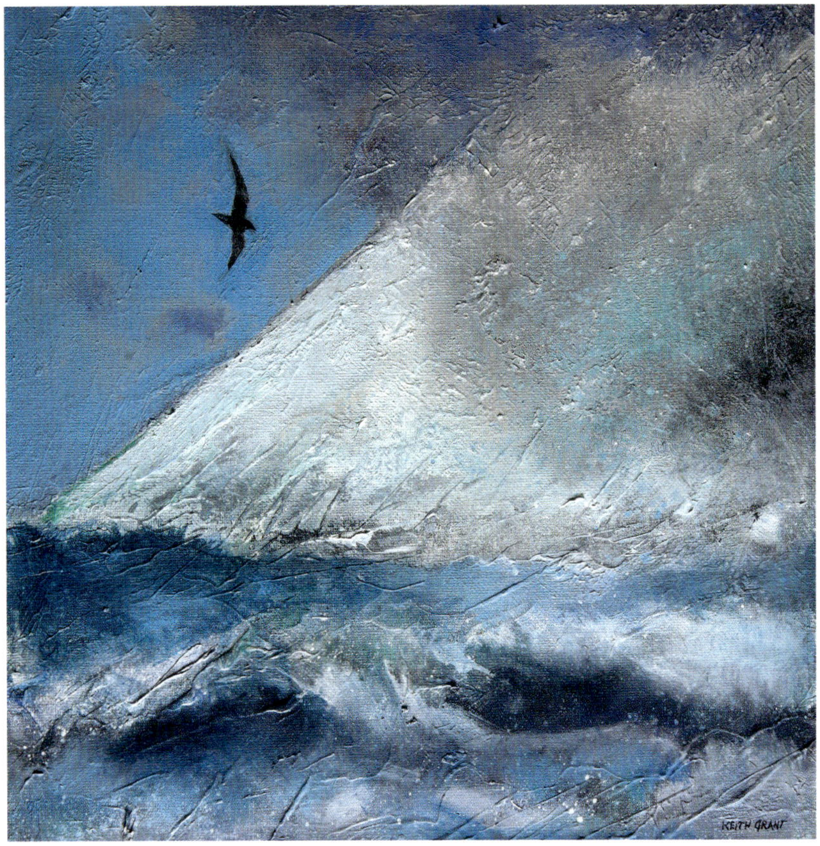

74 (left)
Squall on a Nameless Coast,
2017
Oil on canvas
30 × 30 cm
Private Collection, UK

75 (below)
Small Bergs in Rough Sea, off South Shetlands, 2018
Oil on canvas
35 × 70 cm
Collection of the artist

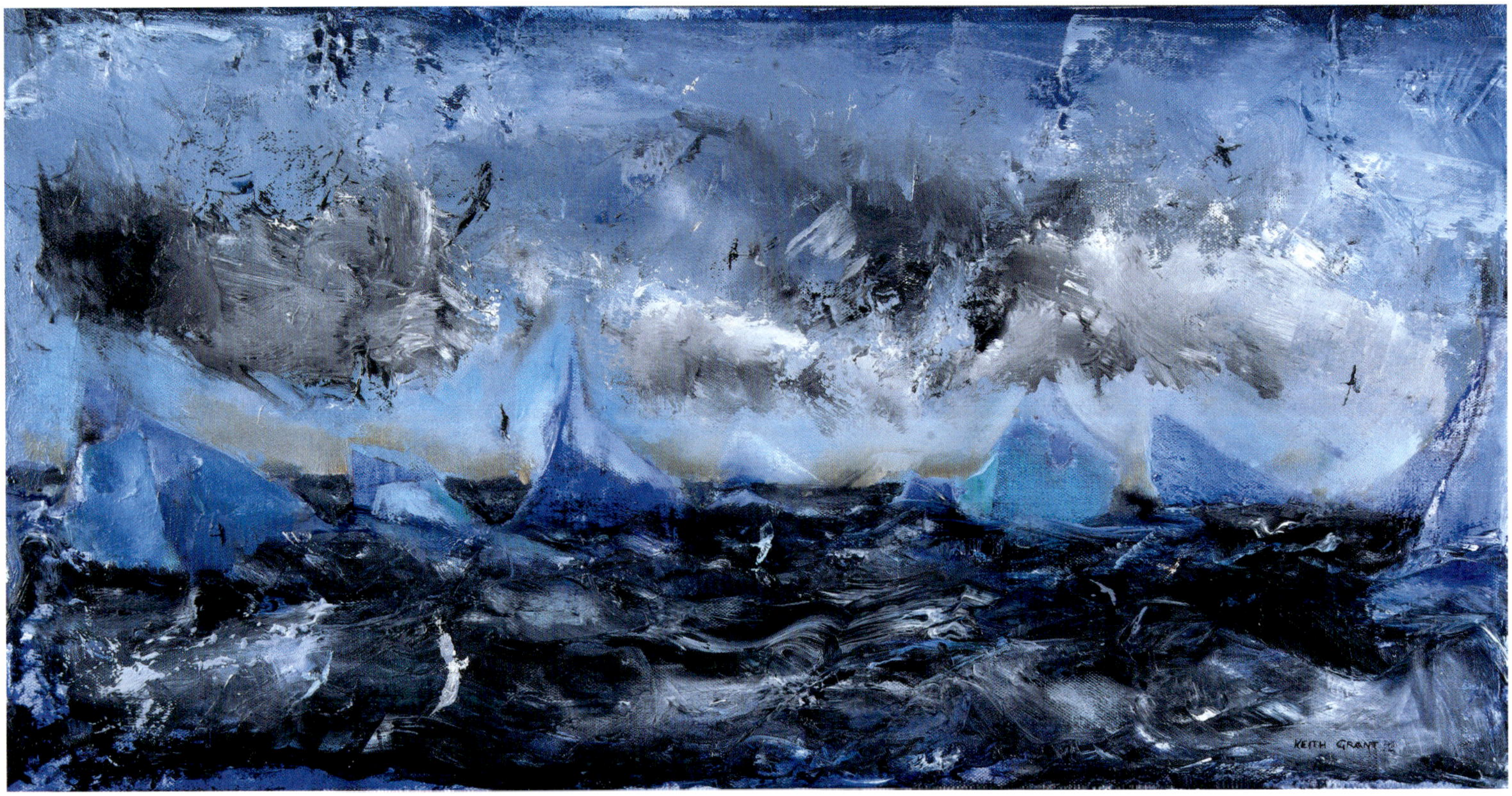

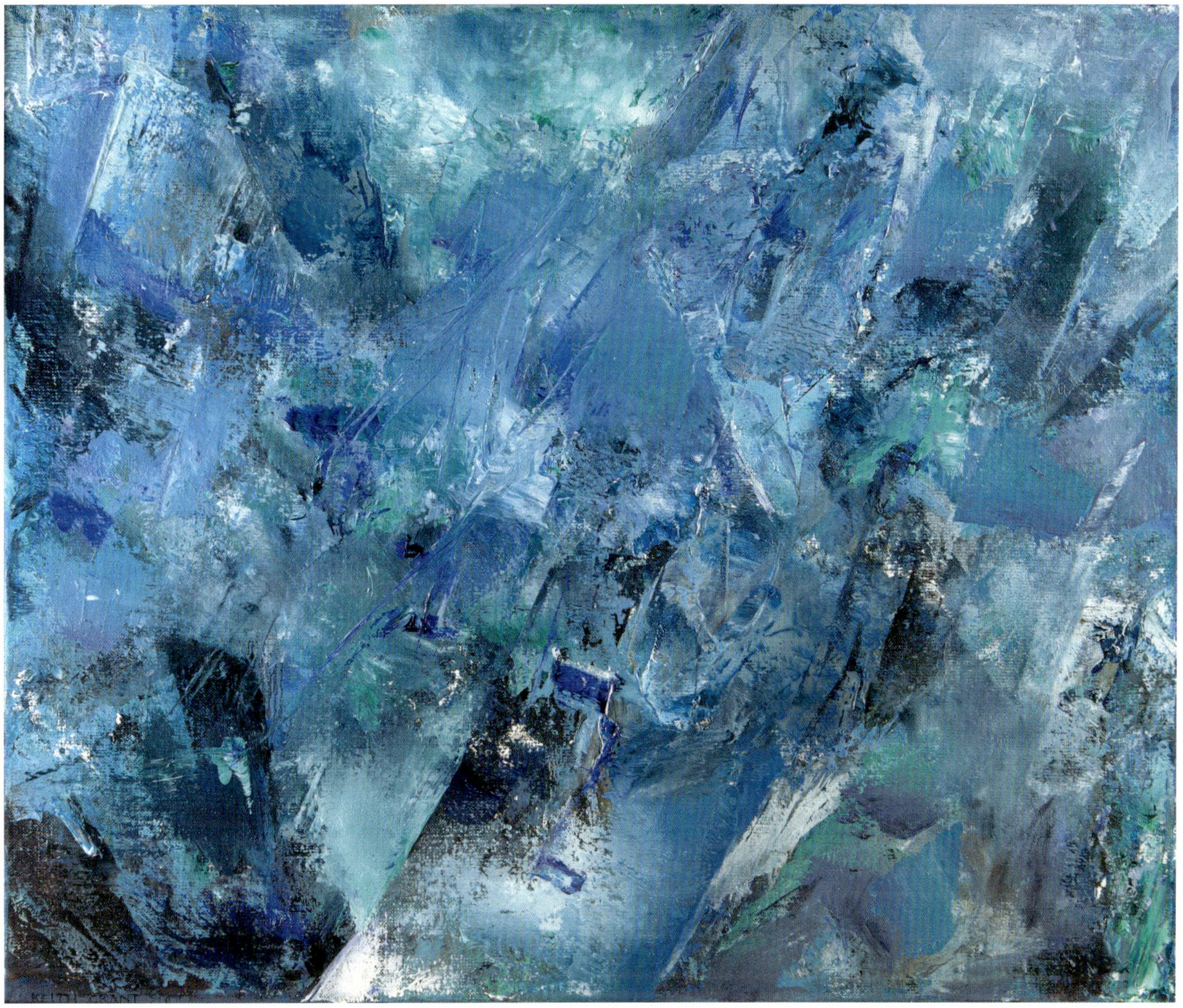

76
Avalanche III, 2018
Oil on linen
50 × 61 cm
Collection of the artist

2018), the storm shifts focus (fig.75). Where *A Nameless Scene* (2002; fig.71) had presented icebergs marooned in isolation, white against black, here they are buffeted and robbed of monumentality: assimilated into the seascape. A heightening of the palette sees the ice stained vivid blue; birds become no more than flecks against the sea and sky. The icebergs are sharpened by wind and rain – literally sculpted by the weather. In the South Shetland Islands the temperature remains below freezing for eight months of the year, with strong westerly winds blowing constantly.

With *Avalanche III* (June 2018), the imagery is approached so closely as to enter its midst (fig.76). Grant had always recalled a comment by a student, in the 1970s, that he should paint as if he were within his subject. At the time Grant was painting volcanoes and could not see how to realise the suggestion. Now he imagined himself 'veritably within the cascading blocks of ice and rock'.[23] The elements are brought directly to the picture plane, which splinters, engulfing the canvas in a torrent of snow. There is no depth, only chaos.

One of the most significant paintings in *Ice and Fire*, Grant's solo exhibition at the Fitzwilliam Museum, Cambridge, in 1994, was *Dissolution* (1993): a study in blue, featuring a single iceberg merging with the

77

Tranquillity, Antarctica, 2018

Oil on canvas

119 × 150 cm

Private Collection, UK

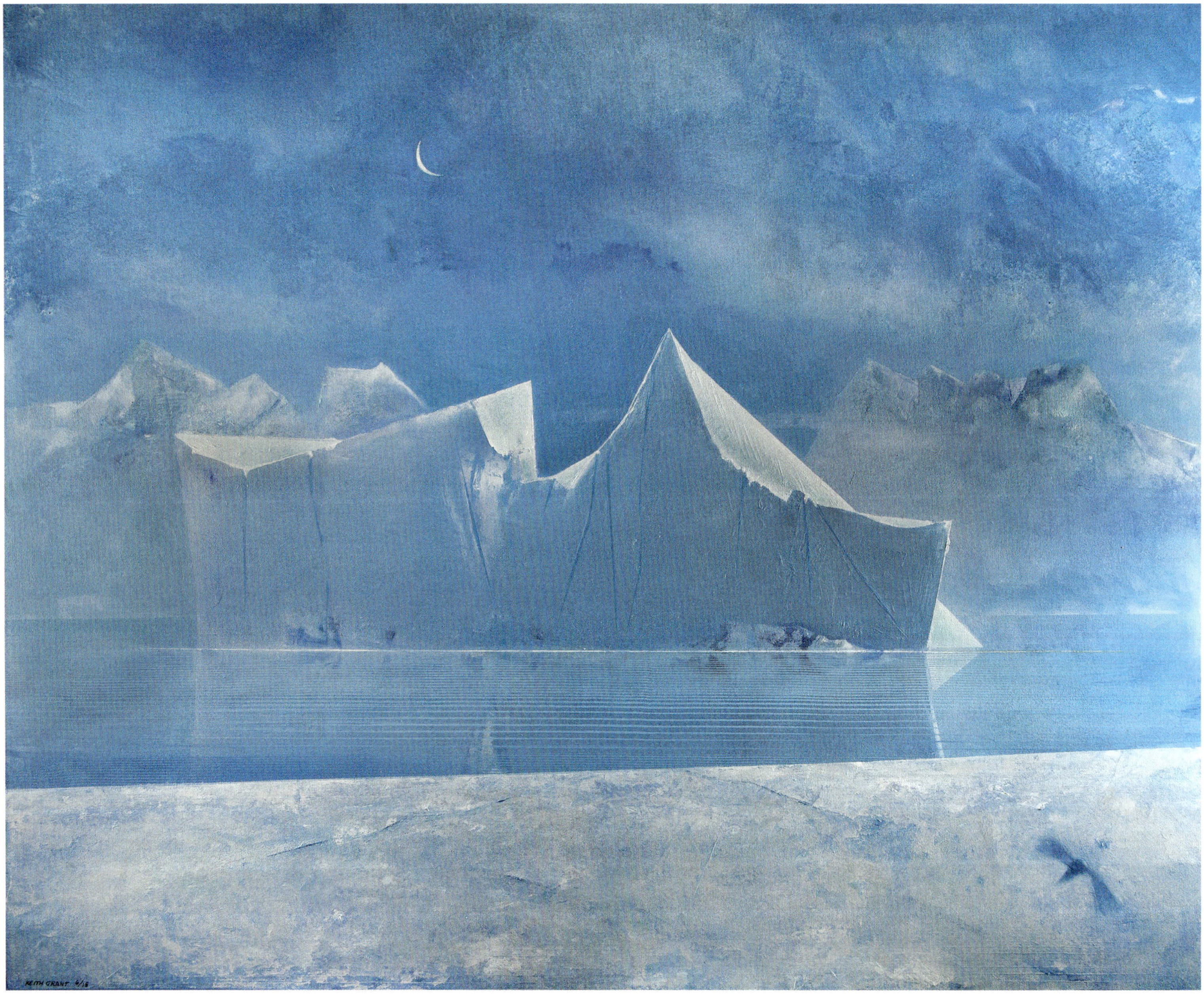

78
Ice, Rock and Glacier by Moonlight, Antarctica, 2018
Oil on linen over board
50 × 60 cm
Private Collection, UK

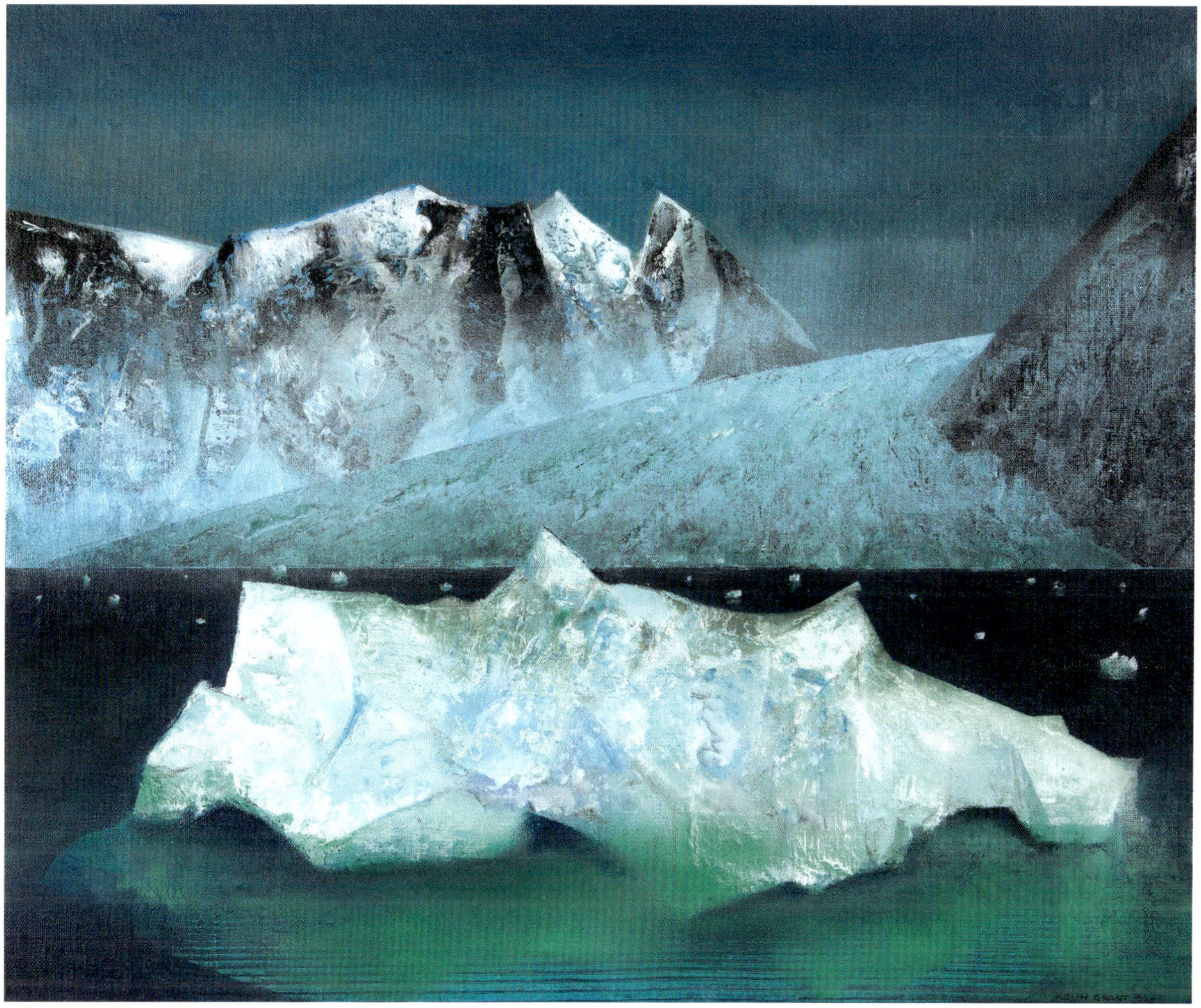

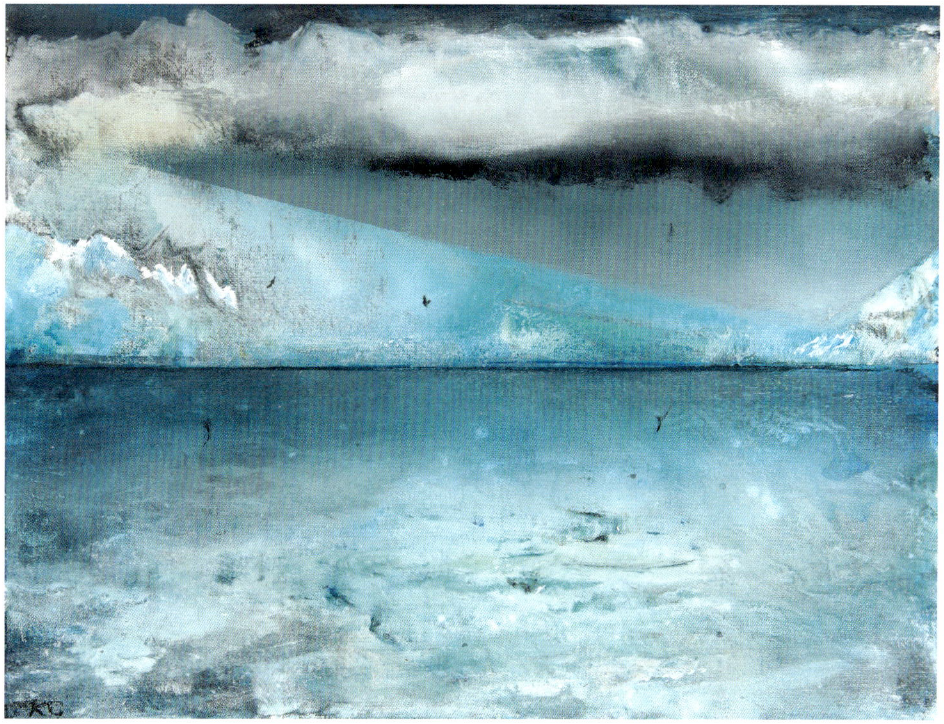

79
Impromptu III: Cloud Triangle, 2018
Oil on linen
21.5 × 26.5 cm
Private Collection, UK

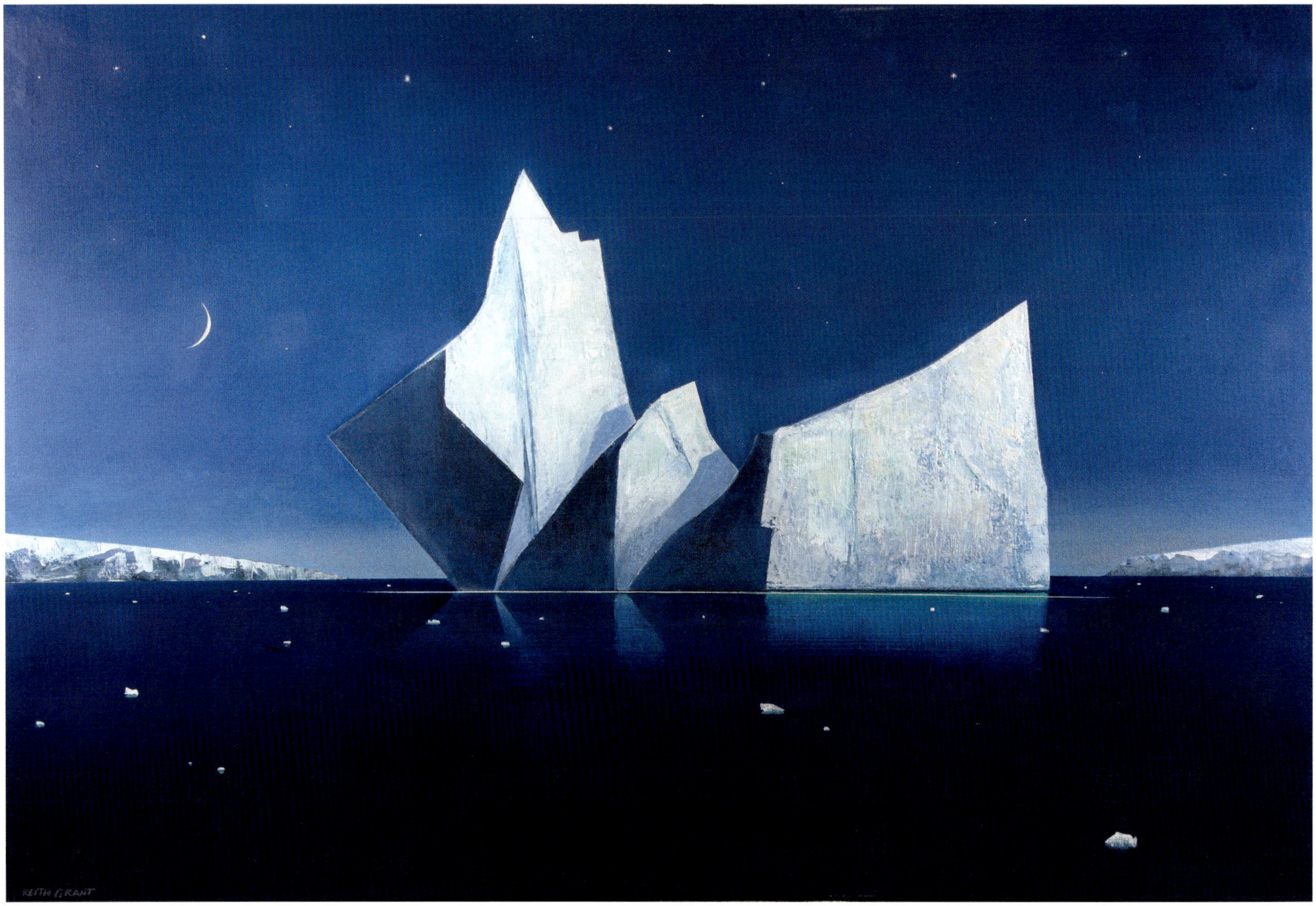

80
Departure, 2018
Oil on linen
97 × 151 cm
Private Collection, UK

sea and air as it passes from one state to another. As Grant was just over midway through his new series of Antarctic paintings, he conceived *Tranquillity, Antarctica* (June 2018) as a 'sister work' to *Dissolution*, emphasising yet separating the elements that fused in the earlier composition (fig.77). Water, ice and air, each clearly defined, are deployed to indicate slow, inexorable movement. The air is vaporous, the iceberg veined with cracks, the water rippled. Above the ice a bird flies, unseen. Uncertainty coexists with clarity, the solid with the fugitive. Studying the exquisite detailing of this texture introduces a further dimension to what is, essentially, a monumental image. The danger in reproduction is to reduce the painting's impact to illustration, a charge unlikely to be levelled when encountering it face to face.

The moon and bird's shadow in *Tranquillity, Antarctica* accentuate the scene's mystery, returning to Grant's fascination with Surrealist imagery and the realm of dreams. In *Ice, Rock and Glacier by Moonlight, Antarctica* (July 2018), the work of Paul Nash is invoked by the 'monster' iceberg in the foreground (fig.78). It appears to levitate, rather than, as Grant knew, to be only the exposed tip of a mass extending deep into the sea. The green haze beneath the iceberg lends an uncanny emphasis to its form, counterpointing the arrested downflow of the glacier above. As Grant worked on this painting, he was working on two other canvases of the same dimension: a tactic essential for the oil paint to dry sufficiently to achieve the effects he sought.

He had just completed a set of nine small canvases he described as impromptus – 'studies in the interpretation of light, movement and mood'.[24] With these, unlike the three larger paintings, Grant sketched the compositions then worked on them individually, concerned to maintain their distinctiveness as well as a harmony within the set. *Impromptu III: Cloud Triangle* (July 2018) shows a phenomenon that haunts Grant's later paintings (fig.79). In his journals he noted having seen such a triangular cloud, then, doubting his memory, checking his photographs for confirmation. None of these impromptus attempts to depict landscape as it was witnessed objectively, but rather to follow the example of the avalanche paintings by reflecting 'a raw poetry as manifested in nature itself'.[25]

Grant set himself a formidable challenge. Returning to the drawing from 2001 that initiated *Stillness, Antarctica* (2002, fig.70), he began work on a large iceberg painting that he hoped would 'suggest characteristics which are applicable to the human experience'.[26] The proposition is intriguing. Titled *Departure*, the painting depicts an iceberg starting its journey towards dissolution (fig.80). Yet Grant explicated its message as manifold:

It may simply state a natural law of the melting and disappearance of the huge masses of ice, or it could be a metaphor for the travel towards that distant horizon, the crossing of which is impossible this side of death. It might be interpreted as imperceptible movement, as silence of solemnity or as the lowest register of sound heard against the background, the whispering of one's own metabolism when everything else is tremorless tranquillity. There is a cosmic significance behind all the paintings for this exhibition, of the one place on earth where the extra-terrestrial transcends the telluric; silence levels silence![27]

The exhibition Grant alluded to was *Antarctica*, at the Chris Beetles Gallery, London, in autumn 2018. Ironically given the subject's bleakness, the private view, opened by Sir David Attenborough, was so crowded that one spectator fainted.

Departure, a crystal-clear reinterpretation of both the drawing and the earlier painting, *Stillness, Antarctica*, is held by Grant to define his experience of the Antarctic. More than that, it constitutes a profoundly personal metaphor, as he recorded:

The work has been unremitting but the sense of discovery and the revelations coming through the use of paint intuitively and spontaneously have led me towards a truth beyond that of representation. I will wait until I see the entire collection on display before confirming or denying that I have achieved a new vision of the natural world. But it is clear that I have not been in thrall to anyone else's Antarctica but my own.[28]

The iceberg symbolises life, and with it Grant's joy and thankfulness for the capacity to respond to the natural world. Grant dedicated *Departure* to his daughter, Thea.

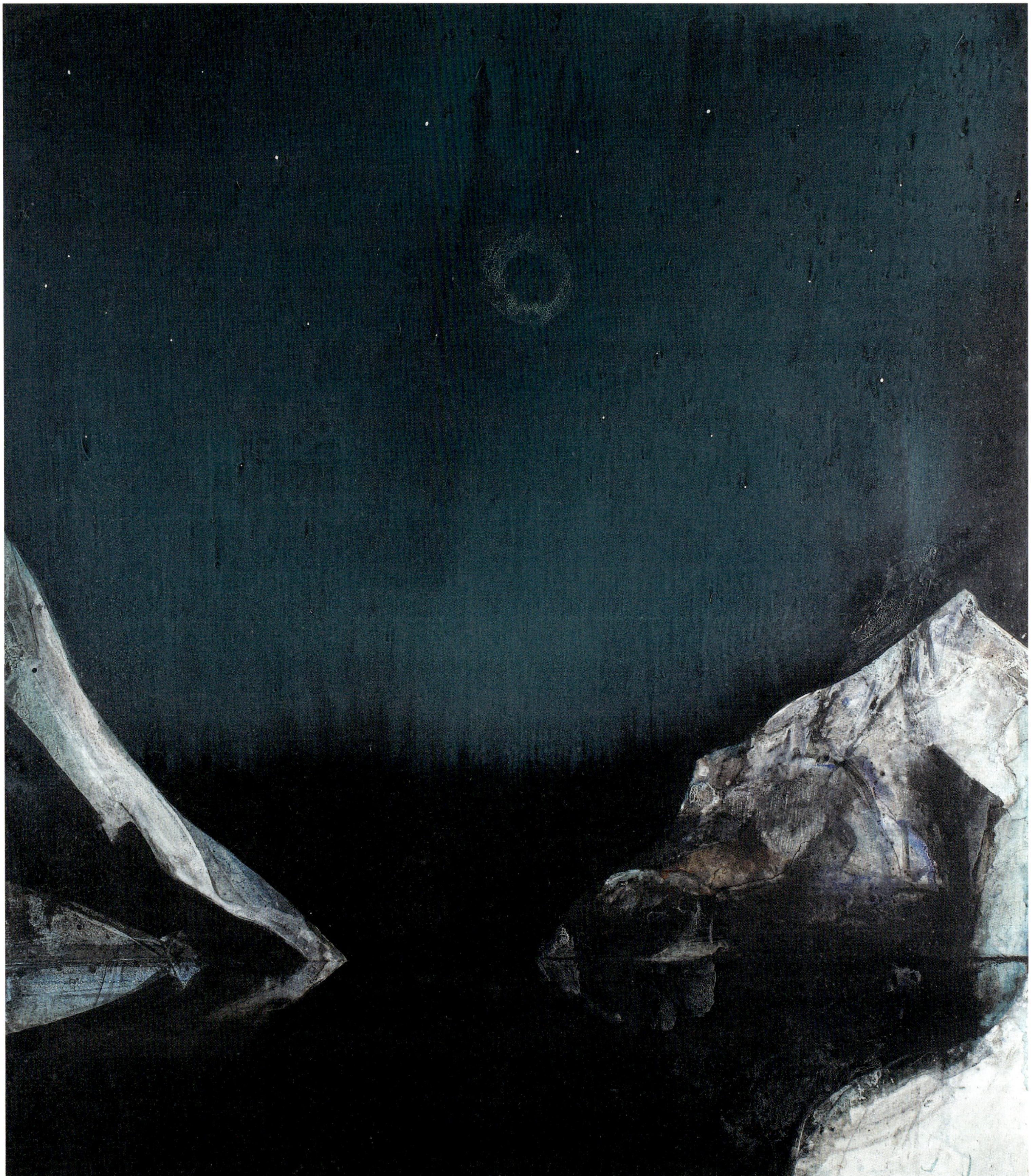

5

Night

81
The Blind Moon, 1978
Acrylic on paper
115.6 × 104.1 cm
Lakeland Arts Trust, Cumbria

On 24 March 1978, the first of two total lunar eclipses that year occurred. Grant was in Svolvær, having recently begun a three-month visit to prepare for his next exhibition. Intending to create a visual and written record, he titled his journal 'The Norwegian Journey: letters to myself from the Corridors of the North', adding, 'Please return if lost – reward a painting of mine'.[1] The entry for 24 March had described the landscape's relentless intensity of light, reflected from snow and ice: a painter's dilemma in its distortion of form and distance. As Grant experienced the eclipse, he was already anticipating the time of the midnight sun:

Now the moon is full and illumines the night sky, but it is a sky that from now on knows no real darkness – just under the rim of the western horizon the sun is shielded by the oblique angle of the turning earth. Night is not far divided from day – there is something restless about the nights now. An impatience for the time when the sun will not set for many weeks. It is cold.[2]

Was the restlessness that Grant ascribed to night his own? If so, it derives from an acute sensitivity to phenomena that shape and alter landscape. The night before the eclipse he looked at the moon through binoculars, seeing the water seething with movement – as if from 'millions of black creatures writhing in a lake of quicksilver' – and the horizon sharply dividing one element from another.[3]

The Blind Moon (1978) depicts the stillness of this landscape (fig.81). The moon pales by comparison with the stars, yet light glows on the icy shore and feathers towards the water. Grant described the depth of the night sky when seen through field glasses, which allowed him to penetrate with clarity 'the folds of darkness'.[4] In the painting, the moon is embossed: an imprint on the firmament. The foreshore is brought forward, while the sky, in washes of cyan to black, recedes to infinity.

Night has grown in significance for Grant since the mid-1970s and continues to retain a special place in his response to landscape. Here it is considered in its broadest remit, including liminal areas such as the midnight sun, dawn or dusk. The cosmos – or night sky, with its stars and planets – formed a particular focus for works created in the early 1990s. Even in 2022, as this book was being written, Grant was creating paintings of exceptional power based on the aurora. To each period of work, a different emphasis is brought.

A pair of experimental works sets the scene. *Icebergs and Particle Storm* (fig.82; 1993, reworked

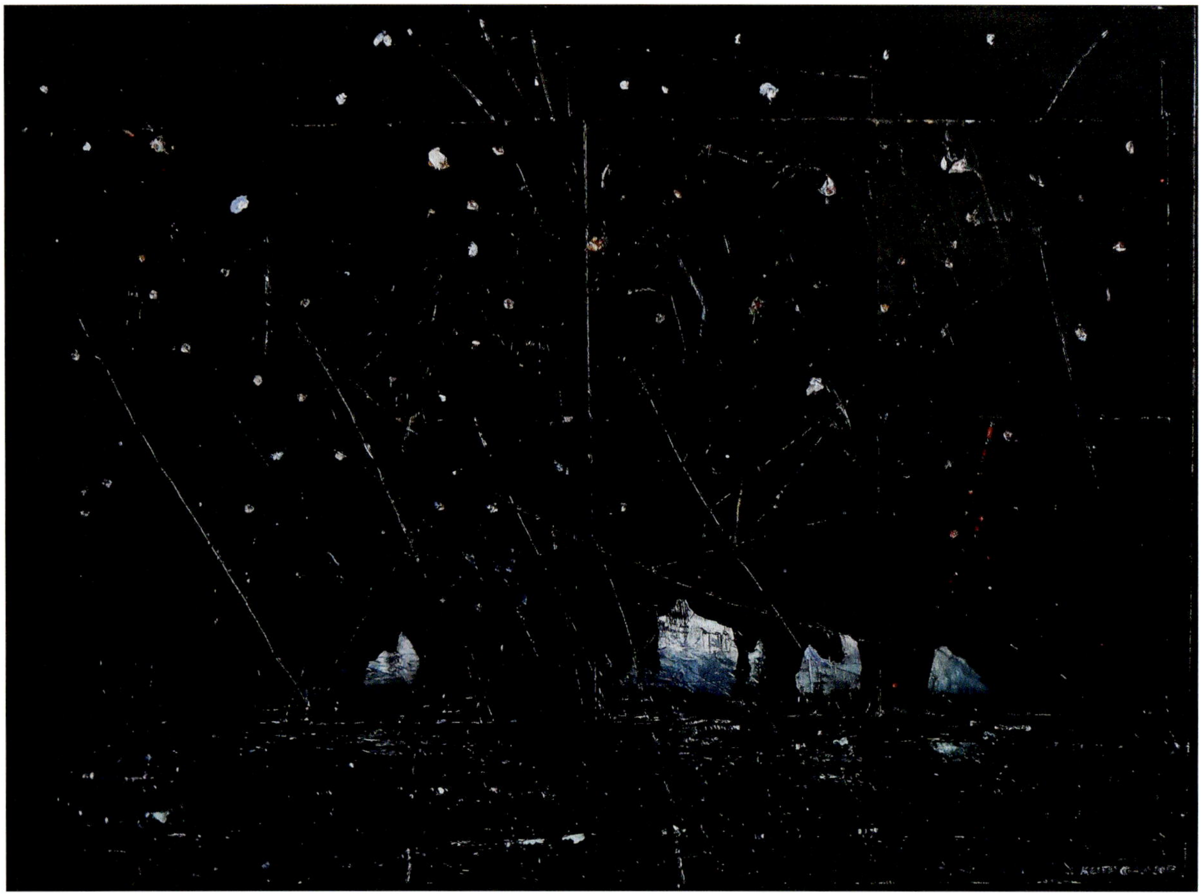

82
Icebergs and Particle Storm, 1993, reworked 1998
Acrylic and ink on paper
36.5 × 51 cm
Collection of the artist

1998) parallels the puma fence studies (see fig.53, p.68) in its use of collage and mixed media. A central raised area again implies that the composition has been enlarged. The harsh black background flickers with stars, particle trails and the white crests of waves, suggesting movement but no warmth. Moreover, the painting's surface implies violence. Scored to reveal pulses of colour, and patched so that the trajectories of light are curtailed or misaligned, it embodies the storm of its title. Within this chaos, the icebergs strike a glassy, spectral presence.

A second painting relates the phenomenon of 'iron night' (*Jernnatt*), the first frost of autumn, to the archetypal pyramid peak (fig.83). The date on the work, indistinct yet appearing to read as '2/95', coincides with a dream recalled in Grant's journals of a 'pyramid peak the pinnacle of which was wreathed in billowing cloud light against an ultimate black sky'.[5] In *Iron Night, Vesterålen*, the 'ultimate black' is created by the addition of carbon to create a ground that alters from dense graphite to silver according to the light. Above this glittering surface, impasto acrylic conveys the layering of cloud – white through midnight blue – and the delineation of fissured snow on the peak. The use of polystyrene board as a support facilitates the texturing of the night sky, slashed and stabbed to suggest a particle storm. 'Iron night' maintains its grip on the Norwegian psyche as the end of summer and herald of the cold, persistent months of darkness. Grant's familiarity with it stems from Knut Hamsun's *Pan*, in which the narrator, Lieutenant Thomas Glahn, leaves his cabin at nightfall in late August, with his dog and gun, and lights a fire amid the forest. There is no frost, however, and Glahn's emphasis on its absence

83
Iron Night, Vesterålen, 1995,
Mixed media on polystyrene board
14 × 30 cm
Private Collection, UK

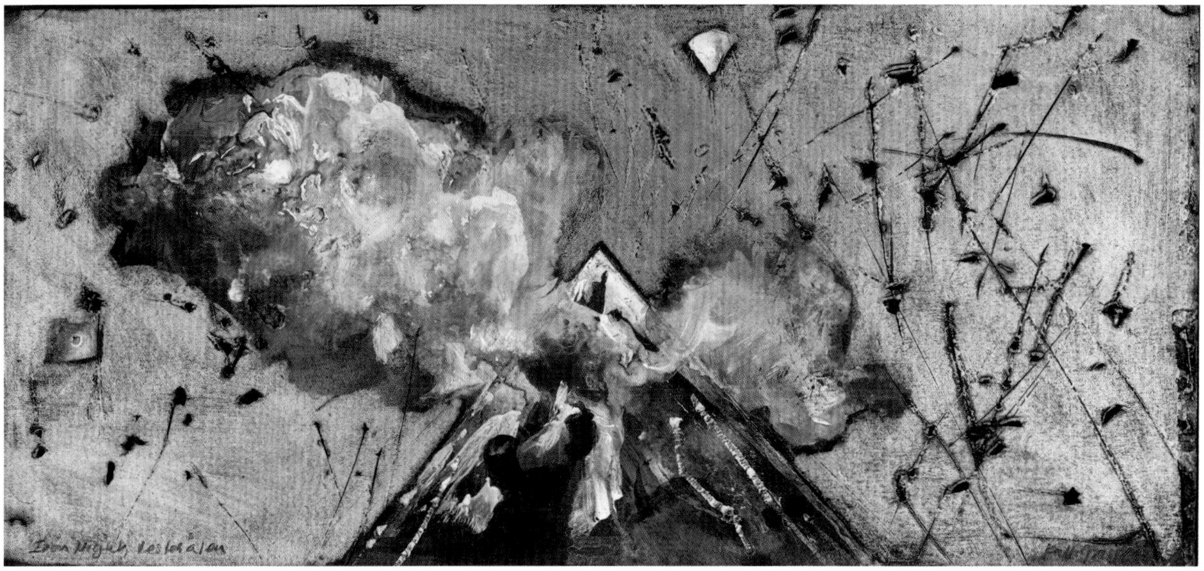

– even on a mild, second 'iron night' – underlines the uncanniness of the passage.[6]

These two studies establish the tenor for considering Grant's paintings of the sky. They are exploratory and unsettling, just as *The Blind Moon* possesses an ill-defined frisson despite its stillness. Watching the launch of the *Ariane* rocket in French Guiana in 1982 had reawakened Grant's interest in space, which continued through studying photographs of the night sky taken from the Mount Wilson observatory in Colorado. As he contemplated a new series of paintings in 1983, he wrote, 'at the present the night sky gives me the greatest opportunity to merge abstraction with reality; technique with poetry'. The specific area he began to consider was the parallel between the universe's visible form and the 'free interaction of paint'.[7] How this might be realised was deferred because of his travels to Malaysia, Israel, Greenland and Venezuela. In 1992, however, he began a series of 24 paintings he identified as the 'cosmos' series.

The *Cosmos* Series

In 1990 the Hubble Space Telescope was launched into low orbit around the earth, relaying photographs that Grant remembers vividly. Among these, in October 1991, was the first true-colour image of Jupiter: a planet banded in rust-red clouds caused by frozen ammonia crystals and compounds of carbon, sulphur and phosphorus. A correction in 1993 to the telescope's main mirror, which had been incorrectly ground, allowed it to work at full capacity – capturing exceptionally detailed images with minimal background light to give a deep view of space.

Cosmos (1993) shows the pulling together of many of these strands (fig.84). Matching process to subject, the surface of the painting is characterised by a 'free interaction of paint', described by Grant in detail:

I have applied the paint by dropping it from the brush and dripped in cans of pre-mixed colour or directly from the palette into a brush charged with clean white spirit. I am excited by some of the qualities which are now emerging, a kind of 'distance autography' the marks and details of which form as a result of the natural laws governing the flow of fluid and viscous liquids. There is an uncanny relevance to my subject created by the chance delivery of paint . . . [Some] has flowed in milky translucency appearing like clouds of interstellar gas and some has coagulated into irregular densities which seem

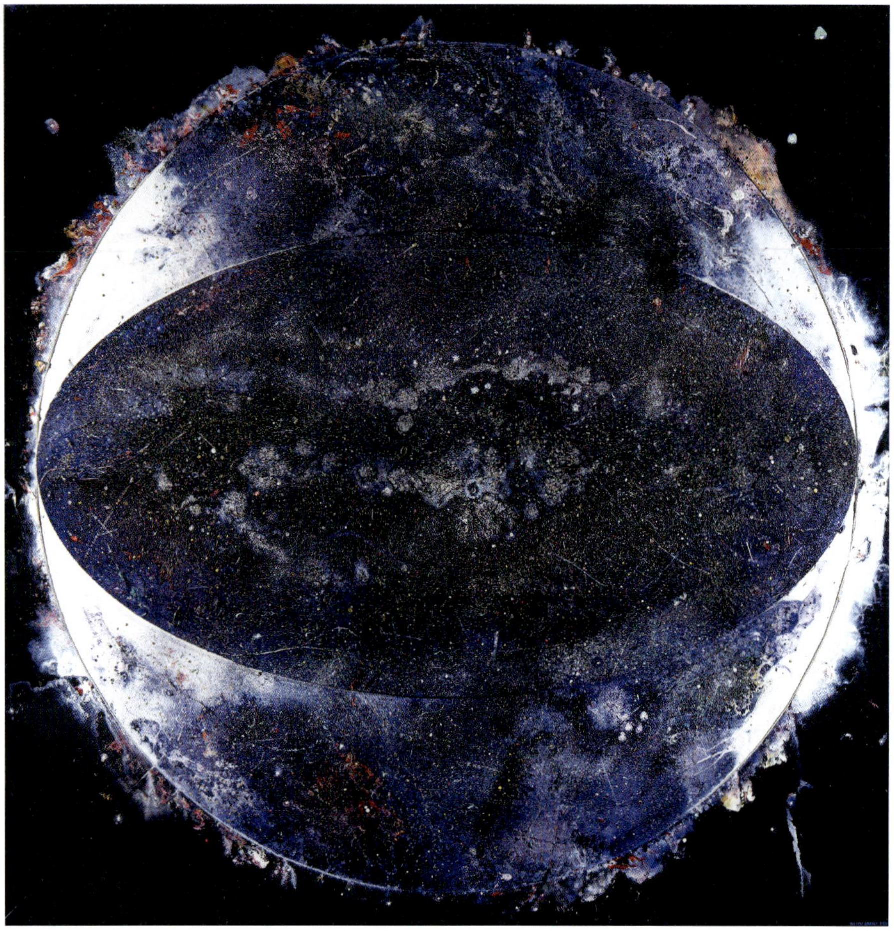

84
Cosmos, 1993
Oil on board
182.5 × 182.5 cm
Paintings in Hospitals, UK

to reflect the inevitable form of matter at different stages of accretion.[8]

Although a primary influence was Grant's interest in photographs of space, he drew formally from a historic source, Hieronymus Bosch's *Garden of Earthly Delights* (1490–1500): a mediaeval triptych that, when folded, reveals a grisaille depiction of *The Third Day of the Creation* as an ellipse within a sphere. This device recurs throughout Grant's 'cosmos' paintings. In some, painted on hardboard, the oval is raised in relief, in others it is set within a frame to suggest a geometrical reading of space. Grant's journals reveal that during this period, especially, he was probing the relationship of spirituality, philosophy and science to painting. His readings included *The Tao of Physics* (1975), by the Austrian-born physicist, systems theorist and ecologist Fritjof Capra. Music, too, formed an essential counterpart. As he worked, he listened to Messiaen, John Tavener, John McLeod and above all Jonathan Harvey, who visited Grant's studio and discussed with him the 'cosmos' paintings as they evolved.

If Grant would later view these works as a diversion or as 'research', at the time they were an intensely serious preoccupation prior to his exhibition at the Fitzwilliam Museum in 1994. They also proved divisive – David Scrase (from the Fitzwilliam) and Lillian Browse among those initially sceptical. Larry Berryman, who watched the paintings evolve, and contributed an essay to the catalogue, considered them his finest work, extending the tradition of Mark Rothko, Mark Tobey and Morris Louis. Chiming with Grant's interest in Capra, Berryman urged viewers to see how 'his triptychs accord with the Taoist conception of the unframed, open-ended universe and, with Barnett Newman, affirm a comparable metaphysics'.[9]

Through these examples, the scope of Grant's paintings concerning the night begins to clarify. Their focus is the sky. They rarely address land without water, except where an isolated peak is depicted, and they almost always relate to cold or northerly environments, where the air is clear and light's effects intensify. It is in these paintings, too, that some of Grant's most radical formal experiments are tried.

Midnight Sun and Moon

Grant's earliest painting in this book shows a view from a bedroom window, although there is no indication within the composition that the scene is observed from indoors (fig.5, p.14). Such a context is made explicit in the view from the RRS *James Clark*

Ross, where a splashed windowpane intervenes between the observer and the seascape (fig.68, p.86). This was an idea Grant developed over the following years, with particular vividness in *Triptych of the Midnight Sun and Midnight Moon* (2006), based on a recollection of his 1961 return voyage from Norway. Each of the three paintings features the curved frame of the porthole, flanked by green and red to suggest port and starboard ship's lights. *Midnight Moon*, illustrated here, combines the effect of the clearview screen, a glass disc rotated by electric motor to disperse rain from the wheelhouse window, with the reflected halo of the moon (fig.85). Fragmented reflections from the cabin's interior merge with the seascape outside to imply an intimation of the cosmos where vapour droplets resemble stars or constellations. The horizon bisects the window, yet it is the moon, with its immense halo, that endows the composition with its compelling force. Using this device, Grant created variations upon the optical effects of the midnight sun, such that 'retinal images move around the disc of light with flares of colour flashing on and off . . . as if staring at the real sun'.[10]

Midnight Moon and *Midnight Sun Refracted through a Cabin Window* recall a specific experience, filtered through memory. Often Grant's recollections accumulate to create composites that might be considered definitive of their type. Another possibility, frequent in his work from the mid-1960s, is the slicing of an image to suggest the passage of time. Rarely, however, is this depicted as graphically as in a small study of the midnight sun, a gift to Benjamin Britten and Peter Pears, which charts the sun's position from low over the horizon to high in the sky (fig.86). In Norway, in summer, the sky remains light even at midnight. Grant folds his landscape so that the sun's fullness remains occluded, cutting through space as the composition cuts through time. The beauty of this landscape lies in its kaleidoscopic fracturing, such that the horizon, like the sun, dips then rises. Is there an implication that landscape is never the same, hour to hour?

Sun Collage: North Norway, near Tromsø, completed in April 1979, is a portent of the midnight sun – too high to be at midnight, yet glacially bright against a darkened sky (fig.87). Using ink, watercolour and gouache to create veils of light, Grant anchored the image with cut-out photographs of mountains to either side of the sun. The technique bears a correlation to John Piper's use of photography, painting and drawing in his *Stones and Bones* and *Eye and Camera* series of lithographs between the late 1960s and early 1980s, although *Sun Collage*, with its archetypal composition

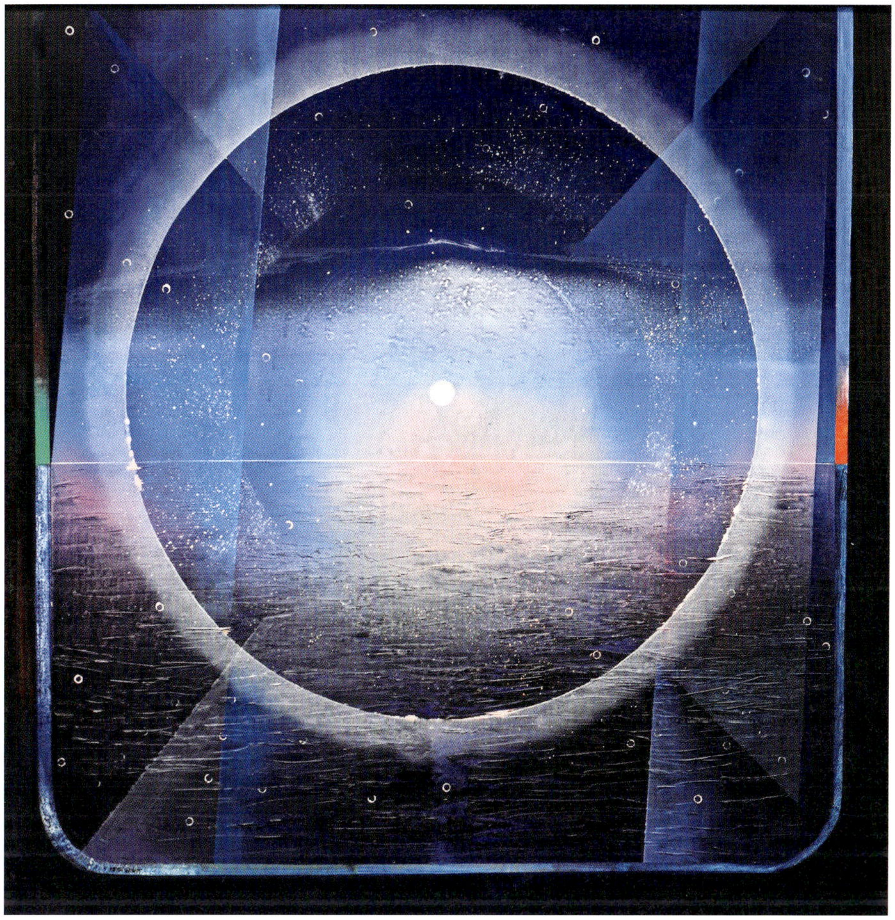

85
Midnight Moon, from *Triptych of the Midnight Sun and Midnight Moon*, 2006
Oil on canvas
120 × 120 cm
Private Collection, UK

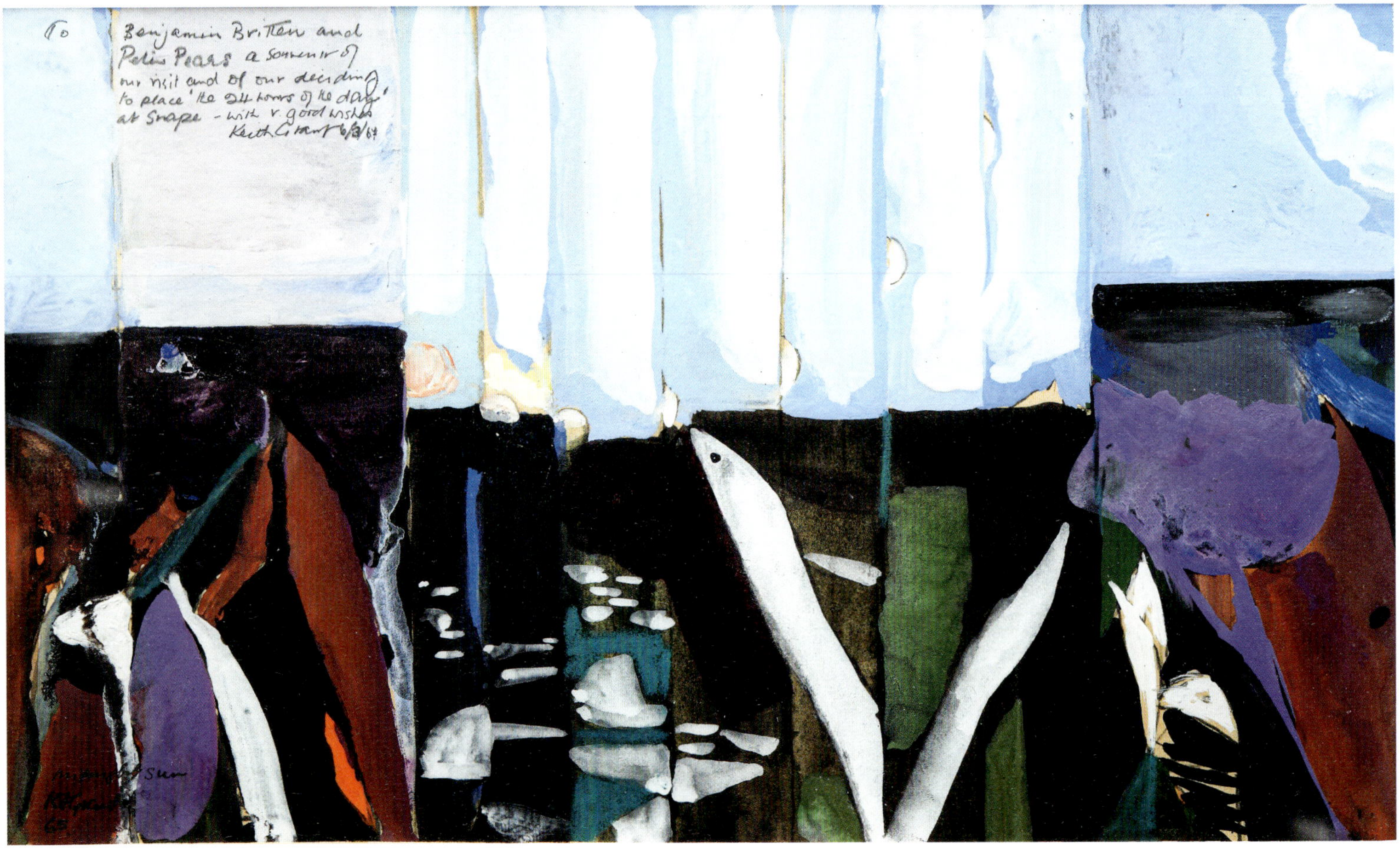

of sun, mountains and water, could be mistaken for the work of no other artist. Despite its limited palette, the effect is blinding: a perfect replication of the sun's intensity in the cold of the far north. Although Grant did not realise it at the time, this painting would preface a series of works in which the sun becomes the sole subject of the imagery.

Northern Lights

Most magical and persistent among Grant's depictions of light, however, are his paintings of the aurora borealis or northern lights. The phenomenon is experienced most vividly near the Arctic Circle, when the interaction between charged particles from the sun and the earth's magnetic field initiates a cycle of fluctuating currents, accelerating electrons into the upper atmosphere of the earth's dark side. As these electrons collide with particles of oxygen and nitrogen, energy is transferred, creating a spectrum of light eerie in its unpredictability. The remainder of this chapter charts Grant's fascination with this spectacle across half a century.

Witnessing the aurora in January 1972, in Svolvær and aboard the MS *Nordstjernen*, Grant described the sight tersely as a sequence that might inform his paintings:

This evening we passed through the Raftsund Channel in darkness. But there was no darkness. Thus huge mountains stood up on either side of water a glassy calm. The snow patterns of infinite variety ghostlike in the deep winter light. The sky was eerily illuminated by the Northern Lights. Shafts of pulsating pallid colour. Phosphor and neon. The stars shone

86
Midnight Sun, 1965
Gouache on paper
16.2 × 27.9 cm
The Red House Aldeburgh Collection (Britten Pears Arts), Aldeburgh

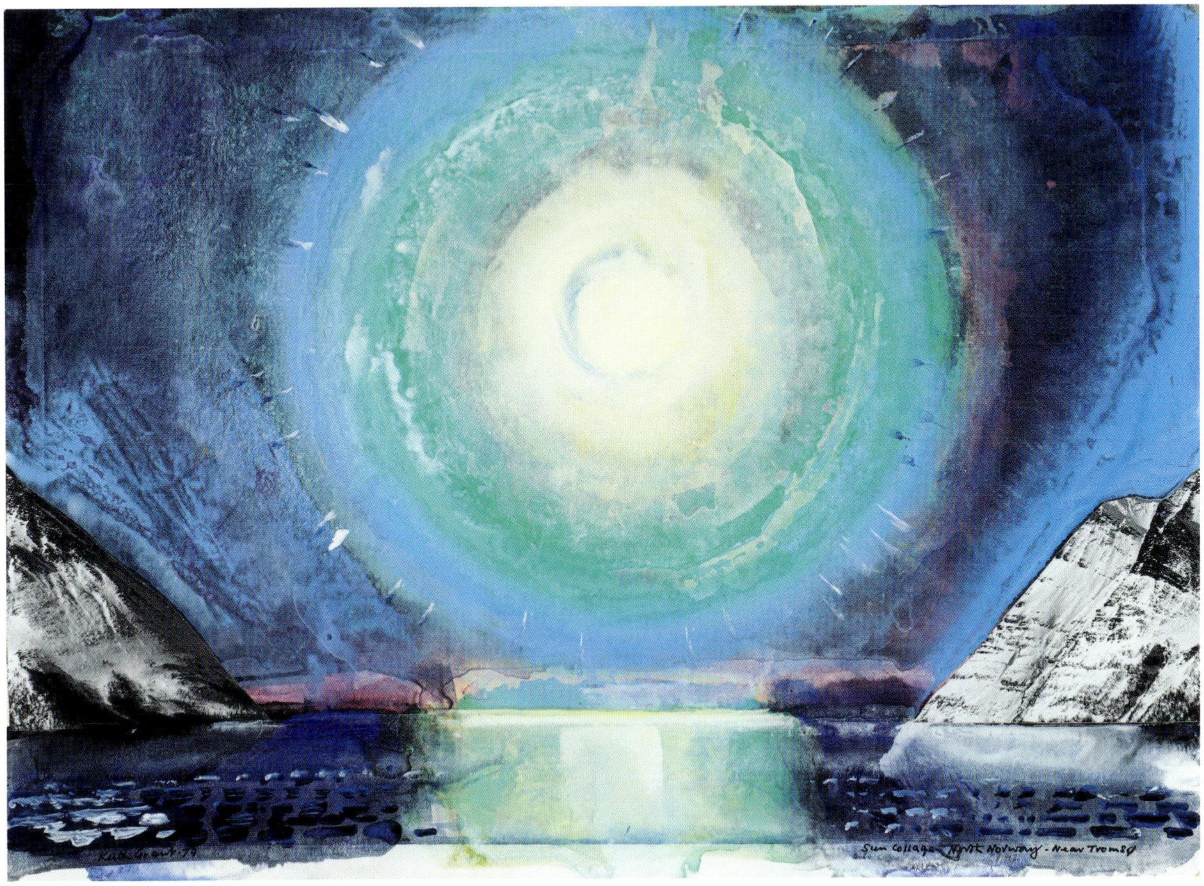

87
Sun Collage: North Norway, near Tromsø, 1979
Acrylic, ink, gouache and collage on paper
36.5 × 52.5 cm
Inverness Museum and Art Gallery

through the bands of light without losing any intensity. The Aurora was reflected in the water. The boat glided past chains of mountains deep in snow. There was a profound depth and intensity of colour – a deep hollow blue-black. The sky pulsating into changing light fold upon fold. Wafting across the entire dome of the heavens. The stars were countless.[11]

Aurora Borealis, Svolvær (1973), originally part of the multi-canvas work *Maritime Polar*, seems a close visual parallel to this description: a composition in which pulses of light wash across the sky (fig.88). The tonality is akin to *The Blind Moon* (fig.81), and indeed the two landscapes are related. Both were acquired by Guy Howard, a doctor, keen explorer and rock climber with a fine collection of paintings.

In *Pyramid Peak with Weak Aurora* (1977), the focus is a mountain, formalised as a triangle against the night sky (fig.89). Grant had recently completed three small works based on this geometry. Painted from imagination, they sought to capture an image with the potency of a volcano: a rock rising above the forests of the North, revealed for one day 'in a mantle of glittering frost'.[12] *Pyramid Peak with Weak Aurora* filled Grant with disquiet, having evolved, he felt, almost without his will: 'It speaks of the night and its archetypal depth – of frost and mist, of the stars and of the architectonic mass of mountains. It is the first painting on the theme of the △ ○ □ which I accept now as a basic element of my designs.'[13]

What was leading Grant towards these night landscapes? In March 1987 he travelled again to northern Norway, where the aurora can be seen particularly vividly above mountains. He was still compelled by geometry, noting with excitement, in a book by Katharine Scherman, an allusion to the

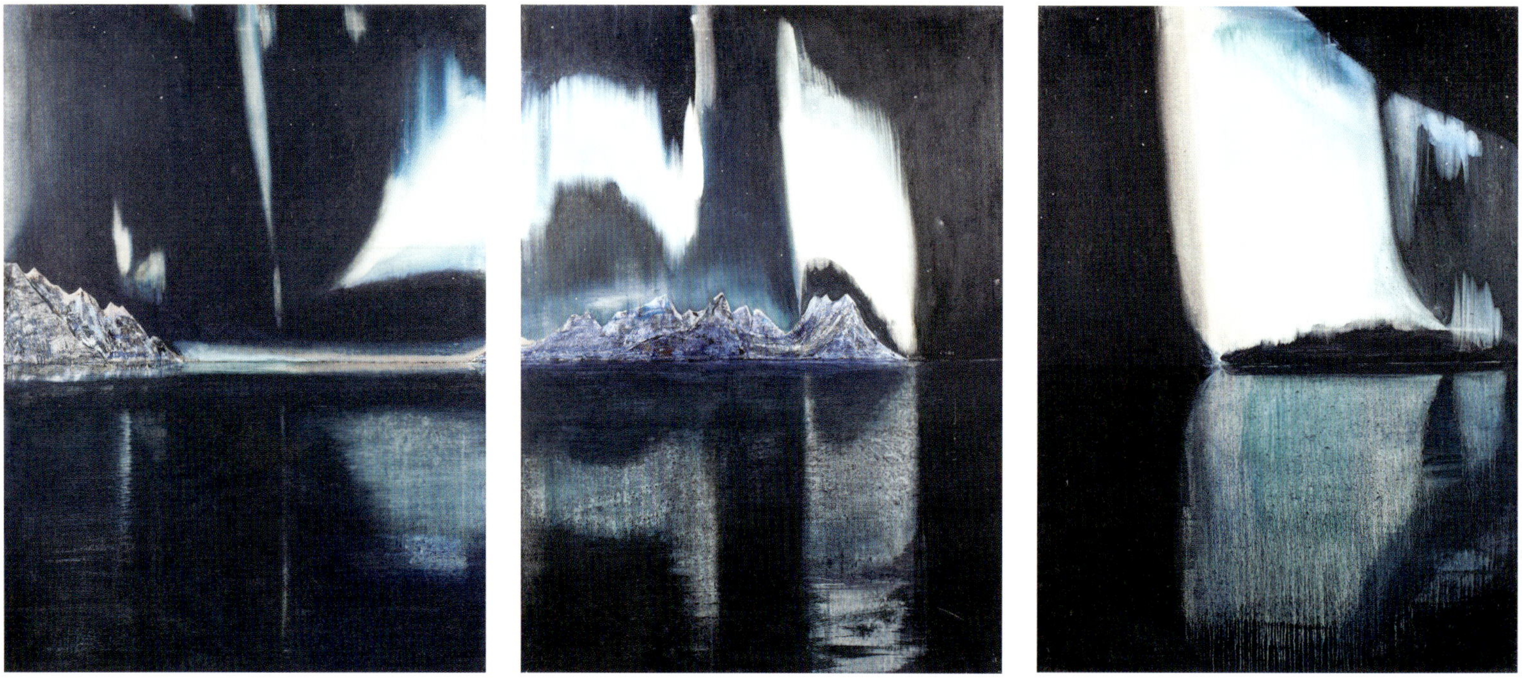

'geometric' nature of land subjected to extreme cold.[14] The descriptions of what he witnessed in Tromsø and Alta abound with colour and texture. Turquoise, emerald, amethyst, steel: 'Everywhere the earth is scratched and scarred – roads covered with sheet ice are like the backs of old whales. I walk upon oiled glass.'[15] A month later, Grant had completed 20 small paintings in acrylics, envisaging at least a hundred. These works are characterised by fluidity – as if, having absorbed the landscape's mood, he was able to communicate it without hesitation. Their colours are exquisite, anchored by the substructure of the mountains.

Describing the haunting impact of the Arctic, David Attenborough drew attention to Grant's paintings of the aurora borealis 'hanging in the sky', and 'the eerie surrealist shapes of icebergs in the bleak polar light'.[16] *Iceberg and Aurora, Ilulíssat* (1990) is a composite of imagery from recent visits to Greenland and north Norway (fig.90). On the day of its completion, Grant recorded the painting as having developed almost accidentally, beginning with precise 'light shafts and arcs', then overpainting in non-waterproof and waterproof blacks: 'Gradually a huge drama in the firmament was revealed in which over-conscious intervention had to be denied.'[17] Concluding with an intimation of how the study might develop, Grant invoked the magisterial precedent of El Greco's *View of Toledo* (*c.*1599–1600), whose sky Rainer Maria Rilke likened to splintered light, tearing and tilling the ground.[18] *Iceberg and Aurora, Ilulíssat* could scarcely be more different. Numinous and otherworldly, the aurora shimmers in turquoise and amethyst, texturing a sky punctuated by stars. Nothing is permanent. Unlike El Greco's landscape of stone and earth, this is a nightscape of water, ice and air.

In the evolution of Grant's aurora paintings, no experience was more important than his journey to Alta in north Norway in February 1990. Near Lakselv, at a temperature of -15°C, the aurora 'undulated in waves as if a huge banner of pale mauve silk was being wafted on an unearthly wind'.[19] He slept one night, during a blizzard, on reindeer skins laid on snow inside a Sami *lavvu*, a conical tent with a hole at its apex to allow smoke to escape. Two days later, at

88
Aurora Borealis, Svolvær, 1973
Acrylic on canvas
Triptych, 122 × 276 cm (each panel 122 × 91 cm)
Lakeland Arts Trust, Cumbria

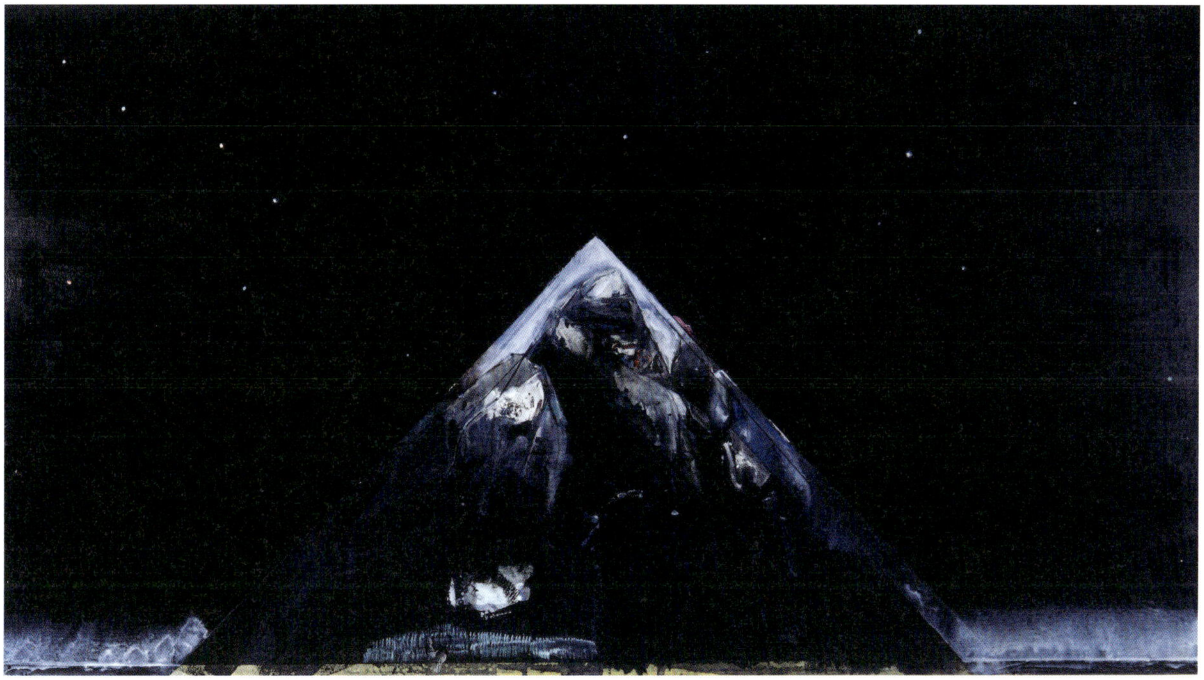

89
Pyramid Peak with Weak Aurora, 1977
Acrylic, gouache and ink on paper
96.5 × 177.8 cm
Private Collection, Norway

Alta, he watched the aurora, sketching its changing form at five-minute intervals. It metamorphosed from vertical flares to horizontal curtains, modulating from rose-purple to whitish green. As the night progressed, Grant's record of the variations shifted from carefully defined forms, sometimes with geometrical lower edges resembling crenellations, to highly schematic images containing the essence of the spectacle. These drawings would provide source material for numerous paintings, as testified by markers identifying pages for future reference.

Certain paintings relate to specific phenomena, however. In 1995 Grant saw a display of the aurora at Stø in Norway that appeared startlingly close. A cloud of visionary brilliance rushed towards him, exploded into the drapery of a vast curtain then broke into vibrating shafts of light, before resuming 'the familiar folded forms of the aurora'. Shaken by the experience, Grant discussed it with Hilde Ellingsen, a musician whom he had met recently and would later marry. Hilde told him how Norwegian children are warned never to look at the aurora or wave a white cloth lest they attract attention. Conversely, another friend described the descending light as a gift from an 'unknown but beneficent force'.[20]

From these experiences, in 2006 Grant painted *Benediction*, a large-scale composition in which the sky is suffused by green- and mauve-tinted light (fig.91). Its mood appears peaceful, ordered by the crisp horizon and reflected diagonal of light that characterise the night paintings of this period. There is an immeasurable depth to the scene, and an expansiveness derived from the softness of the sky, the low placement of the horizon and wide physical format of the canvas.

Space, within painting, was an issue confronted over an extended period through *The Green Aurora* (2007–9; fig.92). A first version, darkened towards the sea, was shown in May 2008 in Grant's solo exhibition, *Snow, Sea and Stars*, at Partridge Fine Art. Subsequently Grant described having removed the implication of land to left and right, 'so that the work will be solely concerned with the elements of water, space and light'.[21] His suggestion is surprising, in that the catalogue illustration includes no sign of land. Was there a further, intermediate version? Either way, with the sea and sky uniformly green, and the introduction

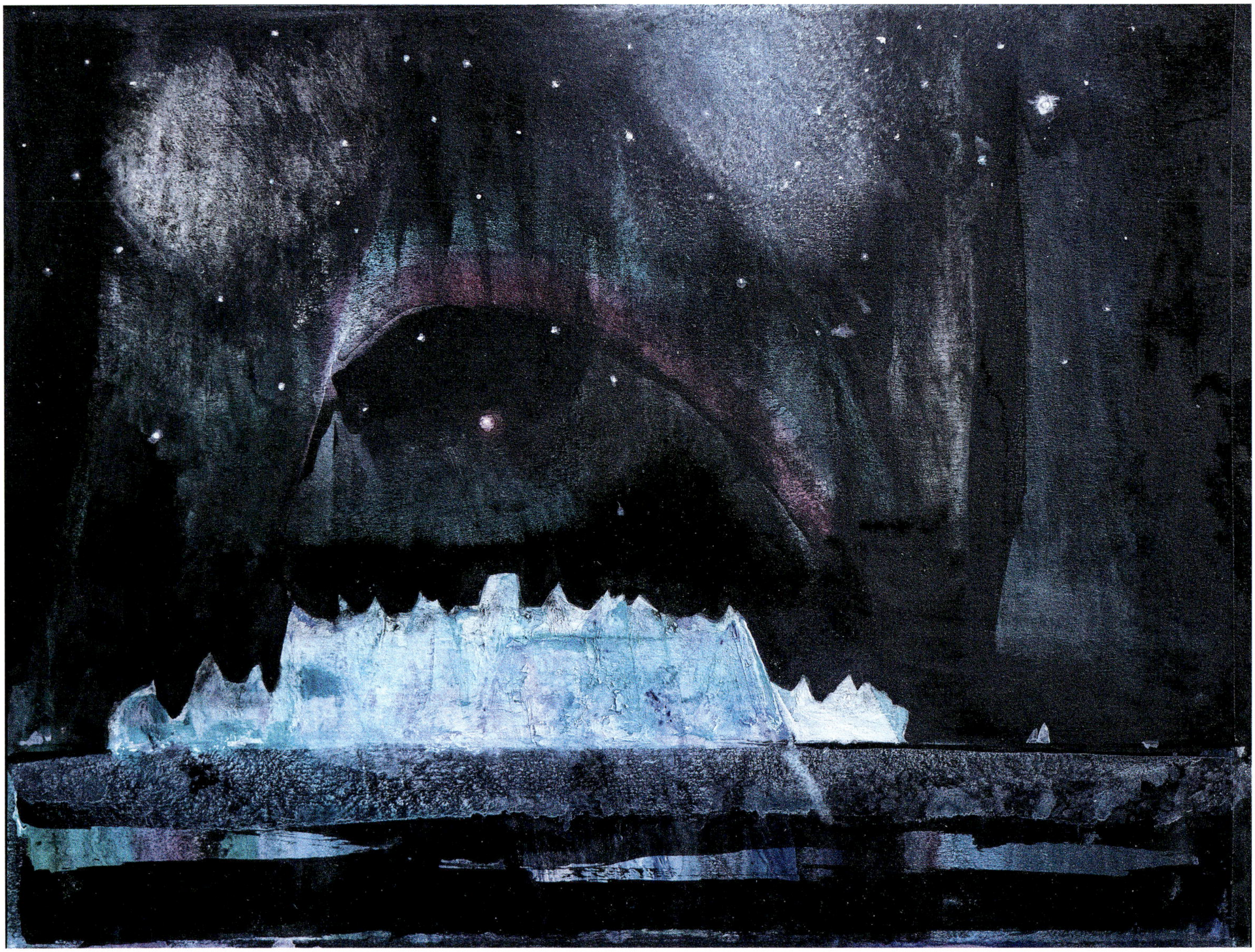

90
Iceberg and Aurora, Ilulíssat,
1990
Acrylic, gouache and ink on
paper
28 × 37.7 cm
Private Collection, Norway

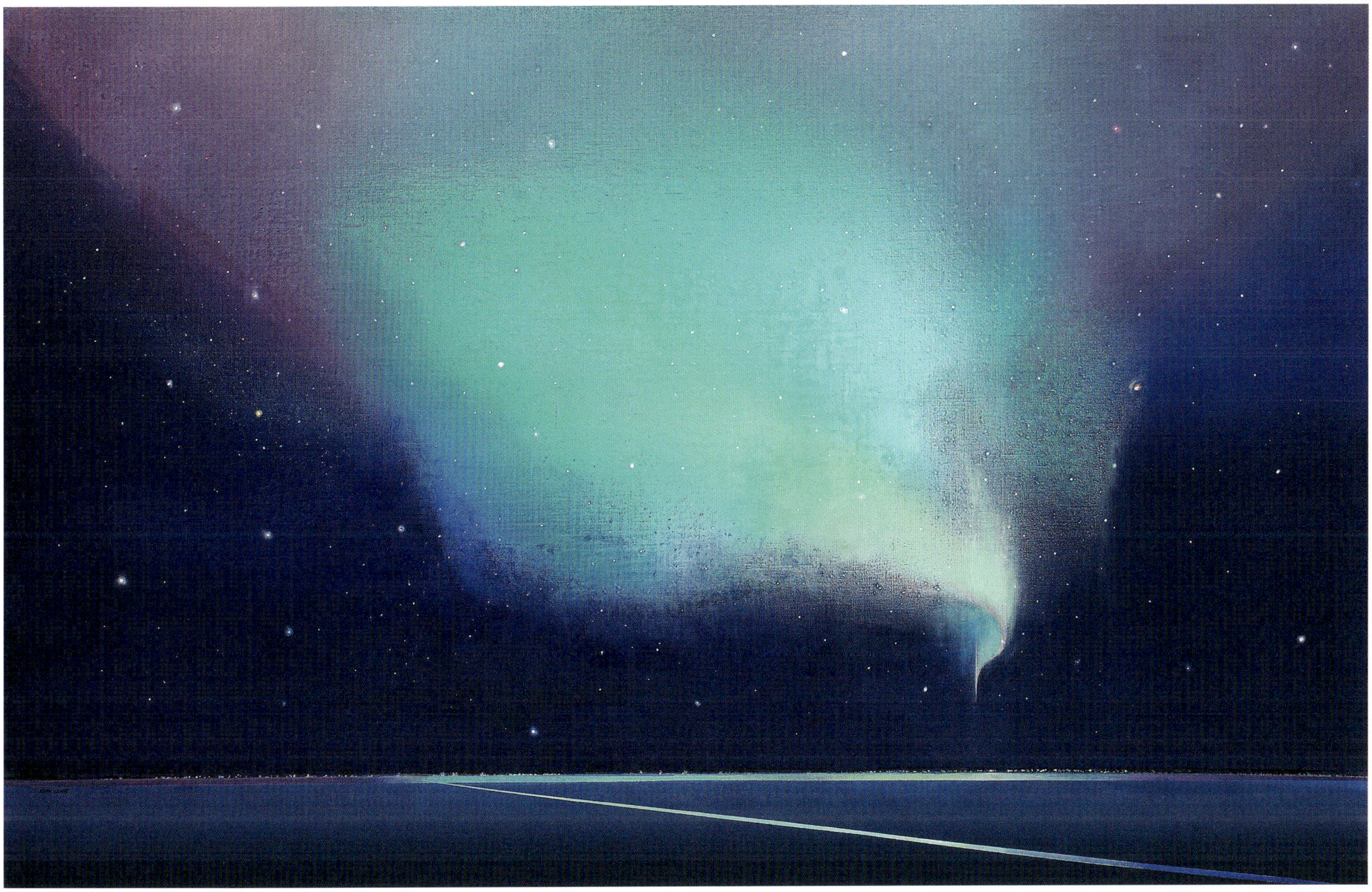

91
Benediction, 2006
Oil on canvas
117 × 190.5 cm
Private Collection, France

of a red buoy, beacons on the horizon and a strongly reflected northern star, Grant was satisfied that he had unified the composition. The aurora itself remained unaltered. A dark wave defines its lower edge, drawing the eye upwards to a midnight blue that seems to hover above the surface. Having striven to recreate the mystery of the northern night, Grant finally felt he had defied the 'two-dimensional reality of the canvas'.[22]

There are many solutions to the same problem, and while *The Green Aurora* fulfilled Grant's current parameters regarding the depiction of space, earlier paintings proposed different answers. *Night, Firmament Divided from the Waters* (1991), in an exhibition of Grant's work as artist-in-residence at Roehampton Institute, impressed Peter Vigar as 'a new departure': a large expanse of colour, containing no apparent landscape motif, with a quality 'altogether more characteristic of Abstract Expressionism' (fig.93).[23] In this and the series that followed, a potent blue is relieved by a tracery of white pinpricks and vapour trails that proves elusive to reproduce in print. The sources behind these paintings – Genesis 6 and Haydn's oratorio *The Creation* – had prompted Grant to reflect deeply on his subject matter and purpose as a painter.

The dilemma Vigar identified from reading Grant's journals – of belief in Nature's divine mystery, yet difficulty in acknowledging God as the force behind it – was one he traced specifically to artists associated with the northern Romantic tradition, who turned to

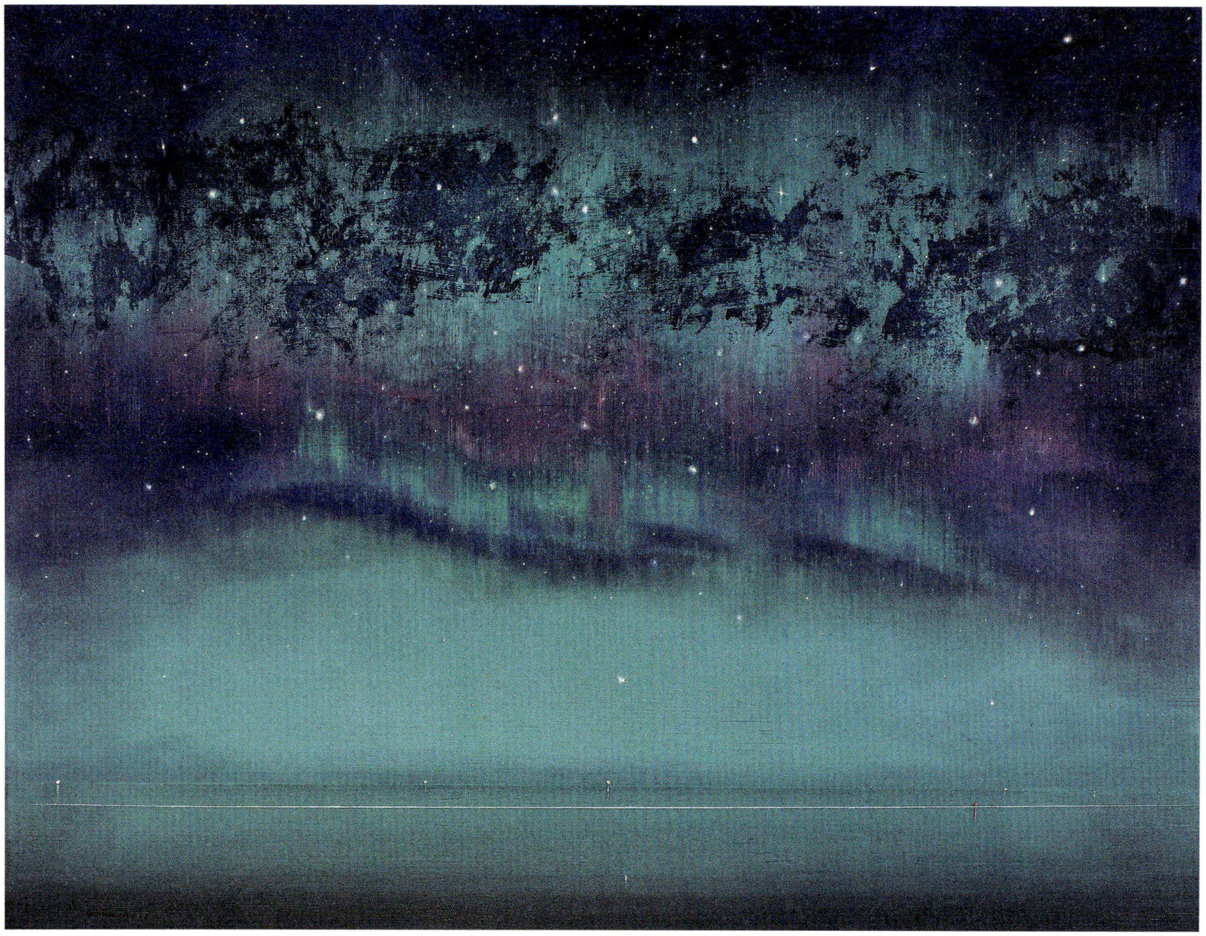

92
The Green Aurora, 2007–9
Oil on canvas
112 × 150 cm
Private Collection, UK

Genesis for a fresh interpretation of the cosmos.[24] Grant, turning the narrative on its head, contemplated humankind having exploited earth's resources to destruction. Would there be greater wisdom in other galaxies? 'Will the particles of man re-form but with a superior intelligence and respect for the will of . . . . Will there be other Edens? Or is this man's only chance?' The ellipsis represents Grant's indecision regarding a higher force. He had no doubt about humankind's capacity for cruelty.[25]

From the starting-point of chaos – the sublime dissonance at the opening of Haydn's *Creation* – he began to structure *Night, Firmament Divided from the Waters*. There would be no defined horizon. Grant in fact envisaged flux, whereby the sea was so 'brightly dark' that it reflected in the firmament, just as the firmament found its own mirror in the waters.[26] The sky appears crumpled like tissue paper or shot silk: a gossamer tracery of stars, infinitely layered. Unlike in *The Green Aurora* or *Benediction*, where depth is implied through an absence of incident, here it is the overwhelming detail that hints at infinity.

The precedent of this work continues to resonate through Grant's paintings of the night sky. He has always said that when returning to a theme he must enlarge upon it. With *Song of the Aurora* (2021), the transformation is masterly (fig.96). From the building blocks of the night paintings, Grant constructs an image that is dynamic yet ambiguous, dreamlike yet clearly defined. The aurora forms an arched portal in the night sky, countering the horizontality of the sea, and tumbling with moon-crescents, primary, reflected

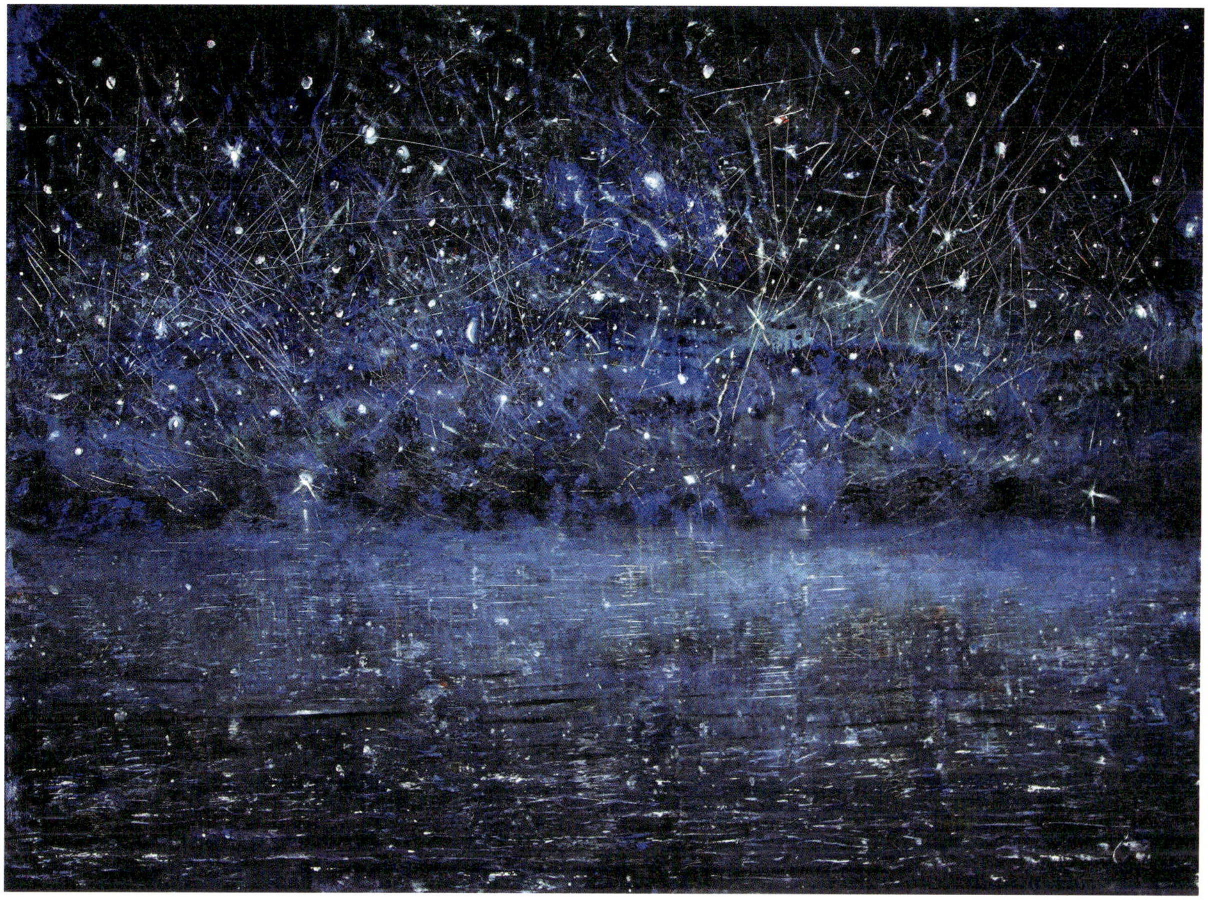

93
Night, Firmament Divided from the Waters, 1991
Oil on canvas over board
156 × 217 cm
Private Collection, UK

and refracted. Above all, this is a painting of joy: a song.

In two further recent paintings, Grant continues to transform his depiction of the aurora. The first, aptly titled *Aurora of the Transfigured Night* (2021; fig.95), recalling sketches made at Alta from 1990, as well as the painting of Svolvær from 1973 (fig.88), demonstrates the power of imagination wedded to an increasingly subtle technique. But first, the echo of the title itself. *Transfigured Night* (*Verklärte Nacht*; 1899) is a string sextet by Arnold Schoenberg based on a poem of the same name by Richard Dehmel. The poem presents a man and woman walking through the cold of the night. The woman is pregnant by another, yet the man forgives her, promising that his love will make the child his own. In Schoenberg's music, an opening tonality of D minor is transformed to D major, as the couple walk towards the light. Grant may not consciously have invoked Schoenberg, or Dehmel, but he was undoubtedly aware of the allusion. The aurora is transformed in his painting into a spectacle more substantive than previous examples: although shimmering, it has weight and opulence. Each detail – from the aurora's frayed or knife-point edges to the ruled perspective of the sea – is transfigured to imply a new experience of night and its mystery.

In August 2022, Grant completed *Night of the Aurora, Tysfjord, North Norway* (fig.94). The landscape, with its inland water and mountains, including the distinctive, twisted peak of Stetind, is among the most spectacular in the country. For Grant, it is also one of the best places to see the night sky. With this new painting, he felt for the first time he had

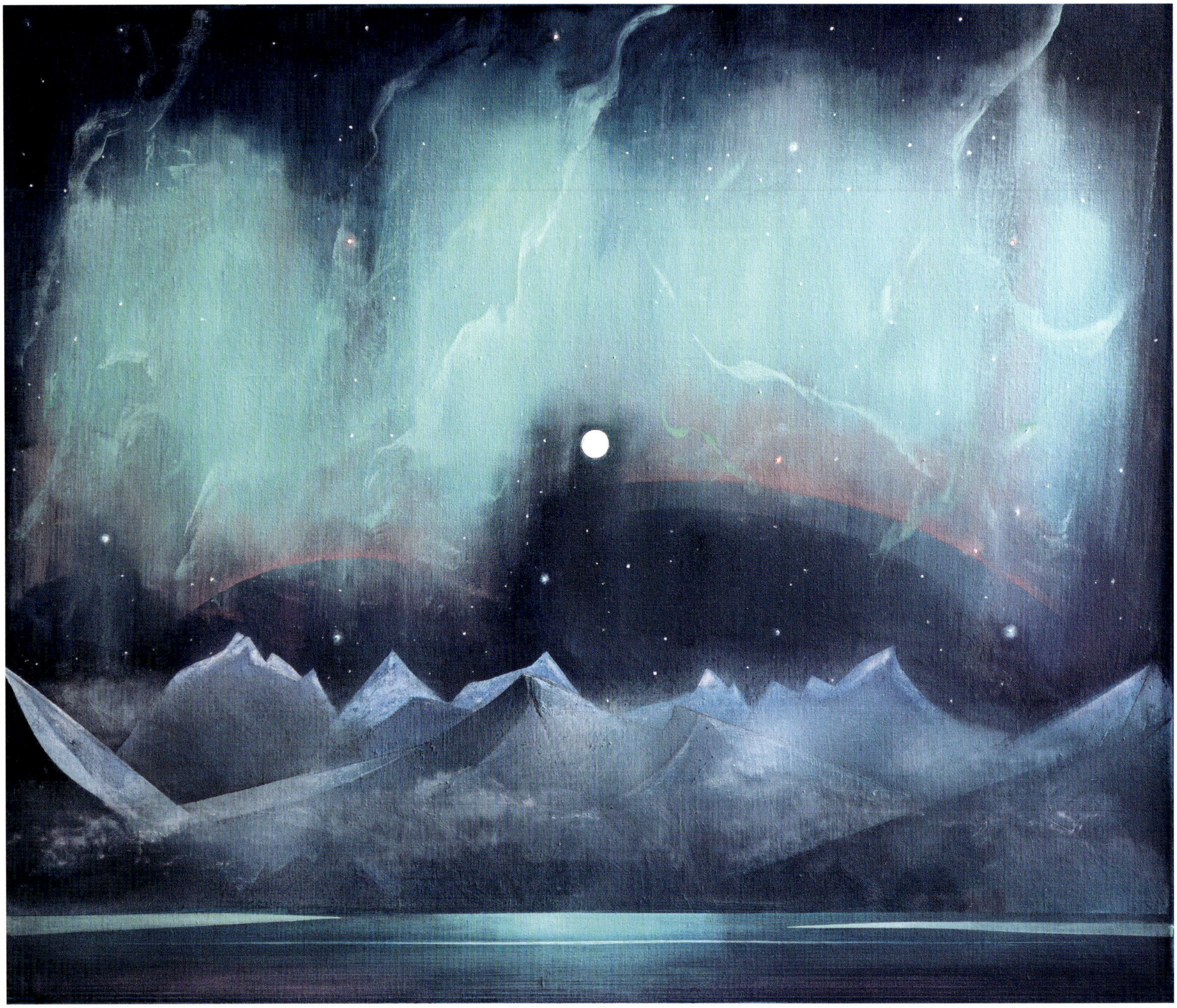

94
Night of the Aurora, Tysfjord, North Norway, 2022
Oil on linen
100 × 120 cm
Private Collection, Norway

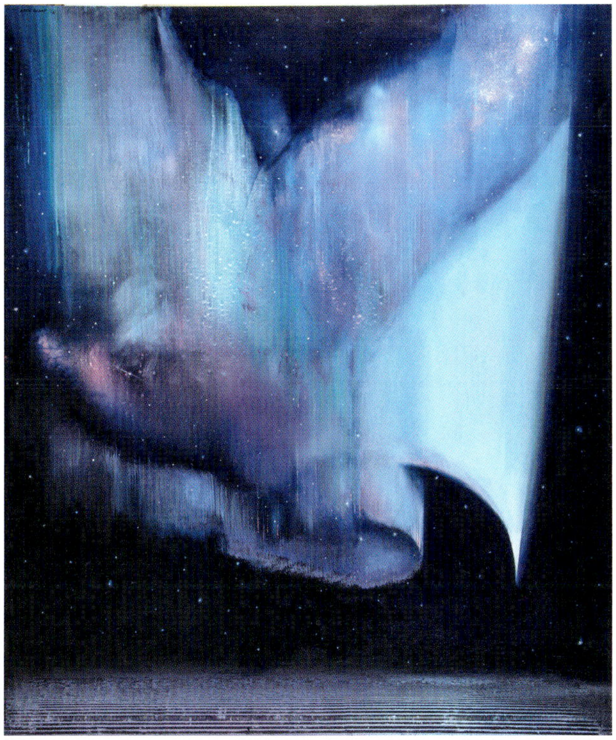

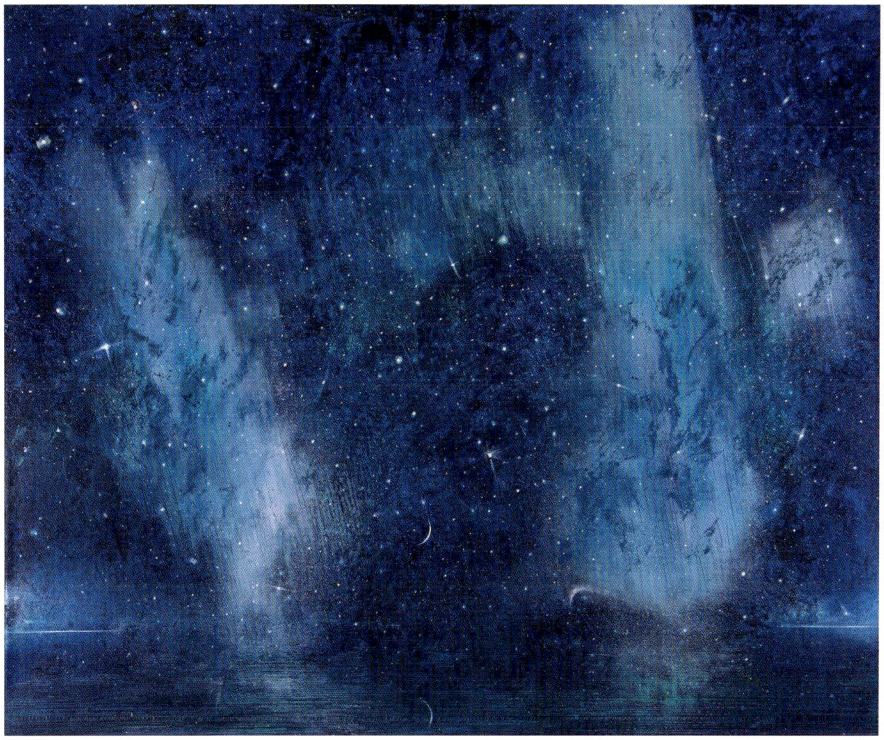

95 (above left)
Aurora of the Transfigured Night, 2021
Oil on linen
150.5 × 130.5 cm
Collection of the artist

96 (above right)
Song of the Aurora, 2021
Oil on linen
120 × 149.75 cm
Private Collection, UK

managed to convey movement within the aurora, based neither on magnetic lines nor a 'curtain' format. Layers of light in the painted sky create several effects simultaneously, rippling and arcing with the delicacy of gauze. The quest to achieve such subtlety – and having achieved it, to surpass it – is what spurs Grant to continue painting.

Yet it is important not to forget the circuit completed by a perceptive viewer: the process described by Britten, in relation to music, as the sacred triangle of composition, performance and listening. When Guy Howard was dying in his fifties from a brain tumour, Grant hung *Blind Moon*, bought but not yet displayed, where he could see and enjoy it. He recorded,

The title intrigued him and he kept repeating it with a wry smile, so typical of him. It was as if the mystery of the title was an echo of that greater mystery into which, he well knew, he was about to enter. I like to feel that his response to my work was because of its hinting at the extra-terrestrial existence of matter and its continuation throughout time, as well as its speaking of the far North, an area of the world especially evocative and mysterious for us both. We had often spoken of nature's miraculous interchange between the inanimate and the animate, and the higher state of consciousness of itself, to which we felt nature was constantly aspiring. We talked of mimicry and melanism and how many forms in nature appeared reflected in each other, of camouflage and of the importance of change. And change on a spiritual level was, I felt, the conviction of Guy before his death. During a disjointed conversation towards the end of his life Guy said, on sensing my distress – 'It comes to us all sooner or later, but nothing is lost, nothing is ever lost.'[27]

Grant's final view was of him sitting at the kitchen table 'opposite my painting and waving to me with his "one good arm" as I left the flat at the end of his corridor lined with books and important paintings.'[28]

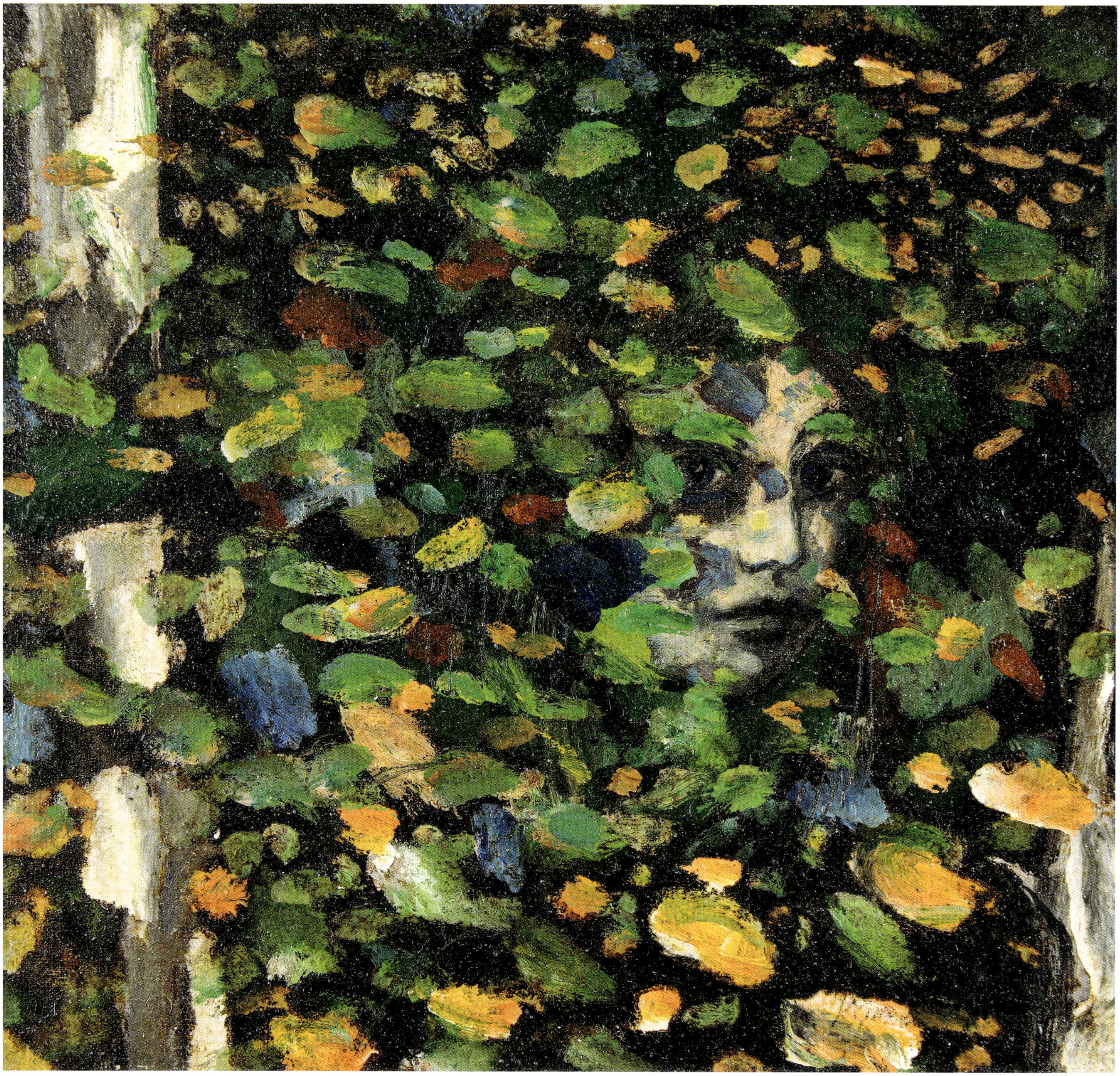

6

Metamorphosis

In September 1969, Grant again met Milada Tashnerova, a young Czech graphic design student introduced to him by the British Council. Grant was in Seljord, in the Telemark region of Norway, to look at a cottage offered by the local council for use as a studio. With Milada he spent a magical few days – 'of Chinese watercolour atmosphere' – among the forests, hills and by the sea, moved by her beauty and innocent response to landscape.[1] At one point he lost sight of her, as she turned, half-hidden by birch trees.

Back in London, worried that he had received no news since Milada discovered her visa to re-enter Czechoslovakia had expired, Grant began a series relating to the forests of Sweden and Norway. One large painting showed Milada entering a dark wood. A smaller composition depicted her turning to face him from behind trees (fig.97). A patterning of leaves dominates, dappling the darkness and only partially disclosing Milada's wide-eyed, serious expression. The moment is one of camouflage and metamorphosis. Milada's face is the colour of birch bark, her dark eyes and lips transmuted into forest shadow.

This incident points to Grant's fascination with change and simulation in nature: the transition from animate to inanimate, or a creature's adaptation to resemble its habitat. If the interest itself was longstanding, Grant's exploration of it did not begin seriously for over forty years after his painting of Milada. In 2012 he began a series specifically predicated on metamorphosis: a theme that effected a radical reorientation of his work.

It is interesting to conjecture why Grant alighted on this idea at this particular time. There is no clue in his preceding landscape paintings, from which the new paintings formed a complete departure. And while mimesis and camouflage were topics he had discussed with his friend, the collector Guy Howard, and experienced at first hand in the rainforest, he had not addressed them in his painting since the 1980s. There seems to have been a broader, incipient interest, of which he could scarcely have been aware. Setting aside nominally related projects (a new film of Kafka's *Metamorphosis*; a trilogy of ballets, *Metamorphosis: Titian 2012*), the most resonant is Carlos Fonseca's *Museo Animal* (2017), reworked in translation as *Natural History* (2020). Into a wide-ranging, polyphonic narrative, Fonseca weaves allusions to Alejo Carpentier's *Lost Steps*, following a voyage to the heart of the jungle. The protagonist, a museum curator, receives an invitation from a fashion designer to collaborate on an exhibition whose content – hinted at through discussions of

97
Milada and Birch Grove,
1969
Oil on board
33 × 35.5 cm
Private Collection, UK

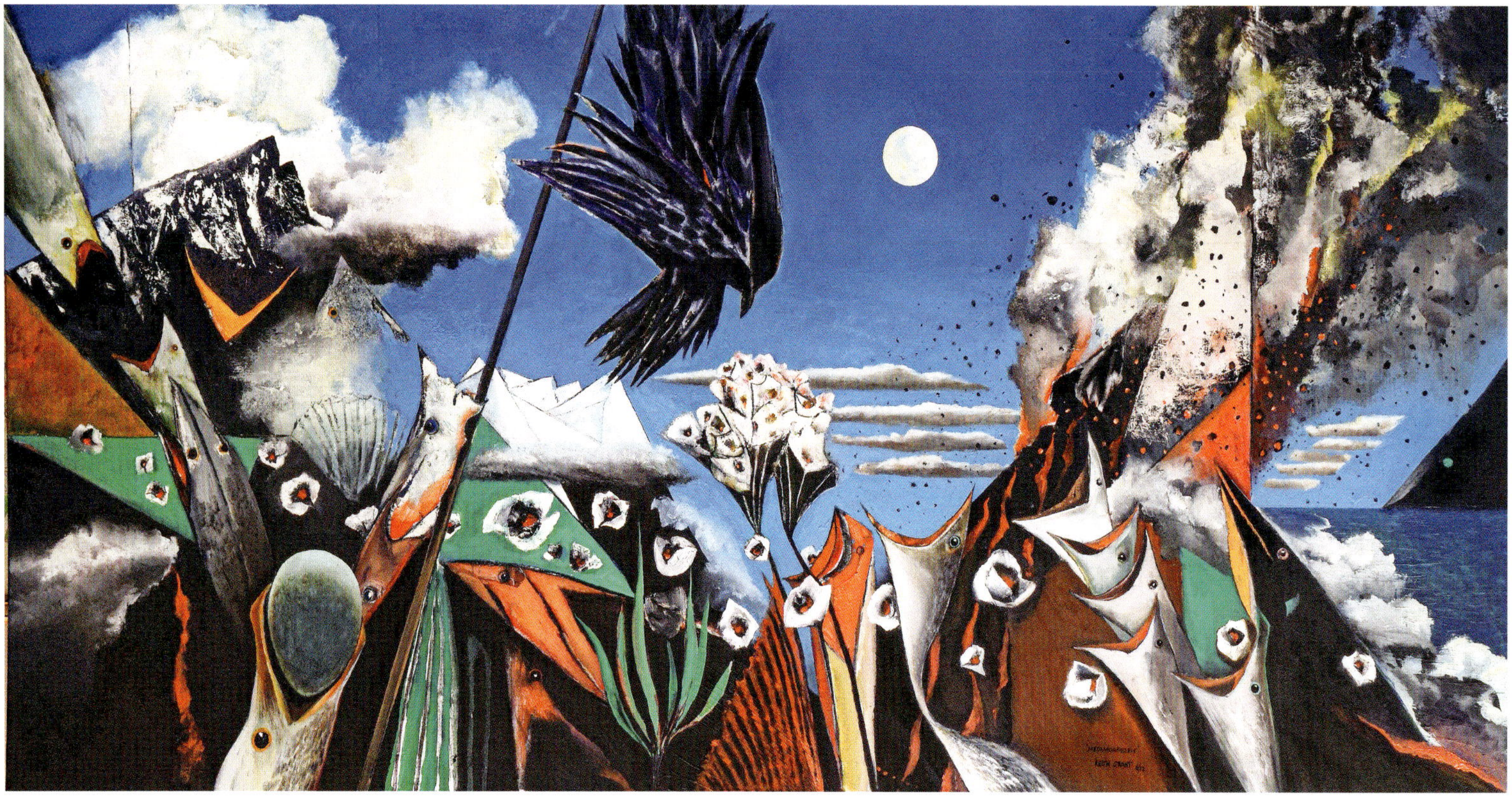

98
Metamorphosis, 2012
Oil on canvas
100 × 300 cm
The David Game Collection, UK

mimicry, masks, sketches of creatures that dissemble as others – remains unclear. A key appears to be the idea, borrowed from Thomas Browne's *The Garden of Cyprus* (1658), that behind all natural patterns is a geometric arrangement of five points, the quincunx. Fonseca's is a beautiful shadowing of ideas central to Grant's work; here, most pertinently, geometry and metamorphosis.

Geometry and Metamorphosis

Grant, returning in 2012 to a photograph he had taken in 1961, showing a crow killed and 'gibbeted' by Norwegian cod fishermen, began a painting of a falling black bird. An azure sky, with full moon and tiers of clouds, offsets a marine landscape. To the right erupts a volcano, and beneath is an array of open-mouthed creatures: ambiguous composites of fish, birds and flowers, straining upwards towards the crow. Recalling the paintings of Hieronymus Bosch, as well as the photograph he had subtitled 'Death in Northern Guise', Grant felt his 'imagined forms owe something to the primal fear of the unknown and the terrors of the sea and the forest'.[2] Completing the composition in June 2012, he titled it *Metamorphosis* (fig.98).

Elements of the painting had occurred in earlier works, yet the bright palette, clarity of definition and internal juxtaposition within *Metamorphosis* was utterly new. Grant listed in his journal a plethora of sources contributing to it, from photography to space-lattices, crystals, rock pools, geology, images of birds in motion 'when it is impossible to ascertain for certain their features or characteristics', light, air, space and the eruptions of volcanoes, ornithology and botany.[3] In the photograph of the gibbeted crow, hung by fishermen to deter birds from feeding on the drying cod, Grant found a resonance with Robert Musil's exquisitely detailed essay, 'Flypaper' (1913), in which insects, in their final struggles, appear totally human.

99 (above)
The Winged Hours of the Seabirds, 2013
Oil on canvas over board
114 cm diameter
Private Collection, UK

100 (below)
Metamorphoses, 2012
Oil on canvas
127 × 127 cm
The David Game Collection, UK

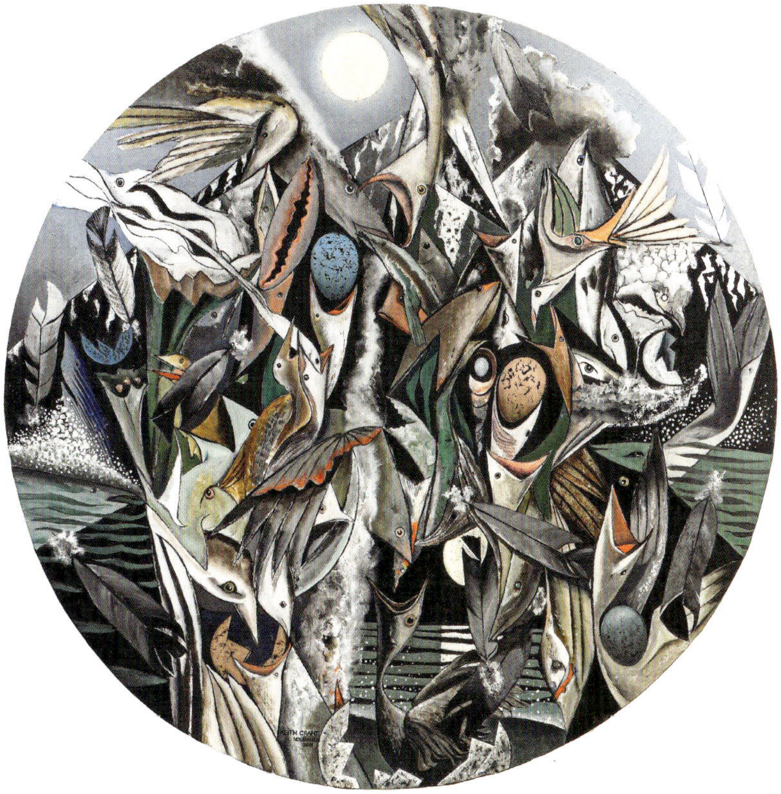

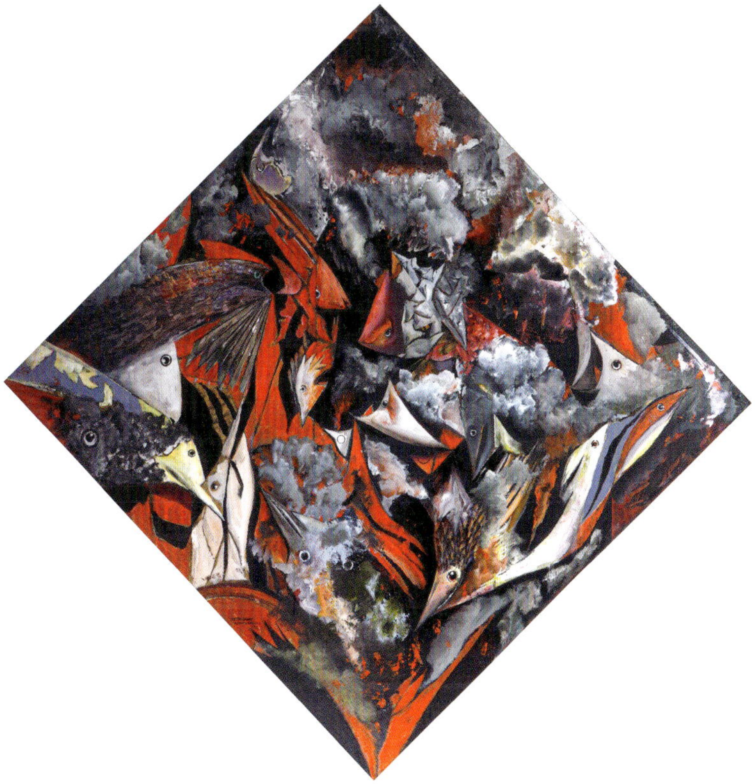

Yet there was also the unseen. Grant noted the depiction of blossoms releasing 'pollen, scent or a fine powder of minutest particles forming a gossamer mist – invisible but none-the-less present'.[4] In *Ragnarok* (2012), a painting also featuring a marine volcano, a thin jet recalls the presence of a humpbacked whale, at close proximity in Greenland in 2006. A fountain of spray passed between Grant and the light to become finely shadowed lace.

The layered references within these new paintings evoke mystery, autobiography, as well as the humanitarian or environmental concerns that will be addressed later. Approaching these themes symbolically, Grant repositioned a deep-rooted attraction to Surrealism in relation to the formalism that reasserts itself periodically throughout his work. Motifs from nature are abstracted and subjected to cubist distortions, sometimes echoing aspects of John Craxton's landscapes, which Grant admired. With *Metamorphoses* (2012), however, he took the theme of a marine volcano and forged it into an apocalyptic, baroque fantasy (fig.100). A diamond format lends sharpness to a chaotic vortex of fish, whose sharp snouts and fins approximate the beaks and wings of birds, in a counterchange of red and black. Grant described it as 'The Firebird's Nest', sensing as he painted it that the North was losing its grip on his imagination. Was he right? In his journals, he immediately questioned his own assertion:

The new work, freed as it is from allusion to reality, releases mystical forms and symbols which I begin to see as no-less expressive of my northern awareness as references to the topography of actual places. Moreover these strange forms and patterns are perhaps a deeper and truer expression of the

101
Persephone (Summer), 2012
Oil on canvas
115.5 × 130 cm
Private Collection, Norway

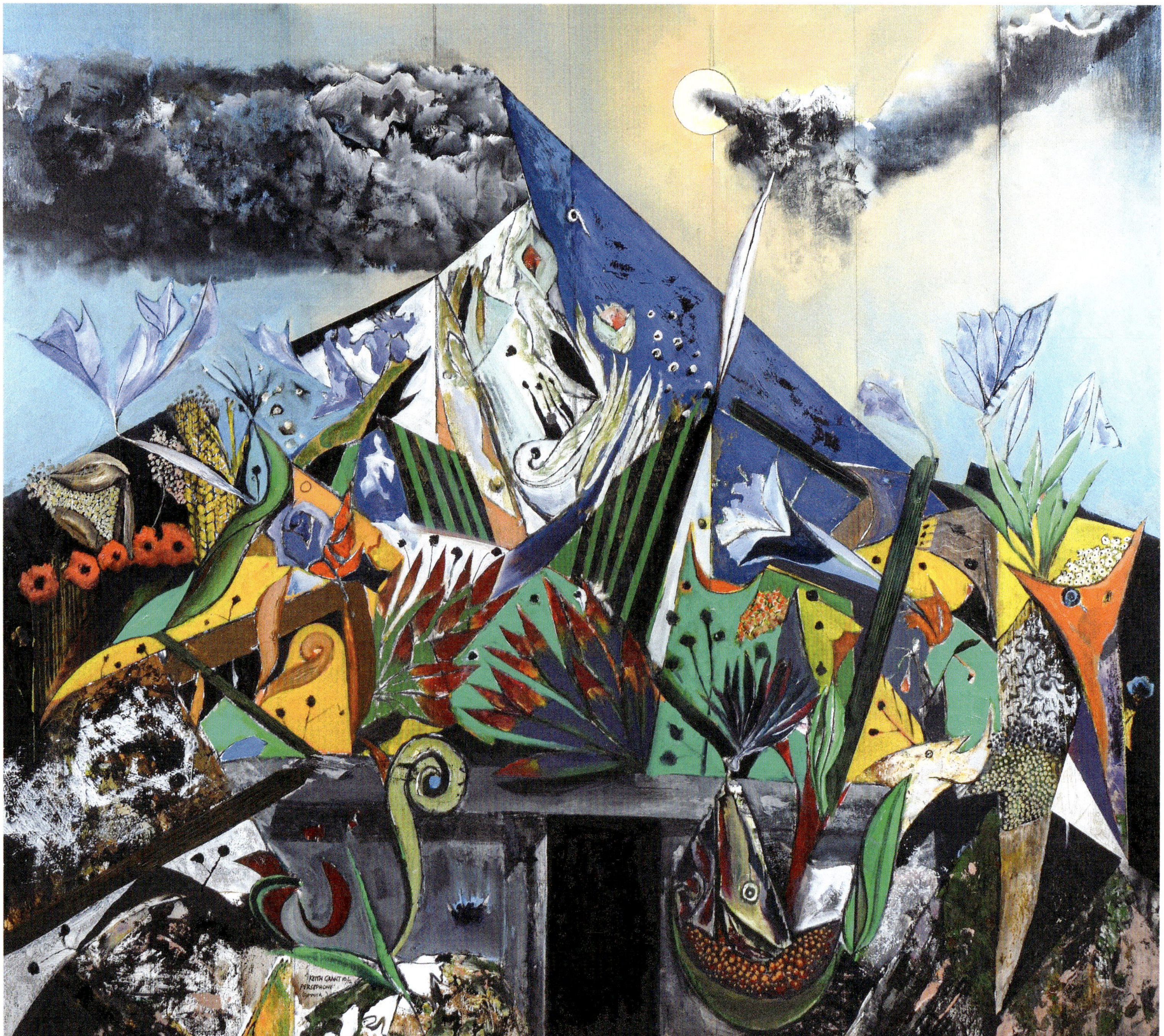

interactive struggle of life, consciousness and of mystical atavism and death as the dark spiritual reality of the North reveals itself.[5]

At a profound level, these new 'metamorphic' paintings reinterpreted rather than supplanted Grant's response to the North.

In *Persephone (Summer)* (2012), a frozen mountain and simmering volcano anchor a melée of mythical references: corn, an entrance to the underworld, seedpods (fig.101). According to Greek mythology, Persephone was rescued after her abduction to Hades, yet was compelled to return there for a third of each year since she had eaten pomegranate seeds whilst underground. These dark months became winter, while her time on earth denoted summertime and harvest. As the painting is studied, ubiquitous warning signs appear. Instantly noticeable is the dark entrance to what resembles a wartime bunker. Less obvious are the eyes that animate fish or birdlike forms, spilling across the landscape and transforming the volcano into a shark, or pomegranate seeds into fish roe. A feather resembles the petals of flowers; fanned foliage appears tipped with blood. And the palette? A conceivably realistic sky, banded to denote the passage of time, jars against the vivid central section whose green tones seem synthetic rather than natural. Perhaps only the lowest section, with its mossy, textured rock, offers reassurance.

The miracle of *Persephone (Summer)* is to hold these elements in tension, such that the tantalisingly sinister never for a moment becomes repellent. Grant achieves this so deftly that the painting could be read quite plausibly as a summer landscape *tout court*: replete with uncurling ferns and a riot of flowers.

The circular format and muted *grisaille* palette of *The Winged Hours of the Seabirds* (2013) alter the terrain instantly (fig.99). Some elements recur, such as triangular peaks, fish-bird forms and feathers, yet the locus is transposed to the marine volcano of Surtsey, complete with waterspout. Among the creatures are a lobster and squid.

Any humorous intent behind these almost 'cartoonish' creatures is countered by the glassy replication of eyes throughout the composition. Grant had recently experienced problems with his sight, manifesting itself as double or zigzag vision. The eyes in these compositions thus assumed an autobiographical resonance, as he contemplated both the vulnerability of these 'quite unbelievable mechanisms' and an anguish at the thought of their destruction. His predicament rekindled a childhood horror at the eyes of cooked fish, the symbol most expressive of blindness, but also a parallel with his night paintings. As he wrote in his journal, 'The eyes of all the creatures that have ever lived have to my mind a direct relationship to the stars of the universe . . . perhaps my projected northern lights work may have "eyes" as planets and the distant suns; the stars.'[6]

Underpinning *The Winged Hours of the Seabirds* is such a tight structural plan – a triangle, a vertical accent and the moon – that its surface elaboration never appears confused. Even more than *Metamorphoses* it possesses an almost childlike identification with the grotesque, traced by Grant to sources of northern decorative art in which invented beasts stand as surrogates for the ferocity of nature. On the sleighs discovered at the Oseberg ship burial in Norway are fantastical carved heads. Was their purpose, Grant wondered, to instil fear, to appease evil forces, or to repel them?[7]

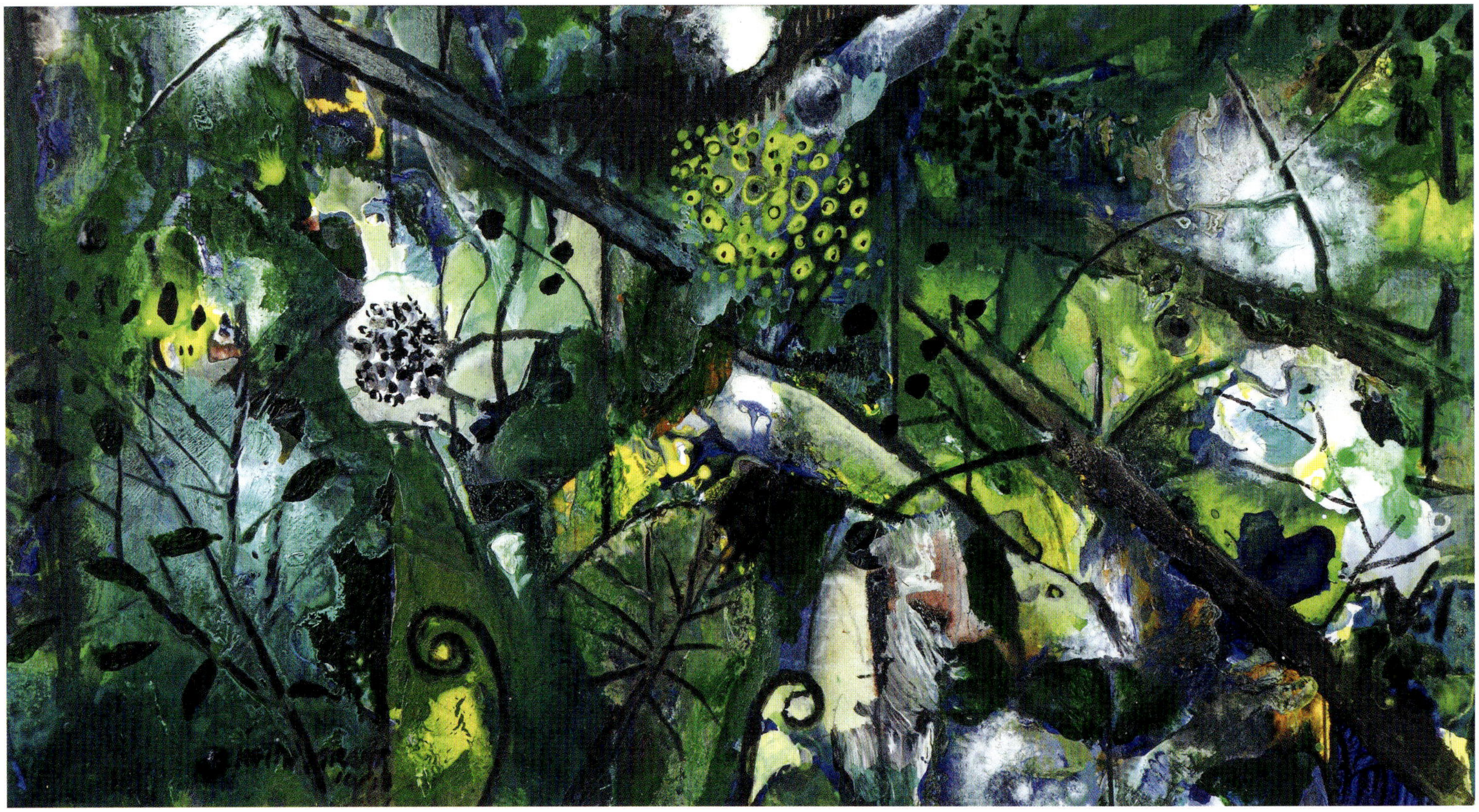

102
Moonlight, Wenlock Wood,
2013
Acrylic and ink on paper
17 × 31 cm
The David Game Collection, UK

Forest Paintings

Towards late summer 2013, Grant's attention turned towards woodland settings, with paintings that would lead to a reconsideration of the British landscape. For the time being, the cast of these new works remained ambiguous. Grant painted golden light at the end of tree tunnels, compositions transforming sunlit foliage into patterns resembling frogspawn, or a flash of kingfisher blue amid aqueous greens and yellows, suggesting a Rorschach test. In a small study such as *Moonlight, Wenlock Wood* (2013; fig.102), there is an intriguing vertical banding, recalling the temporal segmentation of the 1960s' volcano studies. Behind the painting is a memory of A.E. Housman's poem *On Wenlock Edge*, which evokes nature's reclaiming of the once-powerful Roman settlement of Uricon, located beneath the Shropshire landscape of The Wrekin. Grant's composition has an artless quality, overlaying twigs, seedheads and the acid bracts of spurge against lush green foliage.

These paintings of woodland interiors were informed by Grant's experience of taking Patchy, his dog, for walks in the forest. He would climb uphill, then, resting, attempt to analyse the rhythms, forms and spaces around him. The apparently random placing of leaves, husks, berries or twigs, in harmonies of colour, resolved into designs structured by upright, prone or angled shapes – as an 'abstract tapestry'.[8] This close, immersive view of landscape had not been seen in Grant's painting before, despite his having conjectured it in relation to a volcano or the aurora. The approach drew significantly upon his reading of Gaston Bachelard's

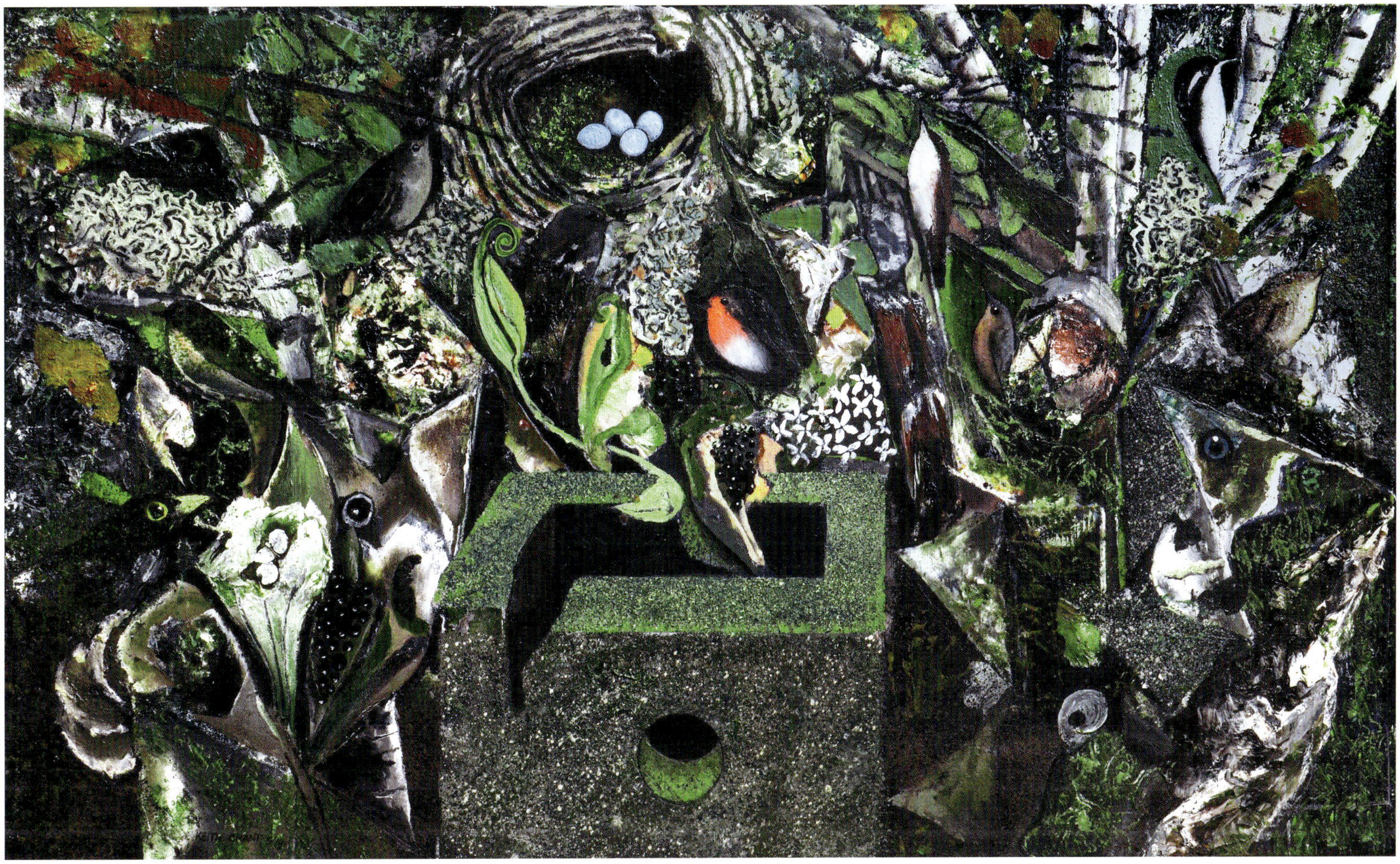

103
The Ruined Cistern, 2014
Oil on canvas over plywood
69.5 × 116 cm
Private Collection, USA

The Poetics of Space (1957), which at this point he numbered as among the four books most important to him (the others being Bashō's *Narrow Road to the Deep North*, Cesare Pavese's *This Business of Living* and Fernando Pessoa's *The Book of Disquiet*).[9] Bachelard, with his perceptive examination of enclosed spaces – forests, nests, shells – as well as the miniature and the immense, gave Grant the 'courage to stand by the images I intuitively create'.[10]

Among the first of these new paintings, *The Ruined Cistern* (2014) is dominated by a water tank discovered by Grant, submerged in a small stream crowded by rotting wood, stones, moss, leaves and twigs (fig.103). Its context within the forest would have been categorised by Bachelard as of 'inner immensity': a space that appears limitless, extended in the imagination by veils of tree-trunks and foliage.[11] Grant depicted the setting as an intermeshing of nature, crossing and colonising every space, such that plants curl through one another and surfaces are textured by lichen, in a cycle of growth and decay. The placement and formation were intuitive, realised in a heavy impasto 'by almost willing the paint to develop its own relations and affinities' to parallel nature's effects.[12] Reading Bachelard's *The Poetics of Reverie*, Grant found a sentence to encapsulate this process: 'The imagination ceaselessly revives and illustrates the memory.'[13]

Grant thus probed the relationship between memory and invention. In the cistern's broken shell

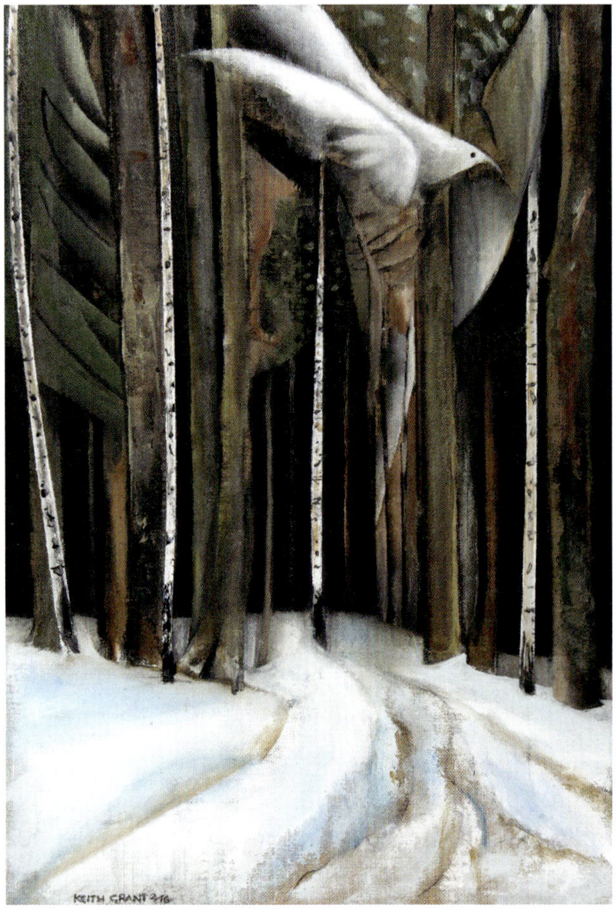

104 (left)
Entrance to the Enchanted Forest, 2016
Oil on board
58 × 38.5 cm
Private Collection, UK

105 (below)
The Elk Fence II, 2022
Oil on linen
45 × 80 cm
Collection of the artist

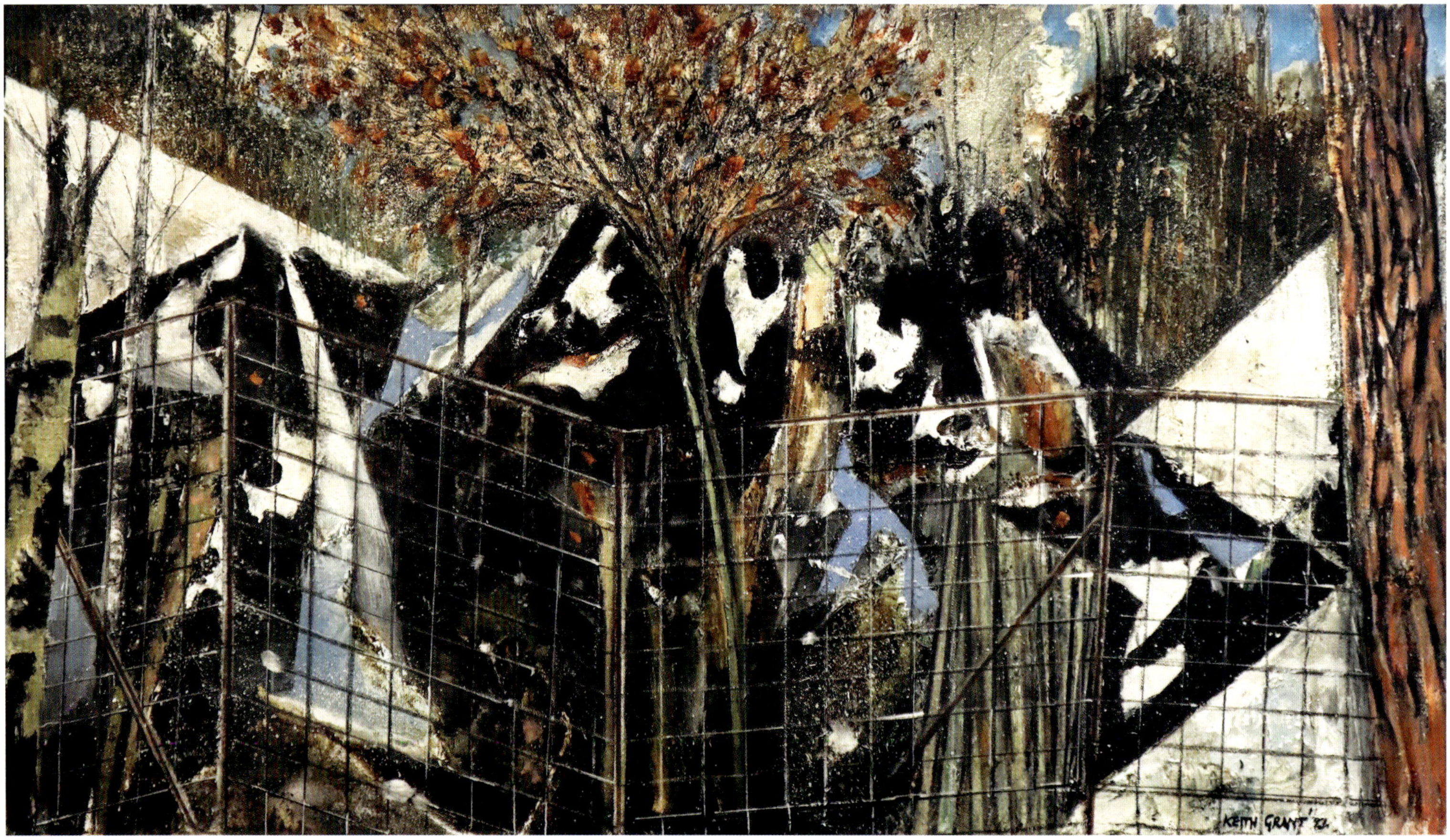

106
Torunn, 1960
Oil on board
approx. 122 × 91 cm
Private Collection, Norway

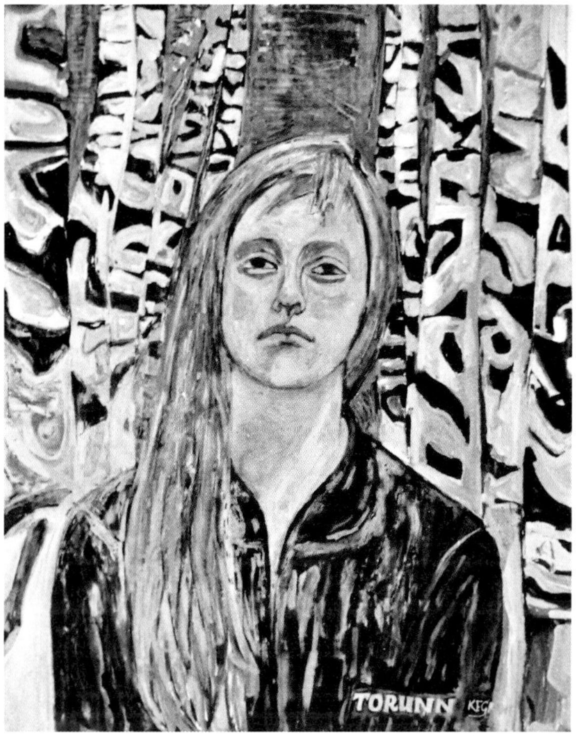

he imagined the voice of an oracle, heralding the mystical renewal of spring amid the decay of human detritus. He made no apology whatsoever for introducing birds into the composition: these were creatures neither of sentiment nor strict scientific ornithology, but, as for the composer Olivier Messiaen, to whom birdsong was so important, 'little servants of immaterial joy'.[14] As the painting progressed, it diverged from the pure abstraction Grant had envisaged to reflect instead the contrapuntal texture of the forest: quick-darting birds, the slower rhythms of plants germinating or rotting, and greens that 'everywhere blink, fluoresce and glimmer in the spaces between'.[15] This latter statement could, in fact, be read as a description of earlier paintings to test the difference between the two. Where *Moonlight, Wenlock Wood* is essentially an abstract study of light, texture and form, *The Ruined Cistern* is an essay on the experience of the forest, juxtaposing recognisable species of bird, berries, flowers and trees with hybrids born from the imagination.

Grant's response to the forest, longstanding and productive in terms of paintings, could sustain an entire study. During his second visit to Norway, in 1960, he painted a portrait of a young Norwegian woman he had met in Oslo, Torunn Busch, against a thicket of birch trees characteristic of the rich forests surrounding the city (fig.106). Immediately behind Torunn is a tree of a different species, its central placement recalling Grant's painting of trees at Verulamium (fig.14; p.24). The birch trees' bark resembles snakeskin. Grant developed such an affection for the birch – regarded as a weed in Norway and often felled – that it has become a personal symbol, often painted in isolation. Here, it vigorously outnumbers the other trees, sparsely interspersed in the background. The painting's subject is, of course, Torunn, yet it is equally a close-framed portrait of the forest.

In *Entrance to the Enchanted Forest* (2016), Grant's focus is the anticipation of penetrating the forest (fig.104). The composition grew from one of several sketches made in January of that year, when Grant accompanied two young filmmakers to the 'frozen forest' near Bø. He drew until his hands became so cold they felt 'paralysed beyond the possibility of pain'.[16] In the resulting painting, the enigma lies in the tracks carved in the snow – who made them? where do they lead? – and in the

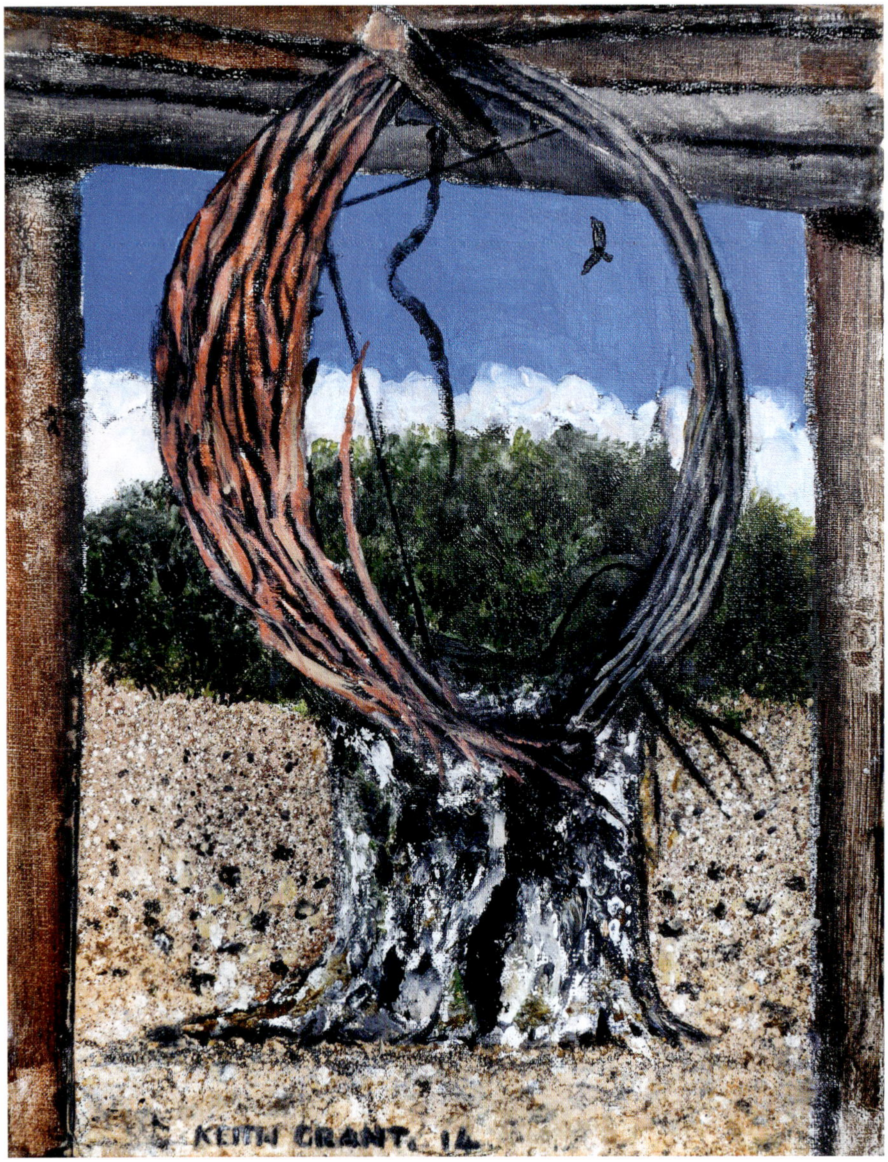

107
The Old Olive Tree behind a Remnant of a Woven Basket, 2014
Oil on canvas
35 × 26.5 cm
Collection of the artist

presence of the white bird hovering above. The fir trees' boughs resemble wings, the flurry of snow feathers. Grant painted the composition thinly, so that the texture of the board suggests bare earth and the underdrawing is present as a smudge within the snowy tracks. The white bird symbolises the spirit of the forest.

In this painting, space is illusory. It appears limitless because of the darkness, while in reality after only a short distance of rocks, rivers and trees the path leads to the open air. There is, however, a sense of confinement implicit in the close-pressed trees. Enclosure has always fascinated Grant in relation to landscape, whether as boundaries imposed by agriculture or landed estates, those that occur naturally as a result of geographical features, or simply looking out through the division of a window. The puma fences in French Guiana inspired landscapes suggesting both humans and animals as subject to captivity (see fig.53, p.68). In 2021 Grant re-envisaged the puma fence as a barrier erected to prevent Norwegian elks from straying onto roads (fig.105). The mesh wreaks a strange distortion on the landscape. Snow camouflages the rocks, in an echo of birch bark, while wedges of blue might equally be water or the sky reflected in ice. The composition is pinioned by the verticals of tree trunks, between which the fence extends as an angled screen. This was the second, perhaps most radically couched, of the *Elk Fence* series.

Sustaining these paintings is the capacity to seize and imaginatively transform an idea. *Entrance to the Enchanted Forest* filters a sketch made *en plein air* through the lens of Bachelard, to become, as Grant wrote in his journal, 'an invitation to enter an area of limitless mystery'.[17] The immediacy of a painting such as *The Old Olive Tree behind a Remnant of a Woven Basket* (2014) stems from Grant's skill at resisting the temptation to overwork its imagery (fig.107). We could imagine it as an artfully composed snapshot in which, for a moment, the olive tree becomes a different creature. A modest wooden structure frames the view; the basket becomes the 'head' of the tree, oracular and surreal. Only later does the viewer consider the strip of foliage as belonging to the olive tree rather than to a distant landscape.

Myth

Grant, in 2014, was increasingly preoccupied with paintings evoking myth. In March he began a composition based on a formation of rocks resembling a horse, seen near the cabin of the photographer Trym Ivar Bergsmo in Lødingen. The discovery rekindled memories of *Landscape of a Landscape, Harstad* (*c.*1961), based on the same northern terrain (fig.22, p.34). Now, Grant enclosed within a transparent box a miscellany of visual incidents from his recent journey, including an otter, transformed into 'a shape more expressive of what I know of the animal than if I had made a figurative study of it'.[18] This first painting, *Rock Horses* (2014), was a complex orchestration of the surreal: a cluster of horses and less identifiable creatures in front of a peak that breaks through the ceiling of a glass box. Behind one ridge of the peak glints an eye, and the whole is set against the night sky. Although Grant described his impasto handling of paint as almost 'modelling', to create a sculptural bas-relief, this aspect would be more acutely visible in the subsequent *Storm Horse Emerging Against the Window* (2014), worked using oil over acrylic and wax pencil, which resembles a classical carving weathered by the elements.

Rock-Horse in the North, completed on 14 April, is a small variation in acrylic, captivating in its apparent spontaneity (fig.108). To harmonise the composition Grant applied a transparent blue wash 'which immediately reticulated, and by intuition or accident created exactly the effects I needed'.[19] The glass-encased horse appears as if through a rain-splashed windowpane. Thus softened, the imagery becomes a more potent evocation of myth than in the surrealistically razor-sharp *Rock Horses*. The peak's eyes, closed in slumber, go almost unnoticed.

Over the course of the next year, Grant completed three 'Atlantis' paintings that constitute in scale and ambition the most significant of his metamorphic works. Their subject is introduced almost casually in his journals, as he recorded having taken 'a step into the dark' by introducing a human face into the preliminary drawing of a sea-piece. Aphrodite, an 'androgynous visage' with sea-waves as hair, presaged Grant's forthcoming visit to the goddess's birthplace, Cyprus.[20] Forty years earlier, in 1974, he had been shown a group of rocks off the coast of Cyprus, where, according to myth, Aphrodite had emerged. The image haunted him, fusing in this new painting with his recollection of Mediterranean light.

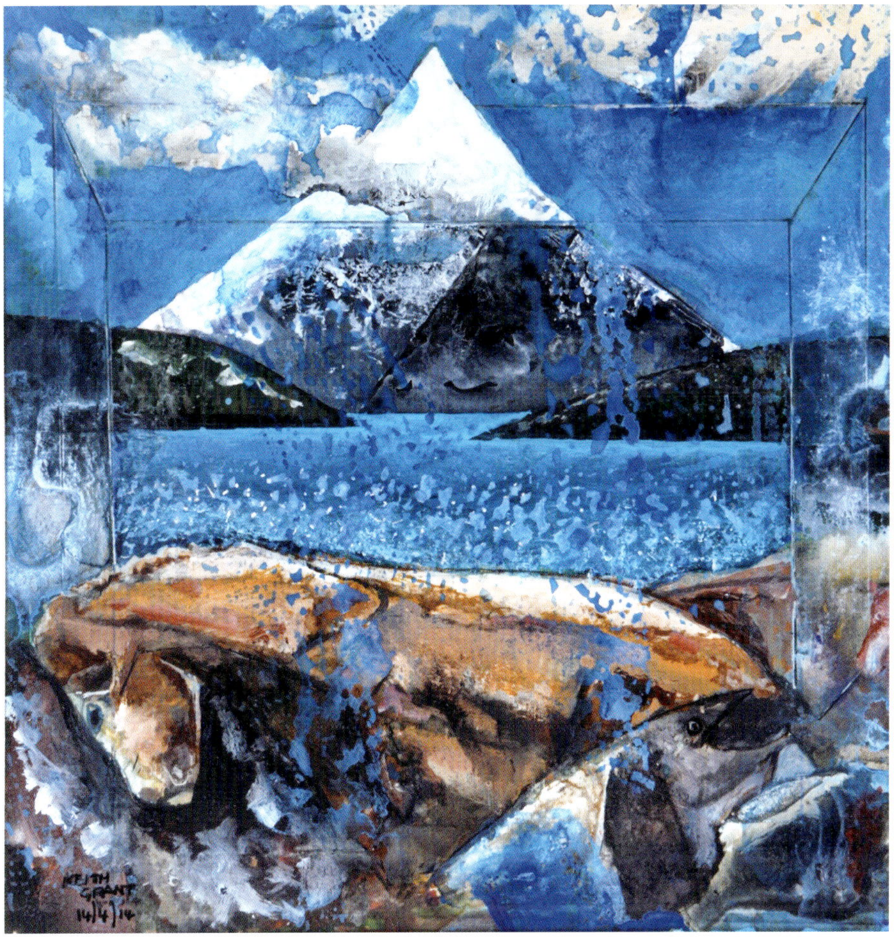

108
Rock-Horse in the North,
2014
Acrylic on paper
25.5 × 25.5 cm
Private Collection, Norway

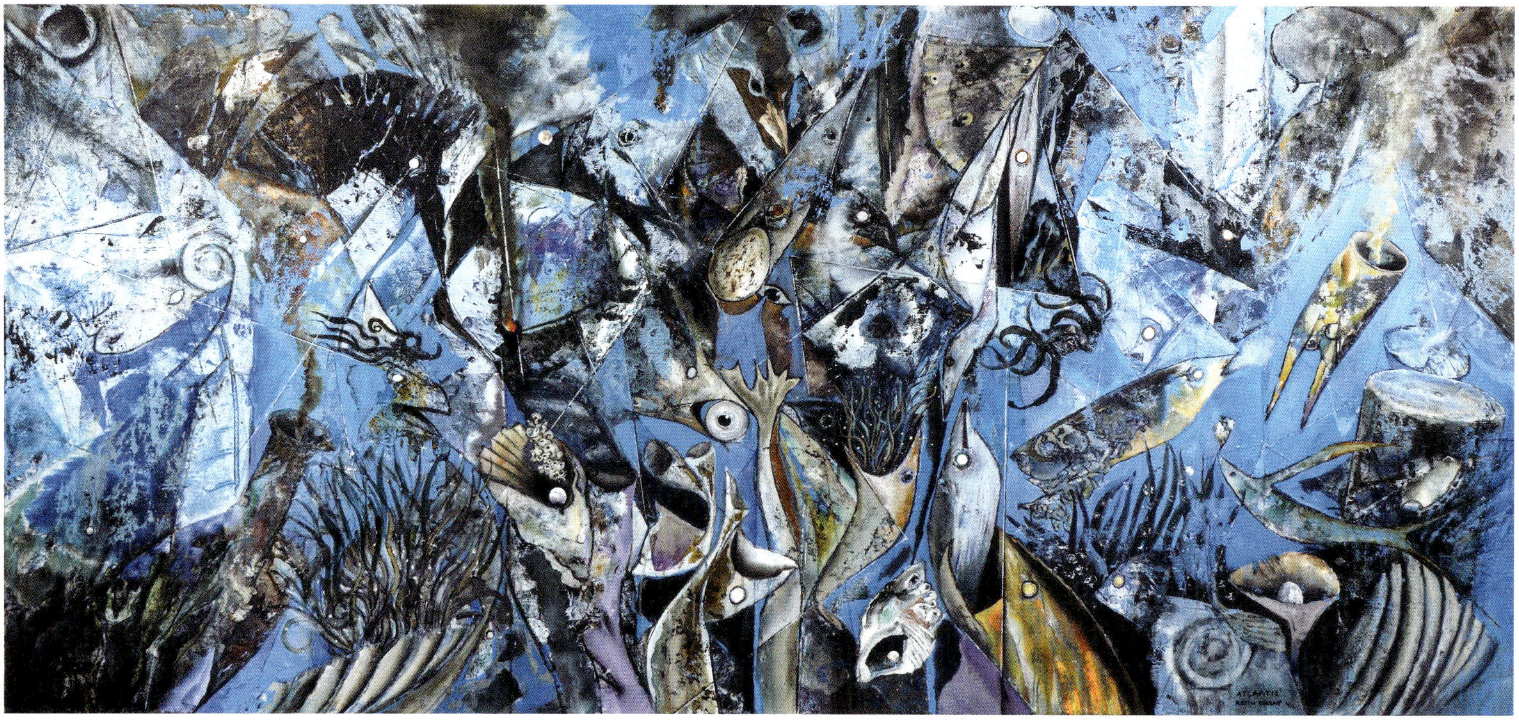

109
Atlantis I: A recreation of myth, 2014
Oil on canvas
100 × 200 cm
Private Collection, UK.

Aphrodite shape-shifted within the new composition. As Grant painted, he was always conscious that she might be eliminated altogether. Indeed, after a week's work, she was distilled to a mask lying 'Brancusi-like in the palm of a fragmented shell'.[21] The visit to Cyprus emphasised for Grant that the essence of the classical lay not in myth – in all its absurdity – but in the stories of the stones themselves. On one stone he noticed a 'sensuous frieze of lyrical shapes' resembling monsters and gods.[22] His focus transferred to Troy, then Atlantis, dredging memories of books and museum visits to recapture 'the mystery and romance' of maritime consciousness, beginning with Homer and Thucydides'.[23]

Atlantis I: A recreation of myth (2014) thus marshals a phantasmagorical marinescape (fig.109). Shells, fish, crab pincers and weed tangle with relics from ancient civilisations. To the left, a ship's prow collides with the head of a stone-carved beast to create a spiral-horned ram; below, an urn emits silted vapour. Everywhere there are signs of nature's metamorphosis and colonisation. Near the centre, the eyes that proliferate appear more human, albeit distinct from any identifiable form. The enchantment of the painting lies in its play of light against solidity, whereby blocks of masonry, abraded and barnacled, seem to dissolve in the water. Looking upwards to the light above the water's surface, the imagery fractures.

Is the composition alive – enacting a slow, balletic movement?

In *Atlantis II* (2015) the composition feels more static: a close-knitted tableau of sea creatures and fragmented stone columns. Grant had just visited Sardinia, returning with a strengthened sense of the water's surface 'as a membrane shielding a world of exotic forms'.[24] Beneath the remains of the Roman amphitheatre at Nora was an ancient amplification system, using bottomless vessels, *dolia*, to collect sound from the stage and project it into the auditorium. Grant incorporated these urns into his design, to evoke sound and its suppression underwater. That this scene alludes to the splendour of a past civilisation is evident in its shattered pillars, the torso of a young girl (in Grant's mind a statue of Tanit, the warrior goddess of dance and fertility) and the remnant of a skull, through which a fish swims.

With *Atlantis III: Le cimetière marin* (2015), based on the poem by Paul Valéry, Grant concluded the series (fig.110). This was a work planned and documented in immense detail. Grant first studied the text, in its original French and in translation, making sketches based on its symbolism. He contemplated the blank canvas as Valéry's 'blank page' ('la feuille blanche'), and the progress from the first charcoal mark that

instantaneously creates a measurable distance between the artist and the position he occupies in infinite space. Beyond the mark infinity, limitlessness. Then the next mark, then a long curvilinear sweep, a serpentine line which spans the 2.60 m. width of the canvas splitting and spinning its virgin purity and defining a measurelessly active, geometrical space into which the shattered absolute of white is absorbed.[25]

He envisaged the imagery as a galaxy, 'the perimeter of which will be the "event-horizon" of the canvas, its extent and its edges'.[26] He wondered, too, if its creation would reawaken the sensation, experienced at times in the past, of colour transcending the resistance of the canvas and force of application by knife or brush. This colour was nearly always blue, causing Grant to 'enter a limitless, dimensionless globe of light and space . . . like writing on the sky'.[27]

Valéry's poem is based on the coastal graveyard at Sète, where he is buried. Visiting in September 2015, Grant was struck by the gulf between Valéry's poetic vision and the present-day accumulation of cheap funerary ornaments. The light was uncannily even. There was no sign of anything – whether blazing sun, harsh shadows, doves or ravens – to evoke Valéry's poem. Gradually, however, a different hierarchy established itself, as Grant became mesmerised by marble pavilions that dissolved into light-reflecting masses, dark cypresses and a solitary gull against the water. Crumbling iron and stone, as well as birds on the brink of migration, became ciphers for the continuum of nature. Grant walked briskly to the sea, holding in his mind Valéry's likening of coastal rocks to altars, dice and upturned tables.

The act of walking from cemetery to sea, where the sea enacted 'a living, elemental dance', pre-empted Grant's realisation that he need not follow Valéry's imagery slavishly but could create his own composition in parallel. Although *Atlantis III* contains multiple references to the text, it does so with sophistication, and a mischievous lightness of touch that renders its subject beguiling rather than macabre. The approach recalls that of Giorgio de Chirico, who in paintings such as *The Uncertainty*

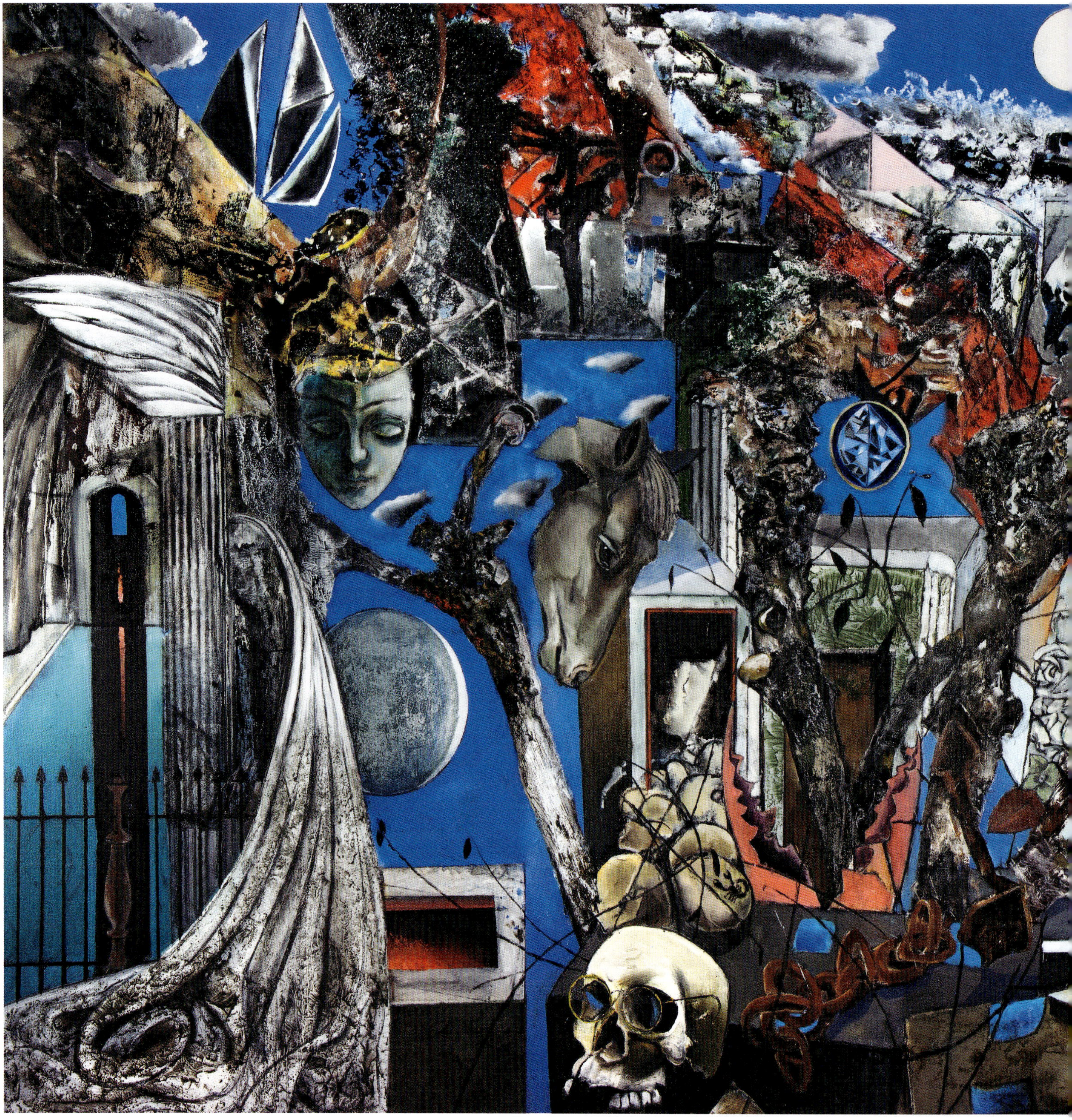

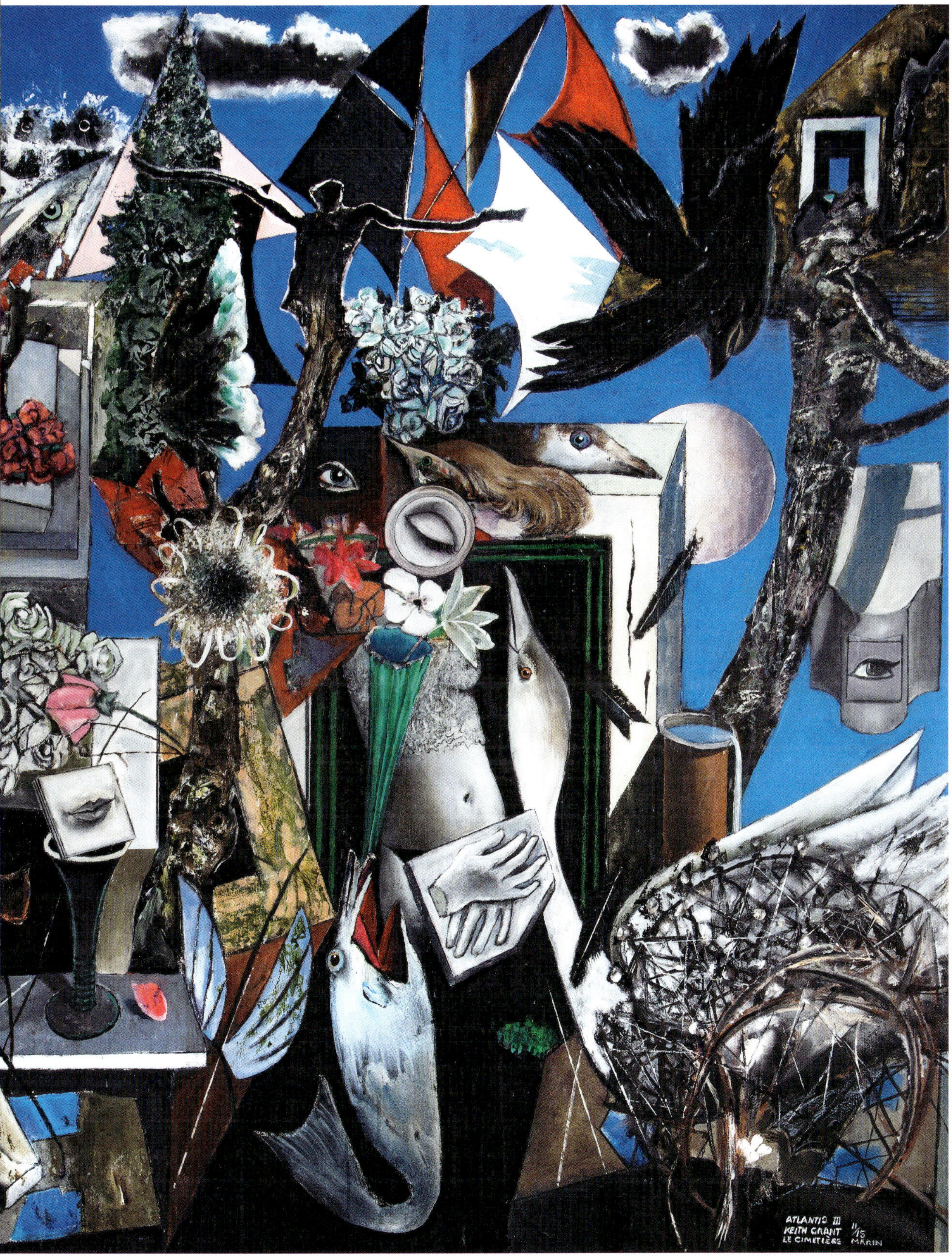

110
Atlantis III: Le cimetière marin, 2015
Oil on canvas
141 × 261 cm
Collection of the artist

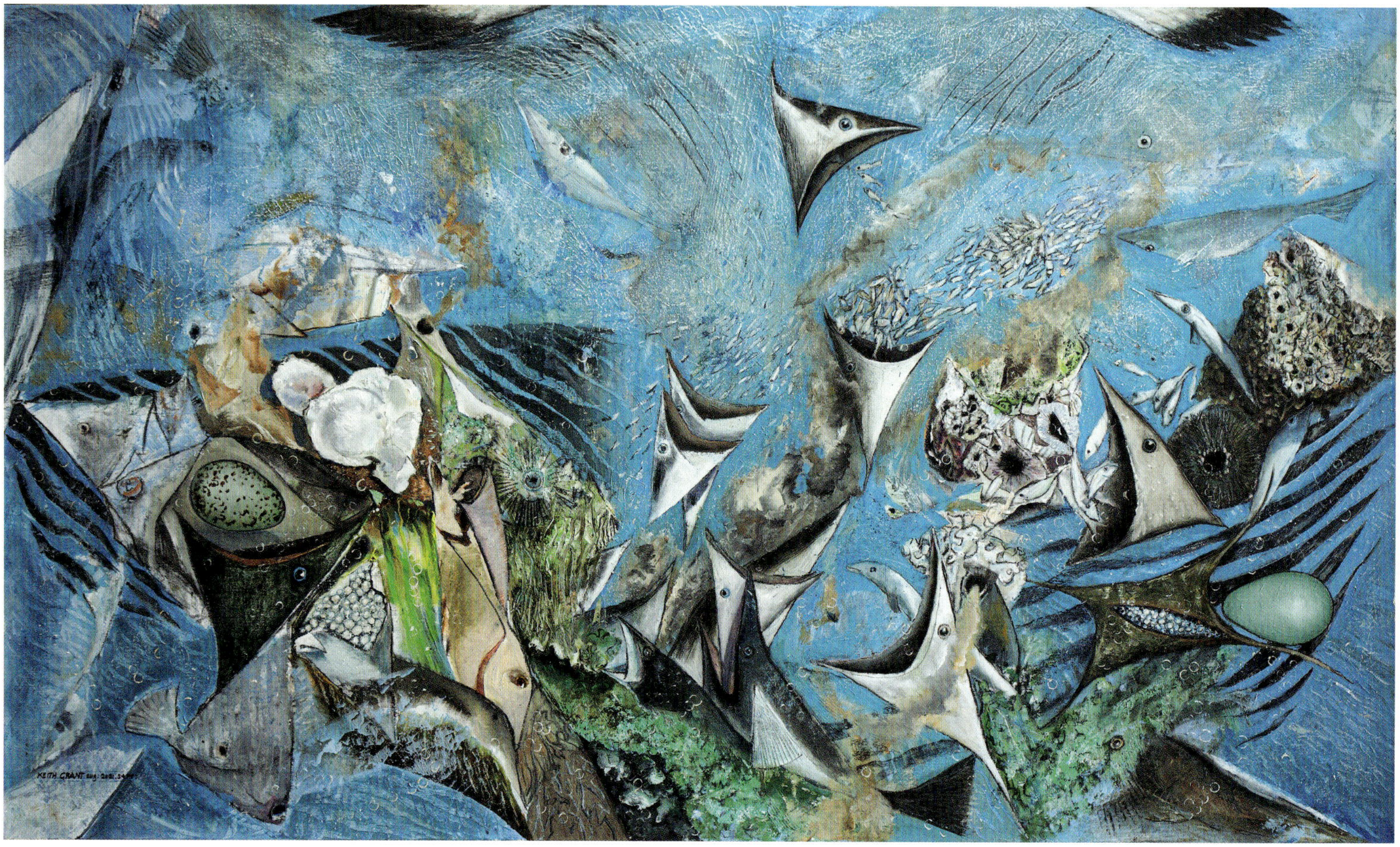

of the Poet (1913) juxtaposes unexpected objects – a torso of Aphrodite, a passing train and bunches of bananas – within a desolate architectural setting. Describing De Chirico's ability to condense feeling through metaphor, critic Robert Hughes observed, 'One can try to dissect these magical nodes of experience, yet not find what makes them cohere.'[28]

Atlantis III erects a scaffolding of imagery from Valéry's poem, the reality of the graveyard at Sète and his own life similarly as a network of mysterious correlations. Scanning the canvas, we see Minerva's temple, faceted diamonds, flowers, the detritus of tombstone kitsch, a nubile torso and winking eyes (a sly reference to Valéry's 'tickled' girls), sails pecking at stone, rusting iron, a scorpion, the crow seen at Svolvær in 1961, Leda's swan and, last but certainly not least, a gold-bespectacled skull, metamorphosing Valéry's 'eternal laughter' through a memory from Sarawak. The final stages of the painting involved a simplification of its design, admitting space into which entered the sea: the principal theme of Valéry's work. By repositioning the coastal graveyard as an underwater cemetery, and landscape as marinescape, Grant committed an act of such audacity that *Atlantis III*, like Valéry's poem, transcends the paraphernalia of death from which it is constructed.

111
Fish Bird Duality VII, 2021
Oil on linen
94.5 × 162.5 cm
Private Collection, Germany

New Dualities

Grant had all but exhausted the intense focus on metamorphosis that characterised his paintings between 2012 and 2015, although not their fundamental concerns. When he returned five years later, following the Covid pandemic and a solo exhibition he had been unable to attend, it was to a differently envisioned world. Circumstances enabled a slower, more contemplative production of work. Plundering subjects that had preoccupied him since the 1960s, Grant began to re-examine equivalences of form through multiple strands of imagery. Most prominent among these was the *Fish Bird Duality* series: seven paintings based on the similarities of two distinct creatures. Their setting was immediately ambiguous: water or air, cloud or sea-foam? Against veiled blue grounds, hybrid creatures – often no more than beaks, jaws or wings – float and overlap. Some of the paintings are loosely painted, suggesting a momentary glimpse into this strange habitat. In *Fish Bird Duality VII* (2021), the largest of the series, Grant approached the subject with an attention to detail comparable with *Atlantis I*. What distinguishes these works? While both are marinescapes, there is a fundamental difference in effect. *Atlantis I* resembles a stilled tableau. *Fish Bird Duality VII*, by contrast, asserts a vital sense of movement across the composition – whose constituents whirl and eddy, tossed by the sea or air currents (fig.111). Shoals of tiny fish are driven towards jaws that need only open to catch their prey; eggs find sanctuary in the arms of a sea purse, or imminent extinction from a yawning gullet. Eyes crowd the composition, disguised as limpets, fish roe, bubbles, pearls. The dark feathering of the water surely mirrors the wings cropped from the top of the painting. This beautiful linking of subject to context can be traced as far back as Grant's *Gull in the North* (fig.23, p.35), 60 years earlier, if only to illustrate how far his painting, and preoccupations, have developed.

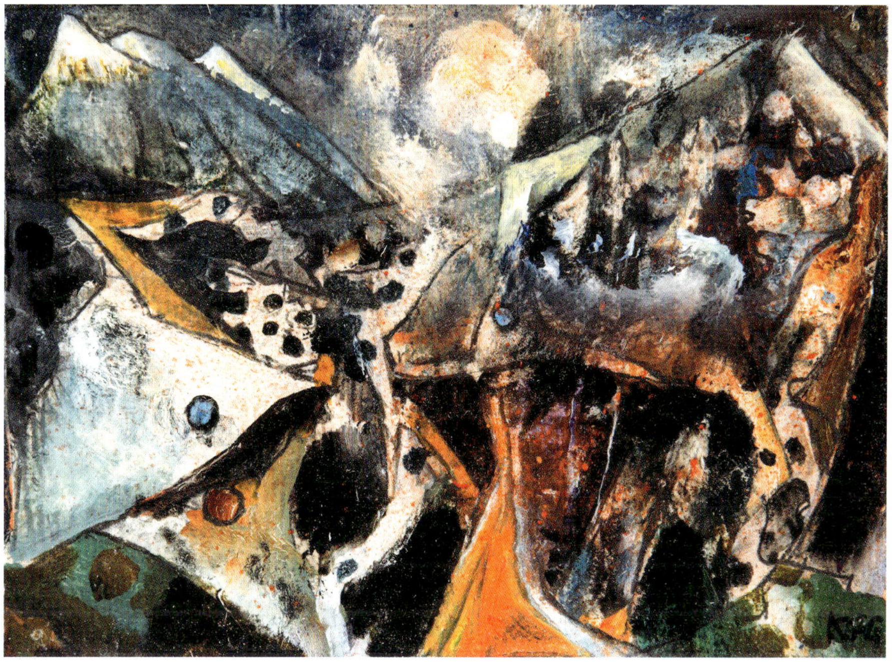

112
Lava Field, 2021
Oil on paper laid on board
14.5 × 20.25 cm
Collection of the artist

Grant similarly reassessed his earlier commitment to Matsuo Bashō's *The Narrow Road to the Deep North* (see Chapter 2), creating a set of small studies derived from its imagery. *Lava Field* (2021), the sixth in the series, addresses the symbol of the volcano (fig.112). Unlike the subdued palette and regimented structure of *Lava Field* (*c.*1965; fig.25, p.39), this new version is visibly active: a chaos of molten lava and spewing rocks. The intimate scale allows its imagery to be presented in haptic, almost unmediated

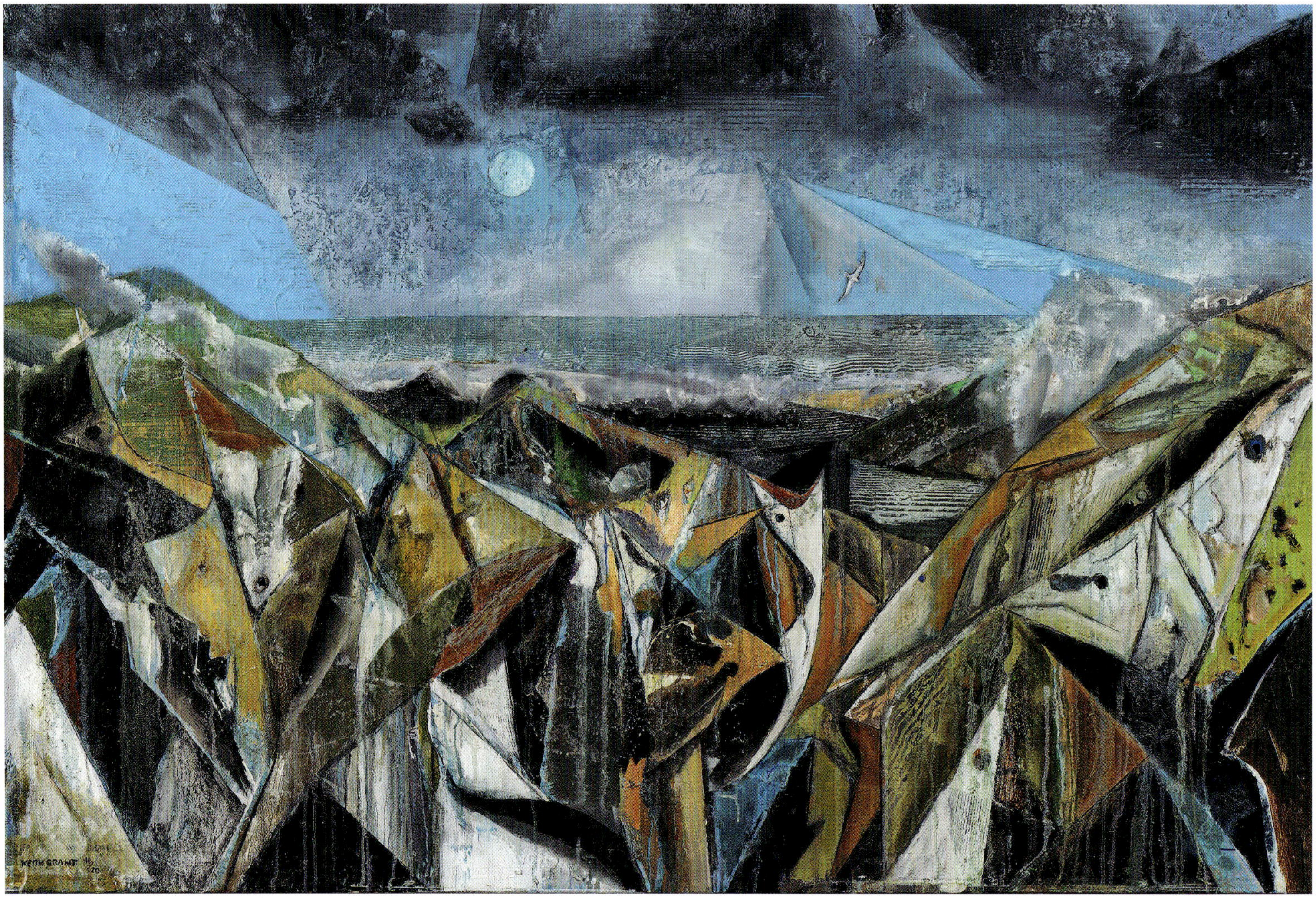

113
Sea Drift by Moonfleet, 2020
Oil on linen
100 × 150 cm
Collection of the artist

fashion. Huge black dots signify the expulsion of matter from the volcano, while snow-capped peaks read indistinctly against the sky. Heat is expressed almost palpably through colour.

Sea Drift by Moonfleet (2020), wrought from sources further back in Grant's memory, was worked on a larger scale and passed through numerous versions before its final state (fig.113). As its title suggests, it refers to two texts long familiar to Grant. Walt Whitman's poem *Sea Drift* (1891–2) contains the haunting image of a seabird whose mate fails to return. *Moonfleet*, a late 19th-century adventure about smuggling on the Dorset coast, by J. Meade Falkner, has long been set as a text for schoolchildren. The visual origin of Grant's painting is the stretch of coast on which Falkner's novel was based, near Chesil Beach, but also the view from which his *Dorset Mural* derived in the early 1960s (fig.18, pp 28–9). Adding a further layer of complexity, Grant had recently completed a series of paintings based on the music of Delius, including a setting of *Sea Drift* (see Chapter 8).

There was an unacknowledged precedent, too, included in Grant's first solo exhibition at Roland, Browse and Delbanco, and reproduced to accompany his 'Declaration of Intent' in *Labour Monthly*, in February 1967. The painting in question, *The North* (1966), presents an Arctic coastline, splintered and striated, 'echoing with the struggle for life and emphasising the passing of time'. The triangular forms at its lower edge suggest whales and seabirds, with 'armadas of clouds' pressing upon the dark cliffs.[29] Through landscape, Grant sought to accentuate the parallels between nature in the North and human life at its extremes of hunger and violence. Which of these two, *The North* or *The Dorset Mural*, is closer to *Sea Drift by Moonfleet*?

Both – and neither. There is a choleric clarity to *The North*, whose linear composition reads as graphically as handwriting. *The Dorset Mural*, by contrast, clothes its subject in painterly effects – blended and dripping across areas of the composition. All three present a geometrical fragmentation of the coastal scene, evident in triangular rocks and forms that more or less nearly approximate to birds or fish. Yet the composition of *Sea Drift by Moonfleet* settles through a sureness of vision resting on experience. The techniques used, specifically the scoring or 'combing' of wet paint to create parallel lines, not only texture the image but unite areas of the composition. Thus lines that appear darkly in the sky shimmer across the sea, through the coastal inlet, to find an echo on the rocks. Similarly a diagonal vector leads from the fractured sky to the coast, while the rocks themselves are the only area where paint is allowed to drip freely, pulling weight to the lower edge of the composition. Most strikingly, the solitary bird is echoed in the keening white form among the rocks, initiating a scimitar of movement towards the moon. This last symbol, so often a feature of Grant's painting, and requisite here to justify the title 'Moonfleet', was absent from the earliest phase of the painting, where the sky was lit only by stars. Balancing such details, in the final painting, Grant effected an impressive transformation of the raw materials of memory.

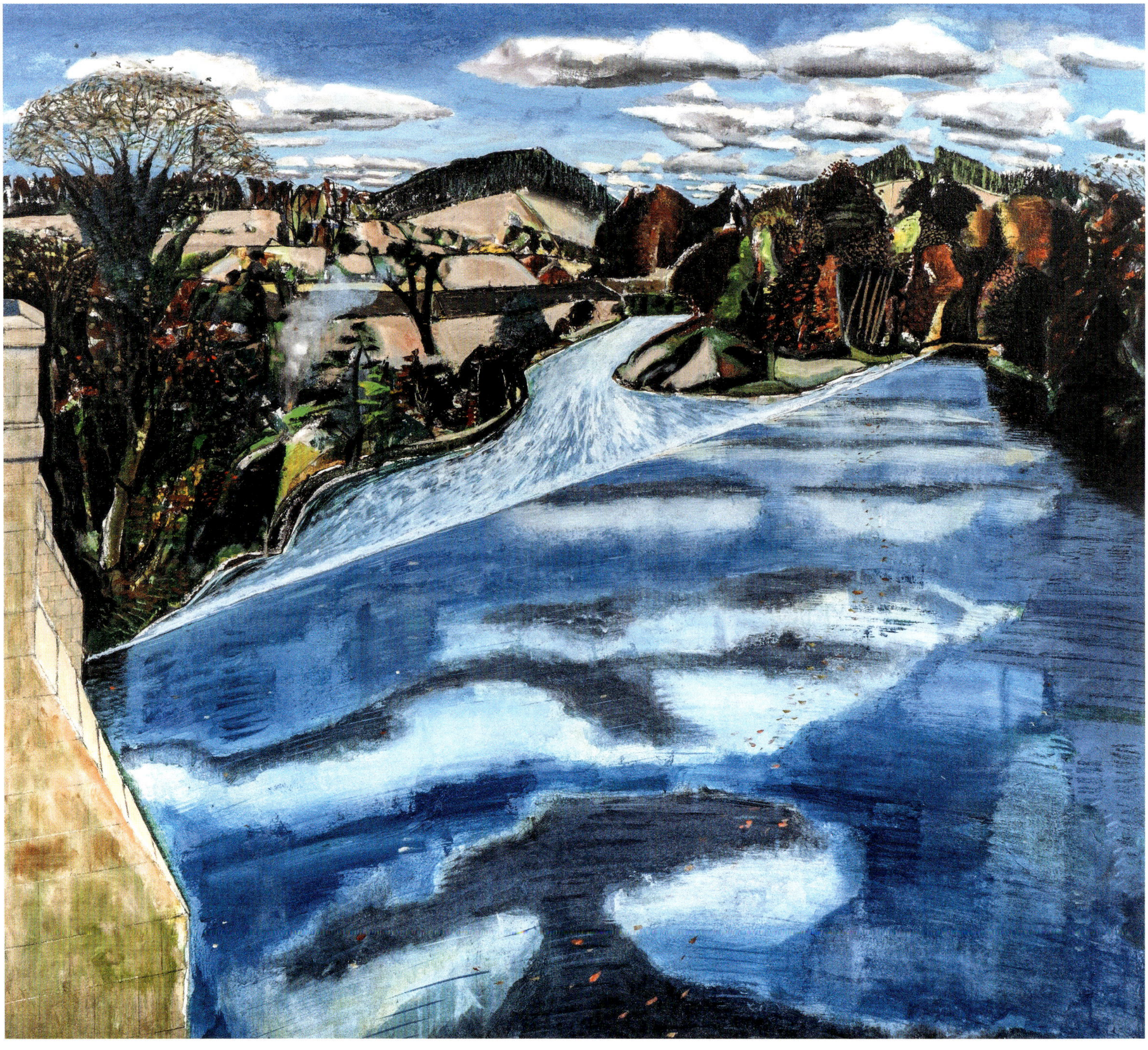

7

Return to a Land

In May 1981, Grant observed, 'I am more and more resolved to give up Norway and to embark on a series of English landscapes . . . I long to re-discover English landscape, to return more intensely to its leafy moodiness, to re-read the *Natural History of Selborne* and explore the nature poets.'[1] He was experiencing a period of turmoil in his life. Why else might he yearn to paint landscapes that were ordinary and optimistic, readable by all, composed from the grey quietness of early mornings?

The North Tyne, Lewes and Yorkshire

Grant's first visit was to Chollerford, in Northumberland, where he made a dispassionate drawing of the setting sun through trees. Chollerford was only a short drive from Newcastle, where in 1979 he had been appointed Head of Painting at the Polytechnic, although it was only now – when he was about to begin a new post at Roehampton Institute – that he started to notice its landscape. The area was alive with a buffeting wind, shafts of rain then sun, and the song of larks.

Jacquetta Hawkes, with whom Grant had developed a close friendship, was nervously intrigued by his change of allegiance. What landscapes would he choose: the wilder chalklands of east Dorset, Elgar's Malvern hills, or perhaps Wales?[2] Yet it was Chollerford that held his attention, and in August 1981 he was developing ideas for a triptych deliberately in the style of Samuel Palmer, Paul Nash and Graham Sutherland. *Spring, the North Tyne, Chollerford* (1981), now in the Leicestershire County Council Artworks Collection, assumes a palette of greens and blues quite different in character from works based on Norway. In the river flowing across the three panels, Grant envisaged a symbol for the continuity of life. At the time, he was hoping the composition might be translated into a tapestry, woven by the studio at West Dean, in Sussex.

The weir at Chollerford was a site Grant studied insistently in the autumn of 1981, waiting for a windless day that would reveal the reflections he imagined. Often the wind was so cold that he could hardly draw, but the drama of the Northumbrian skies mesmerised him. In a short space of time every weather effect was possible, endowing the landscape with a constantly changing tactility – 'a textural richness involving all states, soft to brittle, wet to bone dry, smooth to rough'.[3] The composition of *Autumn: The Weir at Chollerford Bridge* (1981; fig.114) has an expansiveness

114
Autumn: The Weir at Chollerford Bridge, 1981
Oil on canvas over board
106 × 120 cm
Private Collection, UK

115
Spring, The 'Pells', Lewes, 1982
Oil on board
128 × 128 cm
Private Collection, Canada

reminiscent of paintings by the 20th-century Scottish landscape artist William Gillies, whose work Grant would have seen often in Benjamin Britten and Peter Pears's house at Aldeburgh. The water stretches from a mirrorglass plane, cut by a strong diagonal, to the turbulent current below. One side is buttressed by a stone bridge, beyond it the landscape fragments into a patchwork of detail and autumnal colour. But despite the space within the composition, there is also a fascinating sense of compression. Clouds that stack closely in the sky, mushrooming as reflections in the water, arc downwards towards the horizon. This tilt is emphasised by the trajectory of rust-red leaves floating towards a hill-top wood in which there is a cleft. Paradoxically, given Grant's stated quest for the 'ordinariness' of landscape, it is among his most daring compositions.

The return to English landscape developed fitfully. Grant was beset with doubts, weighing the luxuriousness of music by Vaughan Williams and Delius, to which he listened while making his new paintings, against the crack of ice – the 'raw noise of nature', devoid of sentiment.[4] Reading Alejo Carpentier's *The Lost Steps*, in April 1982, he was thinking already about travelling to Latin America. The anticipation of the fecund landscape he might find invigorated a series of English paintings developed in the months prior to departure. Taking North Yorkshire as his subject, he first placed the sun as it appeared above a wooded cliff, with the River Ure at the picture plane. The sun pulsates, illuminating the surrounding foliage in brilliant, pointillist colour. Below, the trees' roots reach for water. Grant saw his painting as commenting upon 'the essential elements for abundant life: sun, earth, water and air'.[5] Two months later, he was finishing an equally detailed work based on the Pells Pool in Lewes, near where he lived (fig.115). Central to the composition is a red willow, whose livid trunk contrasts sharply with acid green foliage. The entire image seems to curl around this form, recalling both the curvature of the Chollerford weir painting and the earlier triptych, whose gnarled biomorphic trees invoke Sutherland or John Craxton. Here, the effect has a strange hyperreality, the reflections defined with such clarity that each leaf appears as an exact replica of its original. Glazing the surface, Grant completed the invention. The whole composition appears, as in an X-ray photograph, to reveal the essence of the view: the willow as skeleton leaf. That this fresh, unpolluted image was a lie was admitted by Grant in his journal. Tossed carelessly into the Pells Pool was all manner of rubbish, from beer cans to the plastic wrappers from stale bread used to feed the ducks. If he could, Grant wanted to exhibit the painting in Lewes as 'propaganda', such was his outrage at the desecration.[6]

The unusually detailed execution of this and the preceding work based on the River Ure meant that Grant completed only two paintings during an entire term at Roehampton. While he responded to the specificity of a landscape and its mood when he encountered it – 'the sense of nature's presence', as he described it – he was affected also by broader spans of influence.[7] The area around Wharfedale in Yorkshire he considered magical, its skies textured with skylarks and curlews, looping and spiralling.[8] It was a landscape painted by Turner and referenced in poetry by Wordsworth, the latter drawing from legends about the The Strid, where unsuspecting travellers, trying to jump across the River Wharfe, had been dragged into caverns and drowned. Combining

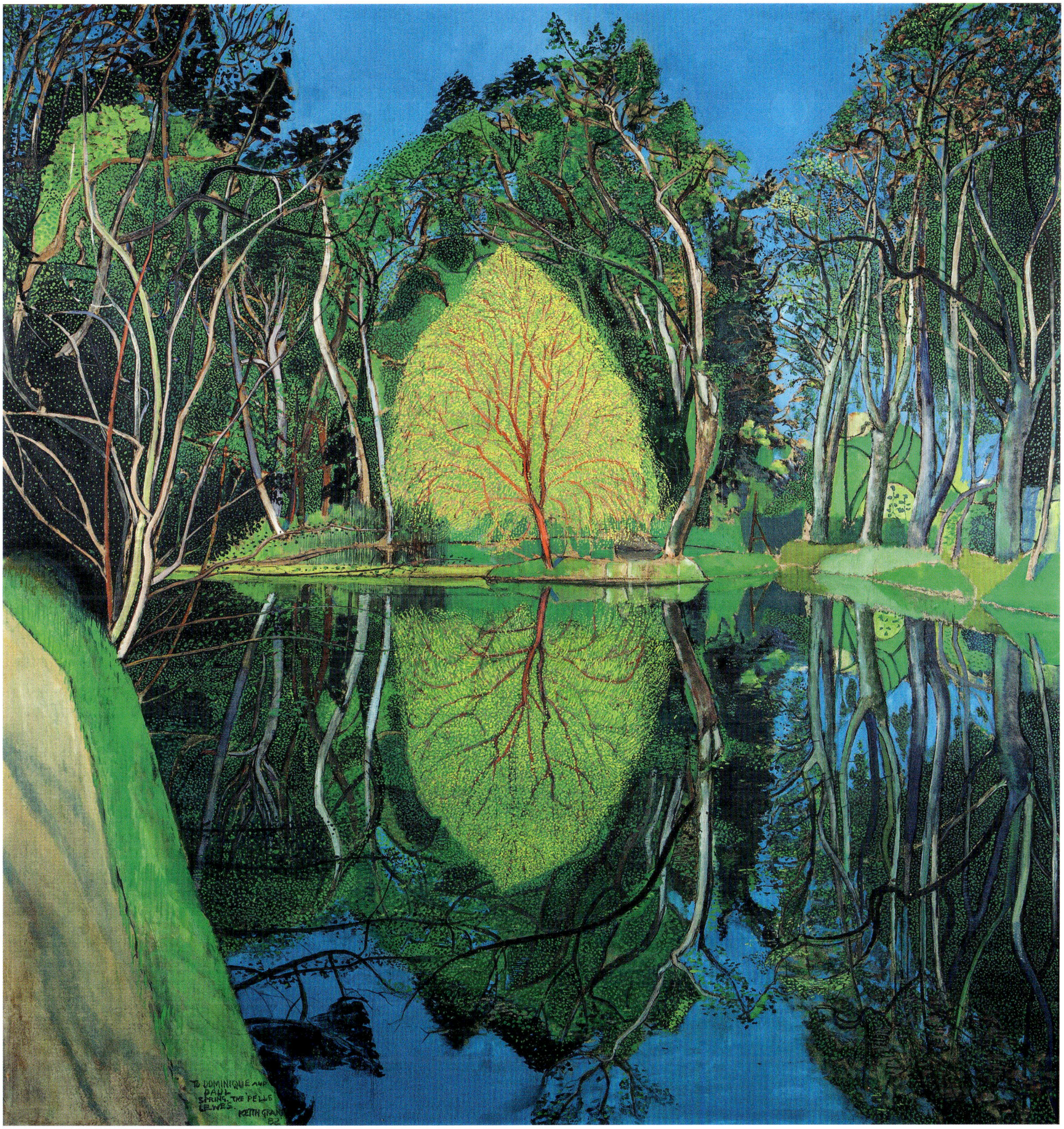
TO DOMINIQUE AND
PAUL
SPRING. THE PELLS
LEWES.
KEITH GRANT
82

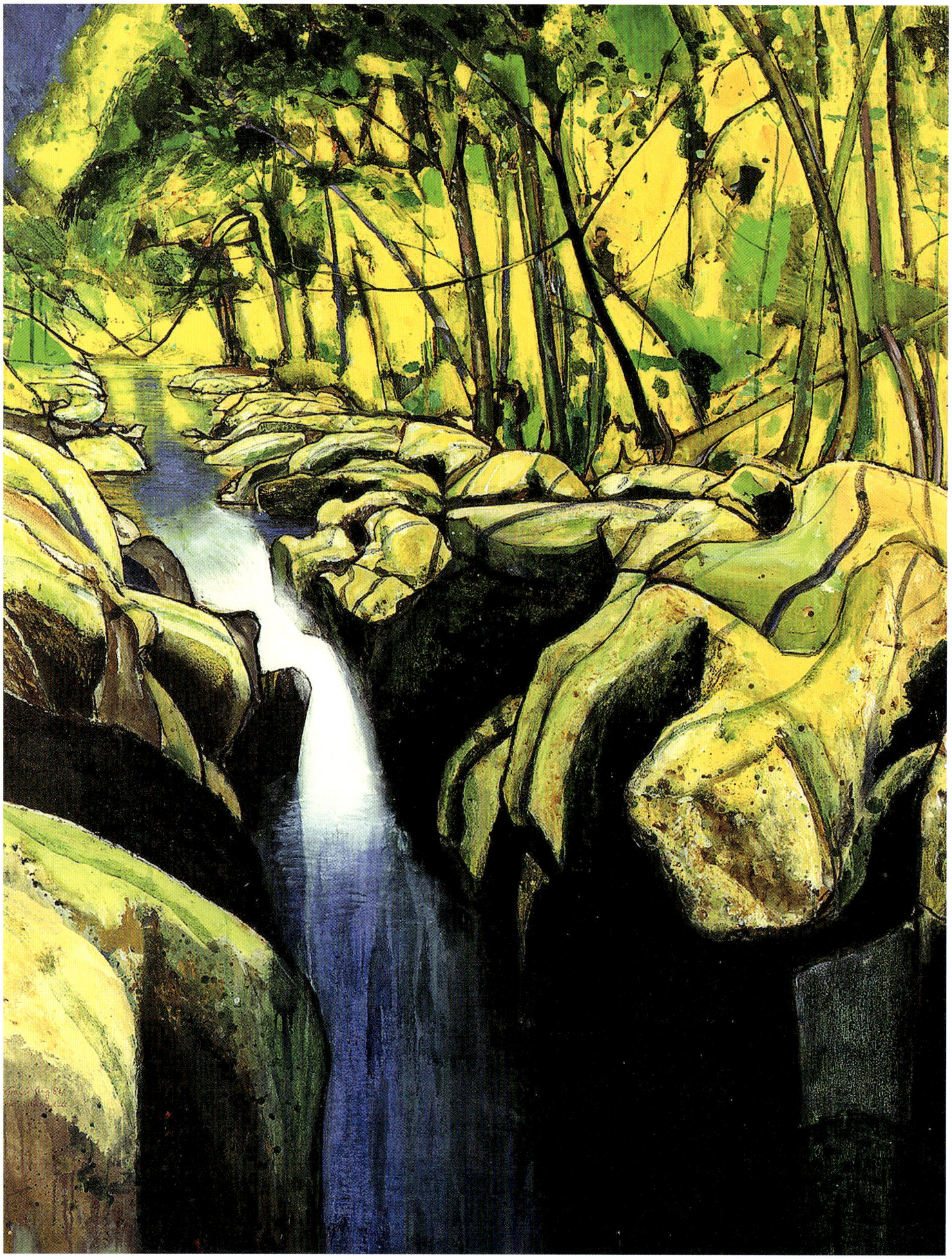

116
The Strid, 1984
Acrylic on board
approx. 122 × 91 cm
Private Collection (location unknown)

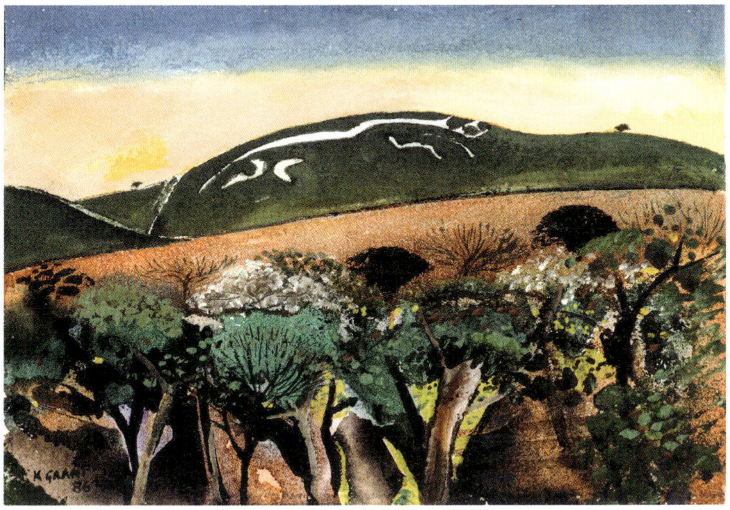

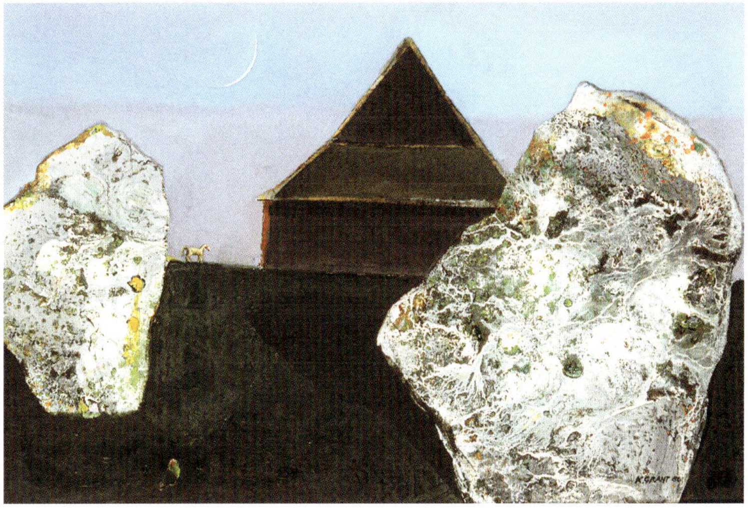

117 (left)
Spring at White Horse Hill, 1986
Acrylic, watercolour and ink on board
26 × 33.5 cm
Private Collection (location unknown)

118 (right)
Monoliths, New Moon, Barn and Horse, 1986
Oil and acrylic on board
approx. 50.5 × 76 cm
Private Collection (location unknown)

his recent experience of the tropics with a lushness of yellow foliage and waterworn rocks he considered 'truly English', Grant's painting *The Strid* (1984) restructures what he saw, transforming it with 'a hint of a more northern metamorphosis' (fig.116).[9] From a drawing made on the spot, two weeks later he began the painting out of doors in his garden at Lewes. The combination of working in daylight and gradually layering the painting, using acrylics then oils, created a luminous effect of light filtered through spring leaves and reflecting on the crystal water.

The Ridgeway

Two years later, in 1986, Grant was one of several artists invited by the Francis Kyle Gallery to create work based on the Ridgeway: a prehistoric route from Avebury to Ivinghoe Beacon in north-west London, known variously as Britain's, or Europe's, oldest road. The project inspired an exhibition, a documentary for the ITV series *Putting on the South*, in which Grant was filmed working from aerial and land views, and a book by Richard Ingrams that reproduced 59 pictures by 13 artists.[10] A tepid review by John McEwen queried whether the book's commercial basis desecrated the tradition of literature inspired by the Ridgeway ('written more for love than gain'), promoting paintings that resembled 'uninspired' colour photographs from 'snapped originals'. He nonetheless commended the work of two artists, Malte Sartorius and Grant.[11]

Towards the end of March 1986 Grant revisited the White Horse at Uffington in Oxfordshire – the oldest chalk-cut hill figure in Britain – finding the landscape unchanged since his student pilgrimages save the removal of more hedges, which intensified its bleakness. His response was muted, the landscape's browns and umbers, untouched as yet by spring, seeming to 'express the tiredness of the earth'.[12] This is the mood that suffuses his acrylic and gouache study of the White Horse, in which the sky darkens with hail clouds, the earth is still bare and the only herald of spring is the sparse touch of blossom above the trees (fig.117). When Eric Ravilious painted the same scene around 1939, from a more distant vantage, he rendered it emptier: a landscape of undulating chalk downs, stippled by grass and lit by a sky scratched with rain. Taking a more frontal view, Grant flattened the landscape to emphasise

119
Portrait of Jacquetta Hawkes,
1990
Oil on canvas
110.5 × 66 cm
The Fitzwilliam Museum,
Cambridge

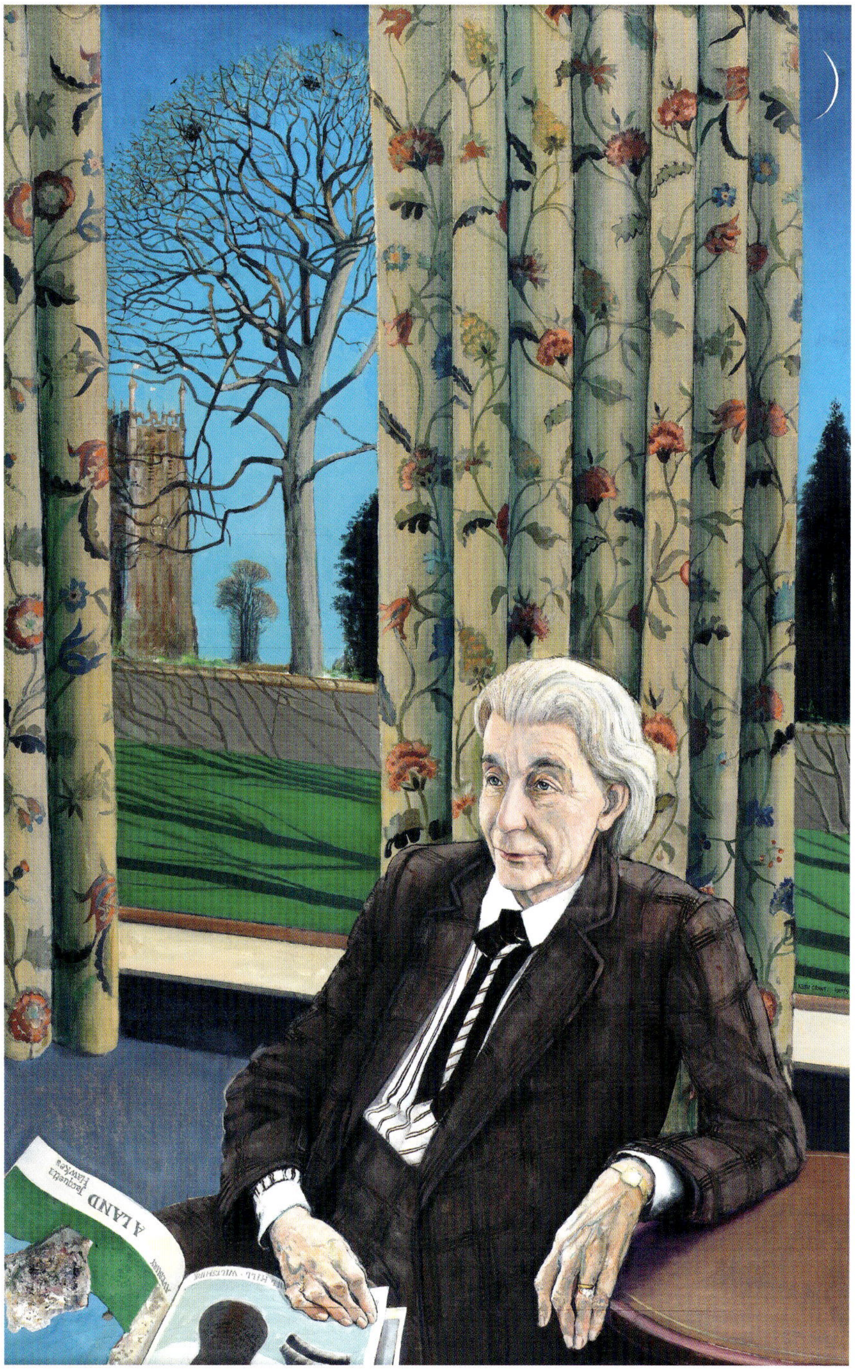

the carving that Paul Nash described as 'more of a dragon than a horse . . . whose bleak character and stark expression accord perfectly with its lonely situation on the summit of the bare downs'.[13] At least three paintings by Grant depict the Uffington horse, in one of which a crescent moon surrealistically echoes the horse's legs. In other paintings the creature becomes animate, standing sentinel adjacent to Avebury's monoliths and barns (fig.118).

Grant's visit to Avebury, two months earlier, reignited the strong connection he had experienced in the 1950s, now – in the mid-1980s – inspiring the enthusiastic response of students he took there. Grant sensed at Avebury the beginning of time. The stones he saw as 'restless wind sculptures', patterned by lichen: he knew almost every one yet felt each afresh. In the volcanic cone of Silbury Hill he saw the angled descent of an Arctic mountain to the sea, noting, 'I believe I can trace back all the preferential forms in most of my work to my 1st experiences as a painter at Avebury and the surrounding countryside.'[14]

Finishing the Ridgeway series, he returned to the Cameroon paintings he had temporarily set aside. Yet he remained committed to English landscape through his friendship with Jacquetta Hawkes. Contemplating Avebury, he mentioned – seemingly at random – that when thinking of her he never considered her age.[15] A year later he began a portrait of Hawkes that would preoccupy him for an extended period of time.

Portraits

Are portraits relevant to a study of Grant's landscapes? The defence is that Grant's finest portraits maintain a connection with landscape,

120
Sir Francis Patrick Neill, 1989
Oil on canvas
142.2 × 97.8 cm
All Souls College, University of Oxford

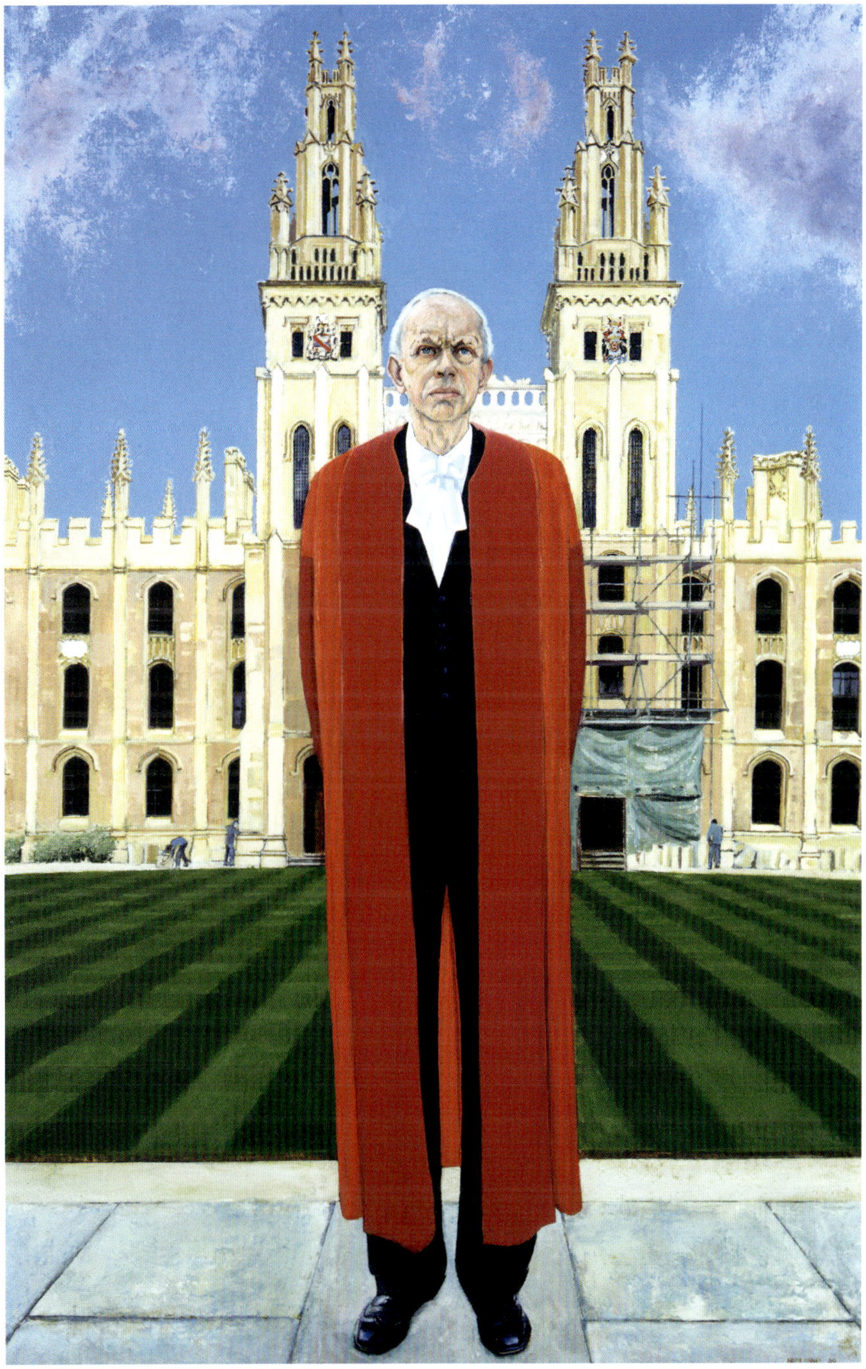

however subtle or seemingly tenuous. With Hawkes, the relationship is intrinsic to her own field of interest as well as to Grant's sympathy with her writings. The preparatory stages of the portrait, as Grant documented, went 'badly'. Seated in a tall chair, Hawkes looked impressive, yet electric light revealed the texture of her skin and emphasised her age – an issue both parties wished to avoid. By June 1988, eighteen months after her first sitting, Hawkes declared Grant 'a portrait painter', yet requested further work on the composition.[16] Finally, in March 1990, Grant made the final adjustments that satisfied him the portrait was complete. It had taken a full three years.

Hawkes is portrayed sitting in front of elaborately patterned floral curtains that half-screen the view from the window. Prominent outside is a large beech tree, to its left the church tower of Chipping Campden, to the right a crescent new moon (fig.119). The church tower, with its clock, symbolises faith and time, the tree life, and the moon hope and renewal. Rooks flying above the tree recall a poem by Hawkes, but also Vincent van Gogh's *Autumn Landscape* (*c*.1885), seen by Grant in the Fitzwilliam Museum in Cambridge. On Hawkes's lap, a copy of *A Land* features on its cover Avebury in the style of Grant's recent paintings. Linear elements unobtrusively unify the composition – from Hawkes's veined hands and time-furrowed face to the curtain design and shadows of the trees stretching across the walled garden. The sitter is not only at one with her environment, but sees percipiently beyond it.

Overlapping with the protracted evolution of Hawkes's portrait was a commission to paint Sir Francis Patrick Neill, Lord Neill of Bladen, the eminent judge, academic, Warden of All Souls College and

Vice-Chancellor of Oxford University. Neill's portrait represented a friendship dating back to the 1960s, when Grant had painted a mural for the music room of the family home in Scotland. Early sketches placed Neill, seated, before an imposing window revealing the distinctive twin towers of Hawksmoor's All Souls quadrangle. To achieve this symmetrical composition Grant effected a painterly sleight of hand, shifting the Warden's Lodgings 'to somewhere in front of the Radcliffe Camera'.[17] The effect troubled him, however. A fortnight later he had resolved to depict Neill in front of the partially scaffolded facade of the College, whose renovation Neill had set in motion (fig.120).

With this grid of scaffolding and square of tarpaulin, Grant both interrupted the sublime symmetry of Hawksmoor's facade and introduced a measure to gauge human endeavour against the warp of nature. One of the last elements introduced into the composition were the clouds, tempering the startling blue of the sky. At ground level the grass, rolled and mowed, reinforces a controlled perspectival space begun in the flagstones and continued in the architecture. Neill, standing on stone, is anchored as firmly as Hawksmoor's towers. His shoes form a minute mirror to the light, his robes an extreme tonal contrast to the grass. The gravity of this context weighs in his expression, although such thoughtfulness unquestionably also qualified him for his position. Having established the composition's principal elements, Grant felt he had achieved 'greater balance and spatial imperatives' than in any previous work: experience that could be brought to bear in future landscape paintings.[18]

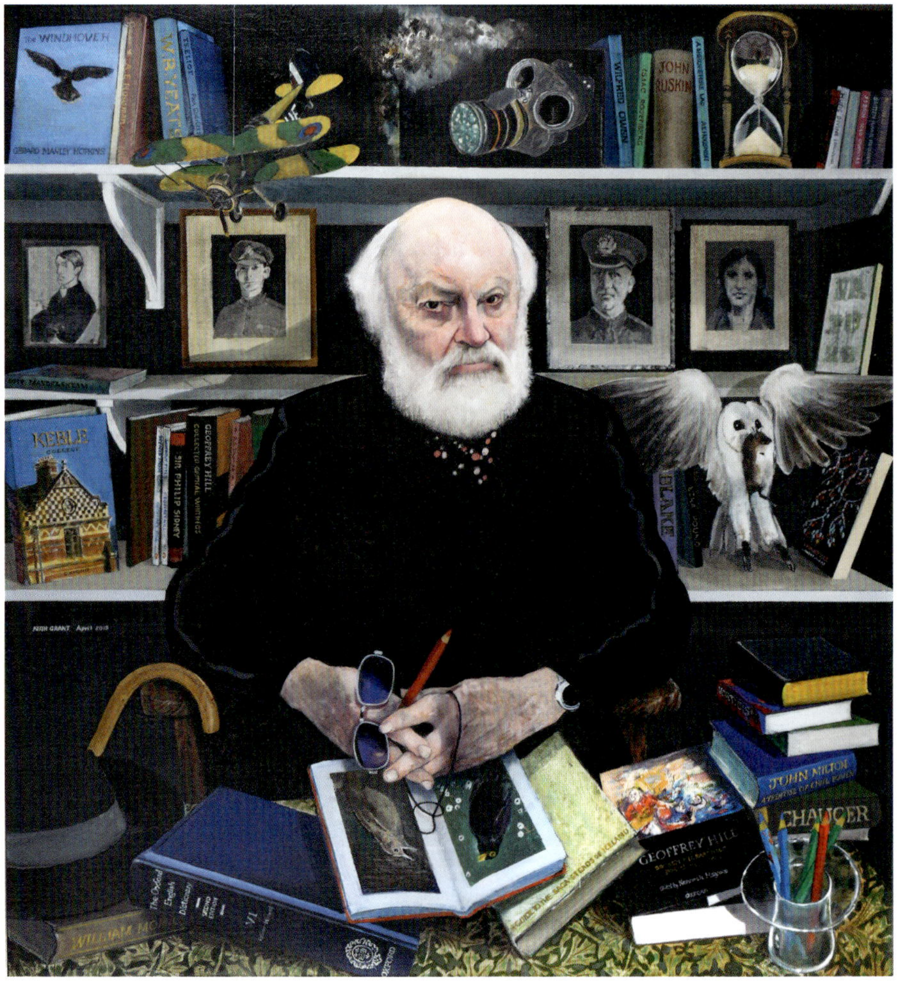

121
Portrait of Sir Geoffrey Hill, 2015
Oil on canvas
119 × 109 cm
Private Collection, UK

While Neill's portrait was created amid paintings of Greenland and the North Sea at Aldeburgh to which it bore no relation, Grant's portrayal of Sir Geoffrey Hill, poet and Professor of Poetry at Oxford University, was again embedded within his current concerns (fig.121). Certain elements, such as the depiction of birds, already a feature in the 'metamorphic' series, would become an important aspect of the new Selborne series and paintings inspired by music. Yet poetry became the principal subject, crowding every corner of the composition and ranging from physical copies of books to more or less obscure symbolic references to Hill's poetry. The portrait is a cornucopia of treasures – those important to Hill and those perceived notable by Grant – comparable to *Le cimetière marin*, painted later that year (fig.110, pp 130–31).

Grant had met Hill in 2012, when taking part in a three-year series of seminars on creativity at Keble College, Oxford. As Grant began the portrait, in February 2015, he identified the themes that would bind the composition as time, old age and death, derived from comments made during conversations. The literary figures important to Hill, represented by books in the painting, are Gerard Manley Hopkins, A.E. Housman, W.B. Yeats, T.S. Eliot, Sir Philip Sidney, Ezra Pound, R.S. Thomas, John Ruskin, William Blake, John Milton and Geoffrey Chaucer, with William Morris signalled also by the design of the tablecloth. Hill's family and early life are symbolised by photographs and a toy aeroplane. His own books are clustered on the first shelf, while on the table is the volume of collected poetry, *Broken Hierarchies* (2013), whose cover illustration by Oskar Kokoschka gave Grant 'some pleasure in making a rather impressionistic interpretation'.[19] The setting is antithetical to Edward McGuire's portrait of Seamus Heaney painted relatively early in the poet's life, in 1974. Heaney sits at a table covered with a white linen cloth, before him a single open book. The room appears unfurnished. Yet like Grant, McGuire includes a nod to the place of nature in Heaney's poetry: through the window, in more of an echo of Morris than a possible view, is a decorative panel of foliage and birds, larger than life.

Portraying Hill, Grant replaced his poetry volume *Clavics* (2011) with a freestanding version of its cover

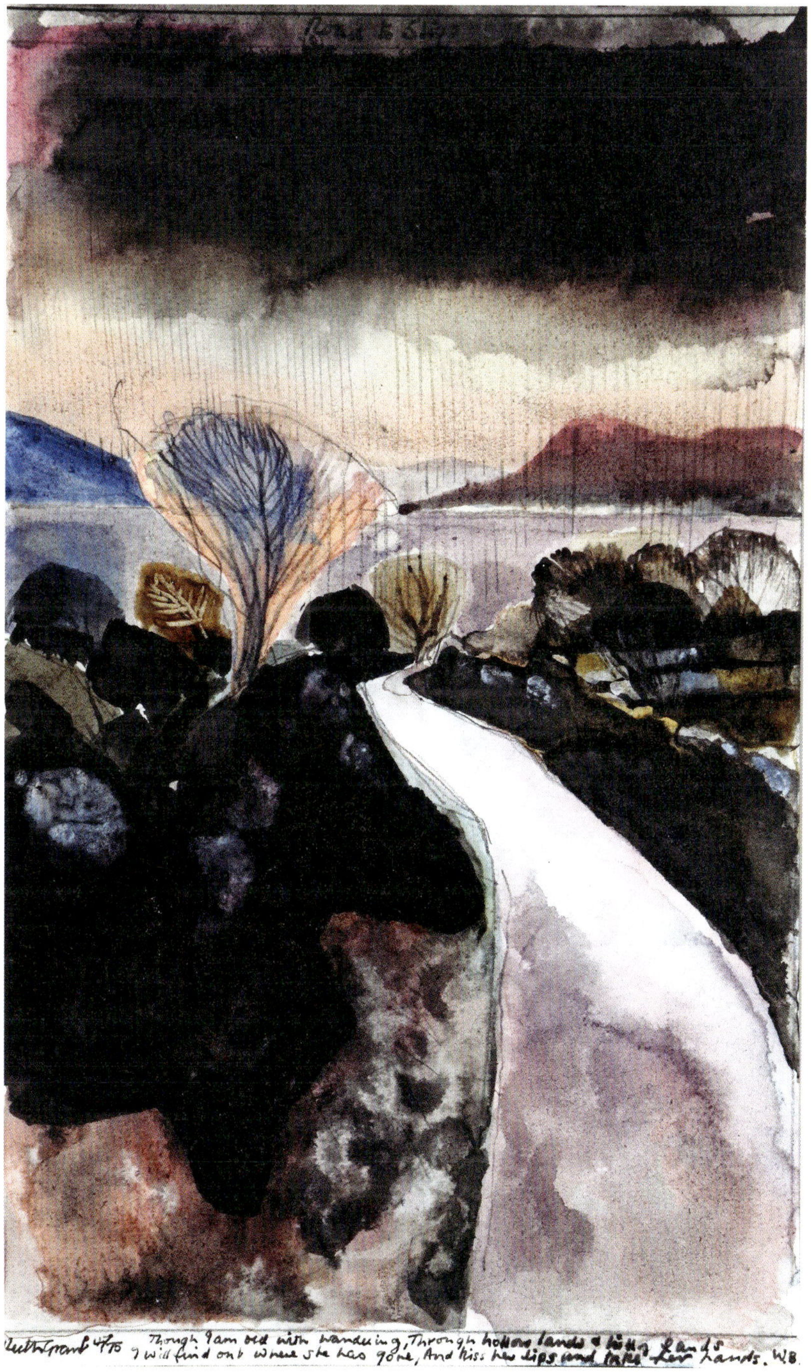

122
Road to Sligo, 1975
Watercolour, ink and pencil on paper
26 × 17 cm
Private Collection, UK

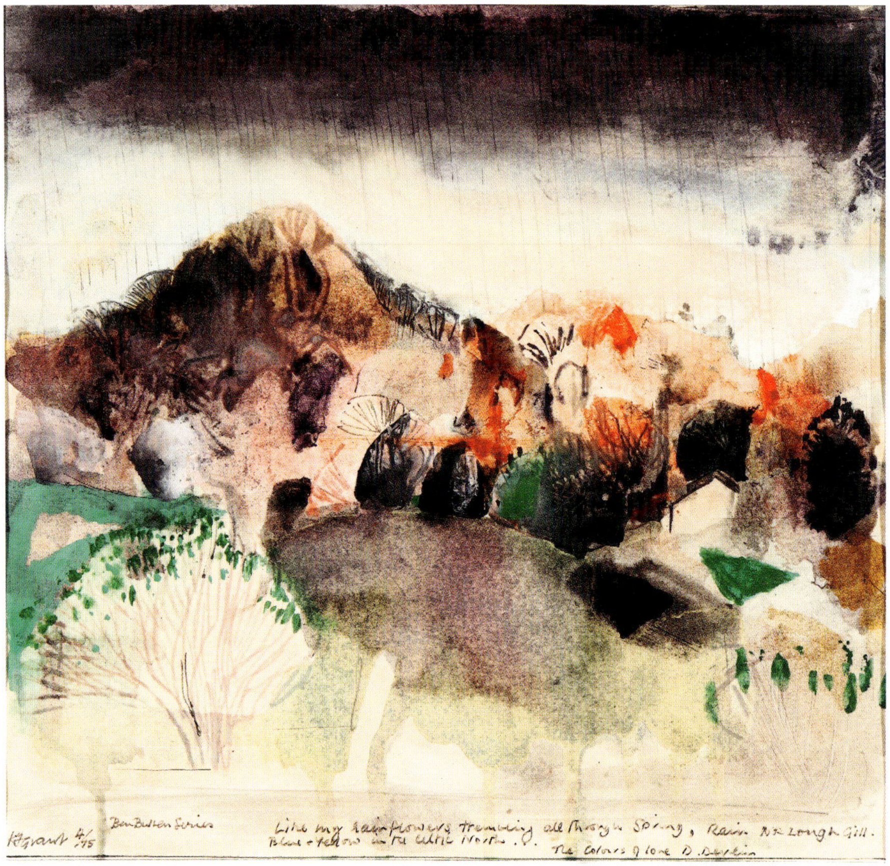

123
Ben Bulben Series: Rain nr Lough Gill, 1975
Watercolour and ink on paper
27.5 × 29 cm
The Red House Aldeburgh Collection (Britten Pears Arts), Aldeburgh

image: a barn owl with prey, captured in flight by the pioneering wildlife photographer Eric Hosking. This called to mind Hill's 'air-treading crucifix-pose struck by that mousing owl', while a reference to an hourglass – paying homage to George Herbert, in the first edition of *Clavics* – prompted its inclusion on the top shelf.[20] To the left is a gas mask (recalling Hill's lines, 'in gas mask awkward, off the record with sifted word'),[21] acting also as surrogate for a skull, after Hans Holbein's *The Ambassadors* (1533). At times, and particularly as Grant struggled to paint following a gall bladder operation, the precision and difficulty of the task seemed overwhelming. Then, its mystery would reassert itself. 'Suddenly', as Grant described, 'a quite irrational action caused me to paint in an exploding anti-aircraft shell as I had seen them during the far-off Blitz in Liverpool.'[22] The shape developed into a cloud of gas associated with the gas-mask skull symbol, whose scale and remoteness from the intention of the work opened an intuitive passage into history. The past is thus not only Hill's, emphasised by the family photographs, the edition of *The Oxford English Dictionary* he had used as a student and the coloured pencils he preferred, but Grant's, through a shared passion for poetry and nature. Is it also a valediction? Hill's stern gaze, captured so signally by Grant, conveys the call for attentiveness – to history, to landscape, to nature's detail – that permeates his writings.

Ireland

Long before meeting Hill, Grant was thinking about landscape through the eyes of a poet whom they both admired, Yeats. In early 1975 Grant spent a fortnight near Sligo, on the west coast of Ireland. Near the beginning of his stay he visited Yeats's grave twice, noting in his journals the lines of poetry inscribed on his memorial stone. Yeats died in France in 1939, yet had requested, after any furore had abated, that his body should be transferred to a final resting place in Sligo. From this narrative, and from the landscape 'under bare Ben Bulben's head',[23] Grant painted *Road to Sligo* (1975), a composition steeped in allegory and symbolism (fig.122). The road disappearing towards the sea, in a landscape washed by ink-black rainclouds, embodies Yeats's yearning for Sligo. Beneath, as with *The Narrow Road to the Deep North*, is a quotation: from Yeats's *The Song of the Wandering Aengus*, written in 1899 when the poet was some ten years older than Grant. The poem tells of a young, restless traveller, 'Aengus', who catches a fish and places it on the fire, only to see it transformed into a beautiful

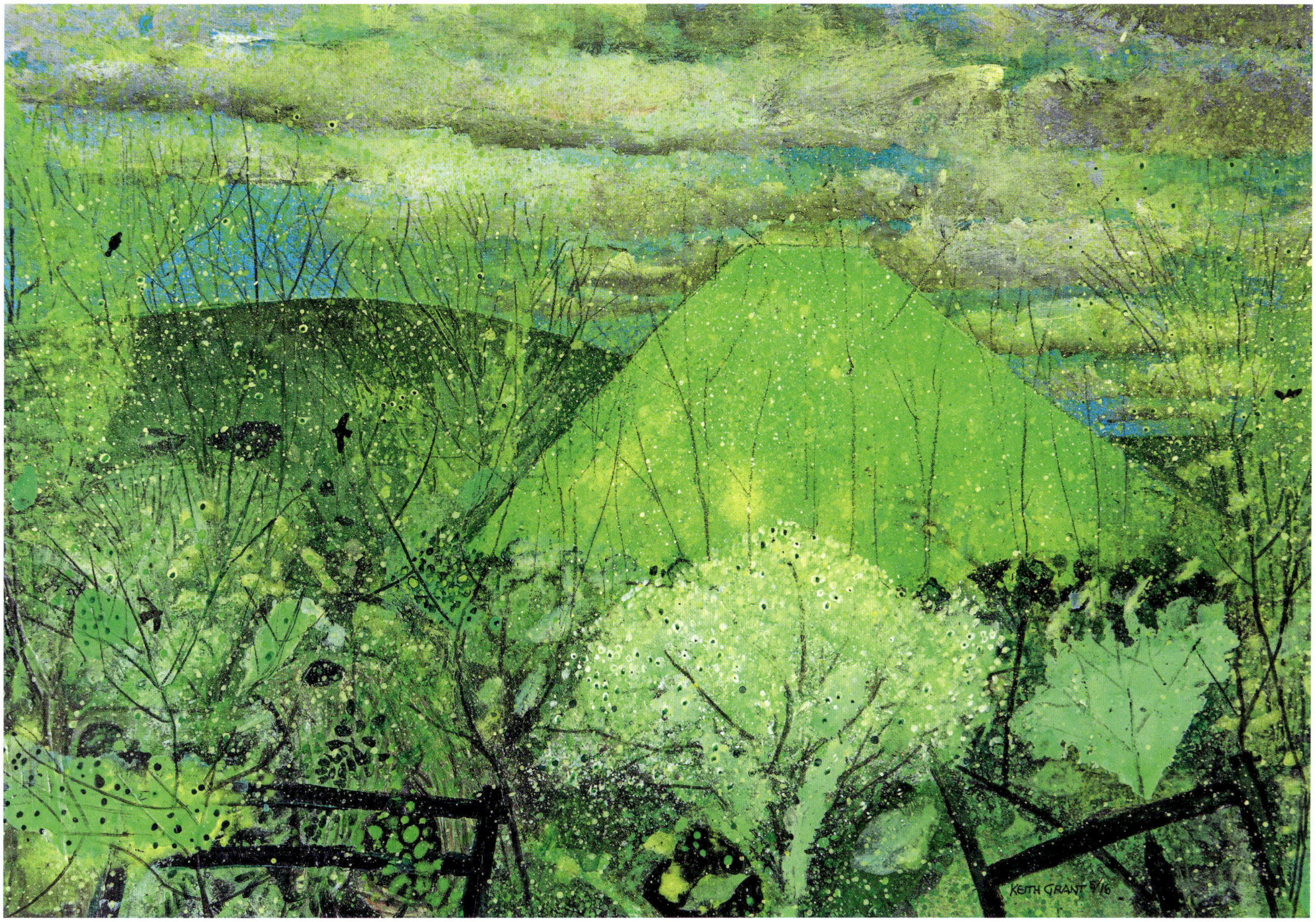

'glimmering girl'. She vanishes instantly and Aengus spends the remainder of his life trying to find her.

Grant's intense identification with Ireland's sea, hills, round forts, cairns and standing stones, in often harsh, lowering spring weather, was shared with Phillida Ball, a young artist and important presence in his life at this time. Together they climbed Ben Bulben and collected 'fractions of eternity rolled up neatly into the fossil worm casts' – heavy stones whose weight Grant did not feel.[24] Two mountains dominated 'this Irish journey' for Grant: Ben Bulben, in whose shadow Yeats is buried, and Croagh Patrick, whose summit has been a site of pilgrimage since the fifth century. The light was unlike that of Norway or Iceland, revealing the strange greens preserved in the Book of Kells that Grant admired early in his visit. On one occasion, Ben Bulben appeared through the mist 'like a fantastic faery kingdom guarded by enormous walls: slowly the cloud obscured the vision again and it was difficult to believe we had seen it'.[25] *Rain nr Lough Gill* (1975) might be imagined as this vision (fig.123). Grant had begun to draw trees again as abstract forms, thinking of the geometrical figures they might assume in oil paintings, on his return. Here, they bristle across the landscape, holding tessellations of colour under the still-raining sky. Underneath

124
Spring, Dovedale, Derbyshire, 2016
Acrylic and fixed wax on board
30 × 45 cm
Private Collection, UK

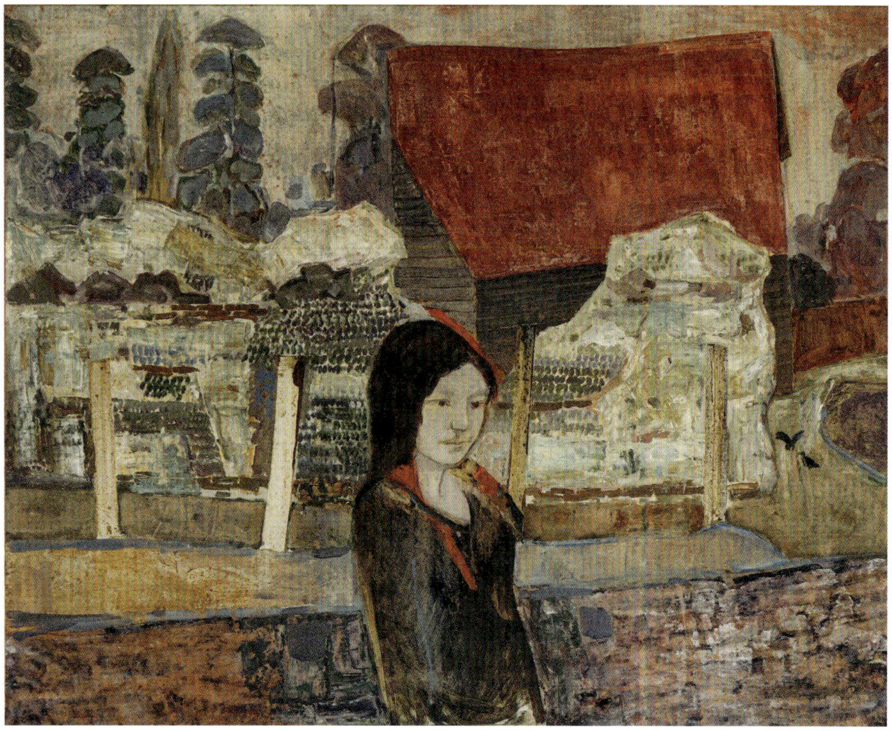

125
Anna and the Roman Wall, 1959
Oil on board
128 × 97 cm
Private Collection, UK

126 (right)
The Falcon and the Dove at Verulamium, 2017
Oil on canvas
70 × 60 cm
Collection of the artist

Grant wrote lines from *The Colours of Love* by the 20th-century Irish poet Denis Devlin that read as a simple evocation of landscape: 'Like my rainflowers trembling all through spring, Blue and yellow in the Celtic North . . .' In its entirety, Devlin's poem addresses failed love and a farewell in 1920s Paris, where boulevard lights resembled the delicate flowers *Zephyranthes*, otherwise known as 'rain' or 'fairy' lilies. The slippage between the poem, the poem's inspiration and Grant's landscape is intriguing. Grant visited Ireland several times between 1973 and 1975, but did not return to it as a subject, despite an exhibition at the Solomon Gallery in Dublin in 1982.

New English Series

In 2016, Grant began a series that would be titled *New English*. He visited Dovedale, near where he and his brother Roy had been evacuated as boys. To Grant's surprise, the Derbyshire landscape was more fertile than he remembered it. *Spring, Dovedale, Derbyshire* (2016) clothes the flat-topped peak of Hope Cloud in a vivid green that permeates the sky and burgeoning foreground (fig.124). Pencil-thin lines indicate branches yet to bud, while the texture is woven with the presence of birds. Within the form of the conical peak is the echo of mining heaps seen in Wales, volcanoes in Iceland, pyramid peaks in Norway, Wiltshire's Silbury Hill or the 'frown' of Ben Bulben.

In 1959, Grant had painted Anna Davidson, a model from Kingston, in front of the Roman wall at Verulamium (fig.125). She stands, pensive, eyes downcast, with a similar faraway expression to one captured in a studio portrait.[26] The background to these works was lost in the burning of Grant's early journals, but what we can see is a reworking of a small area of *Village Landscape* (fig.12, p.24). Taking the section of wall with the distinctive 'V'-shaped gap, Grant alters the perspective so that the fence posts, wall and barn appear in much closer proximity and the sky is all but occluded. The scene is at once humanised and rendered more intimate. Through the figure, it accrues a layer of time.

Anna and the Roman Wall was exhibited at the New Art Centre, from where it was purchased by Lord Timothy Willoughby, a young collector of contemporary art. When Grant returned to the same subject, for the *New English* series, he began by including a female figure, then changed his mind and substituted a peregrine falcon, adding a dove in the distance (fig.126). Altering the context to night, Grant also modified the wall to include a mysterious square recess and an opening through which bare trees can be seen. The falcon is as vigilant as Anna was detached, indicating the renewed significance of birds in Grant's paintings. In *Kestrel and Cloud, over a Path near Abergavenny* (2016) – a Welsh landscape indicating

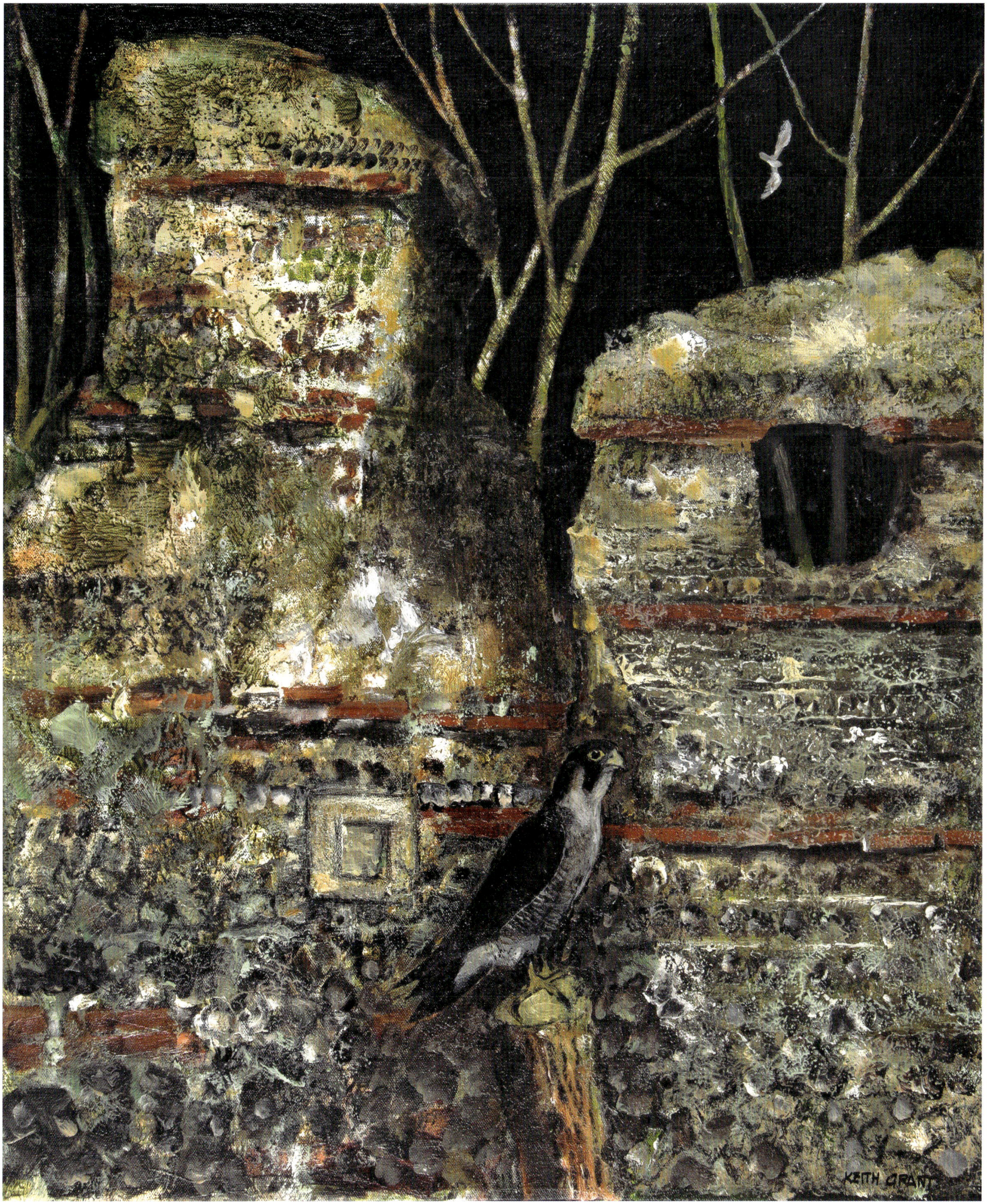
KEITH GRANT

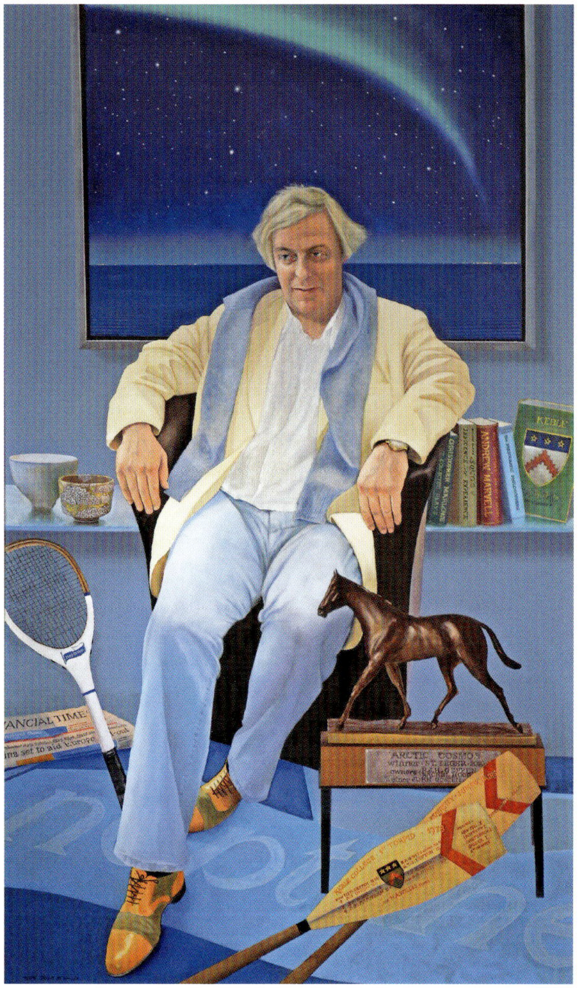

127
Portrait of Robin Geffen, 2011
Oil on canvas
160 x 100 cm
Private Collection, UK

that the new series was not strictly 'English' – a dark kestrel was included as a tribute to Geoffrey Hill, 'who read Hopkins' *Windhover* with such perfection of diction, rhythm and feeling' that it became for Grant the definitive interpretation.[27] The bird's silhouette replicates that on the cover of Hopkins's verse in the top left-hand corner of Hill's portrait (fig.121), forming a mute link to the earlier work. But what were Grant's own feelings, contemplating his new series of paintings? In his journal, he identified exile as the difference between recent work based on the North and the forthcoming 'English' paintings: the separation from his native landscape since moving to Norway in 1996, with all the 'plaintive yearning and sense of loss' entailed.[28] The sentiment is surprising, given the ineluctable magnetism Norway has exerted throughout his life. To what extent does it intensify the mood of the new work?

We have already seen Grant's responses to Dovedale and Verulamium. From early 2016 he visited Uriconium, Ludlow, The Wrekin and Wenlock Edge in Shropshire, important to him through Housman's poetry; Herefordshire; Saltwood Castle in Kent, where Kenneth Clark had lived; and the Vale of Ceiriog he had known when young. Grant's renewed attachment to Wales, as a subject, indicates the extent to which emotion plays a role when responding to landscape. While the new paintings responded unequivocally to the countryside's winding lanes, hills, fields and vales, thirty years earlier, when visiting his foster mother in Ffynnon Bach, the drama of snow and hail against the mountains had functioned as an invidious reminder of Norway, prompting him to write, 'somehow I am not ready to paint in Wales. I am deeply attracted by the profound beauty of the place but it is tempered by an irrational impatience and resentment.'[29] Working on a painting of a lake in Snowdonia, in January 2017, he was reminded of seeing the former Czechoslovakia with Milada Tashnerova, who described the many small areas of water as 'the eyes of the country'.[30] It was a sentiment voiced by Gaston Bachelard, as Grant realised, but also by the American naturalist Henry David Thoreau, for whom lakes were 'landscape's most beautiful and expressive feature . . . earth's eye; looking into which the beholder measures the depth of his own nature'.[31]

In 2011 Grant had painted the portrait of Robin Geffen, an Honorary Fellow of Keble College as well as a highly successful fund manager and racehorse owner (fig.127). It is a perceptive study, uncharacteristically Hockneyesque in palette and register, including in its composition the 'oars' Geffen

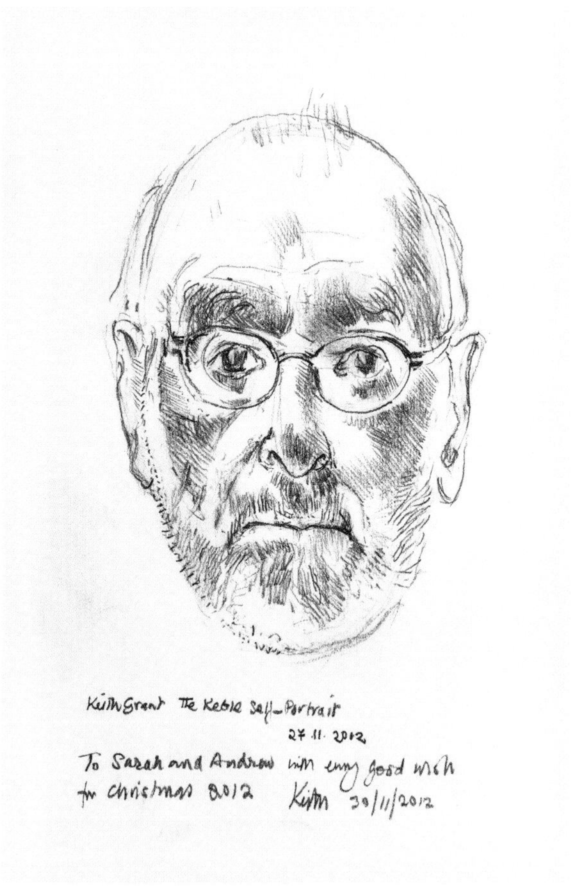

128
The Keble Self-Portrait, 2012
Pencil on paper
16 × 11 cm
The Lambirth Collection, UK

won for rowing at College, a rug emblazoned with 'Neptune', an investment company founded by him, a trophy for his winning racehorse 'Arctic Cosmos', as well as an image of one of Grant's own recent aurora paintings. Four years later this was followed by the portrait of Hill, described above (fig.121). Between these, in 2012, Grant drew his own portrait: a probing likeness in pencil, known as *The Keble Self-Portrait* (fig.128). Look at the eyes – which address the viewer and artist squarely. As Grant was thinking about the symbolism of lakes as eyes, he recalled Gabriele D'Annunzio, again via Bachelard, describing the eyes of a trembling hare which, 'in one torment-free moment', stops to look at the horizon, in so doing conferring peace over the autumnal landscape.[32] It is a complex set of ciphers, to which we might add Grant's own symbolic reiteration of eyes in the paintings predicated on metamorphosis. Grant's *Keble Self-Portrait* is unsparing in depicting his age and unblinking gaze. What does it suggest? Isolation? Experience? We know from Grant's work the many landscapes recorded in his memory. The rest is conjecture.

Selborne

The culmination of the *New English* series, where this vision is most strongly brought to bear, is the set of paintings based on Selborne in Hampshire. Their foundations were laid during a visit at New Year 1959, from which two paintings are known to have resulted: *Landscape with Haystacks* (fig.17, p.27) and *The Hanger, Selborne*, the latter described by Kenneth Clark as 'the most "complete" of the exhibition'.[33] Both of these paintings are beautiful renderings of landscape with a specific sense of order and logic to them. It is not that they are unduly formalised, simply that there are no discordant elements to alert the viewer to remain attentive. Representing absorption in an idyllic landscape, they relay their vision adeptly.

In a statement from 2017 to accompany the new paintings, Grant recorded that Selborne had hardly changed since he visited as a student.[34] So what had happened, to result in such a different vision? One of Grant's favourite analogies when describing the mutability of landscape is the experience of making a return journey: the landscape is the same, but the spectator's vision is transformed through a new perspective. Returning to Selborne, Grant observed different aspects with fresh intensity. He noted the 'dishevelled' nature of woods containing dead trees – 'or seemingly dead since I found it difficult arriving at

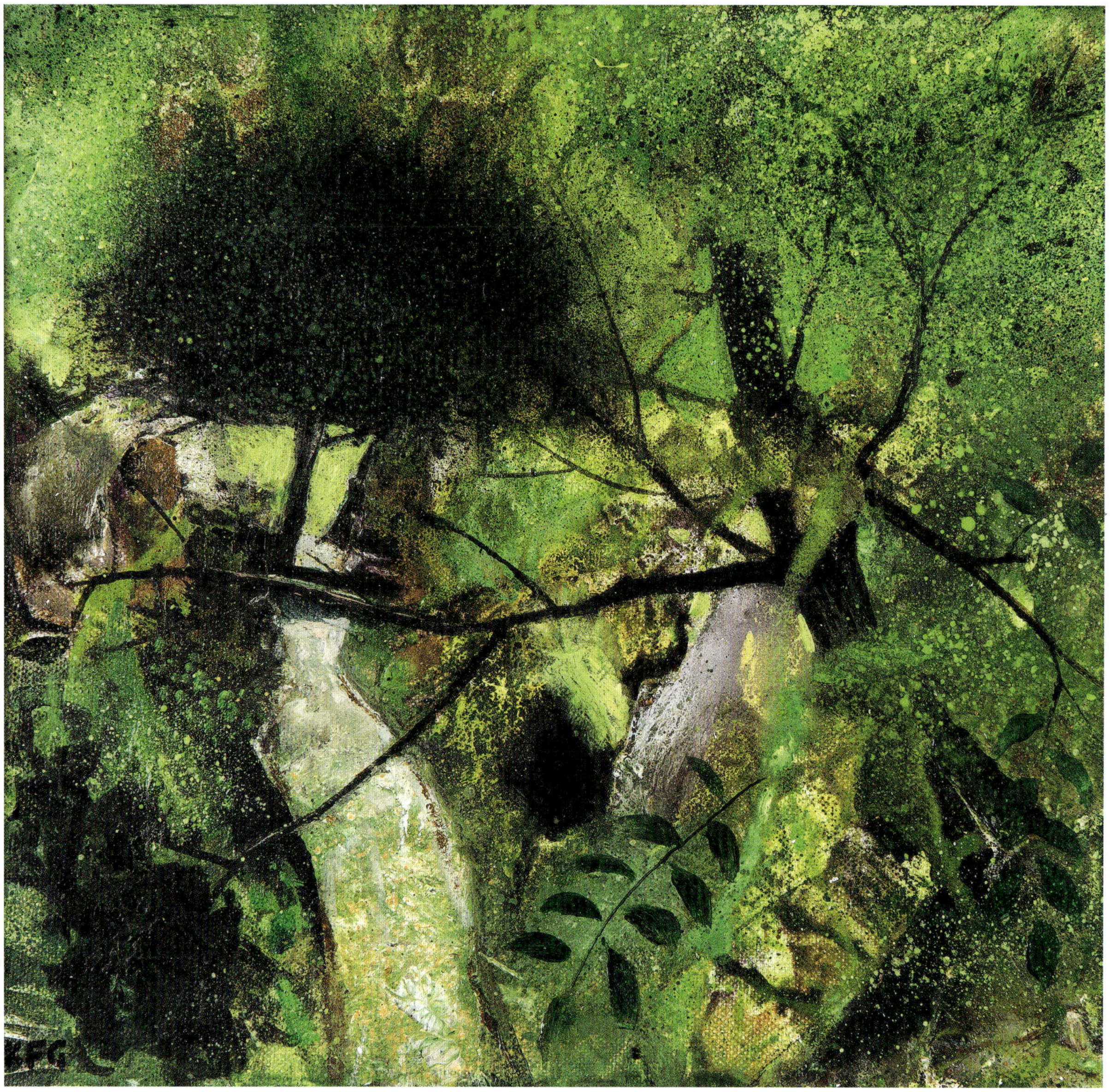

129
The Sunken Road, Selborne, 2017
Oil on canvas laid on board
30 × 31.5 cm
Private Collection, UK

the spring solstice to tell the dead from the living'. The impending spring was expressed not by the pointillism of buds, but by a 'neutral mistiness of pale ochres and browns, umbers and siennas as if reflecting a lambent, slightly milky sheen upon every limb, branch and twig, leaf and blade, petal and stem . . . Close to, branches, trunks and entwined espalier-like hedgework seemed glazed, picking up accents of light in every modulation imaginable.'[35] This closeness of vision was one adjustment, shaped by the experience of walking through woods in Norway and the resultant metamorphic forest paintings.

In *The Sunken Road, Selborne* (2017), Grant depicts one of the ancient 'hollow lanes' worn deep beneath the level of fields by repeated use and the erosion of water (fig.129). After floods or in winter, as Gilbert White recorded in his *Natural History of Selborne*, such lanes 'exhibit very grotesque and wild appearances', with roots, tangled and twisted among the strata, forming fanciful shapes of frost-work. He continued, 'These rugged gloomy scenes affright the ladies when they peep down into them from the paths above, and make timid horsemen shudder while they ride along them; but delight the naturalist with their various botany.'[36] Grant's painting is a confusion of leaves and branches, not gloomy as White intimated, but certainly mysterious in its layering of ill-defined forms. The outline of a dark bush merges with surrounding foliage through flicked and spattered paint, just as the lane assumes the dappled gold of filtered light. Grant is drawn once again to the image of a receding road. In his journals, thinking of the numerous roads in A.E. Housman's poetry, he joked, 'Once, a long time ago, I wrote of my feeling as "a corpuscle in the blood-stream of a whale". I might now say "as a corpuscle in the arteries of tracks, lanes and highways!"'[37]

Have these paths been trodden before? Undoubtedly, and in a wood-engraving by Eric Ravilious, *The Hollow Lane* (1938), just such a scene is depicted. Ravilious shows an owl hovering against the crisply incised textures of leaf and twig, echoing with its wings the enfolding branches of a sunken road. Ravilious's engravings, produced as illustrations for a Nonesuch Press edition of *The Natural History*, illuminate descriptions within White's text, such as the tortoise, hoopoes and the moose hanging in the Duke of Richmond's greenhouse.[38] As part of a lineage of imagery assembled for *Drawn to Nature: Gilbert White and the Artists* (2020), an exhibition at Pallant House in Chichester, Ravilious is testament to the attraction of White's writing from the 1920s to the present day. Grant was not referenced in either the exhibition or subsequent book. Beautiful though the anthology is – including contributions by Gertrude Hermes, Claire Oldham, John Nash, John Piper and, from the present day, Angie Lewin – it is unashamedly a study of illustration, whether historic or newly commissioned for White's tercentenary in 2020.[39] Grant's work differs both in execution (as paintings, rather than graphic or printed media) and in its derivation from the landscape of Selborne: as homage to White but not as illustration of his text.

The geometry that Grant had always detected in nature directed the views he wished to depict. In *Early Spring, Selborne* (2017), he combined the conical roof of a barn, the grid of a wooden fence, and a rectangular water trough (fig.130). Although each of these elements had appeared in the landscape, they could not be seen from a single viewpoint. To the clouds mirrored in the water trough, Grant added the surrealistic touch of a crescent moon. As he wrote to a student, when explaining his approach, 'My practice has changed towards a more formal and a more surrealist means of expression. That comes with age. I have more confidence now – and I live for what I do.'[40] At the top left of *Early Spring* is a brief zigzag, in reference to the path cut through the Hanger by Gilbert White and his brother in 1753. Here it hovers above the trees, seemingly unconnected to the landscape, whereas in the painting from 1959 it occupied a central position, carving a steep ascent to the brow of the hill.

In Grant's new Selborne paintings, objects register as presences in the landscape. A white-painted wooden obelisk becomes a sentinel, clipped evergreens hem the garden or stand isolated and erect. The recurrent motif of a bonfire, itself alive, suggests a further trespassing into the landscape. Grant was conscious of this change, which he described as 'a more disturbing orientation', although he remained unaware of its origin. As he wrote,

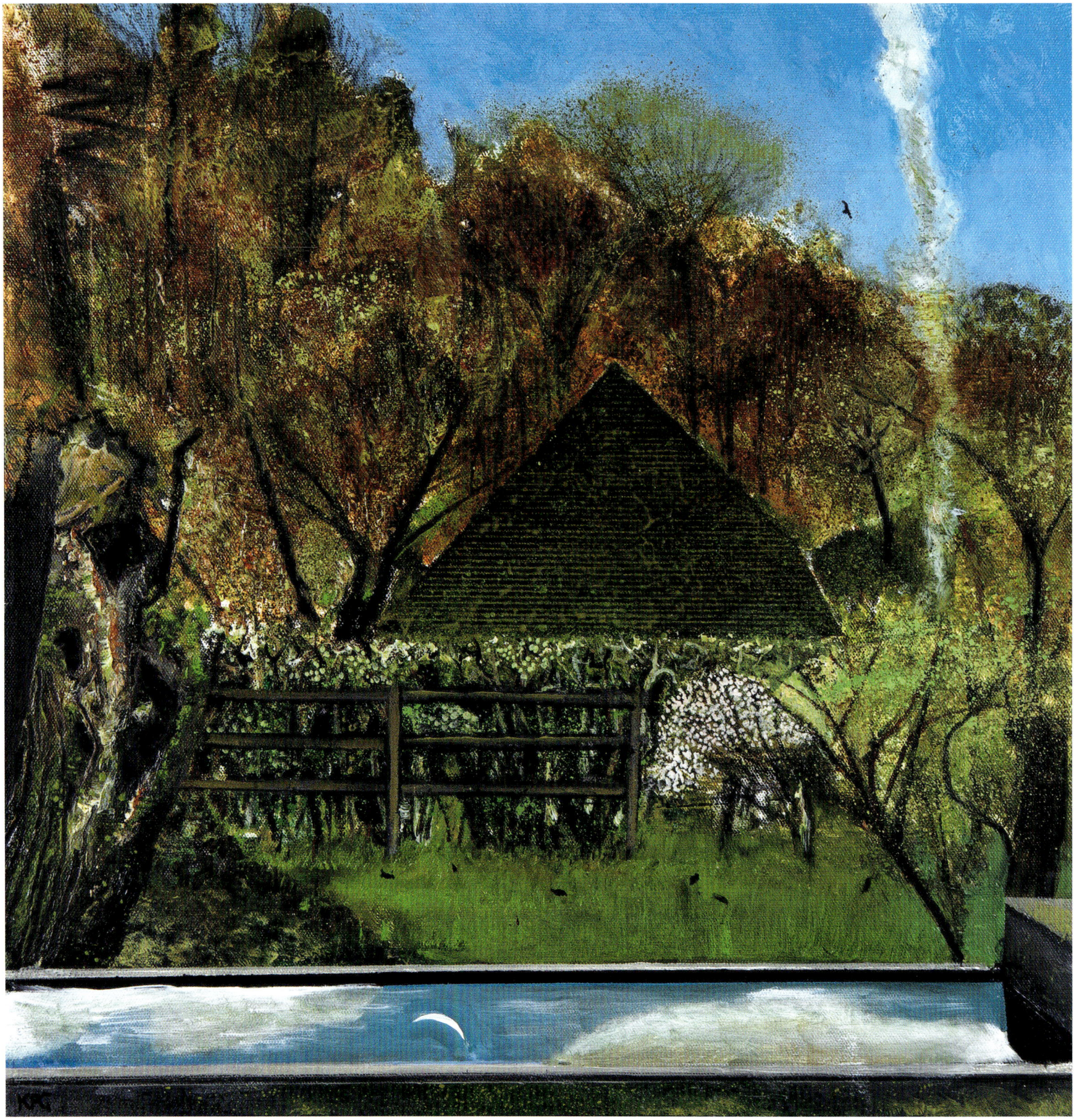

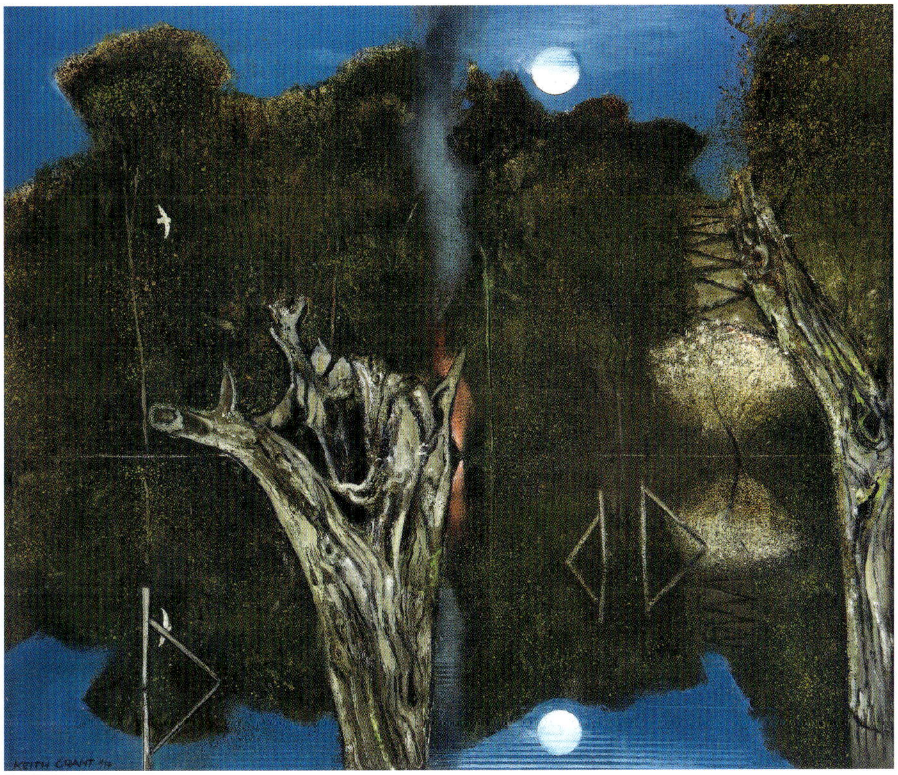

131
The Flooded Meadow, The Hanger, The Moon and the Bonfire, Selborne, 2017
Oil on canvas
50 × 60 cm
Private Collection, UK

130 (left)
Early Spring, Selborne, 2017
Oil on canvas
50 × 50 cm
Collection of the artist

I begin to see in some of the forms arrived at a premonition of something able to communicate soundlessly and lifelessly a kind of ghostly benignity which telescopes the centuries . . . Both Palmer and Nash would have liked to experience Blake's propensity to bona-fide visions but striving after them certainly precluded their appearance and one is forced to find schematic solutions as in Nash or quasi-religious pantheism as with Palmer.[41]

Elsewhere, Grant recorded the still-pervasive influence of Graham Sutherland, whose early work is 'a perfect reflection of the English landscape'.[42]

Is it, then, a landscape of ghosts? The garden and meadows at Selborne are now preserved, restored or recreated, to the extent that the six large flowerbeds, known as 'Quarters', are filled with plants known to have been cultivated by White, that peak at different seasons of the year. Walking in Selborne's main street, Grant watched with astonishment an immaculately dressed man, wearing a cravat, broad-brimmed hat and silver-buckled shoes, 'plainly intending to be Gilbert White'. Passers-by seemed oblivious, leading Grant to wonder what he had, in fact, seen.[43]

The Flooded Meadow, The Hanger, The Moon and the Bonfire, Selborne (2017), the final and among the most evocative of the Selborne series, fuses such sensations into a disquieting image whose dominating motif is the gnarled 'monster' trunk, decayed yet seemingly animate (fig.131). At the absolute centre of the composition, however, is an amber beacon: an oracular flare quite unlike the garden bonfires Grant had already depicted as volcanoes in miniature. This fire, the column of smoke and the bird are the only implications of movement in an otherwise stilled landscape. Grant counterpoints his reflected imagery adroitly: the bird's double is bisected by a wooden hurdle in the pond, blossom dusts the water's surface, below which, as eerily as a water snake, floats the zigzag path.

White, in *The Natural History*, described with delight the discovery, near a hedge, of a large snake's slough. Newly cast, it resembled a peeled stocking or glove, with detached scales appearing at its head 'like a pair of spectacles'.[44] The description, part comical, part sobering, telescopes time. It brings to mind Grant's first sight of a viper, as well as his eye for a surreal juxtaposition: the gold-rimmed spectacles, placed reverently on a skull in Sarawak, which thirty years later would feature in *Atlantis III: Le cimetière marin* (2015; fig.110, pp 130–31). A kinship between Grant and White is rooted not just in nature but in minute, patient and serious observation.

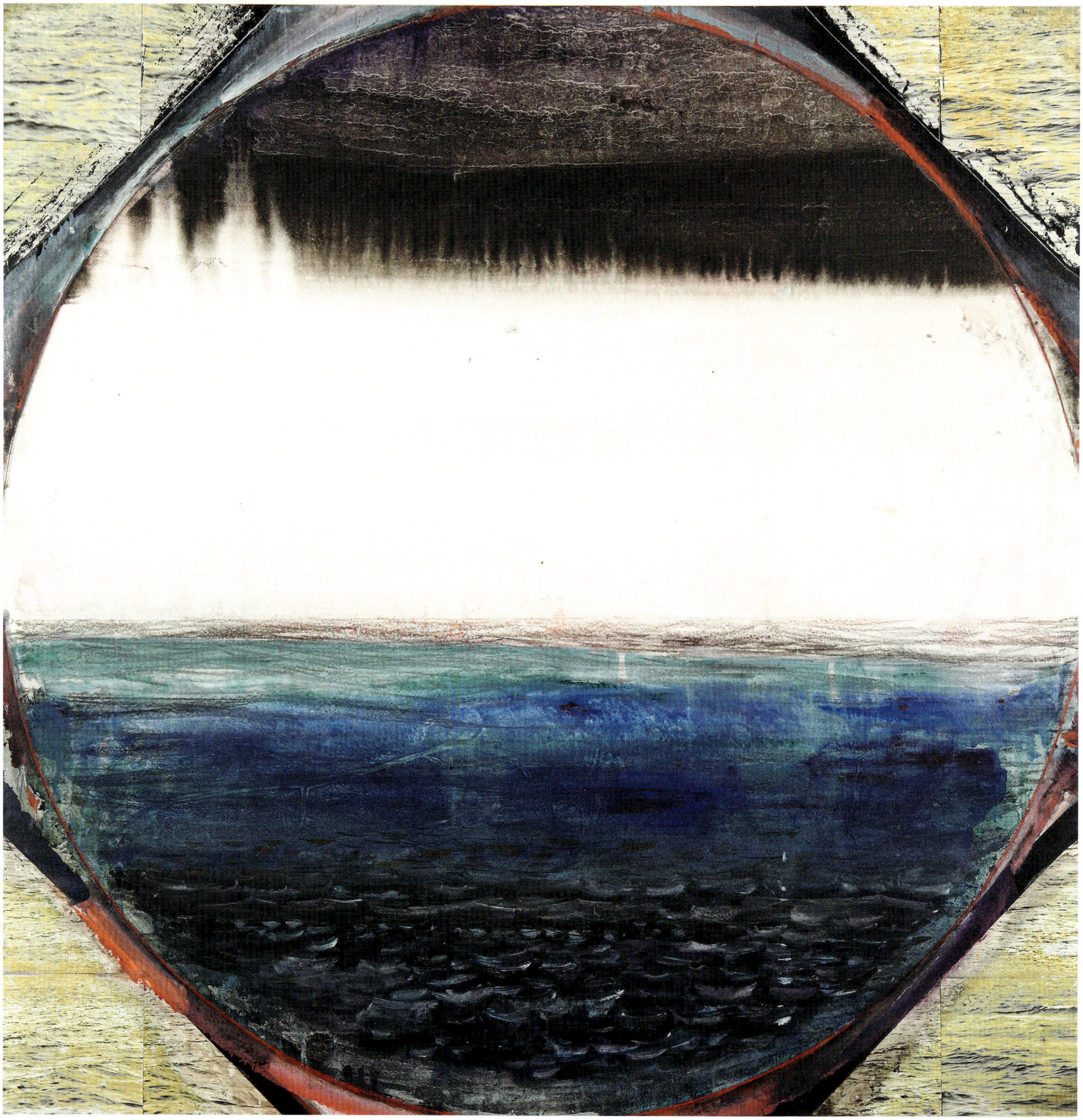

8

Interludes

132
The Sea Interludes, 1977
watercolour, oil, pastel and photograph on paper laid on board
127 × 127 cm
The Red House Aldeburgh Collection (Britten Pears Arts), Aldeburgh

Music holds a privileged place in Grant's life, as inspiration and companion while he paints. Indeed, in his journals he not only questions whether without music he could continue as a painter, but states that music has had a greater impact on him than the work of other artists: 'I seldom am as entranced by a painting as I am by music.'[1] These are extraordinary, thought-provoking claims. Not only does music provide direct inspiration for the subject matter of Grant's painting, it suggests ways in which to approach it. The linking thread is most often landscape, although it should be stressed that this is not always the case. Bach, for instance is a composer whose instrumental music Grant admires for its essentially abstract, formal expression. Here, however, it is Grant's passion for music impelled by or depicting nature that most concerns us.

Grant's interest can be traced from an early love of Vaughan Williams to Benjamin Britten and, most recently, Frederick Delius, source of an entire series of paintings. His interest is intelligent and enquiring, leading to choices that surprise even musicians. In 2012, when Grant was invited to take part in *Private Passions*, the Radio 3 equivalent to *Desert Island Discs*, the composer Michael Berkeley registered the unusualness of his playlist, particularly in its emphasis on contemporary music. Grant's selection included *The Tempest* (1979) by the Norwegian composer Arne Nordheim, *The Gokstad Ship* (1982) by Scottish composer John McLeod and *Cantus Arcticus* (1972) by the Finnish composer Einojuhani Rautavaara. Britten, a friend of Grant's from the late 1960s until the composer's death in 1976, was represented by 'O rose, thou are sick', a setting of William Blake from the *Serenade for Tenor, Horn and Strings* (1943), where it forms a dark interlude. Grant identified the subtext of both poem and music as the corruption of innocence, indicative of the injustice that exists in life and in nature.

Framing Landscape through Music

Framing the *Serenade* is a fanfare-like motif for solo horn. It is a device characteristic of Britten's music: a means of summoning then dismissing attention, in the same way that organ music might preface and conclude a church service. Ritualistic and functional, it provides a contemplative space emphasising music's division from everyday life. When Grant made a series of memorial paintings to Britten, he alluded to the format of J.M.W. Turner's *Peace – Burial at*

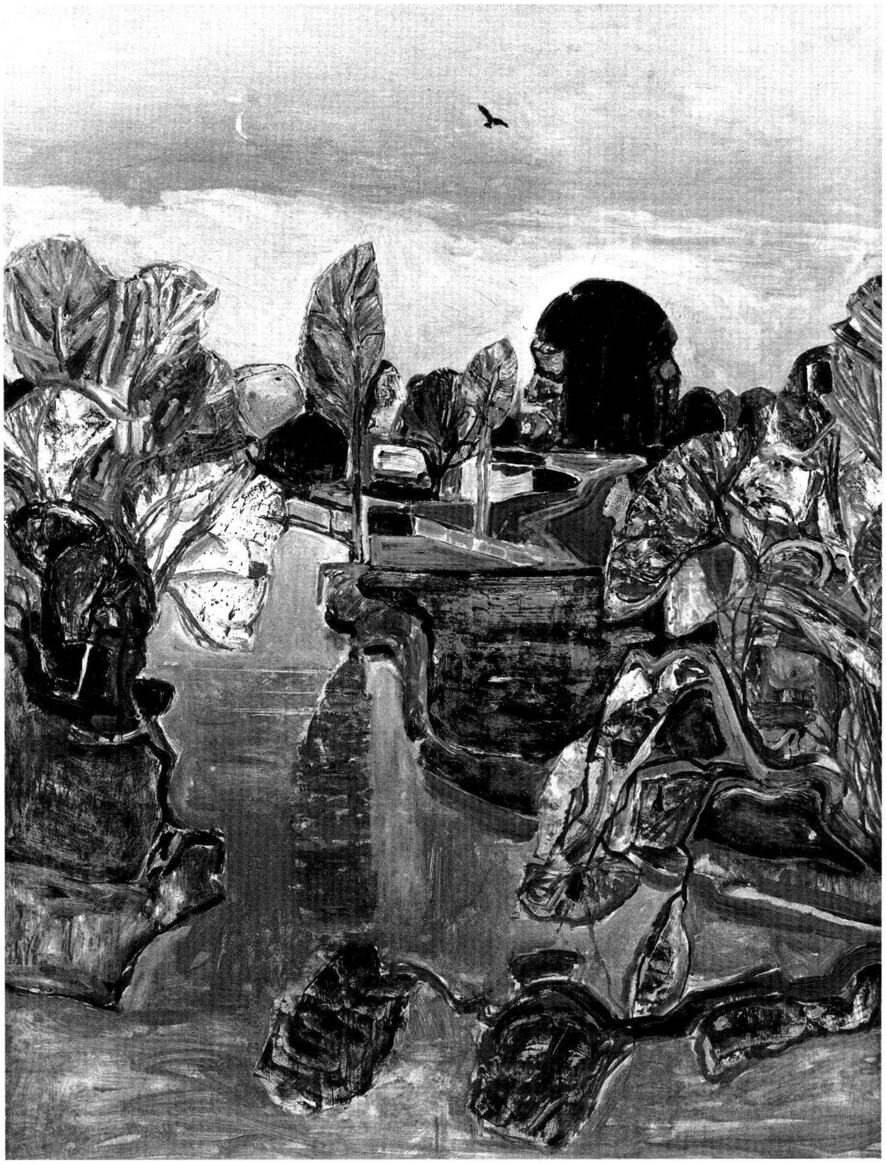

133
The Lark Ascending, 1959
Oil on board
81.5 × 61 cm
Private Collection, UK

Sea (exhibited 1842), painted in tribute to Sir David Wilkie, whose frame originally obscured the corners of a square canvas. Grant blocked the corners of his paintings with black, encapsulating his seascape within an octagonal space and providing an extra barrier, as with Britten's *Serenade*, between content and environment. Double-framed, the paintings function even more powerfully as a symbol of mourning.

The sea was of immense importance to Britten. He was born at Lowestoft, on the Suffolk coast, and lived for most of his life at Aldeburgh, a fishing town characterised by its long, bleak, shingle beach. Grant's large memorial paintings alternate between the sea at Aldeburgh and the coast or fjords of Norway, representing Britten's last journey abroad. The emptiness of *The Sea Interludes* (1977; fig.132), the painting owned by Peter Pears, echoes 'Dawn', the first *Sea Interlude* from Britten's opera *Peter Grimes*, which counterpoints high, ethereal strings against the low undertow of brass and a rippling gesture from woodwinds. Instantly a seascape is conjured, the waves pulling at the beach, gulls wheeling above and an immense sense of space implied through the distancing of instrumental forces. In this instance, Grant collaged photographs of the North Sea over the blackened corners of his painting. Space is conveyed by absence; the sky, an almost featureless white, is weighted darkly to the top. As he was painting, with every brushstroke he was thinking of Britten's music, charging the seascape with a profound sense of loss.

Grant's earliest musical landscape was *The Lark Ascending* (1959), made during post-RCA forays into the countryside when he was searching 'for landscape with "visionary" mood and following in the footsteps of Paul Nash' (fig.133).[2] Uninhabited, the scene depicted is that of the River Thames at Day's Lock near Dorchester. Grant was conscious, as he drew, of the Wittenham Clumps to his left, featured in paintings by Nash. The landscape is composed of verticals, zigzags and the voluptuously full foliage of the nearest tree. High above soars a solitary lark.

Ralph Vaughan Williams's *The Lark Ascending*, inspired by George Meredith's poem, and described by Grant as 'one of the jewels of romantic English musical expression',[3] was written on the brink of the First World War. Once this is known, the high register, trills and melismatic writing of the solo violin, the

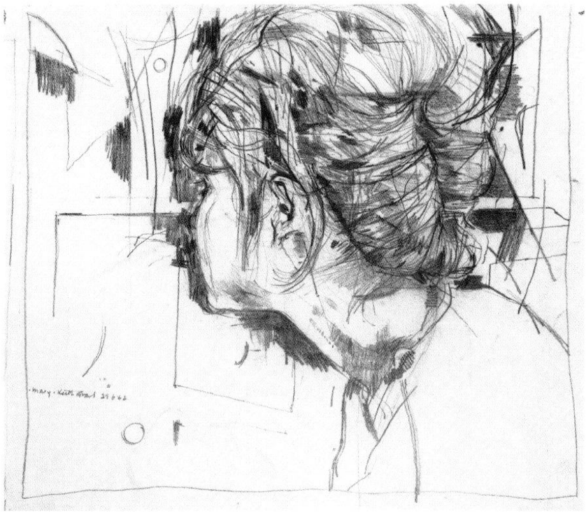

134
Study for Death and the Maiden, 1962
Pencil with chalk on paper
35 × 38 cm
Private Collection (location unknown)

incorporation of folk-like melodies and the use of modal harmonies characteristic of archaic music assume a mantle of nostalgia. Revisiting Grant's landscapes from the 1950s, there is a tendency to see them through a similar lens. Yet there is a firmness and directness of approach that cuts through sentimentality, just as there is a clarity of vision in Vaughan Williams's music. When Grant returned to *The Lark Ascending*, in 1981, he relocated it from Dorchester to Chollerford in Northumberland. He drew and memorised the view before starting work, listening to a 1950s recording of Vaughan Williams played by the violinist Jean Pougnet and conducted by Adrian Boult. In the series of vertical compositions that resulted, more closely detailed than the earlier painting, Grant presented a more conventional view of landscape: the River Tyne, or nearby meadows, curtained by foliage and illuminated by a low sun.

It is characteristic of Grant's working methods to revisit subjects, sometimes at many years' distance. In 1962, he began a series titled *Death and the Maiden*, a theme to which he returned, most notably, in the painting of Tuah in Sarawak (fig.54, p.70). His earliest depictions relate to Schubert's song *Der Tod und das Mädchen* (*Death and the Maiden*), whose insistent rhythm, harmony and minor key recur in the late D minor string quartet of the same name. Pencil studies depict a young woman looking towards a window (fig.134). In a coloured version, he amplified the landscape and introduced a skull so close to the woman's face as to imply a reflection. Beneath, he wrote, 'I intend to develop this theme in the North of the World.'[4] When Grant revisited the subject in 1973, while working at Bosworth College, it was as a series of photographs taken in the context of an anatomy department. A fair-haired girl faces a skull in close proximity, the skull suspended or reflected in a mirror. Printed in black and white, thus emphasising the shadows, reflections and darkened areas, the images possess a chilling premonition of mortality.

What was characteristic about these studies is that they had either a literary or musical resonance, just as when Grant painted young women against the backdrop of fjords, in the 1970s, he was thinking of the character Edvarda from Hamsun's *Pan* (fig.33, p.47). To paint figures with minimal reference to landscape, except in the instance of commissions, was highly unusual. Yet this is what he did in relation to Britten's *The Turn of the* Screw, in 1963, when he based a series of imaginative paintings on the opera's principal characters. Derived from the novella by Henry James, Britten's opera unfolds as a set of tautly devised scenes, separated by variations on a twelve-tone theme that parallel the narrative's devastating trajectory: the corruption of two children and their governesses by a former servant, Peter

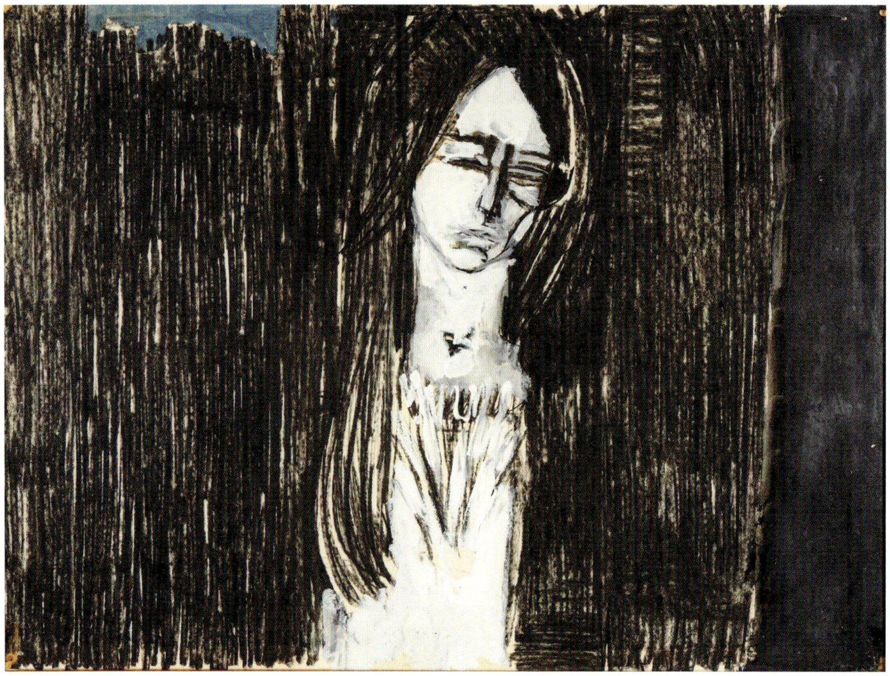

135
Miss Jessel, 1963
Charcoal, white gouache and conte crayon on board
58 × 78.5 cm
The Red House Aldeburgh Collection (Britten Pears Arts), Aldeburgh

Quint. Grant's paintings are sombre, angular portraits against densely scored backdrops. Most suggest the merest outline of a window through which the action is observed. In that of Miss Jessel, however, there is the intimation of an outside setting: a tree trunk to the right, and a sliver of sky (fig.135). Head hung and eyes closed, she resembles the ghost she has become. The claustrophobic framing of her figure, hemmed by darkness, is an apposite mirroring of the stifling atmosphere of the opera.

Invited to exhibit work on the subject of music at Heal's furniture store in Tottenham Court Road, London, in 1965, Grant offered paintings inspired by *Death and the Maiden*, Shostakovich's 8th Symphony (which he had recently heard), and Sibelius's *Swan of Tuonela.* The last of these, sharing its title with Sibelius's music, was highly significant for Grant. Lost soon after its inclusion in an exhibition in Milan, that autumn, it depicted a swan dying amidst reeds, under a sky patterned ominously by clouds. Sibelius's *Swan of Tuonela* is a movement from his *Lemminkäinen Suite*, in which the swan, guarding the entrance to Hades, is given voice by a cor anglais, plangent against shimmering strings. Grant, in the mid-1960s, would take this imagery as the basis for a series of politically motivated landscapes (see pp 196–7).

Debussy and Mallarmé

Music acts as a stimulus for Grant's painting, but equally it may provide a gloss for an idea that has already formed. Grant first travelled to Sicily with Gisèle and her sister in 1964, arriving at Etna towards the end of a particularly volatile period in the volcano's history, when there were spectacular lava fountains from the central crater, coupled with multiple spillages to the south and west. From this experience Grant made a series of gouaches flashed with emerald and crimson under ashen skies. He remained enthralled by the memory of Etna: 'the slow rhythmic beauty of the smoke column against the sky' with the constant threat of explosion – as compelling as 'a snake which is charmed'.[5] When he returned, in 1977, he took with him a group of students from Camberwell School of Art and met the volcanologist John Guest. At night, looking with Guest into the volcano's main crater, they watched a pulsating glow from the magma. The mountain echoed from muffled explosions deep within the volcano's throat; standing back, a meteor flashed over the mountain's horizon.[6] Looking for a theme to link the drawings he was now making, Grant alighted upon Debussy's *Prélude à l'après-midi d'un faune*, based on a text by Stéphane Mallarmé that mentions Etna. Debussy's music is sultry, opening famously with a low-pitched flute solo. Grant witnessed violent thunderstorms with forked lightning, while in Sicily: 'The flashes flickered in degrees of intensity. Sometimes the lightning would be like veins suddenly standing out all over the flank of the cloud – sometimes like a tree.'[7] To Mallarmé's lines, 'upon your lava, when a melancholy slumber rumbles', he painted a lead-black landscape crackling into flashes of iridescent green and blue, inscribing the text underneath (fig.136). He was pleased with the paintings, describing their forms as sensual but 'very English . . . [harking] back to early Sutherland, Vaughan and Palmer'.[8] Even before commencing, he had dedicated them to his six-year-old daughter, Dominique.

Grant's marrying of landscapes to music and literature is exemplified by his painting of Etna. Encountering it for a first time, in 1964, he conveyed the mass of the volcano in paintings possessing an immense sense of weight and history. His second visit elicited a more nimble, mercurial response, seeking to reflect 'an element of surrealism and poetry'.[9] Debussy and Mallarmé provided an irresistible adjunct. Yet, as he admitted, there was something 'English' about the result, which in fact tallied also with his recent studies of Ireland.

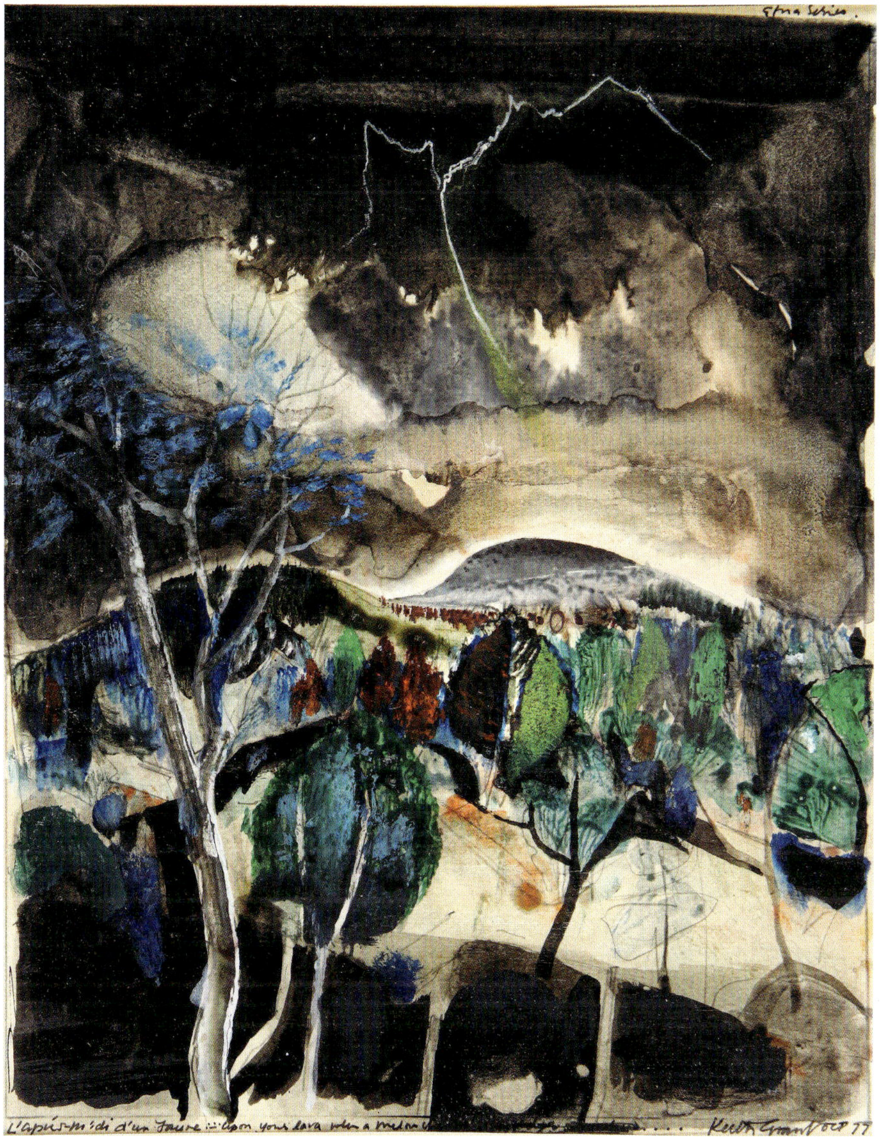

136
Etna Series: L'après-midi d'un faune, 1977
Ink and watercolour with bodycolour and pencil on board
35 × 27 cm
Chris Beetles Gallery, St James's, London

The *Delius* Series

When Grant approached his most extensive series of work relating to music in 2019, based on the work of Frederick Delius, he harnessed a lifetime's experience of painting landscapes to an almost exhaustive level of research. Delius's own biography – his attraction to the mountains and fjords of Norway, and the pastoral setting of Grez-sur-Loing, in France, where he died – chimed with Grant's own. In the ensuing paintings we see familiar landscapes: fjords, rivers, forests. Some include in their titles allusions to specific pieces by Delius, such as *On Hearing the First Cuckoo in Spring*; others are simply named after their location or subject. But there are stranger, more surrealistic or complex sets of reference that distinguish certain paintings from their straightforward landscape counterparts. It is these that will be studied here.[10]

The research that Grant undertook provides an essential grounding for understanding his choice of subjects and why he approached them in specific ways. He already knew Delius's music well, but he now sought anything he could find, however obscure,

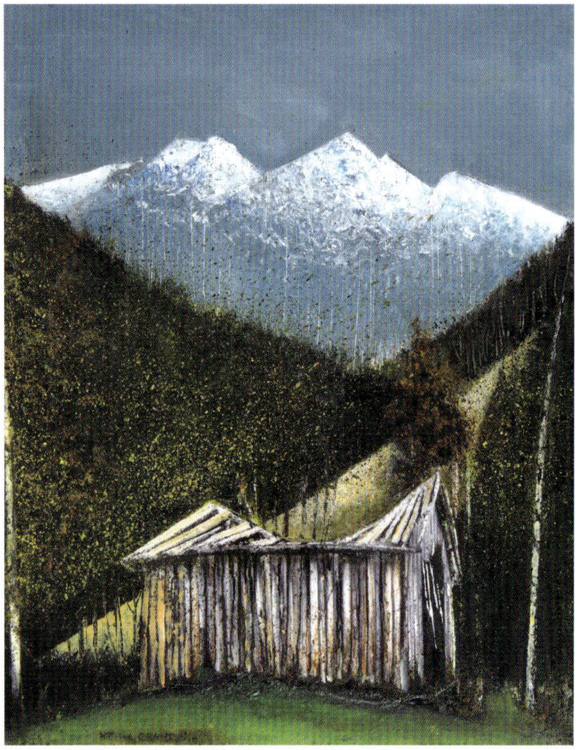

and listened to recordings daily in his studio. He read recent scholarly studies of Delius's music by Andrew Boyle and Daniel Grimley, addressing the significance of 'place', Eric Fenby's account of working with Delius towards the end of his life and watched Ken Russell's film, *Delius: Song of Summer* (1968), based on Fenby's book.[11] He visited the north of England, where Delius grew up, and Grez-sur-Loing, his home for over thirty years. In Grez-sur-Loing, Grant went to the house where Delius lived, made many drawings of the river that was so important to him and walked the road to Marlotte where Delius would think out his compositions. The books Grant read contained photographs of Delius's garden at the time he lived there, as well as cabins where he stayed while walking in the Norwegian mountains. These primary and secondary sources provided fertile material for transformation. Not least, Russell's *Song of Summer*, shot in black and white on 35 mm film, creates an indelible visual imprint of the composer and his landscapes. Seeing it in on its release, Kate Bush found it so haunting that ten years later, aged 20, she wrote her own tribute, *Delius (Song of Summer)* (1978): a mesmeric, harmonically complex song, accompanied subsequently by its own film, in which Bush dances as a swan and her brother, Paddy, is Delius – seated in a bath chair, a sun mask covering his face, gesturing feebly to the music.

Grant had his own potent aural memory from decades earlier: a Norwegian folk song, used by Delius in *On Hearing the First Cuckoo in Spring*, that features also in *Grant North*, sung by Pears. Grant knew already many of the landscapes evoked by Delius's music. He thus had no need to travel to Norway to discover places Delius had visited. Yet he did – refreshing his memory or looking for views or details that might inform or inspire his work. Travelling to Jotunheimen in June 2018, he saw a derelict cabin near the path Delius followed towards the mountains, where the composer might have sheltered, aged 27, when introduced to Jotunheimen by the older Edvard Grieg. From this view, Grant painted *The Derelict Hut, Jotunheimen* (2019), showing a crumpled wooden structure against folded mountains (fig.137). It is a characteristic composition: a mountainscape containing a triangle of snow that recalls both a flower and the crinoid fossil illustrated in Jacquetta Hawkes's *A Land* (1951). But there is something magical about the painting, dusted with the light

137
The Derelict Hut, Jotunheimen, 2019
Oil on linen with collage
40.5 × 33 cm
Collection of the artist

foliage of birch trees. Is it because Delius might have stayed there?

Delius's response to nature was matched by an acute ear for timbre and an often restless, extended approach to harmony that facilitated infinitesimally subtle changes in register. He used unfurling melody to imply journeys across landscape through time, widely separated orchestration to define space, a *decrescendo* or reduced forces to evoke distance, and solo instruments or voices to express solitude. A quickened tempo summons a storm, a timpani roll the rumble of thunder and the harp or celesta, shimmering within an orchestral texture, the appearance of stars. Cold is suggested, instantly, by the tense, crystalline timbre of strings in a high register. *The Song of the High Hills* (1911) opens with a plaintive exchange between violins and violas, closing with a dissonant G sharp minor ninth chord. Between the two, a gamut of effects expresses joy, exhilaration, but also (in Delius's words) 'the loneliness & melancholy of the high Solitudes & the grandeur of the wide far distances'.[12] Grant would paint at least thirty paintings based on Norway, under the sway of Delius's music.

The connection in *The Derelict Hut* is only tangential, through a landscape the composer might have seen. Elsewhere, the titles of Grant's paintings suggest specific pieces, singly or in combination. A painting titled *Ascent to the High Hills* (2018) points to Delius's *Song of the High Hills*, yet owes its imagery also to *A Mass of Life*, which describes a spiritual journey into the mountains through passages selected from Nietzsche's *Also sprach Zarathustra*. Combining the two, Grant emphasised the lonely asceticism of Zarathustra's journey by depicting steps, perilously crooked and uneven, carved from rock and shrouded with mist. His painting contrasts the solid with the transient to suggest – through light, colour and texture – the promise of transcendence. Grant had listened so frequently and attentively to Delius's music as to absorb and make its landscapes his own.

Russell's film, spanning the years when Fenby, a young composer, acted as amanuensis to the terminally ill Delius, contains a climactic flashback. Delius had insisted on seeing the sun set on the mountains of Norway one last time before losing his sight. Carried on an improvised sedan chair by Percy Grainger and a servant, they begin the ascent of Liahovda behind Delius's cabin at Lesjaskog. Cutting back to France, during a visit from Grainger, Delius tells how his wife, Jelka, had to help carry the chair when the servant sprained his wrist. The film reverts to Norway, Jelka and Grainger perspiring, Delius with eyes shut, the landscape disclosed in glimpses of rock and snow. Reaching the summit, the mist that threatened to engulf the view suddenly clears, and – as Delius recalls – 'there was the most glorious sunset'. The climax is relayed swiftly: a close-up of Delius's face cuts to the sun, then back to him, lying in bed, eyes shut. It lasts only ten seconds.

The impact is profound, heightened in the soundtrack by the moment at which voices appear in *The Song of the High Hills*, signifying, as Delius had earlier explained, 'Man in Nature': a presence that becomes increasingly faint, then vanishes.[13] The sunset is ephemeral. Grant's painting *A Song at Sunrise* (2018; fig.138) likewise embodies such a moment, its splendour mirroring the wide-eyed response of Delius (portrayed by Max Adrian) to his last sunset. The sun's aura acts as an inner frame, drawing the eye inward, away from the richly textured landscape. Surrounded by splintered, pearlescent colour, amid the glare

138
A Song at Sunrise, 2018
Oil on linen
115 × 132 cm
Collection of the artist

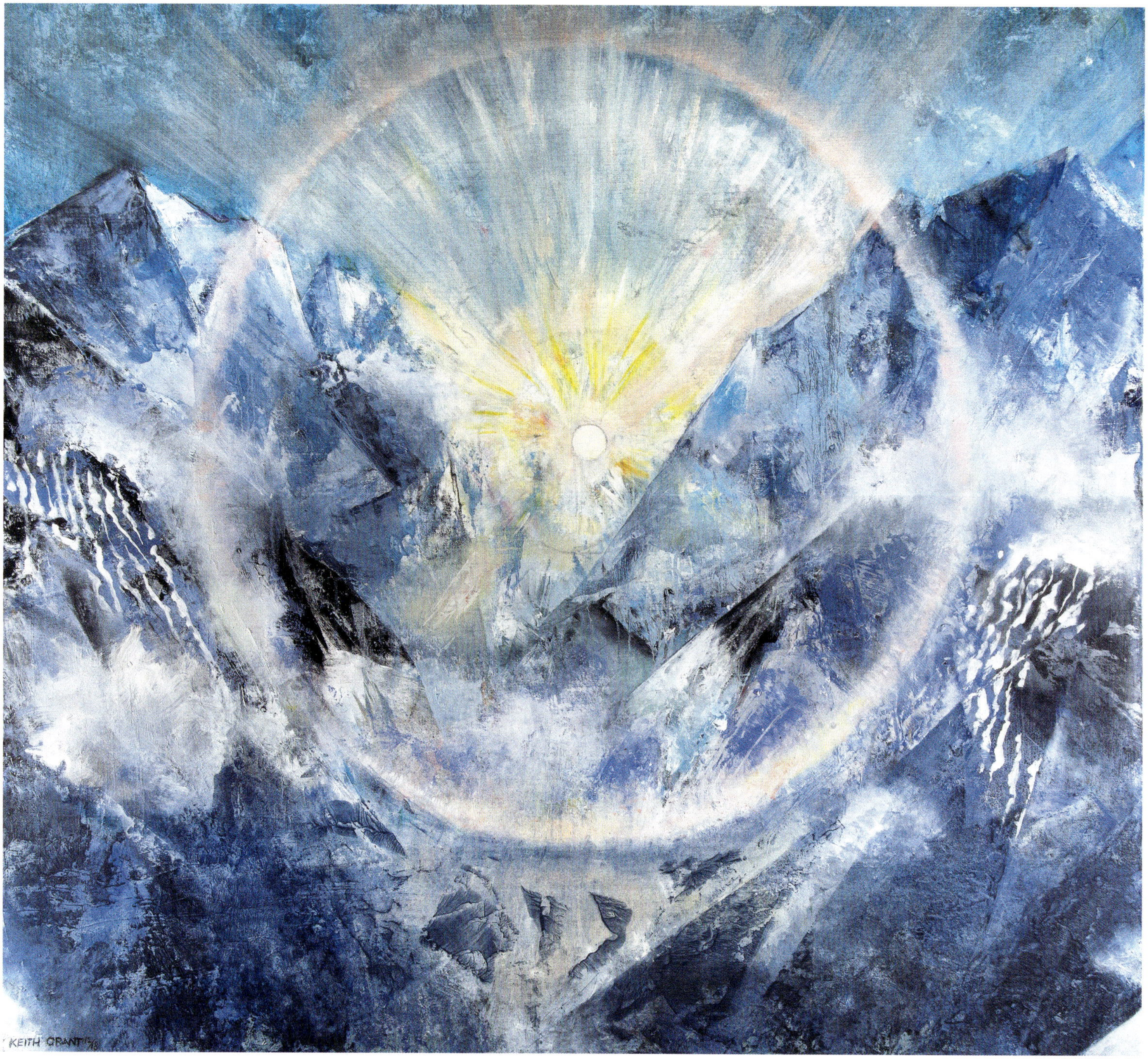

139
Rêverie du jardin de Jelka et Delius, Grez-sur-Loing, 2020
Oil on linen
38 × 45.5 cm
The David Game Collection, UK

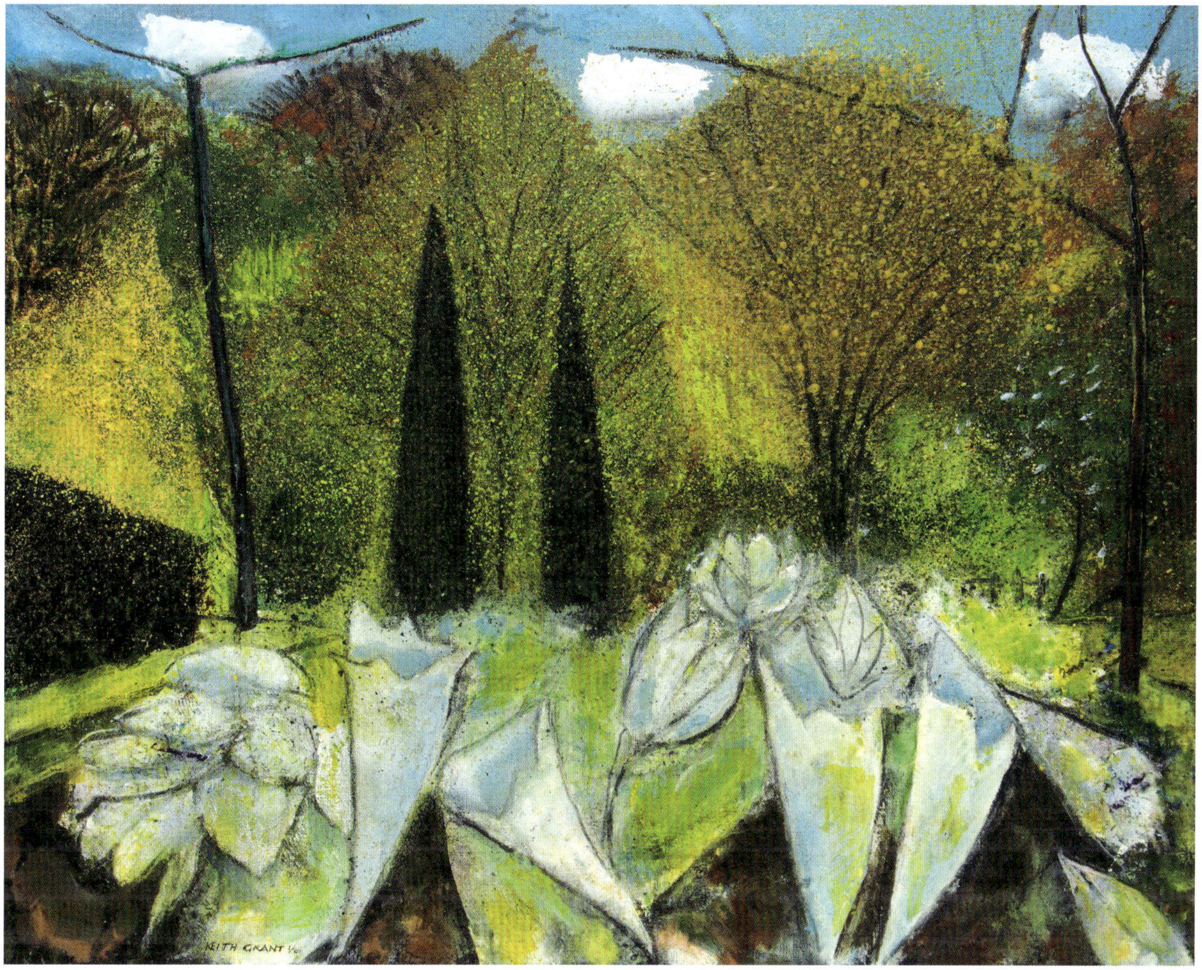

from the snow, the centre is dazzlingly white. While Grant's title references a different work (Delius's *A Song before Sunrise*), his painting stems from a prolonged consideration of *The Song of the High Hills*, which accompanied the mountain ascent in Russell's film, captured so sensitively by the cinematographer Dick Bush. Grant repeatedly simplified his painting to reflect, in his words, the 'geological structures of the mountains' and thus the structure of Delius's *Song of the High Hills*. He added, 'The best of Delius is of a nuanced complexity resulting in a unity with nature and music . . . which I hope to reflect in all the works of my Delius project.'[14]

Grant's paintings of France are different in timbre. Delius lived adjacent to the River Loing, which had attracted painters from artists' colonies nearby at Barbizon, Montigny and Marlotte since the mid-19th century. At Grez, the river Loing was slow-moving, bordered on one side by gardens and on the other by open meadows, characterised by a distinctive grey light in autumn.[15] Visiting in the 1870s, Robert Louis Stevenson described it as 'full of gentle attractions for the navigator: islanded reed-mazes, where, in autumn, the red berries cluster'.[16] Grant stood on the old stone bridge to draw, creating from his sketches a series of large compositions, across the seasons, that seek to distil the essence of Delius's many compositions based on rivers. In one drawing, however, Grant stood to one side, deftly capturing the solidity of the bridge, its geometric structure and canopy of trees.

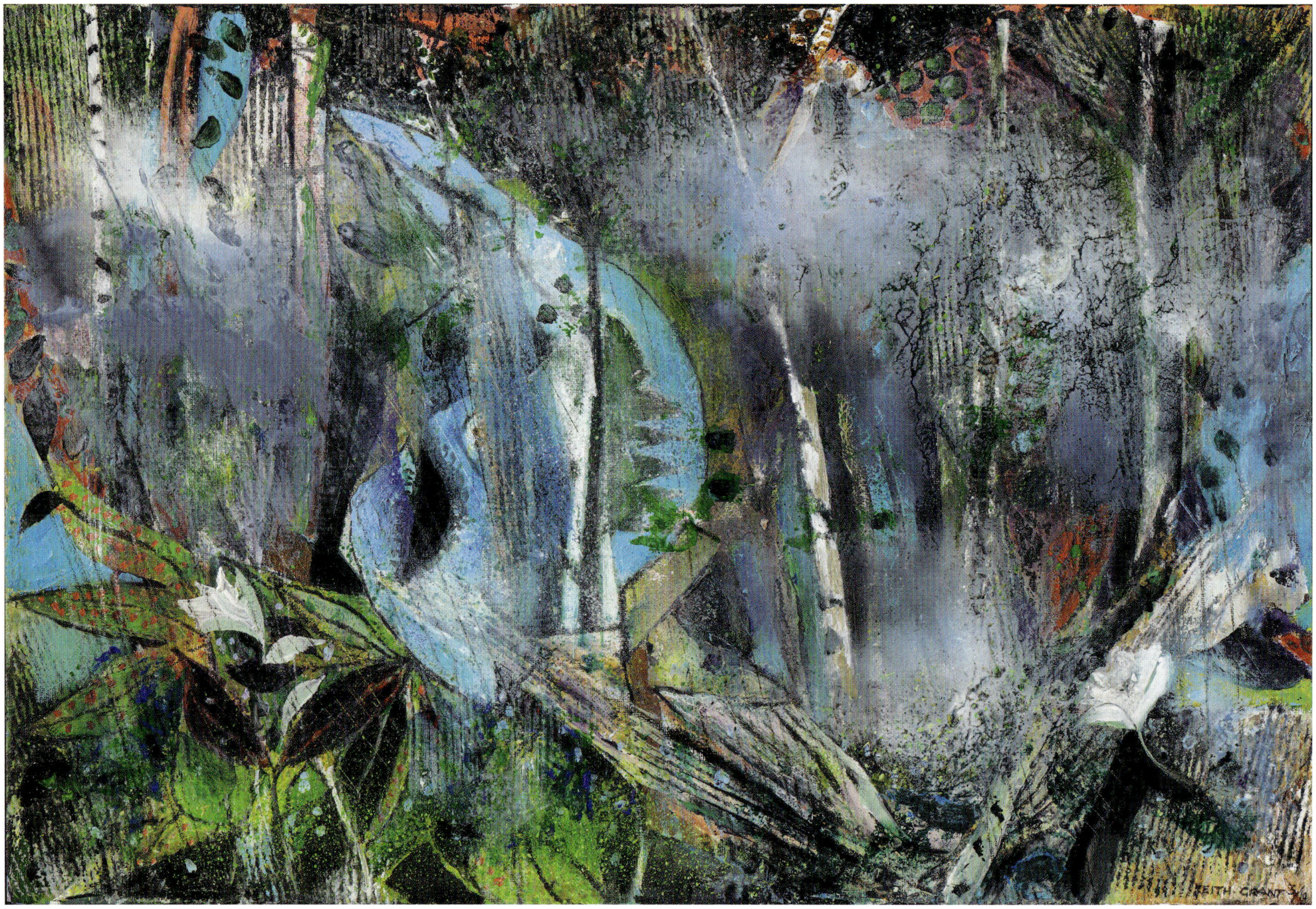

140
Rain in the Paradise Garden,
2019
Oil on linen
39 × 59.5 cm
The David Game Collection,
UK

Grant described his visits to Grez-sur-Loing, in spring and summer 2019, as 'beautiful and deeply poignant' but also 'profoundly disturbing'.[17] He was fortunate to visit the garden created and tended by Delius's wife, Jelka, where there had once been a kitchen garden to provide fruit and vegetables, and where flowers bloomed profusely from spring to summer. The garden had altered. From the terrace where Delius sat, Grant observed two cypresses against a backdrop of deciduous trees. *Rêverie du jardin de Jelka et Delius* (2020) conveys a strange mixture of lilies, convolvulus and 'Gloire de Dijon' roses in the foreground (fig.139). A dense bank of trees to the back, the composition encloses the trees' canopy with skeleton branches at odds with the season.

One of Delius's best-known works, 'The Walk to the Paradise Garden', was conceived to cover a scenery change in his opera, *A Village Romeo and Juliet* (1901). The plot concerns two young lovers, Sali and Vrenchen, who walk from a village fair to the 'Paradise Garden': an inn on a lonely hillside. Delius's luminous score suggests the couple's absorption in one another to the exclusion of the outside world. Yet the opera's overall trajectory is tragic, containing within it a sinister undercurrent that accounts for the force of the narrative. A tract of land, source of a rift between the couple's families, becomes increasingly wild, while the character of the Dark Fiddler appears intermittently, to tempt and threaten. It is this darker side that typifies Grant's paintings related to the work.

Rain in the Paradise Garden (2019) is dominated by a strange bloom, blue and hooded, that flowers amid the birch trees, lilies and forest foliage (fig.140). Grant began the painting with a presentiment of the woodland, followed by rain and mist, as he worked obsessively on the canvas: 'I wanted the notion of blossoms or some mysterious flowers . . . a calyx, or cup, a beaker-type shape, a bit like convolvulus . . . but the picture started to inform me as to what it wanted – what I could get away with next, what I could add to it, or subtract.'[18] Mist became crucial; sometimes high in the branches, sometimes to the sides, re-enclosing a closed world. Grant used the imprint of fabric to create parallel lines, relating them abstractly to tree trunks. In the painting, textures dissolve then coalesce, just as in Delius's 'The Walk to the Paradise Garden' solo lines emerge only to melt away, or be passed to other instruments.

Of all Grant's paintings relating to Delius, *Arabesque* (2020) is undoubtedly the most uncanny, responding to a score brimming with sensuality and latent violence (fig.141). Delius's text, by the Danish poet Jens Peter Jacobsen, equates a destructive passion with the brevity of the northern summer. From the outset he establishes a mood of brooding malevolence located in the forest's darkness. The musical language is intensely chromatic, harmonically unstable, coloured with the metallic glint of triangle and tambourine. Jacobsen describes 'a strange herb' that flowers fleetingly to resemble a frenzied eye. In Grant's painting, the white flower glows against a darkened backdrop, through which light penetrates in orange-green streaks. The flower's eye is equivocal: coolly observing, in a composition as expressively charged as the flower paintings of Georgia O'Keeffe.

With *The Listening Forest* (2019), Grant created an auditory equivalent, suggesting an entire woodland setting as sentient (fig.142). An open sheath crammed

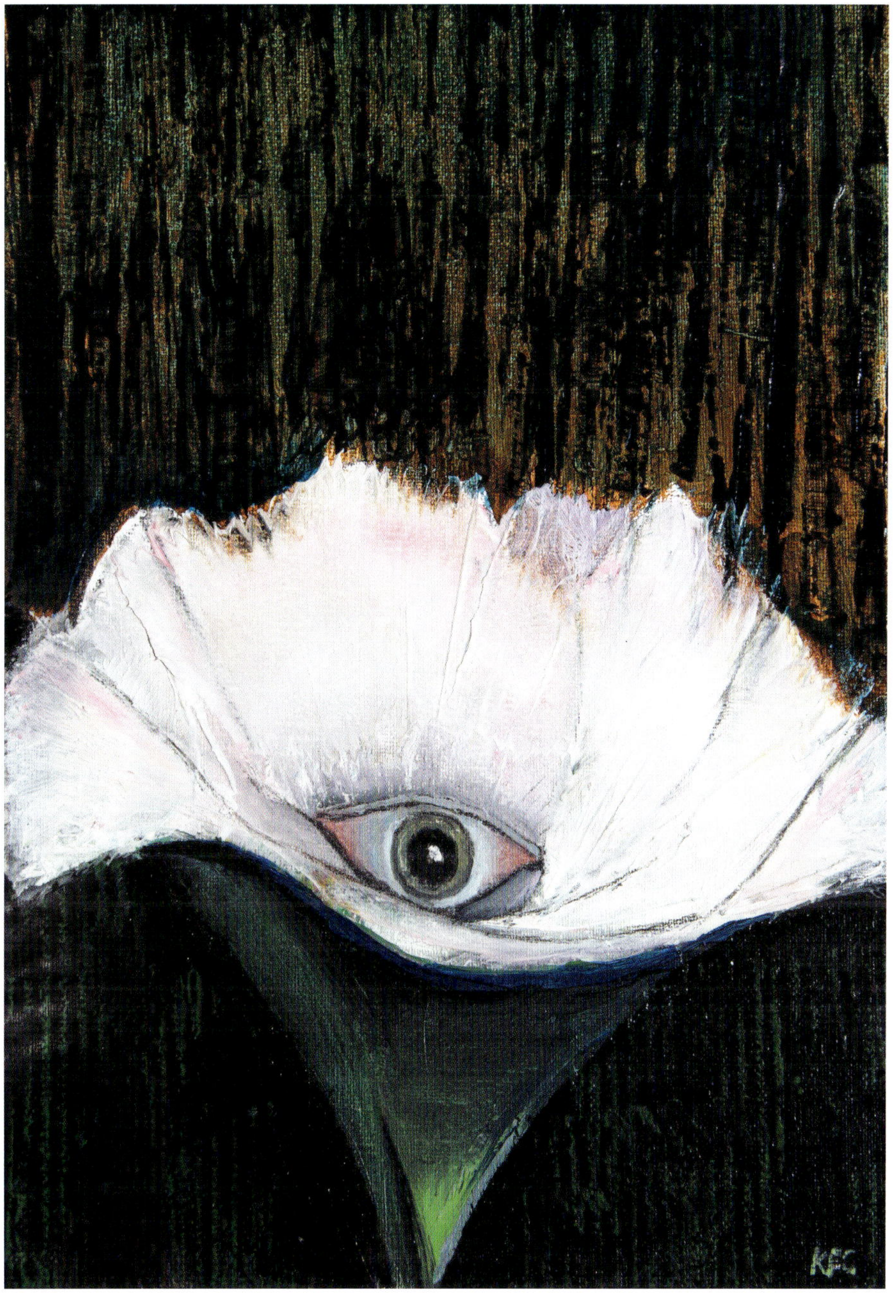

141
Arabesque, 2020
Oil on linen
24 × 19 cm
Private Collection, UK

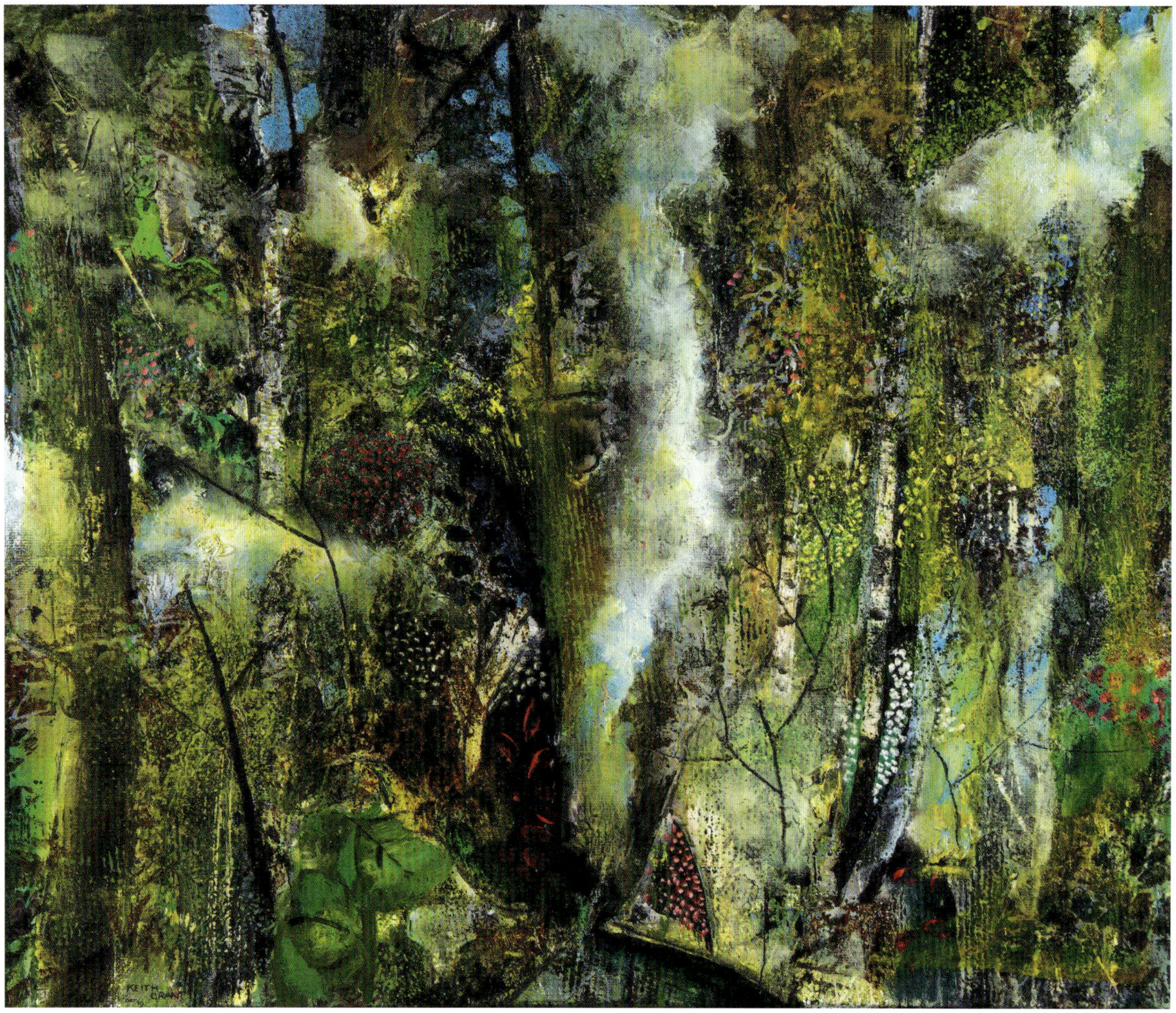

142
The Listening Forest, 2019
Oil on linen
59.5 × 70 cm
Private Collection, Luxembourg

with berries, a filigree of twigs and a lacework of flowers balance against the broader rhythm of repeated verticals. Between birch trunks, punctuated by daylight, weaves smoke from a fire. This is no facile equivalent to Delius's music, rather a tapestry weaving a parallel mystery. But a listening forest? Describing the painting, Grant wrote that 'the forest has anticipated our entrance and listens and looks at us as we attempt to evaluate our passage into or through it'.[19] In a subsequent painting, *The Intruding Forest* (2020), the forest not only looks but advances threateningly. Heavy brocade curtains gape to reveal a forest and thornbush replete with berries, the latter an escapee from other paintings by Grant, and other music by Delius. Curtains feature also in paintings relating to Delius's *Sea Drift*. This hybridising, of transgressing the integrity of his source material if not its spirit, is one of the most compelling, fertile aspects of Grant's *Delius* series.

Messiaen and Birdsong

Threading through Grant's choices of music are allusions to birdsong: Vaughan Williams's *The Lark Ascending*, Delius's *On Hearing the First Cuckoo*,

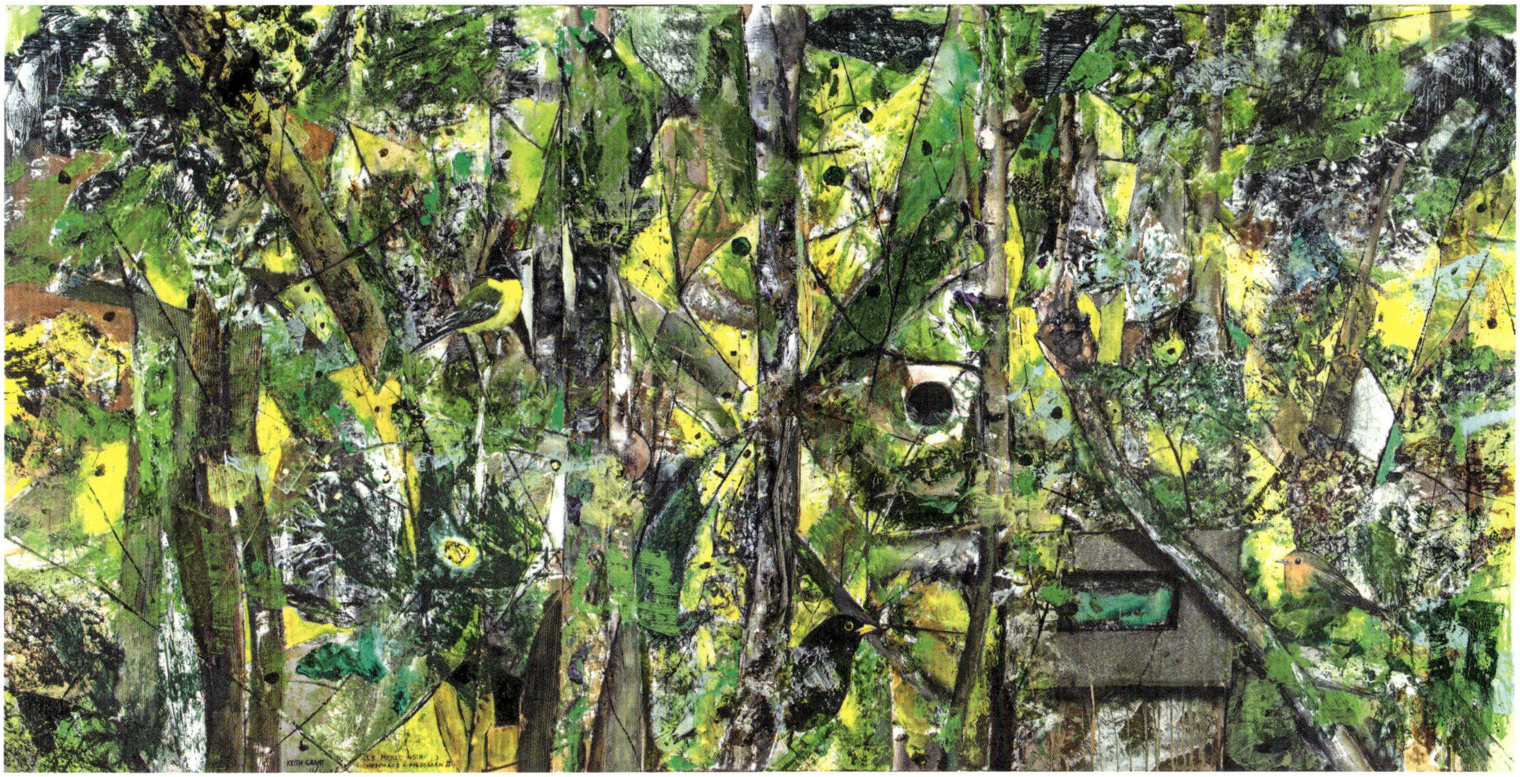

143
Hommage à Messiaen II: Le merle noir, 2015
Oil on canvas
100 × 200 cm
Collection of the artist

as well as *The Birds' Story*, sung by Felicity Lott and conducted by Eric Fenby. The music of Messiaen is first noted in Grant's journals in 1992, as he worked in Lewes on paintings of the night sky. He remarked, 'Messiaen means much to me – I am ignorant of all but a few works and those I know are early like "Quatuor pour la fin du temps".'[20] Two years later, he described 'Louange à l'éternité de Jésus', the fifth movement from *Quatuor pour la fin du temps* (*Quartet for the End of Time*), as at that moment the most beautiful music he knew:

Even if I did not know the composer's research into colour, into birdsong and into the vivid phenomena of nature I would still feel the affinity of his sound with my own subject matter and my own reasoning on the equivalents for the immanence of the spirit within natural forms. There are so many dimensional voices calling and declaiming in the 'Quatuor pour la fin du temps' that they parallel all possible visual exigencies.[21]

Quatuor pour la fin du temps (1941) was written during Messiaen's imprisonment in Silesia, now Poland, using pencils and manuscript paper given to him by a German soldier. The birdsong outside served as inspiration. Titling the third movement of the quartet 'Abîme des oiseaux' ('The Abyss of the Birds'), he included in it his first representation of a blackbird's song. A decade later, in 1951, he composed *Le merle noir* (*The Blackbird*) for flute and piano. Birdsong permeates Messiaen's music, as the result of memorising and transcription, eventually also studying recordings made by his wife, Yvonne Loriod. Messiaen could identify more than 500 birds by sound alone. He considered his transcriptions to be interpretations, 'just as a painting captures the essence rather than the surface of its subject', but moreover that the blackbird's song surpasses 'human imagination in fantasy'.[22] *Le merle noir* derives fundamentally from this song, containing flutter-tonguing, cadenzas, rhythms and phrases

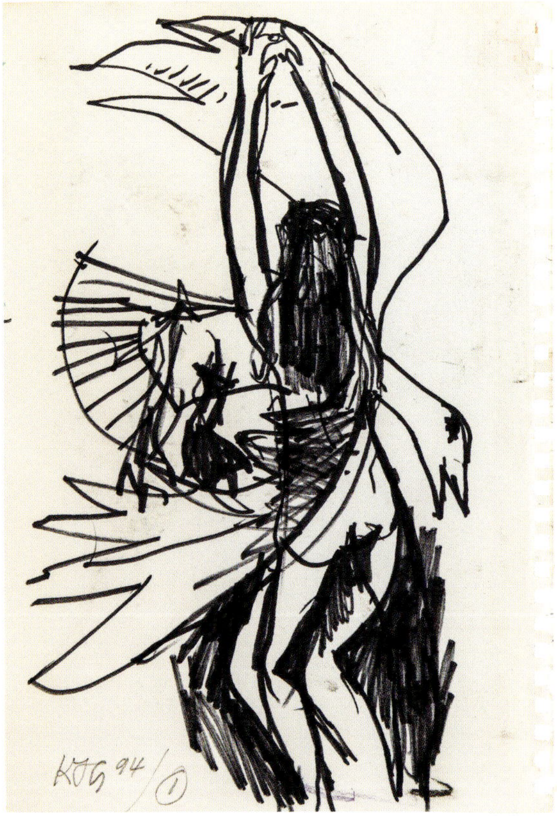

that tally with the length of the bird's iterations. It is an extraordinarily evocative piece, distilled into little more than five minutes in performance.

Grant's love of birds and birdsong make it almost inevitable that he would be drawn to Messiaen's music. Around the time of the metamorphosis series, in 2012, his inclusion of birds in his paintings altered from abstractions to quite specific depictions of British birds, especially wrens, blackbirds, bluetits or robins. In 2017, he painted *A Convocation of Birds* in homage to the naturalist Gilbert White: 84 precisely depicted birds in the setting of the Hanger at Selborne. Preceding this, however, were two homages to Messiaen. The first, *Catalogue des oiseaux* (2015), named after Messiaen's piano pieces, includes 15 small birds. The second, *Le merle noir* (2015), includes three: a blackbird, robin and yellow wagtail (fig.143). Setting these birds within a northern forest, Grant created a less surrealistic, more formalised counterpart to *The Ruined Cistern* (2014; fig.103, p.123). The cistern reappears to the lower right, yet it is the overall patterning of the composition, articulated with the black lines, matted textures and limpid tessellation of glass, that is so remarkable about this painting. Where Messiaen used techniques such as serialism, canon, ancient Greek and Hindu rhythms to structure his music, while perfectly conveying the plaintive 'cadence' of a blackbird's song, so Grant ordered his composition tautly without compromising its imagery's naturalness.

The *Kalevala*, Wagner and Sibelius

Myth reasserts itself intermittently in Grant's work, almost always in relation to the North. A key source, familiar to him since the 1960s, is the *Kalevala*: an epic of aural tradition that has inspired innumerable writers, artists and composers, not least Wagner. In the mid-1990s, Grant was involved in plans for a millennium production of Wagner's *Ring* for Opera North. The intermediary was his friend, Sir John Tomlinson, one of the finest operatic singers of his generation and a consummate interpreter of Wagner, particularly the role of Wotan. (Berkeley, explaining that it was Tomlinson who recommended Grant for *Private Passions*, joked that he had received a phone

144
Luonnotar, 1994
Pencil on paper
25 × 18 cm
The Lambirth Collection, UK

call 'from Wotan himself'.)[23] Among the designs Grant made for the projected *Ring* cycle was a model for *Das Rheingold*, showing the entrance to the Nibelung's cave as a triangular aperture in the rock face, behind a veil of suspended gold nuggets. He envisaged lighting effects inspired by the aurora, as a corollary to his night paintings. Despite enthusiasm for the project, it proved worryingly time-consuming. Grant was thus relieved when it foundered because of a change of directorship, freeing him to concentrate on painting.

Grant considered Sibelius's *Luonnotar*, inspired by the first canto of the *Kalevala*, over a span of several years. Its subject is essentially a creation myth: a young girl, 'bride of the air', descends to the sea where she swims for seven hundred years, before raising her knee above water. A teal, seeing it as a nest, lands and lays an egg. Yet the egg is too warm to bear: the girl lets it tumble and it breaks, the upper part becoming the dome of the heavens, the lower becoming the earth, with all its creatures. Sibelius's tone poem is visionary, juxtaposing an unsettled orchestral texture, for the sea, against a vocal line based on Finnish runic singing, simulating weeping. In autumn 1986, Grant mused, 'How could it be possible to make large pictures of the 1st Runo of the Kalevala? – only by not painting the descriptive imagery no matter how enchanting, no matter how easily the young female form may ebb and flow in the waves, with glimmers of lustrous white.'[24] Inspired by Picasso's sketchbooks in a recent exhibition at the Royal Academy, he made drawings he almost instantly rejected as too illustrative, needing to be pared of sentimentality without a loss of sensuality. The drawings were not developed further. At the time, he was painting works based on the lagoon at Venice amidst still-unfinished paintings of Korup.

A subsequent set of drawings from 1994, although annotated 'Luonnotar', appear to depict a girl and swan, rather than a teal. Indeed, Grant later identified them as relating to Yeats's poem *Leda and the Swan*, as well as to Sidney Nolan's paintings on the same subject.[25] Grant's drawings are both sensual and ambiguous: counterparts to Sibelius's music while referencing the violent sexual encounter between Leda and Zeus, disguised as a swan (fig.144). Nolan's own *Leda* series, exhibited in 1960 at the Matthiesen Gallery in London, and consisting of 45 works executed fluidly and abstractly, was as remarkable as his Ned Kelly paintings at the Redfern Gallery in 1955. Again, Grant did not develop his drawings, having several times thought of destroying them as expressions of 'juvenile desire'.[26] That *Luonnotar* was significant, nonetheless, can be inferred from the symbolic inclusion of an egg, often in situations of threat, in paintings from early and later periods of Grant's career.

Myth provided the motivation, too, for works on the subject of Baldur: the Viking sun god, protected by nature. Loki, the fire god, deciding to kill Baldur, wielded an 'unnatural' object – a mistletoe bough. Baldur's body was placed in a boat, pushed out to sea and set alight. The whole of nature wept for him as the sun set, symbolising the day's cycle and the yearly melting of ice and snow in the thaw. In 2016, Grant painted a set of seascapes titled *Baldur's Death*, in which smoke indicates the floating funeral pyre. Preceding these, however, was a composition in which Baldur's boat features as a tiny emblem in the top right-hand corner. *Transfiguration* (2015) juxtaposes memories of the blockhouses at

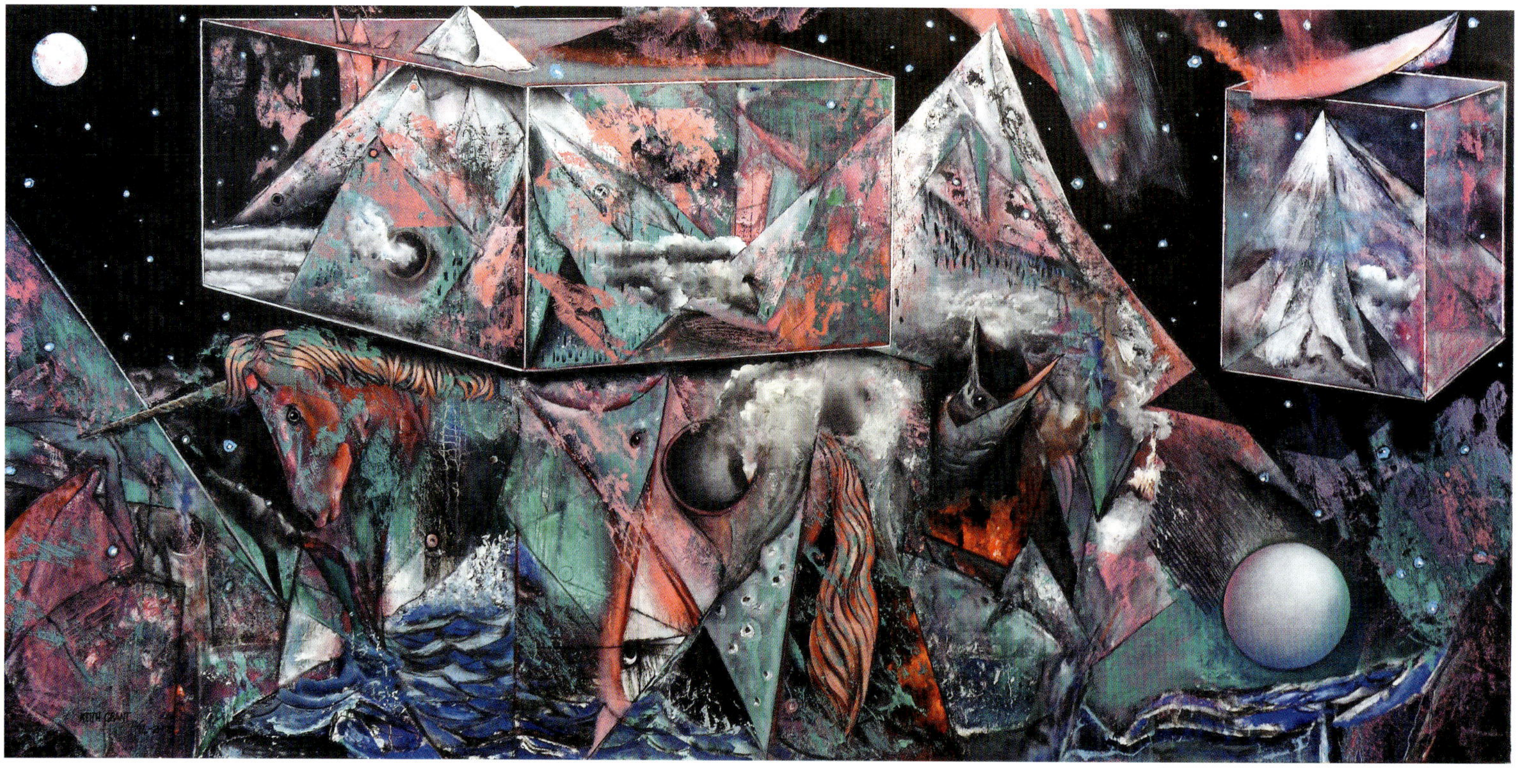

Lødingen with a mythical unicorn, long admired by Grant from French tapestries (fig.145). A white sphere alludes to Goethe's description of an artist as one who stoops 'above a fast-running stream and [lifts] a perfect sphere from the clear water'.[27] Yet there are Wagnerian references too, in admiration for Tomlinson: a memory of Surtsey that is also Brünnhilde's ring of fire, and a mysterious exhalation from a cave, perhaps from the dragon guarding the Nibelung's treasure. One of Tomlinson's most celebrated moments as Wotan is his singing 'farewell', as he kisses his daughter, Brünnhilde, to sleep and encircles her with flames.

Interviewed for *Private Passions*, Grant related Baldur to John McLeod's *The Gokstad Ship* (1982), based on a beautifully constructed vessel preserved in the Viking Ship Museum in Oslo. McLeod's composition uses 16-note patterns to reflect the ship's 32 planks: 16 on either side. Listening to this music, echoes of Britten's tonal and melodic language inevitably complete a circle. The Gokstad ship recalls Baldur's death, but also the fisherman Peter Grimes, who, having been judged guilty of murdering his apprentice, was ordered to sail out to sea and sink his boat.

145
Transfiguration, 2015
Oil on canvas
100 × 200 cm
Collection of the artist

Coda

Can pictures, like landscapes, have ghosts? The last, perhaps most unexpected choice in Grant's *Private Passions* was a movement from *Cantus Arcticus* by Rautavaara. The movement in question, 'The Bog', splices recordings of wild birds in counterpoint with the orchestra, which also imitates bird sounds to evoke a disturbingly alien landscape: one described by Grant as 'the most wonderful expression of the North'.[28] A painting titled *Proscenium Arcticus* developed between 2012 and 2013 from an island seascape at night to a version with stars as 'strings of jewels or pearls', after a line from Arthur Rimbaud's 'Phrases', in *Les Illuminations*.[29] In 2016 Grant removed the islands, substituting a harbour 'as a kind of marine "sanctuary" garden', with the sky and distance suggesting the tenuous nature of humankind's 'possession' of the earth.[30] Overlaying the night sky with a mauve-green aurora, he titled this third version *Cantus Arcticus*, echoing the work by Rautavaara. Yet this was not the end: a fourth version, in 2021, transformed the work irrevocably to *Song of the Aurora* (fig.96, p.115). Listening to Rautavaara, it is tempting to imagine that a visual equivalent to *Cantus Arcticus* remains beyond reach, resisting a fixed countenance.

There is always capacity for change in the search for a definitive expression, needing only a prompt to release it. In 2020 Grant discovered Karol Szymanowski's Third Symphony, 'Song of the Night', having known works such as his *Stabat Mater* and *Love Songs of Hafiz* for years. He was instantly enthused, playing the recording incessantly. The music formed the perfect accompaniment to the text of the ancient Persian poem by the Sufi poet Jalal al-Din Rumi, as Grant wrote:

I knew that I had come upon a perfect matrix of sound full of the sonorities and all-pervading spatial enigma of the Night and because this music . . . was for me a 'cosmic' expression, I felt I could find within it an abstract dimensionality. A further thought-provoking aspect of Song of the Night was its association with Islamic culture and its long history of astronomical investigations and discoveries.[31]

Grant's triptych, *Song of the Night*, takes its title from Szymanowski's Third Symphony. The first painting, *The Cosmos Touches the Sea*, is a freer interpretation of *Night, Firmament Divided from the Waters* (fig.93, p.113) – an abstracted evocation of the universe benefiting from the many observations Grant had made in sub-Arctic Norway, Greenland and the tropics. The second, *Star Mirror*, derives from sketches made while crossing the Tysfjord in north Norway, seeking to convey its 'surreal stillness and visual purity' through peaks that resemble icebergs, a shimmering reflection of the largest island, and darkness contrasting with the snow-covered mountains (fig.146). Lastly, *Winter Landscape Illuminated by the Moon, Geilo, Norway* recalls a night of intense cold, when the sky blazed with starlight.[32] None of these paintings breaks compositional new ground; rather, as with Bach's music, they build upon earlier expressions to create works of greater depth and refinement.

Returning in 2023 to the subject of the river in Grez-sur-Loing, Grant sharpened his vision (fig.147). For the first time he included both the edge of the bridge and a stone buttress, projecting into the water. The riverbanks are subject to their most geometrical rendering yet, the sky and reflections executed flawlessly. Across the composition falls a perfect stillness.

146

Song of the Night II: Star Mirror, Tysfjord, Norway, 2020
Oil on linen
111 × 121 cm
The David Game Collection, UK

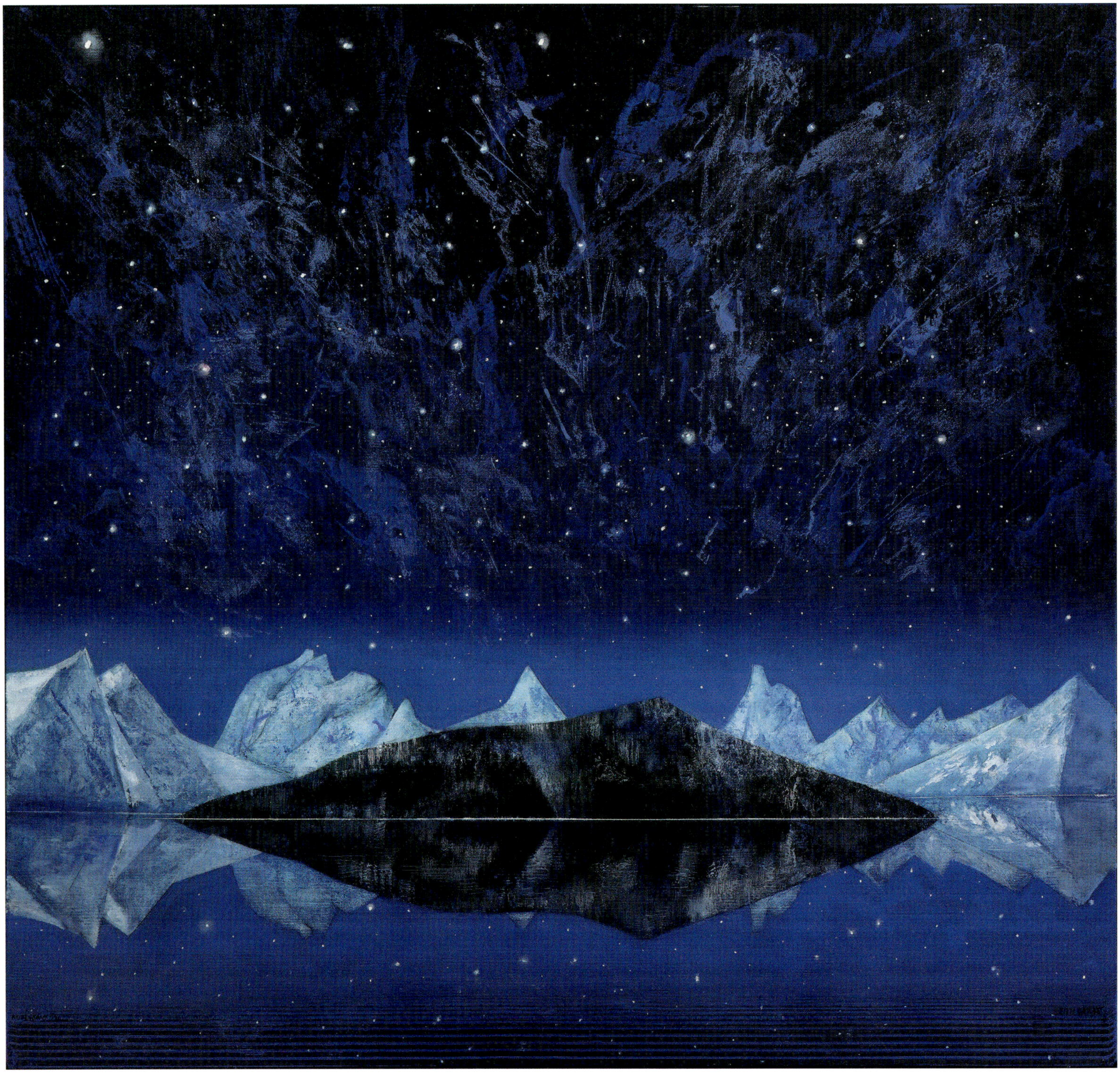

147
From the Old Bridge,
Grez-sur-Loing, France, 2023
Oil on linen
80 × 100 cm
Collection of the artist

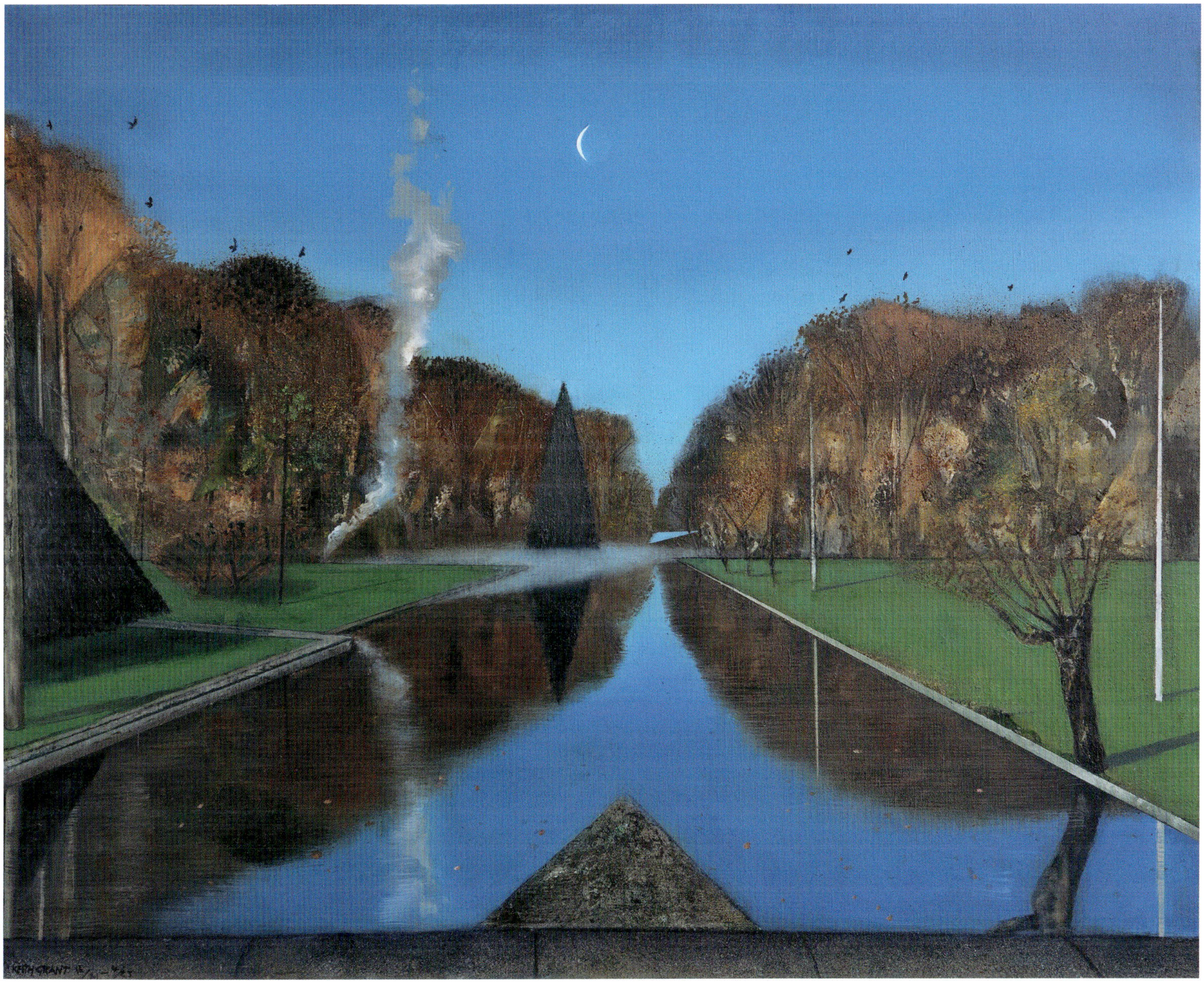

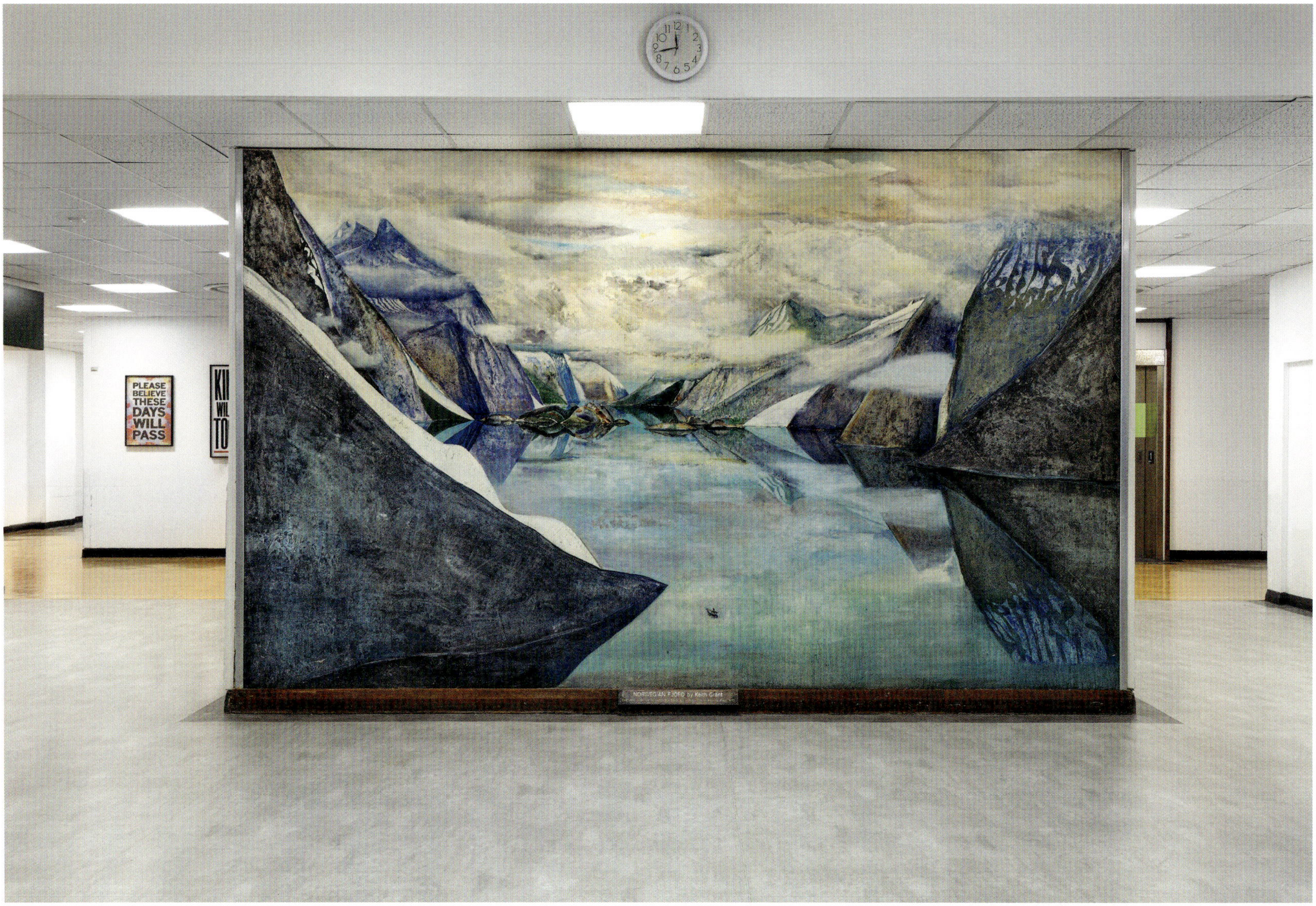
PLEASE BELIEVE THESE DAYS WILL PASS
NORWEGIAN FJORD by Keith Grant

9

Beyond the Gallery

148
Norwegian Fjord, 1975
Oil on panel
252 × 434 cm
Charing Cross Hospital, Imperial Health Charity Art Collection, London

In early November 1964, Grant accompanied Dr Richard Hunter to the Friern Hospital at Barnet in north London, with a view to placing paintings in the wards. Hunter had emigrated from Germany with his family in the 1930s and qualified as a doctor in 1946. Despite initially wanting to become a surgeon, he became increasingly interested in psychiatry. The Friern Hospital, where he was appointed consultant psychiatrist in 1963, was described in contemporary accounts as forbidding: a long, dimly lit corridor (apparently the longest in Europe, at a quarter of a mile), along which were thirty or forty open-plan wards crammed with beds. The patients were segregated into wards or cells in a building that was unclean, dilapidated and in winter so cold that bedpans would freeze.[1] Grant was appalled. The experience recalled for him the seven weeks he spent in a polio ward following his ill-fated attempt to sail to Norway in 1960, where he witnessed patients unable to move and articulated by machines, yet striving to continue a fragile existence. Faced with the conditions at Friern, he recorded in his journal, 'I have not been more shaken, more full of sympathy and more unable to give any help – help that I would love to give – to ease my anger and sadness.'[2]

Art in Hospitals

It was a full decade before Grant was commissioned to make his first site-specific work for a hospital. In June 1975, following discussions with Nigel Weaver, District Administrator and Chief Officer of Charing Cross Hospital, Grant recorded plans for a large 'life affirmative' painting, in colours to suggest space, stillness and a reverence for the miracle and majesty of nature.[3]

The commission was supported by the Edwin Austin Abbey Memorial Trust Fund for Mural Painting, whose previous recipients included Richard Eurich, Leonard Rosoman and Carel Weight. Grant based his design on reflections in a Norwegian fjord. Working in the hospital itself, he began to feel that his presence was making a contribution beyond the final painting. One day he had an audience of patients with speech difficulties, whom he was able to engage in response to his work, although ironically when the BBC filmed Grant, for a documentary on art in the community, onlookers were conspicuously absent.[4]

Norwegian Fjord (1975) is permanently installed on the first floor of Charing Cross Hospital (fig.148). Sited near the top of the main escalator, at the centre of a concourse serving the adjacent cafe, lifts

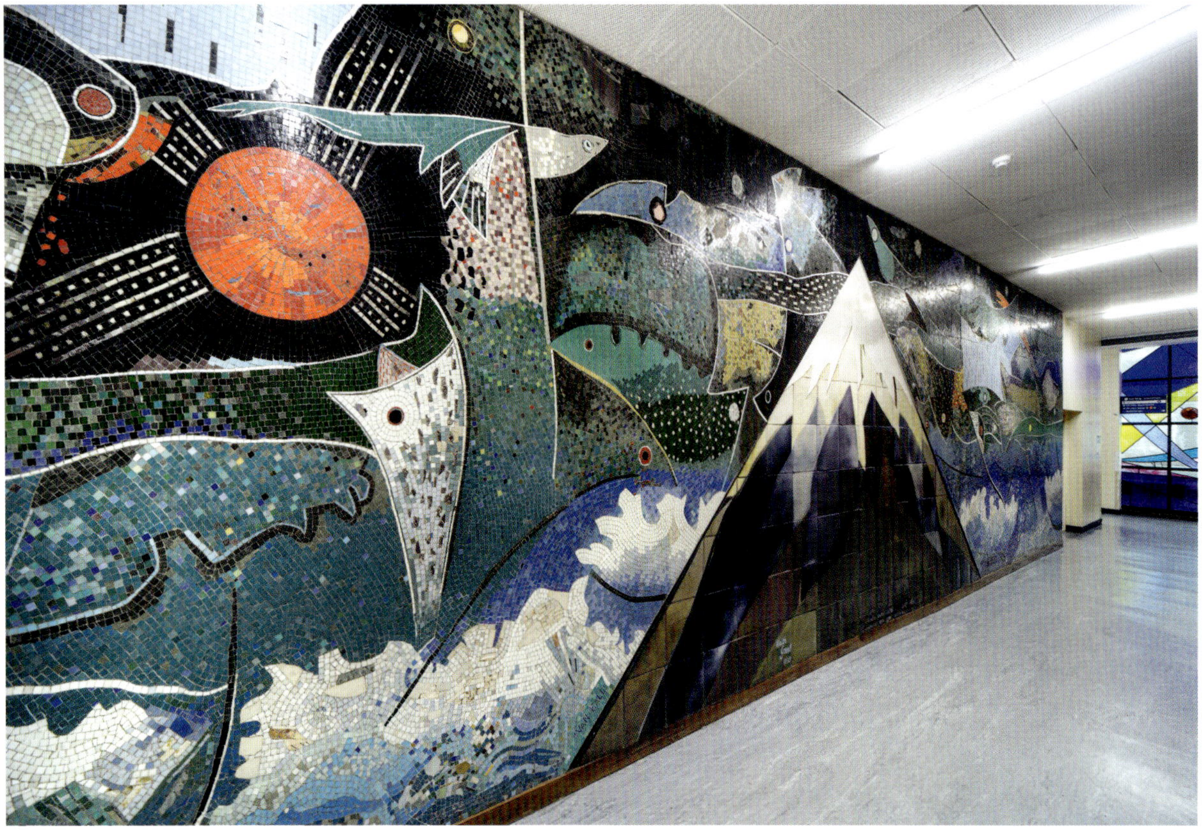

149
The Magic Mountain, 1979, installed in 1980
Mosaic
2.3 x 20 m
Charing Cross Hospital, Imperial Health Charity Art Collection, London

and corridors, it provides a point for contemplation – a cool, expansive landscape amid the bustle and distraction of the hospital. The colour blue is especially calming in this context; red, conversely, being a colour that patients can find upsetting. In 2022, when the mural was photographed, it made a reassuring contrast with Mark Titchner's poster-style artwork *Please Believe These Days Will Pass*, as well as the still mandatory wearing of face masks by visitors and staff.

The collections of the Imperial Health Charity are particularly rich in works by Grant. In late 1980, a mosaic mural was installed in a ground floor corridor at Charing Cross Hospital, instantly brightening the environment (fig.149). *The Magic Mountain* extended the idea of community art, being made by local unemployed young people under Grant's supervision, with funding from the Government's Manpower Services Commission. Those involved, whose names were credited in the mural's design, were encouraged to consider further studies in art.[5] *Norwegian Fjord* and *The Magic Mountain* each relate to work Grant was creating at the time, the former representative of his 'reflection' paintings, the latter his 'pyramid peaks'. This would be the case with all Grant's commissions, whose subject matter – landscape and nature – is indivisible from his painting.

The gestation of *The Magic Mountain* was relatively slow, however. In February 1978, when Grant was in the National Gallery in Oslo, he studied mosaics by the 20th-century German artist Rolf Nesch. Nesch's use of mica and copper, as well as the variety of depth introduced into his compositions, distinguishes his mosaics, or *Material-Bilde* ('material images'), from more traditional examples of the medium. Although Grant had never used mosaic before, he interpreted his design inventively, combining different materials, sizes of tesserae and glazes. At the centre, the magic mountain stands proud in relief, assembled from cut marble as well as a grid of the largest tiles in the composition, subtly glazed to create the effect of mist. Around the mountain swirls a maelstrom of mythically inspired imagery: fish, a sun, birds, fossils, clouds and sea. The work's title derives from Thomas Mann's *The Magic Mountain* (1924), a novel whose narrative takes place at a sanatorium high in the Swiss Alps.

The reiteration of the pyramid peak, a powerful symbol within Grant's work, caused him to reflect on repetition through a statement from Cesare Pavese's diaries:

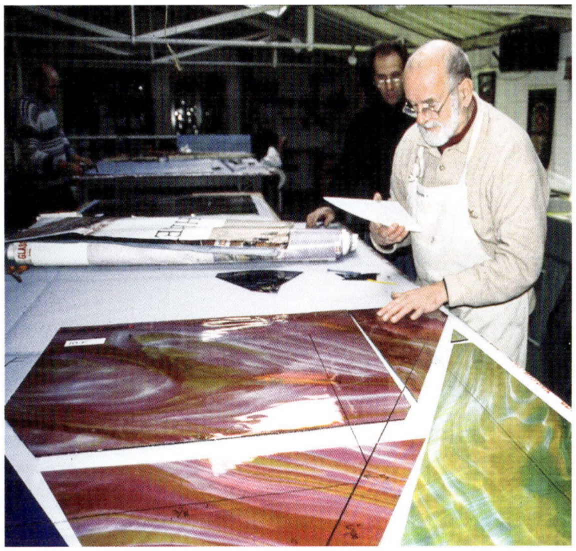

150
Keith Grant making *Millennium Window I*, 1999, for Charing Cross Hospital, London, with Marc Gerstein in the Lead & Light workshop, Camden

If, as Pavese says 'the story of an artist is the successive improvement upon the technique employed in his previous work, with a fresh creation that imposes a more complex aesthetic law', excitement with one's subject . . . could lead to 'static technique'. Perhaps my work has been too scornful of process – and perhaps there is a point at which to stop re-searching into a well known subject and allow the experiences of the past to operate as they should from the vast reserve of visual data I have, I hope, accumulated in the north.

The design of the Pyramid for Charing + mosaic seems to imply this – there is a simplicity which I think I have married to the scale exactly. The rich textures of the glazes express the essence of the absent detail.[6]

The counterplay between experience and renewal was demonstrated on its largest scale in two further site-specific commissions for Charing Cross Hospital. A proposal was made to enhance the entrance to the building, where large windows overlook a central loading bay and refuse area. Grant's suggestion was to obscure this view with stained glass, with the result that a window 12 x 7.5 m was commissioned, costing £100,000 and taking five people seven weeks to complete. Grant and his wife, Hilde, travelled to the north of England to select glass and Grant undertook the minimal painting required. The design was cut and assembled by the Lead & Light workshop in Camden, whose director, Marc Gerstein, described the result as an 'ocean of glass' (fig.150).[7]

Grant's design, an abstract interpretation of the cosmos, was installed in December 1999 as the first of two millennium windows at the hospital (fig.151). Too large to be apprehended from a single viewpoint, it forms a wall of coloured light seen partially from the ground floor, via the escalators that cut across it, or at greater leisure from the first-floor balcony, near where *Norwegian Fjord* is

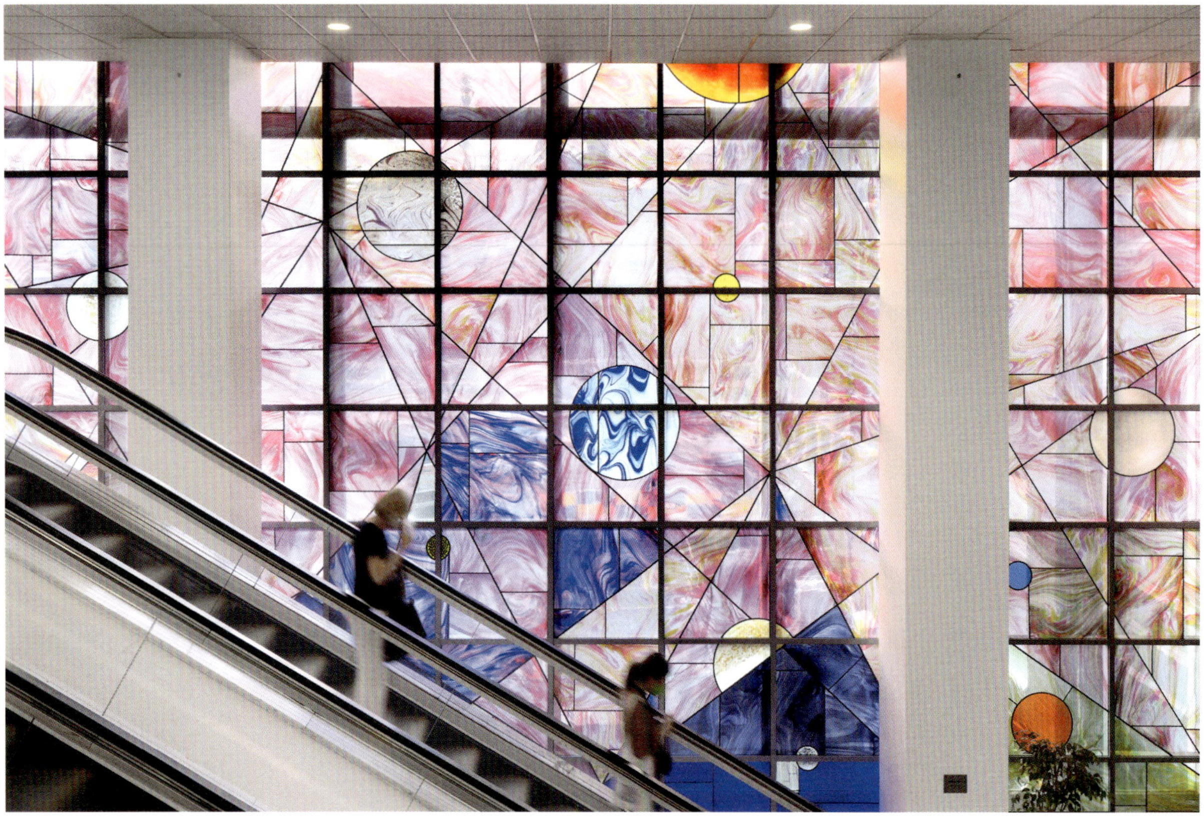

151
Millennium New World I, 2000
Stained glass
7.5 x 12.5 m
Charing Cross Hospital, Imperial Health Charity Art Collection, London

installed. The imagery can be traced back to Grant's particle storm and cosmos paintings. Here, however, the design is both magnified and simplified to maximise the impact of the 'streaky' glass, in which colour, as well as gold, is swirled into the mix. The medium is beautifully handled, the effect ethereal, emphasising the sense of space within the atrium.

A second window, located at right-angles to *The Magic Mountain*, demanded a greater intensity of colour to screen the outside view (fig.152). Grant used tones of blue, red and purple, allied to a more directional design flowing in parallel with the corridor. Watching patients, sometimes with crutches or walking slowly, it becomes clear that the window is more than decorative. Pausing, it becomes a welcome distraction. Through its vibrancy it provides motivation to continue along a route that might otherwise seem interminable.

Tyne & Wear Metro

The Magic Mountain created an important precedent for Grant. Commissioned to make a mosaic for the new Metro in Gateshead, he devised a project to involve students at Newcastle Polytechnic as well as young people employed through the Manpower Services Commission. Grant had acted as catalyst for this commission through an approach to the Public Transport Executive. Not only was it the first example of public art in Gateshead, but it opened opportunities for artists to create work for a further 14 stations in the Tyne & Wear Metro system. As the initiative gained momentum it became one of the largest schemes to date in the UK, with support from the Arts Council of Great Britain, Northern Arts, the Crafts Council, Newcastle Polytechnic and the vitreous enamelling company ESCOL Ltd, who supplied studio space and technical facilities.[8] Gateshead Metro

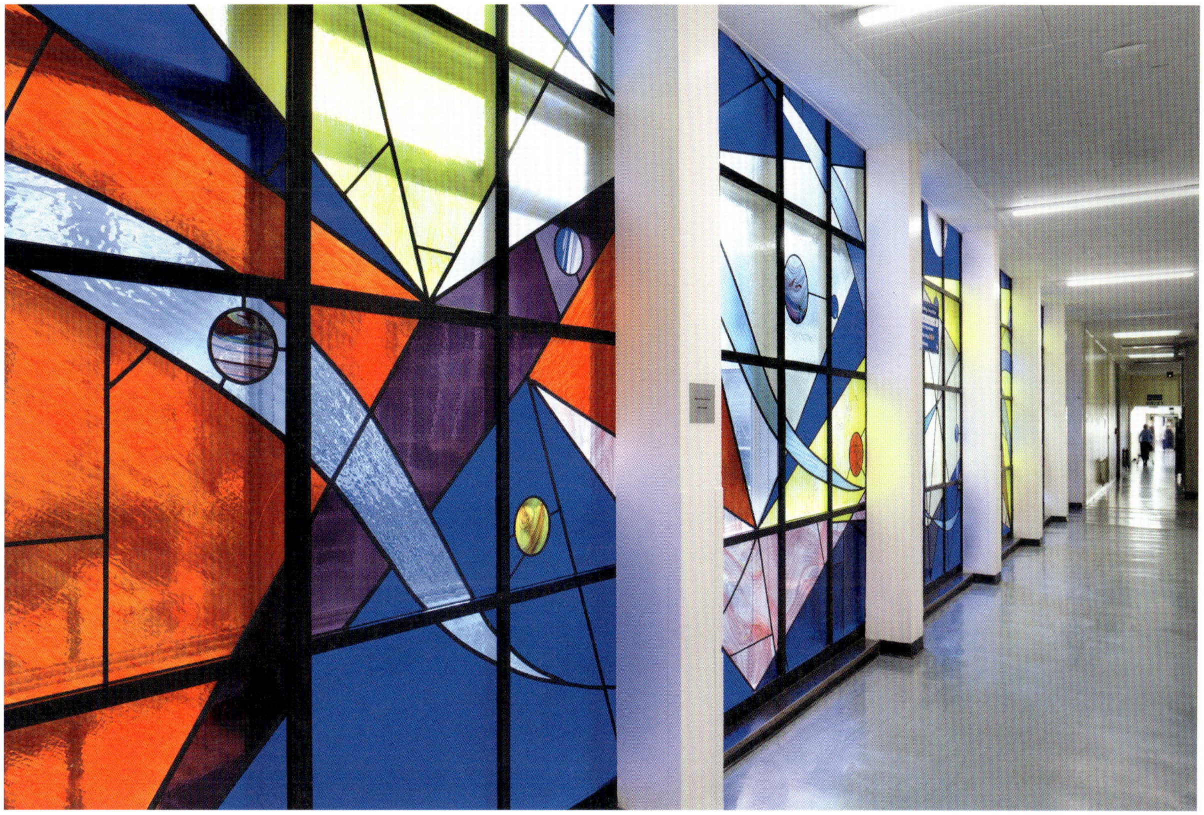

152
Millennium New World II, 2000
Stained glass
2.3 x 20 m
Charing Cross Hospital, Imperial Health Charity Art Collection, London

was officially opened on 6 November 1980 by Queen Elizabeth II, standing in front of Grant's mosaic, *Nocturnal Landscape*. Two months earlier, as part of the festival 'Newcastle 900', celebrating the centuries-long connection between Norway and Northumbria, Newcastle Polytechnic Gallery held an exhibition of Edvard Munch's paintings, selected by Grant from the Munch Museum in Oslo.

Nocturnal Landscape (1980) drew inspiration from a 19th-century Japanese woodblock print, elided with Grant's vision of an archetypal Norwegian landscape. Skilfully and sensitively translated to mosaic, it creates a work so apt for its medium that it exceeds the possibility of painting. The water is textured mysteriously in knots, the mountains sculpted as if from soapstone, while the moonlight shimmers and glints. The mosaic tesserae were imported from Italy and laid onto nine plywood panels, to facilitate transport and installation. Grant designed and oversaw the realisation of two further panels, for the platforms below at Gateshead Metro. *Night* and *Day* (1982–3) symbolise a transport system that never stops. Each features a pyramid peak: *Night* against a midnight sky and *Day*, a particularly Japanese-inspired design, with a foreground of stylised clouds (fig.153).

Art in the Community

Grant's three Metro mosaics, made between 1980 and 1983, straddled his teaching appointments at Newcastle Polytechnic and Roehampton Institute. Later at Roehampton, when he was artist-in-residence, Grant led a programme entitled 'Art in a Community Context', which taught students skills such as mosaic-making as well as the processes of researching, securing and realising public commissions. Grant's

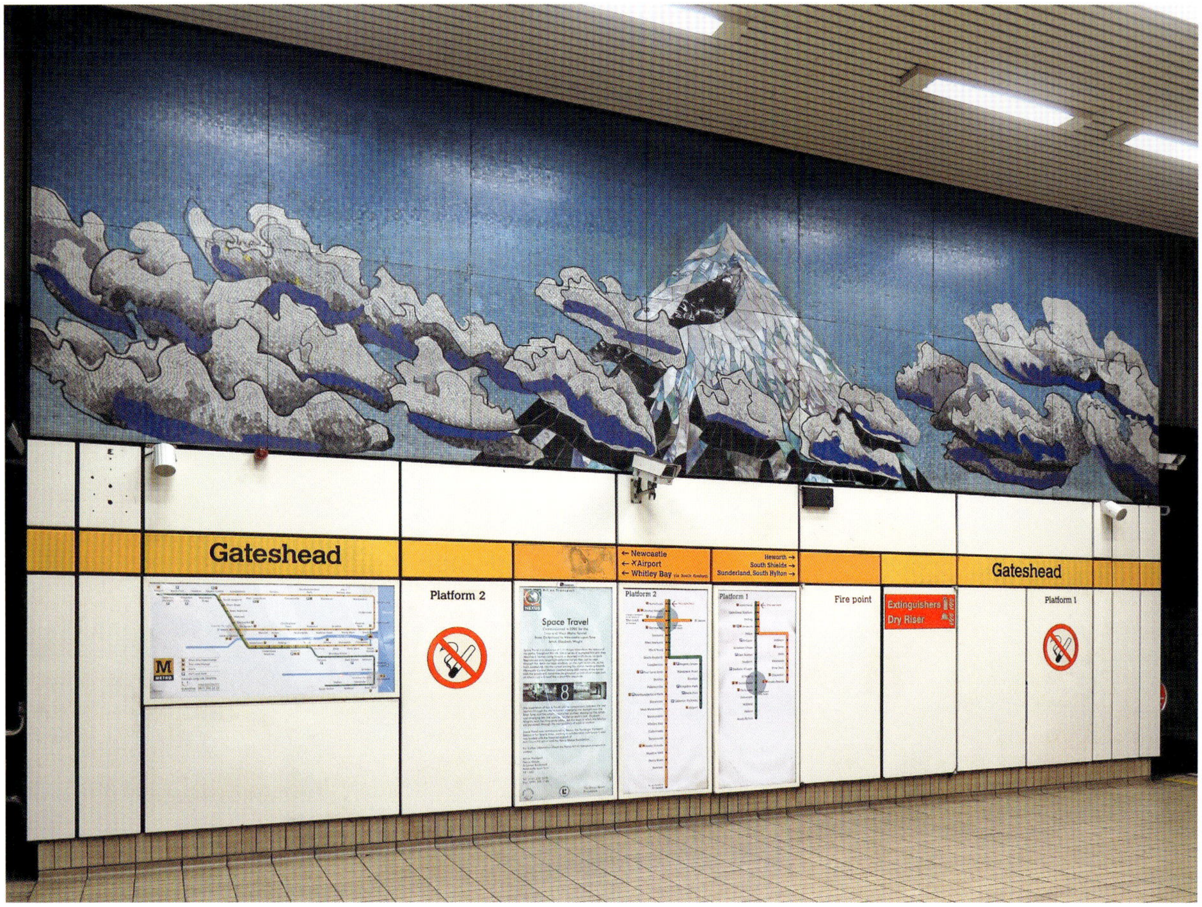

153
Day, from *Night and Day*,
1982–3
Mosaic
2 x 7 m
Gateshead Metro

own practical expertise had begun through tuition at Willesden School of Art, although it was informed more fundamentally by his own interests. Archaeology led to his knowledge of the construction of Roman mosaics, while his curiosity about the techniques of stained glass encouraged him to visit the studio of Patrick Reyntiens, maker of John Piper's stained glass and one of the foremost artist-craftsmen of the 20th century. The course at Roehampton focused on materials such as ceramic tiles and laminated glass for their intrinsic beauty, durability and ease of maintenance. As Grant emphasised, once art is introduced into a public context it often leads to a sense of pride, encouraging residents and local authorities to improve the surrounding areas.

Aside from the Charing Cross and Gateshead mosaics, Grant worked as a community artist in a more fundamental sense than is often understood today, where a project might 'buy in' the services of an artist to work with sectors of the public. From the time of his studies at the Working Men's College in St Pancras, London, in the early 1950s, Grant was strongly connected with one particular location: Camden. He lived at Camden Studios, with its own artistic community, from 1966, but he also arranged or took part in exhibitions for the Camden Festival, Camden Artists and on behalf of the Medical Aid Committee for Vietnam. For the Camden Festival in 1968, he organised the exhibition *25 Camden Artists*, including sculpture by Robert Adams, David Annesley, Anthony Caro and Bernard Meadows, constructions by Anthony Hill, Kenneth and Mary Martin, and paintings by Frank Auerbach, John Craxton, Tess Jaray, Michael Kidner, Marc Vaux and Keith Vaughan. As

154
Idomeneo, 1969–70
Mild steel, stainless steel and Perspex
426 × 240 × 240 cm
Unisa, Pretoria, South Africa

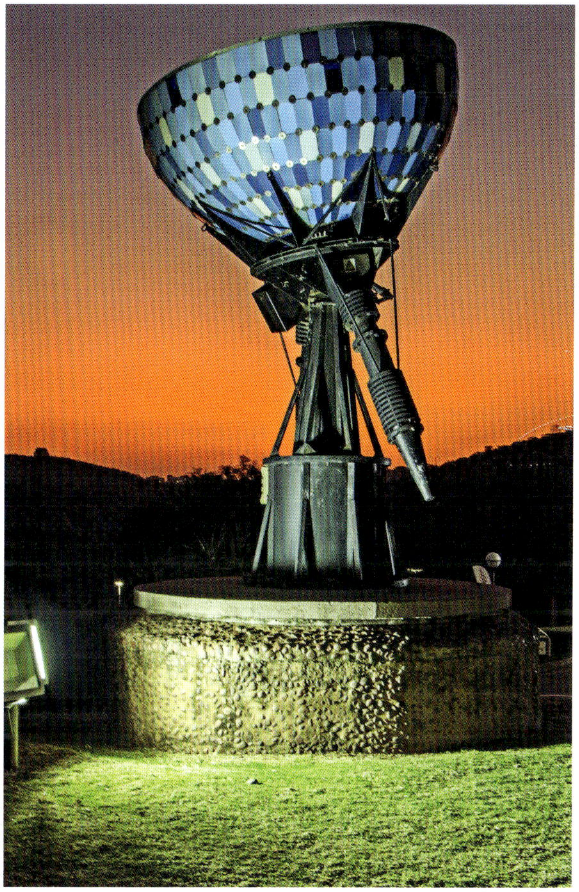

Grant stated at the time, 'Camden really is unique. So many leading contemporary artists are living and working here that the exhibition will truly represent contemporary art in Britain today.'[9] The only notable absentee was Phillip King, who was preparing to exhibit at the Venice Biennale.

In 1968, having constructed a small stainless steel fountain – which he described as 'pretty but has taken so much time that I am resolved to resist the temptation to be always making things' – Grant led an approach to the Borough Council of Camden to offer the services of artists.[10] An ideal scenario, he suggested, might be that a professional artist, in consultation with architects and ideally local residents, would supervise students to make a sculpture, environmental work, landscaped area, wall relief, mural or screen. The scheme was not taken further, yet it was characteristic of the five years from 1967 to 1971 that Grant describes self-deprecatingly as 'his Meccano period', when he focused on designing or making mechanical constructions.

'Social' Sculptures

Spanning this period were three large-scale works. The first, *Earth Time Space – The North* (1967–9; fig.29), was exhibited at Snape Maltings in Suffolk, then relocated to Bath. The second, *Idomeneo* (1969–70), was conceived with the assistance of Arts Council funding for the international exhibition, *Kinetics*, that opened at the Hayward Gallery in September 1970. *Idomeneo* was made literally at the heart of Camden Studios, in the central courtyard. Grant would work often noisily until midnight, without – as he recalled – any complaint from residents. The process was detached, slow and painstaking: more in the spirit of a fabricator than an artist. In August 1969, having worked for at least three months without any clear end in sight, he suggested variously that he might call the construction 'Idomeneo' (after Mozart's opera, in admiration of Anne Pashley's performance as Idamante in the year that Snape Maltings burnt down), 'Revolution' (by incorporating badges featuring Mao Tse Tung into its mosaic), or simply

155
St Joan, 1971/2002, adjacent to the Shaw Theatre, Ossulston Street, London
Steel, coloured acrylic
762 cm (height)
London Borough of Camden Council

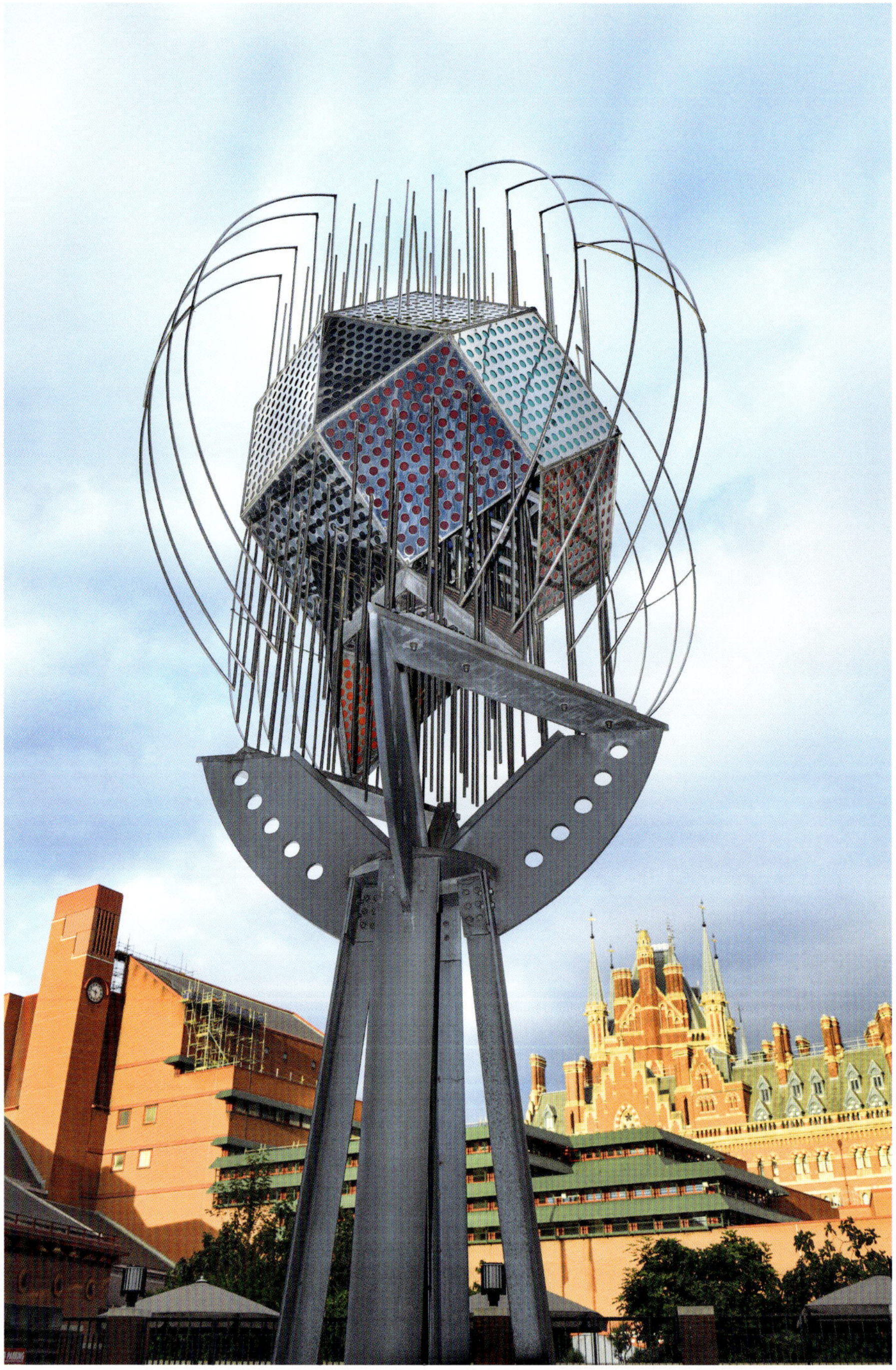

'Cuba'. He viewed it as a 'social' sculpture, and was delighted when, having demonstrated it to friends shortly after its completion in July 1970, a chorus of 'thank you' echoed from the council flats above.[11] Not long afterwards, *Idomeneo* was lifted by crane out of the courtyard to be transported to the South Bank.

Kinetics received mixed reviews. Historical examples were represented by projected images, in addition to works by well-known artists such as the American Alexander Calder and younger artists who had received support from the Arts Council. Grant's construction consisted of a hydraulically powered hemisphere, iridescent in tiles of blue, green and gold, mounted on a tall pedestal. The construction's dished 'head' tilted vertically and rotated horizontally, emitting light modulated by coloured Perspex panels and revolving discs. It featured at the outset of a documentary film about the exhibition: an imposing robotic sentinel adjacent to Jean Tinguely's *Fontaine*, around which children scampered, dodging jets of water.[12] *Kinetics* proved so popular with the public that Bryan Robertson, in a delightfully mischievous review for the *Spectator*, condemned it as 'doubly dangerous because . . . it is undeniably entertaining'.[13] Grant envisaged offering *Idomeneo* to the Borough of Camden on long-term loan, to be placed on the sun deck of the outdoor Oasis swimming pool in Holborn, whose history dates back to 18th-century Turkish baths. No such provision was necessary. Henry Roland (of Roland, Browse and Delbanco) showed *Idomeneo* to Dr Anton Rupert, Chair of the Rembrandt Tobacco Corporation, who immediately bought and presented it to the University of South Africa in Pretoria (fig.154). Located on the Muckleneuk Campus at Unisa, and extensively restored in 2012, it continues to act as a beacon for the university.[14]

156
Model for St Joan, 1970
Metal, cardboard and wire
75 × 45 × 37 cm
Private Collection, UK

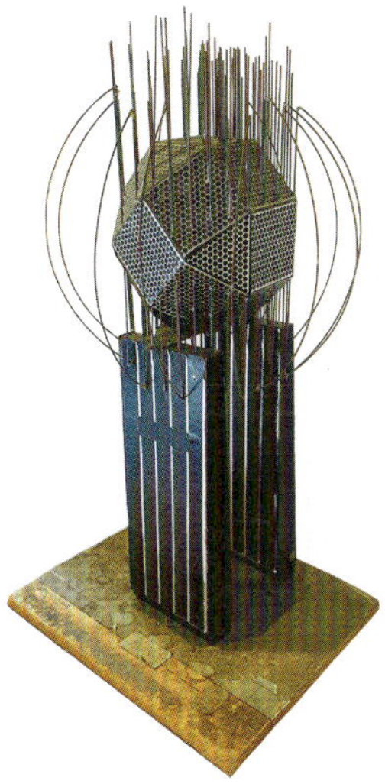

Grant's third and final large-scale construction made a tentative appearance in November 1970, when the *North London Press* illustrated a model, based again on the geometrical form of the rhombicuboctahedron, proposed to stand outside the new St Pancras Library and Shaw Theatre in Euston Road (fig.156). The subject was *St Joan*: title of a play by George Bernard Shaw, who was himself a former resident of St Pancras. Grant envisaged the construction's steel arcs as symbolising crossbows, its black columns as representing imprisonment, and grooves upon them as suggesting the River Loire, where Joan waged battle. While the explanation was sufficiently convoluted to merit mention in *Private Eye*'s Pseuds Corner, the construction was both contemporary in appearance and impacted upon its environment. Perforated and bristling with stainless steel rods, the 'head' contained an optical encoder that beamed then dimmed coloured light in pulses suggesting a heartbeat. The effect was so arresting that soon after its installation a taxi crashed, its driver momentarily distracted by the sight.

Richard Cork, reviewing *St Joan*, considered it to be 'a quirky hybrid, neither woman nor machine'. It was indeed an intriguing alliance of technology and the loaded symbolism of post-war public sculpture. Cork nonetheless praised everyone responsible for introducing it into the brutal landscape of contemporary architecture, creating a landmark the public would surely grow to love.[15] Documented in the BBC feature, *Together they made it on Euston Road* (1971, directed by Bridget Winter), *St Joan* was removed to storage for six years in the 1990s during the redevelopment of the area, finally being returned, with a new base designed by Grant, in 2002 (fig.155).

Stage Design

If Grant's constructions, *St Joan* apart, were transient presences in the landscape, still more ephemeral were his stage designs. In 1965 Grant received a commission from Jean-Pierre Voos, Director of the International Theatre Club, to design two short plays by Ingmar Bergman. The intermediary was the composer Sandy Wilson, best known for his musical *The Boy Friend* (1953), in whose London flat Voos had first encountered Grant's work. The plays were due to receive their London premiere at the relatively new theatre for LAMDA (London Academy of Music and Dramatic Art). Voos considered that a straightforward enlargement of a painting would suffice as backdrop, although Wilson suggested that Grant might be prepared to provide considerably more.[16]

The first play was *A Painting on Wood* (1954), later adapted as the film *The Seventh Seal* (1957). Based on the imagery of mediaeval paintings and frescoes seen by Bergman as a child when accompanying his father, a Lutheran minister, to preach in churches around Stockholm, its cast includes a knight, squire, pregnant woman, witch, jester and blacksmith, threatened by plague. The sequence of tableaux concludes with a dance of death, the characters being led to hell at the command of a skeleton. Grant based his set on a vertically segmented painting of a volcano and midnight sun at Surtsey in Iceland. Enlarged as a monumental triptych, the design invoked a landscape burning and blackened with ash (figs 158–9). The backdrop was painted, flat on the floor, with assistance from students at Hornsey College of Art. Among those who helped was the Icelandic sculptor Jón Gunnar Árnason, whom Grant

157 (above)
Set model for Ingmar Bergman's *The City*, 1965
Mixed media
Approx. width 91 cm
(destroyed)

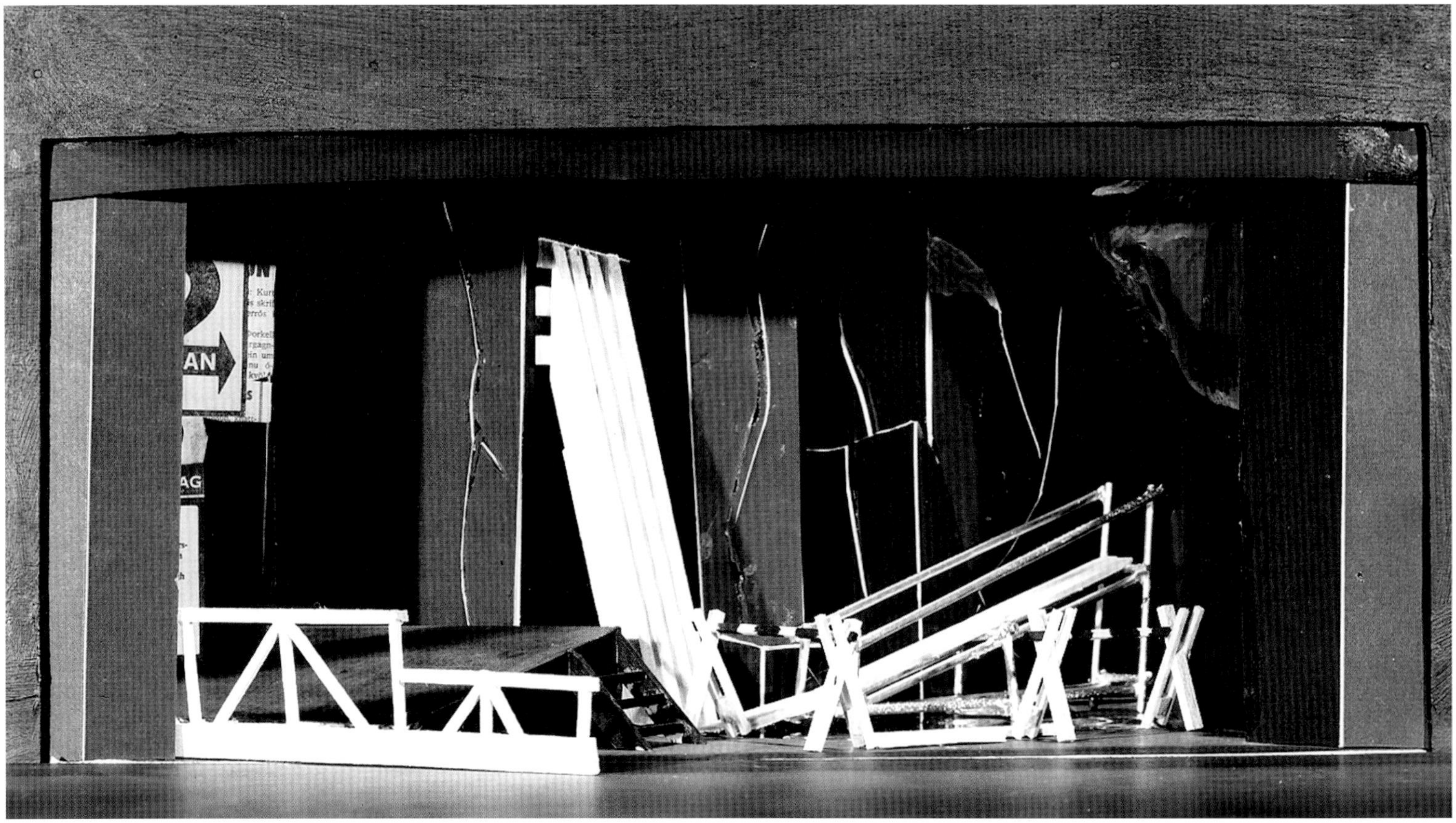

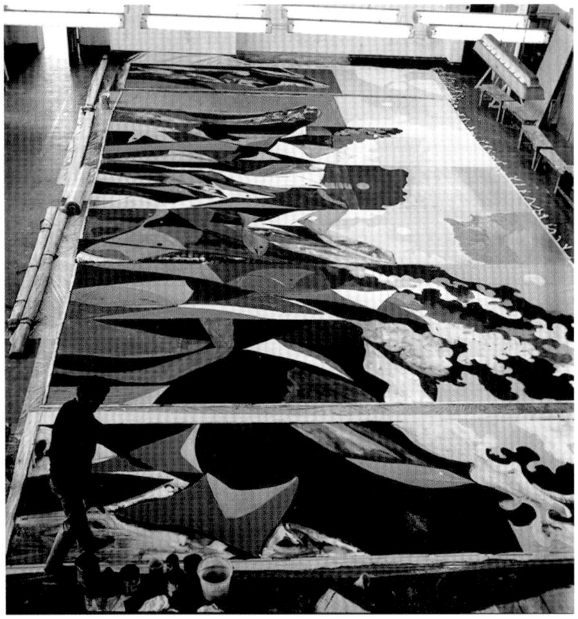

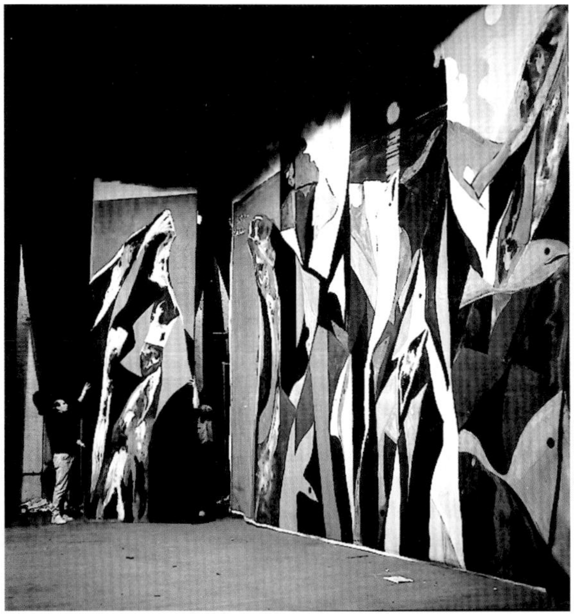

158 (left)
Backcloth for Ingmar Bergman's *A Painting on Wood*, 1965, under construction, photograph by Peter C. Amsden

159 (right)
Backcloth for Ingmar Bergman's *A Painting on Wood*, 1965, during installation, photograph by Peter C. Amsden

had met in Reykjavik and who was continuing his postgraduate studies in London.

The experience of Iceland was fresh in Grant's mind when designing the sets, which are among his first responses to the country's extraordinary landscapes. In late May 1965, shortly before returning from Iceland, he was interviewed by the Icelandic newspaper *Vísir*.[17] Grant arrived at the reporter's house carrying a large file of paintings, photographs and newspaper cuttings: he discussed his visit to Iceland, the Icelandic sagas, and inscribed a painting with a promise to return. Grant's decision to base the depiction of hell on Surtsey roused considerable interest, with *Morgunblaðið*, one of Iceland's leading national newspapers, featuring a cartoon of him, brushes and palette tucked under his arm, nonchalantly approaching a volcano from which the Devil proclaims, 'Everyone welcome!'[18] Grant's design extended from floor to ceiling, angling across the wings to present the volcano as a flickering, encompassing inferno. *The Times* commended the production for its 'incantatory unity of mood, and Mr. Keith Grant's apocalyptic backcloth, given very imaginative lighting, [as] both appropriate and exciting'.[19]

While this first design enlarged a painting, aptly enough given the play's origins in mediaeval frescoes, Grant's second Bergman set was sculptural; an intimation of the constructions he would shortly begin. *The City* (1951) represents a journey into the subconscious, after its principal character, Joakim Naken ('Joachim Naked'), discovers that the city of his childhood has been reduced to ruins. In Grant's set model we see the beginnings of scaffolding that would spread across the stage, and the cracked, angled back panels that represent the collapsing city (fig.157). Realised in the theatre, lighting caused the aluminium scaffolding to fluoresce against a dark background. Sections were illuminated to throw others into darkness, while the set's muted colours emphasised the glitter of city lights. The concept was praised as 'ingeniously simple', although one reviewer noted that film cameras, or at least 'all the technical paraphernalia of an elaborately equipped stage' might have better facilitated the abrupt transitions required.[20] It was an impressive achievement with minimal resources, the same actors providing the cast of the two plays.

Grant's experience in stage design began over a decade earlier, in 1951, at the Mountview Theatre Club, Crouch Hill, in Hornsey, a precursor to the Mountview Academy of Theatre Arts. Established by Peter Coxhead as an amateur company in 1945, two years later it staged its first production, Oscar Wilde's *The Importance of Being Earnest*, in a theatre converted from the gymnasium and basement of a former school. A new production was presented every fortnight. One of the highlights, designed by Grant in 1953, was Eugene O'Neill's *Mourning Becomes Electra*: a multi-part drama staged in two parts during the week, and on the last night in its five-hour entirety.[21] The repertory covered at Mountview gave Grant an excellent introduction to stage design. For a production of Wilde's *Salome* in 1977 at the Collegiate Theatre, in Bloomsbury, Grant created a set whose principal feature was a row of monumental pillars topped with grotesque, mask-like heads. The colours were gold, red and lacquered black, suggesting the Symbolist opulence of Wilde's original conception.

Yet it was not until 1982, when Grant designed *Hamlet* for the Young Vic at the Roundhouse, with Edward Fox in the leading role, that he made his first venture into professional theatre. He received

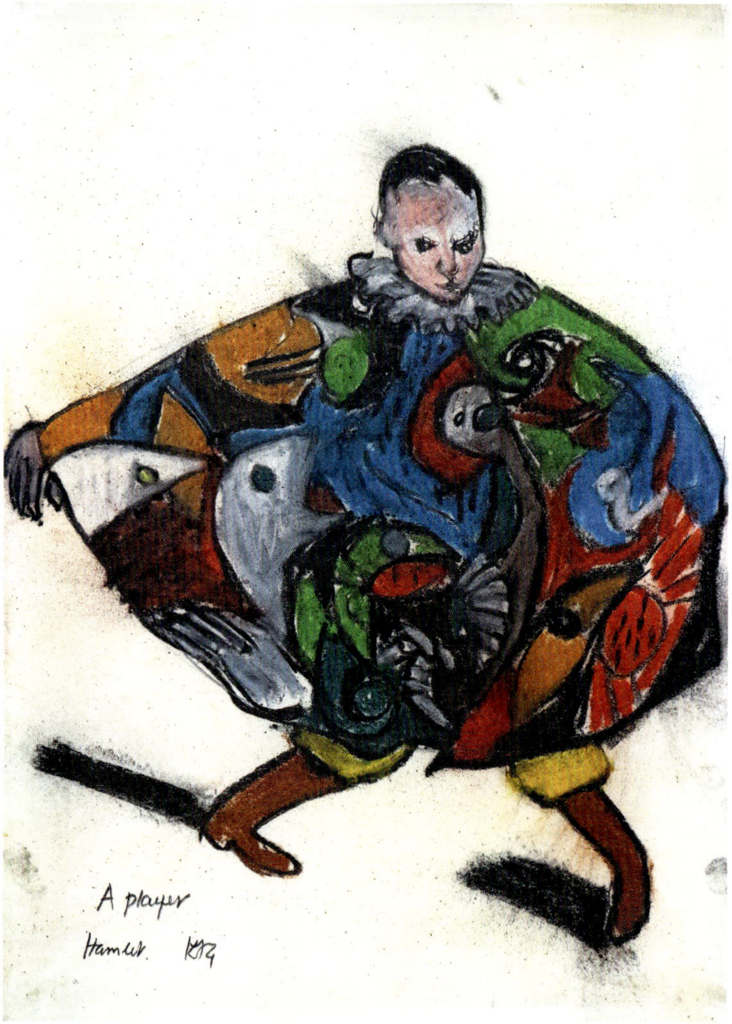

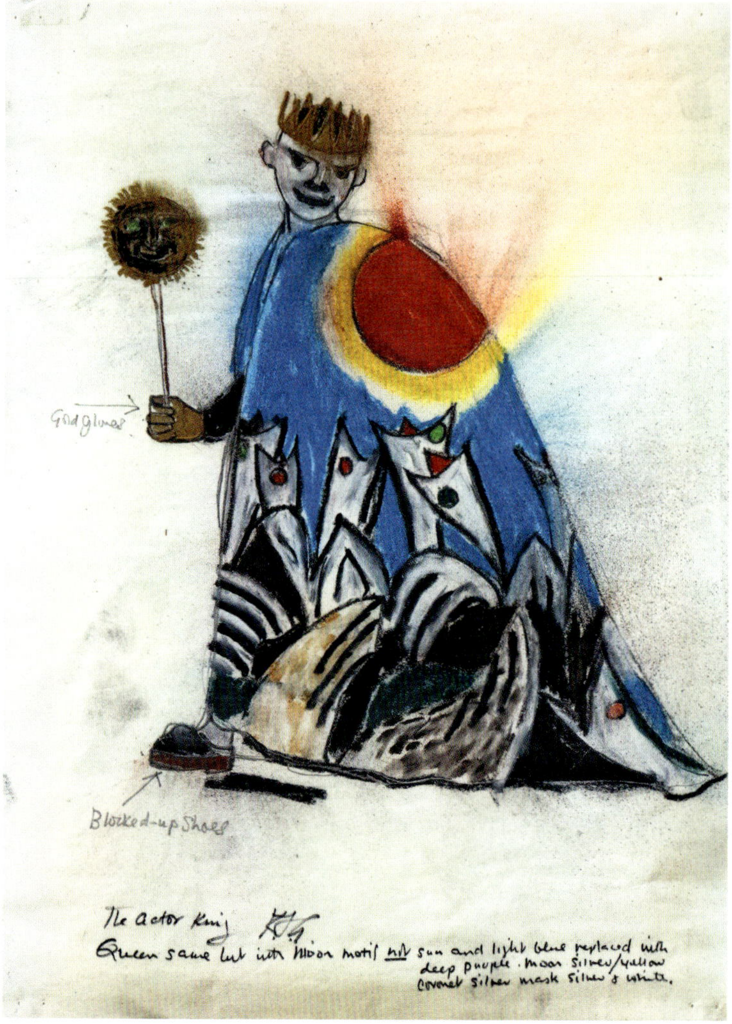

the commission a year earlier, while working on the landscape paintings based on Chollerford. Describing how the bric-a-brac of visual experience, collected and 'jealously' guarded from architecture and the spirit of place, was 'only too adaptable' to the stage, he wrote,

That is to admit that my work has always had a theatrical element and that this element is related to the intrinsic multi-dimensional nature of my thoughts but the limited two-dimensional method of my making them visible.

Whenever the apprehension of the universe becomes conditioned by the mortal inability to give it real artistic expression the result is: theatricality?[22]

The question is fascinating in its hinting at the no-man's land between painting and sculpture. Grant's constructions had taken landscape painting towards the three-dimensionality of kinetic work. Could a parallel case be made for discerning 'the theatrical' in his painting?

Grant was bitterly disappointed that his original set design for *Hamlet*, although received enthusiastically, was considered too costly to build. There is no record of this model, but the design that was approved was in many respects traditional. Grant returned the location squarely to Elsinore, with a painted panel intended to invoke Viking imagery as the principal embellishment. Bryan Robertson described the set as 'simple and useful', facilitating

160 (left)
Costume design for ***Hamlet: A Player***, 1981
Oil pastel on paper, under plastic laminate
42 × 29.5 cm
Collection of the artist

161 (right)
Costume design for ***Hamlet: The Actor King***, 1980
Oil pastel on paper, under plastic laminate
42 × 29.5 cm
Collection of the artist

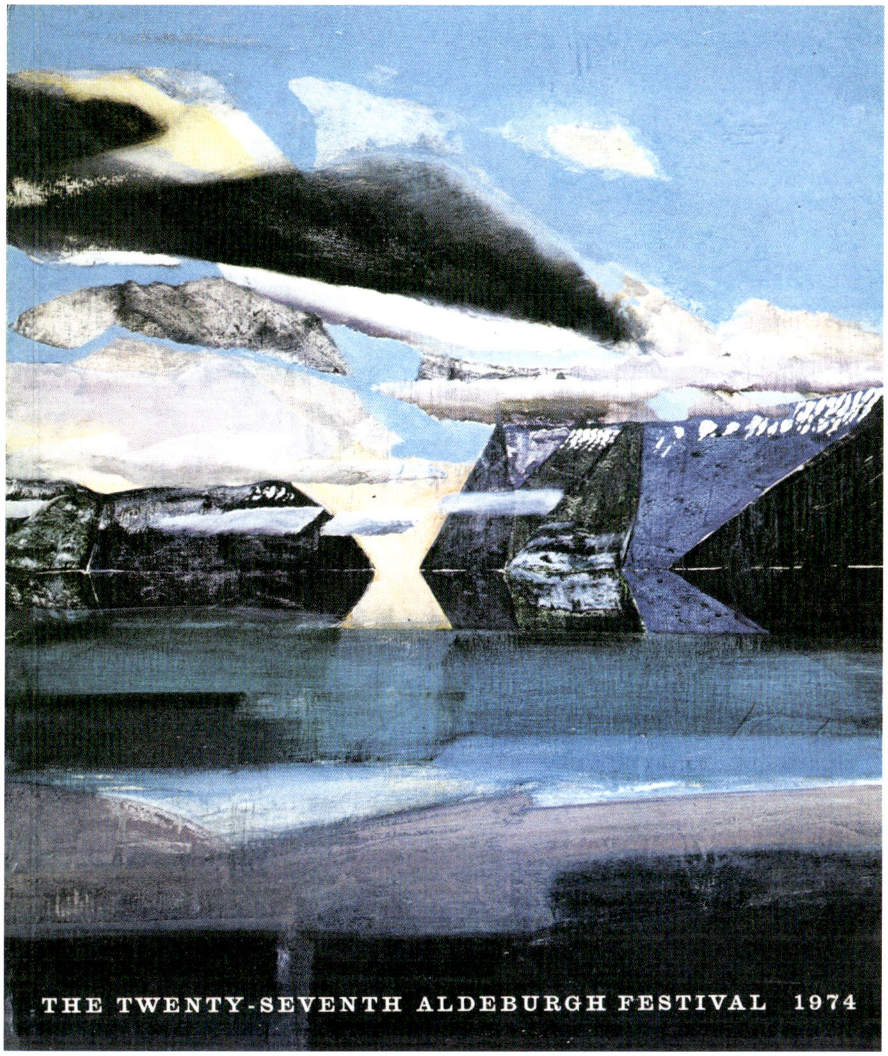

162
Cover for the Aldeburgh Festival Programme Book, 1974, featuring *Midnight Sunrise*, from the *24 Hours Series*, 1974
24.5 × 18.5 cm

action at different levels, although Nicholas de Jongh considered it to function more as a 'picture than a design', its openness precluding a 'sense of court intrigue, corruption or grandeur'.[23] Most striking, perhaps, were the costumes. As a foil to the subdued background, Grant introduced the mobile dimension of colour through costumes blazing with the imagery of the northern landscape. The most elaborate example, made by the Young Vic costume department, was the cloak of the Actor King: sky blue, shimmering with the sun and fringed with the upward-straining birds so characteristic of Grant's paintings (fig.161). Ophelia's dress was muted, raggedly stained with grass and moss, while the cloak of a Player was envisaged as sumptuously embellished in primary colours (fig.160).

Grant's vision of *Hamlet* is documented principally by the costume designs and slides in his archive, professional photographers having preferred to concentrate on Fox in the title role. Ephemeral, too, was an international 'happening' in which Grant participated in Sortland, Norway. Travelling to Vesterålen to work over Christmas 1994, he spent time with the photographer Trym Ivar Bergsmo, and by early January was '99% resolved' to return for an event scheduled for the following March.[24] The intention was to collaborate with Bergsmo on an installation combining a large cosmos painting with a *fiskehjell*, a traditional pyramidal or rectangular structure used to dry cod. Grant chose the pyramid as reflecting the geometry of mountain slopes descending steeply to fjords.[25] By early January he had decided some aspects of the project through a scale model and was about to begin work on the large (6 x 1.75 m) painting, formed of smaller squares, to reduce his workload in Norway. He recorded his dream of a pyramid peak 'wreathed in cloud against an ultimate black sky', which inspired *Iron Night, Vesterålen* (1995; fig.83, p.103), before countering defensively, 'No I am not returning to a former imagery but recognising that there is a lexicon of motifs that has been with me subconsciously for the whole of my life.'[26]

In Sortland, in mid-March 1995, the construction proved exhausting yet exhilarating to work on alongside younger artists. The weather was atrocious, with rain and high temperatures turning the ice into a treacherously slippery surface. When the exhibition opened, for a single day, it was crowded. A display of installations made from local materials such as wood, fish, snow, salt and cow hide struck Grant as 'appropriate to the rawness of the environment'.[27] His painting was well received and would ultimately be installed permanently in a new cultural centre in Sortland. The pyramid peak, made from thick compressed wooden board, 2.5 m high, was made singlehandedly, after Bergsmo became unwell and was unable to complete the area Grant designed for the display of his photographs. The pyramid's surface was worked with plaster that refused to set in the cold, humid environment. Failing to realise its apex as sharply as he desired, Grant resorted to plaster of Paris, which he painted black, pouring the remaining powder over the wet acrylic paint. It cascaded downwards in four separate avalanches, to create 'a phenomenal effect of snow clinging to the dark rocky sides of the cubistic geometrical solids which [are] the structure of the mountains of Vesterålen'. The effect surprised Grant as much as those who saw it.[28] When he conceived the work in his Lewes studio, he had been steeped in Wagner's music amid the possibility of designing *The Ring*.

Cover Designs

Grant's openness to working with environments beyond the gallery has always fostered an eclectic range of projects. In the mid-1960s, his paintings were associated briefly with The Creation, a band described as 'a unique hybrid of pop, rock, psychedelia and the avant garde'.[29] An early version of a mural commissioned by Grant's friend, Francis Patrick Neill, combining mythical Norwegian and Icelandic symbols with an abstract depiction of the creation, caught the eye of the band's manager, Tony Stratton-Smith. Precisely what happened next varies in different accounts, one recalling that Grant reproduced a section of his painting on the band's bass drum, another that a painting by Grant was destroyed on stage during a performance. What is incontrovertible is that Grant's painting, *The Swan of Vietnam* (1965; fig.168, p.197), was reproduced in the *Record Mirror*, in June 1966, to advertise The Creation's new single, *Making Time*.[30]

Grant's paintings have been reproduced as record covers, ranging from an Argo LP of contemporary music by Gordon Crosse and Hugh Wood, using a detail from *Gulbenkian Triptych: Symphony of Voices* (1974), to a CD of music by John McLeod, including *The Gokstad Ship*, which was illustrated by *Arctic Evening, The Ice Fjord, Jakobshavn* (1989–92). An extended association with publishers Collins Harvill saw Grant's landscape paintings, whether Norwegian mountains, the tropics or the sea, reproduced as covers for books by Peter Matthiessen, including *The Snow Leopard, Far Tortuga, Under the Mountain Wall, The Cloud Forest* and *At Play in the Fields of the Lord*. In 1974, *Midnight Sunrise*, from the *24 Hours Series*, was used as an elegantly simple cover design for the Aldeburgh Festival Programme Book, in the same year that Grant held a solo exhibition in the New Gallery at Snape Maltings (fig.162). Perhaps most intriguingly, in the early 1970s, Grant's paintings and constructions were shown alongside work by David Leverett and Derek Boshier at the King's Road showroom of Adel Rootstein, a designer famous for basing her mannequins on celebrities such as Twiggy and Cher.

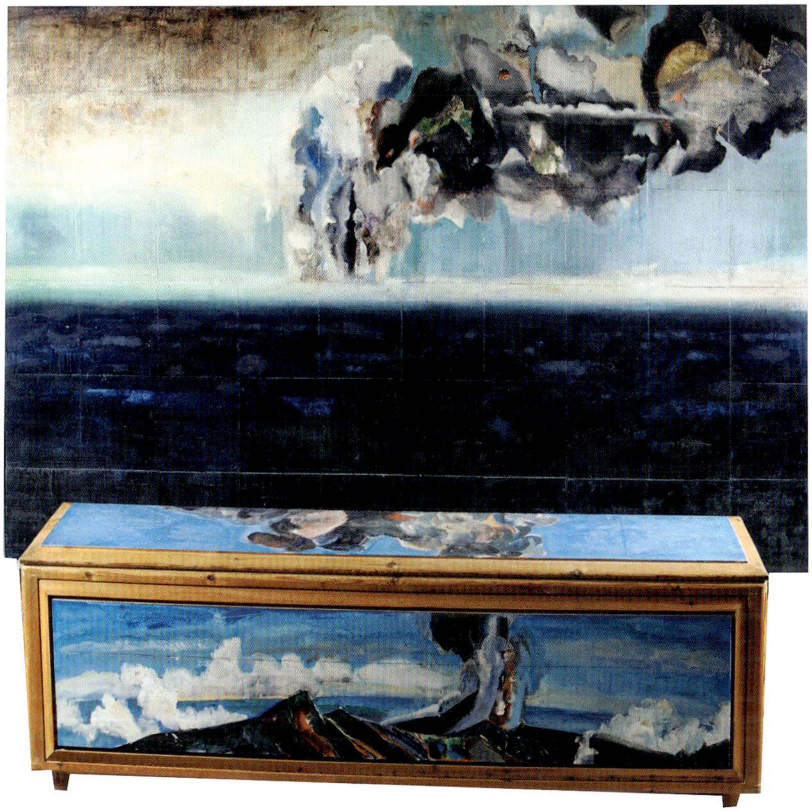

163
Volcano in the North, 1976,
Mixed media
Chest: 71 × 241 × 45 cm
Painting: 181 × 302.5 cm
Portsmouth Museums,
Portsmouth City Council

Functional, Devotional and Memorial Commissions

Less frequently, Grant has made works for domestic environments, some of which have since entered public collections. A triptych commissioned for the new home of Arthur White, head of Midland Dairies, now hangs in New Cross Hospital, Wolverhampton. Similarly, a wooden chest painted for Colin Hamilton and Kulgin Duval was acquired by Portsmouth Museum and Art Gallery (fig.163). The latter was commissioned after a pine tree blew down near Hamilton and Duval's home near Pitlochry in Scotland: a local carpenter made the chest and Grant was invited to decorate it. He completed the task in July 1976, alone in their house, listening to their collection of music and watching the clear night skies. The imagery relates to the *Volcano in the North* series (see Chapter 2; fig.40, p.58) and in particular to two works in the Fitzwilliam Museum: *Volcano and White Bird* (1974–5) and *Eruption Column at 20,000 Feet, Heimæy, Iceland* (1976). On the chest, a livid plume of smoke billows over the lid, continuing, after some interruption, on a painting hanging behind.
The painting and chest were combined in 1977 when both were acquired by Portsmouth Museum and Art Gallery, the shared imagery making it an apt juxtaposition.

Decorative yet functional, the chest has always been described by Grant as a *cassone* chest, after the ornate wedding chests made in Italy from the 14th to 16th centuries that might be carved, gilded or painted with scenes from mythology or the Bible. Grant's only work for a church similarly straddled boundaries, presenting landscape in the context of a votive altarpiece. When the wooden church of Kopervik was set alight in 2001, its altarpiece, a copy by August Eiebakke of a resurrection painting by Adolph Tidemand, was destroyed. Grant was commissioned to create a replacement. Yet the project proved controversial, provoking objections to Grant's proposed design. His triptych combined imagery central to his work – the sun, a reflected landscape, the aurora, a rainbow, fish – with the Christian symbols of corn, a dove and the lamb (fig.164). When closed, for Lent, it showed a night sky and seascape, overlaid with a cross. Consecrated in June 2005, the painting was destroyed just five years

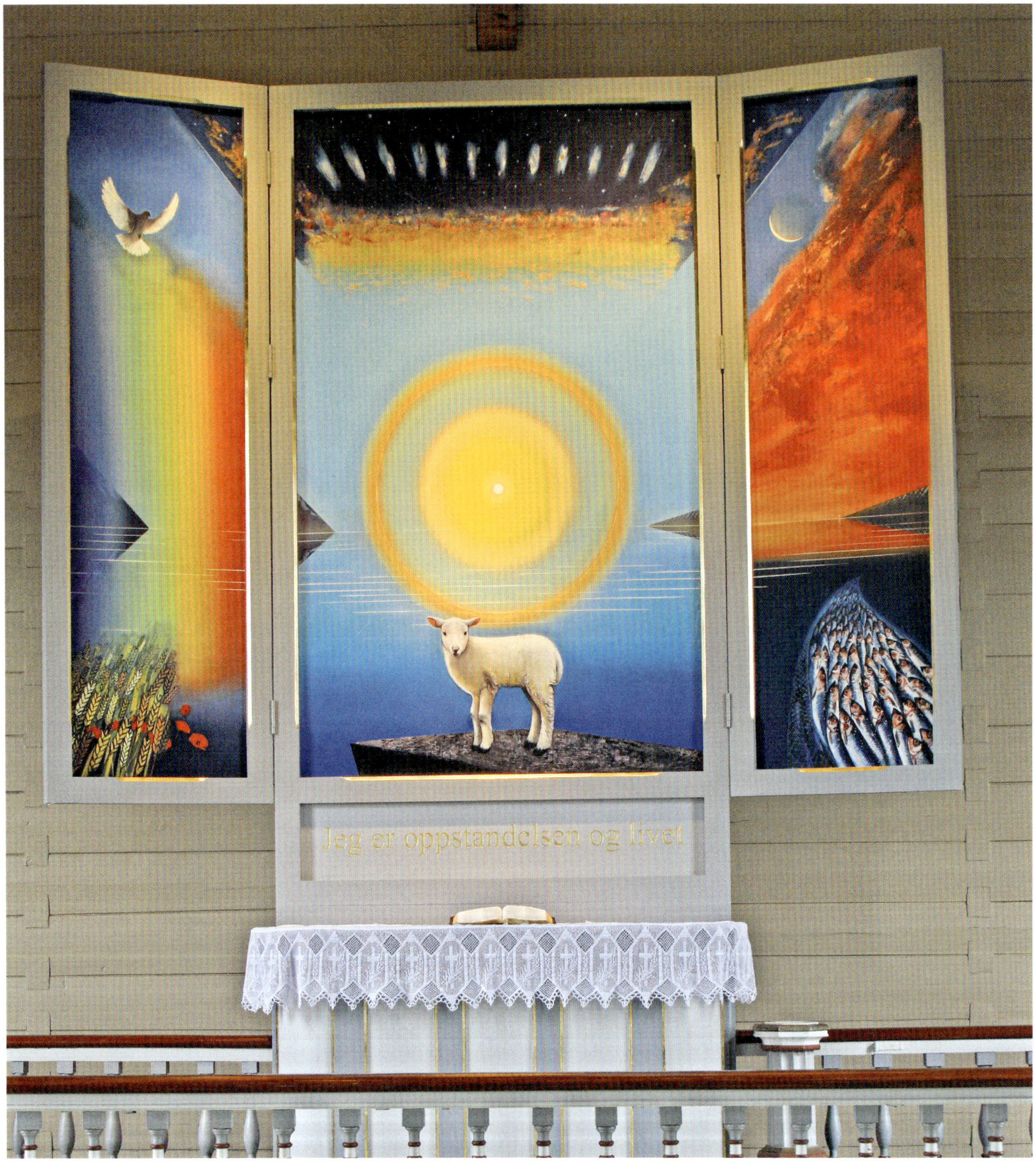

164
Altar Painting, Kopervik Church, Karmøy, Norway, 2005
Oil on board
originally 225 × 280 cm
(destroyed by fire)

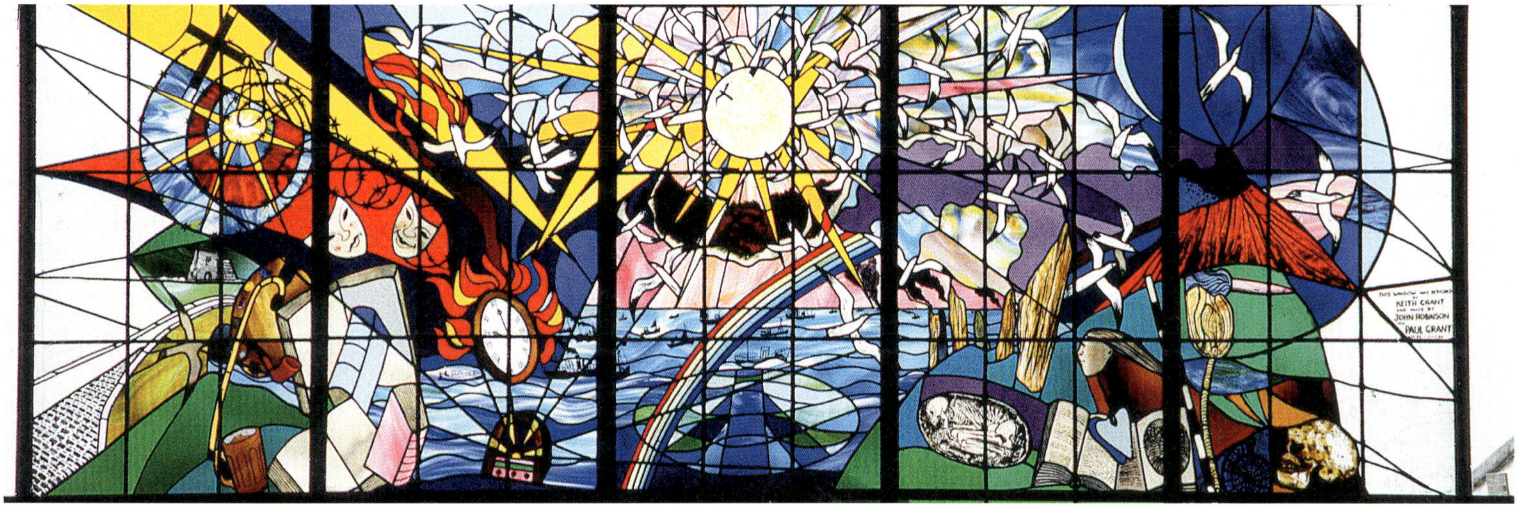

165
Window Dedicated to J.B. Priestley and Jacquetta Hawkes, during construction, Belle Vue Boys School, Heaton, 1994 (detail)
Stained glass
Originally 1.7 x 7 m

later, when an accident caused the church to burn to the ground.

Destruction, or at the very least relocation, is not uncommon for commissioned work. In early 2022, it came to Grant's attention that his first stained-glass window, designed as a joint tribute to J.B. Priestley and his wife, Jacquetta Hawkes, had been moved from its original location at Belle Vue Boys School in Heaton (Priestley's former school) to the library of Beckfoot Upper Heaton School. The window, proposed by Hawkes in 1992 and completed in 1994, features, in Grant's words, an 'illuminated manuscript' of imagery (fig.165).[31] On the left, actors' masks, books and a wireless set represent Priestley's work as author, playwright and broadcaster, with a walking cane, pipe and beer glass to indicate his character. To the right, ciphers from landscape and history represent Hawkes: standing stones, an ancient burial, an archaeologist's measuring stick, book and crinoid fossil. The two halves are united by landscape, blessed by sun, gulls, the sea, hills and a rainbow. Dependent on natural light to bring out its vivid colours, the window originally contained panels on either side with quotations from Priestley and Hawkes, in lettering by Larry Berryman. For Grant, there were further resonances. A volcano, a symbol crucial to his own work, reflected Hawkes's description, in *A Land*, of Ailsa Craig, south of Arran in Scotland: a rock 'stained white by thousands of nesting gannets, aloof, pale-eyed birds pressing their warm feathers against the once boiling granite'.[32] To the right of the volcano, an inscription identifying Grant as designer names his two assistants as John Robinson and Paul Grant.

When the window was relocated, it was mounted without the two endmost panels and within a lightbox. Its colours no longer alter with daylight or the weather, appearing unnaturally even. The omission of the panels containing quotations from Priestley and Hawkes is, at the time of writing, unexplained. Grant feels his work to be compromised, but senses most keenly this loss in relation to his friend, Larry Berryman, and his son, Paul.

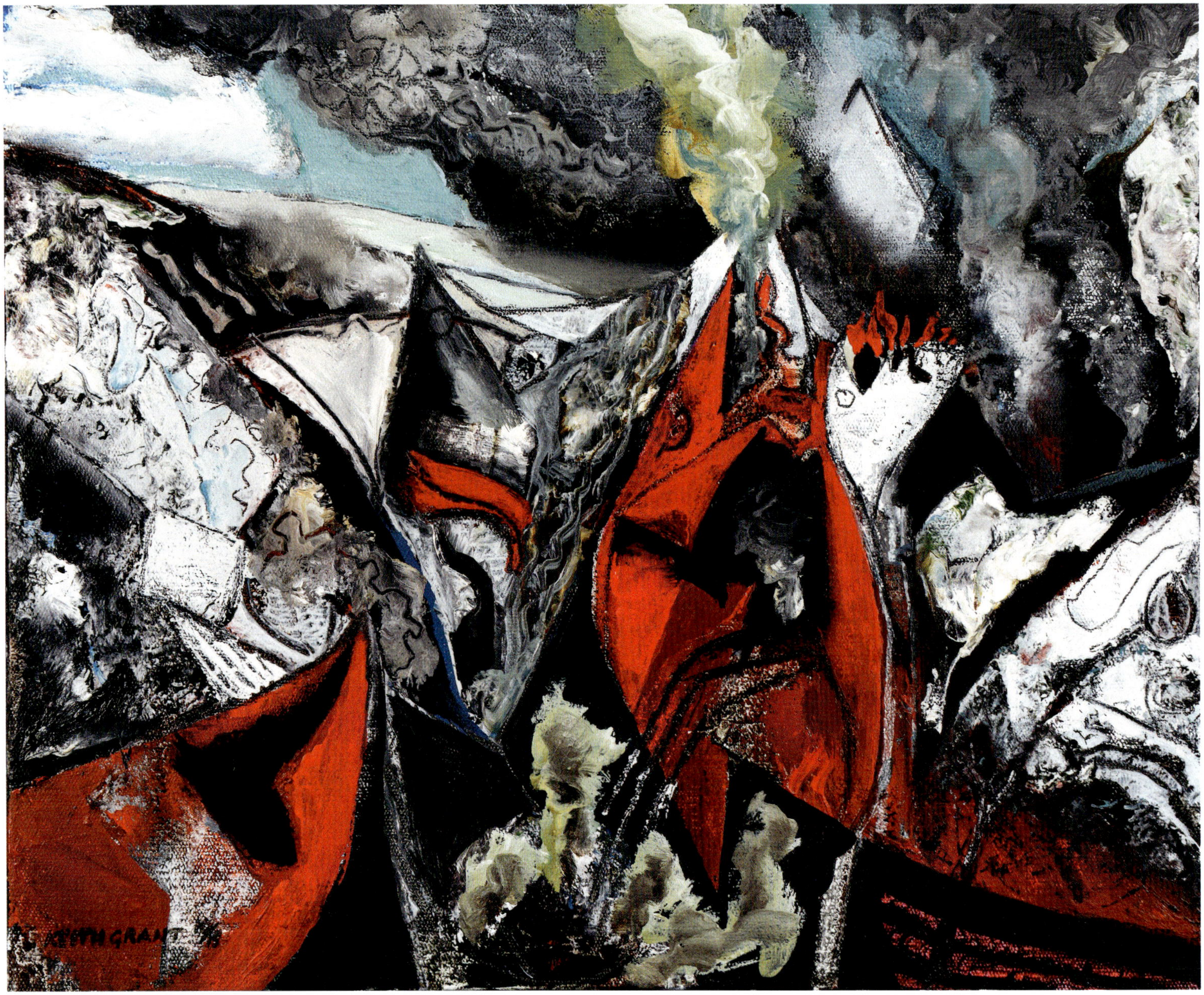
KEITH GRANT

10

Landscapes of Protest and Memory

166
Catastrophe, 2015
Oil with oil pastel on canvas
40 × 49.5 cm
The David Game Collection, UK

Grant describes the imagery of *Catastrophe* (2015) as 'spontaneous', 'accidental' (fig.166). Worked over a previous landscape, it related originally to a series of demolition paintings. It then began to suggest something more primal, erupting across the surface of the canvas. Unpacked, it consists of elements that Grant could indeed paint subconsciously: a pyramid peak, volcano, ice, metamorphic fish-bird forms. Yet the composition is both structured and disturbingly fractured. Threefold gashes gouge the image, while the ice is textured with serpentine cracks. From the open mouths of strange creatures issue flames. There is an unconscious equivalence with Carlos Fonseca, whose novel *Colonel Lágrimas* (2015; English translation, 2016), written in tandem with a thesis on the representation of catastrophe in art and literature, features an artist obsessed with painting the same volcano. Modelled on the Mexican artist and revolutionary Dr Atl, Fonseca's character embodies a view of the 20th century as a series of catastrophes: from the October Revolution in the Soviet Union, to the Spanish Civil War, to Vietnam.

The landscapes addressed here are among Grant's most urgent, painted to express sorrow, anger or foreboding through the lens of elemental change. Each example commemorates the destruction of life, principally, tangentially, personally or universally. Grant states, perhaps misleadingly, that the paintings are created not to make a political point but through a need to voice deeply felt emotions. To examine their themes, it is imperative to consider what gave rise to them, first, in the mid-1960s.

The 1960s

The symbol Grant uses consistently to represent suffering and empathy is that of the bird. Returning to *The Swan of Tuonela* (1964), introduced earlier in relation to Sibelius's music, we can now propose a different interpretation. Having just completed the painting, in December 1964, Grant wrote,

It is my poor comment on the barbarities of the Congo – the swan – a sort of embodiment of human consciousness and beauty despoiled and engorged with blood – moving into the rushes bordering the great lake. A dispassionate horizon with menacing clouds – the swan dies before breaking through the last resistance to its progress of death and does not find itself a part of the unthinking cruelty and primitiveness of the world.[1]

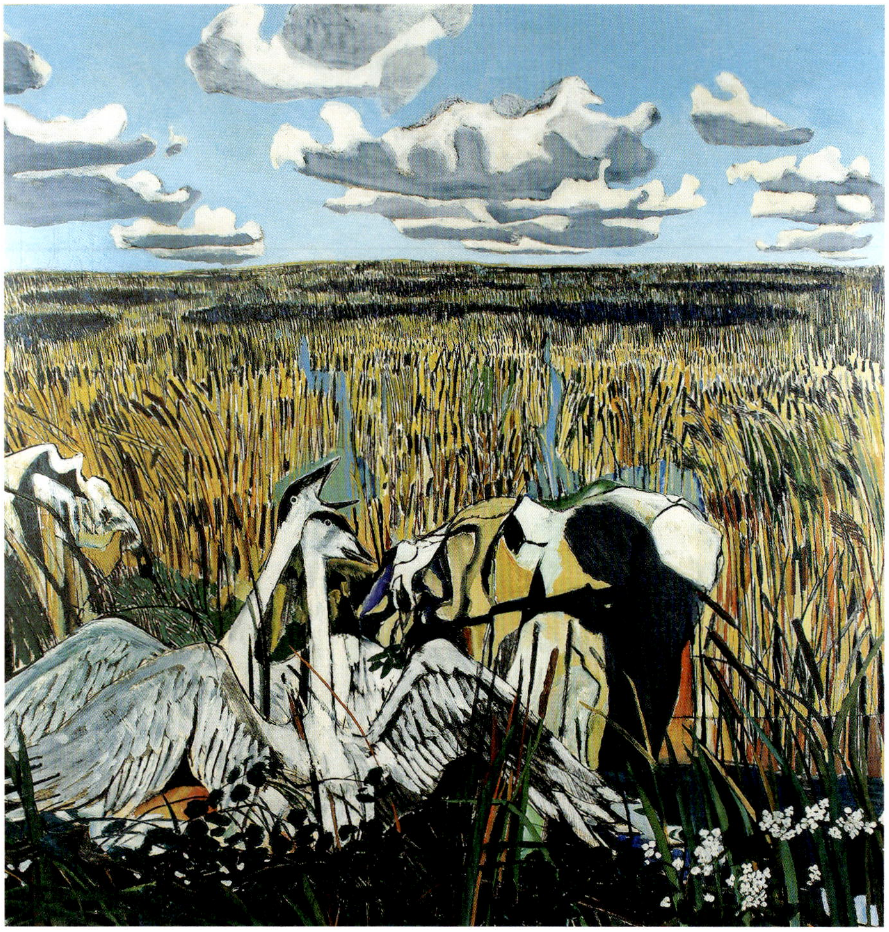

167
Death of the Swans, 1965
Oil on board
183 × 183 cm
Private Collection (location unknown)

The unrest that lasted for five years, during which 100,000 people are thought to have died, began almost as soon as the Congo gained independence from Belgium in 1960, the conflict becoming a proxy for the Cold War when the Soviet Union and United States intervened in support of opposing factions. Grant painted *The Swan of Tuonela* at the time of the hostage-taking and massacres in Stanleyville (renamed Kisangani in 1966), not knowing that the bloody conflict was nearing its close. He wanted to show that artists 'may comment on the inhumanity of our times', not simply by showing 'what is', but what might be done: 'how we might liberate ourselves from apathy and convention'.[2] Why, then, did he title the painting *The Swan of Tuonela*?

Wanting his symbolism to be read on numerous levels, Grant distracted attention from any political agenda through its title and by exhibiting it with a group of paintings connected to music, at Heal's furniture store in the summer of 1965. In his next two paintings, imagery and message became increasingly overt. *Death of the Swans* (1965) depicts a hunter whose shadow falls on a lava rock (fig.167). Two swans recoil, their wings arching protectively; reeds mottled with shadow stretch to the horizon. Low clouds compress and stifle a landscape that appears unnaturally still. Even the swan's open beak implies a mute cry. Grant initially included the gun's barrel to the right of the composition but removed it as too obvious, leaving the hunter's shadow – almost camouflaged – to speak for itself.

Grant was reading William Morris's journals in preparation for travelling to Iceland, and described the painting as perhaps 'a little Morrissian' as a result, drawing upon Morris's accounts of lakes so populated with swans that no water was visible. Grant sensed his work moving towards greater realism. While not deliberately positioning himself in opposition to the emerging dominance of New Generation painting, as exhibited at the Whitechapel Art Gallery in 1964, or the various influences of painting from the United States, he was acutely conscious of differences in style and motivation. Alluding to the 'inevitable fate of South Africa', he questioned, 'what real point has pop art? What escapism! I want each picture from now to point to this great sadness but I also want to show optimism.'[3] In *Death of the Swans*, life – cradled in the immensity of the landscape – is balanced at the moment before all is lost.

Grant's journals situate this gesture in the quotidian context of an artist's life. He was debating (without decision) whether to exhibit work at the Royal Academy and experiencing the petty frustrations of showing with commercial galleries. Fixing the painting, made on two pieces of paper, onto hardboard required assistance from a caretaker at Hornsey College of Art, where he was teaching. It snowed – transforming the view from Alexandra Palace into one that lifted his spirits, as snow had always done since he was a child.

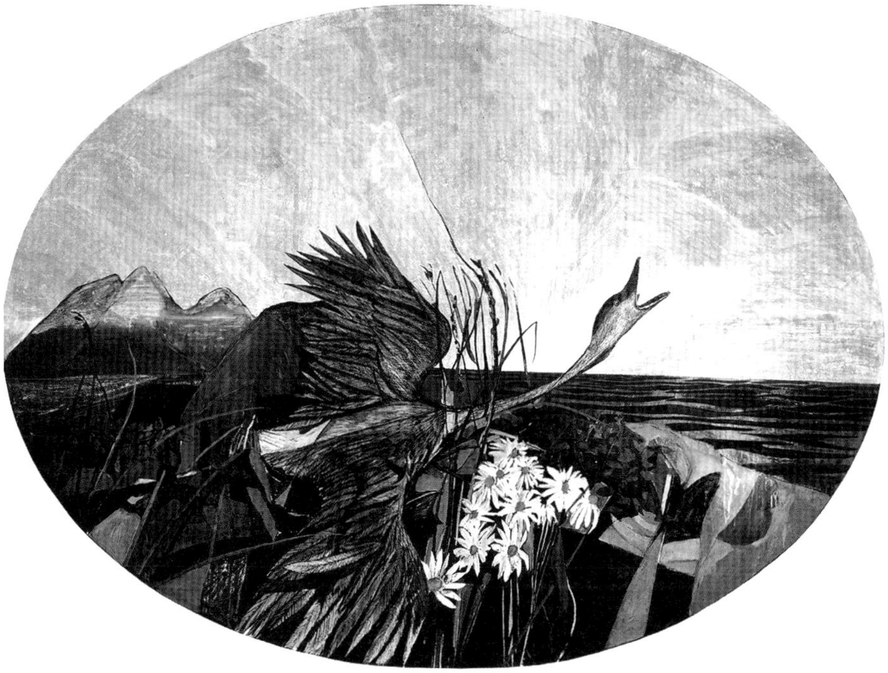

168
The Swan of Vietnam, 1965
Acrylic and ink on paper laid on board
122 × 152 cm
Private Collection (location unknown)

Vietnam

A new painting of a black swan, injured and at the point of death, took shape. Again a protest against murder, this time Grant explicitly titled it *The Swan of Vietnam* (1965; fig.168), and made plain, in his journals, the dichotomy of using a style attractive to 'non-artists' to express a theme that might just as easily repel for being 'too socialist, too pacifist, perhaps a little red'.[4] His journal entries railed against injustice and brutality. When *The Death of the Swans* was accepted for the Royal Academy's *Summer Exhibition*, Roger Berthoud commented that in poor company Grant had acquitted himself 'creditably'.[5] He made a further diptych juxtaposing a gull newly hatched against a collage of headlines about Vietnam: first he overpainted the headlines, then destroyed the painting. In January 1966 he renewed his acquaintance with John Berger, whom he had first met at the Royal College of Art in the 1950s, seeing him at 'Marxism & the Arts', the following day at the Royal Academy's Bonnard exhibition, then sending a letter and a recent watercolour as a gift.

Against this backdrop, Grant was preparing for an exhibition at the New Art Centre to feature work based on Iceland. Were the two strands related? Among the new canvases were aerial views of volcanoes superimposed, according to the title of one example, with the circles of an aeroplane's drift indicator (fig.169). Arthur Moyse, artist, anarchist and critic for *Freedom*, viewed the device instead as 'the black ringed veins of the bomber's camera's eye'.[6] His interpretation was corroborated by Jack Hazan's film, *Especially at My Time of Life* (1969). Footage of *Drift Indicator*, hung in the window of the New Art Centre in 1966, is cut against the eruption of Surtsey in Iceland, seen from the air. Speaking to camera, Grant states,

When you have something that is very different from normal experience you can use it to say so many different things. I'd like it to mean a lot more than just a landscape. I'd like it to mean . . . all sorts of things, based on my reaction to Vietnam.[7]

Later, at Camden Studios, Grant describes using a large triptych of Surtsey to parallel his ideas about human nature. There is no mistaking the violence of these landscapes, a point that Hazan underlined through the film's harrowing soundtrack, splicing detonations with the cries of children and seabirds. Grant instils an aerial view of Surtsey, distanced 'in

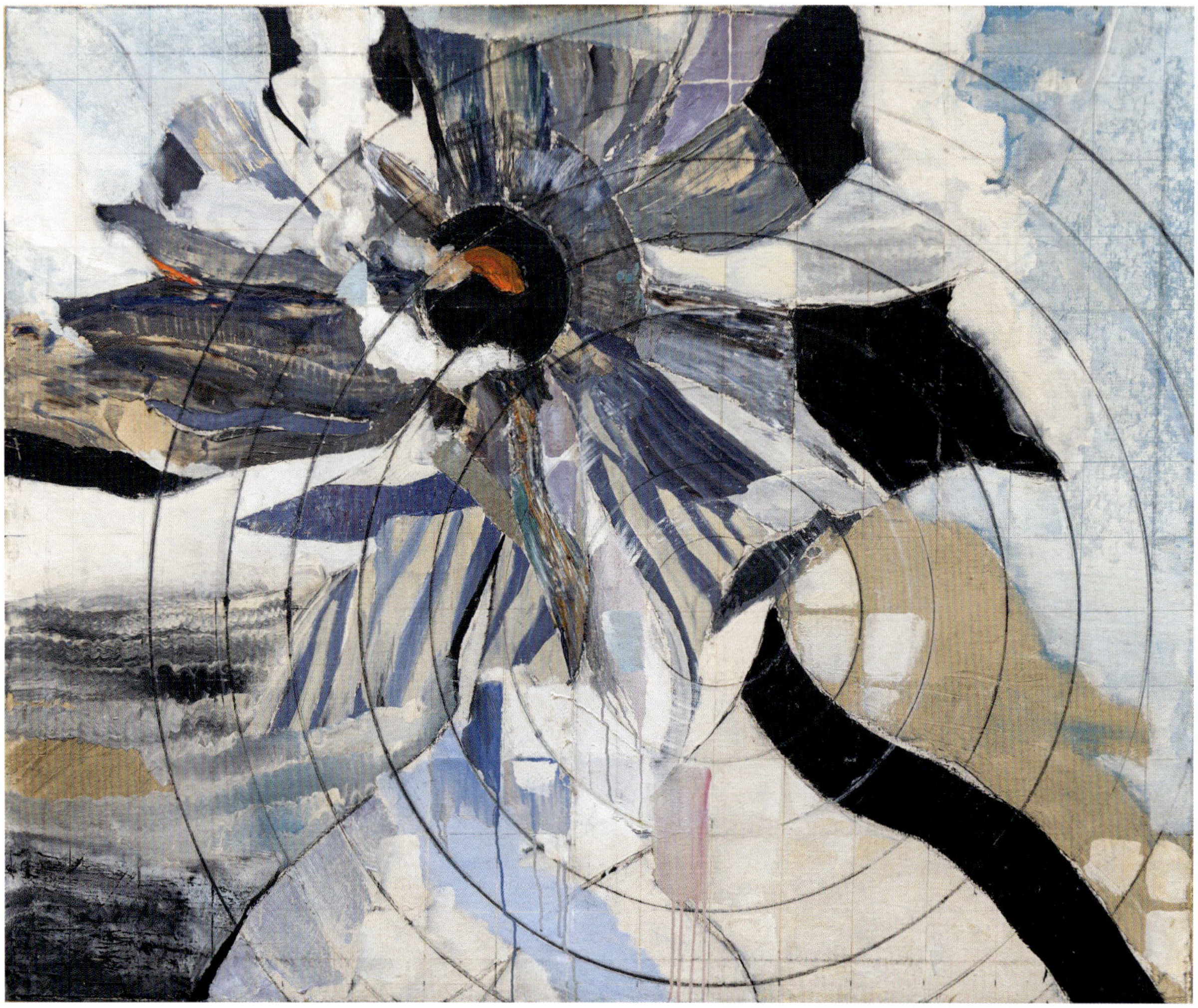

169
Drift Indicator, 1966
Oil on canvas
101 × 127 cm
Collection Jack Hazan

order to know it better', with the emotional content of 'another American bombing of a Vietnamese village'. He had already described how fish are disgorged, ready cooked, from the mouth of a volcano; the red tints of his paintings suggesting the glint of submarine fire.[8]

Instead of the oval format used for *The Swan of Vietnam*, Grant often now adopted a circular frame, implying the selective view of field glasses. Taking a circular oil painting, *Steam and Lava* (*c.*1965), as exemplar, he began a series of oil, acrylic and gouache paintings titled *Another Country*. From the vantage of a promontory they depict a land veiled in smoke: the Hebrides (seen from the air when returning from Iceland) or Vietnam, smoke and distance hiding the atrocities. Two days later, Grant finished *Another Country II* (1966), denoting by its title 'an area nationally or spiritually or morally accepted not to be our responsibility'.[9]

Grant, for perhaps the only period in his life, was acting as a politically engaged artist. He despaired of art he considered trivial, especially when related to popular culture. Watching a television documentary about the five artists selected to represent Britain at the Venice Biennale in 1966, in private he registered sympathy only for Richard Smith. His chief reproach was on the grounds of detachment – 'I don't know whether they experience life & I suspect they just

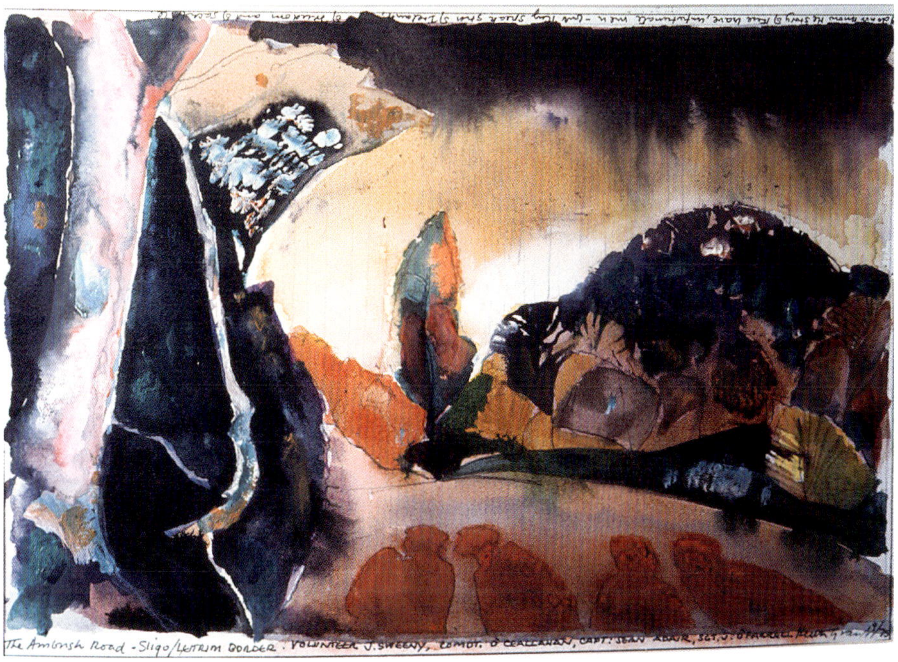

170
The Ambush Road, Sligo, Leitrim Border, 1975
Watercolour, ink and pencil on paper
20 × 27 cm
Private Collection, Norway

doodle it away.'[10] In February 1967, concurrently with his first solo exhibition at Roland, Browse and Delbanco, he organised the first of several exhibitions on behalf of the Medical Aid Committee for Vietnam, at a new exhibition hall attached to Camden Studios. More than 100 artists participated, some, including Patrick Heron and Bernard Cohen, waiving their percentage of sales. Over £1000 was raised. As the *Tribune* review commented, the exhibition in a small way filled the gap of 'What Can The Individual Do About Vietnam' while including artists of national stature, such as Michael Ayrton, Kenneth Armitage, Ceri Richards and Joe Tilson.[11] That summer, in France, Grant visited Berger, who spoke particularly encouragingly about Grant's 'new mobiles or landscapes in movement', since he considered that 'the easel painting as such is finished'. They explored together whether kinetic art might prove more effective at engaging the interest of the layman, who 'without the knowledge of the trends . . . [is] strict about what he permits himself to like.'[12] On 17 March 1968, having attended the anti-Vietnam protest outside the American Embassy in London, which notoriously (and to his horror) turned violent, Grant contacted the BBC to complain of the misrepresentation of events. Meanwhile, Berger applauded the written reports Grant sent him, which, he stated, provided inspiration for the 'Don Juan' novel he was writing, *G.*[13] Two years later, on 30 August 1970, Grant briefly joined the Communist Party, observing 'It was very much easier to join than it was to remain outside it.'[14]

Memorials

While Grant preferred to remain isolated from news while travelling, in order to experience landscape undisturbed, this was as impossible in practice as to ring-fence the creative space of his studio. North of Narvik in Norway, in 1966, surrounded by snow and mountains, Grant had watched an enormous convoy of lorries, tanks, light guns and machine gun carriers pass on the E6, on its way home from Vietnam, bringing 'in this remote place the sadness and horror . . . Even here we cannot escape.'[15] Returning from France in September 1971, a letter from Milada Tashnerova interrupted his focus on a new series of work based on French rivers. With Milada, Grant had explored Europe, inspiring paintings in which she featured against a fjord or amid trees (fig.97, p.116). Milada's letter caused him to revisit the reflection photographs taken in Czechoslovakia in 1970 and to contemplate a memorial to her brother's suicide, depicting an empty boat on a lake surrounded by pines. The cycle of connections this triggered ranged from the literary – Palinarus, Ophelia, Bertolt Brecht's *Drowned Girl*, George Eliot's *The Mill on the Floss*, Henrik Ibsen's *Rosmersholm* – to the actual. Uppermost in Grant's mind were the deaths of Jan

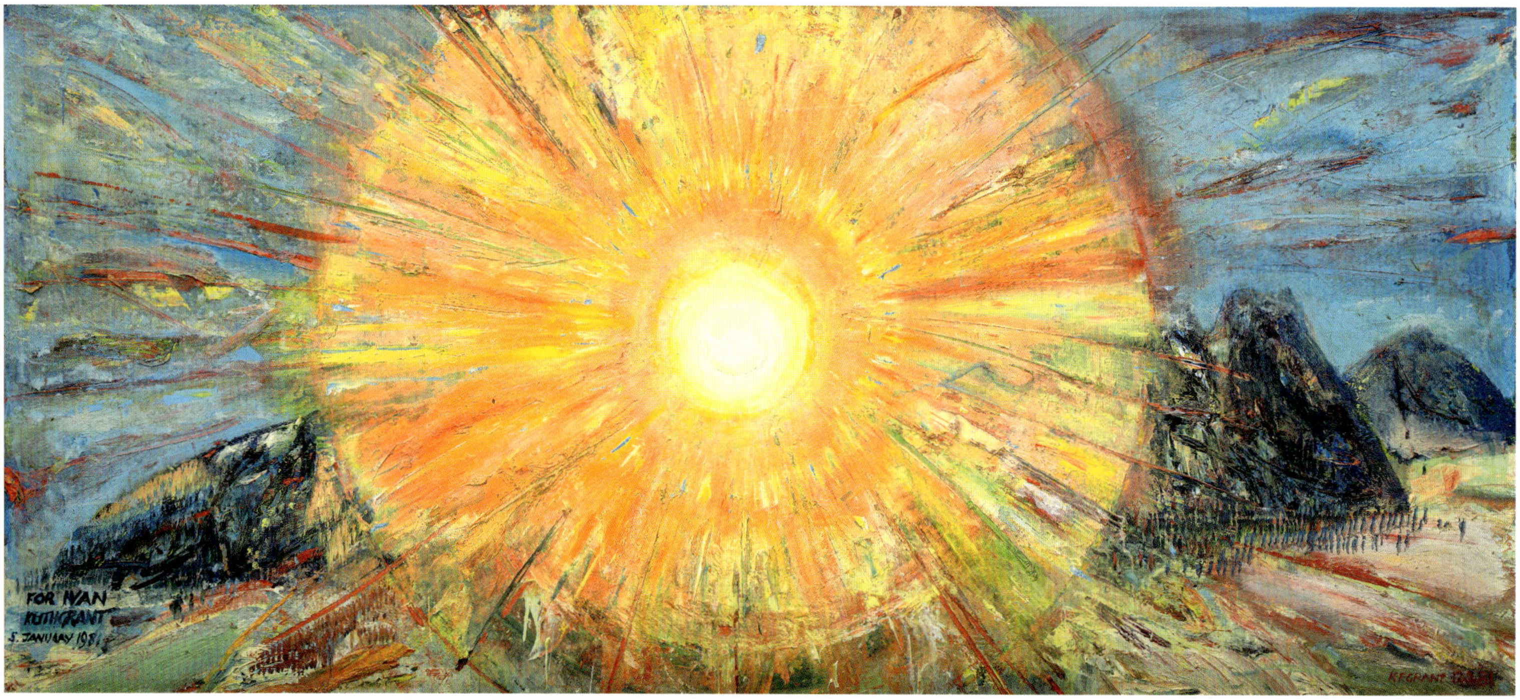

171
A Sun for Ivan, 1981
Oil on board
90 × 201.5 cm
Private Collection, UK

Palach, a young protester against the 1968 invasion of Czechoslovakia, of 'old Paul', a neighbour who drowned in Vereux, and most recently the American writer and activist George Jackson. He sensed in the paintings of rivers he was making a transferred uneasiness.[16] Accepting his inability to express himself except through the medium of his work, Grant questioned,

How can my landscapes disturb, how can my constructions teach? . . . if I achieve any distinction in my field . . . [it is because] my work speaks with another voice. It blandly shows the face of the earth, but behind that countenance there is tumult . . . I will protest that I am a socialist artist, and my love of the stolen earth, the polluted earth, is an identification of all that is denied the people, all that is devalued and decried by the capitalist mentality.[17]

The duality of Grant's landscapes can be explored by placing *Rain nr Lough Gill* (1975; fig.123, p.146) alongside *The Ambush Road* (1975; fig.170), painted five months later. Both address the same location: Lough Gill, County Sligo, in Ireland. The first is an uninhabited landscape, showing the peak of Ben Bulben under a grey, rain-washed sky. The second was painted following Grant's discovery of a rusted sign at Dooney Rock, commemorating the ambush and killing of four members of the National Army on 13 July 1922. As in *Death of the Swans* (fig.167), figures are present only through shadows; here, poignantly because of their death. Underneath, Grant commemorated their names as they appeared on the sign – Volunteer J. Sweeny, Comdt P. O'Ceallahan, Capt. Sean Adair, Segt J. O'Farrell – with at the top, 'I do not know the story of these brave, unfortunate men, but they speak still of Ireland, of freedom and of sacrifice.'

With Grant in Ireland had been Phillida Ball, whose brother, Ivan, was among the young people who helped construct the Charing Cross Hospital mural. In January 1981, Ivan took his own life at the age of 31. Dedicating to him a painting of the sun he had just finished, Grant described it as 'large and crude . . . a reflection of my shock and anger

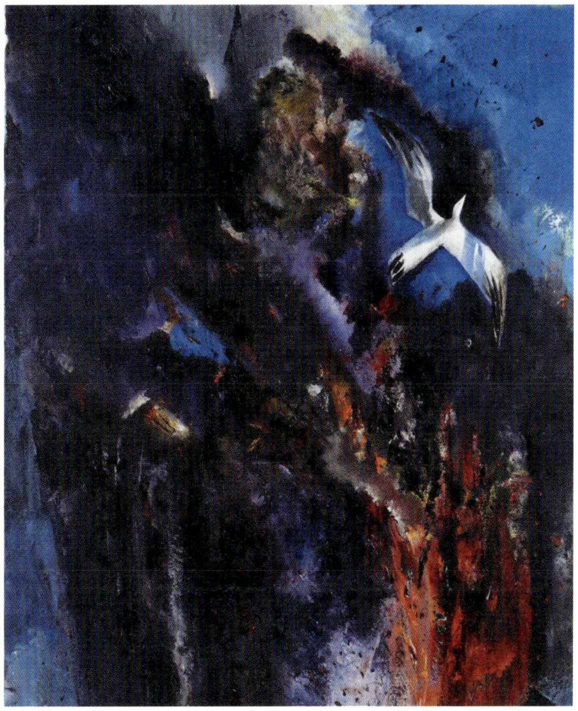

172
Volcano and White Bird, 1994
Oil on canvas
122 × 91 cm
Private Collection, Portugal

at the news' (fig.171).[18] *A Sun for Ivan* (1981) was a continuation of a series made for an exhibition at Roland, Browse & Darby that would open in less than a week's time. Reviewing the exhibition for the *Daily Telegraph*, Terence Mullaly described it as 'a violent explosion . . . one of the most impressive London one-man shows of recent years'. He focused on one sun painting in particular, which he considered 'a tour de force of which few living artists are capable . . . Almost the entire surface of the picture is taken up by a great erupting sun', white at the centre, radiating to yellow, touches of pink and the surrounding blue sky.[19] This painting, which has an intense, positive energy, is now in the collection of the Imperial Health Charity. *A Sun for Ivan* is altogether different. Livid and expressionistic, its brushstrokes are welts of red and yellow, its landscape furiously stippled in cyan and crimson to evoke pine forests. A memorial, it is one that burns with energy.

Near the beginning of his essay, 'Aesthetics and Nuclear Anaesthesia' (1981), the critic Peter Fuller alluded to Grant's recent sun paintings. The context was the devastating potential of a nuclear bomb, which would not only annihilate life but blind anyone who glimpsed its flare up to 200 miles away. Compared with this, Grant's practice of glancing at the sun with the naked eye, for his paintings, was mere child's play. Fuller was passionately involved with artists' peace initiatives. His article illustrated Peter Kennard's *The Haywain – Cruise Missiles* (1981), a subversive collaging of a Cruise missile onto John Constable's landscape, which Fuller considered flawed yet fascinating in its reference to 'two utterly irreconcilable opposites'.[20] Fuller and Grant were close during the 1980s, with Fuller due to write on Grant's paintings of Greenland before his premature death in a car accident in 1990. Grant wrote in defence of Fuller following Waldemar Januszczak's obituary in the *Guardian*, praising him as a 'courageous exponent of the validity of landscape painting at a time when it was deemed culturally valueless in the opinion of much of the influential art establishment'.[21]

Many of Grant's paintings are commemorations: not always conceived as such, but dedicated after completion to a friend or colleague who has died, or as a collective memorial, such as to crew of the three English trawlers lost off the coast of Iceland in 1968.[22] Each year Grant paints a silver birch tree, one of which commemorated his twin brother, Roy. Equally potent is the symbol of a single bird, usually white, often a gull, that Grant identifies as 'the white forager'. Although this bird appeared both before and after his son Paul's death, it is often linked in Grant's mind to his son's spirit. Such is the case with *Volcano and White Bird* (1994), an intensely rendered image of a marine volcano, in which a vortex of forces is set in motion by the eruption (fig.172). Pressed to the edges of the canvas, the sea churns, sending up a vertical spout; the blast from the crater ricochets splinters of rock into the blackened

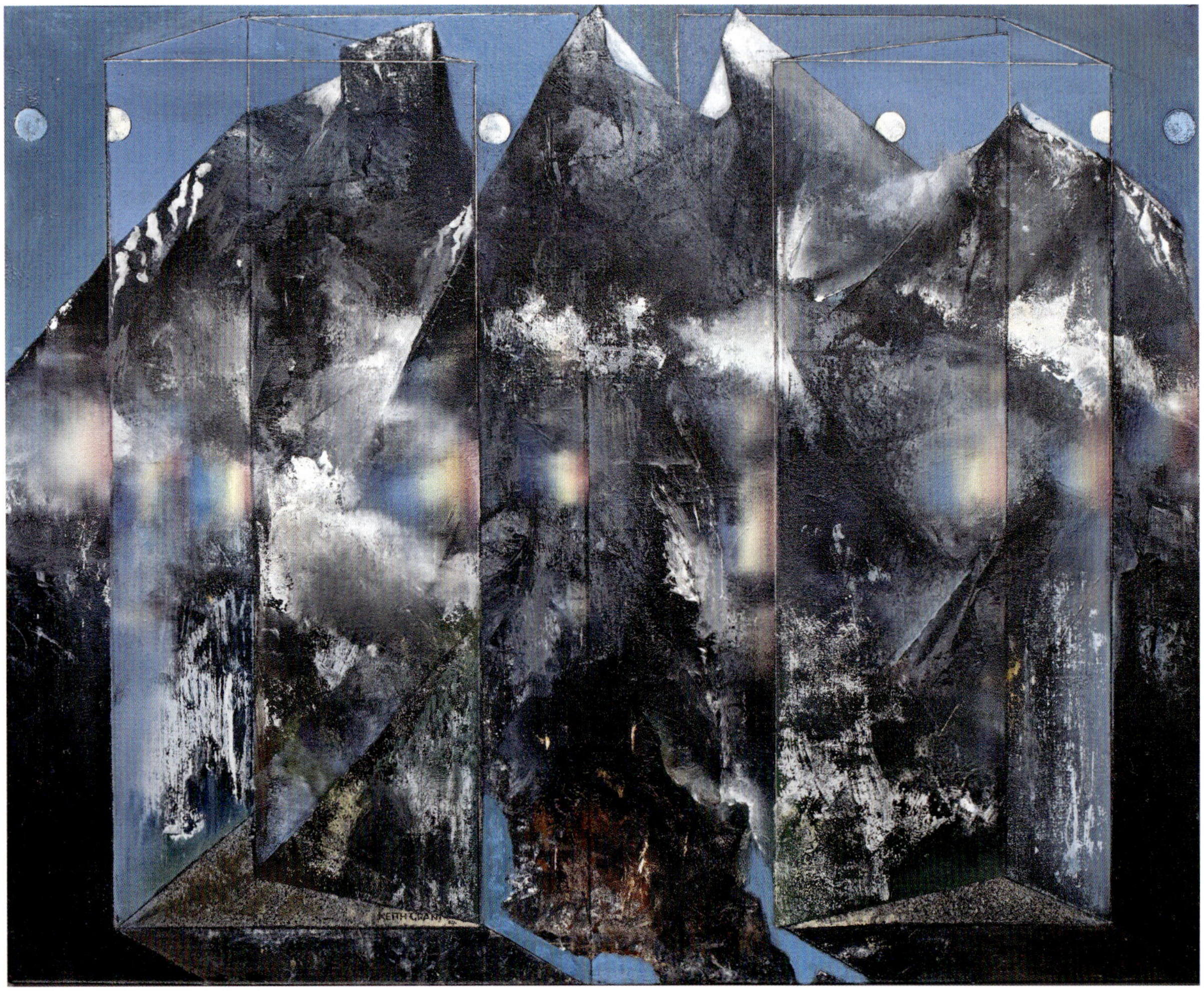

173
My Himalayas, 2014
Oil on canvas
61 × 91.5 cm
Private Collection, Norway

air. At the fulcrum is the bird, frail, white, possibly injured. An immolation? In 1968 Grant stood before Matthias Grünewald's *Crucifixion* (*c.*1515), absorbing the darkness behind Christ that threw its contemporary drama into light – 'darkness that has permeated the world ever since'. Of the painting itself, he wrote, 'I will not say anything about it as a work of art, but I want to say that I understood it very well.'[23]

The landscapes that Grant painted as symbols of protest or memory were capable of multiple resonances. *My Himalayas* (2014), for instance, is both a tribute to his friend, Trond Eilertsen, who had successfully climbed Everest a year earlier and a memorial to the 16 Sherpas killed in an avalanche on 18 April 2014, one of whom Eilertsen knew well (fig.173). It depicts a dark, brooding mountainscape seen through a structure resembling a folding glass screen. Grant observed how the wildness of the mountains was 'somehow measured and subdued' by the enclosure, while remaining, he felt, 'very disturbing'.[24] As the painting neared completion, it changed in character as Grant introduced reflections into the prism of the glass. The effect was no longer what he had envisaged as 'an oppressive masquerade' but extraordinarily beautiful and mysterious: a dance of light and texture.[25]

At Lødingen, north Norway, in 2015, Grant was struck by the extent of German fortifications, partially destroyed or used as storerooms, that formed a honeycomb across the peninsula. He conceived

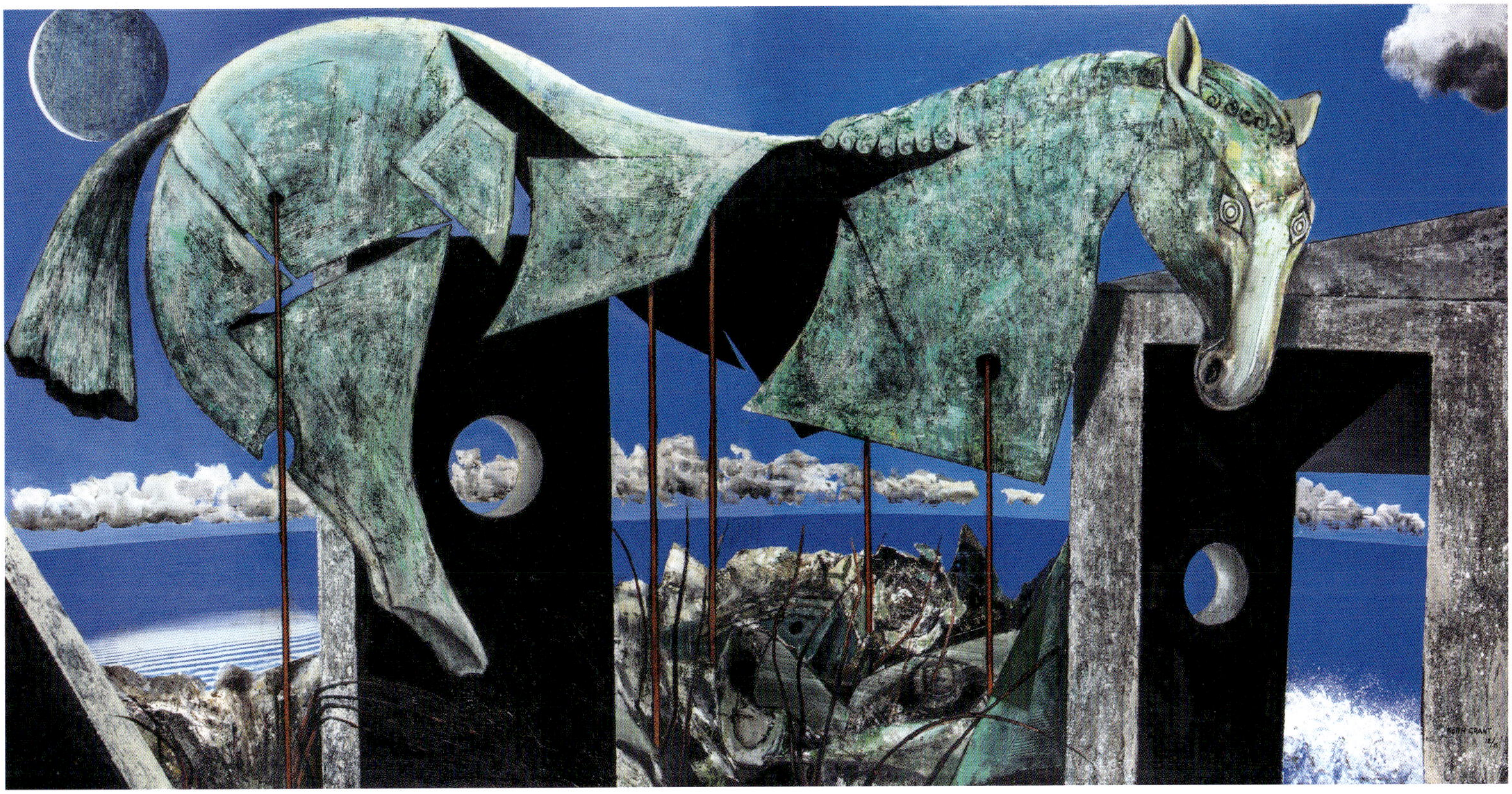

174
Demolition of the Trojan Horse, 2015
Oil on canvas
100 × 200 cm
Private Collection, Norway

an idea to develop the 'rock horse' series. Wood supplanted stone, then bronze replaced wood, as Grant explored versions of a Trojan horse being dismantled above the concrete bunkers. In the largest version, rusted iron rods support the remaining bronze plates of the horse to reveal it as the puppet, or hollow pretence, that it was (fig.174). The composition is superbly ordered and executed – from the textures of bronze and concrete to the echoes of eyes, moons and lookouts, or oxide-red grasses that claw and mimic the rods. It is a landscape of myth and memory, in which the apparatus of war may degrade, but will never be eradicated.

Destruction of the Environment

Rarely visible in Grant's paintings, landscape's pollution is a theme that has featured in his journals since the 1980s. It lies behind the unmarred spectacle of *Spring, 'The Pells', Lewes*, painted in 1982 (fig.115, p.139). Four years later, working on a series of sea paintings, Grant recalled first becoming aware of the 'vast quantities' of plastic washed onto Britain's coastlines when walking at Worbarrow Bay in Dorset with the actor Edward Fox. At the time, he thought of converting the floating plastic bottles into marks of paint, commenting 'Perhaps in one way the careless gestural behaviour which produces pollution . . . is part of the harmonious pattern of our interaction with nature.' His comments were not without censure, but he did underline the 'elegant insensate justification' of the sea returning waste to the feet (or shorelines) of those who abandon it.[26] To an artist preoccupied with the surrealistic transformation of found objects, any happenstance event in the landscape is a gift.

In 2015, when Grant received a commission for a painting related to the work of the demolition company John F. Hunt, he visited five of their sites

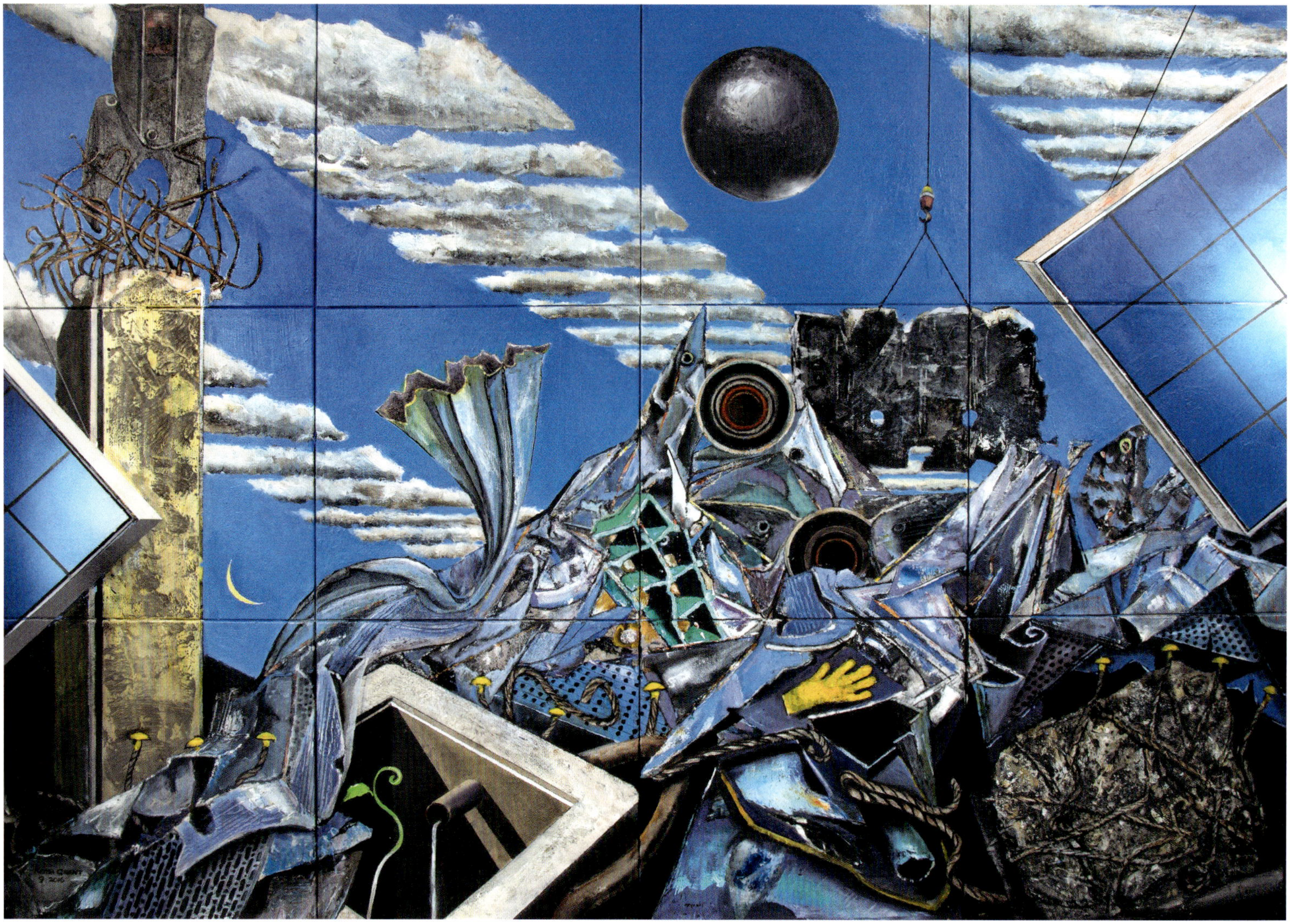

to collect data. The original intention was to make a series entitled *12 Stanzas of Demolition*, for reproduction as a company calendar. Sifting the imagery of rubble, scrap metal and machinery designed to 'rend, tear, bend, crush and pulverise', he began to associate it with the parallel behaviour of nature in its struggle to survive.[27] The evolving versions of the work recorded as photographs in Grant's journal bear witness to the work's genesis, from a mosaic of images, including a mechanical digger, to an apocalyptic vision of humankind's legacy (fig.175). Concrete is torn to show its writhing armatures, polythene rears as a poison-chaliced flower, a perforated concrete slab suggests the eyes of a death mask. This is one way of interpreting the composition. Yet Grant effects it with such surrealistic sophistication that it is hard to decide whether the effect is malevolent or otherwise. Panes of glass dangle modishly, mirroring an azure sky stacked rhythmically with clouds. The wrecking ball metamorphoses into a gleaming graphite sun – a glitter ball in the sky – while the moon appears as a jaunty crescent below.

What Grant has created, far beyond any corporate image, is a companion piece to the

175
The Discarded Glove: A Demolition Allegory, 2016
Oil on board
122 × 162.5 cm
Private Collection, UK

metamorphic forest paintings (see fig.103, p.123) and to *Atlantis III* (fig.110, pp 130–31), in the company of which it evolved. The image of a cistern (or oracle) appears at the perimeter. Sharp points of metal resemble fish or birds. Nature, implied in the mushrooming yellow bolts, is present in a tentative green shoot, fostered by the cistern's dripping spout. At the centre, a yellow plastic glove is virtually the only element to have survived from the original scheme, denoting the human agency for the destruction. How did Grant see the composition? It was a job, a commission, an opportunity that grew into an inspiring, creative challenge. Writing to Andrew Lambirth, Grant alluded to Paul Nash's *Totes Meer* (1940–41), in which Nash transformed the sight of wrecked aircraft in a field in Oxfordshire into 'a great inundating sea', static and dead, yet appearing to twist in *rigor mortis* in the moonlight.[28] A contemporary resonance, mentioned only briefly in Grant's journals at this point, was the startling similarity of elements in the painting to the destruction seen daily in news from Syria.[29]

Visiting Cyprus in 2014, Grant had bought a book from which a photograph of a golden oriole, caught illegally by trappers, continued to haunt him. As an image of cruelty against an innocent creature, it encapsulated, for him, the merciless bombardment of eastern Aleppo. Returning to the subject in 2016, he hesitated, questioning the motivation of using human tragedy as the basis for art. He resolved in favour of attempting 'a visual damnation of those that kill other human beings', while acknowledging that 'such passions are not supposed to be experienced by a pastoralist such as myself'.[30] The self-portrait of the artist as 'pastoralist' might be justified as a reflection upon the English and Selborne landscapes Grant was currently painting. Otherwise, it is a curious mellowing of spirit from one who fifty years earlier attended the demonstration against the war in Vietnam.

Aleppo and Ukraine

As it transpired, paintings based on Aleppo would be the first of a new body of paintings precipitated by humanitarian concerns. A sketch for *Aleppo*, completed in October 2016, shows a city aflame and crumbling. From this, Grant deduced that a much larger canvas was needed: a scale analogous to the *Iliad* or *War and Peace*, upon which to express war's 'vileness, cruelty and dispassion'.[31] In the *Aleppo* sketch, using acrylic on board, a golden oriole is depicted almost as in the photograph from the book, with golden-brown plumage and distinctive markings. In *Aleppo*, painted in oil on canvas, the bird's stricken posture is retained but rendered almost in sepia or *grisaille*, harrowed in death (fig.176). The backdrop is drastically simplified, recalling the flames in Nicholas Hilliard's portrait miniature, *An Unknown Man* (*c.*1600). In the foreground, a precariously balanced egg denotes the fragility of life. Grant ensures there is no mistaking the subject by printing 'ALEPPO' boldly in the corner of the canvas.

In February 2022, the Russian invasion of Ukraine provided an impulse for three further works in which landscape serves as a medium to express Grant's anger and sadness. The first, *The Birch Tree of Ukraine* (2022), depicts a single tree, resolute and upright against a forest of fire (figs 177–8). The trunks glow red, suggesting the advance of Russian troops from darkness. In the second painting, *From a Ukrainian*

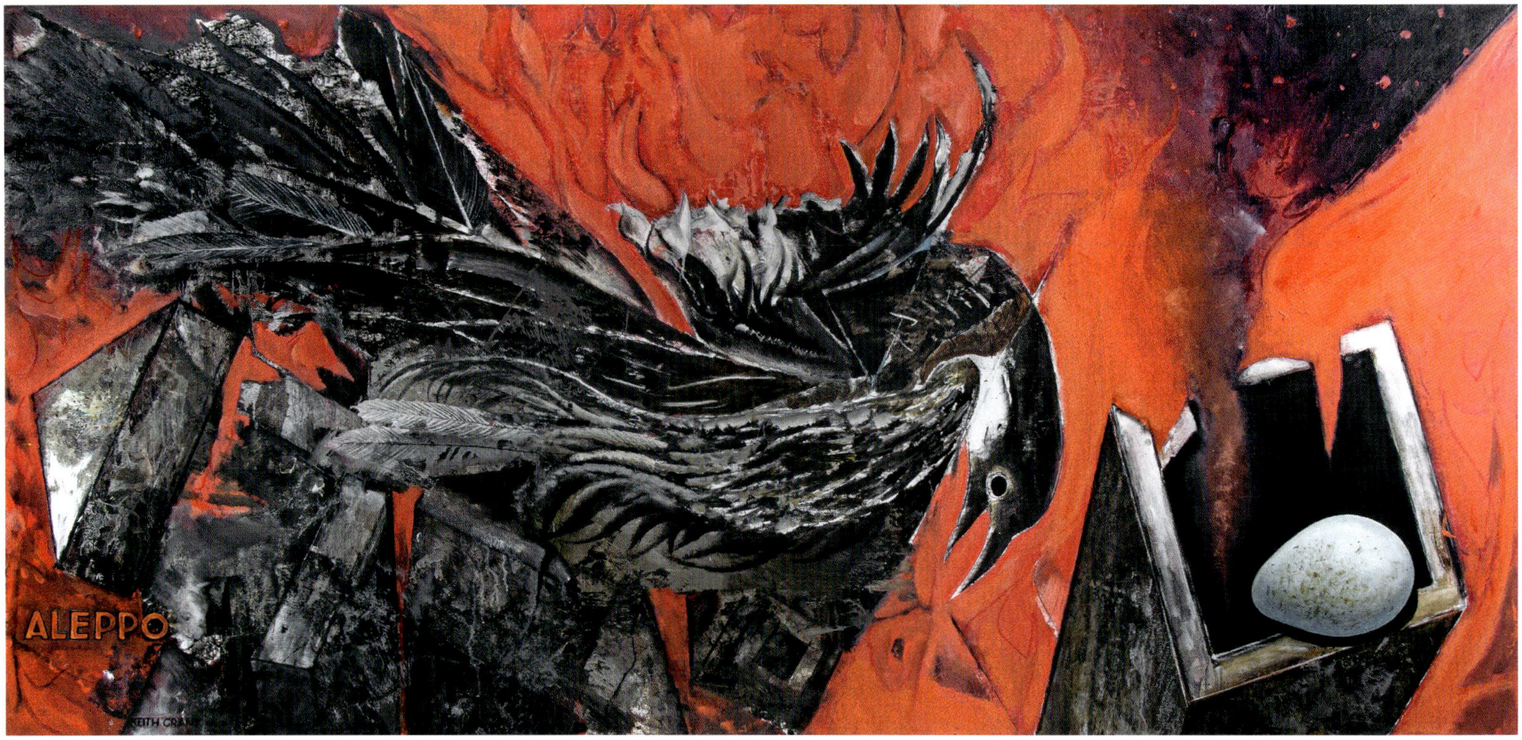

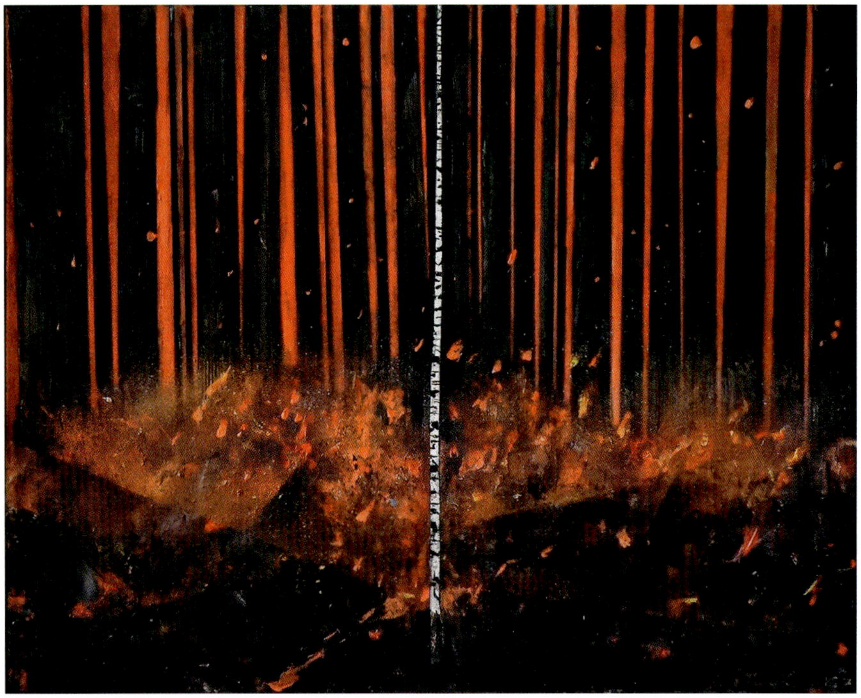

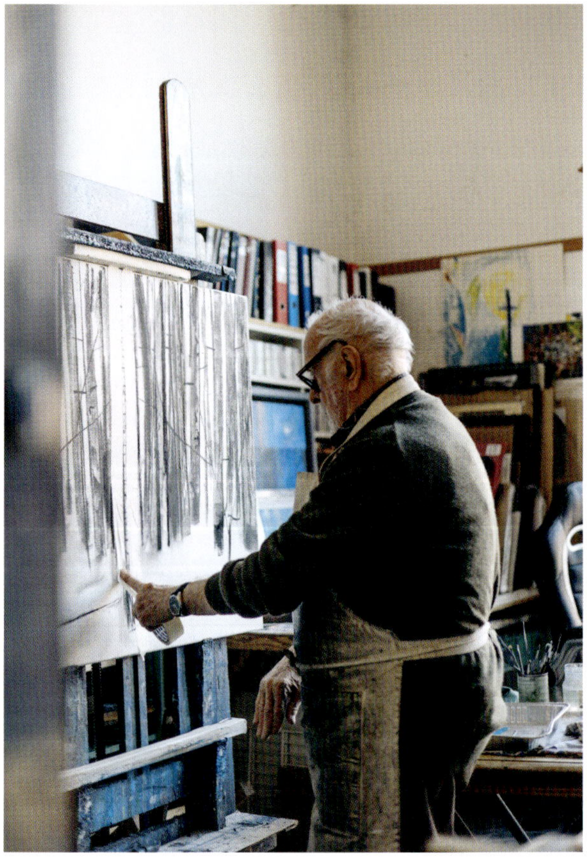

176 (above)
Aleppo, 2016
Oil on canvas
110 × 221 cm
Collection of the artist

177 (below left)
The Birch Tree of Ukraine, 2022
Oil on linen
80 × 100 cm
Ukrainian Cultural Centre, Luxembourg

178 (below right)
Keith Grant painting *The Birch Tree of Ukraine* in his studio in Norway, 2022
Photograph by Luca Jahn

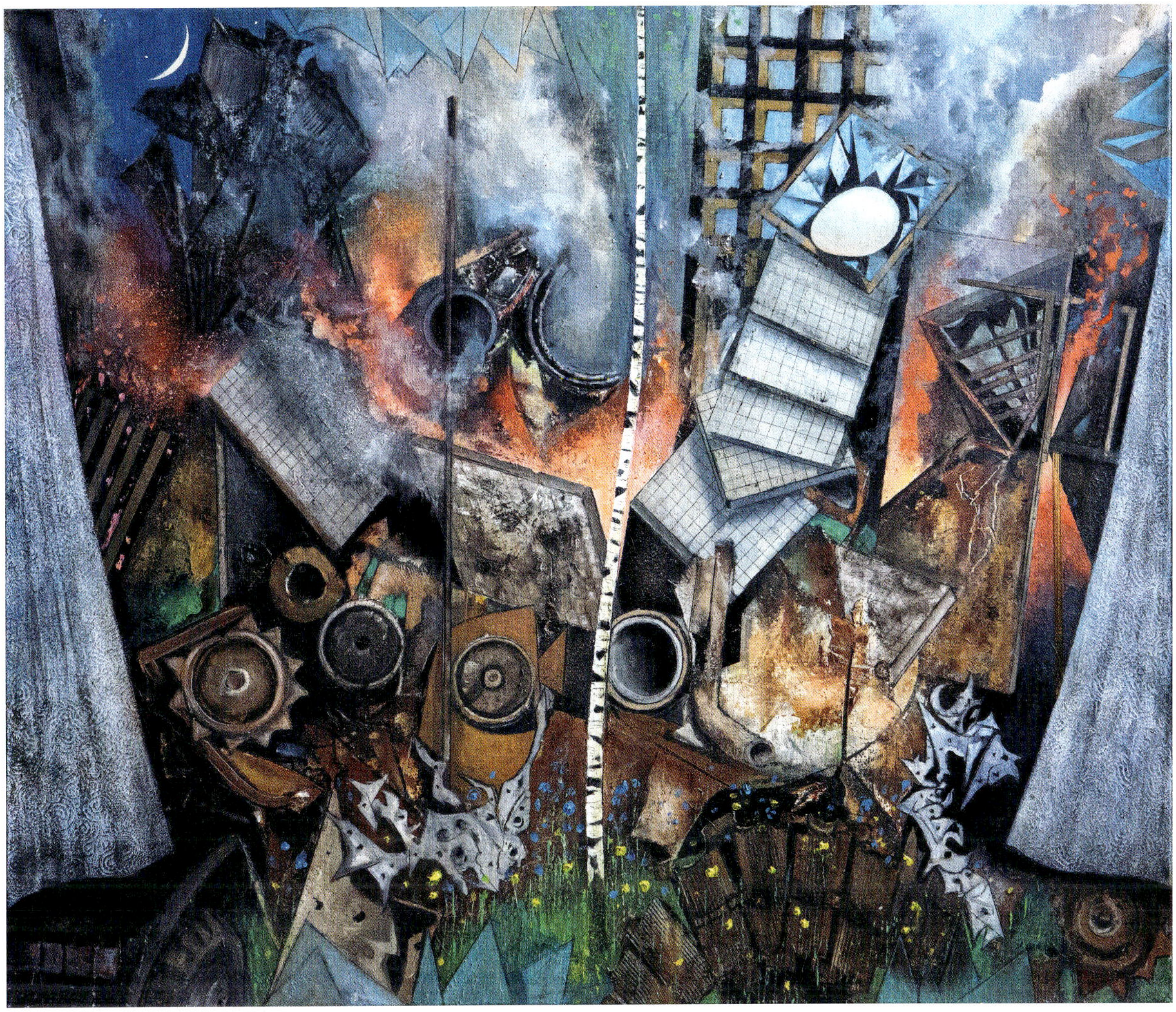

179
From a Ukrainian Child's Room, 2022
Oil on linen
100 × 120 cm
Collection of the artist

Child's Room (2022), Grant shifts to a metamorphic, surrealistic mode (fig.179). Beyond the curtains is a scene of catastrophic destruction. Windows shatter and cascade amid a cacophony of weaponry. The landscape burns, yet the egg appears unbroken and the birch stands as a symbol of resistance, undercarpeted by delicate yellow and blue flowers. Finally, *When you are gone* (2022) suggests the reclaiming of landscape (fig.180). In this, perhaps the closest equivalent to Nash's *Totes Meer*, twisted metal rusts on the forest floor, softened by snow and moonlight. There is a depth and stillness that, unlike Nash's landscape, suggests the enclosure of a cathedral.

These paintings are particularly arresting in their suggestion of new registers for considering landscape. *From a Ukrainian Child's Room* takes as its starting point a scene glimpsed through curtains, a device used already in the *Delius* series (see Chapter 8). Derived from a memory of Edvard Munch's *The Sick Child*, in which a curtain blows across the edge of the painting, it references also the bizarre conjoining of events in Paul Nash's *Harbour and Room* (1932–6), where a ship and seascape enter, via mirrored reflections, into the bedroom. Grant dissolves any division between outer and inner, but further complicates his composition by assembling within it a miscellany of events. By comparison, the

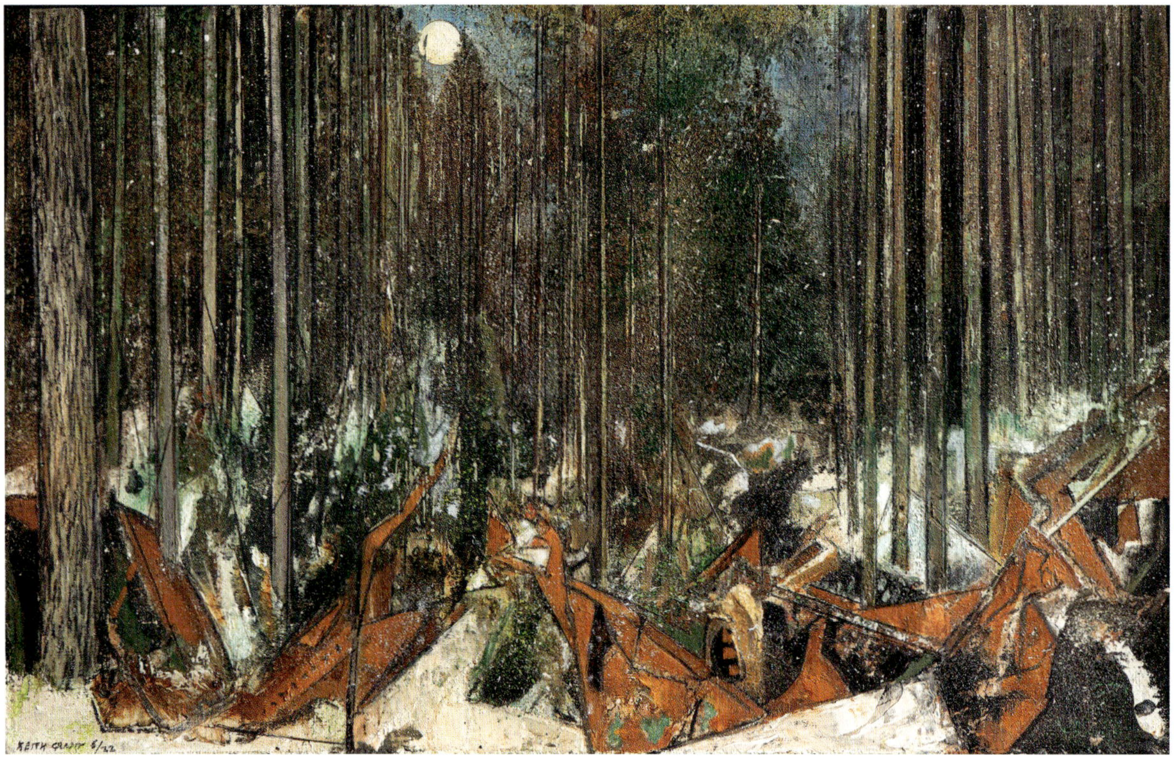

180
When you are gone, 2022
Oil on linen
55.5 × 83 cm
Collection of the artist

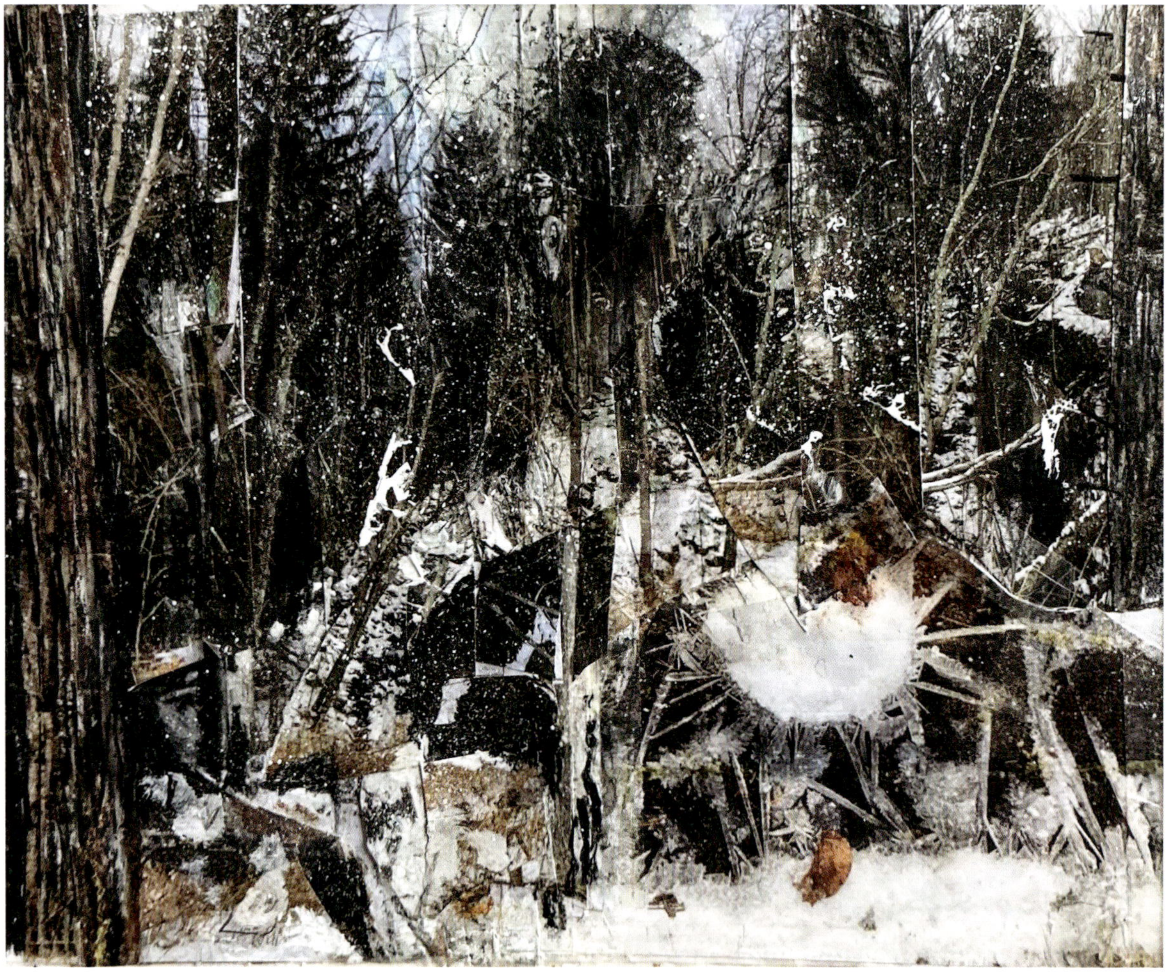

181
Once you are gone, 2022
Collage and acrylic on paper,
laid on board
25 × 32 cm
Collection of the artist

182
Keith Grant drawing, Norway, November 2018, photograph by Anne-Katrin Purkiss

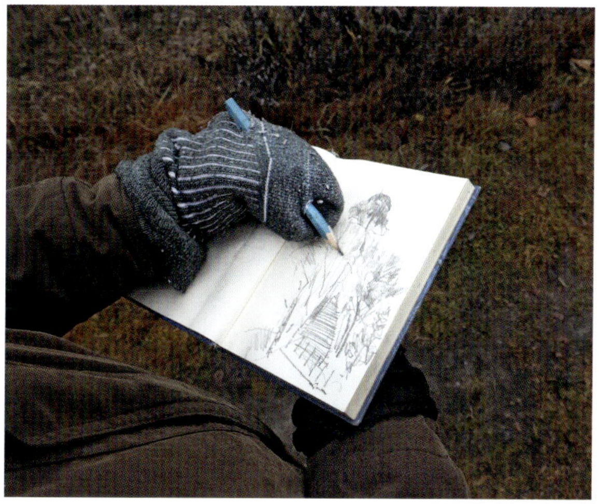

symbolism of *The Birch Tree of Ukraine* appears relatively straightforward. But turning to a collage, made as a study for *When you are gone*, Grant's lens shifts. Cutting and collaging photographs of the forest in Norway, before painting over them, he creates an image deconstructing the landscape: snow resembling birch bark splinters into ice crystals (fig.181). A white detonation, originally intended to feature in the painting, too, was abandoned. And what of the birch tree?

The transfiguration of the birch is one of the most intriguing aspects of Grant's work. He has always identified it with Norway, as a symbol of resilience. A study written by Tom Jeffreys, *The White Birch* (2021), takes a different slant; principally – and ironically, in the context of Grant's recent paintings – by addressing the significance of the birch to Russia. Jeffreys casts his net widely, exploring the birch in art, history, as a symbol of protest and of contested borders. The trees, of course, respect no geographical divisions. They are relatively short lived, with a lifespan comparable with that of humans. They are almost impossible to classify. *Betula klokovii*, claimed by one botanist to be represented by as few as fifty specimens in a tiny area of western Ukraine, is not recognised by other experts. ('In some countries there is a nationalistic wish to have endemic species which only occur in that country – even though they may not be distinguishable from similar plants in neighbouring countries.')[32] Birch trees flower and produce seed quickly, often being the first to colonise new land, adapting to poor soils, inhospitable climates and high altitudes. They occupy patches of seemingly barren soil, reducing acidity, encouraging earthworms and increasing fertility. Transformed, the earth may foster hungrier plants, while the birch forests die and regenerate elsewhere. It is a narrative, as Jeffreys concludes, that challenges the notion of landscape as fixed. The birch represents 'something temporal, fragile, in need perhaps of protection. Yet it is also flexible, adaptable, and maybe even hardier than species such as the oak or elm more traditionally associated with strength.'[33]

At Mogritsa, where a Ukrainian land art festival was first held in 1997, close to the Russian border, an artist threaded red fabric between the birch trees on the Ukrainian side in memory of the millions who died in the Holodomor, a famine induced in 1932–3 by the Soviet authorities. As Anna Gidora, the festival's founder, explained, 'birch trees are associated with Russia, the red with aggression and blood'.[34] Grant's blazing forest is thus in all senses a radical landscape, reclaiming the birch, with its powers to resist, transform and heal, for Ukraine. While it is premature to anticipate the outcome of this particular conflict, Grant's message is that in nature – and landscape – there is always hope for renewal.

Chronology

1930

Born 10 August, Liverpool

1948–50

National Service, RAF

1950–58

Studied at Working Men's College, St Pancras (1950–52); Willesden School of Art (1952–5); Royal College of Art (1955–8)

1956–61

Married to Valerie Owen

1957

First visit to Norway

1964–96

Married to Gisèle Barka Djouadi

1971

Daughter, Dominique, born

1974

Son, Paul, born (died 1995)

1996

Settled in Norway

2000

Married Hilde Ellingsen. Together they have a daughter, Thea

Teaching

1958–60

Kingston School of Art

1961–2

Gravesend School of Art

1962–3

Goldsmiths' College of Art

1963–8

Lecturer, Hornsey College of Art

1968–71

Head of Fine Art Department, Maidstone

1971

Byam Shaw School and St Martin's School of Art

1973–5

Gulbenkian Award Artist-in-Residence, Bosworth College, Leicester

1975–9

Camberwell School of Art and St Martin's School of Art

1979–81

Head of Painting Department, Newcastle Polytechnic

1981–90

Head of Department of Art, Roehampton Institute

Exhibitions, Commissions and Collections

Select Solo and Two-Person Exhibitions

1955 *A Students [sic] Progress*, Bootle Art Gallery
1960 New Art Centre, London
1962 New Art Centre, London
1964 New Art Centre, London
1965 Galleria Montenapoleone, Milan (with John Grome)
1966 New Art Centre, London
1967 *The North Lands*, Roland, Browse & Delbanco, London
1969 *Paintings of the North*, Geffrye Museum, London
1970 *Recent Paintings of the Northlands*, Roland, Browse & Delbanco, London
1972 *Recent Paintings*, Roland, Browse & Delbanco, London
Paintings of Norway, Folkestone Arts Centre
1973 *The Narrow Road to the Deep North*, Scottish Arts Council Gallery, Edinburgh (and tour)
Icelandair, London (opened by Sir Kenneth Clark)
1974 *Recent Paintings – Norway and Iceland*, Roland, Browse & Delbanco, London
Loans and New Works, Folkestone Arts Centre
National Gallery of Iceland, Reykjavik
Paintings of Norway, Aldeburgh Festival, The New Gallery, Snape Maltings
1976 *Recent Paintings – Iceland and Ireland*, Roland, Browse & Delbanco, London
The Way to Cold Mountain, Rochdale Art Gallery
The Paintings and Drawings of Keith Grant at Bosworth, Leicestershire Museum and Art Gallery
1977 *The Volcano in the North*, Portsmouth Museum & Art Gallery
Roland, Browse & Delbanco, London
1978 Town Hall, Svolvær, Lofoten Islands, Norway
1979 *A Winter Journey*, Browse & Darby, London
Landscapes of the North, Compass Gallery, Glasgow
Ibsenhuset, Skien, Norway
1980 Polytechnic Art Gallery, Newcastle upon Tyne (touring to Loughborough College of Art and Design)
Keith Grant: Paintings, Metropole Arts Centre, Folkestone
The Festival of North Norway: Keith Grant, Harstad, Norway (supported by the British Council)
1981 *The Sun*, Browse & Darby, London
The Elements: Paintings of Iceland, Norway and England, Elizabethan Exhibition Gallery, Wakefield
City Art Gallery, Trondheim, Norway
1982 Solomon Gallery, Dublin
Yehudi Menuhin School, Stoke D'Abernon, Surrey
1983 *Paintings from French Guiana*, Logica Holdings Ltd, London
E.S.A. Pavilion, International Air Show, Le Bourget, Paris
1984 *Recent Landscapes of England and South America*, Browse & Darby, London
1985 *Paintings and Drawings of Sarawak*, Francis Kyle Gallery, London
Recent Painting, Aldeburgh Festival, Aldeburgh Cinema
1986 *Between Two Extremes: Painting and Drawings of French Guiana and Sarawak*, Metropole Arts Centre, Folkestone
1987 *Paintings of the North and the Tropics*, Abbot Hall Art Gallery, Kendal
Landscapes of the Frozen North, Francis Kyle Gallery, London
1988 Cadogan Contemporary, London
Touring exhibition to Alta, Tromsø, North Norway
1989 Cadogan Contemporary, London
1990 *Paintings of the Arctic and the Desert*, Crane Kalman Gallery, London
1991 *Keith Grant, Artist in Residence: Recent Paintings*, Roehampton Institute, London
1992 *Recent Paintings: Rainforest and the Kaieteur Falls, Guyana; Arctic Night Skies*, Gillian Jason Gallery, London
1993 *Farther North: Paintings of the Arctic*, The First Gallery, Southampton
1994 *Ice and Fire*, Fitzwilliam Museum, Cambridge
Ice and Fire, Rocket Gallery, London
Glyndebourne Opera House
1995 *Paintings and Drawings*, Cassian de Vere Cole, London

1996 Cadogan Contemporary, London
Cercle Munster, Luxembourg
Star Gallery, Lewes
1997 *The Northern Element: Landscape Paintings*, St John's International School Art Gallery, Waterloo, Belgium
Malerier, Ibsenhuset, Skiens Kunstforening, Norway (supported by the British Council)
Galleri Amare, Stavanger, Norway
1998 Cadogan Contemporary, London
Haugesund Art Gallery, Norway
2000 *Recent Paintings*, Cadogan Contemporary, London
2003 *Antarctica*, Cadogan Contemporary, London
Antarctic Landscapes, Churchill College, Cambridge
2004 *In Antarctica*, Number Nine the Gallery, Birmingham
2005 *Recent Paintings*, Cadogan Contemporary, London
2006 Galleri Arctandria, Oslo, Norway
2008 *Snow, Sea and Stars*, Partridge Gallery, London
Galleri Arctandria, Oslo, Norway
2010 *Elements of the Earth*, Chris Beetles Gallery, London
2016 *Metamorphosis*, Chris Beetles Gallery, London
2017 *North by New English*, Chris Beetles Gallery, London
2018 *Antarctica*, Chris Beetles Gallery, London
2020 *Invention and Variation*, Chris Beetles Gallery, London
2022 *Visions of Nature*, Biodiversum, Luxembourg

Select Group Exhibitions

1954 *Young Contemporaries*, Royal Society of British Artists, London (and Arts Council tour)
Six Young Contemporaries and Hubert Dalwood, Gimpel Fils, London
Thirty Contemporary Paintings, Arts Council (tour)
1955 *Daily Express Young Artists' Exhibition*, New Burlington Galleries, London
1957 *Summer Exhibition*, Royal Academy, London
1958 *Young Contemporaries*, Royal Society of British Artists, London (and Arts Council tour, 1959)
Summer Exhibition, Royal Academy, London
1959 *St Pancras Artists*, St Pancras Festival, St Pancras Town Hall, London
Summer Exhibition, Royal Academy, London
September Selection, New Art Centre, London
1960 *Summer Exhibition*, Royal Academy, London
Contemporary Painting and Sculpture for Leicestershire Schools, Arts Council (tour)
1961 *Spring Exhibition*, Bradford City Art Gallery
London Group, RBA Galleries, London
1962 *Keith Grant, Terry Lee, Donald Pass. Pictures for Offices*, New Art Centre, London
Towards Art?, Royal College of Art, London
1965 *Contemporary Drawings and Watercolours*, New Art Centre, London
St Pancras Artists, St Pancras Town Hall, London
Summer Exhibition, Royal Academy, London
1968 *25 Camden Artists*, 1968 Camden Festival, Central Library, Swiss Cottage, London
Exhibition of Contemporary Art, Camden Studios, London; proceeds to Medical Aid Committee for Vietnam
Sculpture Exhibition: City of London Festival
1969 *Summer Exhibition*, Royal Academy, London
1970 *Summer Exhibition*, Royal Academy, London
Kinetics, Hayward Gallery, London
1971 *British Paintings and Drawings*, Roland, Browse & Delbanco
1972 *Summer Exhibition*, Royal Academy, London
1973 *Peter Coker; Alfred Cohen; Keith Grant; Barbara Tribe*, Fieldborne Galleries, London
1974 *Ludlow Festival*
1976 *The Roland Collection*, Camden Arts Centre, London
1980 *Festival of North Norway*, Harstad, Norway

1983 *Pintura británica contemporánea*, Museo Municipal, Madrid
Modern Art and Nature, Scottish National Gallery of Modern Art, Edinburgh
1986 *The Ridgeway*, Swindon Art Gallery
1987 *Susan Foster; Keith Grant; Bill Wilkinson; Don Wilkinson*, Abbot Hall Art Gallery, Kendal
1989 *Ten Contemporary Scottish Painters*, Thackeray Gallery, London
Images of Paradise, for Survival International, Harewood House, Leeds
The Late Dr Guy Howard's Collection, Abbot Hall Art Gallery, Kendal
1990 *Rainforest Art*, Natural History Museum, London
1995 *SPENN*, Sortland, North Norway
1996 Kunstnerhuset, Sortland, North Norway
2000 *Summer Exhibition*, Haugesund Art Gallery, Norway
2010 *Volcano*, Compton Verney, Warwickshire

Public Commissions

1957 Murals for Verulamium Museum, St Albans (destroyed)
1959 Mural for Rhodesia House, London (destroyed)
Shell Guide to Wiltshire
1961 Shell Guide to Cardiganshire and Breconshire
1962 Shell Guide to Shetland
1964 Mural for Silver Springs Hotel, Cork (destroyed)
1965 Stage designs for Ingmar Bergman's *A Painting on Wood* and *The City*, LAMDA, London
1970 *Idomeneo* (Arts Council grant)
1971 *St Joan*, Shaw Theatre, Euston Road
1972 Mural for Middlesex Hospital (destroyed)
1975 Mural for Charing Cross Hospital, London
1977 Stage designs for *Salomé*, Collegiate Theatre, London
1979 Mosaic for Charing Cross Hospital, London (installed 1980)
1980 Mosaic for Gateshead Metro
1981 Stage designs for Hamlet
1994 Stained-glass window dedicated to J.B. Priestley and Jacquetta Hawkes, Belle Vue Boys' School, Bradford (relocated to Beckfoot Upper Heaton School)
1999/2000 Stained-glass windows for Charing Cross Hospital
2005 Altarpiece for Kopervik Church, Karnøy, Norway (destroyed)

Public Collections

Abbot Alfred East Art Gallery, North Northamptonshire Council; All Souls College, University of Oxford; Art Gallery of Hamilton, Ontario, Canada; Art Gallery of South Australia, Adelaide; Arts Council Collection, Southbank Centre; Atkinson Art Gallery, Southport; Beaverbrook Art Gallery, Fredericton, Canada; Britten Pears Arts, Aldeburgh; The Fitzwilliam Museum, Cambridge; Fundacíon Alejo Carpentier, Cuba; Government Art Collection; Hatton Gallery, Newcastle; Haugesund Art Gallery, Norway; The Hepworth, Wakefield; Imperial College of Science and Technology, London; Imperial Health Charity Art Collection; Lakeland Arts (Abbot Hall Gallery, Kendal); Leamington Spa Art Gallery & Museum; Leicestershire County Council Artworks Collection; London Borough of Camden Council; Manchester City Art Gallery; National Gallery, Guyana; National Gallery of Iceland; New Cross Hospital, Wolverhampton; North Lincolnshire Museums Service; Portsmouth Museums, Portsmouth City Council; Royal College of Art; Sainsbury Centre for Visual Arts, Norwich; Te Papa Tongarewa Museum of New Zealand; Touchstones, Rochdale; Towner, Eastbourne; Trondheim City Art Gallery, Norway; University of Birmingham; University of Surrey; Victoria and Albert Museum, London.

Sources and Notes

Sources

The majority of Grant's surviving sketchbooks and journals, from 1961 to 2003, are in the collection of the Fitzwilliam Museum, Cambridge. The remainder are located in the artist's archive, Norway.

Notes

Introduction: Elemental, Radical – The Landscape Paintings of Keith Grant

1 Corinne Fowler, 'Landscape and Empire: colonial contexts and legacies', in *Radical Landscapes*, exh. cat., Tate Publishing, London, 2022, p.46.

2 Keith Grant, *Maratime Polar* [*sic*], c.1972, unpublished manuscript. Fitzwilliam, GRANT 2a.

3 David Attenborough, *Keith Grant: Recent Paintings: Rainforest and the Kaieteur Falls, Guyana, Arctic Night Skies*, exh.cat., Gillian Jason Gallery, London, 1992.

4 Four extracts from Grant's journals were published, with illustrations, in *The London Magazine*: 'May in Iceland: a painter's journal', vol.10, no.2, May 1970, pp 5–18; 'Norway: some images from a notebook', vol.13, no.2, June 1973, pp 29–36; 'Notes from Kourou, F.G.: the launching of Ariane', vol.24, no.7, October 1984, pp 43–52; 'Extracts from a Sarawak Journal', vol.30, no.1, April–May 1990, pp 47–65.

5 Gerald Forty, 'The Painting of Keith Grant: introduction for the catalogue of Keith Grant's exhibition – Norway 1980', typescript. Artist's Archive, Norway.

6 Jack Hazan, conversation with the author, June 2022.

7 Keith Grant, Journals, 13 August 1987. Fitzwilliam, GRANT 2/21.

8 Grant, Journals, 20 August 1987. Fitzwilliam, GRANT 2/21.

9 William Shakespeare, *Hamlet*, Act II, Scene I.

1 A Land

1 Keith Grant, interview with the author, 10 October 2021.

2 Grant, interview with the author, 28 September 2021.

3 Grant, interviews with the author, 19 January and 28 September 2021.

4 F. Cromwell Cooke, 'Post-war Teachers – Working Men's College', *St Pancras Artists*, exh.cat., 11th St Pancras Arts Festival, London, 1965, pp 3–4.

5 'Extract from Lowes Dickinson Report – June 1952', annotated typescript. Artist's Archive, Norway.

6 Grant, 'The Journey to the South of France', Lowes Dickinson Scholarship Lecture, given at the Working Men's College, 22 February 1954, handwritten script. Artist's Archive, Norway.

7 'Young Contemporaries', BBC Television, 8.15 pm, 12 February 1954, and 'The Critics', The Third Programme, February 1954.

8 *Six Young Contemporaries and Hubert Dalwood*, Gimpel Fils, London, August 1954. Other student artists included Craigie Aitchison (1928–2009) and Bernard Cohen (b.1933).

9 Stephen Bone, 'Darkness visible: striving for romance by young artists', *Manchester Guardian*, 3 May 1955, p.5.

10 James Hyman, *The Battle for Realism: Figurative Art in Britain During the Cold War 1945–1960*, Yale University Press, London, 2001, p.42.

11 Royal College of Art, *Annual Report*, 1956, p.53.

12 'Back to Boadicea with the artist's eye: murals for Verulamium Museum', *Guardian*, 22 August 1957.

13 Keith Grant, 'Modern Mural Decoration', *The Artist*, vol.59, no.3, issue 351, May 1960, p.61.

14 Terence Mullaly, 'Mural with a triple theme', *Daily Telegraph*, 5 November 1958, p.10.

15 Grant, 'Above Verulamium', *ARK*, no.21, spring 1958, pp 27–9.

16 See Scott Anthony, Oliver Green and Margaret Timmers, *Shell Art & Advertising*, Lund Humphries, London, 2021.

17 'Summer exhibitions', *The Times*, 13 August 1962.

18 See Margaret Garlake, *Artists Making Landscapes in Post-war Britain*, Modern Art Press, London, 2021, pp 70–71.

19 Kenneth Clark, 'The End of Landscape Painting', lecture notes, Oxford, 16 June 1947, quoted in Catherine Jolivette, *Landscape, Art and Identity in 1950s Britain*, Routledge, Abingdon, 2016, p.156.

20 Kenneth Clark, at the opening of Sutherland's 1951 retrospective at the ICA, quoted in Douglas Cooper, *The Work of Graham Sutherland*, Lund Humphries, London, 1961, p.149.

21 Peter Lanyon, recorded talk for the British Council, 1963, quoted in Toby Treves and Barnaby Wright (eds), *Soaring Flight: Peter Lanyon's Gliding Paintings*, exh.cat., The Courtauld Gallery in association with Paul Holberton Publishing, London, 2015, p.130.

22 John Russell, 'Getting down to scale', undated press cutting in Grant's journals, March 1964.

2 The North

1 Peter Davidson, *The Idea of North* (first published 2005), Reaktion Books, London, 2016.

2 Grant, Journals, 23 November 1964. Fitzwilliam, GRANT 2/1.

3 Grant, Journals, 6 October 1987. Fitzwilliam, GRANT 2/21.

4 'Roger Berthoud, 'The Briton who found inspiration in Norway', *Evening Standard*, April 1962, undated cutting. Artist's Archive, Norway.

5 John E. Blake, 'Chiefly concerning Landscape', *ARK*, summer 1952, pp 34, 31.

6 Richard Jefferies, *The Story of My Heart: An Autobiography*, Constable and Company Ltd, London, 1947.

7 Grant, Journals, 9 June 1963. Fitzwilliam, GRANT 2/1.

8 Although Grant inscribed the painting 'Brixdal, Norway', the standard spelling 'Briksdal' is preferred.

9 *Volcano in the Sea* (1963), oil on canvas, 120.5 x 90 cm, Government Art Collection, GAC 6424.

10 Joseph Wright, *Vesuvius in Eruption, with a View over the Islands in the Bay of Naples*, c.1776–80, oil on canvas, 122 x 176 cm, Tate Collection.

11 Eric Ravilious, letter to his wife, Tirzah, 31 August 1942, in Anne Ullmann, *Ravilious at War*, Fleece Press, Upper Denby, 2002, p.261.

12 Grant, Journals, 13 May 1965. Fitzwilliam, GRANT 2/1; W.G. Collingwood and Jón Stefánnson, *A Pilgrimage to the Saga-Steads of Iceland*, W. Holmes, Ulverston, 1899.

13 Grant, Journals, 14 May 1965. Fitzwilliam, GRANT 2/1.

14 ibid.

15 Grant, Journals, 25 May 1965. Fitzwilliam, GRANT 2/1.

16 Anon., 'A painter's revolving landscape', *The Times*, 3 April 1967.

17 Max Wykes-Joyce, 'Keith Grant', *Arts Review*, vol.XVII, no.9., 14 May 1966, p.218.

18 ibid.

19 Peter Amsden, email to the author, 8 September 2022.

20 Grant, Journals, 21 May 1966. Fitzwilliam, GRANT 2/1.

21 *Especially at My Time of Life*, 1969, directed and filmed by Jack Hazan, music by Colin Richards and The Creation, black & white, 37 minutes.

22 Grant, description of *Twenty-Four Hours of the Day* (1967) for the City of London Festival, 1968. Artist's Archive, Norway.

23 Anon., 'A painter's revolving landscape', *The Times*, 3 April 1967; Grant, Journals, 3 June 1967. Fitzwilliam, GRANT 2/3.

24 Soundtrack, *Grant North*, 1969.

25 Grant, Journals, 23 January 1969. Fitzwilliam, GRANT 2/3.

26 Anon., 'Dual role', *Evening Standard*, 7 February 1967.

27 Terence Mullaly, 'Artists' shows offer sharp contrasts in styles', *Daily Telegraph*, 1 February 1967, p.17; Bruce Laughton, 'Keith Grant – Bernard Dunstan', unidentified press cutting, Grant, Journals, February 1967, Fitzwilliam, GRANT 2/1.

28 James Burr, 'The Agony of a People', *Apollo*, February 1967, p.136.

29 Grant, Journals, 29 May 1967. Fitzwilliam, GRANT 2/3.

30 ibid.

31 ibid.

32 Grant, Journals, 4 March 1971. Fitzwilliam, GRANT 2/3.

33 Grant, Journals, 24 June 1971. Fitzwilliam, GRANT 2/3.

34 Grant, in *Paintings of Norway, oils, mixed media by Keith Grant*, exh.cat., Arts Centre, New Metropole, Folkestone, 1972.

35 Robert Melville, 'Flemings', *New Statesman*, 1 October 1971, p.454.

36 Grant, Journals, 3 October 1971. Fitzwilliam, GRANT 2/4.

37 Grant, Journals, 4 October 1971. Fitzwilliam, GRANT 2/4.

38 William Blake, *Selected Poems*, edited with an introduction and explanatory notes by F.W. Bateson, Heinemann Educational Books Ltd, London, 1961, endpaper.

39 'I was amazed by the greenness of the western fjords and by their subtle mistiness which evoked Chinese landscapes.' Grant, Journals, 29 May 1967. Fitzwilliam, GRANT 2/3.

40 Matsuo Bashō, *The Narrow Road to the Deep North and Other Travel Sketches*, trans. Nobuyuki Yuasa, Penguin Books Ltd, London, 1966, p.165.

41 Grant, Journals, 20 November 1971. Fitzwilliam, GRANT 2/4.

42 Grant, Journals, 11 December 1971. Fitzwilliam, GRANT 2/4. *Snow Country*, by the Japanese writer Yasunari Kawabata (1899–1972), was first published in English in 1956.

43 Grant, Journals, 15 January 1972. Fitzwilliam, GRANT 2/5. Grant quotes a different translation of Bashō's text.

44 Grant, Journals, 3 December 1971. Fitzwilliam, GRANT 2/4.

45 Bashō, *The Narrow Road to the Deep North*, p.52.

46 Yasunari Kawabata, *Snow Country*, trans. Edward G. Seidensticker (Penguin Books Ltd, London, 1956), Penguin Classics, 2011, p.8.

47 Grant, Journals, 19 April 1965. Fitzwilliam, GRANT 2/1.

48 Grant, Journals, 25 June 1967. Fitzwilliam, GRANT 2/3.

49 Alan Roger, in *Keith Grant*, exhibition leaflet, Cadogan Contemporary, London, 1988.

50 Grant, in *The Way to Cold Mountain: an exhibition of paintings by Keith Grant*, exh.cat., Rochdale Art Gallery, 1976.

51 Jack Kerouac, *The Dharma Bums*, Penguin Classics, London, 2007, p.19. Kerouac dedicated his book to Han Shan.

52 Grant, Journals, 10 June 1973. Fitzwilliam, GRANT 2/8.

53 Grant, Journals, 20 August 1973. Fitzwilliam, GRANT 2/8.

54 ibid.

55 Grant, Journals, 23 May 1973. Fitzwilliam, GRANT 2/7.

56 D.H. Lawrence, *Monologue of a Mother*, from *Amores*, Duckworth and Company, London, 1916.

57 Grant, Journals, 30 April 1972. Fitzwilliam, GRANT 2/6.

58 Grant, Journals, 19 June 1973. Fitzwilliam, GRANT 2/8.

59 In 2022, despite extensive enquiries, its location could not be traced.

60 Patrick Procktor, *Self-Portrait*, Weidenfeld & Nicolson, London, 1991, p.172.

61 'The mountain of fire that threatens a town', *Yorkshire Post*, 19 February 1973. The photographs of Eldfell erupting were taken by Grant.

62 Grant, Journals, 12 February 1973. Fitzwilliam, GRANT 2/7.

63 J.E. Guest, in *The Volcano in the North*, exh.cat., Portsmouth Museum and Art Gallery, 1973.

64 Grant, Journals, 9 March 1973. Fitzwilliam, GRANT 2/7.

65 Grant, Journals, 9 December 1975. Fitzwilliam, GRANT 2/9.

66 Grant, Journals, 26 December 1975. Fitzwilliam, GRANT 2/9.

67 Grant, Journals, 13 March 1978. Fitzwilliam, GRANT 2/12.

68 Grant, Journals, 9 April 1978. Fitzwilliam, GRANT 2/12.

69 Grant, Journals, 20 April 1978. Fitzwilliam, GRANT 2/12.

70 Grant, Journals, 23 April 1978. Fitzwilliam, GRANT 2/12.

71 Letters to Grant from Ronald Alley, 2 May 1983, and Alan Bowness, 21 July 1983, Tate Gallery. Fitzwilliam, GRANT 2/15.

72 Grant, Journals, 11 January 1989. Fitzwilliam, GRANT 2/22.

73 Grant, Journals, 19 January 1989. Fitzwilliam, GRANT 2/22.

74 Grant, Journals, 2 May 1989. Fitzwilliam, GRANT 2/22.

75 Grant, Journals, 21 June 2008, quoted in *Keith Grant: Elements of the Earth*, exh.cat., Chris Beetles Gallery, London, 2010, p.50.

76 Grant, Journals, 17 May 2016. Artist's Archive, Norway.

77 ibid.

78 Grant, Journals, 21 February 1973, Fitzwilliam, GRANT 2/7, includes a reproduction of *The Monk by the Sea*.

3 The Tropics and Desert

1 Grant, 'Notes from Kourou, F.G.: the launching of Ariane', *The London Magazine*, vol.24, no.7, October 1984, p.50. These extracts are the only record of a journal that is lost.

2 Alejo Carpentier, *The Lost Steps*, trans. Harriet de Onís (Harmondsworth: Penguin Books, 1956), reprinted 1980.

3 ibid., pp 149–50.

4 Grant, 'Notes from Kourou', p.46.

5 Grant, Journals, 4 September 1982, pasted into Journals, July–August 1983. Fitzwilliam, GRANT 2/15.

6 Grant, Journals, 28 February 1983. Fitzwilliam, GRANT 2/15.

7 Grant, Journals, 4 January 1983. Fitzwilliam, GRANT 2/15.

8 Grant, 'Notes from Kourou', p.44.

9 ibid., p.46.

10 Copy of Hawkes's text, intended as an introduction to the Logica exhibition but not printed, in Grant, Journals, 4 March 1983.

11 Terence Mullaly, *The Daily Telegraph*, 16 January 1984, p.10.

12 John Minton, 'Vogue's Travelogue', *Vogue*, British Edition, November 1951, pp 132–4.

13 *Manchester Guardian*, 13 September 1951.

14 John Berger, review of Minton's Lefevre Gallery exhibition, *Art News & Review*, 22 September 1951.

15 Grant, 'Extracts from a Sarawak Journal', *The London Magazine*, vol.30, no.1, April–May 1990, p.53.

16 Carole Buchan, 'To the ends of the earth in search of an artistic ideal', *Sussex Express*, 9 August 1985.

17 Grant, 'Extracts from a Sarawak Journal', p.54.

18 Grant, Journals, 17 July 1985. Fitzwilliam, GRANT 2/17.

19 Jacquetta Hawkes, in *Paintings and Drawings of Sarawak*, exh.cat., Francis Kyle Gallery, London, 1985.

20 Grant, Journals, 25 July 1985. Fitzwilliam, GRANT 2/17.

21 Grant, Journals, 18 September 1984. Fitzwilliam, GRANT 2/16.

22 Grant, Journals, 10 April 1986. Fitzwilliam, GRANT 2/19.

23 Grant, Journals, 16 April 1986. Fitzwilliam, GRANT 2/19.

24 Grant, Journals, 13 April 1986. Fitzwilliam, GRANT 2/19.

25 Grant, Journals, 18 April 1986. Fitzwilliam, GRANT 2/19.

26 Grant, Journals, 22 April 1988. Fitzwilliam, GRANT 2/22.

27 Grant, Journals, 26 April 1988. Fitzwilliam, GRANT 2/22.

28 Albert Schweitzer, *The Quest of the Historical Jesus*, Adam and Charles Black, London, 1911, p.181.

29 Grant, Journals, 7 May 1988. Fitzwilliam, GRANT 2/22.

30 Grant, Journals, 13 May 1988. Fitzwilliam, GRANT 2/22.

31 Grant, Journals, 21 May 1988. Fitzwilliam, GRANT 2/22.

32 Grant, Journals, 22 April 1988. Fitzwilliam, GRANT 2/22.

33 Grant, Journals, 10 May 1988. Fitzwilliam, GRANT 2/22.

34 Grant, Journals, 20 April 1988. Fitzwilliam, GRANT 2/22.

35 Jacquetta Hawkes, in *Keith Grant: Paintings of the Arctic and the Desert*, exh.cat., Crane Kalman Gallery, London, 1990.

36 Grant, Journals, 26 July 1991; re-written 29 September 1991. Fitzwilliam, GRANT 2/26.

37 Grant, Journals, 9 October 1991. Fitzwilliam, GRANT 2/26.

38 David Attenborough, *Keith Grant: Recent Paintings*, exh.cat., Gillian Jason Gallery, London, 1992.

39 Attenborough, in Linda Talbot, 'Grant's "green hell" and high water', *Ham and High*, 21 February 1992, p.84.

4 Ice

1 Grant, Journals, 30 August 1989. Fitzwilliam, GRANT 2/23.

2 Grant, Journals, 5 August 1989. Fitzwilliam, GRANT 2/23.

3 A reproduction of this painting, titled *The Wreck of the 'Hope'*, was included in Grant's journal entry for 20 August 1973.

4 Grant, Journals, 4 August 1989. Fitzwilliam, GRANT 2/23.

5 Wally Herbert, letter to Grant, 8 August 1987, pasted into Grant's Journals. Fitzwilliam, GRANT 2/21.

6 Grant, Journals, 3 September 1989. Fitzwilliam, GRANT 2/23.

7 Grant, Journals, 2 September 1989. Fitzwilliam, GRANT 2/23.

8 Grant, Journals, 5 August 1989. Fitzwilliam, GRANT 2/23.

9 Jacquetta Hawkes, 'Keith Grant', in *Keith Grant: Paintings of the Arctic and the Desert*, exh.cat., Crane Kalman Gallery, London, 1990.

10 Grant, 'Antarctic Journal' (2001–2), typescript, p.2, entry for 19.11.01. Artist's Archive, Norway.

11 ibid., p.8, entry for 21.11.01.

12 ibid., p.21, entry for 28.11.01; Alejo Carpentier, *Explosion in a Cathedral*, Penguin Books Ltd, Harmondsworth, 1971, p.9.

13 Grant, Journals, 17 September 2002. Fitzwilliam, GRANT 2/34.

14 Grant, 'Antarctic Journal', p.44, entry for 11.12.01.

15 Grant, Journals, 13 July 2002. Fitzwilliam, GRANT 2/34

16 Grant, 'Antarctic Journal', p.23, entry for 29.11001.

17 ibid., p.72, entry for 25.12.01.

18 ibid., p.28, entry for 1.12.01.

19 ibid., p.78, entry for 27.12.01.

20 ibid., p.113, entry for 13.1.02.

21 Gerard Manley Hopkins, *The Blessed Virgin compared to the Air we Breathe* (1883).

22 Grant, Journals, 13 December 2007. Artist's Archive, Norway.

23 Grant, Journals, 26 June 2018. Artist's Archive, Norway.

24 Grant, Journals, 2 July 2018. Artist's Archive, Norway.

25 ibid.

26 Grant, Journals, 21 August 2018. Artist's Archive, Norway.

27 ibid.

28 Grant, Journals, 25 August 2018. Artist's Archive, Norway.

5 Night

1 Grant, Journals, 1978–80, flyleaf. Fitzwilliam, GRANT 2/12.

2 Grant, Journals, 24 March 1978. Fitzwilliam, GRANT 2/12.

3 Grant, Journals, 23 March 1978. Fitzwilliam, GRANT 2/12.

4 ibid.

5 Grant, Journals, 14 February 1995. Fitzwilliam, GRANT 2/30.

6 Knut Hamsun, *Pan*, trans. James W. McFarlane, Alkin Books, London, 1994, pp 122–3.

7 Grant, Journals, 15 September 1983. Fitzwilliam, GRANT 2/15.

8 Grant, Journals, 21 December 1992. Fitzwilliam, GRANT 2/28.

9 Larry Berryman, 'Keith Grant and the Enlargement of the Landscape Tradition', in *Ice and Fire: paintings by Keith Grant*, exh.cat., Fitzwilliam Museum, Cambridge, 1994, pp 8, 10.

10 Grant, Journals, 16 December 2008, reproduced in *Keith Grant: Elements of the Earth*, exh.cat., Chris Beetles Gallery, London, 2010, p.27.

11 Grant, Journals, 12 January 1972. Fitzwilliam, GRANT 2/5.

12 Grant, Journals, 19 October 1977. Fitzwilliam, GRANT 2/11.

13 Grant, Journals, 13 November 1977. Fitzwilliam, GRANT 2/11.

14 Katharine Scherman, *Spring on an Arctic Island*, Little, Brown and Company, Boston and Toronto, 1956.

15 Grant, Journals, 25 March 1987. Fitzwilliam, GRANT 2/18.

16 Attenborough, *Keith Grant: Recent Paintings*, exh.cat., Gillian Jason Gallery, London, 1992.

17 Grant, Journals, 8 July 1990. Fitzwilliam, GRANT 2/25.

18 Rainer Maria Rilke, letter to Auguste Rodin, 16 October 1908, in Rilke, *Rodin: ein Vortrag Die Briefe an Rodin*, Fischer Bücherei, Frankfurt, 1956, p.104.

19 Grant, Journals, 14 February 1990. Fitzwilliam, GRANT 2/24.

20 Grant, Journals, 11 March 1995. Fitzwilliam, GRANT 2/30.

21 Grant, Journals, 24 January 2009. Artist's Archive, Norway.

22 ibid.

23 Peter Vigar, 'Keith Grant and the Cosmic Element', in *Ice and Fire: paintings by Keith Grant*, exh.cat., Fitzwilliam Museum, Cambridge, 1994, p.19.

24 ibid. Vigar was referencing Robert Rosenblum's *Modern Painting in the Northern Romantic Tradition*, Harper & Row, New York, 1975.

25 Grant, Journals, 10 April 1991. Fitzwilliam, GRANT 2/25.

26 Grant, Journals, 12 April 1991. Fitzwilliam, GRANT 2/25.

27 Grant, 'Appreciation of Dr Guy Howard', *The Late Dr. Guy Howard's Collection of Contemporary British Paintings and Works from Abbot Hall Art Gallery's Collection*, exh.cat., Abbot Hall Art Gallery, Kendal, 1989, p.5.

28 Grant, Journals, 10 January 1988. Fitzwilliam, GRANT 2/21.

6 Metamorphosis

1 Grant, Journals, 19 September 1969. Fitzwilliam, GRANT 2/3.

2 Grant, Journals, 25 May 2012. Artist's Archive, Norway.

3 Grant, Journals, 2 June 2012. Artist's Archive, Norway.

4 ibid.

5 Grant, Journals, 15 December 2012. Artist's Archive, Norway.

6 Grant, Journals, 21 December 2012. Artist's Archive, Norway.

7 ibid.

8 Grant, Journals, 20 August 2012. Artist's Archive, Norway.

9 Grant, Journals, 18 June 2014. Artist's Archive, Norway.

10 Grant, Journals, 26 May 2014. Artist's Archive, Norway.

11 Gaston Bachelard, *The Poetics of Space*, trans. Maria Jolas, Beacon Press, Boston Massachusetts, 1994, p.185.

12 Grant, Journals, 27 May 2014. Artist's Archive, Norway.

13 Gaston Bachelard, *The Poetics of Reverie*, trans. Daniel Russell, Beacon Press, Boston Massachusetts, 1971, p.20; copied into Grant, Journals, 9 August 2014. Artist's Archive, Norway.

14 Olivier Messiaen, *The Technique of My Musical Language*, trans. John Satterfield, Alphonse Leduc, Paris, 1956, p.34.

15 Grant, Journals, 19–30 May 2014. Artist's Archive, Norway.

16 Grant, Journals, 28 January 2016. Artist's Archive, Norway.

17 Grant, Journals, 29 February 2016. Artist's Archive, Norway.

18 Grant, Journals, 25 March 2014. Artist's Archive, Norway.

19 Grant, Journals, 14 April 2014. Artist's Archive, Norway.

20 Grant, Journals, 2 September 2014. Artist's Archive, Norway.

21 Grant, Journals, 10 September 2014. Artist's Archive, Norway.

22 Grant, Journals, 30 September 2014. A photograph of the 'stone frieze' is included in this entry. Artist's Archive, Norway.

23 Grant, Journals, 3 October 2013. Artist's Archive, Norway.

24 Grant, Journals, 9 July 2015. Artist's Archive, Norway.

25 Grant, Journals, 24 September 2015. Artist's Archive, Norway.

26 ibid.

27 ibid.

28 Robert Hughes, 'The Enigmas of De Chirico', *Time*, 12 April 1982, p.2.

29 Grant, 'Declaration of Intent', *Labour Monthly*, February 1967, pp 72–3.

7 Return to a Land

1 Grant, Journals, 28 May 1981. Fitzwilliam, GRANT 2/14.

2 Jacquetta Hawkes, letter to Grant, 17 August 1981. Fitzwilliam, GRANT 2/14.

3 Grant, Journals, 29 October 1981. Fitzwilliam, GRANT 2/15.

4 Grant, Journals, 9 January 1982. Fitzwilliam, GRANT 2/15.

5 Grant, Journals, 8 April 1982. Fitzwilliam, GRANT 2/15.

6 Grant, Journals, 31 May 1982. Fitzwilliam, GRANT 2/15.

7 Grant, 'Painter with Passion', *The Artist*, April 1985, p.14.

8 Grant, Journals, 21 June 1984. Fitzwilliam, GRANT 2/15.

9 Grant, 'Painter with Passion', p.14.

10 *Putting on the South*, ITV, 29 May 1986; Richard Ingrams, with a foreword by Francis Kyle, *The Ridgeway: Europe's Oldest Road*, Phaidon, Oxford, 1988.

11 John McEwen, 'Does the Road Wind Uphill All the Way?', *The Spectator*, vol.260, no.8341, 21 May 1988, p.33.

12 Grant, Journals, 31 March 1986. Fitzwilliam, GRANT 2/18.

13 Paul Nash, 'Unseen Landscapes', 1938, quoted in Ingrams, *The Ridgeway*, pp 36, 38.

14 Grant, Journals, 20 January 1986. Fitzwilliam, GRANT 2/18.

15 Grant, Journals, 23 January 1986. Fitzwilliam, GRANT 2/18.

16 Grant, Journals, 11 June 1988. Fitzwilliam, GRANT 2/22.

17 Grant, Journals, 2 July 1989. Fitzwilliam, GRANT 2/23.

18 Grant, Journals, 16 August 1989. Fitzwilliam, GRANT 2/23.

19 Grant, Journals, 2 March 2015. Artist's Archive, Norway.

20 Geoffrey Hill, *Liber Illustrium Virorum LII*, in Hill, *Broken Hierarchies: Poems 1952–2012*, ed. Kenneth Haynes, Oxford University Press, Oxford, 2013, p.736; Geoffrey Hill, *Clavics*, Enitharmon Press, London, 2011, p.30.

21 Hill, *Ludo 24*, in *Broken Hierarchies*, p.612.

22 Grant, Journals, 24 March 2015. Artist's Archive, Norway.

23 W.B. Yeats, *Under Ben Bulben*, 1938.

24 Grant, Journals, 17 May 1975. Fitzwilliam, GRANT 2/8.

25 Grant, Journals, 30 March 1975. Fitzwilliam, GRANT 2/23.

26 Grant, *Portrait of Anna Davidson* (July 1960), location unknown. A photograph exists in the Artist's Archive, Norway.

27 Grant, Journals, 23 December 2016. Artist's Archive, Norway.

28 Grant, Journals, 17 July 2016. Artist's Archive, Norway.

29 Grant, Journals, 28 March 1986. Fitzwilliam, GRANT 2/23.

30 Grant, Journals, 18 January 2017. Artist's Archive, Norway.

31 Bachelard, *The Poetics of Space*, p.210; the extract cited by Bachelard is from Thoreau's *Walden; or, Life in the Woods*, Dover Publications, New York, 1995, p.121.

32 ibid., pp 208–9.

33 Grant, annotation in photograph album of early paintings. Artist's Archive, Norway.

34 Grant, 'Selborne, 2017', in *Keith Grant: North by New English*, Chris Beetles Gallery, London, 2017, p.50.

35 Grant, Journals, 3 April 2017. Artist's Archive, Norway.

36 Gilbert White, *The Natural History of Selborne*, Oxford University Press, London, 1937, p.26.

37 Grant, Journals, 20 July 2016. Artist's Archive, Norway.

38 *The Writings of Gilbert White of Selborne*, selected and edited with an introduction by H.G. Massingham, with wood-engravings by Eric Ravilious, Nonesuch Press, London, 1938.

39 Simon Martin, with an introduction by Sir David Attenborough, *Drawn to Nature: Gilbert White and the Artists*, Pallant House Gallery, Chichester, 2021.

40 Grant, Journals, 18 August 2016. Artist's Archive, Norway.

41 Grant, Journals, 3 April 2017. Artist's Archive, Norway.

42 Grant, Journals, 18 August 2016. Artist's Archive, Norway.

43 Grant, Journals, 24 February 2017. Artist's Archive, Norway.

44 Gilbert White, *The Natural History of Selborne, with its Antiquities; Naturalist's Calendar, &c.*, Orr & Smith, London, 1836, p.294.

8 Interludes

1 Keith Grant, Journals, 14 and 29 October 1967. Fitzwilliam, GRANT 2/3.

2 Grant, 'Painter with Passion', *The Artist*, April 1985, p.14.

3 ibid.

4 Grant, *Death and the Maiden* (1962), bodycolour and pencil, 12.5 x 20 cm.

5 Grant, Journals, 3 March 1965. Fitzwilliam, GRANT 2/1.

6 Grant, Journals, 15 September 1977, Fitzwilliam, GRANT 2/11.

7 Grant, Journals, 19 September 1977, Fitzwilliam, GRANT 2/11.

8 Grant, Journals, 12 October 1977, Fitzwilliam, GRANT 2/11.

9 Grant, Journals, 15 September 1977, Fitzwilliam, GRANT 2/11.

10 A fuller account of Grant's *Delius* paintings has been published in Judith LeGrove, 'Framing Nature: Keith Grant and the music of Frederick Delius', in *Keith Grant: Invention and Variation*, exh.cat., Chris Beetles Gallery, London, 2020, pp 17–28.

11 Andrew J. Boyle, *Delius and Norway*, The Boydell Press, Woodbridge, 2017; Daniel M. Grimley, *Delius and the Sound of Place*, Cambridge University Press, Cambridge, 2018; Eric Fenby, *Delius as I Knew Him*, G. Bell & Sons Ltd, London, 1936.

12 Delius, letter to Norman O'Neill, 10 February 1920, in Lionel Carley, ed., *A Life in Letters, II: 1909–1934*, Scolar Press, London, 1988 [1994], p.79.

13 ibid.

14 Grant, Journals, 24 December 2018. Artist's Archive, Norway.

15 Alexandra Herlitz, *Grez-sur-Loing Revisited: the international artists' colony in a different light*, Makadam Förlag, Göteborg, 2013.

16 Robert Louis Stevenson, *Across the Plains, with other Memories and Essays*, Bernhard Tauchnitz, Leipzig: 1892, p.128.

17 Grant, interview with the author, September 2019.

18 ibid.

19 Grant, in *Keith Grant: Invention and Variation*, p.51.

20 Grant, Journals, 8 May 1992. Fitzwilliam, GRANT 2/27.

21 Grant, Journals, 14 February 1994. Fitzwilliam, GRANT 2/29.

22 David Kraft, 'Birdsong in the Music of Olivier Messiaen', PhD thesis, Middlesex University, 2000, p.24; Messiaen, *The Technique of My Musical Language*, trans. John Satterfield, Alphonse Leduc, Paris, 1956, p.34.

23 Michael Berkeley, *Private Passions*, BBC Radio 3, 15 April 2012.

24 Grant, Journals, 22 October 1986. Fitzwilliam, GRANT 2/20.

25 Keith Grant, note accompanying the *Luonnotar* drawings, 2013, The Lambirth Collection.

26 Grant, Journals, 5 February 2013. Artist's Archive, Norway.

27 Grant, Journals, 22 December 2014. Artist's Archive, Norway.

28 Grant, *Private Passions*, BBC Radio 3, 15 April 2012.

29 Grant, Journals, 19 September 2016. Artist's Archive, Norway.

30 Grant, Journals, 18 September 2016. Artist's Archive, Norway.

31 Grant, in *The Figurative Tradition*, exh.cat., Chris Beetles Gallery, London, 2020, p.30.

32 ibid.

9 Beyond the Gallery

1 Claire Hilton and Tom Stephenson (eds), *Psychiatric Hospitals in the UK in the 1960s* (Witness Seminar), Royal College of Psychiatrists, London, 2020, p.25.

2 Grant, Journals, 4 November 1964, Fitzwilliam, GRANT 2/1.

3 Grant, Journals, 16 June 1976, Fitzwilliam, GRANT 2/8.

4 'Art and Design', *Arena*, broadcast 11 February 1976.
5 Jeremy Hugh Baron and Nigel Weaver, *Art in the Hammersmith Hospitals and Medical Schools*, 1996, p.9.
6 Grant, Journals, 19 September 1980. Fitzwilliam, GRANT 2/14; Cesare Pavese, '12 December 1939', *This Business of Living*, World Distributors, London, Consul Edition, 1964, p.91.
7 'Hospital glass needs plenty of patience', *H&H Series* [*Ham & High Express*], 17 December 1999.
8 Deanna Petherbridge, 'Commissions: the one percent', *Art & Architecture*, vol.52, December 1981, p.31.
9 Unidentified press cutting, in Grant, Journals, 13 February 1968. Fitzwilliam, GRANT 2/3.
10 Grant, Journals, 27 December 1967; Grant, letter to S.A.G. Cook, Borough Architect, London Borough of Camden, 9 February 1968. Fitzwilliam, GRANT 2/3.
11 Grant, Journals, 28 July 1970. Fitzwilliam, GRANT 2/3.
12 *Kinetics* (1972), a documentary filmed by Lutz Becker, 23 minutes, colour.
13 Richard Cork, 'The fallacy of kinetic art', *Evening Standard*, 30 September 1970, reprinted in Cork, *Everything Seemed Possible: art in the 1970s*, Yale University Press, New Haven and London, 2003, p.434; Bryan Robertson, 'Dark Dangers', *The Spectator*, 3 October 1970, p.376.
14 Theo van Wijk, Principal and Vice Chancellor of Unisa, speech at the installation of *Idomeneo* in 1974.
15 Richard Cork, 'This Joan is neither woman nor machine', *Evening Standard*, 3 April 1971.
16 Sandy Wilson, letter to Grant, 11 May 1965, in Grant, Journals. Fitzwilliam, GRANT 2/1.
17 '"Komdu aftur –" viðtal við Keith Grant' ['"Come back again –" an interview with Keith Grant'], *Vísir*, 3 June 1965.
18 Sigmúnd [Sigmúnd Jóhannsson], 'Surtsey og víti', *Morgunblaðið*, 11 October 1965, in Grant, Journals. Fitzwilliam, GRANT 2/1.
19 'Pessimism impressively interpreted', *The Times*, 22 September 1965, p.14.
20 ibid.
21 George Taylor, *History of the Amateur Theatre*, Colin Venton White Horse Library, Melksham, 1976, p.72.
22 Grant, Journals, 28 September 1981. Fitzwilliam, GRANT 2/15.
23 Bryan Robertson, 'Bright Revivals', *The Spectator*, 4 September 1982, p.25; Nicholas de Jongh, 'Young Vic: Hamlet', *The Guardian*, 10 August 1982, p.7.
24 Grant, Journals, 5 January 1995. Fitzwilliam, GRANT 2/30.
25 ibid.
26 Grant, Journals, 14 February 1995. Fitzwilliam, GRANT 2/30.
27 Grant, Journals, 20 March 1995. Fitzwilliam, GRANT 2/30.
28 ibid.
29 Sean Egan, *Our Music is Red with Purple Flashes: the story of The Creation*, Cherry Red Books Ltd, London, 2004, p.9.
30 *Record Mirror*, no.275, week ending 18 June 1966, p.2.
31 Grant, Journals, 28 June 1992. Fitzwilliam, GRANT 2/28.
32 Hawkes, *A Land* (first published 1951), Collins, London, 2012, pp 13–14.

10 Landscapes of Protest and Memory

1 Grant, Journals, 14 December 1964. Fitzwilliam, GRANT 2/1.
2 ibid.
3 Grant, Journals, 18 January 1965. Fitzwilliam, GRANT 2/1.
4 Grant, Journals, 12 February 1965. Fitzwilliam, GRANT 2/1.
5 Roger Berthoud, 'This attempt to be "with it" – what a sad flop!', *Evening Standard*, [31 April 1965] (undated press cutting in Grant's journals). Fitzwilliam, GRANT 2/1.
6 Arthur Moyse, 'Round the Galleries', *Freedom*, vol.27 no.17, 28 May 1966.
7 Grant, in *Especially at My Time of Life*, 1969, directed and filmed by Jack Hazan, music by Colin Richards and The Creation, black & white, 37 minutes.
8 ibid.
9 Grant, Journals, 18 June 1966. Fitzwilliam, GRANT 2/1.
10 Grant, Journals, 25 September 1966. Fitzwilliam, GRANT 2/1.
11 Margaret Richards, 'Artists and Vietnam', *Tribune*, 10 February 1967, p.11.
12 Grant, Journals, 14 August 1967. Fitzwilliam, GRANT 2/3.
13 John Berger, letter to Grant, 26 March 1968. Fitzwilliam, GRANT 2/3.
14 Grant, Journals, 30 August 1970. Fitzwilliam, GRANT 2/3.
15 Grant, Journals, 10 September 1966. Fitzwilliam, GRANT 2/2.
16 Grant, Journals, 9 September 1971. Fitzwilliam, GRANT 2/4.
17 Grant, Journals, 29 September 1971. Fitzwilliam, GRANT 2/4.
18 Grant, Journals, 16 January 1981. Fitzwilliam, GRANT 2/14.
19 Terence Mullaly, 'Land of midnight sun', *Daily Telegraph*, 4 February 1981, p.11.
20 Peter Fuller, 'Aesthetics and Nuclear Anaesthesia' (1981), in *The Naked Artist: 'Art and Biology' & other essays*, Writers and Readers, London, 1983, p.41.
21 Grant, draft letter to the *Guardian*, 2 May 1990. Fitzwilliam, GRANT 2/24.
22 Grant, Journals, 13 February 1968. Fitzwilliam, GRANT 2/16.
23 Grant, Journals, 23 August 1968. Fitzwilliam, GRANT 2/3.
24 Grant, Journals, 8 May 2014. Artist's Archive, Norway.
25 Grant, Journals, 8 May 2014. Artist's Archive, Norway.
26 Grant, Journals, 18 January 1986. Fitzwilliam, GRANT 2/16.
27 Grant, Journals, 15 August 2016. Artist's Archive, Norway.
28 Paul Nash, letter to Kenneth Clark, 11 March 1941, in Anthony Bertram, *Paul Nash: the portrait of an artist*, Faber and Faber, London, 1955, pp 172–3.
29 Grant, Journals, 12 September 2016. Artist's Archive, Norway.
30 Grant, Journals, 7 October 2016. Artist's Archive, Norway.
31 Grant, Journals, 8 October 2016. Artist's Archive, Norway.
32 Tom Jeffreys, *The White Birch: a Russian reflection*, Corsair, London, 2021, p.30.
33 ibid., p.34.
34 ibid., p.190.

Acknowledgements

Thanks are due above all to Keith Grant and his wife, Hilde Ellingsen-Grant: this book could not have been written without their friendship and support. I would like also to thank Peter Amsden, Douglas Atfield, Lindsay Badenoch, Chris Beetles Gallery, Trym Ivar Bergsmo, Madeleine Bessborough and Luke Sainsbury (New Art Centre), Brigitta and Michael Best, Kjell Bitusøyl, Olwyn Bowey, Cadogan Gallery, Alyson Charles, Nick Clark (Britten Pears Arts), Ana and Jeff Davies and family, John and Anna Edwards, Karin and Trond Eilertsen, Pierre Fowell, David Game, Thea Ellingsen-Grant, Dominique Grant, Jack Hazan, Jean Henderson, Adina Holmes, Þorbjörg Jónsdóttir, John Kimpton, Andrew Lambirth, Peter, Sandra and Clare Lancaster, John LeGrove, Susan, Kate and Rachel Mahaffy, Amy Marquis and Suzanne Reynolds (Fitzwilliam Museum), Joey Mason (Imperial Health Charity), Emma Miller, Hattie Neill, Timothy Neill, Paddy O'Connor, Fred Olsen, Neil Parkinson (RCA Library), Stephen Parnell, Anne-Katrin Purkiss, Ingram Reid, Lady Tia and Sir Stephen Sedley, Phillida and John Sillince, Abi Shapiro (Hepworth Wakefield), Lady Moya and Sir John Tomlinson, Sissel Walum, Nigel and Iris Weaver.

This book is dedicated to the memory of Mark Henderson: a fearless explorer, historian and reader.

Image Credits

The publisher would like to thank the copyright holders for granting permission to reproduce the images illustrated. Every attempt has been made to trace accurate ownership of copyrighted images in this book. Any errors or omissions will be corrected in subsequent editions provided notification is sent to the publisher.

Alfred East Gallery, North Northamptonshire Council: fig.20; Peter C. Amsden ARPS, ABIPP: frontispiece, figs 28, 157–9, 168; Arctandria, Oslo: fig.91; Artist's Archive (photographer unknown): figs 19, 29, 41, 56, 57, 116, 150; Art Gallery of South Australia, Adelaide, South Australian Government Grant 1964, 0.2042: fig.2; Douglas Atfield: figs 14, 21, 23, 24, 26, 34, 35, 43, 113, 140, 146, 148, 149, 151, 152, 155; © The Atkinson, Southport: fig.5; The Beaverbrook Art Gallery, gift of the Second Beaverbrook Foundation, collection of the Beaverbrook Art Gallery, 1959.87: fig.8; Kjell Bitustøyl: figs 6, 54, 55, 59, 64, 82, 90, 94, 105, 111, 147, 160, 161, 179–81; Courtesy of Bonhams: fig.167; Courtesy of Olwyn Bowey: fig.10; Britten Pears Arts, The Red House Aldeburgh Collection, 5-9700292, 5-9400042, 5-9700408, 5-9400132, 5-20170087: figs 31, 86, 123, 132, 135; Courtesy of Britten Pears Arts: fig.162; Cadogan Gallery: figs 68–71, 85; Courtesy of the Chris Beetles Gallery, St James's, London: figs 13, 15, 18, 22, 37, 42, 47, 49, 50, 74–80, 95–104, 107–110, 112, 121, 122, 124, 126, 127, 129–31, 134, 137–9, 141–3, 145, 166, 174–6; Andrew Curtis: fig.153; © Dreweatts 1759: fig.12; Marius Els: fig.93; © The Fitzwilliam Museum, Cambridge. PD.47-2996, PD.44-2007: figs 67, 119; Kenneth Ginn: figs 44, 115; Gorringe's Auction House: fig.114; Nuno Manuel Martins Graça: fig.172; Keith Grant: figs 9, 30, 33, 38, 40, 52, 53, 58, 60, 62, 63, 66, 106, 117, 118, 120, 133, 165, 170; Richard Gray: fig.65; Helge Hovland, Studio Technika: fig.173; Imperial Health Charity Art Collection: fig.39; Inverness Museum & Art Gallery. Photograph: Ewen Weatherspoon: fig.87; Paul Jackson: fig.156; Luca Jahn: figs 177, 178; Lakeland Arts Trust: accepted in Lieu of Tax by HM Government and allocated to Lakeland Arts Trust in 1990. Reproduced courtesy of Abbot Hall, Lakeland Arts Trust, England: figs 81, 88; Leamington Spa Art Gallery & Museum (Warwick District Council): fig.73; Leicestershire County Council Artworks Collection: fig.51; Bill MacKinnon: fig.169; Ian Marshall: fig.171; Courtesy of the New Art Centre, Wiltshire: fig.17; Paul Paiewonsky: fig.4; Portsmouth Museums, Portsmouth City Council: fig.163; Private Collection, courtesy of the owner: fig.125; Quantum Photography: fig.154; Anne-Katrin Purkiss: fig.182; Bill Robertson: figs 61, 84, 89; Courtesy of the Royal College of Art archive; photographer unknown: fig.11; Royal College of Art collection: fig.16; Peter Stone: figs 128, 144; Robert Stopford, courtesy of the Chris Beetles Gallery, St James's, London: figs 3, 46, 72, 92, 136; Te Papa Tongarewa Museum of New Zealand, Wellington, New Zealand: fig.25; Sergiu Timar & India Stewart: fig.7; Touchstones Rochdale, Lancashire, UK© Touchstones Rochdale Art Gallery/Bridgeman Images: fig.36; Towner Eastbourne: fig.1; Ole Jakob Voraa: fig.164; Wakefield Permanent Art Collection (The Hepworth Wakefield). Transferred from The Education Resource Service. Image Courtesy: The Hepworth Wakefield. Photographer: Anna Bridson: fig.27; © Jonty Wilde: figs 32, 45, 48, 83.

Index

Note: italic page numbers indicate figures; Keith Grant is abbreviated to KG in headings and subheadings.